Beyond Marx

Historical Materialism Book Series

The Historical Materialism Book Series is a major publishing initiative of the radical left. The capitalist crisis of the twenty-first century has been met by a resurgence of interest in critical Marxist theory. At the same time, the publishing institutions committed to Marxism have contracted markedly since the high point of the 1970s. The Historical Materialism Book Series is dedicated to addressing this situation by making available important works of Marxist theory. The aim of the series is to publish important theoretical contributions as the basis for vigorous intellectual debate and exchange on the left.

The peer-reviewed series publishes original monographs, translated texts, and reprints of classics across the bounds of academic disciplinary agendas and across the divisions of the left. The series is particularly concerned to encourage the internationalization of Marxist debate and aims to translate significant studies from beyond the English-speaking world.

For a full list of titles in the Historical Materialism Book Series
available in paperback from Haymarket Books, visit:
www.haymarketbooks.org/category/hm-series

Beyond Marx

Theorising the Global Labour Relations of the Twenty-First Century

Edited by
Marcel van der Linden and Karl Heinz Roth

In collaboration with
Max Henninger

Haymarket Books
Chicago, IL

First published in 2014 by Brill Academic Publishers, The Netherlands
© 2014 Koninklijke Brill NV, Leiden, The Netherlands

Published in paperback in 2014 by
Haymarket Books
P.O. Box 180165
Chicago, IL 60618
773-583-7884
www.haymarketbooks.org

ISBN: 978-1-60846-410-4

Trade distribution:
In the US, Consortium Book Sales, www.cbsd.com
In Canada, Publishers Group Canada, www.pgcbooks.ca
In the UK, Turnaround Publisher Services, www.turnaround-psl.com
In all other countries, Publishers Group Worldwide, www.pgw.com

Cover design by Ragina Johnson.

This book was published with the generous support of
Lannan Foundation and the Wallace Global Fund.

Printed in Canada by union labor.

10 9 8 7 6 5 4 3 2 1

Library of Congress Cataloging-in-Publication data is available.

Contents

Notes on Contributors

Riccardo Bellofiore lectures in the history of economic thought at the University of Bergamo. He is the editor of numerous books, including *Global Money, Capital Restructuring, and the Changing Patterns of Labour* (Cheltenham: Edward Elgar, 1999), *Rereading Marx: New Perspectives after the Critical Edition* (New York: Palgrave Macmillan, 2009; with Roberto Fineschi), and *Rosa Luxemburg and the Critique of Political Economy* (New York: Routledge, 2009).

Sergio Bologna, historian and social scientist, was one of the chief exponents of Italian workerism during the 1960s and 1970s. In 1973, he founded *Primo Maggio*, a journal for militant historians. During the 1980s, he lectured at the University of Bremen, Germany. He is co-author, with Cesare Bermani and Brunello Mantelli, of *Proletarier der 'Achse': Sozialgeschichte der italienischen Fremdarbeit in NS-Deutschland 1937 bis 1943* (Berlin: Akademie Verlag, 1997). His most recent book is *Vita da freelance: i lavoratori della conoscenza e il loro futuro* (Milan: Feltrinelli, 2011; with Dario Banfi).

C. George Caffentzis teaches philosophy at the University of Southern Maine and is a member of the Midnight Notes Collective. He is the author of *Clipped Coins, Abused Words, and Civil Government: John Locke's Philosophy of Money* (Brooklyn: Autonomedia, 1989), *Exciting the Industry of Mankind: George Berkeley's Philosophy of Money* (Boston and Dordrecht: Kluwer Academic Publishers, 2000), and *In Letters of Blood and Fire: Work, Machines, and Value in the Bad Infinity of Capitalism* (Oakland: PM Press, 2012).

Silvia Federici teaches political philosophy at Hofstra University in the USA. She is a co-founder of the Committee for Academic Freedom in Africa and of the Radical Philosophy Association's campaign against the death-penalty. She is the author, with Leopoldina Fortunati, of *Il grande Calibano: storia del corpo sociale ribelle nella prima fase del capitale* (Milan: FrancoAngeli, 1984) and *Revolution at Point Zero: Housework, Reproduction, and Feminist Struggle* (Oakland: PM Press, 2012). She is also one of the editors of *Enduring Western Civilization: The Construction of the Concept of Western Civilization and Its 'Others'* (Westport: Praeger, 1995).

Niklas Frykman teaches history at Claremont McKenna College, Claremont, California. He is currently writing a book on mutinies and other forms of transnational maritime radicalism during the age of Atlantic revolution.

Ferruccio Gambino, lectures on international migrations at the University of Padua. He has taught in the United States and in France. He was a co-editor of the journal *altreragioni* (1992–2000). His publications include: *Migranti nella tempesta* (Verona: Ombre corte, 2003), and 'The transgression of a Laborer: Malcolm X in the Wilderness of America', *Radical History Review*, No. 55 (1993). He is co-editor, with Devi Sacchetto, of *Un arcipelago produttivo. Migranti e imprenditori tra Italia e Romania* (Rome: Carocci, 2007), and a contributor to Pier Paolo Poggio (ed.), *Comunismi eretici. Vol. 3* (Milan: Jaca Book, 2013 forthcoming).

Sebastian Gerhardt is a freelance writer and resides in Berlin. He earns a living as a tour-guide at the 'Topography of Terror' museum and the German-Russian Museum Berlin-Karlshorst. He devotes part of his free time to various projects (the Berlin 'House of Democracy and Human Rights', the journal *Lunapark21*). He is currently working on a teaching unit for the SALZ educational association: 'No Revolution is no Solution Either: On the Critique of the Political Economy of the twenty-first Century'.

Detlef Hartmann is co-editor of the book series *Materialien für einen neuen Antiimperialismus*. His books include *Leben als Sabotage. Zur Krise der technologischen Gewalt* (Tübingen: IVA, 1981), *'Empire': Linkes Ticket für die Reise nach rechts* (Berlin and Hamburg: Assoziation A, 2002), *Cluster: Die neue Etappe des Kapitalismus* (Berlin and Hamburg: Assoziation A, 2008; with Gerald Geppert), and *Krisenlabor Griechenland: Finanzmärkte, Kämpfe und die Neuordnung Europas* (Berlin and Hamburg: Assoziation A, 2011; with John Malamatinas).

Max Henninger lives in Berlin and works as a translator and author. He is the coordinating editor, with Peter Birke, of the online journal *Sozial.Geschichte Online*. He has contributed to the *International Encyclopaedia of Revolution and Protest, 1500 to the Present* (Oxford: Blackwell, 2009; edited by Immanuel Ness) and the edited volume *Banlieues: Die Zeit der Forderungen ist vorbei* (Berlin und Hamburg: Assoziation A, 2009).

Thomas Kuczynski, economist and author, worked at the Institute for Economic History of East Germany's Academy of Sciences from 1972 until 1991. His publications since 1990 include *Das Kommunistische Manifest (Manifest der Kommunistischen Partei) von Karl Marx und Friedrich Engels: Von der Erstausgabe zur Leseausgabe. Mit einem Editionsbericht* (Trier: Karl-Marx-Haus, 1995) and

Brosamen vom Herrentisch. Hintergründe der Entschädigungszahlungen an die im Zweiten Weltkrieg nach Deutschland verschleppten Zwangsarbeitskräfte (Berlin: Verbrecher-Verlag, 2004).

Marcel van der Linden is research director of the International Institute of Social History and professor of social movement history at the University of Amsterdam. His recent books include *Transnational Labour History: Explorations* (Aldershot: Ashgate, 2003), *Workers of the World. Essays toward a Global Labor History* (Leiden: Brill, 2008), and *Western Marxism and the Soviet Union: A Survey of Critical Theories and Debates since 1917* (Leiden: Brill, 2007; Chicago: Haymarket, 2009).

Peter Linebaugh is professor of history at the University of Toledo and author of *The London Hanged: Crime and Civil Society in the Eighteenth Century* (Cambridge: Cambridge University Press, 1992) and *The Magna Carta Manifesto: Liberties and Commons for All* (Berkeley: University of California Press, 2008). He is co-author, with Marcus Rediker, of *The Many-Headed Hydra: Sailors, Slaves, Commoners, and the Hidden History of the Revolutionary Atlantic* (Boston: Beacon Press, 2000). He co-edits the journal *CounterPunch*.

Ahlrich Meyer is professor-emeritus of political science at the Carl von Ossietzky University in Oldenburg. He was co-editor of the journal *Autonomie. Materialien gegen die Fabrikgesellschaft* (1975–9, new series 1979–85). His books include *Die Logik der Revolten: Studien zur Sozialgeschichte 1789–1848* (Berlin and Hamburg: Verlag der Buchläden Schwarze Risse und Rote Straße, 1999); *L'Occupation allemande en France* (Toulouse: Editions Privat, 2002), and *Das Wissen um Auschwitz. Täter und Opfer der 'Endlösung' in Westeuropa* (Paderborn: Ferdinand Schöningh, 2010).

Maria Mies is a sociologist and retired professor at the Cologne University of Applied Sciences. Her many publications include *The Lace Makers of Narsapur: Indian Housewives Produce for the World Market* (London: Zed Books, 1982), *Patriarchy and Accumulation on a World Scale: Women in the International Division of Labour* (London: Zed Books, 1986), *Women: The Last Colony* (London: Zed Books, 1998; with Veronika Bennholdt-Thomsen and Claudia von Werlhof), *Krieg ohne Grenzen. Die neue Kolonialisierung der Welt* (Cologne: Papyrossa-Verlag, 2004), and *Das Dorf und die Welt: Lebensgeschichten – Zeitgeschichten* (Cologne: Papyrossa-Verlag, 2008).

Jean-Louis Prat is a philosopher and co-editor of the *Revue du MAUSS* (*Mouvement Anti Utilitariste dans les Sciences Sociales*). His publications include *Introduction à Castoriadis* (Paris: La Découverte, 2007).

Marcus Rediker is professor of history at the University of Pittsburgh. His books include *Between the Devil and the Deep Blue Sea: Merchant Seamen, Pirates, and the Anglo-American Maritime World, 1700–1750* (Cambridge: Cambridge University Press, 1987), *The Slave Ship: A Human History* (New York: Viking, 2007), and, with Peter Linebaugh, *The Many-Headed Hydra: Sailors, Slaves, Commoners, and the Hidden History of the Revolutionary Atlantic* (Boston: Beacon Press, 2000).

Karl Heinz Roth, medical doctor and historian, is an associate of the Foundation for Social History in Bremen, Germany. He was co-editor of the journals *Autonomie* (1975–9, new series 1979–85), *1999* (1986–2002) and *Sozial.Geschichte* (2003–7). His recent publications include *Facetten des Terrors: Der Geheimdienst der Deutschen Arbeitsfront und die Zerstörung der Arbeiterbewegung 1933 bis 1938* (Bremen: Edition Temmen, 2000), *Die globale Krise* (Hamburg: VSA, 2009), and *Reemtsma auf der Krim. Tabakproduktion und Zwangsarbeit unter der deutschen Besatzungsherrschaft 1941–44* (Hamburg: Edition Nautilus, 2011; with Jan-Peter Abraham).

Devi Sacchetto lectures in the Sociology of Labour at the University of Padua. He was a co-editor of *altreragioni* (1994–2000). His publications include: *Fabbriche galleggianti. Solitudine e sfruttamento tra i nuovi marinai* (Milan: Jaca Book, 2009). He is co-editor with Gianni Sbrogiò of *Pouvoir ouvrier à Porto Marghera. Du Comité d'usine à l'Assemblée régionale (Vénétie—1960–1980)* (Paris: Les nuits rouges, 2012) and with Ferruccio Gambino of Pun Ngai, *Cina, la società armoniosa. Sfruttamento e resistenza degli operai migranti* (Milan: Jaca book, 2012). Together with Rutvica Andrijasevic he recently published: "Integration verschiedener Arbeitsrégime? Foxconn in Tschechien", in Pun Ngai (ed.), *iSlave. Ausbeutung und Widerstand in Chinas Foxconn Fabriken* (Vienna: Mandelbaum, 2013).

Subir Sinha, a historian and political scientist, lectures in the Department of Development Studies at the School of Oriental and African Studies, London. He publishes on the history of Indian planning, and of the lineages of political subjectivity expressed in contemporary social movements of the rural poor on question of natural resource use.

Massimiliano Tomba lectures in the philosophy of human rights at the University of Padua. His publications include *Crisi e critica in Bruno Bauer: Il principio di esclusione come fundamento del politico* (Naples: Bibliopolis, 2002) and *La 'vera politica': Kant e Benjamin – la possibilità della giustizia* (Macerata: Quodlibet, 2006). He is co-editor, with Devi Sacchetto, of *La lunga accumulazione originaria: Politica e lavoro nel mercato mondiale* (Verona: Ombre corte, 2008).

Carlo Vercellone is Maître de conférences in the economic sciences at Université de Paris I (Panthéon-Sorbonne). He recently co-edited *Cognitive Capitalism and its Reflections in South-Eastern Europe* (Bern: Peter Lang, 2010).

Peter Way is professor of history at the University of Windsor in Canada. He is the author of *Common Labour: Workers and the Digging of North American Canals* (Cambridge: Cambridge University Press, 1993) and has published articles in a range of academic journals and edited volumes. He is currently working on a book-length project titled *Making War: Common Soldiers and the Building of Britain's American Empire in the Seven Years' War.*

Steve Wright teaches information-management at the Caulfield School of Information Technology, Monash University, Australia. He is the author of *Storming Heaven: Class Composition and Struggle in Italian Autonomist Marxism* (London: Pluto Press, 2002).

Introduction
Marcel van der Linden and Karl Heinz Roth

I

For the past five years, the world economic crisis has kept us holding our breath.[1] It is the first global crisis of the century. Its impact is tremendous, and it has now reached every corner of the planet. The ruling elites were entirely unprepared for it. They responded by means of countermeasures that are in some cases without historical precedent. In doing so, they have so far been able to prevent the collapse of the world-economy, but they have not been able to master the crisis itself. Significant indicators suggest that the crisis will lead into a long depression.

The current crisis began in late 2006 and early 2007. It began as a real-estate crisis in the transatlantic region; its focal points were the USA and the European periphery. Its global expansion was due to four factors. First, the subprime crisis directly impacted international financial markets, as these had distributed the associated risks across the world. Second, the crisis led to the collapse of mass-consumption in the USA. This prompted a recession, as well as the contraction of global export-markets and transportation-chains. Third, the entire industrial sector was affected, starting with the automobile-industry: profits shrank and investment was curtailed. Fourth, global investors withdrew their capital from newly industrialising

---

1. On the origins, the expansion and the further development of the crisis to date, see Roth 2009, Stiglitz 2010 and Panitch 2010; see also the ongoing coverage in *The Economist* and *Neue Zürcher Zeitung.*

countries. These factors mutually reinforced one another and caused the crisis to smoulder the world over. International trade contracted by 12 percent. In the developed national economies, GNP dropped by between five and ten percent. The growth-rates of the leading newly industrialising countries dropped by half. The trough of the crisis was reached in the spring of 2009.

This was followed by an intermediate phase that lasted until the summer of 2011. Three different developments were evident. Some newly industrialising countries underwent a striking recovery-process, a second group of national economies remained in crisis and a third began to experience stagnation. As a result, serious imbalances developed, masked by the temporary recovery of world-trade and global commodity-markets and overshadowed by a worldwide rise in food-prices: in 2010 alone, food-prices rose by 29 percent. In addition to this, the anti-crisis measures adopted within monetary and fiscal policy in the autumn of 2008 led to worldwide state-debt. The countries of the triad-region (Japan, USA, Europe) were especially affected; their total debt of fifty trillion US dollars is now roughly equivalent to the world's annual economic output. These three factors mark the road into a long depression, characterised by a rapid succession of downturns and recovery-phases and by the further aggravation of regional imbalances. The most recent downturn, in the autumn of 2011, has been accentuated by the intensification of the European debt- and banking-crisis.

The leading elites responded to these developments with remarkable energy and stamina. In doing so, they were less concerned with ameliorating the social effects of the crisis than with rescuing the global 'financial architecture' and stabilising the structural core of the world-system. Following the outbreak of the debt-crisis in late 2009 and early 2010, they have even proceeded to transfer the costs of the crisis directly to the lower classes, implementing austerity-programmes within their national economies and economic blocs. These programmes combine the slashing of welfare-state transfer-benefits with restrictive monetary policies and comprehensive deregulation and privatisation. This change of course has accelerated the social decline that the lower classes have been experiencing since the onset of the worldwide recession, turning that decline into an outright process of pauperisation and proletarisation, especially in crisis-areas. Current reports and analyses allow one to identify six particularly significant aspects of this process.

(1) Mass-unemployment – at about two hundred million persons before the crisis – has increased by another fifty million persons, of whom twenty-five million are Chinese migrant-workers. During the intermediate phase, mass unemployment dropped by between twenty and twenty-five million, but it has begun rising markedly again as a result of the implementation of austerity-programmes and the current second downturn.[2]

---

2. International Labour Organization 2009, 2010.

(2) Significant parts of the world's lower classes are once again facing absolute poverty, hunger and chronic malnutrition. So far, the crisis has caused the number of persons who dispose of less than one US dollar per day to increase to 1.7 billion people. The drastic rise in food-prices means that almost two-thirds of the persons in this group suffer from chronic malnutrition.[3]

(3) In the course of the crisis, precarious working- and living-conditions have become the norm.[4] They have now become visible even in the developed national economies and economic blocs – in the form of street-hawkers, beggars, courier-services, and so on. In addition to this, there are the invisible precarious working-conditions in the factory-halls and office-wings: fixed-term workers, temp-workers and poorly remunerated, often highly qualified, pseudo-self-employed contract-workers.

(4) Young persons (up to the age of 24) have been especially affected by the effects of the crisis.[5] Their unemployment-rate is approaching the fifty-percent mark, even in the countries of the European periphery. The jobs that they find – when they find any – are almost always fixed-term and poorly remunerated, making it impossible for these young people to become independent of their parents and set up families of their own. This development can be observed the world over. Far from concerning only poorly qualified young persons with an immigrant-background, it also affects highly qualified persons, including university-graduates.

(5) Substantial parts of the middle-classes have experienced marked social decline.[6] Medical doctors, journalists, lawyers and teachers now also have difficulty finding long-term employment, and they are losing their traditional systems of social security. Particularly dramatic cases of social decline can be seen in the domain of so-called micro-enterprises, where millions of self-employed persons are being degraded to the status of pseudo-self-employed contract-workers. Deprived of secure incomes, they live from hand to mouth.

(6) All of these developments are overshadowed by a clear polarisation of the social structure, with pauperisation on one side and enrichment on the other.[7] This development is especially dramatic in those national economies that have seen the implementation of harsh austerity-programmes despite persistent tendencies toward crisis and stagnation, such as Great Britain, Greece, Italy and Spain. Within these regions, we are seeing dramatic cases of decline. They are

---

3. United Nations 2009, 2010; Food and Agriculture Organization of the United Nations 2011.
4. Jütting and de Laiglesia 2009.
5. International Labour Office 2010.
6. Bologna 2007; Vogel 2009.
7. OECD 2008.

occurring throughout the various segments of the lower classes, and they are now reminiscent of events that occurred during the Great Depression of the 1930s.

These tendencies toward the (re-)proletarisation of growing parts of world-society were, however, already becoming evident during the decades of the previous economic cycle.[8] Since the 1970s, manifold processes of expulsion from land and separation from the means of production and the means of subsistence have meshed with the devalorisation of qualifications and the elimination of social-security guarantees against the vicissitudes of individual and/or family-life, producing comprehensive processes of impoverishment. Hundreds of millions of peasant-subsistence economies have lost their means of existence. The expelled and expropriated have escaped to urban areas, with about one billion people being absorbed by the shadow-economies of the slum-cities. At the same time, those young persons who were especially mobile went on the tramp, triggering continental and transcontinental mass-migrations; hundreds of millions of persons had already participated in these mass-migrations by the time when the crisis began. Meanwhile, new labour-markets emerged in the fields of care-work, domestic services, transportation and highly qualified communication- and knowledge-work – the first such labour-markets to display a genuinely global structure. Other segments of the changing global working class were subjected to rigorous exploitation in the special economic zones that emerged with the development of the new international division of labour. In addition to this, there were massive relocations of the industrial working class: from the developed centres of the past to the new emerging economies, especially China, India and southeast Asia. Caught within the interrelated processes of dispossession, impoverishment and the imposition of work, the world's lower classes found themselves inside the complex crucible of global restructuring. Since the crisis began, they have again been exposed to tremendous shocks.

II

Most people were unable to avoid deterioration of their working- and living-conditions, which has been going on for years and is now coming to a head in the crisis. But they have engaged in resistance, and continue to do so. With increasing frequency, they search for strategies of defence. This is not easy, as many allowed themselves, during past decades, to be led astray by the promises of a new market-radicalism, commonly referred to as 'neoliberalism'. According to this doctrine, the development of wealth is guaranteed only when labour-

---

8. Weisbrot 2010; Roth 1994, 2005; Van der Linden and Lieber 2007.

and production-relations are left to the self-regulating interplay of supply and demand; those whose income from work is too low can be helped by extensive credit. But the promises associated with the 'deregulation' and 'flexibilisation' of work, the privatisation of public goods, the dismantling of social-security systems and the lure of cheap money and speculative enrichment dissolved into thin air during the first months of the crisis. The search for new reference-points began. Politicians and economic experts hurried to close the resulting gap by invoking new concepts. They invoked a 'renewal of capitalism', to be achieved by the restoration of economic policy's regulatory systems. But their half-hearted promises and one-sided operations for rescuing the financial sector merely reinforced the sense of mistrust and the spread of insecurity. While the claim that the manifest systemic crisis can be mastered by state-interventionist practices says much about the conflicting interests of the political classes, economic elites and owners of capital-assets, the survival and security needs of the lower classes were hardly considered. *Qua* victims of the crisis, they were taken into account only to the extent that they might cause 'social unrest' – which was, and continues to be, unwanted. Policy-makers do not want the lower classes to contribute actively to the handling of the crisis. The lower classes are seen as needing to be pacified – by means of extended short-time compensation and unemployment-benefits, as well as by the curbing of compulsory auctions of houses and owner-occupied apartments. They are to remain objects of crisis-management.

These efforts to bring about a 'renewal of capitalism' and the social concessions that have been made (albeit only within the developed national economies) have certainly not been a complete failure. But they have not been able to prevent the search for a new compass by which to understand the systemic crisis – all the more so as they have been thoroughly disavowed with the adoption of austerity-programmes in 2010. To be sure, the available alternatives were few and far between. Parts of the Left referred back to British economist John Maynard Keynes, whose ideas about the mobilisation of public credit and the 'socialisation of investment', understood as instruments for the anti-cyclical regulation of the economy, had for decades been condemned wholesale by economic decision-makers. But another economist, who had spent more than half of his life in British exile, was also rediscovered as an analyst of the capitalist cycle of crisis – Karl Marx.

The European Marx renaissance is, without doubt, one of the most remarkable cultural epiphenomena of the current world economic crisis. The London *Times* insisted on paying homage to the 'old man from London'. The *New York Times* praised Marx as a 'prognosticator' who 'foresaw the contours of today's financial crisis'. And the *Economist* called Marx's *Capital* the 'first book to describe the relentless, all-consuming and global nature of capitalism'. The world over, Marx reading-groups have sprung up among left-wing students. Those participating in these groups expect Marx's texts to provide them not just with a convincing analysis of socio-economic problems, but also with feasible approaches to the solution of those problems. In this, they resemble us, the editors and older authors of this volume: in the 1960s and 1970s, we joined work-groups in which to collectively read and discuss the *Grundrisse, Capital* and the *Results of the Direct Production Process*.

Thus we all have a common teacher, one who gave conceptual expression to the ruthlessness and coldness of the capitalist dynamic like no other. And he has given everyone a great deal. The systems of the great economists are, to a significant extent, built on Marxian foundations, even if few of these economists – such as Joseph A. Schumpeter – have explicitly acknowledged this heritage.[9]

III

But have we seen and understood Marx correctly? Was his critique of political economy really as stringently developed and monolithic as orthodox Marxists have claimed, and as tends to be suggested within the most recent Marx renaissance as well? In reflecting on this issue, we should distinguish between, first, the deficits of the reception history to date and, second, the errors inherent in Marx's overall approach. The latter have been exposed both empirically, by the historical process since Marx's death, and by scholarly criticism.

It is only in recent years that the second *Marx-Engels Gesamtausgabe (MEGA²)* has provided us with an (almost) complete edition of Marx's writings and studies on the critique of political economy.[10] We are now forced to acknowledge that we are dealing not with a self-contained analytic system, but rather with a giant torso of fragments and preliminary studies.[11] At bottom, we always knew that Marx had meant to write a six-volume work whose central topics were to be '1. On Capital. 2. Landed Property. 3. Wage Labour. 4. State. 5. International Trade. 6. World Market',[12] but that he had never got beyond the first book, *Capital*, with only the first of its three volumes published during his lifetime. It simply remains impossible to analyse the competition-driven processes and cycles of the world-economy on a genuinely Marxian basis. Moreover, we have been

---

9. Schumpeter 1942, Part I.

10. Marx 1976–2008. Further volumes are forthcoming, but a first overview of the inner development of Marx's critique of political economy has become possible since the publication of Volume 14.

11. See the preliminary editor's report and the discussion of its implications in Musto 2007.

12. Marx 1975–2004a, Letter to Friedrich Engels, 2 April, 1858; also Marx 1975–2004b, pp. 268–71; and Marx 1975–2004c, p. 261.

forced to recognise that Marx's original manuscripts for *Capital* Volumes II and III differ significantly from the editions of the two volumes studied by us during the 1960s and 1970s, editions from which most of us continue to quote.[13] It would, surely, be an exaggeration to attribute revisionist intentions to the editor and publisher of *Capital* Volumes II and III, Friedrich Engels. But he was not up to the task of editing Marx's papers, which were fragmentary and far from ready for publication. He doubtless did the best that could be done in his day and age. He deciphered the handwriting that only he was able to read, omitted passages in order to smooth over contradictions, closed obvious gaps in the argument by contributions of his own and inserted references to recent events. But readers had to pay a high price for the resulting printed editions. They – and we – were largely prevented from seeing that the late Marx was increasingly plagued by scholarly doubts about the stringency of his conceptual approach and desisted from publishing *Capital* Volumes II and III despite being pressured from all sides.[14] Most of us remained unaware of this, despite Marx's iconisation within central-European social democracy and the later planned economies, a development that ought to have made us wary. To be sure, we already attempted to read and interpret Marx against the grain back then, which is why we seized eagerly on the available manuscripts and fragments – especially the *Grundrisse* and the *Results of the Direct Production Process*. But we tended to think of Marx's work as a sort of theoretical quarry that lent itself excellently to heretical escapes from the swaged maxims of scientific socialism, rather than as the legacy of a precarious private scholar who was plagued by self-doubt and scruples and never got past the first stage of his critique of political economy.

This new state of our knowledge, which we owe to the achievements of the *MEGA*², needs always to be borne in mind when engaging with the limitations, errors and immanent contradictions of Marx's approach to the critique of political economy. We should not, however, allow ourselves to be inhibited by this new perspective on Marx. Today, only a handful of experts are able to engage with Marx's genuine legacy on the basis of the enormous textual torso that is his oeuvre. Only a few contributors to this volume will refer to the new *MEGA*

---

13. This emerges especially clearly from a comparison of *Capital* Volume III as edited and published by Friedrich Engels with the original, which has been available in print under the title 'Hauptmanuskript' ['main manuscript'] since 1992: Marx 1976–2008, 4.2. The editors have provided a comprehensive list of the contentual and formal changes made by Engels: Einführung der Bearbeiter 1992, pp. 381ff., especially pp. 393ff., 407ff.

14. Marx had originally meant to publish what we have come to think of as *Capital* Volumes II and III as a second book. But he kept postponing its publication, because he wanted first to observe the effects of the long economic depression of the 1870s; he also wanted to test the cornerstones of his theory by reference to the ongoing development of economic policy in the USA and tsarist Russia. On the details, see Einführung der Bearbeiter 1992, p. 9ff.

and the mutually-exclusive proposals that can already be found in Marx's own writings, and they will do so only rarely. Thomas Kuczynski's contribution is a laudable exception and demonstrates in an exemplary manner that Marx often contradicted himself even when developing his system's most elementary concepts, or that he considered a range of possible solutions. In general, the Penguin edition of *Capital* and the *Marx-Engels Collected Works* (*MECW*) will serve as the basis for our critical engagement with Marx. Overcoming the empirically and/or theoretically refuted axioms and conceptual systems of the Marxian approach by referring back to the questions and interpretive variants already found in Marx's own work will be the privilege of a later generation.

IV

But let us turn now to the empirical and methodologico-conceptual problems that engagement with the Marxian critique of political economy has raised during the past decades. We urgently require a critical theory that allows us to analyse the development of the capitalist world-system and work out prospects for a comprehensive reordering of society. Such a theory must be historical. It should put us in a position to understand the history of world-capitalism in all its complexities. It should allow us to explain capitalism's uneven development and the interdependencies inherent therein.[15] And it should allow us to indicate the transcontinental possibilities for action open to a new anticapitalist International. At the same time, history should be defined as an open process.

Marxian theory provides important elements for such a reorientation. But it is not sufficient, as it leaves open, or fails to comprehensively address, too many questions. This is already true of the longevity of the capitalist system. Karl Marx thought that he would live to see the transition to a socialist order. For example, he drafted the *Grundrisse* because he expected the 1857–8 economic crisis to mark the beginning of the great transformation. In late 1857, he wrote to Engels: 'I am working like mad all night and every night collating my economic studies so that I at least get the outlines clear before the *déluge*'.[16] The fact that capitalism has proven more resilient than its enemies thought and hoped has often induced Marxists to resort to the most varied intellectual constructs. One need think only of Fritz Sternberg's theory of the 'reprieve', by which he hoped to explain capitalism's recovery from the depression of the 1880s and 1890s, or of the theory of the 'rising surplus', developed by Paul Baran and Paul Sweezy to

---

15. On the difficulties associated with a 'combined' analysis of developments in various parts of the world, see Van der Linden 2007b.

16. Marx 1975–2004d, p. 217.

account for the boom of the 1950s and 1960s.[17] The 'socialist' experiments in the Soviet Union, the People's Republic of China, and elsewhere are also difficult to understand from a Marxian perspective: these social formations were characterised by structural exploitation, but they lacked consolidated ruling classes. In other words, they did not constitute a real alternative to capitalism, and they could, in many cases, be toppled relatively quickly.[18] This is, of course, related to the ineluctable question concerning the working class as revolutionary subject. Why has it, until now, hardly lived up to the hopes of Marx and the Marxists? In the present volume, we want to focus especially on discussing this last question. What is the working class? What might a critique of the political economy of labour look like, critically reviewing the experiences of the past two hundred years while moving beyond the Eurocentrism that continues to dominate Marxism?

To begin with, we need to note that Marx neglected studying the working class in favour of studying capital. As we pointed out above, Marx conceived of *Capital* as the first part of a six-part work; the 'Book on Wage-Labour' was to be another such part, but it was never written. To be sure, there are some rough indications of what Marx would have said in this book.[19] Nevertheless, much remains entirely unclear. The well-known British social historian Edward P. Thompson rightly observed that *Capital* discusses the logic of capital, but not capitalism; it neglects the social and political dimensions of history, the anger and outrage that become apparent in class struggle. This anger and outrage must remain incomprehensible for as long as one considers only the closed system of economic logic. The 'human experience' is neglected, even though it expresses something essential:

> Men and women also return as subjects, within this term – not as autonomous subjects, 'free individuals', but as persons experiencing their determinate productive situations and relationships, as needs and interests, and as antagonisms, and then 'handling' this experience with their consciousness and their culture... in the most complex... ways, and then (often but not always through the ensuing structures of class) acting upon their determinate situation in their turn.[20]

For example, Marx convincingly explains why capital repeatedly attempts 'to extend the working day to its physical maximum', but he leaves it unclear why

---

17. Sternberg 1926; Baran and Sweezy 1966.
18. The extensive debates on this question have been reconstructed in Van der Linden 2007a.
19. Lebowitz 1992.
20. Thompson 1978, p. 164.

'the working man constantly presses in the opposite direction'.[21] Michael A. Lebowitz has pointed out that *Capital* has nothing to say about the way in which ever-new needs are created for workers. Marx does point out, in the *Grundrisse*, that the capitalist attempts to spur the workers on 'to consumption, to give his wares new charms, to inspire them with new needs by constant chatter etc'. He notes that 'the contemporary power of capital' rests on these ever-new needs.[22] But *Capital* is silent on the golden chains binding workers to capitalism.[23]

After all, *Capital* assumes that 'in a given country at a given period, the average amount of the means of subsistence necessary for the worker is a known datum'[24] and should be treated as 'a constant magnitude'.[25] Marx had already noted in the *Grundrisse* that the general study of the changes undergone by proletarian needs belonged in the chapter on wage-labour.[26] Moreover, Marx hardly took note, analytically, of worker-organisations (trade-unions). In *Capital*, historical developments are consistently initiated by the capitalists – to the point that Marx even explains the wage-level in terms of capital's needs. Since the worker is mortal, Marx argues, he must reproduce himself.

> The labour-power withdrawn from the market by wear and tear, and by death, must be continually replaced by, at the very least, an equal amount of fresh labour-power. Hence the sum of means of subsistence necessary for the production of labour-power must include the means necessary for the worker's replacements, i.e. his children, in order that this race of peculiar commodity-owners may perpetuate its presence on the market.[27]

Just like a machine, the worker 'will wear out', which is why he needs the means 'to bring up a certain quota of children'.[28] Michael Lebowitz comments on this as follows:

> Frankly, to propose that the value of labour-power contains provisions for the maintenance of children because capital wants future recruits twenty years hence – rather than because workers have struggled to secure such requirements – is a teleological absurdity! However, it is a logical result of the disappearance of wage-labour-for-itself from *Capital*. Marx himself must bear responsibility for some of the functionalist absurdities of his disciples.[29]

---

21. Marx 1975–2004e, p. 146.
22. Marx 1973, p. 287.
23. Lebowitz 2009, p. 308. We will also be following Lebowitz in the sections that follow.
24. Marx 1976, p. 275.
25. Marx 1976, p. 655.
26. Marx 1973, p. 817.
27. Marx 1976, p. 275.
28. Marx 1975–2004e, p. 129.
29. Lebowitz 2009, p. 311.

These sorts of tacit assumptions are precisely what we should discuss critically.

A second point, closely related to the first, concerns objectivism. When Marx wrote *Capital*, he was politically isolated. To be sure, his plan to write a book on the critique of politics and political economy goes back to the 1840s.[30] But when he began his studies in earnest, during the 1850s, the young European labour-movements had suffered serious setbacks, and Marx had withdrawn from public life. The link between 'scientific socialism' and labour-organisations had been lost. Karl Korsch already stated in 1929:

> The materialist view of history grew out of a revolutionary period prior to 1850 as an integral part of the subjective action of a revolutionary class, which continually criticizes in theory and overthrows in practice the false illusions and transient appearances of all existing social relationships. In the succeeding period, it developed into a purely abstract and contemplative theory dealing with the objective course of social development as determined by external laws.
>
> Marxist economy was originally formulated as a radical critique of bourgeois political economy, a critique which was to have found both theoretical and practical culmination in a real revolution. This original schema was later changed by Marx and altered even more by Engels. Today the apologists as well as the critics of Marxism view Marxist economics as little more than a scientific system in which all economic phenomena of bourgeois society are deduced theoretically from an uncritical, axiomatic concept of "value".[31]

The preface to the first German edition of *Capital* is one expression of this process of scientification. There, Marx compares himself to a physician. He speaks of the 'natural laws of capitalist production', laws that impose themselves 'with iron necessity'.[32] A few pages later, he speaks again and more precisely of his 'standpoint, from which the development of the economic formation of society is viewed as a process of natural history'.[33] In this passage, Marx is fully in the thrall of objectivism. As a scientific socialist, he has, as it were, risen above reality: he studies it and hopes to discover its 'natural laws'. Subjects that resist these laws never feature in this view of history, except as Don Quixotes. This objectivist tendency in Marx's thought, which became dominant after 1850, was

---

30. As a 27 year-old, Marx had signed a contract with the publisher Leske in Darmstadt, agreeing to write a book on this subject. In August 1846, he promised to complete the first volume by the end of November. 'The 2nd volume, of a more historical nature, will be able to follow soon after it', he added overconfidently: Marx 1975–2004f, p. 51. As we know, this never happened, and the revolutionary struggles of 1848–9 delayed the project further.

31. Korsch 1974, p. 9. Translation corrected on the basis of the German text (Korsch 1996a, p. 144).

32. Marx 1976, p. 91.

33. Marx 1976, p. 92.

already criticised by the communist workers of London in 1846. They wrote the following to Marx and Engels:

> You are right to combat the philosophical and sentimental tendency in communism as soon as they are, or become, one-sided and strive to impose themselves exclusively, but you too must avoid becoming one-sided – and you become thus when you reduce the possibility of communism to nothing but the growing distress of the workers and the improvement of machinery etc.... You cannot want to suffocate sentiment – the human heart.[34]

Like Hegel before him, Marx situated himself 'within history only in order to get out of it, they try to have a look at themselves from outside, they believe that they can inspect their own backs'.[35] This sort of objectivism leads either to vanguardism or to passivity. Vanguardism comes about when groups who have discovered the 'natural laws' of society, thereby disposing of absolute 'truth', feel justified in deciding for others.

> If and to the extent that revolutionaries succumb to the fanciful notion that they can rationally dominate history and society, they naturally set themselves up, from that very moment, as the subjects of both. One can then be certain that this is the possible beginning of a totalitarian development.[36]

Passivity results when one rejects all intervention in social struggles, arguing – like the Dutch council-communists – that the working class will liberate itself and that outsiders can only delay and confuse the process of emancipation.[37]

This leads us to a third point. Within the Marxian/Marxist tradition, a certain segment of the global working class is privileged vis-à-vis other segments. The core of this privileged segment is represented by the doubly-free wage-worker, who 'as a free individual can dispose of his labour-power as his own commodity' and who 'has no other commodity for sale'.[38] The privileged status of the doubly-free wage-worker originates in the early nineteenth century, when workers, and in particular highly qualified artisans, began to organise in trade-unions, thereby establishing the 'modern' labour-movement. Within these early organisations, there was a strong need for self-legitimation and distinction. The theorists who sympathised with these workers reinforced this need and attempted to draw a clear dividing-line between 'real' proletarians and other workers. This can be seen very clearly in Karl Marx. In the *Manifesto of the Communist Party*, written

---

34. Kommunistisches Korrespondenzkomitee 1979, p. 252. Na'aman 1979 has systematically engaged with this problem. Lucas 1983 also provides important suggestions.
35. Castoriadis 1984, p. xxi.
36. Castoriadis 1990, p. 203.
37. Pannekoek 2003; Brendel 2008.
38. Marx 1976, p. 272.

with Engels in December 1847 and January 1848, exclusionary thinking can be clearly discerned. As is well known, the *Manifesto* features the statement that the bourgeoisie has engendered the men who will dig its grave: 'the modern working class – the proletarians', 'who live only so long as they find work, and who find work only so long as their labour increases capital'.[39] The proletarians are fundamentally different from other lower classes: 'Of all the classes that stand face to face with the bourgeoisie today, the proletariat alone is a really revolutionary class. The other classes decay and finally disappear in the face of modern industry; the proletariat is its special and essential product'.[40] Small merchants, artisans, peasants – they are all reactionary, 'for they try to roll back the wheel of history'.[41] And the lumpenproletariat, 'that passively rotting mass thrown off by the lowest layers of old society' also has a tendency to become 'a bribed tool of reactionary intrigue'.[42] Marx's need to set the proletariat apart from other lower classes also emerges very clearly in his later writings on the critique of political economy. There, however, he is concerned mainly with the opposition between proletarians and slaves. (We will return to this issue in the final chapter of this volume.) Such a policy of exclusion is misleading. First, 'impure' elements have played an enormously important role even in the history of the European labour-movement – witness the Silesian weavers, who were employed according to the putting-out system, and whose 1844 revolt marked the birth of the German working class, according to Friedrich Engels.[43] The early social-democratic 'labour-parties' are another case in point; they were often dominated by small entrepreneurs (such as August Bebel) and academics. Second, from a global perspective, doubly-free wage-workers have always been a rather insignificant minority within the proletariat.

A fourth weakness of Marxian and Marxist thought lies in their methodological nationalism. Marx and the Marxists have tended to assume, and still tend to assume today, that the nation-state is the logical unit of analysis. In Marx, this is obvious. To him, history revolves around a handful of states (especially large states), whose working classes and labour-movements act in concert or against one another. Most labour-historians have also specialised in the history of a specific country; typically, they remain within this framework even when drawing international comparisons. There now exist countless studies comparing aspects of the labour-relations or labour-movements of two or three countries. There is nothing to be said against this approach, as long as one bears in mind that

---

39. Marx and Engels 1973a, p. 73.
40. Marx and Engels 1973a, p. 77.
41. *Ibid.*
42. *Ibid.*
43. Engels 1975–2004a, p. 11.

the nation-state is a historical product that needs to be explained and contextualised. What makes this difficult is that we tend not to have learned how to do this. We have been taught that the world is made up of national societies that are linked to one another. Wallerstein has rightly pointed out that this is a nineteenth-century assumption: 'it reifies and therefore crystallises social phenomena whose real significance lies not in their solidity but precisely in their fluidity and malleability'.[44]

Methodological nationalists fall victim to two basic intellectual errors. First, they declare the nation-state to be something natural. While they recognise that nation-states only developed during the nineteenth and twentieth centuries, they continue to interpret earlier history as the prehistory of the later nation-state and view processes that play out above or below its boundaries as deviations from the 'pure' model. We are, therefore, dealing with a teleology that we should abandon completely. Within a global perspective, the existence of nation-states remains an essential aspect of the world-system, but it is an aspect that needs to be thoroughly historicised and linked to other, subnational, supranational and transnational aspects. Second, methodological nationalists conflate society with the state and a national territory.[45] They believe that societies are geographically identical with nation-states. The United States have their own society, and so do Mexico, China, and so on. Here too, we obviously need an entirely new approach.

A fifth and final problem is represented by Eurocentrism, which is demonstrably a feature of almost all of Marx's work. There are at least three variants of Eurocentrism. The first variant is simply neglect: attention is only paid to one part of the world, and the author assumes that the history of 'his piece of the world' can be written without considering the rest. This attitude is well-expressed by the popular distinction between 'the West' and 'the Rest', mentioned by Samuel Huntington and others. The second variant is prejudice: the authors do consider global connections, but nevertheless believe that Greater Europe (including North America and Australasia) 'shows the way'. This Eurocentrism is especially evident among modernisation-theorists. Robert Nisbet characterised this approach to development as follows:

> Mankind is likened to a vast procession, with all, or at least a very large number of peoples made into the members of the procession . . . Naturally, Western Europe and its specific, historically acquired pattern of economic, political, moral, and religious values was regarded as being at the head, in the vanguard, of the procession. All other peoples, however rich in their own civilization, such as China and India, were regarded as, so to speak, 'steps' in a procession

---

44. Wallerstein 1986, p. 9.
45. In fact, they often function as opposites, for instance in Germany *circa* 1848, when the concept of 'society' was used to demonstrate opposition to the state.

that would some day bring them too into the fulfilment of development that was the sacred West.[46]

The third variant consists of empirical beliefs. This is the variant that is most difficult to recognise and combat. We are dealing, here, with scientific viewpoints which have seemingly been confirmed time-and-again by research. Empirical Eurocentrists make assertions because they think that all of this is fact. They believe, for instance, that trade-unions are always most effective if they concentrate on some form of collective bargaining. This, they think, has been proven repeatedly. Historians defending such a view would deny emphatically that they harbour any Eurocentric prejudices, and very few of them actually do hold such prejudices. Attacking the first two variants (neglect and prejudice) is relatively straightforward, but the third variant presents a bigger obstacle. As the late Jim Blaut wrote: 'Eurocentrism...is a very complex thing. We can banish all the value meanings of the word, all the prejudices, and we still have Eurocentrism as a set of empirical beliefs'.[47]

In Marx, we encounter all of these forms of Eurocentrism, even though he began, in his late period, to think openly about non-European variants of development. Aside from one important exception (his letter to Vera Zasulich, which features the well-known statement that the 'commune is the fulcrum of social regeneration in Russia'),[48] Marx always adhered to the view that (Western) Europe embodies progress, which spreads across the world from there.[49]

It is our main hypothesis that the five limitations of radical theory discussed here need to be overcome if theory is to provide useful orientation in the years to come. We therefore wish to demonstrate that these five key problems have led to fundamental logjams in key areas of Marx's work. As early as the 1970s, Hans-Georg Backhaus observed 'that a whole range of weighty problems is now characterised by their veritably antinomian character. Some of them were already discussed more than seventy years ago, and attempts to solve them have been

---

46. Nisbet 1971, p. 101.
47. Blaut 1993, p. 9.
48. Marx 1975–2004g, p. 72. On this, see also Max Henninger's contribution to this volume.
49. This is expressed most clearly in Marx's essays on colonial India, where one reads that India's 'social condition has remained unaltered since its remotest antiquity, until the first decennium of the 19th century', and that the peasants lived a 'stagnatory, and vegetative life' (Marx 1975–2004h, p. 128). Further considerations on this can be found in Blaut 1999. August Nimtz (2002) has attempted to deny Marxian Eurocentrism by pointing out that Marx thought in global terms, but Eurocentrism and cosmopolitanism go together quite well. It is doutbful whether the letter to Zasulich can be interpreted as venturing toward a more comprehensive, multilinear theory of development, as argued by Kevin Anderson (2010).

made time and again, but to no avail'.[50] Even today, 145 years after the publication of the first volume of *Capital*, it remains the case that Marxist authors can 'only read Marx in contradictory ways'.[51] It is a matter of developing an alternative that sublates the achievements of Marxian thought into a new theoretical perspective.

All the core concepts of traditional labour-history are primarily based on experiences in the north-Atlantic region, and should, therefore, be critically reconsidered. This applies to the concept of 'labour' itself. In the most important Western languages (English, French, Spanish, Italian, and so on), a distinction is often made between 'labour' and 'work', in which 'labour' refers to toil and effort (as in 'women's labour'), while 'work' refers more to creative processes. This binary meaning – to which a philosopher like Hannah Arendt attached far-reaching analytical consequences – simply does not exist in many other languages, and sometimes there is even no single word for 'labour' or 'work', because these concepts abstract from the specific characteristics of separate labour-processes.[52] We ought, therefore, to investigate carefully to what extent the concepts 'labour' and 'work' are transculturally usable, or at the very least, we should define their content much more precisely than we are used to doing. Where does 'labour' begin, and where does it finish? How exactly do we draw the boundary between 'labour' and 'work', or is that boundary less obvious than is often assumed?

The concept of the 'working class' also merits a critical survey. It looks like this term was invented in the nineteenth century to identify a group of so-called 'respectable' workers, in contrast to slaves and other unfree labourers, the self-employed (the 'petty bourgeoisie') and poor outcasts, the lumpenproletariat. For many reasons, which lack of space does not permit us to discuss, this interpretation is simply not appropriate in the global South. The social groups which, in the eyes of old and new labour-history, are quantitatively not significant – exceptions which prove the rule – are the rule in large parts of Asia, Africa and Latin America. We will have to devise a new conceptualisation, oriented less to the exclusion than to the inclusion of various dependent or marginalised groups of workers. We have to recognise that the 'real' wage-workers who were the centre of attention for Marx, workers who, as free individuals, can dispose of their own labour-power as their commodity and have no other commodity for sale, are only one kind of way in which capitalism transforms labour-power into a commodity.[53] There are numerous other forms that deserve as much

---

50. Backhaus 1978, p. 27.
51. Backhaus 1978, p. 29.
52. Arendt 1958.
53. Marx 1976, p. 272.

attention, such as slaves, contract-workers, indentured servants, sharecroppers, self-employed workers, and so on.

Yet if we assume that the Marxian 'doubly-free' wage-workers are no longer the strategically privileged part of the global working class, and that slaves, contract-workers, (pseudo-)self-employed workers and others within capitalism are equipped with 'equal rights' theoretically, then this has far-reaching consequences for the development of theory. It probably means not only that the Marxian theory of value is obsolete, but also that the theory of revolution needs to be thoroughly reconceptualised.

V

In addressing these five fundamental problem-areas, we realised that in addition to being a multilayered and inherently contradictory textual torso, Marx's work is only of limited use – and perhaps of no use at all – to efforts to give conceptual expression to the overwhelming complexity of global labour-relations, because of the determinist narrowness of its conceptual approach. But what did our friends and colleagues think of this? Were we mistaken, or did they share our doubts? Did they perhaps have suggestions about how the deficits of the labour-theory of value and the associated limitations of the Marxian concept of labour, with its fixation on doubly-free wage-labour, could be developed further, in such a way as to make them stand up to the empirical findings of labour-history? And if they felt that such remedial work is impossible, what alternative would they propose? Should we respectfully place Marx's labour-theory of value in the pantheon of great social models and then get back to business as usual, striving to develop a new theory of exploitation and emancipation, one that takes account of earlier critiques of the Marxian system but focuses mainly on addressing contemporary relations of exploitation?

In early 2007, we decided to present these questions to a group of intellectuals situated on the heterodox margins of Marxism, intellectuals who had not severed the link between their historical, socio-scientific and economic analyses and emancipatory practice. Aside from members of our own generation who have been shaped by the 'red decades' of the 1960s and 1970s, we were thinking of those who spearheaded radical theoretical approaches during the 1950s and early 1960s. We also had in mind the remarkably active group of 'younger persons' who have either joined the heterodox camp or are searching for approaches of their own. This heterodox camp is extraordinarily multifaceted. It consists, first, of exponents of the feminist movement who have criticised the lack of attention paid to reproductive work, going on to dismantle the orthodox concept of labour by analysing the 'housewifisation' of contemporary labour-relations and presenting new models of subsistence and reproductive economics (Maria Mies and Silvia Federici). Second, it consists of the French group *Socialisme ou Barbarie*, which was born from the critique of Trotskyism and should probably be considered the first laboratory of Marxist heterodoxy to emerge after the Second World-War. Its exponents, Cornelius Castoriadis in particular, formulated a stimulating critique of Marx's labour-theory of value[54] and exercised a decisive influence on workerism during the latter's gestational phase in the early 1960s.[55] In the present volume, Jean-Louis Prat presents a concise summary of Castoriadis's critique of Marx. Related to these two approaches is a third current that also struck us as significant: associated with the German journal *Autonomie – Materialien gegen die Fabrikgesellschaft*, its exponents have worked to develop a social-revolutionary concept of emancipation whose cornerstones are the right to subsistence and the antagonistic subjectivity of the exploited (Ahlrich Meyer and Detlef Hartmann). Fourth, there is the archipelago of Italian and North American workerism, whose exponents have moved in separate directions since the 1970s. The 'Padua school' has concentrated on the old and new phenomena of migrant-labour (Ferruccio Gambino). Sergio Bologna and his Milanese associates have worked to analyse self-employed labour, and Antonio Negri and his comrades have devoted themselves to engaging with the new forms of 'immaterial', cognitive labour-relations. But workerism has also given rise to significant new efforts to extend the temporal and geographical scope of labour-history, with Peter Linebaugh, Marcus Rediker and Peter Way doing most to bring about a consequential paradigm-shift. Finally, there are the economists of the earlier workerist spectrum, such as Riccardo Bellofiore and C. George Caffentzis. They have been striving for new insights into the histories of theory and money, as well as into the effects of those histories on the working class.

We did not, however, want to limit ourselves to inviting exponents of heterodoxy active at the transatlantic core of the world-system. We wanted their views to be supplemented and corrected by an authentic perspective on the history of the working class and labour-organisations of the periphery. We chose to focus on India, and were able to convince Subir Sinha to participate in our project. It seemed equally important to us to include the heterodox currents that developed within the nooks of Eastern Europe's planned economies, as these currents have produced significant contributions to the critical development of the Marxian approach (Thomas Kuczynski). It is a testament to the vitality of

---

54. Castoriadis's most important writings are available in English: Castoradis 1984, 1987, 1988–93, 1997a, 1997b, 2007, 2010, 2011.

55. The most important 'transmitter' was Danilo Montaldi. See Sergio Bologna's contribution to this volume and also the remarks by Romano Alquati in Trotta and Milana 2008, pp. 95–8, 631–5.

all these tendencies that they have been able to bring about a dialogue with the younger generation. For some years now, this younger generation has been producing remarkable contributions to the critical assessment, development and/or superation of the Marxian approach. In the present volume, it is represented by Niklas Frykman, Sebastian Gerhardt, Max Henninger, Devi Sacchetto, Massimiliano Tomba and Steve Wright.

VI

The contributions to this volume revolve around two closely-related key themes: empirical labour-history and its theoretical conceptualisation. They do not focus equally on both sides of the interplay between labour-history and the concept of labour; instead, they either confront empirico-historical findings with the problems of conceptual and methodological generalisation, or they proceed in the opposite direction. In accordance with these different emphases, we have organised the contributions in two sections.

In Part I, historical perspectives are dominant. Peter Linebaugh, Marcus Rediker, Niklas Frykman and Peter Way present their findings on the global multiverse of proletarians during the pre-industrial eighteenth century. Ferruccio Gambino's and Devi Sacchetto's broadly-framed essay on the development of migrant-labour establishes a link between the labour-history of capitalism's entire pre-industrial period and the labour-relations of the nineteenth and twentieth centuries. A third group of contributors – Sergio Bologna, Subir Sinha and Detlef Hartmann – discuss the labour-relations of the present, albeit from different perspectives. They refer to their own experiences in order to discuss the road that has led from mass-labour to self-employed labour (Bologna), address the tensions between the Indian working class and Indian labour-organisations (Sinha) and reflect on how contemporary management-strategies target the subjectivity of the exploited, assessing the antagonistic prospects that result from this (Hartmann). The section is concluded by the contributions of Maria Mies and Silvia Federici, which address contemporary issues of reproductive work by reference to care-work (Federici) and to a subsistence-economy that superates the 'housewifisation' of labour-relations (Mies).

We have arranged the contributions to Part II based on the extent to which they refer critically to Marx's labour-theory of value. The first group contains analyses that reject the conception of class implicit in Marx's labour-theory of value. They do so by invoking a different logic of social struggles (Jean-Louis Prat), discussing the history of Marx's own time (Ahlrich Meyer) or addressing today's global relations of work and poverty (Max Henninger). These contributions call – explicitly or implicitly – for the conceptualisation of an emancipatory theory that is situated beyond Marx. The second bloc is constituted by three essays that also point to serious deficits within Marxian theory, proposing either an immanent methodological correction (Thomas Kuczynski), the theory's conceptual extension (Sebastian Gerhardt), or the theorisation of the global coexistence of several interlinked régimes of exploitation (Massimiliano Tomba and Riccardo Bellofiore). In the third group, Steve Wright and C. George Caffentzis introduce the monetary aspects of the exploitation of living labour-power into the discussion: Wright engages with earlier debates on a workerist monetary theory and Caffentzis discusses the consequences of the 1971 dropping of the gold-standard for Marxian theory. The last group consists of one author who retains the Marxian approach: Carlo Vercellone limits Marx's labour-theory of value to the processes by which labour is rendered increasingly abstract: processes that result from the substance of value. From this, Vercellone derives a genealogy of labour-relations that ranges from industrial labour to mass-labour and on to the 'cognitive labour' of our own day. Vercellone has written his contribution in close consultation with Antonio Negri, the originator of this conceptual framework, and it can, therefore, be read as a synthesis and synopsis of the internal intellectual development of this approach.

Acknowledgment

This volume could not have been published without the unrelenting support and good advice of Max Henninger, who – with only two exceptions – also provided the English translations of all French, German and Italian chapters.

Amsterdam and Bremen, December 2011
Marcel van der Linden and Karl Heinz Roth

Part One

The Many-Headed Hydra: Reflections on History from Below
Peter Linebaugh and Marcus Rediker

Who built the seven gates of Thebes?
The books are filled with the names of kings.
Was it kings who hauled the craggy blocks of
    stone?
And Babylon, so many times destroyed,
Who built the city up each time? In which of
    Lima's houses,
The city glittering with gold, lived those who built
    it?
In the evening when the Chinese wall was finished
Where did the masons go? Imperial Rome
Is full of arcs of triumph. Who reared then up?
    Over whom
Did the Caesars triumph? Byzantium lives in song.
Were all her dwellings palaces? And even in
    Atlantis of the legend
The night the sea rushed in,
The drowning men still bellowed for their slaves.

Young Alexander conquered India.
He alone?

Caesar beat the Gauls,
Was there not even a cook in his army?
Philip of Spain wept as his fleet
Was sunk and destroyed. Were there no other
    tears?
Frederick the Great triumphed in the Seven Years
    War. Who
Triumphed with him?

> Each page a victory,
> At whose expense the victory ball?
> Every ten years a great man,
> Who paid the piper?
>
> So many particulars.
> So many questions.
>
> Bertolt Brecht, 'A Worker Reads History'

The first third of the poem is about builders, the middle-third is about destroyers, and the last third, as the worker looks up from his reading, invites us to reflect upon the classes of people and the writing of history. We wish to use Brecht's poem to reflect on these themes and others as they appeared in our book *The Many-Headed Hydra: Sailors, Slaves, Commoners, and the Hidden History of the Revolutionary Atlantic*.[1] A central concern of the book is a central theme of this volume: what is the working class?

Brecht's geographical range is planetary, and his chronological depth is four millennia; in contrast, we confine ourselves in *The Many-Headed Hydra* to the north Atlantic and two centuries. Modestly, we salute Brecht, the champion of 'history from below', who wrote its anthem. We, as historians of below, come after those who came after him. Three traditions of history from below have influenced us: the Black-radical tradition, the English tradition, and the American tradition.

Brecht put Africa first. He placed Thebes, the Ethiopian capital of the Egyptian Middle-Kingdom, at the origin of civilisation. Writing the poem in 1935, as Italian Fascists bombed Ethiopia, Brecht recalled to building-workers their universality, a proletarian internationalism. In the pan-African milieu of the 1930s, which encompassed the Harlem Renaissance, the *négritude* movement, and the International African Service Bureau, Thebes was well-known. The African-American nationalists of the Garvey movement observed that the Nilotic empires began in Thebes, the original cradle of mankind's arts and sciences, deep like the rivers. 'A race of men now rejected from society for their *sable skin and frizzled hair*, founded on the study of the laws of nature, those civil and religious systems which still govern the universe', wrote Volney, the French revolutionary *savant*, referring specifically to astronomy, commerce, geometry, and agriculture.[2]

African-American historians from below have concentrated on the study of slavery and the struggle against it, when others did not. W.E.B. DuBois taught us to study the colour-line and the insidious ideology of white-supremacy.

---

1. Linebaugh and Rediker 2000.
2. Volney 1991.

He published *Black Reconstruction in America* in the same year as Brecht's poem appeared. 'The emancipation of man is the emancipation of labor and the emancipation of labor is the freeing of that basic majority of workers who are yellow, brown and black'. C.L.R. James's *The Black Jacobins: Toussaint L'Ouverture and the San Domingo Revolution*, published soon after 'A Worker Reads History' (in 1938), explained the first victorious workers' revolution in modern history – and that what the plantation-slaves began, the European urban masses completed. James taught us his theoretical axiom, 'The more capital organizes itself, the more it is forced to organize for itself the working class'. George Rawick introduced to us the notion of self-activity. After Rawick and the 20 volumes of the *Slave Narratives*, it was impossible not to think of the slave as a historical actor. Walter Rodney always held forth to us the supreme example of the scholar, theorist, and activist. He urged a 'radical break with the international capitalist system'.[3] In sum, the African-American tradition of history from below necessarily adopted an Atlantic or internationalist perspective; and it was necessarily concerned with slavery and its abolition. The 'Black Atlantic' invented by DuBois, James, George Padmore, Eric Williams, and the Fifth Pan-African Congress between 1935 and 1945 was also red.

The strength of English history from below was a notion of the working class that was theoretically deep and historically specific, such as E.P. Thompson provided in *The Making of the English Working Class*. The specificity brought a methodological corollary – archival discovery – and a rule of interpretation – documents 'must be held up to a satanic light and read backwards'.[4] Its emphasis on workers as agents of history renewed the 'voluntarist' side of Marxism, as against the doctrine of economic determinism. A second strength of the Anglo-tradition of history from below was its emphasis on alternative ideas to those of the dominating class. Of the radical ideas of the English Revolution described by Christopher Hill in *The World Turned Upside Down*,[5] the one that has signified most to us has been antinomianism. Raphael Samuel introduced a volume of papers from the 1979 People's History and Socialist Theory conference at Ruskin College, Oxford, with Brecht's poem 'A Worker Reads History'.[6] To Samuel, the poem 'interestingly explains why Marxism and people's history – for all the theoretical differences between them – have so often had occasion to converge'. Indeed, the historians of below in England – the country of Marx's long exile, the country which provided capitalism with its classic form – treat the ideas of Marx with special confidence.

---

3. Rodney 1972.
4. Thompson 1963, p. 58.
5. Hill 1972.
6. Samuel 1981, p. xxxiii.

In America, Brecht's poem had the declaratory effect of a manifesto. Jesse Lemisch abridged the poem in 1968 to begin his essay, 'The American Revolution as Seen from the Bottom Up'.[7] Herbert Gutman and his colleagues at the American Social History Project used the poem to introduce and give title to their two-volume history of workers in America, *Who Built America?* This history from below challenged the Cold War's history of great men, championed the inclusion of diverse historical subjects, and cracked the conservative consensus that was dominant in American historical writing. Staughton Lynd relied on 'oral history from the bottom up' to explain that the 'history of poor and working people is a history of dreams, of reaping, of unexpected divinity, and of memorable death'.[8]

These traditions have tended, as Paul Gilroy notes, to be *völkisch* in their approaches, whether Afrocentric, Anglocentric, or 'American-exceptionalist'. They have been found wanting, first, for parochialism or insularity, often nationalist in nature, and second, for disregarding the wageless. They tend in some incarnations to be 'histories from the lower middle up', concentrating on artisans and people of small property. Questions were raised by 'herstory', or women's history; questions were raised by liberation-theology, in its Hispanic inflection. 'So many particulars, so many questions' remain.

Some of these questions, we posed in our earlier work, *Between the Devil and the Deep Blue Sea*[9] and *The London Hanged*,[10] whose similarity is expressed by the proverb, 'The sea and the gallows refuse none'. The former book analysed the class-struggle of the sailors and port-workers, providing an alternative to the artisanal labour-history of the nineteenth century and moving the history of the proletariat back to an earlier time of capitalism. The latter book expatiated on the criminalisation that was a necessary complement to the waging of labour. Both books concerned the uprooted; they both concerned fugitives; they expressed movement by people on a move. We crossed the Atlantic in opposite directions. Marcus had been in Philadelphia, where social history meant not history from below but social science, so he crossed eastwards to refresh himself at the fountain of English radical historians. Peter, satiated by a long draught from the cup of Anglotude, crossed westwards searching for groundings in the Black revolution. We met, and shared a determination to study and learn from, C.L.R. James. We discovered that our passage was part of a longstanding historical pattern from America to England and back, via the Caribbean.

---

7. Bernstein 1970, p. 3.
8. Remarks, Annual Dinner of the Friends of the Kent State University Libraries, 15 April 1998.
9. Rediker 1987.
10. Linebaugh 1991.

The book had its beginning in 1981, when Margaret Thatcher and Ronald Reagan were red in tooth and claw, and the Brixton riot erupted. We organised a conference through the Philadelphia Center for Early American Studies at the University of Pennsylvania entitled 'The World Turned Upside Down: Working People in England and America, 1660–1790'. Here, we began our effort to bring together the Black-radical and Anglo-American histories from below, as if to explore Brecht's worker's astonishment that

> ... even in Atlantis of the legend
> The night the sea rushed in,
> The drowning men still bellowed for their slaves.

What was this Atlantis? We looked to William Blake, who had used the legend of Atlantis in his revolutionary prophecy, *America*, published in 1793. Inspired by the Haitian Revolution, Blake rejected the 'new Atlantis' of Francis Bacon, in whose ceremonial, patriarchal laboratory the 'meaner sort' played no role, the women kissed the hem of the garments of the men, the 'little foul ugly Æthiop' was banished, and the exploration of nature was described in the imagery of conquest and rape. Blake blended geography, history, morality, sexual generation, and mythology, pointing us toward something not yet described:

> On those vast shady hills between America & Albion's shore,
> Now barr'd out by the Atlantic sea, call'd atlantean hills,
> Because from their bright summits you may pass to the Golden world,
> An ancient palace, archetype of mighty Emperies,
> Rears its immortal pinnacles, built in the forest of God.

His belief that the Earth once had a different arrangement of continents and oceans became the basis for imagining the anti-imperialist peaceable kingdom where generosity was no longer fouled by science as a means of conquest, nor by the 'laws' of political economy, nor by racial doctrines of superiority. We sought to describe the relationships among the divided, and to avoid Afrocentrism, Eurocentrism, and American exceptionalism as we did so. We thought to draw upon the several traditions of history from below, each of which, we felt, was impoverished – and to some extent falsified – without the other. To tell the tale of the slaves, we grew pensive, like Brecht's worker, and searched afar – to a time before the theory of race, before the 'making of the working class' – we went way back to Hercules and the many-headed hydra.

Hercules was the mythical hero of the ancients, and of mixed birth – his father Zeus, was a god, his mother Alcmene, was mortal. As a suckling, he was so violent that his nurse, the goddess Hera, flung him from her breast, which spurted milk to form the Milky Way. Angered, Hera sent serpents to his cradle, but the infant strangled them. Later, Hera made Hercules insane; he killed his children. To atone, he undertook twelve labours. One of these was the destruction of the venomous, many-headed hydra of Lerna. This creature, born of Typhon (a tempest or hurricane) and Echidne (half-woman and half-snake), was one in a brood of monsters – Cerberus the three-headed dog, Chæmera the lion-headed goat with a snake's tale, Geryon the triple-bodied giant, and Sphinx the woman with a lion's body. Confronted with the many-headed hydra, Hercules found that as soon as he cut off one head, two grew in its place. With the help of his nephew Iolaus, he used a flaming branch to cauterise the stump of the beast's neck, and so they killed the hydra. Hercules dipped his arrows in the gall of the slain beast, providing him with projectiles of such fatal power that he was able to complete his remaining labours. He freed Prometheus. He performed feats of strength, voyaging with the Argonauts, wrestling down Antæus, and bearing up the heavens for Atlas. He rent asunder the African and European continents, with one hand offering seafaring-enterprise to the Phoenicians, and with the other protecting the Mediterranean from the monsters of the ocean. The *ne plus ultra* of the world were the Pillars of Hercules, the Rock of Gibraltar in Europe and Mount Hacho in Ceuta, Africa.

Hercules and the hydra are a variant of a near-universal combat-myth, in which a demi-god fights a dreadful, monstrous enemy, defeats chaos and creates *nomos*, or social order. Diodorus of Sicily wrote in the first century BC that the cult of Hercules appeared universal. He was worshiped on the eastern banks of the Indus as a founder of cities and bringer of agriculture. Herodotus wrote that Hercules was by birth an Egyptian, that he was the oldest man known on Earth. Charles DuPuis argued in his 1795 *Origine de tous les cultes, ou la religion universelle* that all religions were one and that Hercules proved the point: 'wherever the blessings of the Sun were experienced, there the worship of Hercules is found established...' We are inclined to agree with Volney that his origin, like mankind's, lies in east Africa. The twelve labours of Hercules correspond to the signs of the zodiac: thus knowledge of the labours of Hercules informed agriculturalists and navigators. According to the magi of seventeenth-century capitalism, the Hercules-myth undergirded the planet: the Flemish instrument-maker, Mercator, made an image of Atlas holding up the world the frontispiece of his book of maps, and he was among the first who named the ocean 'Atlantic' on the basis of the Hercules cycle.

But what did the heads mean? How would we interpret them? Did they express the evolving division of labour? The producers of different commodities? The practitioners of different skills? The workers of different regions? Or, did they stand for different beings, of gender, of race, of ethnicity, of geography, and of type, of species? The first interpretation suggested an economistic hydra, roughly parallel to the social division of labour between various work-ers. The second interpretation led to a biological hydra, a taxonomy of diverse organisms. The former had undertones of class, the latter of race. The ambiguity would prove useful.

The hydra-heads did not often share 'class'-consciousness, certainly not of the class 'for itself'. And if they were not class-conscious, neither were they race-conscious, gender-conscious, or nation-conscious to any advanced degree. The heads of the hydra were, at times, incoherent, they bit each other, yet they did not always yap at one another with red-eyed rage. Often they talked, as people will. These were the wild men and rimers of Ireland with their glib and mantle pluck-ing the forbidden harp-string; the obstinate craftsman of London with tankard and tool singing a ballad under Tyburn tree; the skilled hunting, surfing teen-ager shivering with unknown companions on the middle-passage preserving and creating deep, percussive rhythms of home; the lined countenance of the wise-woman and healer entering trances with her keening and lullaby; the chained men and boys spirited away with the glinty-eyed former commoner singing a Jubilee-hymn; the Jamaican maroon in the bush and the cockpits studying the Englishman and signalling by conch. Slowly, what began as a metaphor became a concept: the hydra allowed us to consider the histories of such people, each in relation to the other, and to discover surprising connections. The second labour of Hercules became a way of exploring the class-struggle.

Our book is organised around two related themes: 1) the development of capi-talism in the countries of the Anglophone north Atlantic, and 2) an historical series of challenges to it commencing with the English Revolution and ending with the Age of Revolution, 1760–1835. Its primary subjects are the workers of northwest Europe, West Africa, the Caribbean, and North America. Each chapter of our book concerns the cooperation of African, African-American, or Carib-bean workers with those from Ireland, England, and northwest Europe. We hope that this is one of its main contributions. In addition to the many-headed hydra, we have discovered other contemporary designations of the multitudes to be pregnant with meaning – 'hewers of wood and drawers of water', 'outcasts of the nations of the Earth', 'the motley crew', and 'the human race' – each of which suggests analytical possibilities. We now summarise *The Many-Headed Hydra* in order to reflect on the history of the proletariat as a class.

Section I consists of two chapters covering the years 1600–40. They explore the simultaneous development of capitalism in England and colonisation in America. The motley, many-headed proletariat performed the labour.

In Chapter One, 'The Wreck of the *Sea Venture*', we argue that the central issue both in Shakespeare's play, *The Tempest*, and in this era of history, was expro-priation, or the separation of people from the land, their means of subsistence.

This is the starting-point of all capitalist development. Shakespeare's protagonist, Prospero, confronts and overcomes the commonism of Caliban, his 'savage
and deformed slave' and likewise defeats the multi-racial conspiracy of Caliban, Stephano the sailor, and Trinculo the jester. Shakespeare presents them
comically for the rulers to laugh and to scorn. Exploitation and slavery follow.
The geographical locus of the chapter is as multiple as that of the original play,
encompassing Europe, Africa, and the Americas, Blake's 'atlantean hills'.

Chapter Two, 'Hewers of Wood and Drawers of Water', shows how the expropriated were set to work to drain the marshes and the fenlands, clear-cut the
forests, dig the canals, deepen the riverways, and build the roads. Described by a
Biblical phrase with connotations of degradation and slavery, this mass of wood-
land- and hydraulic-workers were expropriated from the ecological commons of
Africa, Ireland, England, Barbados, and Virginia, and subsequently exploited in
the transformation of these economies. 'Since civilisation began, there has always
been a working-class', wrote Mark Starr of the South Wales Miners' Federation in
A Worker Reads History,[11] in a book that might have inspired Brecht. The phrase,
'hewers of wood and drawers of water', acquired ethnic connotations, as suggested by Osborne Ward in his book *The Ancient Lowly* in 1888: 'They were not
only slaves but they formed, as it were, another race. They were the plebeians,
the proletariat; "hewers of wood and drawers of water"'.[12] Subjected to terror and
required to work in large numbers, they carved the plantations from the American wilderness, expanded the arable farmlands of England and Ireland, and built
the docks, ships, and warehouses of the port-cities. Their labours in wood and
water, in workplace- and family-settings, made life possible. The hewers of wood
and drawers of water built the infrastructure of Atlantic capitalism.

Section II covers the years 1640–80. During these years, English capitalism
experienced a series of challenges – originally in the metropolis, then in the
colonies – that collectively constituted its first major crisis, beginning with the
English Revolution. Overcoming the crisis made possible a breakthrough for
capitalist development. Mancipation as enslavement and mancipation as selling
labour, became the rule, resulting in the plantation and ship at the material level
and the labour-theory of value at the ideological level. These were extra-insular
developments: in England, a pause ensued in the development of industrialism
and of development of political freedom, alike.

Thomas Edwards studied the popular heresies in revolutionary England in
1646 and called for war against the hydra. Edwards was especially concerned
about antinomians, religious radicals who believed that they were no longer

---

11. Starr 1917.
12. Ward 1888.

subject to the law and were free, divinely-inspired, and self-organised to raise up an egalitarian Jerusalem against the wicked Babylon. In Chapter Three, we study one antinomian, 'A Blackymore Maid named Francis'. She was an African, or African-American, servant and member of a radical religious congregation in Bristol. Here was the stone the builders rejected: could it be the cornerstone? Although few traces of her life remain, they nonetheless reveal the power of female prophecy in the English Revolution to raise an egalitarian conception of humanity based on the Biblical precept, 'God is no respecter of persons'. They also allow us to study the historic defeat of women, who suffered not only the loss of political and moral standing as religious radicalism was suppressed, but also the violent terror of widespread burning-alive in simultaneous prosecutions for witchcraft. Once women were defeated and forced by violence back into the male-controlled realm of reproduction, the rulers of the day began to use the term 'proletariat' to describe the class of workers who had nothing to contribute to the state but their children. The debate about the nature of a human being turned on the clash between the elevated view that all people were worthy of respect and the degrading belief that masses of people were beneath respect.

Chapter Four, 'The Divarication of the Putney Debates', begins at the peak of the antinomian challenge in 1647. Here, revolutionary soldiers defended the commons by name, attacked expropriation, denounced slavery, and promoted jubilee. Thus they challenged the fundaments of capitalism in England and abroad. Yet Cromwell defeated the Levellers, Diggers, and Ranters in England, opening the way to Ireland, to Jamaica, and to West Africa, where transoceanic slaving becomes the middle-passage between expropriation and exploitation. The defeated radicals were dispersed to American plantations, the setting of continued opposition to slavery. But the defeat of the antinomians a second time, in Barbados and Virginia, consolidated the breakthrough for English Atlantic capitalism, securing the plantation as a foundation of the new economic order and ensuring that racism would be an essential element of it. Although much of the action in Section II takes place in England, it is demonstrated that the crisis had Atlantic origins and consequences, as its resolution closed the era of the English Revolution and ushered in years of accumulated exploitation, terror, slavery, conquest: in short, accumulation of capital.

Section III consists of two chapters, and covers the years between the two revolutionary eras, 1680–1760. The challenges to capitalism in this era came from the ships, ports, and plantations of the Caribbean and American colonies. Money became a sensitive political tool in creating divisions within the 'labour-market'. This was the era about which DuBois concluded, 'The most magnificent drama in the last thousand years of human history is the transportation of ten million human beings out of the dark beauty of their mother continent into the new-found Eldorado of the West...It was a tragedy that beggared the Greek'. Transoceanic slaving became the middle-passage both among continents and between expropriation and exploitation, upon which were built the imperial structures of economic concupiscence.

As the plantation-economies of the New World evolved in relation to continuing expropriations and expansion of agriculture and manufacturing in the Old, rulers understood immediately the importance of ships and sailors. Chapter Five, 'Hydrarchy: Sailors, Pirates, and the Maritime State', explores the organisation of the seafaring state and the self-organisation of sailors. As the British navy and the merchant-shipping industry expanded, sailors were forced to cooperate in ways that anticipated the factory. This cooperation quickly turned to opposition, as sailors and pirates rejected the practices of the maritime state and organised themselves on different principles, combining the experience of Native-American communism, the English Revolution, and slave-resistance in the West Indies, to build among the 'outcasts of the Earth' an autonomous, democratic, multi-racial social order at sea. The ruling class recognised the subversive power of this alternative way of life and responded with extermination, hanging pirates in the hundreds, thus removing an obstacle to the African slave-trade.

The western Atlantic remained the setting for a new challenge to the development of transatlantic capitalism, as seen in Chapter Six, 'The Outcasts of the Nations of the Earth', about the New York Conspiracy of 1741. As a culmination of a cycle of rebellion that raged through the slave-societies of the Americas in the 1730s, African, Irish, Caribbean, and Hispanic maritime workers organised an insurrectionary plot to burn the imperial garrison Fort George to the ground, seize one of the Atlantic's leading port-cities, abolish slavery, and declare a new kind of 'motley government'. The circulation of subversive experience – from the Gold Coast of Africa, the famine-ravaged land of Ireland, the Spanish military outpost of Havana, and the Blue Mountains of Jamaica to the waterfront of New York – made the rising possible, as did the antinomian messages of the Great Awakening. The outcasts developed the idea and practice of the urban insurrection, suggesting that the city, like the ship, could be captured and made autonomous, thus pointing toward revolution. The authorities of New York responded to this possibility with characteristic hangings, burnings, and banishments as they attacked the multi-racial taverns, restructured the slave-trade, and promoted white-supremacy.

Section IV consists of three chapters covering the years 1760–1835, the age of the American, French, and Haitian revolutions. The challenges of this period moved from west to east, as the ideas and practices of the workers of the Americas migrated to the European metropolis, with the effect of turning the world upside-down. The pause in development is concluded by hinges such as Equiano and Cugoano, who swing the door of history wide open.

The section begins with Chapter Seven, 'A Motley Crew in the American Revolution', which shows how sailors and slaves launched a new cycle of rebellion, created a new crisis, and inaugurated another era of revolution in the Atlantic. Tacky's Rebellion in Jamaica in 1760 triggered a series of revolts throughout the hemisphere. Hydrarchy and urban insurrection came together as the motley crew, denounced as 'monstrous hydras', animated multi-racial, anti-government mobs in the port-cities; they burned vessels, protested against slavery, and intimidated royal officials, thereby creating a crisis of authority, destabilising society, and propelling a movement towards revolution. The mass-actions of the motley crew also created breakthroughs in revolutionary thought – the 'rights of mankind', the strike, the 'higher-law' doctrine – that would help to abolish impressment and plantation-slavery. Against the revolt from below, the American counter-revolution advanced quickly, expressing itself in the political science of the Founding Fathers, who used notions of race, nation, and citizenship to discipline, divide, and exclude the motley crew who had contributed so much to the revolutionary cause in the first place.

Many of the slaves who were denied freedom within the American Revolution made their way into the British Army, some of them into the regiment of the Irish Colonel Edward Marcus Despard. In Chapter Eight, 'The Conspiracy of Edward and Catherine Despard', we show how the struggles of the motley crew against slavery in America returned to England, intensifying a crisis in London in the 1790s. Working in America as a military officer and a colonial superintendent, Despard defended his poor African-American soldiers against a wealthy oligarchy in British Honduras, and, indeed, redistributed land to them in a jubilee, for which he was removed from office. Returning to London, he brought with him his African-American wife Catherine, experiences of cooperation with the Mayan and Zambo-Miskito Indians, and opposition to slavery. The Despards joined the struggle of the United Irish. In London they organised an insurrectionary coup in 1802, the objective of which was to capture the city, seize the Bank of England, take Parliament, and support the creation of independent republics in Britain and Ireland. The plot was foiled. Edward Despard and six others were hanged in 1803. He declared to the assembled crowd that he had been 'a friend to the poor and the oppressed'.

By the early nineteenth century, the Atlantic proletariat had its own theorists, one of whom is discussed in Chapter Nine, 'Robert Wedderburn and Atlantic Jubilee'. Wedderburn was born to a Scottish plantation-owner and a slave-woman in Jamaica in 1762. He became a sailor, a prisoner, a writer, and a revolutionary Spencean, connecting different kinds and moments of proletarian resistance on both sides of the Atlantic – those of Jamaican maroons, Gordon rioters, Black Baptists, naval (Nore) mutineers, and machine-breakers. Wedderburn, following Thomas Spence and an African-American Biblical tradition, preached jubilee, which promised freedom to slaves and servants, restitution of land to those who had lost it, the cancellation of debt, and a year of rest for the land and the worker. He believed that jubilee, when enacted through slave-revolt and urban insurrection, could be revolutionary on an Atlantic scale, and he creatively designed a proletarian intellectual tradition to prove the point. He synthesised antinomian Christianity, Painite republicanism, and abolitionism as he constructed a common history of the communist Christians in antiquity, the Levellers in the English Revolution, the slaves in the Haitian Revolution, and a multi-ethnic insurrectionary working class in England as it underwent industrialisation. His life and work illuminate the moment in which some workers flooded into the factory as others, after abolition and jubilee, fled the plantations. Wedderburn, an organic intellectual of the Atlantic proletariat, was a strategically-central figure in the formation and dissemination of revolutionary traditions.

Brecht asked us to consider the classes of people and the writing of history, how the past has been remembered and how it might be remembered differently. 'Who paid the piper?', his worker asks. In Brecht's day and since, the pipers have been paid to play the tune of the great men. NATO pipers made some erasures and the smudges in its writing of history, as Toni Morrison pointed out.[13] Can we conceive of civilisation as something more than great, vain men and great monuments to their vainglory? Brecht's worker seems to ask for the impossible: there were millions of sailors, and builders, and parents, and cooks! How can we find out all those names? Yet, who can say that justice does not demand it? While we do not know everybody's name, we know more than we used to, and we added a few in this book. 'History from below' is no longer as inarticulate, anonymous, spectral, or invisible as it once was.

If we cannot name every individual, what is the *class* of people to whom Brecht's worker refers, and can we put a name to it? The *naming* of the revolutionary class is an act of uncertainty, risk, danger. The salt of the earth, it seemed, had lost its savour. Communism seems finished. The working class seems dead. And yet...and yet, as Galileo said in another context, 'it moves'. *The Many-Headed Hydra* expressed a depth and multiplicity of our class which the predators of neo-liberalism had not destroyed, but which Karl Marx seems to have anticipated: this revolution 'abolishes the rule of all classes with the classes themselves, because it is carried through by the class which no longer counts as a class in society, is not recognised as a class, and is in itself the expression of the dissolution of all classes, nationalities, &c., within present society'.[14]

The Many-Headed Hydra was meant as a challenge to labour-histories based on prevailing orthodoxies of *subject*, *time*, and *place*. To the traditional *subjects* of

13. Morrison 1992.
14. Marx and Engels 1975–2004a, p. 94.

labour-history – the minority of mostly white, male, waged, skilled, artisanal or industrial workers – we wished to add the majority who were variously motley, female, unwaged, and located in other settings within a capitalist economy. Even though the 'new labour-history' had expanded the range of historical subjects, many remained left out, especially the sailors, slaves, and commoners named in our subtitle. We sought to break down the polarity between what has been called 'slave-labour' and 'free labour' by studying the cooperation and connections between people who had been trapped and falsely isolated in blinding ideal-types. It follows that the artisan-to-industrial-worker paradigm, long dominant in labour-histories around the world, is woefully inadequate to explain the rise of capitalism and the experiences of working people within it.[15]

The orthodoxy of *time* imposes another set of limitations on the story of labour-history as it has long been told. Many labour-historians still accept the paleo-Marxist postulate that there was no working class until the factory-system was established in the 1830s. The largely unexamined assumption is that 'merchant-capital' could never generate a working class; only 'industrial capital' could do so. Brecht would ask: if the world-market was established in the seventeenth and eighteenth centuries, who built it? The answer provided by *The Many-Headed Hydra* is a motley proletariat, which was, as Brecht knew, ancient, much older than the factory. This is why *The Many-Headed Hydra* ends in the 1830s, just when most labour-histories begin. We proposed, as outlined above, a different chronology, periodisation, and process of class-formation in relation to a longer history of capitalism.[16]

The orthodoxy of *space* constitutes a third major limitation, making labour-history, like most history, a national story. It takes place on land, *terra firma*, the proper place of the nation. But, of course, class 'happens' – and history happens – in spaces beyond the nation, on vessels, at sea, on oceans far from the nation, as we were at pains to emphasise in *The Many-Headed Hydra*. On slave-ships, captains employed extreme violence to stamp the commodity-form on human beings, making a profound kind of labour-history in the process. Those against whom the violence was aimed resisted, responding with an astounding cultural creativity that also shaped the history of labour. All of this happened, not in England, Senegal, Jamaica, or the United States, but at sea, and it would, over time, affect, even transform, the histories of those landed regions. Nations remain profound modalities of power, but they are, nonetheless, constituted

---

15. Important comments on the connections between enslaved and free labour can be found in Gutman 1987, p. 45. For a sophisticated treatment of the labour-history of slavery, see Berlin 1998. Two excellent critiques of, and alternatives to, the artisan-to-worker paradigm are Way 1993 and Rockman 2008.

16. Rediker 2004.

by events, processes, people, and ideas from afar. Labour-history cannot be a national story.

We sought in *The Many-Headed Hydra* to escape these limitations and the narrow, tendentious definition of the 'working class' that they imposed. We offered a new conception of class that was broader in subject, time, and space – more inclusive of labouring subjects, longer in its chronological sweep, and wider in its spatial settings. It does not make productive relations the sole determinant of class, nor does it depend for its existence or power on the specific consciousness of those involved in it. Rather, the definition emphasises the process of change over time in the constitution and experience of class – from expropriation through a middle-passage to a new reality of exploitation. This conception would, of necessity, have motion built into it, as against the sedentary bias that has informed most labour-history. Ours was an effort to capture the lives, thoughts, and actions of footloose people as they connected the local, the national, the Atlantic, and the global. Their internationalism would be something quite different from the cooperation of nationally-organised blocs of workers operating through a union or political organisation.[17]

We reached back to the term 'proletariat' to try to capture these complexities of subject, time, space, and motion. We traced the etymology of proletariat, which means the lowest class of the community, back to the Roman Republic, when Marius Gaius implemented military reforms that severed the traditional relationship between the property-owning citizen and military service, making it possible for people without property (including barbarians) to join the Roman army. Proletarians had no property, paid no taxes, and had no clear allegiance to the Roman state. All they had to contribute was labour power: their own and that of their children. We also showed that the concept is no anachronism in the early-modern era: 'proletariat' entered common usage in Europe 'at the end of the fifteenth century and the beginning of the sixteenth with the rise of international trade, the colonial system, banking, and state and private manufacture'. In England, the term became common in the 1660s, after the defeat of the popular movement in the English Revolution and the restoration of the monarchy. It described the poor and the vanquished, chiefly women, as in ancient Rome. This was before Karl Marx seized upon the concept in 1844.[18]

If the proletariat is older and broader than the working class, it follows that scholars and activists should consider a transition that Marx himself mentioned but never analysed: from proletariat to working class. The formation of an Atlantic proletariat was a necessary backdrop to, and an influential process upon, various national 'makings' and racialisations. Working-class formations that took

---

17. Linebaugh 1982; Clifford 1992.
18. Godelier 1980; Linebaugh and Rediker 2000, p. 93.

place around the Atlantic, in Britain, France, and the United States, in the 1830s, drew selectively but profoundly upon Atlantic ideas, practices, and symbols such as the strike, the jubilee, and the red flag. The history of the Atlantic proletariat thus overlapped with and influenced the histories of nation-states. The age of revolution signaled the ascent of the modern nation-state and a movement from the Atlantic proletariat towards the national working class.[19]

In analysing the Putney Debates, a highpoint of the English Revolution, we followed Colonel Thomas Rainsborough in emphasising the historic connection between the subsistence and relative autonomy of the commons, on the one hand, and the violence and terror of expropriation and slavery, on the other. These themes found both resonance and dissonance among our readers. John Donoghue has now broadened and confirmed our suggestion that the abolition of slavery was central to the revolutionary thought and practice of the Levellers, Ranters, Diggers, Quakers, and others in the English Revolution.[20] Others, including David Brion Davis, Nicholas Rogers, and Bryan Palmer, were upset by our treatment of violence and the commons.[21] We ourselves went on to pursue both subjects, Peter writing about the long historic struggle over the commons (in *Magna Carta Manifesto*), Marcus about the long historic struggle over the violence and terror of the slave ship (in *The Slave Ship*), both in relation to the making of modern capitalism.[22] Against our critics, we are convinced that these twin themes are even more important than we were able to show when we published *The Many-Headed Hydra* in the year 2000.

One of the theses of *The Many-Headed Hydra* was that the Atlantic proletariat was '*terrorized, subject to coercion*. Its hide was calloused by indentured labor, galley slavery, plantation slavery, convict transportation, the workhouse, the house of correction. Its origins were often traumatic; enclosure, capture, and imprisonment left lasting marks'.[23] We suggested that, despite important work on European expansion around the globe, we have yet to come to grips with the degree, variety, and breadth of violence and terror involved in the making of modern capitalism. For example, it is rarely noted that *all* of the main transatlantic institutions of labour were built upon violence: armies, navies, merchant-shipping, indentured servitude, plantation-slavery. Such violence, planned at the highest levels of the maritime state, was fundamental to, and formative of, the social and economic processes of Atlantic capitalism. We suggest four basic

---

19. These issues and more are being studied in pathbreaking ways by Niklas Frykman. See his essay in this volume.
20. Donoghue (forthcoming).
21. Davis 2001; Palmer 2003; Rogers 2002.
22. Linebaugh 2008; Rediker 2007.
23. Rediker 2003, p. 120.

types of violence, which had straightforward, interrelated purposes: they were instrumental to the formation, shipment, use, and control of labour-power.[24]

The original form was the violence of expropriation, meant to separate people from the land, often ancestral holdings, and thereby to create proletarians – people who had no productive property, and hence nothing to sell but their labour. This is what Karl Marx described as 'primary', 'original', or 'primitive' accumulation, which took place by many means, through enclosure of the commons, military action, Indian war, and slave-raiding. The Afro-Jamaican revolutionary Robert Wedderburn described the violence of expropriation in 1817 and linked it to slavery: 'He that first thrust his brother from his right [to the land] was a tyrant, a robber, and a murderer; a tyrant because he invades the rights of his brother, a robber, because he seized upon that which was not his own, a murderer, because he deprives his brother of the means of subsistence. The weak must then solicit to become the villain's slave'. Such violence, as we showed in *The Many-Headed Hydra*, made colonisation and capitalism possible.[25]

Second came the violence of the middle-passage, understood as the temporal and spatial interlude between expropriation from the land and the exploitation of labour in a new setting. Carceral violence was enacted in and through the ship's hold, the tender-boat, the prison-hulk, the crimp-house, the press-room, the cookhouse, the storehouse, the barracoon, the factory, the trading-post, the fort, the trunk, the cage, the city- or county-gaol, the bridewell, the house of correction, and finally the modern prison. There were many slaveries and many middle-passages: Africans in their millions, as well as spirited indentured servants, kidnapped children, transported convicts, trepanned maidens, 'barbadosed' labourers, banished 'breeders', deported vagrants, press-ganged sailors, and exiled rebels. The violence of the middle-passage was essential to the labour-systems of the Atlantic.[26]

Third was the violence of exploitation, the brutal physical discipline practiced by the slave-overseer with his whip; the boatswain with his rattan; the factory-foreman with his cane; the ship-captain with his cat-o'-nine-tails; the schoolmaster with his birch; the regimental staff-sergeant with his triangle and lash; the naval lieutenant followed by his club-wielding press-gang of bullies; the hangman with his various instruments of torture – the 'heavy-iron chains', the muzzles and thumbscrews, the handcuffs, manacles, and irons – in short, the hardware of bondage. The bodies of vagrants, servants, sailors, and slaves were routinely mutilated and chained. The long-term trend, beginning in the middle of the seventeenth century, was to racialise the violence of exploitation, targeting people

24. Rediker 2003.
25. Wedderburn, quoted in Linebaugh and Rediker 2000, p. 314.
26. Christianson 1998, pp. 16, 18; Christopher, Pybus and Rediker 2007.

of African descent, but it would take more than two centuries to abolish flogging in the navies of the Atlantic. What William Blake called the 'furrows of the whip' marked the corporal history of the capitalism.

A final type was the violence of repression, employed to maintain control over the various régimes of accumulation that were built by the force of the other three, usually in the aftermath of resistance by the Atlantic proletariat. Repressive violence took many forms, within which capital punishment was especially important, following, for example, the cycles of rebellion that exploded around the Atlantic in the 1640s, the 1730s, the 1760s, and the 1790s. It was also used against the expropriated and exploited at those moments when they sought out alternative, anticapitalist ways of organising themselves, especially when this involved a reappropriation of material life through commoning. This violence attempted to restore the social order of capitalism.[27]

The accumulation of the proletariat is also the accumulation of its experiences. Proletarians the world over share an experience of loss. Hence the more the proletariat grows, the more the experience of commonism – 'primitive communism', it has sometimes been called – accumulates. Expropriation, by definition, consists of defeat, but that does not necessarily entail the loss of the *experience.* For that reason, we cannot adhere rigidly to a stadial view of historical development. We know that terror is essential to expropriation, whether that is the West African village, the English commons, or the Irish *clachan.* Furthermore, we know that terror is essential to criminalisation, or the maintenance of the separation of the proletariat from subsistence. We recognise a third effect: terror is necessary to forgetting, or the work of denial. A colossal amount of repressive social energy is necessary to obliterate knowledge of alternatives. It does not pay to remember.

The word 'commons' has an extraordinary range of meanings in English: as the name of the people or the community; as the name of the third estate of the constitution after the king and the lords; as provisions to be shared by all community-members; as the name of the table from which victuals are supplied; or as the name of the victuals themselves. It is the relationship of the lofty, political and social meanings to the domestic, gustatory meaning that interests the historian from below. Often in the past, the relation is mediated by practices that remain to be discovered, but which phrases such as 'common right' or 'commonwealth' or, indeed, 'primitive communism' gesture towards. When the

---

27. Although there is a logic and an order to these four types of violence (many thousands of people experienced them in precisely this order), it should be emphasised that they overlapped and co-existed in time. The violence of expropriation, for example, spanned the entire seventeenth, eighteenth, and early nineteenth centuries (indeed, it continues to the present), and the violence of repression was closely linked to it (and to the other two types) at every historic step.

former meanings are drained of human hopefulness by defeat or betrayal, the latter meanings may come alive. Thus, Lewis Henry Morgan, after the horrific repression of the 1871 Paris Commune recorded the experience of 'Montezuma's Dinner', in which 'The dinner in question was the usual single daily meal of a communal household, prepared in a common cookhouse from common stores, and divided, Indian fashion, from the kettle'.[28] Olaudah Equiano wrote similarly after the repression of the middle-passage, remembering his youth in West Africa, 'Whatever was gained by any member of the household on hunting or fishing expeditions, or raised in cultivation, was made a common stock'. Remembering is essential to working-class self-activity. Hence, we write as people's remembrancers[29] attempting to remember that, for three centuries prior to the Marxist proclamation of communism in 1848, experiences in unprivatised, pre-commodified, non-enclosed social relations – call it 'commons' – provided a profound and coeval alternative to capitalism.

28. Morgan 1876.
29. Following Gwyn Williams, the Welsh 'historian from below'.

Seamen on Late Eighteenth-Century European Warships
Niklas Frykman

When the inter-imperial arms-race accelerated in the late eighteenth century, European navies entered a three-decade long period of vast expansion. Measured in terms of total displacement, the French navy increased by 107 percent between 1760 and 1790; the Dutch navy by 98 percent; the Spanish by 85 percent; the Danish-Norwegian by 34 percent; and the British navy by 26 percent.[1] Admiralties ordered both more ships and bigger ships, and then crammed more guns into them. They built larger dockyards and more complex bureaucracies, hired more workers, produced and purchased more timber, iron, hemp, and provisions, cast more guns, cannon-balls, and nails, constructed docks and warehouses, and raised barracks and offices. The state-financial effort was immense.

Building and arming ships was, however, only part of the challenge. The larger fleets and the near-permanent warfare that raged between them also required far more men than were available. By the 1780s, the French and British warfleets both had manpower-needs that were equivalent to all domestically-available supply, thus theoretically stripping all non-military shipping of its workers if they were to man all of their warships.[2] The Dutch navy barely managed to scrape together two-thirds of its manpower-requirements for the Fourth Anglo-Dutch War in 1780–4, and Sweden suffered acute shortages of men during its war with Russia between 1788 and 1790.[3]

---

1. Glete 1993, Vol. I, p. 311.
2. Meyer 1980, p. 78.
3. Lybeck 1945, p. 420; Bruijn 1993, pp. 195–6.

European navies met this emergency by expanding their coercive recruitment-systems to include groups previously safe from non-voluntary service at sea, and by allowing the proportion of foreign-born seamen on-board their ships to expand. But greater numbers of forced workers, as well as more men without any reason to be loyal to the country under whose flag they sailed, drove up desertion-rates to previously unimaginable heights. Then came a massive, international wave of mutiny, the like of which had never been seen in Europe's armed forces before, or since. Hundreds of crews revolted, at times disabling whole fleets in the midst of the annual fighting-season. By the second half of the 1790s, mutineers were executed by the dozen, prompting more violent, more disloyal, more treasonous revolts from below-deck. At the end of the century, class-war was no longer a metaphor in the wooden world of European warships.

Mobilising manpower

Late eighteenth-century Atlantic Europe is estimated to have been home to around three to four hundred thousand skilled seafarers.[4] The British Isles, with a hundred to a hundred and fifty thousand men, had the largest concentration, followed by France, Spain, and the United Provinces, each with around sixty thousand, and Denmark-Norway with approximately forty thousand.[5] These were the men who made up the basic pool of naval manpower. Since no major state could afford to maintain a permanently armed fleet, they were mobilised and released as the rhythms of imperial warfare dictated. Whenever peace broke out, hundreds of warships were laid up, and tens of thousands were released onto the maritime labour-market. Conversely, when armed conflict was again imminent, European admiralties activated their recruitment-systems, and tens of thousands were rapidly sucked back into war-work.

The failure to develop a specialised workforce meant that the ability to wage war at sea hinged on the efficiency of the mechanism by which manpower was shifted between the civilian and military sectors. Since demand and supply tended to move in counter-cyclical directions – that is to say, many seafarers were drawn to naval service in peacetime, whereas the merchant-fleet attracted them during wartime – this was largely a question of how best to capture and coerce men into service. European navies developed three basic solutions: conscription, impressment, and crimping.

---

4. Meyer 1980, p. 79.
5. Palmer and Williams 1997, pp. 93–118, 102; Rodger 1995, p. 369; Le Goff 1997, p. 300; Meyer 1980, p. 78; Bruijn and Van Eyck van Heslinga 1984; Sætra 1997, p. 183; Johansen 1997, p. 242; Kiær 1970, p. 248.

France, Spain, Denmark-Norway, and Sweden relied predominantly on systems of conscription. Every maritime worker in these countries had to register his name with local state-officials, and, in return for a number of benefits, was ordered to be ready for service whenever called up. Frequency of actual service differed from country to country. In France, registered men served every few years for twelve months, while in Denmark-Norway conscripts were only mobilised in times of acute crisis to supplement the small permanent force that was stationed in Copenhagen.[6]

Britain several times attempted the establishment of such a register, but its mariners refused cooperation, and so the navy continued to rely on the more haphazard, yet astonishingly efficient, system of impressment: whenever war threatened, the admiralty issued warrants, and His Majesty's press-gangs came sweeping through port-towns and roadsteads, forcefully abducting as many men as they could get their hands on, and then distributing them to whatever ship stood in need of manpower.[7]

In the United Provinces, the navy outsourced recruitment. Crimps, commonly known as *zielverkopers* [sellers-of-souls], preyed on the destitute and desperate, offered them an advance on room and board, and then forced them into the first available warship. The navy then paid the man's wages to the crimp until all his accumulated debts had been cleared. If this system failed to bring in enough manpower, the government sometimes resorted to embargoing all outgoing shipping, a crude but devastatingly effective mechanism for quickly swelling the pool of unemployed and easily recruited workers in the port-towns.[8]

The near-permanent cycle of warfare that commenced in the 1750s put considerable pressure on these manning-systems. War not only increased the demand for seamen, it also killed them by the tens of thousands. Peacetime-seafaring itself already had exceptionally high mortality-rates. Alain Cabantous has found that between 1737 and 1790, twenty-five percent of all Dunkirk seamen died while in their twenties, a proportion broadly equivalent to that of Salem, Massachusetts in the late eighteenth century.[9] Certain trades, of course, were far more dangerous than others. Workers in local trading and fishing-industries only had marginally higher death-rates than their shorebound colleagues, but slave-ship sailors customarily lost twenty to twenty-five percent of their fellow crewmen on a single voyage.[10] But navies were the biggest killers. Between 1774 and 1780, the British navy lost 0.7 percent of all its seamen in combat, and 10.5 percent to

---

6. Cabantous 1984, pp. 82–4; Phillips 1997, p. 343; Nørlit 1942–3; Kiær 1970, pp. 246–52; Berg 2000, pp. 101–4.

7. Bromley 1976; Hutchinson 1914.

8. Bruijn 1979, pp. 331–2; Boxer 1973, p. 74; Davids 1997, p. 64.

9. Cabantous 1980, p. 109; Vickers 2005, p. 108.

10. Christopher 2006, pp. 183–4; Rediker 2007, p. 244.

disease – nearly twenty thousand men.[11] The numbers grew worse: during the French-Revolutionary and Napoleonic wars almost ninety thousand Royal Navy seamen died, up to twenty-four thousand of them in the Caribbean theatre alone between 1793 and 1801.[12] In France, the administrative and financial collapse of the old navy took an immense human toll: over eight thousand men died when typhus tore through Brest in 1793–4, and this was not the only time or place an epidemic raged out of control.[13] Several thousand more died in the notoriously lethal British prison-hulks.[14]

Most governments preferred their own country's mariners to man the navy, but by the late eighteenth century, that was no longer a viable option. Some provincial ports were ravaged so thoroughly by naval recruiters that they had practically come to a standstill. Seaman William Richardson remembered the huge cost his hometown of Shields was made to bear: 'My brother and I went on shore, but found Shields not that merry place we had hitherto known it; every one looked gloomy and sad on account of nearly all the young men being pressed and taken away;...'[15] This was in 1795, a mere two years into a war that was to last for twenty more.

One way out of this crisis, adopted especially by the British and Dutch navies, was to recruit foreign-born workers in ever-larger numbers. On the *Hermione*, in most respects an ordinary British frigate, only fifty percent of the crew came from England, twenty percent from within the Empire, another twenty percent from Ireland, and ten percent from eleven different countries around the Atlantic rim.[16] Such a distribution appears to have become common in the late eighteenth-century British navy, but it was nothing compared to the role foreign-born workers played in the Dutch service.[17] In 1799, for example, Captain van Grootenray of the *Kortenaar* complained that he was unable to communicate with his crew, for almost all of them were fresh recruits from Eastern Europe. Worse still, their efforts at Dutch language-acquisition had apparently ceased with the word *sold* [wages], but that, Van Grootenray reported, they repeated over and over again.[18] Perhaps the *Kortenaar* was an extreme case, but indications are that proportions

11. Kemp 1970, p. 139.
12. Pope 1981, p. 131; Duffy 1987, p. 334.
13. Taillemite 2003, p. 284.
14. LeGoff 1985, p. 103; Roos 1953, pp. 17–19.
15. Childers 1908, p. 121.
16. *Hermione* muster-book, April to July 1797, The National Archives: Public Records Office (UK) ADM 36/12011; *Adventure* muster book, January to February 1797, TNA: PRO (UK) ADM 36/12931; *Success* muster-book, December 1796 to September 1797, TNA: PRO (UK) ADM 36/14745.
17. Rodger 1992, pp. 29–30.
18. Captain van Grootenray to Admiral de Winter, 14 July 1799, Nationaal Archief, Den Haag, Departement van Marine, 1795–1813, nummer toegang 2.01.29.01, inventariesnummer 236.

of foreign-born crewmen on Dutch warships of up to seventy percent were not unusual at the time.[19]

It was nothing new for the Dutch to recruit migratory labour from the North Sea and Baltic Sea regions to work in their deep-sea industries, and the navy utilised these centuries-old networks to the fullest.[20] This went so far that, even while fighting a war against Britain, there were recruiters doing the rounds in London's sailortown, busily sending men to Amsterdam by way of the Dutch embassy in Hamburg.[21] Likewise, the Dutch East India Company had a longstanding tradition of recruiting manpower from deep within the rural heartlands of the Holy Roman Empire, and the eighteenth-century navy drew heavily on these sources as well.[22] Finally, there seems to have been an increase in the number of south, south east Asian and African-descended seamen on-board Dutch warships.[23]

In the British navy, too, there was a rise in the number of 'Black Jacks' and lascars, but the bulk of foreign-born labour-power here clearly came from the north-Atlantic region. Americans had always been important, and they continued to be pressed with impunity even after independence.[24] Their numbers were dwarfed, however, by the tens of thousands harvested in Ireland: if, as Rodger plausibly suggests, a proportion of twenty-five to thirty percent had become common on most British warships in the late 1790s, than somewhere around thirty thousand Irishmen were serving in the Royal Navy at any one time.[25]

France largely avoided this trend towards increasing the number of foreign-born men in the navy, and in 1795 even fixed an upper limit of twenty-percent foreigners on any one ship.[26] In order to expand the pool of recruits, the French navy chose to make new social groups targets for coerced recruitment instead. The officially defined area where maritime workers might be found – that is, men subject to conscription – was extended far up the riverine systems, and the number of potential recruits was swelled still-further by including economic sectors

---

19. Davids 1997, p. 50.

20. Lucassen 1997. It is interesting to note that when the commander of the Swedish archipelagean fleet Mikäl Amkarsvärd denounced the practices of a local recruiter he used the German translation of the Dutch word for crimp: *Seelenverkäufer*. Quoted in Lybeck 1945, p. 420.

21. Extract from a letter from Gravesend, forwarded to Evan Nepean, 26 July 1797, TNA: PRO (UK) ADM 1/4173; Interrogation of Peter Strouck, NA (NL), Hoge Militaire Rechspraak, 1795–1813 (1818), 2.01.11, inv. nr. 239.

22. van Gelder 1997, pp. 53–70; Davids 1997, p. 51.

23. Bruijn 1993, p. 202.

24. Selement 1973.

25. Rodger 1992, p. 30.

26. 'Arrêté du comité de salut public, concernant l'enrôlement des marins étrangers. Du 25 Prairial an III', in *Recueil* 1797–8, Vol. V, pp. 337–40.

that only had very indirect connections to the sea.[27] In Britain, the Quota-Acts had a similar effect. Each county, whether maritime or not, was required to send a certain number of men for service in the fleet. Approximately 30,000 came, many of them landsmen who had never set foot on a ship before.[28]

This increased reliance on landsmen was part of a long-term trend in the eighteenth-century maritime industries. By the 1780s, more than half of all registered seamen in France were first-generation mariners, and in the deep-sea trades, their proportion was higher still.[29] This was a consequence of technical changes, foremost to the arrangement of the rigging on ocean-going vessels, which had devalued the skills and experience of seamen, and, instead, put an increased premium on their muscle-power. The number of able seamen on-board transatlantic merchantmen consequently declined by as much as a third to a half in the middle of the century, and in their place came cheap, unskilled workers without much or any experience of the sea.[30] Work-processes were increasingly standardised throughout the industry, and that depreciated the value of the seamen's craft-skills still further.[31] Another set of changes, among them the removal of armaments from merchantmen following the defeat of Atlantic piracy, caused average crew-sizes in relation to tonnage to shrink: the organic composition of capital in the deep-sea industries was rising, and fast.[32]

On warships, the situation was slightly different. While average crew-sizes shrunk on merchantmen, navies crammed more and more guns into their ships and, therefore, required ever-more men to fight its battles. In the late seventeenth century, a ship of the line had a crew of approximately five hundred men; a hundred years later, crews of seven hundred and fifty were common, and up to nine hundred far from unheard-of.[33] Since few of these men were needed to sail the ship, and the skills necessary for firing the guns were easily learned, navies had no difficulty absorbing and training large numbers of landsmen. There was, of course, an upper limit. Commander Evertsen found nearly eighty German and Polish landsmen amongst his crew of a hundred and twenty when he assumed his position on the *Scipio* in the summer of 1797. To put to sea, Evertsen estimated, he needed around sixteen more seamen, plus a handful of petty officers.[34] That still would have left him with nearly sixty percent landsmen, a figure far

---

27. 'Décret sur les classes des gens de mer, 31 Décembre 1790', in *Recueil*, Vol. I, pp. 219–27.
28. Rodger 2006, pp. 443–4; Emsley 1978, pp. 16–21.
29. LeGoff 1984.
30. LeGoff 1980, pp. 104–5; Rodger 1992, p. 30.
31. Rediker 1987, p. 83.
32. Unger 1980, pp. 104–5.
33. Meyer 1980, p. 80.
34. C.G. Evertsen to the committee for naval affairs, 30 July 1797, NA (NL), Departement van Marine, 1795–1813, 2.01.29.01, inv. nr. 236.

higher than was considered desirable in the British navy. There, it seems, the proportion of landsmen and boys was kept below twenty-five percent. At the same time, it was only considered necessary to have another twenty-five percent experienced and able seamen on-board, while the remaining fifty percent could safely be made up of low-skilled common ratings, often recent landsmen themselves.[35]

The largest group of new recruits that washed onto warships in the 1790s were the sons of the European peasantry.[36] Massive population-growth, coupled with the enclosure of common land, the monetisation of rural social relations, and the commercialisation of agricultural production, brought forth a vast landless surplus-population, highly mobile, and desperate for work and sustenance. Europe's roads were clogged with men and women seeking a living, and while most of these roads led into the rapidly expanding slums of the cities, there were others that led to the coast. There is a striking correlation, for instance, between the astonishing numbers of landless peasants in Bohemia in the last quarter of the eighteenth century – estimated at forty to sixty percent of the total population – and the substantial presence of Bohemians in the Dutch navy at the same time.[37] This is, of course, merely suggestive, but similar developments can be observed in Ireland, where peasants flooded into the British navy, and rural France, where they filled the lower decks of their own country's fleet.

Many new seafarers also came from Europe's urban centres, where capitalist deregulation, together with the imposition of the wage-form, smashed the moral economy of the guild-system and released artisans, journeymen, labourers, and low-level intellectual workers into market-freedom by the hundreds of thousands.[38] Wartime recession drove them into unemployment and to the brink of starvation. They were easy targets for naval recruiters.

The largest group on-board European warships, however, remained the men who were born and bred to the sea.[39] But these came from two relatively distinct sectors. One was made up of the men of the deep-sea trades who sailed out across the world's oceans to carry back capital and commodities to Europe's major port-cities. These were the proletarianised mariners whose dreary lives were essentialised into the well-known stereotype of Jack Tar: deracinated, spendthrift, and impulsive. Their working conditions had been steadily deteriorating since the late Middle-Ages and, by the late eighteenth century, co-ownership of the cargo had been replaced with straightforward wage-payments and limited collective

---

35. Bromley 1980, p. 40; Neal 1978, p. 52.
36. Davids 1997, pp. 62–5; LeGoff 1997, pp. 300–1.
37. Klíma 1979, p. 54; for the number of Bohemians in the Dutch navy, see various muster-books in NA (NL), Departement van Marine: Monsterrollen, 1795–1810, 2.01.30.
38. Linebaugh 1992, pp. 402–41.
39. LeGoff 1984, p. 368.

decision-making, given the captain's almost boundless powers.[40] In the other sector, however, that of local fishing and short-distance merchant-shipping, the patriarchal relations of old-régime rural Europe still prevailed. Crews were small, hierarchies flat, cargo-ownership shared, and the powers of the captain limited both by custom and the force of communal disapproval in the home-port, usually a small town or village where most of the crewmen lived with their families.[41] Movement between these two sectors was limited, but it appears that an increasing number of men shifted from the shallow to the deep-sea trades in the later eighteenth century. Long years of naval service, with its socially corrosive and individualising effects, often made this move one of permanent proletarianisation. Many old seafarers struggled to reintegrate into landed society when the wars drew to a close.[42]

Life and death on a man-of-war

Whatever their life may have been before – experienced mariner, landless peasant, or unemployed artisan – new naval recruits found themselves in a profoundly alien environment. Only very rarely in the eighteenth century did hundreds of men work together in one place, let alone at a single machine as they did on-board of a warship. Few people had experience of industrial labour-discipline, and most barely accepted that the clock might have anything to do with when they ought to be working.[43] But coming into a warship, new recruits suddenly found themselves in a miniature mass-society, physically isolated for long periods of time, with extraordinary levels of internal stratification, complex organisational structures, twenty-four hour work-cycles, constant, close surveillance, and a terroristic justice-system. This régime shock-proletarianised tens of thousands.

While a vast number of finely graded social distinctions separated an admiral from the lowliest seaman, shipboard society basically consisted of only four groups. On top were the commissioned officers, the inhabitants of the quarterdeck, who, under the leadership of the ship's commander, enjoyed virtually unlimited powers on-board. They were of mixed competence and usually drawn from the prosperous middle-classes or the aristocracy, although in post-revolutionary France and the Netherlands, where most of the old officer-corps was judged politically unreliable, they were sometimes drafted from the ranks.[44]

---

40. Unger 1980, pp. 66–8.
41. Welke 1997, pp. 14–24.
42. See, for example, Forester 1954.
43. Thompson 1991b.
44. Cormack 1995, p. 109; Roodhuyzen 1998, p. 123.

Below the commissioned officer-corps came the warrant- and petty officers, largely specialist seamen and trained craftsmen, such as caulkers, coopers, carpenters, gunners, and sailmakers. These were career navy-men who had slowly built up their position through years of service. Socially, most of them belonged to the lower deck, but thanks to their experience, skill, and strategic position within shipboard society, they were generally treated with respect by the commissioned officer-corps. The same could not be said about the largest group on-board, the common seamen. These were, at best, seen as dumb instruments of the officers' will, at worst as unruly, drunken saboteurs. They were usually divided into two or three ranks, depending on their experience and training, and though some advanced up into the petty officer-corps, shipboard social mobility was very limited once a man had become a *loup de mer* [sea-wolf], or as he was less poetically known in the British navy, an able seaman. The fourth and final group on-board were the marines, the onboard police-force that protected the quarterdeck. These were generally of proletarian and often foreign origin, unskilled, and widely disrespected by all others on-board. Their basic task was to stand guard and look menacing.[45]

Most ships at sea operated a two-watch system: the crew, excepting the shipboard artisan-classes, were divided into two identical groups that came on- and off-duty every four hours. Within both watches, the men were assigned to a part of the ship, reflecting their predominant area of labour. The highest-skilled men were sent up into the tops, where they spent long hours in wind and weather bending, loosing, and furling sails. When a man grew too old for the tops, he usually migrated to the forecastle, where duties included handling the frontmost set of sails and the anchor. Less experienced seamen and landsmen were ordered either into the waist or the afterguard, where they pulled the heavy ropes and braces that lifted and lowered the major yards and sails of the ship, looked after the livestock, and pumped bilge-water. In addition to a watch and a part of the ship, each man also had a number of stations which clearly defined his exact duty for a large number of standard manoeuvres, such as mooring and unmooring, weighing, tacking and wearing, lowering and squaring yards, and so forth. In battle, nearly the entire crew was assigned to the gundeck, each man again fulfilling a clearly defined role at a specific gun.[46]

From about mid-century onwards, some navies introduced divisions and squads to facilitate social control on their larger vessels. Under this system, the crew was broken up into small groups of men and put under the immediate supervision of an officer who was held responsible for their good behaviour,

---

45. Seamen sometimes referred to empty bottles as marine officers, indicating just how useful they thought them. Egan 1823.

46. Harland 1985, pp. 91–4; Lavery 1989, pp. 194–9.

cleanliness, and general seaman-like development.[47] The Swedish navy went one step further towards individualised surveillance, issuing each man with a *förhåll-ningsbok* [behaviour-book], in which was recorded his experience, training, rating, and disciplinary history. He was expected to carry it with him throughout his naval career and always present it to a new commander upon first mustering.[48]

Yet despite these innovations, the primary mechanism for social control remained the unceasing rounds of never-ending labour on-board. The day's work on a typical battleship began at four in the morning, when one of the two watches was ordered to commence holy-stoning the deck, one of the most odious activities on-board: 'Here the men suffer from being obliged to kneel down on the wetted deck, and a gravelly sort of sand strewed over it. To perform this work, they kneel with their bare knees, rubbing the deck with a stone and the sand, the grit of which is often very injurious'.[49] This continued for three-and-a-half hours until breakfast, after which the other watch was set to holy-stoning for four hours. The crew detested this incessant cleaning of the decks, especially in the winter-months – one new recruit was even driven to thoughts of desertion after only a single day of it – but captains, nevertheless, continued to order it, because there was, quite simply, little else for the crew to do.[50] A warship had up to ten times as many men onboard as most merchantmen of similar size, and that meant that, in nearly all situations except for battle, they were excessively overcrewed. This was a problem:

> For a sailor to have a moment's leisure is, by many officers, dreaded more than a pestilence. As the real duties of the ship can never occupy the time of half the men employed, the captain has recourse to his invention to find seamen work; for so conscious are the officers that the seamen cannot reflect without being sensible that they have been unmeritedly punished, that they have received almost unlimited injury, that they are fearful reflection should make them compare their situation with the rest of their countrymen, with what they themselves once were, and that this reflection should rouse them to vengeance for oppression.[51]

As the majority of the men were impressed, conscripted, or crimped, there was plenty of disgruntlement on the lower deck, and the threat of open disaffection never far away. And so they were kept busy with make-work like holy-stoning or

---

47. Marcus 1975, p. 117.
48. Lybeck 1945, p. 434.
49. Robinson 1973, p. 32.
50. A British Seaman 1829, pp. 28–9.
51. Hodgskin 1813, p. 44.

endless drills at small arms or the great guns, both of which the men found only marginally less objectionable.[52]

Dinner was served between noon and one, after which one of the watches went back on duty, usually attending to various necessary maintenance-work, or more drilling, while the other watch was given leisure-time until supper at four. Two half-watches of two hours' length followed, making sure that the order of on-duty, off-duty was reversed for the following twenty-four-hour period. Finally, between eight and nine, the hammocks were ordered down and the men of one watch sent to sleep. The watches changed at midnight, and again at four in the morning, when the first watch of the day began scrubbing the decks again.[53]

Except for a few hours of eating, drinking, and yarning in the late afternoon, seamen's daily lives were thus mostly consumed by disagreeable tasks, or by mind-numbing boredom. When writing his autobiography, Samuel Leech vividly remembered the many lonely hours that he had spent on duty as a topman: 'Often have I stood two hours, and, sometimes, when my shipmates have forgotten to relieve me, four long, tedious hours, on the royal yard, or the top-gallant yard, without a man to converse with. Here, overcome with fatigue and want of sleep, I have fallen into a dreamy, dozy state, from which I was roused by a lee lurch of the ship'. The only thing worse than this boredom, he concluded, was 'to be compelled to stand on these crazy elevations, when half dead with sea-sickness'.[54]

Even these discomforts, however, were nothing when compared to 'the King of Terrors', those short bursts of intense violence that ruptured the tedium of everyday life and left men traumatised, wounded, and dead.[55] When battle commenced, the ships' gundecks became an inferno: broadsides were unleashed with eardrum-bursting roars, the smoke and fire from dozens of great guns saturating the air. When cannon-balls struck the hull of a ship, wooden splinters the size of men's thighs tore loose on the inside, severing arms and legs, smashing skulls, and cutting torsos in two as they slashed and hurtled their way across the tightly-packed deck. If the battle lasted for several hours, the gundeck took on the look of a 'slaughterhouse': scores of men dead and dying, heaps of unrecognisable human flesh piled high, blood streaming out from the scuppers and into the sea.[56] Down in the hold, the ship's doctor tried to salvage what he could: 'The stifled groans, the figures of the surgeon and his mates, their bare arms and faces smeared with blood, the dead and dying all round, some in the last agonies of

---

52. Melville 1990, pp. 66–7.
53. Robinson 1973, pp. 31–8; Lavery 1989, pp. 200–3.
54. Leech 1999, pp. 141–2.
55. Leech 1999, p. 77.
56. Nicol 1997, p. 174; Moreau de Jonnès 1929, p. 66.

death, and others screaming under the amputating knife, formed a horrid scene of misery, and made a hideous contrast to the "pomp, pride, and circumstance of glorious war" '.[57] Brian Lavery has estimated that serious mental illness was seven times more common on warships than in society at large, and though it may very well be true that drunken seamen more often knocked their heads against wooden beams than did the rest of the population, it seems likely that post-traumatic stress-disorder also played a role.[58]

The maintenance of discipline on-board warships was never an easy matter. Naval theorists found comfort in thinking of shipboard society with its hundreds of tightly-organised workers as 'a great machine', operated by a single human agent, the captain.[59] Seamen, in this vision, were nothing more than 'a wheel, a band, or a crank, all moving with wonderful regularity and precision'.[60] Reality, of course, was rather different, and, instead of the interlocking wheels of discipline imagined by the theorists, 'one universal system of terror' prevailed on most ships.[61] The men were either unwilling or unable to function like cogs in a machine, they made mistakes, they were slow, they grumbled and complained. Orders, therefore, were frequently accompanied by the 'flesh-carpenters' – the boatswain and his mates – liberally beating the crew with their rattan-canes and rope-ends to speed up execution.[62]

If seamen actually committed a breach of the ship's many rules, the most common punishment in most navies was flogging with the cat-o'-nine-tails, a whip with nine separate two-foot-long cords, each reinforced with several knots. The legal maximum-amount of lashes the captain could order without a court martial varied from navy to navy (in the British navy, it was 12, and in the Danish navy, 27), but, with a little creativity, violations could be broken down into many constituent parts, and each punished with that number of lashes.[63] The frequency of these floggings varied from ship to ship, but if we assumed an average of approximately once every ten to fifteen days, we would not be far wrong.

The articles of war required that serious violations, ranging from derelictions of duty via 'buggery' to mutiny, be tried by courts martial, and these had a terrifying arsenal of punishments available to them: solitary confinement, hard labour, pillorying, ducking, branding, pulling out of tongues, severing of hands, keel-hauling, running the gauntlet, flogging round the fleet, hanging, gibbeting,

---

57. A British Seaman 1829, p. 142.
58. Lavery 1989, p. 215.
59. A Captain in the Royal Navy 1804, p. 36.
60. Leech 1999, p. 22.
61. Hodgskin 1813, p. ix.
62. A British Seaman 1829, p. 35.
63. Borring 1998, pp. 39–43; Pope 1981, p. 62.

drowning, decapitation, decimation, arquebusing, and breaking on the wheel.[64] There were several more. It is not clear, however, how frequently the more outrageous of these punishments were actually ordered, but, at least in the British navy, hangings and floggings round the fleet with up to eight hundred lashes were quite common, as was ducking and hard labour in the Dutch navy.[65]

Generally, punishments were carefully orchestrated public events, with mandatory attendance to maximise the spectacular impact of terror. When a man was flogged through the fleet, for instance, he was taken in a boat from ship to ship, and given a certain number of lashes next to each. After a few dozen lashes with the cat-o'-nine-tails, 'the lacerated back looks inhuman; it resembles roasted meat burnt nearly black before a scorching fire'.[66] Another eyewitness described it as resembling 'so much putrified liver'.[67] Still, the lashes kept falling, and often the victim was beaten within an inch of his life. Survivors were left severely traumatised:

> Like the scar, that time may heal, but not remove, the flogged man forgets not that he has been degraded; the whip, when it scarred the flesh, went farther: it wounded the spirit; it struck the *man*; it begat a sense of degradation he must carry with him to the grave. We had many such on board our frigate; their laugh sounded empty, and sometimes their look became suddenly vacant in the midst of hilarity. It was the whip entering the soul anew.[68]

If the sentence called for several hundred lashes, the victim often died halfway through. But the full sentence could be carried out regardless, and the man's comrades were then forced to watch as his dead body continued to be mutilated:

> Our captain ordered the doctor to feel his pulse, and found that the man was dead. Our boatswain's mate was then told to give him fifty lashes; 'but', says the Captain, 'lay them lightly on his back.' He might as well have said put them lightly on his *bones*, for I could not see any flesh on him, from his neck to his waist. After this he was carried to two other ships, and received fifty lashes at each, and then carried to low water mark, and there buried in the mud.[69]

---

64. Falconer 1784; Lybeck 1945, p. 436; Pürschel 1961; 'Décret concernant le code pénal maritime (16, 19 et 21 Août 1790)', in *Recueil*, vol. I, pp. 122–40; Robinson 1973, pp. 138–51.

65. For the British navy, see Digest of the Admiralty Records of Trials by Court-Martial, From the 1st January 1755 to 1st January 1806, TNA: PRO (UK) ADM 12/24; for the Dutch navy, see various trial records in NA (NL), Hoge Krijgsraad en Zeekrijgsraden, 1607–1794, 1.01.45; and NA (NL), Hoge Militaire Rechtspraak, 1795–1813 (1818), 2.01.11.

66. Leech 1999, p. 28.

67. Robinson 1973, p. 141.

68. Leech 1999, p. 60.

69. Davis 1811, p. 68. Emphasis in the original.

These, clearly, were not spectacles meant to instill respect for the service; these were calculated acts of terror designed to cow the lower orders into obedience. They were singularly ineffective.

Frontline-resistance

Some men were extremely eager to meet with an enemy-ship, for combat was considered a great opportunity for 'a poor fellow ... of squaring yards with some of his tyrants'.[70] In the chaos of an engagement, it was easy to swing around with the musket, take aim, and 'sweep the quarterdeck of the quality'.[71] Of course, it is impossible to know how many such 'fraggings' actually occurred, but mention thereof is frequent enough to conclude that it was not completely unknown. More common, however, was less lethal violence against individual officers. The ship-environment itself offered many possibilities – a tackle dropped from aloft or an iron-shot rolled across the deck at night smashed plenty of bones – but most often, men out for this type of vengeance appear to have waited for an opportunity to jump their victim on land, preferably as he left a tavern late at night, too befuddled to identify his attackers or put up much resistance.[72]

Nevertheless, individual or small-group violence against officers was rare. The risks involved were simply too great. If men found a particular situation growing intolerable, they preferred simply to run away instead. It was the mariner's traditional response. Since most of his long-standing social bonds were severed when recruiters forced him into a ship that sailed halfway around the world, leaping overboard and making a run for it when opportunity offered came easily. And judging from the numbers of men who ran, there was no shortage of such opportunities. According to Admiral Nelson's calculations, some forty-two thousand British seamen took 'French leave' between 1793 and 1802, a figure that is all the more impressive when recalling that the overall strength of the service in 1800 was just under one hundred and twenty thousand.[73] On some ships, the lower deck apparently had a revolving door: on the *Hermione* frigate, for example, with a regular complement of approximately 180 men, there were 129 desertions between 1793 and 1797.[74]

In the French and Dutch navies, the situation was even more extreme, in part because the British blockade kept their fleets bottled up in port for long periods

---

70. A British Seaman 1829, p. 128.

71. Court martial against men from the *Diomede*, TNA: PRO (UK) ADM 1/5347; Steele 1840, pp. 205–6.

72. Davis 1811, p. 71; Dann 1988, p. 76.

73. Lloyd 1970, p. 265.

74. *Hermione* muster-book, April to July 1797, TNA: PRO (UK) ADM 36/12011.

of time, thus giving their seamen plenty of opportunities to desert. The Dutch navy had already been haemorrhaging seamen since the early 1780s, but with the combined French invasion and revolution of 1795, desertion became a mass-phenomenon. On many warships, the entire lower deck simply walked away, while on others, only skeleton-crews remained. On the *Staaten Generaal*, with a regular complement of 550, only 122 men were left on-board; on the *Delft*, with 350 men, only 10; on the *Castor*, with 270 men, only 22; on the *Maasnymph*, with 75 men, only 29. And so the list continued.[75] Throughout 1796, the navy slowly rebuilt manpower-levels, but by the following year ,desertions were once-again rampant. Men kept running in vast numbers until Batavian naval power finally collapsed with the Texel surrender of 1799.

French seamen were just as footloose, especially during the counter-revolutionary years of the late 1790s. Thousands deserted to the interior, rejoined their families, or linked up with brigand-bands.[76] Mass-desertions in Brest grew to such proportions that the commune periodically felt compelled to close the city's gates in order to prevent anyone from leaving town. It did not help. Deserting seamen simply landed outside of the walls.[77] By 1799, the Atlantic fleet was over eight thousand men short, while the Mediterranean fleet at Toulon was missing a full third of its regular complement.[78] Eventually, the back-country harboured so many deserters that the government sent the hated '*Colonnes Mobiles*' against them, but even that proved completely ineffectual. Mass-desertions continued unabated until the end of the wars.[79]

Seamen in the deep-sea trades had always been enthusiastic deserters, but never before on this scale. In part, perhaps, the spike in desertions, especially to the interior, was due not to seamen, but to the vastly increased number of forcibly recruited landsmen who found life at sea intolerable and tried to make their way home. But this was often difficult, unless they happened to be stationed in

---

75. Various court-martial cases for desertion, NA (NL), Hoge Krijgrsraad en Zeekrijg-sraden, 1607–1794, 1.01.45, inv. nr. 377; List of ships still in service, February 1795, report of the ships lying at Flushing, 8 March 1795, and general report on the ships belonging to the central division, 15 March 1795, NA (NL), Departement van Marine, 1795–1813, 2.01.29.01, inv. nr. 227.

76. Court martial against André Monfroy *et al.* Service historique de la Défense, Marine, Vincennes, CC/3/1728, Personnel, Troupes et équipages, Conseils de Guerre, Lorient, 1799; Memorandum on insufficient punishments of naval deserters, SHD Marine, Vincennes, CC/3/1471, Personnel, Troupes et équipages, Mémoirs sur les jurys militaires etc.

77. Captain D'Auvergne, Prince of Bouillon to Secretary Dundas, Jersey, 31 May 1797, TNA: PRO (UK) ADM 1/4172.

78. Vice-Admiral Morard de Galles to the Minister of the Navy and Colonies, Brest, 14 Nivôse Year VII, SHD Marine, Vincennes, BB/3/153, Service Général, Correspondance, Brest, 1799; Manning levels during Germinal, Year VII, SHD Marine, Vincennes, BB/3/158, Service Général, Correspondance, Toulon, 1799.

79. Substance of the last information which has reached me directly from my correspondents in the sea ports, Brest, 20 Floréal Year V, TNA: PRO (UK) ADM 1/4172.

their home-countries. Having lost their wages by running away, they had few resources to sustain themselves for long, and so, in most cases, economic pressure or predatory recruitment soon forced them back into service on the first available ship. Frequently that ship sailed under a foreign flag. The men who ran from the British *Hermione* after the famous mutiny, for instance, variously ended up on Danish, Spanish, American, Dutch, and British merchantmen, in South American coastal shipping, on French privateers, and in American and even British naval vessels.[80]

Some men consciously chose to switch sides, and some only dreamed of it. John Daley, sergeant of marines on the British *Thames*, hoped one day to desert to the French, for he wrongfully believed them 'to have no flogging at all'.[81] Others did run. William Jetking served as a British soldier in the Low Countries, but as the French army moved north and brought revolution to the United Provinces, he crossed the lines and soon afterwards signed-on with the new Batavian navy. When Britain again invaded in 1799, Jetking stood ready to defend his adopted Republic at sea.[82] There were many more like him.[83]

More unusual even than the lower deck's high level of cross-border mobility was the astonishing explosion of mutiny that followed in their tracks. In navy after navy, the common seamen refused obedience on a massive scale, and before the decade was out, hundreds of ships' crews had risen on their officers. It began, as with so much else in these years, in France.

By the time that the Committee of Public Safety dispatched Jean-Bon Saint-André to reimpose order on the fleet in 1793, the lower deck had become almost ungovernable. Revolutionary seamen habitually disregarded their commanders; they organised autonomous councils; they struck for higher wages, for higher invalid-compensation, and for better treatment of war-widows and their children; they rioted through port-towns, wandered on and off their ships at will, threw admirals into prison, sabotaged their ships, refused to put to sea, and soon drove virtually the entire officer-corps into exile.

---

80. John Slenison's declaration, TNA: PRO (UK) ADM 1/397; John Duncan's declaration, TNA: PRO (UK) ADM 1/731; Petition of John Williams, TNA: PRO (UK) ADM 1/1031; Courts martial against men from the *Hermione*, TNA: PRO (UK) ADM 1/5343 and 1/5344; various letters relating to unrest on the *Malta*, TNA: PRO ADM 1/1048; 'Extract from Captain Thomas Truxtun's journal, U.S. Frigate *Constellation*, at Hampton Roads, 31 August 1798, Friday', in *Naval Documents* 1935, p. 365.

81. Court martial against men from the *Thames*, TNA: PRO (UK) ADM 1/5341.

82. Interrogation of William Jetking, NA (NL), Hoge Militaire Rechtspraak, 1795–1813 (1818), 2.01.11, inv. nr. 238.

83. List of individuals disembarked at Calais and demanding to serve the Republic, Thermidor, Year X – Brumaire, Year XI, Archives Nationales, Paris, F/7/3050, Police Générale, Year IV–1816.

The first major battle erupted in Brest in 1790. In August, the National Assembly passed a new *code pénal maritime* (articles of war) into law, one, it hoped, that would be more compatible with a 'free constitution' than the old one had been.[84] The new principle was to match every conceivable violation with a precise punishment, thus replacing the arbitrary powers of the captain with the predictability of the law. But the crews greeted it only 'with contempt', rose up in mutiny, and forced a more thorough revision of the sections dealing with corporeal punishments.[85]

The revolution in Saint-Domingue, meanwhile, radicalised seamen in the West-Indian fleet. Mutineers on the *Léopard* sided with the rebel-assembly in Saint-Marc, embarked its members, as well as a number of disobedient soldiers from the Port-au-Prince regiment, and sailed for Brest, where they were greeted as revolutionary heroes.[86] Suspicion now turned on the role of the officer-corps – already unpopular in Brest after the conflict over the new articles – and it became common wisdom that they sought to use the navy as a counter-revolutionary force in the colonies. Seamen were disinclined to be collaborators, and to get that message across, they erected gallows in Vice-Admiral Marigny's front-yard one night.[87]

In Toulon, three years of conflict between the commune, naval authorities, arsenal-workers, and seamen culminated in 'the treason' of 1793: a combination of counter-revolutionary plotting and paralysing internal struggle left port and fleet wide open for the British to seize, and they held onto it until they were driven out by a young Corsican artillery-commander, Buonaparte.[88] The temporary loss of Toulon, the country's second most important naval station, triggered a mass-mutiny by radical republicans in the Atlantic fleet, at the time cruising in Quiberon Bay. Afraid that traitors were about to hand Brest to the enemy, they formed an autonomous fleet-committee and demanded, in the name of popular sovereignty, that Admiral Morard de Galles take them home. The lower deck had come to consider themselves the guardians of the Revolution.[89]

---

84. 'Décret concernant le code pénal maritime (16, 19 et 21 Août 1790)', in *Recueil*, I, pp. 122–40.
85. 'Rapport sur l'insurrection qui a eu lieu à bord du vaisseau le Léopard', in *Recueil*, I, p. 166; 'Rapport et extrait d'une lettre des commissaries envoyés à Brest, 22 Octobre 1790', in *Recueil*, I, pp. 180–84.
86. Various letters and reports in SHD Marine, Vincennes, BB/4/3, Service Général, Campagnes (1790–1913), Iles Sous le Vent, 1790; Cormack 1995, pp. 86–7.
87. '17 Septembre 1790', in Esquieu and Delourmel 1909, pp. 206–8.
88. Saint-André n.d.; Cormack 1995, pp. 173–214.
89. Revolutionary tribunal of Brest, regarding the insurrection which took place at Quiberon on 13 and 14 September 1793, SHD Marine, Vincennes, BB/4/3, Service Général, Campagnes (1790–1913), 1793.

But then came the Terror. In a republic, seamen were reminded, obedience to the state is the first duty of the citizen, and henceforth any unruly behaviour, any questioning of authority, any collective petitioning, any refusal of orders, was counter-revolutionary, and it would be dealt with as such.[90] Mutinous seamen were suddenly redefined as standing outside and against the nation, and to make clear what that meant, Jean-Bon Saint-André ordered a floating guillotine to be constructed, rowed it out into the middle of the Brest roadstead, and there beheaded four mutineers in front of the entire fleet.[91] A flurry of organisational changes followed, rolling back many of the gains that seamen had won since the beginning of the Revolution. Despite occasional outbreaks of major unrest in the coming years – notably at Toulon in 1795, Brest and Cadiz in 1796, and on several ships in 1797 – the back of lower-deck insurrectionism was broken.[92] It was now that mass-desertions commenced in earnest.

Just as serious collective unrest was winding down in the French navy, it got underway in the British service. Beginning in 1793, British seamen launched a series of single-ship mutinies that all, in some way or other, concerned their working conditions. The men of the *Winchelsea* judged their ship unseaworthy, the *Windsor Castle*s wanted less brutal officers, the *Culloden*s also demanded a new ship, the *Terrible*s requested better provisions, and the crew of the *Defiance* more alcohol in their grog.[93] All of these mutinies took the form of the 'armed strike': the men went below, turned the guns towards the quarterdeck, and then opened negotiations.[94] But the officer-corps, perhaps with an eye towards the aristocrats dangling from lamp-posts across the Channel, was unresponsive. All five strikes were broken, 19 men were executed, and 13 flogged with up to three hundred lashes.

The British lower deck was not about to cave in just yet. In the spring and early summer of 1797, they organised the largest, most sustained working-class offensive of the century: around thirty-five thousand seamen in the home-command

---

90. 'Décret qui approuve un arrêté pris par les représentans du peuple, pour le rétablissement de la discipline à bord des vaisseaux de la République. Du 16 Nivôse an II', in *Recueil*, vol. I, pp. 279–88.

91. Cormack 1995, p. 253.

92. Various letters in SHD Marine, Vincennes, BB/3/85, Service Général, Correspondance, Réprésentans en mission, 1795; various letters in SHD Marine, Vincennes, BB/3/93, Service Général, Correspondance, Brest, 1796; various letters in SHD Marine, Vincennes, BB/3/114, Service Général, Correspondance, Brest, 1797; various letters and reports in SHD Marine, Vincennes, BB/3/119, Service Général, Correspondance, Rochefort, 1797.

93. Court martial against men from the *Winchelsea*, TNA: PRO (UK) ADM 1/5330; court martial against men from the *Windsor Castle*, TNA: PRO (UK) ADM 1/5331; court martial against men from the *Culloden*, TNA: PRO (UK) ADM 1/5331; court martial against men from the *Terrible*, TNA: PRO (UK) ADM 1/ 5331; court martial against men from the *Defiance*, TNA: PRO (UK) ADM 1/5334.

94. The phrase 'armed strike' is from Neale 1990.

ran up the red flag of mutiny, asked their officers to leave the ships, and then set about choosing delegates, forming ship- and fleet-committees, and even electing a president. Then they issued their demands. They wanted guaranteed shore-leave and freedom from press-gangs; they requested an increase in their wages; they demanded the abolition of officers' disproportionate privileges in regard to prize-money; they demanded the right to oust tyrannous commanders; and, when in breach of the articles of war, they wanted to be tried by a jury of their peers, not by a court martial made up only of officers.[95] Perhaps it was only a coincidence that most of these demands were among the concessions that seamen in the French navy had managed to wrest from the state early in the Revolution, but perhaps not.

The admiralty was only prepared to offer an increase in wages – the first in nearly a hundred and fifty years – and that proved unacceptable to the more militant wing of the mutineers. After two months, therefore, the government sent troops to suppress the mutiny: just over four hundred men were arrested, around sixty put on trial, 29 executed, dozens more imprisoned, a number flogged round the fleet, and a handful transported to the penal colony in New South Wales.[96]

Both the form and content of mutinies in the British navy now changed dramatically. Strike-like mutinies nearly disappeared entirely, and were, instead, replaced with shipboard seizures of power. In September 1797, the crew of the *Hermione*, having just learnt of the suppression of the fleet mutiny, seized the ship, killed 10 of their officers, and then handed the ship over to the enemy.[97] In the next two years, there were at least twelve serious conspiracies uncovered, all with more or less the same treasonous aims.[98] Then, in March 1800, the men on the *Danae* revolted and sailed the ship to France.[99] In November of that year, the crew of the *Albanaise* rose and took her to Spain.[100] In July 1801, the crew of the *Gaza* mutinied and escaped to Italy.[101] Finally, in February 1802, one month

---

95. Papers found on-board of the *Repulse*, 12 June 1797, TNA: PRO (UK) ADM 1/727.

96. Draft list of mutineers, TNA: PRO (UK) ADM 3/137; List of pardoned mutineers sent to Cold Bath Fields prison in preparation of their being sent to the hulks, TNA: PRO (UK) ADM 1/4173; Convicts transported, 1787–1809, TNA: PRO (UK) HO 11/1.

97. Statement of service, 1789–1839, of Lt. David O'Brien Casey (1779–1853), National Maritime Museum (UK), BGR/12.

98. Courts martial against men from the *Tremendous, Diana, Renomee, Caesar, Princess Royal, Haughty, Defiance, Glory, Ramillies, Queen Charlotte, Diomede,* and *Hope*, TNA: PRO (UK) ADM 1/5343, 1/5345, 1/5346, 1/5347, 1/5348, 1/5350, and 1/5351.

99. Courts martial against men from the *Danae*, TNA: PRO (UK) ADM 1/5353, 1/5354, and 1/5358.

100. Courts martial against men from the *Albanaise*, TNA: PRO (UK) ADM 1/5356, 1/5360, 1/5361, and 1/5362.

101. Courts martial against the men from the *Gaza*, TNA: PRO (UK) ADM 1/5359 and 1/5360.

before the Treaty of Amiens, the captain of the *Syren* uncovered what turned out to be the last treasonous shipboard conspiracy of the war.[102]

If British mutineers gradually turned towards treason, their counterparts in the Batavian navy were exceptionally disloyal from the start. It began with the *Jason* in 1796. The crew rose on their officers, explained to Captain Donckum that they felt the conditions under which they were expected to work were intolerable, and, since they had not signed up to serve under the flag of the Republic anyway, they felt no compelling reason to stay in Batavian service. They took the ship to Greenock in Scotland and handed it over to the enemy. Many of the mutineers joined the British Army, but the most active among them went into the Navy, and, no doubt, enjoyed the fleet-mutinies in the following year.[103]

Only a few weeks after the *Jason*, mutiny exploded in Vice-Admiral Lucas's squadron at Saldanha Bay in the Cape Colony. Within days of entering the bay, the squadron was surrounded by several thousand British land-troops and 13 Royal-Navy warships. On half of the Dutch ships, the crews now rose on their officers, broke into the spirit-rooms, and nearly beat to death several of their shipmates who were known as Patriots. Lucas called a council of war, and it was its unanimous decision to surrender the squadron to the British. Had it come to an engagement, the council was careful to note in its minutes, the crews of the ships would have been as likely to shoot their own officers as fire on the enemy.[104] Lower-deck morale probably improved only a little when, in October of the following year, the Texel fleet was ordered out to sea to get slaughtered by the British for no apparent reason. As expected, it was one of the bloodiest and most thorough defeats in Dutch naval history, and a substantial number of Saldanha-Bay mutineers contributed to it on the British side.[105]

The next year, one of the ships that had been lucky enough to escape the slaughter at Camperdown became the scene of one of the most bloody-minded conspiracies of the decade. Around forty men on the *Utrecht* – nearly all of them hardened veterans, nearly all of them foreign-born, and nearly all of them former deserters – planned to kill every officer on-board save for one lieutenant, cut the cable, run up a Danish flag for decoy, and then, if necessary, fight their way past

---

102. Courts martial against men from the *Syren*, TNA: PRO (UK) ADM 1/5360.

103. Captain Donckum's report, NA (NL), Inventaries van de Archieven van het Departement van Marine, 1795–1813, 2.01.29.01, inv. nr. 451; various letters concerning the *Jason*, TNA: PRO (UK) ADM 98/107 and 99/94.

104. Vice-Admiral Engelbertus Lucas, Dispatches, 20 August 1796, Captain Adjoint A.J. Knok's report, conclusions of the council of war, 16 August 1796, NA (NL), Hoge Militaire Rechtspraak, 1795–1813 (1818), 2.01.11, inv. nr. 221.

105. Captain-Lieutenant Ruijsch to Vice-Admiral de Winter, 12 July 1797, NA (NL), Departement van Marine, 1795–1813, 2.01.29.01, inv. nr. 236.

the batteries guarding the entrance to the Texel roadstead. Their aim was to plunder the ship, and then head for either England or Hamburg.[106]

The *Utrecht* was also involved in the last, catastrophic explosion of unrest in the Batavian navy: the mutiny and surrender of the Texel fleet in the summer of 1799. After an overwhelming British force had moved into the Dutch roadstead, all the tensions, all the frustrations, all the mutual hatreds and suspicions – between commissioned and petty officers, between officers and men, between Patriots and Orangists, between Dutch and foreign-born, between seamen and landsmen, ultimately, between men in war and revolution – suddenly, violently broke loose in the Dutch fleet. On some ships, the lower deck – possibly recalling the senseless slaughter at Camperdown two years before – refused to fight, and went Patriot-hunting instead. On others, they did the opposite, instead attacking their officers for acting cowardly in the face of the enemy. On yet others, they suspected, not without reason, that their commanders had ordered the ships to be blown up rather than surrendered. On nearly all of them, large-scale violence broke out, and several men – most of them known Patriots – were brutally murdered. The fleet was paralysed, and easy prey for the British.[107]

Conclusion

As fighting-season dragged into fighting-season, and desertion-rates remained high and kept rising, an ever-larger number of men grew into hardened veterans with experience of service in several different fleets. Biographies like Carl Ortmann's became common: born in Danzig, he had served in the French navy, been imprisoned by the British, and was hanged for plotting a violent, treasonous mutiny on a Dutch warship. One of his co-conspirators, Louwrens Perinai, was born in Hungary, served in the Imperial navy in the war against the Ottoman Empire, and after that had made his way to the Low Countries. A third conspirator, Daniel Thulander, came from Sweden and had served in the war against Russia between 1788 and 1790, after which he had signed-on with a merchantman that left him in Amsterdam.[108] How many such men were drifting around in the Atlantic naval world is difficult to determine, but even if one assumes only a very cautious average of somewhere between ten and thirty percent foreign-born

---

106. Courts martial against the men from the *Utrecht*, NA (NL), Hoge Militaire Rechtspraak, 1795–1813 (1818), 2.01.11, inv. nr. 234.

107. Various interrogation minutes and reports, NA (NL), Hoge Militaire Rechtspraak, 1795–1813 (1818), 2.01.11, inv. nrs. 236–42.

108. Sentence against Carl Ortmann, sentence against Louwrens Perinai, and second interrogation of Daniel Thulander, NA (NL), Hoge Militaire Rechtspraak, 1795–1813 (1818), 2.01.11, inv. nr. 234.

men in the major fleets, it is clear that their numbers were significant, probably in the tens of thousands.

On many ships, men from a dozen or more countries served together, and even though some of these countries were officially at war with each other, there is surprisingly little evidence of mutual animosity on the lower deck. On the contrary, seamen were renowned for their strong sense of brotherhood, a trait that they learnt to prize after spending years working, living, and fighting together in fragile wooden structures on storm-tossed, war-torn seas. Men who were sent up into the yards together during a gale or down onto the gundeck in a battle had no choice but to learn to trust each other implicitly. Just as importantly, seamen loved to talk about their lives – 'a subject', noted Melville, 'upon which most high-bred castaways in a man-of-war are very diffuse' – and the boredom of naval service gave them plenty of opportunity to do so.[109] As they sat together night after night, year after year, comparing and collating their experiences, it cannot have failed to escape their notice how similar many of their stories were.

Deracination, followed by coerced servitude and savage discipline, were broadly shared experiences on the lower deck. Regardless of their native country, regardless of the flag they served under, regardless of whether they had once been 'outcasts, convicts, foreigners, mechanics, husbandmen, labourers, fishermen, [or] watermen', after a few years of service at sea they became naval warworkers, Atlantic proletarians.[110] Without the emergence of this shared identity, rooted in their collective, border-hopping experience, it is difficult to understand why disgruntled seamen across the Atlantic naval world suddenly stopped running away, instead turning to mutiny on such a vast scale.

Naval authorities were quick to suspect foreign-born men when they contemplated the eruption of increasingly disloyal mutinies and mass-desertions in the later 1790s. In France, they worried that their port – towns were swamped with '*hommes de tous les pays, peu disciplinés, difficilement surveillés*' (men of all countries, undisciplined, difficult to monitor), and they constantly suspected them of stirring up trouble.[111] Their colleagues in Britain agreed: to them, 'Irish & Foreigners' was simply a way of describing potential mutineers.[112]

It probably appeared comforting to frame the problem in such national terms, but the reality was rather different. Foreign-born men were neither more nor less prone to rebel than the native-born, but they did have a particular kind of dangerous influence. Their presence on-board built bridges between the lower decks

---

109. Melville 1990, p. 53.
110. A Captain in the Royal Navy 1804, p. 36.
111. Prefect maritime Caffarelli to the minister of the navy, Brest, 12 Messidor Year IX, SHD Marine, Vincennes, BB/3/181, Service Général, Correspondance, Brest, 1801.
112. Vice Admiral Sir Thomas Pasley to the Lords of the Admiralty, Hamoaze, 9 May 1799, TNA: PRO (UK) ADM 1/814.

of different navies, and so demystified the enemy. This, in turn, intensified the conflict between forecastle and quarterdeck, for not only were the men brutalised in order to kill and be killed, but they realised that they were sent into battle against men very much like themselves. When the men on the British *Pompée* conspired to rise on their officers in June 1797, hoping thereby to trigger a second fleet-mutiny, this time with the aim of forcing the government to make peace, the dangerous potential of this insight became fully apparent. Shortly before the planned insurrection, one of the chief-conspirators, William Guthrie, 'pointed his hand through the Port towards France and said it is not our Enemies that live there it is our Friends'. Such internationalism was intolerable on the frontlines. Three men were sentenced to death, two recommended for mercy, and one condemned to twelve months' solitary confinement in Marshalsea prison.[113]

---

113. Court martial against the men from the *Pompée*, TNA: PRO (UK) ADM 1/5339.

Class-Warfare: Primitive Accumulation, Military Revolution and the British War-Worker
Peter Way

'Force is the midwife of every old society which is pregnant with a new one', Karl Marx avowed in *Capital*. 'It is itself an economic power'. He was referring in particular to the actions taken by the state that contributed to the process that he termed 'the so-called primitive accumulation' in which capital and labour initially formed. With regard to Britain, he addressed the conversion of feudal lands to private property, the enclosure of the commons, the vagrancy- and Poor-Law acts, and wage- and anti-combination measures: the whole coercive apparatus that constituted the infrastructure of capitalism and freed workers from feudal relations for participation in the market. Such 'idyllic methods of primitive accumulation...conquered the field for capitalist agriculture, incorporated the soil into capital, and created for the urban industries the necessary supplies of free and rightless proletarians'. In the colonies, the expropriation of native lands and of indigenous peoples, the extraction of staple-commodities, and the enslavement and transshipment of Africans received his attention. These proceedings are 'the chief moments of primitive accumulation', he recited. 'Hard on their heels follows the commercial war of the European nations, with has the globe as its battlefield'.[1]

This essay departs from Marx's observations to explore the army's role in the transition to capitalism,

---

1. Marx 1976, pp. 916, 895, and 873–940 *passim*.

to place state-sponsored armed conflict in the context of imperial aggrandise-ment in the interests of merchant-capital, which led directly to modern colonial-ism and the social formation of capitalism. For, if force is necessary for change, and is itself economic in nature, then the courts, customs-collectors and colonial officials constituted but implied threats. Ultimate force came in the form of mili-tary action, which flowed from, and proved essential to, the process of primitive accumulation at home and abroad. Further, if the military is central to – and, in fact, productive of – these profound economic changes, it is necessary to re-conceptualise soldiers as war-workers, indeed, as transnational labourers whose martial toil around the globe proved integral to the development of inter-national capitalism.

The early-modern era witnessed what historians of warfare have called a military revolution, involving relatively swift technological and organisational innovation and marked growth in the scale and intensity of armed conflict, developments which had profound implications for both state and society. Often discussed in the curiously bloodless terms of military innovation or state-formation, military revolution was actually part and parcel of the very bloody enterprise of primitive accumulation through the pacification of a nation's gen-eral populace; the subordination of feudal or regional opponents to state-power; state-formation and the creation of fiscal structures to support the military; and the conquest of formerly autonomous states or pre-state polities, as well as the subjugation of their indigenous peoples. Empire comprised the larger theatre of military revolution. The war-machine provided the means necessary for the cre-ation of international capital and its protection within the imperial sphere, the soldiers being the requisite force. Thus warfare must be liberated from national-ist discourses of diplomacy, nation-building and the formation of national iden-tities, in order to reveal the fundamental role of state-sponsored armed conflict in the accumulation of capital antecedent to modern capitalism. Moreover, our understanding of the state and state-power needs to expand beyond confining national boundaries: this was a time in which commerce defined the accessible globe, but the state, through its transnational projection of military and naval power, secured the domains, trading-routes, and human labour upon which merchant-capital depended. State, capital and armed forces formed a triad, a military-commercial complex, so to speak, that lay at the heart of the interna-tional process of primitive accumulation.

That understanding alone proves insufficient, however. War is not some abstract process; it is work – at times hellish, other times banal – performed by a peculiar type of worker. Viewed on his own, it is hard to see a soldier as a worker whose hands produce tangible value. But conceived as a collectivity, an army, cogs in the war machine, soldiers acquire power to wrought fundamental change. The paid labour of soldiers aggregated contributed directly to the political economic project of the imperial state. Such labour won new territories, eliminated or expropriated indigenous peoples, built the infrastructure of empire and defended the new boundaries within which merchant capital could safely pursue economic interest. Soldiers' Herculean labours must be understood in relation to the experiences of other labourers; that is, in terms of proletarianisation, work discipline, class formation and class conflict. At the same time, military labour departed from more traditional forms of labour in its normative separation from civil society due to its engagement in bloodletting, work at once taboo and naturally deemed destructive rather than productive. Soldiers have been made to stand aside from the working class, but their labour in the service of the state is no less a part of capitalism than other 'service' industries, and in the context of the early-modern era, more central to the entire enterprise.

Warfare constituted both a cause and an effect of primitive accumulation, non-mercenary soldiers the martial proletariat thrown up by the process. To engage fully with these ideas, we must move beyond a narrow reading of class rooted in an age of industrial machinofacture. First, our understanding of the transition to capitalism should be expanded beyond the economic and legalistic means by which capital accumulated to incorporate warfare as a central engine of the process of capital and state formation, as well as of the related phenomenon of colonisation. Second, production needs to be less narrowly construed as the generation of a commodity for market consumption. While actively engaged in a destructive enterprise, the military labour-process also creates social and political formations and produces infrastructure as essential to the emergence and operation of the international market as were the sugar and tobacco produced by slaves or indentured servants on plantations. Third, the worker needs to be re-imagined so that military labour is understood in terms of proletarian labour. As Marcel van der Linden argues, 'We have to recognise, that the "real" wage-workers, which were the centre of attention for Marx, that is, workers who as free individuals can dispose of their own labour-power as their own commodity, and have no other commodity for sale... are only one kind of way in which capitalism transforms labour power into a commodity. There are many other forms which demand equal attention, such as chattel slaves, indentured labourers, sharecroppers, etc'.[2] I would add martial workers to this list. Wage-workers, but bound by their oath to serve ostensibly for life, subject to work discipline far more punitive than in civil society, the blood they purged in performing their duties became the currency of commercial empire.

---

2. Van der Linden 2007c, p. 176.

This essay focuses on the British experience in the Seven Years' War, a seminal period in Anglo-American history, when the British Empire came of age, the groundwork of modern imperialism was laid, and the seeds were sown for colonialist revolts by Native Americans and American colonists. The military history of merchant-capital, however, was not peculiar to the British, nor confined to the Atlantic. Wherever European nations fought for territory and access to trade across the globe, the labour of soldiers and sailors comprised crucial components to empire building.

Military revolution and the fiscal-military state

Early-modern states were fundamentally geared to engaging in armed conflict. Michael Duffy observed, 'the governments of Ancien Régime Europe were really giant war-making machines devoting their main efforts to the maintenance of large armed forces'.[3] This situation arose as the result of a military revolution, which according to its originator, Michael Roberts, occurred between 1560 and 1660. Geoffrey Parker updated and globalised the concept, arguing that fortification, firepower, and swelling numbers of armies comprised the three key elements to the revolution, allowing western powers to dominate the world. Infantry eclipsed cavalry and the size of armies mushroomed to maximise firepower. The intensification of warfare required greater coordination and thus training and discipline, and contributed to the decline of private military forces and the rise of professional armies.[4] By the eighteenth century soldiers rarely were mercenaries fighting for a fee and booty under a military enterpriser,[5] but more commonly the paid employees of the state, subject to its disciplines and instruments of its political economic objectives. The era of the Seven Years' War marked the culmination of the military revolution for Parker.[6]

The expansion of military-power proved integral to state-formation.[7] One of the central strands of the military revolution and of modern state-formation, according to Peter Wilson, proved to be the struggle over who had the right to exercise armed force. The centralisation of fiscal-military power to one authority,

---

3. Duffy 1980a, p. 4.
4. Roberts 1956; Parker 1996, pp. 3–4, 10–11, 19–20, 24, 43.
5. A military enterpriser was a military contractor who raised a company of troops and contracted their services to a state or nobleman. Redlich 1964.
6. Parker 1996, pp. 149–51.
7. This is not a new correlation. Max Weber, in *Economy and Society*, maintained that it 'was most often needs arising from the creation of standing armies called forth by power politics, and the development of financial systems connected with them, that more often than anything else has furthered the trend towards bureaucratization'. Cited in Ertman 1994, p. 34.

usually a monarch, constituted the first stage in the process, and was achieved by most European states by the mid-fifteenth century. A key component of this stage was the state's struggle to assert exclusive control over the exercise of military-power in their own lands, having to repress quasi-feudal claims to military rights. The second stage, covering much of the sixteenth and seventeenth centuries, involved internal power-struggles over the extent of these powers, and ended with the acceptance of centralised authority but with powers dispersed to varying extents, accounting for the different constitutions adopted by European states.[8] This monopoly of military force empowered states to pursue the types of social and economic change Marx enumerated in his discussion of primitive accumulation, and to attempt to project that change internationally by dint of armed might.

The struggle for monopoly rights to military-force and the concomitant engagement in increasingly intensive armed conflict caused political changes leading to the development of the modern state, while laying the foundations of economic development. The growth in the size and professionalism of standing armies in the sixteenth and seventeenth centuries, increasing tenfold in just Two hundred years,[9] necessitated an expansion in the state-apparatus to maintain and finance the military. The military revolution also fostered significant state-intervention in the economy, with the state becoming a large producer and consumer of goods and provisions, for example in the shipbuilding- and construction-industries.[10] The state emerged to service the military and the military waxed in strength to protect the nurturing state. This incestuous relationship in most cases led to absolutist rule and the privileging of a military caste (particularly so in eastern Europe). England departed from this trajectory, most argue, managing both to maintain powerful combined military and naval forces, and to develop the most liberal of governing systems of its time.

John Brewer, however, refuted this view that the military was not a dominant force in British society. Instead, he proposed the model of 'the fiscal-military state', by which he meant a state with the main function of waging war and a fiscal policy and administrative apparatus geared to that end. War constituted 'the main business of the state' for Brewer, moreover he argued (unwittingly echoing Marx) '[w]ar was an economic as well as a military activity: its causes, conduct and consequences as much a matter of money as martial prowess'.[11] From the late seventeenth to early eighteenth century, Britain waged war repeatedly with France and her allies in what some scholars call the second Hundred Years' War.

---

8. Wilson 1998, p. 7; Anderson 1988, pp. 29–30.
9. Brewer 1989, p. 8.
10. Duffy 1980a, pp. 5–6.
11. Brewer 1989, pp. xi, xv, xvii, xx.

And the scale of war grew exponentially; between 1689 and 1780, Britain's army and navy grew by Three hundred percent. In addition to funding masses of armed personnel, the state also had to construct a support infrastructure, such as tax collectors, bureaucrats, contractors and victuallers, makers of armaments, dockyard workers, paymasters and commissaries. Consequently, the fiscal-military state 'dwarfed any civilian enterprise'.[12] Needless to say, it entailed great expense. Military expenditure during the major wars of 1688–1783 amounted to 61–74 percent of public spending; and when costs of servicing debt are included, 75–85 percent of annual expenditure went to fund Britain's war-making capabilities.[13] England was able to wage war on this scale due to its wealth, and the state was able to raise this money due to its undisputed powers of national taxation, the fluidity of capital in a commercial economy, and the development of fiscal knowledge enabling borrowing against tax income.[14]

British government-powers expanded in the late seventeenth and early eighteenth centuries to enhance the nation's war-making abilities. It was able to fund its expanding military commitments by sharply increasing taxation, engaging in 'public deficit finance (a national debt)' in an unprecedented fashion, and creating an administrative structure for military and fiscal needs.[15] The Treasury emerged after the Restoration as the controlling body over government-expenditure and tax-collection, particularly of customs, excise and the land-tax.[16] The utilisation of public debt constituted the other key to funding the fiscal-military state. Public debt in this period transformed from short-term to long-term borrowing. Debt rose quickly during war, meaning often a discounting of government bills, thus making it harder to secure credit. The solution was to convert this short-term liability to long-term funded debt in the form of interest-bearing stocks to be paid for from indirect taxes (customs, excise and stamp-duties) determined by parliament.[17] Thus, from 1688–1714, the British state transformed into a fiscal-military state with elevated taxation, sophisticated government-administration, a standing army, and the desire to be a major European power.

The literature on military revolution and state-building, for all its differences, agrees on the central role of war in the formation of states. But a strong tendency exists to treat warfare as a closed loop of advances in military technique and technology and corollary state-development. From one perspective, the military revolution arises *sui generis*, cultured by the battlefield and logistical needs. From another, state-formation precipitates martial innovation through its

---

12. Brewer 1989, pp. 29, 34.
13. Brewer 1989, pp. 27, 40–1.
14. Brewer 1989, p. 42.
15. Brewer 1989, pp. xi, xv, 42, 65.
16. Brewer 1989, pp. 91–8, 128–9, 91.
17. Brewer 1989, pp. 117–19.

defence-requirements. Yet both posit a process that operates at a level divorced from the main historical actors – the soldiers – and in some instances from the social and economic transformations making Europe modern. Even in its most fully – realised form, Brewer's fiscal-military state, there is little acknowledgement that what is actually being documented is the emergence of the capitalist state with its instruments of wealth-accumulation and the development of the associated fiscal infrastructure of banks and insurers populated by a burgeoning bourgeoisie, both reinforced by an expansive military. What military 'revolutionaries' take for granted as a natural development was actually a restructuring of society along commercial lines in which many in Britain and its colonies paid a heavy price for economic and military competitiveness. The very things that Brewer denotes as marking the formation of Britain's fiscal-military state at the turn of the eighteenth century – the expansion of a system of taxation, the notion of public credit and creation of a national debt, the founding of the Bank of England in 1694 – Marx argued marks the era as one of the consolidation of capital. He traced these developments back to the 'colonial system, with its maritime trade and its commercial wars'.[18]

The imperial setting receives little attention from most historians of the military revolution.[19] Yet the fiscal-military state derived in large part from colonial sources – in the need to extend and protect commerce, to keep the colonies free of threats from other colonisers, and to ensure the flow of commodities that, through customs-payments and the spur they provided to the domestic economy, fuelled the war-machine. England's exploration and settlement of new territories necessitated military support, fuelling growth in armies and navies that required unprecedented amounts of capital, which colonial trade provided through customs-collection and taxation of the wealth generated, while the state-apparatus grew in size and activity as a means of managing the military, trade and colonies. Not only did the fiscal-military state have its roots in the colonies, it would reach its logical fulfilment there in the form of militarily-dominated dependencies productive of the economic resources requisite to the perpetuation of the fiscal-military state at home. A supranational accumulative structure developed – funding military expeditions, manufacturing trade-goods, building ships to wage sea-battle or ply trade-routes, producing textiles for

---

18. Marx 1976, p. 919.

19. 'The Age of Discovery called for an increase in both land and sea forces to take advantage of the new overseas opportunities', Michael Duffy prefaced his *The Military Revolution and the State* (Duffy 1980a, p. 1), but this collection of essays did not do much to interrogate the nature of colonial endeavors or the roots of military expansion. For Geoffrey Parker, the West's superior military power allowed it to dominate the world (Parker 1996, pp. 3–4). But Parker's concentration on military tactics and technology tends to dim the role played by political and economic motivations.

soldiers' uniforms, engrossing lands, freeing people from their cultural roots and reallocating them to where their labour was needed, colonising new territories, and engaging in wars to protect the whole structure – a whirlpool of economic activity that spun and spun. Hardly apart from civil concerns or the hell-bent pursuit of profit, the military, under the guise of national interests, helped propel merchant-capital's cyclotron.

> [A]t the end the end of the seventeenth century in England, the different moments of primitive accumulation are systematically combined, embracing the colonies, the national debt, the modern tax system, and the system of protection. These methods depend in part on brute force, for instance the colonial system. But they all employ the power of the state, the concentrated and organized force of society, to hasten, as in a hothouse, the process of transformation of the feudal mode of production into the capitalist mode, and to shorten the transition.[20]

The army comprised the most visceral embodiment of the brutish power of the state, its muscles and sinews the essential apparatus of the colonial system.

The conjoining of militarism and colonialism entered a new era when Britain exported the military revolution to the New World in the Seven Years' War. Historians have characterised the Empire in the seventeenth and eighteenth centuries as commercial in nature, a broad and loosely connected mercantile market ultimately made more systematic by what Daniel Baugh calls Britain's 'blue-water' policy. The main tenets of this policy were: the defence of Britain received first priority; naval control of the English Channel and the North Sea constituted the basic military objective; trade and shipping were the keys to paying for defence and providing the infrastructure to naval prowess; and colonies were important insomuch as they contributed to trade.[21] The 'Atlantic system' that began to take shape under this blue-water policy required a large navy and a growing bureaucracy to pay for it by managing taxation.[22] Valuing colonies primarily for their exports, Britain largely left them to fend for themselves in times of war, instead concentrating its resources on the Royal Navy to protect the British Isles and keep seas open for commerce. Militias and armies raised by the colonies, crisis by crisis, waged the land-war in North America. By the mid eighteenth century, however, the causes of war shifted from issues of succession and alliance in Europe to the acquisition and defence of territories abroad. Just as at home, lands were being enclosed, their former inhabitants removed, and their perimeters fenced and protected by an increasingly punitive and violent

---

20. Marx 1976, pp. 915–16.
21. Baugh 1988, pp. 40–1.
22. Baugh 1994, pp. 185–8.

legal system, foreign lands were coming to be seen as the personal property of the British people, as embodied by the king, to be forcibly taken from those who formerly used them, converted into the private property of those who secured their ownership by the legal process, tilled by labour bonded and free, and to be ringed by a chain of forts manned by the king's troops. The army occupied the centre of this empire-building process.

The Seven Years' War constituted an important catalyst to these processes. The War marked a significant turning point in the nature of empire from being distinctly commercial to being increasingly territorial.[23] Two decisions undergirded this transformation: the unprecedented commitment of tens of thousands of troops to the American theatre; and the stationing of a standing army in North America at the war's end to protect the new acquisitions. The army was an essential player in the winning of this territorial empire, and the empire was increasingly dependent on the army for its defence. The military revolution that had transformed European warfare and the nature of the state was exported to the New World. From Braddock's failed expedition to the Ohio Valley in 1755 to the British capture of Havana in 1762, tens of thousands of men laboured to make Britain the preeminent imperial power in the New World. To deny their efforts, to shroud their work by the red coat, is to buy into the nationalist mystification of military life and the concomitant conjuring of death as the lifeblood of the fatherland.

Freeing the war-worker

Manpower constituted the *sine qua non* for warfare in the era of the military revolution. Technology and strategy might propel, but flesh and blood bore the brunt of the assault. And soldiers, like workers, had to be created, either uprooted from the soil or exiled from the workshop, but certainly severed from the means of production. This was a drawn-out process. Military labour itself did not remain static in nature, in fact undergoing a transformation as part of the military revolution that paralleled primitive accumulation's 'freeing' of the worker; in general terms evolving (in a messily overlapping fashion) from a serf's military-service owed a feudal lord, to the selling of labour-power by a mercenary (or martial journeyman) to a captain who contracted it to a general or state;

---

23. The Seven Years' War was 'the watershed', argued P.J. Marshall (Marshall 1998, p. 1). 'The war revealed that most of those who ruled Britain were investing Empire with a new significance. It was seen as vital to Britain's economic wellbeing, to her standing as a great power, and even to her national survival. British governments began to concern themselves with colonial issues and to commit resources to overseas war on an unprecedented scale'.

to the professional soldier who voluntarily enlisted or was coerced to serve in the army of a particular nation-state. This process was part of the growing control of the state over armed conflict, which witnessed a transition from local militias and 'feudal and quasi-feudal' forces, to professional armies largely manned by mercenaries and officered by military enterprisers, to standing armies raised and administered by the nation-state.[24] Even within that last formation, the state-based army, soldiers of the eighteenth century occupied various labour-relations, ranging from the coerced military labour in wartime of, for example, Frederick the Great's Prussia, to the more voluntary levying of France.[25] In every instance, however, an army had to be raised; labour had to be extracted from the civil economy and fed into the war-industry as armies became engines of primitive accumulation's freeing of the worker.

The connection between proletarianisation and military mobilisation can be seen at work in the Seven Years' War. The strength of the British army in America rose from about 3,000 men in 1754 to a peak of 25,000–30,000 troops in 1761 (exclusive of the thousands of provincial troops raised by the colonies); and when high rates of attrition as a result of incapacitation, death and desertion are taken into consideration, it means that the army's labour needs likely figured in the 50,000–75,000 range for the American theatre alone over the course of the war, the largest concentration of European military resources in North America up to that time. These numbers were no small matter for any society, especially considering that the overwhelming majority of recruits were raised in Britain.

How did the army manage to meet these labour-demands? Coercion offered one obvious solution. The press-gang and the crimp resonated in contemporary popular culture, but the naval service more often pursued these methods of mobilisation. The legacy of the army's role in the Civil War made the English leery of soldiers practicing strongarm tactics on the populace. Thus while the state routinely adopted impressment for the army during wartime, it functioned in a more limited fashion than did the naval press-gang. It targeted those on the margins of society, 'such able-bodied men, as have not any lawful employment or calling, or visible means for their maintenance and livelihood' in the words of the first Press Act of 1704, and local civic officials administered the press not the military. Even so, when the government adopted a press act for the Seven Years' War, popular resistance meant that it only operated for two years (1756–8), meaning that only a very small minority of those who served in the army during the war had been pressed into service.[26] As a result, Britain primarily relied on volunteers to man its army.

---

24. Anderson 2000, pp. 16–32.
25. Wilson 1998, p. 277; Corvisier 1979.
26. Gilbert 1976a, p. 9; Gilbert 1978, p. 7; Gilbert 1976b, p. 705.

What prompted men to volunteer for such an extraordinary enterprise as overseas service in the colonies? When looking at individual cases – and this is difficult to do as common soldiers left few self-reflective records behind – military historians typically point to recruits enlisting out of a sense of adventure, and a desire to escape the humdrum of labouring life or the clutches of local legal authorities for some indiscretion as motivation, as well as heartfelt patriotic feelings. One should not underestimate the power of patriotism in this era, as it has been observed that the eighteenth century witnessed the emergence of strong nationalist and imperialist currents in British culture, and that the Seven Years' War may have been the first to produce recognisably modern forms of war-jingoism.[27]

People no doubt could be caught up in the anti-French, anti-Catholic fervour, and enlist to defend English liberties and the Protestant faith, especially when duty was wedded to the promise of adventure. But Britain proved able to wage war according to the principles of the military revolution, and to do so primarily with a voluntary army, not as a result of youthful exuberance or patriotism's siren-call but for the very same reasons that necessitated such military operations: the economic changes associated with the primitive accumulation of capital. E.A. Wrigley asserted 'the acid test of the strength of an economy is its ability to mobilize sufficient resources to conduct warfare successfully'. As warfare grew in dimension, in terms of material required, size of armies and length of conflict, and as taxation became the basis for military expansion, a nation's economic strength became more important as a factor in military success. The amount of national income that could be mobilised effectively was equally important as the absolute wealth available. Peasant-type economies based largely on subsistence produced less mobile resources that are more easily taxed than did numerically smaller populations operating within a commercial economy. But equally important to the equation is a society's ability to harvest fighting bodies in abundance without unduly harming the economy's productivity. The English economy differed most from those on the continent in the amount of the labour-force in agriculture. Roughly one-third of males worked the land (compared to two-thirds and above on the continent), and were productive enough to feed the rest of the population. '[T]he release of labour from the agricultural sector was such a prominent and unusual feature of modern England', affirmed Wrigley. Those freed from the land were available to work in commerce, manufacturing, service or transportation.[28] This highly mobile society also made England ripe for military mobilisation. While Wrigley broadly accepted the 'progressive' nature of

---

27. Colley 1996; Wilson 1994.
28. Wrigley 1994, pp. 72–3, 76–81, 89–91 (quotations on pp. 72, 83); Marx 1976, pp. 916–17.

the English agricultural economy and its 'release' of labour-power, from a more traditional-Marxian perspective, primitive, accumulation created a proletariat that could not be fully absorbed by industry, and the surplus flowed into tramping labour, indentured servitude, and the army and navy. Merchant-capital required armed forces to secure and defend its interests, and the changes initiated by capital-accumulation, in the freeing of labour-power, generated its own martial labour-force. The fact that Britain rose to the status of most advanced economic power and the dominant military power in the mid-eighteenth century derived from no mere coincidence.

We can get a clearer idea of exactly what lay behind that mobility by looking at the timing and character of mobilisation for the war, as well as the composition of the army. British soldiers of the eighteenth century were commonly referred to as 'the scum of the earth'. But as I have reported elsewhere, data drawn from the Chelsea Hospital Out-Pension Books suggests that the British army in America during the Seven Years' War came from a more skilled occupational background than implied by that sobriquet. While those who had been unskilled labourers, the classic proletariat, accounted for over four-tenths of the sample, almost half unexpectedly came from skilled craft backgrounds. Within these gross categories, four occupations in particular stood out: labourers (37 percent of the total), textile-workers (15 per cent), shoemakers (7 percent), and tailors (4 percent).[29] This data reflects the mobile nature of the English labour-market, as Wrigley would have it, but also points to an underlying current. The occupations that were at the forefront of the organisational changes in the relations of production associated with primitive accumulation (deskilling, piecework, casualisation of labour) – weaving, shoemaking and tailoring – comprised the vanguard of military labour alongside the anticipated manual labourers. The unexpected higher representation of men with skill among recruits for military service can be explained by specific economic factors at work in the English economy. The years in which army-recruitment spiked, from 1756, were years of depression with high prices and stagnant wages accompanied by food-riots and strikes, most significantly in the 1756 bread-riots cum wage-disputes in the Gloucester textile-trades.[30] Economic change, both in the long-term proletarianisation of the labouring classes associated with primitive accumulation, and the short-term swings of an increasingly capitalistic economy, directed thousands into martial wage-work, both those already proletarianised and those who had been holding onto the last shreds of the means of production in the form of

---

29. This analysis is based on the records of 845 soldiers granted pensions between March 1757 and December 1760 from regiments that had served in North America. See Way 2000.

30. Rule 1992, pp. 102–4, 110, 147–8; Rule 1986, pp. 256–9; Malcolmson 1981, pp. 113, 125.

their skill. Enlistment, ostensibly voluntary but enforced by structural change, sundered those last ties.

The picture is even more complex than this, for viewing the *British* army as the product of internal *English* economic developments obscures the heterogeneity of the very institution. Fighting on the scale that William Pitt aspired to in the Seven Years' War required manpower beyond the means of England alone. England looked elsewhere in its dominions to man its army, to domains already compromised by English imperialism rather than developed by proto-industrialisation, Scotland and Ireland. One could argue that the British army was the most *British* of institutions by the mideighteenth century, as revealed by the ethnic composition of the army in America. The English-born accounted for 30.3 percent of the whole, Scots 27.8 percent, Irish 27.2 percent, and continental Europeans 4.4 percent. Colonials made up 4.9 percent of the army, while foreign-born residents of America equaled 5.4 percent.[31] Given the relative populations of these elements of Great Britain, it is clear that Ireland and Scotland disproportionately manned the army, and they did so as a result of specific historical developments.

In Scotland, the series of Jacobite uprisings were finally laid to rest on Culloden field in 1746, and many of the Stuarts's Highland supporters were offered the option of enlisting in the regulars or execution for treason. Many who fought on either side in 1745 also served in America during the Seven Years' War, at least part of the time under the command of the Duke of Cumberland, the Bloody Butcher of the Scots and Commander General of the King's forces at the beginning of the war, and Lord Loudoun, one of his generals in the Scottish campaign and commander-in-chief in America (1756–8). Those Scots who were not involved in the uprising were indirectly affected. Britain established the Board of Annexed Estates to manage confiscated lands after the failed Jacobite uprising of 1745. Tasked with 'improving' the Highland agricultural economy by converting clan-patterns of land-management to more commercial bases, the Board first met in June 1755 and set about shortening leases, promoting single-tenant farms of sufficient size to produce market-surpluses, establishing the security of tenure, removing surplus farm-labour, restricting subtenure and evicting unwanted tenantry, better managing husbandry, and developing new villages. These acts led to large-scale eviction in some areas and sparked fears of depopulation among the Commissioners by 1760 and a reassessment of practices. This surplus-labour

---

31. This representation of the ethnic composition of the army in America derives from regimental returns made in 1757, which can be found in the Loudoun Papers, North American Series, Huntington Library, San Marino California, boxes 88 and 90. See: LO 4011/no. 1/90; LO 6695/99; LO 2533/no. 4/90; LO 2529/no. 1/90; LO 4012/no. 1/90; LO 1944 no. 5/90; LO 6616/88; LO 1683/no. 1/90; LO 5661/85; LO 1391/no. 1/90; LO 1384/no. 2/90; LO 3936/no. 1/90; LO 6639/89; LO 1345/no. 5/90; LO 6616/88; LO 4068/no. 2/90.

was destined for military service. In 1760, the Commissioners proposed in *Hints Towards a Plan for Managing the Forfeited Estates*, 'the propagation of a hardy and industrious race, fit for serving the public in war'.[32] Andrew Mackillop argues that England 'ghettoized' the region commercially and set it aside as a 'military reservation'.[33] And, fortuitously, just as economic depression in England had facilitated mobilisation, famine in Scotland in 1757 assisted the raising of Highland battalions.[34] Dating from the enlistment of highlanders for service in America during the Seven Years' War, the tartan became as much a fixture of the British army as did the redcoat.

Unlike Scotland or Wales, Ireland was a colony. More so than other British colonies, however, its history involved successive invasions and military conquest.[35] First came the wave of Anglo-Norman invaders, followed by 'New English' colonisers of Ireland in the period 1560–1660. The rebellion of 1641 led to the Cromwellian re-conquest and the imposition of a Protestant ascendancy.[36] The English Revolution and the defeat of James II and VII by William of Orange's Protestant armies handed control of provincial power and land to the Anglo-Irish. The Treaty of Limerick of 1692 initiated a series of anti-Catholic penal laws restricting the political, economic and social rights of Catholics.[37] The British fiscal-military state not coincidentally made its presence felt acutely in Ireland. English military build-up had only been allowed by promising to protect the Protestant succession, and offering guarantees against the creation of a standing army within Albion's borders. Both objectives were secured by transplanting the bulk of the British military to Ireland, a predominantly Catholic colony that required an occupying military presence, which was located across a sea from England but conveniently close to the strategic English Channel and North Sea. Hibernia functioned as a stationary troop-carrier for British security-interests. It also served as a prime source of the excessive manpower demanded by England's militarily-revolutionised army. The Treaty of Limerick established a standing army of 12,000 in the country, the only major part of the Empire to accept such a military presence. Taxes set by the Irish Parliament, dominated by the Anglo-Irish, paid for the army. English regiments subject to the English Mutiny Act of 1701 composed the army, whose primary functions entailed the defence of England and to provide a reserve of military labour for deployment elsewhere at the expense of the Irish. The British government profited substantially.[38] Wary

---

32. Mackillop 2000, pp. 77–83; *Hints* cited on pp. 89–90.
33. Mackillop 2000, p. 218.
34. Mackillop 2000, p. 229.
35. James 1973, pp. 289–91.
36. Canny 1987, pp. 159–60.
37. Pittock 1997, p. 49; James 1973, pp. 22–5, 201–3, 203 n. 45, 219–20, 234–6.
38. Mackillop 2000, pp. 23–4; James 1973, pp. 174–8, 181–2, 210–1, quotation on p. 177.

of the majority population and wanting to maintain the Protestant Ascendancy, the British government proscribed Catholics from the British army. Catholics did join the army unofficially, and this did lead to a conflict of loyalties for some in the Seven Years' War when confronting the French Catholic forces, but they had to abjure their faith when enlisting.[39] Britain proved almost equally loathe to enlist Irish Protestants. The regiments, though in Ireland, did not assume the character of 'Irish' regiments. The soldiers in the Irish regiments typically were not Irish. By 1715, the army had adopted a policy of recruiting in England. This rule held until 1745, when the need to mobilise sufficient men to fight the French and the Jacobites led to the recruiting of Irish Protestants from Ulster. The army's manpower-needs in the Seven Years' War again led to the large-scale enlistment of Irish Protestants (and, unofficially, Catholics).[40] In summer of 1756 alone, 1,100 troops destined for America were gleaned from Ireland.[41] The British army acquired a Celtic fringe.

The scale of conflict in the Seven Years' War – fought on three continents across the globe – strained British manpower-resources to such a point that other sources were tapped. Ultimately, Britain decided to fight the war in North America with its own army and to fight in Europe by proxy by purchasing the martial labour-power of another state. Since the Glorious Revolution, the British had depended on a largely voluntary army. It was only able to do this, however, by extensively utilising foreign soldiers and materials.[42] Peter Taylor argued that the fear of a standing army led the English to 'subcontracting the defense of their liberties and privileges to Germans, Native Americans, and Africans'. The 'tributary overlords of German territorial states' secured most of English business in supplying troops from within Europe.[43] The 'military-subsidy relationship' England had with Hesse-Cassel, a part of the Holy Roman Empire, sheds light on the phenomenon. Subsidy-treaties usually took the form of mutual defence-pacts, with arrangements for payments made per man supplied, a subsidy to the state for the duration of the war, and pay for the soldiers. The soldier's food would be paid for out of his 'subsistence' (or pay). The British received soldiers who

39. James 1973, pp. 264–5.

40. James 1973, pp. 178–80; Mackillop 2000, pp. 23–4.

41. George Brereton [to Loudoun], 8 April 1756, LO 1026/23; Dunk [George Montagu, 2nd Earl of] Halifax, 13 Aug. 1756, LO 1478/33.

42. D.W. Jones estimated that foreign troops accounted for 41 percent of British military forces as early as the Nine Years' War and almost 60 percent in the Wars of the Spanish Succession. Thereafter the foreign representation declined, but still comprised more than 14 percent of British forces and nearly one-third of military expenditures in the eighteenth century. Jones cited in Taylor 1994, p. 11.

43. Taylor 1994, pp. 9, 21.

were trained and equipped in return.[44] The Hessian state raised subsidy armies by developing a military tax, *Kontribution*, for training, equipping and payment of troops. It targeted 'marginal' people – the masterless, indolent, those deemed the most expendable – and effectively forced them to perform military-service.[45] This labour it sold on the international market for service in wars, and in the process the nature of the state, society and economy of Hesse-Cassel became attached to the dictates of the British fiscal-military state. Such bartering for coerced military labour in the eighteenth century allowed Britain to maintain its national army proper as an overwhelmingly voluntary force.

Artisans of war

Reorienting military history so that it can be brought to bear on the transition-to-capitalism debate is but the first objective. The second is to realign traditional-Marxian theory to allow for a reading of soldiering as work. 'The starting-point of the development that gave rise to the wage-labourer and to the capitalist was the enslavement of the worker', wrote Marx. 'So-called primitive accumulation, therefore, is nothing else than the historical process of divorcing the producer from the means of production'.[46] Marx's formulation seems to leave little room to manoeuvre. Formerly labourers experienced the servitude of feudalism, and the worker only emerged when freed from the means of production. The teleology imbedded in this formulation, canted as it is to industrial capitalism, obscures the long drawn-out 'process of divorcing the producer from the means of production', as well as the varying forms of 'unfreedom' that arose along the way. Partial freedom as experienced by family-labourers, household-servants, apprentices, tied agricultural workers, indentured servants, and so on, proved more common than free labour in the early-modern era, and arguably until the nineteenth century. Moreover, in its presumption of a linear pathway from serf to worker, the Marxian construct ignores the chronological evanescence of unfreedom, extinguishing in one place only to alight anew elsewhere at another time in another form. Military service constitutes one form of servitude that challenges hard-and-fast notions of bondage and freedom, and belies the Whiggish certitude in the triumph of the worker. By acknowledging the soldier as a worker, accepting his atypicality, and keeping an open mind on the nature of work, we can circumvent

---

44. Taylor 1994, pp. 1, 21–2. During the Seven Years' War, Britain contracted with Hesse-Cassel for 12,000 men in 1755, almost 19,000 in 1757, 12,000 two years later, and over 15,000 in 1760. Taylor 1994, pp. 24–25, Table 1. From 1751–60, English subsidies accounted for 40 per cent of all state revenue for Hesse-Cassel. Taylor 1994, pp. 36–7.

45. Taylor 1994, pp. 49–51, 68–70.

46. Marx 1976, pp. 874–5.

these conventions and place military labour in the centre of the development of the conditions that led to modern labour-forms, in the process opening the door to more flexible readings of contemporary global workers who function in a maze of labour-relations and modulations of unfreedom.

If anything, the kaleidoscope of labour-forms that inhabited the early-modern world reminds us how the nature of labour-exploitation in its finer workings was situational and complexioned by relations of power in specific contexts, including both the power of those who controlled labour and the undeniable agency of those very same labourers. The modern distinction drawn between free and unfree labour is far too rigid. Thus, engaging in a more nuanced reading of free and unfree labour would be productive. While slavery occupied one pole and proletarian labour another, a variety of labour-forms inhabited the rest of the globe. Robert Steinfeld contested the assumption that free labour constituted the norm in Anglo-America once feudal villeinage had disappeared in England, instead arguing that unfree labour proved the norm in early-modern England and its colonies. Free labour, at least as defined in its modern sense as 'labor undertaken under legal rules that did not give employers either the right to invoke criminal penalties for departure or the right to specific performance', first emerged in America in the early eighteenth century, but as 'a special rather than universal form of contractual labor'.[47] Labourers and artificers, as well as servants, were subject to punishment and imprisonment for violating the labour-contract by early departure, and most labour-law concerned the legal control exercised by masters over their workers.

Looking more closely at the different iterations of the unequal labour-relationship will help to situate military labour in the broader spectrum of working relationships. Labourers and artificers most closely approached a modern understanding of free labour. They worked casually, by the day, week or other term, or by the task, but were still subject to the legal restrictions obligating them to fulfil their contract as those who contracted for longer terms. Both types tended to be married and to head a household, which entailed leasing a cottage and small parcel of land or acquiring a right to common land. This access to land gave them the ability to exercise more control over the selling of their labour-power.[48] The ubiquitous servant comprised another labour-form. The term servant typically applied to household-servants who resided with their master and served for a contractual amount of time, normally a year. Servants tended to be unmarried, and left service around the age of 26 (men) and 24 (women), after they had accumulated sufficient wages to marry and establish a household, though some

47. Steinfeld 1991, pp. 3–4.
48. Steinfeld 1991, pp. 34–41.

laboured into their 30s.[49] Apprentices comprised another labour-form, youths contracted to masters for a number of years in return for being taught a trade. An apprentice by law had to obey his master who could 'correct' him if he did not perform his duties properly, although he could not beat him without going to civil authorities and to make his case. If the apprentice was found wanting in his duty, these authorities would have him punished. Apprentices differed from servants in that theirs was an educative relationship, they received no wages for their labour, and they served multi-year terms.[50] The statutes of labourers and Statute of Artificers compelled service from artificers, labourers, servants and apprentices alike. If they left before their term expired, they could be forcibly brought back to their master.[51] The prohibition against leaving a position before the contract was fulfilled was, in fact, tightened in eighteenth-century English law, and in particular applied to those occupations that had been most commercialised, like tailors and shoemakers, so as to ensure the labour-supply.[52]

American colonial practices and labour-law essentially followed English patterns, with the exception of indentured servitude, although English precedent existed for this form of labour. Indentures in the colonies were for longer terms, and the servants subject to harsher discipline, while servants also could be sold in colonies. The intensification of indentured labour resulted from the nature of the colonial labour-market, where scarcity prevailed and relatively easy access to the land existed. Over time the harshness of indentured servitude led to its differentiation from regular household-service, but it still only amounted to a variation of other forms of voluntary wage-labour.[53] By the eighteenth century, Americans viewed indentured servitude in terms of property, a commercial model that at its extreme posited a relationship between a person and a thing untempered by anything other than market forces, the indentured servant being but 'the dehumanized instrument of the other'.[54]

Where does military labour fit within the spectrum of labour-types drawn by Steinfeld? Soldiers were least like artificers and labourers. They did not work casually by day, week or task, but served for a long term, technically for life, but for a majority just for the duration of the war. They did not tend to be married and were not the heads of independent households. Unlike adult artificers and labourers from the beginning of the eighteenth century, officers could punish

---

49. Steinfeld 1991, pp. 17–21, 34.
50. Steinfeld 1991, pp. 25–7.
51. Steinfeld 1991, pp. 22–4.
52. Steinfeld 1991, pp. 113–4, 121.
53. Steinfeld 1991, pp. 40–54.
54. Steinfeld 1991, pp. 87–93; quotation on p. 91. For other studies of indentured servitude, see: Galenson 1981; Salinger 1987; Fogleman 1996; Tomlins 2001.

soldiers corporally for not following orders. Like these workers, however, soldiers were compelled to complete the term of their contract or face legal punishment, although in the American colonies from the beginning of the eighteenth century, this seemed to be no longer the case for civilian workers. Military labourers did share a number of features with servants. They resided with their masters, they were disallowed from leaving their employ for the duration of the labour-contract, and they were unlikely to marry. Soldiers, like servants, would be deemed adults but certainly not independent adults. Servants, however, escaped this status by leaving service by their mid-20s as a prelude to getting married and setting up a household. While some soldiers, particularly noncommissioned officers were allowed to marry and, less frequently, set up home, it was at the sufferance of their commanding officer. Most soldiers were not so favoured, so if they stayed in the military, they did so without a wife, family or house to call their own, making them adults but in perpetuated servitude. Military labour would seemingly have the least to do with apprenticeship, which after all was for educating youth in a particular trade without other remuneration. Soldiers were, for the most part, adults who worked for a wage. But there are rough correlations between the two labour-forms. Soldiers, like apprentices, served multi-year terms and remained subject to corporal punishment throughout that term. And many soldiers entered service as youths, and all those in the army were trained in the skills of warfare. But apprenticeship was seen as a stage in one's work-life, to be left behind by one's early 20s, whereas soldiering led nowhere but to more soldiering and prolonged dependence, or to work in a totally unrelated type of labour once out of the army. War-work offered soldiers a form of perennial youth, but in its unemancipated sense.

Military labour shared a number of features with indentured servitude. Indentured servants voluntarily exchanged a number of years of their labour in return for the costs of their transportation to the American colonies, care, food and clothing. They were wholly under the authority of their masters, subject to corporal punishment, and increasingly came to be seen as a commodity that could be traded in a labour-market. Most British soldiers voluntarily enlisted, nominally for life, but except for a core of professional soldiers, typically for war's duration. For their military service they received a wage, minus deductions to pay for clothing, equipment, food, and health-care. Soldiers were also subject to physical punishment, and punishment that proved far more brutal than that applied in civilian-service, with punishments of 1000 lashes being not unusual and loss of life regularly being exacted as penalty for flight from work. While soldiers were not viewed by the military as commodities to be acquired or exchanged with economic profit the overriding objective, they were transferable or expendable components of the war-machine that could be drafted from one regiment to another.

What is developing is a picture of martial labour as being an occupation in the early-modern Anglo-American world exhibiting less freedom relative to others, with the possible exception of indentured servitude. The unfree nature of soldiers' work constituted the central feature it shared with all these other forms of labour. And martial labour's unfreedom was compounded by the fact that it likely lasted longer than these other forms, rendering soldiers subordinate for an indeterminate period subject to the fortunes of war and the whims of their officers. While all the other forms of labour, even indentured servitude, seemed to offer a way out, a means of advancement, soldiering only seemed to promise more of the same, death, or perhaps life as a crippled begger. Military servitude appears more galling in that it threatened to consume one's life in a way that approached too close to slavery. Human capital to be accumulated and expended in the state's interest, even more so than indentured servants, thus, soldiers were 'the dehumanized instrument' of their masters,[55] although their dehumanisation did not result from their commodification but from their amalgamation with national interests. Soldiers constituted both instruments and objects of imperial authority. As soldiers, they freely enlisted in an occupation that involved taking from others their lands, their freedom and very lives. As workers in the war-industry, they were regimented and rendered unfree for the duration of their enlistment, subordinated as labourers and subjected to a cruel work-discipline, their alienated labour producing value by accumulating land and subordinating others. Unless we confront the elements of bondage in military service we can never fully comprehend the soldier's experience, or recognise yet another stream of unfreedom in merchant-capital's imperial project. The scope of this paper precludes an extensive examination of the production-process of warfare, but some broad strokes should limn the outlines of empire upon the canvass.

Empire-building

Youths did not enlist to become bonded labour to perform the routinised rounds of common labour, drill and drudgery that soldiers' work involved (as I have recounted elsewhere).[56] But it was precisely such productive activities as digging trenches, cutting and hauling wood, and erecting walls of stockades that contributed to the making of the empire in North America. The building of forts and garrisons such as Fort Pitt in Pennsylvania or Crown Point in New York not only acted as defensive military positions, they marked out and made concrete the expanding perimeter of state *imperium*, making safe new lands for

---

55. Steinfeld 1991, p. 91.
56. Way 2003.

settlement and ultimately conversion to commercial agriculture, while demonstrating to indigenous peoples that the land had changed hands and they had been reduced to client-status. The building of roads, such as Braddock's Road heading west from Cumberland Maryland, and Forbes's Road establishing connections between Philadelphia and Fort Pitt, laid the infrastructure of commercial growth, allowing not only for the movement of troops but also of agricultural produce in one direction and consumer-goods in another. These are but two examples of the more material products of Soldiers' labour.

On a more exalted height, one usually occupied by military historians, one can see how the true 'art' of war, fighting, in the acquisition of territories, key cities, and trade-routes led directly to the advancement of the British state and produced its superpower-status in the eighteenth century. In the Seven Years' War, several key victories can be said to have achieved exactly this objective: Louisbourg, Quebec, and Montreal evicted the French from North America. With the continent secure, Albion shifted its military might to the Caribbean. Martinique fell, followed by the capitulations of St. Lucia, Grenada, and St. Vincent. Next, with Spain now in the war, came the siege and fall of Havana. With the Treaty of Paris, these islands were exchanged for the title to Canada and Florida, making North America British east of the Mississippi. The Americas comprised but one theatre of the Seven Years' War, albeit the most hotly contested. As well as the war in Europe, conflict transited the globe to West Africa, India and the Far East.

William Pitt authorised an attack on the French stations on the West coast of Africa, the centre of its trade in slaves, gold-dust, ivory and, particularly, gum Arabic (essential to silk production). A small naval squadron manned with marines took Fort Louis on the Senegal River in April 1758, and a second expedition later in the year took Fort St. Michaels on the island of Goree and a slave-trading factory on the Gambia River. French slave trading and silk-production was disrupted, and British manufacturers and planters profited by their loss. At the end of the war, Britain would return Goree to the French, but hold onto the Senegal base for its African trade, securing direct access to the gum Arabic for its textile-manufacturers and cementing its preeminent position in the trade of human flesh.[57]

The Indian subcontinent would prove even more central to the British imperial project, as can be seen by the increasing commitment of military-resources to the region. British interests in India were served by the East India Company rather than a colonial government, but, as state involvement increased, the British transformed from traders to rulers of densely populated provinces during the eighteenth century. The shift began with the Seven Years' War and, for the first

---

57. Anderson 2000, p. 306.

time to any extent, a larger commitment of state military and naval resources to the subcontinent. Regular soldiers and a naval squadron went with Robert Clive to India in 1754. In 1757, Clive retook Calcutta from the nawab of Bengal and captured the French *Compagnie des Indes* factory at Chandernagore, and established control in Bengal. In January 1760, the British victory at the Battle of Wandiwash ended the influence of the French in India. At the peace, France surrendered all fortifications and territories settled since 1749. British dominance of East Indian trade was secured.[58] India was next used as a base to project British interests to the Far East. When Spain entered the war belatedly, Whitehall decided to target Manila in the Philippines, the centre of Spanish trade in the region. An expedition left Madras in 1762, reaching Manila in September, and soon took the city and fort. However, the Spanish withdrew across Manila Bay, established a base for a provisional government, and continued to harry the British forces until the end of war when Manila was returned to Spain.[59]

The global scale of the Seven Years' War made clear the extent of Britain's imperial ambitions and might of arms, but it should also illuminate for the historian that the 'nation of shopkeepers' meant to bring as much of the world as possible within the embrace of British merchant-capital. Soldiers and sailors constituted the instruments of this engrossment, and, while they could take pride in their martial achievements, they were not unaware of the price they paid for the advancement of the interests of others. James Miller, a common soldier in the 15th regiment, had fought from Louisbourg to Quebec to Montreal to Marintique to Cuba. After the fall of Havana he noted: 'By the above conquest the key to all the riches, in america were in our hands'.[60] Yet all but a few coins fell through the hands of the rank-and-file and into the purses of commanding officers, ledgers of military contractors, and coin-boxes of the Exchequer, enriching the ruling classes and their protecting state. This led to discontent among the troops. It was no mere coincidence that after the regiments returned from Cuba to North America in 1763, a general mutiny broke out in the British army over issues of pay and provision, infecting nearly every unit in North America from Louisbourg to Florida, and lasting in some outposts until the late spring of 1764.[61] Miller was in Quebec at the time of the mutiny. While speaking of the 'bad men' who wished to do violence to the officers, he also clearly expressed his sympathy for the cause of the uprising. After the mutiny was suppressed, Miller's regiment served in Canada for three years before the regiment's repatriation in 1768. Miller recorded that only 150 officers and men survived to return, and that the regiment had been brought up to strength four times in the ten years it had served in the

58. Anderson 2000, pp. 417–18.
59. Anderson 2000, pp. 490, 515–17.
60. Miller (undated), pp. 68–9.
61. For a fuller treatment of this mutiny, see Way 2000.

Americas, meaning a loss of twenty men for every one that survived. 'Is the population of Britain and Ireland adequate to such waste of men?' he ruminated.[62] Unfortunately, the nation proved all too capable of such waste.

Martial labour was not slavery and for many it was a voluntary occupation, but it was also a form of servitude, a bondage to the state and its imperial ambitions. Martial labour was coerced and cruelly corrected, and put to that most loathsome of human professions, bloodletting. Only force could compel such blood-work. Soldiers were held captive by the cruel logic of the military revolution that held that wars could only be won by hurling as many bodies as possible against one another, and by the cold calculations of merchant-capital that cared not what bodies it consumed in its pursuit of gain.

At once free and unfree, soldiers occupied a marchland of labour-relations that, while not that unusual in the eighteenth-century Anglo-American world, were drawn to an extreme in the military due to the unusual nature of 'production' in warfare. Early-modern historians have given much attention to the slave-factory, plantation, merchant-ship, craft-shop, and the household as significant sites where labour-forms were produced and reproduced by Janus-faced merchant-capital, but the military garrison has largely been ignored by other than military historians. Yet, the army was a central player in the making of capitalism; in the securing of the nation-state, in the appropriation of colonial territories and pacification of indigenous peoples, and in the protection of commerce. The triangle-trade may have coursed around the Atlantic on the sails of merchant- and naval ships, but it was anchored in every colonial setting by a military presence. The military revolution that has received so much attention from military historians intertwined with the process of primitive accumulation, together making for the bloody road that led to modern industrial capitalism, a broad pathway of human toil and suffering trodden by slaves, servants, labourers, and artisans alike with soldiers and sailors, every mile in this forced march marked by a resistive act, with the stocks, the whipping-post, the gallows that met this resistance comprising the mileposts. Living now as we do in another era, in which the interests of state and capital fuse with military power, and soldiers and civilians alike suffer, it is fitting that more attention be paid to a historical precursor of this unholy congress.

Editorial note: Subsequent to its publication in German, parts of this essay appeared in English in the author's "'black service ... white money': The Peculiar Institution of Military Labor in the British Army during the Seven Years' War", in: Leon Fink (ed.) *Workers Across the Americas: The Transnational Turn in Labor History* (New York: Oxford University Press, 2011), pp. 57–81.

---

62. Miller (undated), p. 86.

The Shifting Maelstrom: From Plantations to Assembly-Lines

Ferruccio Gambino and Devi Sacchetto

1. Introduction

The modern age saw migrants making their appearance on the world-scene in chains, and their liberty remains a conditioned one almost everywhere today. Generally speaking, capital has not so much followed in the footsteps of migrants as exercised its centripetal force in order to lure them with the promise of a wage or enchain them after destroying the preceding forms of subsistence. In what follows, we wish to draw attention to certain salient features of this process, which has combined elements of freedom and bondage, playing out largely on the terrain of employment-systems that have combined for four centuries the *free* trafficking of slaves and indentured servants with the contested liberty of wage-workers to abandon their employer. Contrary to what is affirmed or implied in many a manual of political economy, the waged individual's right to abandon his or her employer does not necessarily entail the power to choose a different, less unfavourable employer; if systems of employment can be described as battlefields, then *Monsieur Le Capital* usually has the advantage of acting from the higher ground.

According to the International Labour Organisation (ILO), in 2005 the world's immigrants – defined as those living outside their country of birth for longer than a year – numbered 191 million (49.6 percent of them women), a figure corresponding to 2.9 percent of the world's population.[1] This is not a very high percentage, even though the number of immigrants corresponds to more than 10 percent of the indigenous population in some countries, such as Switzerland and Saudi Arabia. These 191 million individuals, to which one should probably add another 10 percent of refugees, can be disaggregrated into five principal categories: permanent immigrants, or those who intend to remain in the country they have migrated to; contract-workers, who receive a temporary residence-permit (valid for the duration of a few months or years) and are denied the right to bring their family-members into the country of residence, as is the case for most such workers in the Gulf states; professionals, who are normally employed by transnational corporations or hold qualified positions within local firms; undocumented workers, so-called irregular immigrants (sometimes also called illegal immigrants), who have either entered the country illegally or outstayed their visa; the fifth category is that of refugees, or of those with a 'well-founded fear of being persecuted for reasons of race, religion, nationality, membership of a particular social group or political opinion', in the words of the Geneva Convention. There is of course a certain overlap between each of these five categories; generally speaking, the most frequent overlap is that between people who outstay the duration of their tourist-visa and people who occupy an irregular position within the national system of employment. Moreover, qualified professionals are not always immune to forms of constraint; in the United States, for example, many of them work under fixed-term contracts and do not have the right to bring their family members into the country.

The early twenty-first century has seen various attempts to rediscipline migrant-flows: in North America, in Asia and in Europe. We can describe these attempts in terms of a twofold selection-process. Immigrants deemed a threat to society face the most explicit and severe barriers; the populations of entire subcontinents may be subject to such barriers. A more opaque selection-process operates by granting a certain leeway to persons acting as formal and informal recruiters of labour for the target-countries. The regimentation of migrant-flows through bureaucratic procedures is driven by production-interests that would apply the 'just-in-time' principle not only to stocks but also to so-called human resources. This embeddedness accords well with a strategy of fostering the indigenous population's illusion that the presence of immigrants is only temporary.[2] The strategies autonomously developed by migrants[3] are frequently confronted with state- and institutional structures that tend towards imposing a rigid itinerary on

---

1. About 10–15 percent of the world's migrants do not dispose of valid documents: IOM 2008, pp. 2, 9.
2. Gambino 2003.
3. Papastergiadis 2000.

migrant-flows. This pattern is one of the principal means of regimenting the mobility of migrants, forcing it into as unitary as possible a framework. Within the apparently orderly process of labour-recruitment, one finds agencies that negotiate *ad personam*, but also recruiters of entire work-teams, as well as public or sectoral institutions that act as intermediaries between employers and migrant-workers, maintaining recruitment-offices in areas of out-migration. Recruiters respond to short-term manpower-demands that may be out of step with governmental immigration-policy. International recruitment fulfils a necessary function within the productive apparatus; it extends to sectors beyond those traditionally reliant on immigrant labour (agriculture and construction) and plays a role wherever production cannot easily be relocated and wherever unattractive working conditions and low wages cause the rate of labour turnover to rise.[4]

Formal and informal recruiters of migrant-labour have thus progressively extended their reach. The process of selecting and transferring labour is largely driven by potential employers and their demand for labour. There is a tendency within this international management of the labour-force to segment the labour-force by allocating specific types of workers to specific jobs. Employers consider such segmentation a reduction of their production-costs. On the level of society, the allocation of migrants to specific jobs presents itself as a double process: on the one hand, certain procedures are institutionalised; on the other hand, immigrants are disciplined to behave in a certain way. In Asia's urban peripheries, along the Southern border of the United States and along the edge of the European Union, centres and camps built to discipline undocumented migrants can be converted into informal recruitment-offices whenever the demand for manpower requires it. Such a lowering of the guard remains unheard of in migrant detention-centres located within the EU and the United States.

In the now lengthy history of modern migration, the intersections of free and bonded migration continue to cast their long shadow over the various trajectories of departure, transit and arrival. In what follows, we wish to contribute especially to the debate on the turnover of free and bonded labour.

2. One turnover-cycle comprises many others

The circumstances in which emigration occurs are determined not only by wage-differentials, the relative ease or difficulty of relocating to another country and the absence or presence of support-networks, but also by the rate of labour-turnover in places of employment characterised by insalubrious working

---

4. Stalker 2000.

conditions, repetitive tasks and externally determined work-paces,[5] as well as in the personal-services sector. More specifically, one needs to examine how externally determined and insalubrious work-paces are related, first, to the turnover of the labour force and to labour-migration and, second, to the mobility of capital. Historically, the imposition of externally determined and insalubrious work paces has generated conspicuous degrees of labour-mobility, thereby forcing the productive apparatus to extend its social and territorial recruitment-areas. The mobility of industrial capital can also be explained, at least in part, by reference to the imposition of such work-paces. Externally determined work-paces and repetitive tasks induce forms of relocation. Firms will frequently (although not inevitably) respond to this labour mobility by adopting a strategy of bifurcation. In brief, they will occasionally attempt to attract workers by raising wages; more frequently, they will extend the reach of their recruitment-practices.

The frequent practice of relocating the site of production (be it within a single nation or across borders) results from a distinctive secular trend: firms go in search of new sources of manpower and flee industrial conflict.[6] But geographically relocating production is often no more than a form of spatial fix that does no more than 'retemporalise the crisis'.[7] In his treatment of the theme of temporality, Marx returns to the theme of production, stressing that production-time exceeds labour-time:

> The production time includes, of course, the period of the labour process; but this is not all. We should first recall that a part of the constant capital exists in means of labour, such as machines, buildings, etc. which serve for constant repetitions of the same labour process until they are worn out. The periodic interruption of the labour process, at night for example, may interrupt the function of these means of labour, but it does not affect their stay in the place of production. They belong to this not only when they function, but also when they do not function.[8]

In this way, slaves and servants – and, more generally, the so-called institutional population, or those deprived of the right to mobility – *belong* to the site of production even when they are not working, as Erving Goffman has succinctly explained in *Asylums*.[9] Industrial capitalism expects the migrant to be prepared to sell his or her labour-power, centre his or her working life on production for profit and disappear off the horizon once he or she is no longer available for working. The migrant, on the other hand, develops strategies for escaping the

---

5. MES/DARES 2000.
6. Silver 2003.
7. Harvey 1993.
8. Marx 1978, p. 200.
9. Goffmann 1968, pp. 15–22.

vortex that has so often overwhelmed those forced into unfree labour. The problem can be posed as follows: Is it possible to formulate a concrete account of the circuit of variable capital? A 'concrete' account would be one that does not focus merely on the quantities of variable capital circulating over time, but on the content of these circuits, the modalities assumed and the consequences entailed by the alienation of labour-power as it occurs for the purpose of accumulation.

In Chapter VIII of *Capital* Volume II, following his discussion of the 'turnover of capital', Marx examines the relationship between 'fixed capital and circulating capital'.[10] As large industry develops, capitalists' control over fixed capital orients the whole of society towards accumulation (notwithstanding the fact that fixed capital is of negligible value compared to the wealth produced by labour-power). In the words of William Thompson,[11] whom Marx will go on to cite later in Volume II: 'By means of the possession of this fixed, permanent, or slowly consumed, part of national wealth, of the land and materials to work upon, the tools to work with, the houses to shelter whilst working, the holders of these articles command for their own benefit the yearly productive powers of all the really efficient productive labourers of society, though these articles may bear ever so small a proportion to the recurring products of that labour'.[12]

In a world thus arranged, it is 'of the utmost importance to treat every ailment of the machinery immediately', while the ills of those operating the machines are of secondary importance.[13] Once fixed capital and accumulation come to dominate a society, labour-power is reduced to its wage-aspect. As Marx notes: 'Thus it is not the worker's means of subsistence that acquire the characteristic of fluid capital in contrast to fixed capital. And it is also not his labour-power, but rather the portion of the value of the productive capital that is spent on it, that has this characteristic in the turnover in common with some components of the constant part of the capital, and in contrast with other parts'.[14]

Marx also observes that the 'turnover of the fixed component of capital, and thus also the turnover time needed by it, encompasses several turnovers of the fluid components of capital'.[15] Unlike fixed capital, the elements of circulating capital 'are steadily renewed in kind', and 'just as constantly is there labour-power in the production process, but only in association with a constant repetition of its purchase, and often with a change in persons'.[16] From capital's perspective, this motion is nothing but a money-circuit; money acts as circulating capital,

---

10. Marx 1978, pp. 237–61.
11. Thompson 1850, pp. 440–3.
12. Quoted in Marx 1978, p. 397.
13. Marx 1978, p. 255.
14. Marx 1978, p. 245.
15. Marx 1978, p. 246.
16. Marx 1978, p. 248.

activating for itself the labour-power of a certain number of individuals and consuming it. Marx notes: 'In calculating the overall turnover of the productive capital advanced, we therefore take all its elements in the money form, so that the return to the money form concludes the turnover'.[17]

The entire movement appears smooth as far as money is concerned, but it is of course a turbulent one when the alienation of labour-power is considered. We can begin to discern the movement's limits: the interchangeability of persons (labour-turnover) and the exhaustion of labour-power, which intensifies as the rhythm of production becomes more demanding. How does Marx conceptualise manufacture in order to explain the relocation of manufacturing capital? Marx's concept of manufacture is an odd one, that of a weak capital constrained to follow the migrations of labour-power: manufactures are 'short-lived, changing their locality from one country to another with the emigration or immigration of workers'.[18] But the manufacturing capital of modernity's first several centuries is a two-faced one: in Europe, it combines the domestic advantages of enclosure, the workhouse and the poorhouse with the grudging pursuit of *its* workers, while on other continents its coercive aspect assumes a manifestly ferocious character, with much of the Americas and large parts of Asia and Africa being transformed into an enormous manufacture cum plantation with its specific hierarchies of slaves, servants and freemen. We are dealing, then, with a capital that is as accommodating when faced with labour-scarcity as it becomes cruel when seeking to establish for itself an apparently unlimited labour-pool.

3. Some specific features of the first centuries of modern migration

Slavery was a feature of a large number of sedentary societies up until the modern era, but its intensification during the period leading up to the transoceanic expeditions and the first four centuries of Europe's invasion of the two Americas is a special case. It gives the lie to notions of irresistible historical process, having developed within a civilisation where slavery had seemed, towards the end of the Middle Ages, to dissolve into forms of bondage less severe than those inherited from the decline of the Roman Empire.

During the second half of the fifteenth century there unfolded two almost concomitant processes, whose centre of gravity lay on the Iberian peninsula: the expulsion of religious minorities (Jews and Muslims) and the extension, first to Europe and then to the Americas, of the African slave-trade, which had hitherto been a local phenomenon, limited to West Africa. Portuguese merchants

---

17. Marx 1978, p. 263.
18. Marx 1976, p. 490.

hold a monopoly on the African slave-trade from the 1440s until the end of the sixteenth century, when English and Dutch merchants begin to enter the business. The diffusion of European slave trading in Africa, particularly West Africa, caused the trade in Slavic slaves to decline progressively during the sixteenth century; it also caused the slave-raids conducted by Christians and Muslims on one another in the Mediterranean to decline during the seventeenth century. *In brief, Western-European practices of subjugation began to be directed at sub-Saharan Africa, where they would continue to strike like a lash for centuries.*

The organised coercion of the African population expanded enormously with the colonisation of the two Americas. Western-European migration to the so-called New World was quite modest in the seventeenth century; generally speaking, the migrants were men-of-arms and adventurers originating mainly from the Iberian peninsula, France, Great Britain and the Netherlands. A distinguishing feature of the British and Dutch migrants was the presence of small but tightly knit Christian sects; these sects settled in the still rather inhospitable territories of North America and did not yet participate in the slave-trade. Notwithstanding the admonitions and appeals uttered by one or the other voice in the desert, the trans-Atlantic slave-trade continued virtually undisturbed until the victorious Haitian slave-revolt of 1801 and the subsequent abolition of the slave-trade by Great Britain in 1807.

When one examines the ratio of deportees to free migrants in the two Americas between the late fifteenth and early nineteenth centuries, one finds that slaves (most of them African) far outnumbered freemen (almost exclusively European) – a fact many white scholars never even mentioned until a few decades ago. The Africans deported between 1450 and 1807 numbered about 11.7 million (one-third of them women); of those deported, close to two million perished *en route*, while 9.8 million reached their destination. European migration to the Americas was quite modest by comparison to these figures: European migrants numbered about 2.3 million, making the ratio of Europeans to Africans about one to five. About eight hundred thousand Europeans migrated to southern North America and the Caribbean, more than half of them as indentured servants. Slightly more than half a million went to Latin America. To them should be added about a million Europeans who migrated to Brazil during the late eighteenth-century gold-rush.[19] The colonial invasion perpetrated by the white lords entailed lethal epidemics for a substantial part of the Native American population; meanwhile, the Africans deported to the so-called New World were held as slaves. By the economic calculus of the European invaders, Africans were more valuable than

---

19. Curin 1969.

Native Americans because they were more resistant to the various diseases introduced by Europeans.

Nevertheless, the working and living conditions under which the Africans were held during the sixteenth and seventeenth centuries were too harsh to allow for stable reproduction. This instability explains in part the ongoing hunt for additional manpower to deport to the Americas. Colonialism's wheel continued turning for four centuries, dragging ever new deportees away with it – both from West Africa and from inside the Americas – in order to sacrifice them on accumulation's altar. Exposure to European diseases and forced labour sounded the death-knell for a substantial part of the indigenous American population, triggering a demographic disaster unparalleled in human history. In 1492, the indigenous inhabitants of the two Americas numbered somewhere between 90 and 112 million. The time of first contact with Europeans varied regionally, but one can say that within the first century of such contact and until the 1880s the indigenous population was repeatedly decimated until it had been reduced to a mere ten percent of its size prior to the 'discovery of America.'[20] As for the African slaves put to work on Brazil's sugar-plantations, they could not expect to live for more than between six and eight years following their arrival. The fate of the African slaves put to work in the Caribbean and in Louisiana was no different.

It was only in the US South of the early eighteenth century, where African slaves did not make up the majority of the population,[21] that conditions were more favourable to stable reproduction and to the formation of a slave-community properly speaking. In any case, the assumption that the two Americas were dominated demographically by people of European origin from the days of Columbus onward is a fairy-tale, and the fact that it is presented as an obvious truth in many a historical manual does not make it any more true. The demographic predominance of Europeans is generally presented as a fact holding for the entire modern era, when it is actually a relatively recent phenomenon. Between 1820 and 1920, about fifty million Europeans emigrated to the Americas, three-fifths of them to the United States. As David Eltis has noted: "Not until 1840 did arrivals from Europe permanently surpass those from Africa. Indeed, in every year from about the mid-Sixteenth century to 1831, more Africans than Europeans quite likely came to the Americas, and not until the second wave of mass migration began in the 1880s did the sum of net European immigration start to match and then exceed the cumulative influx from Africa."[22]

---

20. Hoerder 2002, pp. 189–90.
21. With the exception of South Carolina, where African slaves constituted the majority of the population until the 1720s.
22. Eltis 1983, p. 255.

In the colonies, the liberty of white men was less severely restricted than that of white women, although all those who had nothing to sell but their labour-power were exposed to dangers such as that of falling into temporary bondage.[23] It was only following the first two decades of the nineteenth century that white freemen dominated the Americas demographically, thanks to the mass-migrations from Southern, central and eventually Northern Europe. This demographic predominance rested on the appalling tragedy of some one hundred million Native Americans and Africans sacrificed to colonial development and to the triangular trade between Europe, Africa and the Americas during the preceding three centuries.

Still very much in its prime, colonialism was far from remaining inactive and searched out new sources of enslaveable manpower. Spanish colonialism's functionaries, for example, were quite ingenious in this respect. During the second half of the sixteenth century, silver extracted by the forced labour of indigenous Peruvians was used by the Spanish Crown to finance its first Pacific outposts, particularly those in the Philippines; Chinese, Filipino and (to a lesser extent) Japanese men and women were then forcibly transferred to Mexico and Peru. The Spanish crown eventually abandoned this path to the development of Asian slavery in Latin America, although the illegal sale of Filipino and Chinese slaves to Mexico increased and was accompanied by the migration of freemen until the second half of the eighteenth century. Despite such developments, it was Africa that bore the main burden of the slave-trade.

In short, those leaving sub-Saharan Africa tend to do so in chains. This holds true for a protracted historical period ranging from the mid-fifteenth century to the decline of colonialism around the middle of the twentieth century.[24] People could leave Asia only sporadically and under the oversight of the colonial powers and their armed forces; those leaving tsarist Russia were few and far between and could do so only with a passport issued by the authorities. From the late eighteenth century onward, those residents of the Russian Empire considered 'deviant' faced the threat of exile or forced labour in Siberia, with about a million people being sentenced to the latter throughout the nineteenth century.

Where are the fault-lines in this landscape of widespread subjugation? First and foremost, there is the everyday resistance of the enslaved and the bonded. Then there are their strikes and revolts, on the same wavelength as the high

---

23. Moulier-Boutang 1998.

24. Throughout the first half of the nineteenth century and up until the 'scramble for Africa' during the last quarter of the century, it was wiser for liberated slaves to return to Africa than it was for free Africans to emigrate to the Americas. Slaves liberated by the British navy were taken to Sierra Leone, and some African Americans travelled from the United States to Liberia, a state founded, in what amounted to an act of condescendence, in 1821.

points of the French Revolution and leading up to the victory of the Haitian slaves over two Napoleonic armies and the subsequent proclamation of the Haitian republic.[25] The developments in Haiti inspired terror in slaveholders on both sides of the Atlantic, and the campaigns of the abolitionists became similarly widespread. The British government was thus prompted to soften its stance on slavery, eventually abolishing its African slave-trade (1806–8). Countries that had participated in the slave-trade for centuries responded slowly and reluctantly to its formal abolition, continuing to tolerate clandestine shipments of slaves to the Americas until the 1860s. More than 100,000 slaves were traded in this way; 94,000 of them were liberated by the British navy between 1808 and 1861.[26] Between 1844 and 1848, however, the British government bowed to the pressure of white plantation-owners on the Antilles by confiscating the slaves liberated by its own navy and forcing them to work on the Antilles for 15 years. Between 1848 and 1866, some 40,000 African slaves liberated by the British navy were put to work on the islands of the Caribbean and in British Guyana; they were made to perform indentured labour for periods ranging from one to three years, as compensation for their passage on British vessels. When plantation-owners in the Caribbean began to require additional manpower, they attempted to recruit African workers in Sierra Leone, but they were forced to abandon this practice towards the end of the 1860s, when the first emigrants returned to Sierra Leone and spread the word about living and working conditions on the plantations.[27]

The second fault-line is the abolition of slavery on the British Antilles in 1834. Former slaves readily left the plantations and began to clear uncultivated land where they settled independently; others evaded wage-labour by joining the alternative rural micro-societies established by fugitive slaves (maroons).[28] The plantation-owners, and in particular the owners of sugar-plantations, resorted to the tried and tested practice of employing migrants as indentured servants. This time, labour-power was recruited not from Central and Northern Europe but from the southern coast of China and from Western India.[29] As slavery gradually went into crisis during the nineteenth century, the trade in 'coolies' or temporary servants picked up; the coolie-trade would continue until the 1920s. Within this so-called 'Asian Contract Labour System', 'contract' referred to indentured labour. By the end of the nineteenth century, some 2.5 million Chinese and

25. James 1980.
26. Asiegbu 1969, pp. 191–214; Moulier-Boutang 1998, pp. 418–40.
27. Schuler 1986; Asiegbu 1969, p. 71.
28. Linebaugh and Rediker 2000.
29. The expression 'to shanghai' was coined in this context. Derived from the name of China's large port-city, it refers to the act of kidnapping a person, placing them on a ship and taking them far away, generally to perform forced labour on a plantation.

1.5 million Indians had been taken to the Antilles, various Pacific islands and Southern Africa in this way.[30] Meanwhile, common and political prisoners from the United Kingdom were deported to Australia and massacres were perpetrated on the indigenous population – the beginning of a programme that would go on to become the policy of 'keeping Australia white'.

The third fault-line was the resistance of US slaves to their exploitation and isolation, a resistance that sped the escalation of the conflict between slaveholders and abolitionists into the American Civil War, whose outbreak in 1861 coincided with the abolition of serfdom in Russia. *The progress of nineteenth-century globalisation in no way attenuated the isolation of slaves in the Southern United States; on the contrary, the isolation of the slaves increased to the extent that the world-market developed and the demand for cotton rose in the commercial centres of Europe and the Americas.* As the area of cultivation expanded, slaves were dispersed ever further south and put to work on new plantations catering to the international demand for cotton. New plantations in Alabama, Mississippi and Texas required new slaves, leading to the forced migration of half a million African Americans whose families were torn apart to be sold 'down the river', that is, along the Southern Mississippi River.[31] They were effectively forced into the position of unqualified workers, or deprived of the abilities they had developed in other social contexts. Reduced to growing cotton, they remained largely invisible to so-called public opinion, that is, to newspapers written for readers more familiar with cotton than with slaves. The American Civil War was the product of two conflicting ways of life, but the main reason these ways of life conflicted was that the slaves were social contradiction made flesh. The slaves' everyday struggle to survive and improve their lot was fundamental to the forms of subversion by which the isolation of the plantations was overcome, putting those still enslaved in contact with the abolitionist public. Such contact was typically established by the arrival of fugitive-slaves in the North. No one but the fugitive-slave was in a position to break the spell – thanks in part to the fact that he/she was not immediately placed in a detention-centre, as has become common practice in our mature democracies. The outstanding historian and activist C.L.R. James, a native of the Antilles, offers this account of the fugitive-slave's impact on US public debate during the decades prior to the outbreak of the Civil War: 'The runaway slave heightened the powers of the popular imagination. Here was a figure who not only fled oppressive institutions, but successfully outwitted and defied them. And his flight was to the heart of civilization, not away

---

30. Potts 1990; Hoerder 2002.
31. Gutman 1977.

from it; he was a universal figure whose life was in turn adventurous, tragic, and humorous'.[32]

The fugitive-slave's entry into the political arena caused turmoil there, notwithstanding the fact that he was constrained to operate from within a legal limbo. North of the Mason-Dixon Line, the slave's existence was sometimes semi-clandestine, sometimes highly public, as when he appeared on the political stage to demand another liberation. 'Without the self-expressive presence of the free blacks in the cities, embodying in their persons the nationally traumatic experience of bondage and freedom, antislavery would have been a sentiment only, a movement remote and genteel in a country known as impetuous and volatile'.[33]

The US abolitionists were 'involved in a crucial way in the most significant struggles for human emancipation that were going on in the United States'.[34] They established channels of solidarity to other parts of the world, contributing to a redefinition of the political with repercussions not only for the United States but for the entire world. On the international level, opposition to slavery served as the litmus-test for membership in what Malcolm X would later sardonically call the 'John Brown school of liberals'. 'If ... the flight of the runaway slave from the South is seen as setting in motion a whole series of forces, which no other class of people, no mere party or political sect, no church or newspaper could succeed in animating, then the whole configuration of America as a civilization automatically changes before our eyes'.[35]

Notwithstanding the abolition of slavery in the Americas, free migration from Africa remained a mirage for the rest of the nineteenth and the first half of the twentieth century. The 'scramble for Africa' certainly did not begin with the Berlin Conference of 1884–5. From the first decades of the nineteenth century onwards, *European colonialism's insistence on the evils of the slave-trade and its pleas for 'civilising' the Africans by putting them to work in Africa go hand in hand with the emergence of new prospects for the exploitation of African resources.* Congo, the personal property of King Leopold (1884–1908) before it became a Belgian colony, is a case in point. The country became a vast school of horrors for its neighbours, from Angola to Cameroon: the slave-trade and the subsequent exploitation of ivory, caoutchouc, palm-oil and minerals required by European industry claimed ten million victims between 1885 and 1920, reducing the overall population by 50 percent in the course of 35 years.[36] Such bloodletting has been

---

32. James 1970, p. 140.
33. James 1970, p. 142.
34. James 1970, p. 147.
35. James 1970, p. 151.
36. Hochschild 2008.

a recurrent experience in Congo, right up to the wars raging there since 1997. Fought over coltane, diamonds, gold and wood, these wars have claimed another four million victims.

The opening of the Suez Canal in 1869 heralded the diffusion of forced labour across Africa's East coast and the intensification of human trafficking around Aden.[37] The imperialist nations of the European *Belle Époque* split up Africa between themselves according to their relative might. The Western socialist movement was on the rise, but the freedom of Africans to emigrate was never even debated within it, notwithstanding the fact that such debates were long being held within the African-American communities of the Caribbean and the Southern United States.[38]

4. The great transatlantic migrations from Europe

Early in the twentieth century, Georg Simmel waxed eloquent on the theme of 'the stranger' but chose rather prudently not to pursue that figure's history any further than the late Middle Ages.[39] One of the most significant episodes in the history of European migration was just playing out: a migratory movement destined to continue until the outbreak of the war of 1914–18. The movement would gradually pick up again during the 1930s and continue, this time, until the late 1940s, but in a bifurcated fashion: as free migration on the one hand and unfree (first regimented and then coerced) migration on the other.

The great European migrations to the two Americas that developed between the 1840s and the beginning of the First World War were the result of grave European crises, mainly in agriculture: from the Irish famine of the mid-1840s to the immiseration of Italy's peasants following Italian unification and the exodus of Russian Jews fleeing discrimination and pogroms. The prosperous agriculture of the two Americas spelled ruin for those Europeans who had either always been landless or had lost their land during the second half of the nineteenth century; these Europeans were left with no choice but transatlantic migration. Such migration acted as a kind of pressure-valve, relieving Europe's social tensions, and was therefore encouraged by governments (although these governments also kept a close eye on the activities of the émigrés abroad). European trans-Atlantic migration also constituted the cordon of white residents that kept African Americans in the United States – and, to a point, in South America – bound to the Southern plantation-system, caught within relations of peonage between the vigilante violence of local notables and the armed incursions of the

37. Ewald 2000.
38. Jacobs 1981.
39. Simmel 1950.

Ku Klux Klan. The 1880s also saw Chinese migration to the United States being blocked by specific legislation (1882, 1884, 1888); migration from elsewhere in Asia was discouraged or deflected to other American countries.

During the half-century between the American Civil War and the outbreak of the war of 1914–18, the stream of European immigrants provided the industrial North and West of the United States with fresh manpower, allowing the plantation-owners of the South to continue imposing their apartheid-system on the African American population (the bulk of which remained segregated in the South). The alliance between industrial capital and the political representatives of the plantation-economy was maintained. However, corporate managers found it increasingly difficult to curb the restiveness of the immigrant working class, which bore the burden of economic development in the form of arduous working conditions, and the plantation-system's politicians failed outright in their attempt to impede the north- and westward migration of half a million African Americans between 1910 and 1920. This biblical exodus, known as the 'Great Migration', gained additional momentum in 1917, the year the United States entered the First World War, and continued for another half century. It contributed significantly to the crisis of segregation in the United States.

Within a dozen years, the balance of interests that governed US race-relations was destabilised on two fronts: on the one hand, the founding of the Industrial Workers of the World (1905), the intensification of worker-revolts in industry and the spread of revolutionary trade-unionism cracked the white working-class's complicity in the maintenance of apartheid; on the other hand, there was the entry, however fragmentary and temporary, of tens of thousands of African Americans into industry. Later, discrimination and the post-war recession caused these African Americans to lose the industrial employment they had successfully struggled to obtain during the exceptional wartime-situation, but the laid off African-American workers refused to simply return to the South. As for US industry, it began integrating white European migrants into its vast productive apparatus. The simplification of work-tasks brought about by Taylorism during the last two decades of the nineteenth century and the automobile-industry's introduction of the assembly-line in 1912 created a pressing demand for immigrant-labour. Working conditions were harsh, even if the pay was higher than in Europe. Taylorism and Fordism drastically tightened the vice of the work-pace and factory-discipline. Only a relatively small number of immigrants, most of them British and German, found qualified work. *European migrants were destined for simplified and serialised work, which remained white and European, even if it was precarious, often seasonal and almost everywhere non-unionised.* The urban African-American population and the relatively small number of Asians living on the East and West coasts had to take menial jobs, cleaning jobs and jobs in the lower strata of the personal-services sector; they worked for low wages and were generally bereft of all forms of welfare. Industrial employment was not yet for them.

The urgent need to earn a wage tied immigrant industrial workers to the harsh pace of serial work and to insalubrious working conditions. Between 1899 and 1910, the average immigrant to the United States arrived with 21.5 dollars to his or her name.[40] It was a question of finding work immediately, saving money and getting by with no more than the most elementary forms of everyday reproduction. Workers lived in boarding houses where a waged female domestic worker typically looked after a dozen or more men. The constitution of class-solidarity was slowed by the immigrants' diffidence towards the dominant culture and the conflicts between different national groups. The latter were frequently promoted by employers, in addition to being exacerbated by endemic racism. Moreover, the fact that workers frequently lived away from the great urban centres precluded them from organising collectively.

Female labour-power was constrained, in the penumbral world of domesticity, to keep step with the rhythms of industrial production, reproducing the spent labour-power of white male workers one day at a time. More and more frequently, these white male workers chose to 'vote with their feet', abandoning work that imposed on them its mortiferous pace. As has been noted, the first two decades of the twentieth century saw the productive cycle move largely in syntony with the flux and reflux of migration.[41] While the correlation is not perfect, there are 'general similarities in the appearance of the curves'.[42] The period's high turnover-rates reflect a social restiveness; workers seized the rare opportunity for 'job shopping' and went in search of better employment. By contrast, within single enterprises, labour-mobility continued to be governed by the arbitrary decisions of employers.

The early twentieth century saw US industry developing rapidly; the new employees were mainly European immigrants who did not always hold up to the rapid pace of work. Between 1890 and 1914, about 30 percent of migrants to the United States returned to their countries of origin. The returnees were mainly Italian and Spanish; Russians tended to remain, especially after 1917.[43] On the eve of the war of 1914–18, industrial capital was already beginning to understand that it could not continue to rely on purely local recruitment of its assembly-line workers (who were almost exclusively male and white). Moreover, the European recruitment-pool dried up during the war: 'In 1914 over 1 million Europeans had

---

40. Hoerder 2002, p. 345.
41. Jerome 1926.
42. Jerome 1926, p. 240.
43. Hatton and Williamson 1994, pp. 5–6.

come to America; in 1915 the number fell to under 200,000, and in 1918 to just 31,000. By 1918 the unemployment rate had fallen to 2.4 percent, down from over 15 percent just three years earlier'.[44]

Notwithstanding the decelerating effects of the immediate postwar period's turnover-rates, the labour-force became relatively stable from the mid-1920s onward – a break with the more transient labour-force of previous decades. In effect, the first 20 years of the twentieth century were characterised by elevated turnover-rates all over the United States: 'In 1917–18 the following industries had a turnover rate of over 200 percent: automobiles, chemicals, leather and rubber, miscellaneous metal products, slaughtering and meat packing and furniture and milling'.[45] The best-known case is doubtless that of Ford, where in 1913, when the Highland Park factory had almost been completed, the annual turnover-rate was 370 percent. In January of 1914, management responded by shortening the workday from nine to eight hours and doubling the average daily wage from 2.50 dollars to five dollars for a small section of the labour-force.[46]

The replacement of old by new workers proceeded on a considerable scale, and workers were recruited from ever more distant areas. African Americans continued to be excluded, with the exception of some Ford departments, notably the foundries, welding shops and forges. It is only with reference to whites that one can speak of a widespread expansion of US (and Central-European) employment-systems. Then, Ford quietly began supplementing its masses of European immigrant-workers, most of whom did not speak fluent English, with African-American workers, taking care to maintain a rigid 'colour-line'. In January of 1916, a mere 50 African American employees worked at Ford's Detroit factories. By 1920, their number had risen to 2,500. And it continued to rise, reaching almost 9,000 in 1922, 10,632 in 1930 and 17,653 in 1940.[47] Large-scale recruitment of African-American workers began in 1921–2 and relied on the recruitment-efforts of

44. Gutman and Brier, p. 227.

45. Douglas 1959, p. 710.

46. The same year (1914), Ford set up the Sociological Department: 'A worker could qualify for the five-dollar day only after his or her home was inspected by a member of the Sociological Department. The inspectors came with an interpreter, because the worker usually didn't speak much English, and they examined the home for cleanliness. They checked whether the employee was legally married and whether he kept boarders, which was frowned on. They checked on whether the employee was in debt, whether he drank too much, and on and on'. Staudenmaier 1994. According to another scholar, the labour turnover-rate at Ford was 416 percent between October 1912 and October 1913: Fisher 1917, p. 15, cited in Douglas 1918, p. 309.

47. The percentage of African Americans employed by Ford at its Detroit factories (River Rouge, Lincoln and Highland Park) climbed from 11.45 percent in 1920–2 to 20.88 percent in 1940: Meier and Rudwick 1979, p. 6; Maloney and Whatley 1995, p. 468. It should be noted, however, that another study arrives at a slightly lower estimate for the same years: Foote, Whatley and Wright 2003, p. 499.

Christian ministers, policemen and other notables from the African-American community.[48] Ford sought out and actively recruited African-American workers; during the same years, the company 'abolished the Sociological Department and instituted a régime of speed-up and continuous insecurity'.[49] Black workers were given the worst work, in the foundries and other insalubrious departments. As one African American from Detroit who steered clear of the assembly-lines explained, Ford factories were 'the house of murder.... Every worker could identify Ford workers on the streetcars going home at night. You'd see twenty asleep on the cars and everyone would say "Ford workers".'[50]

Yet although working for Ford meant dire working conditions and wage-discrimination, such work nevertheless represented an opportunity for African Americans. Between 1920 and 1922, 45.2 percent of all African-American industrial workers in Detroit and 19.1 percent of white industrial workers worked for Ford; the figures for 1940 are 52.6 and 14.1 percent, respectively.[51] This high number of black workers – and in particular of *young married* black workers – in the Ford factories is related both to the racist exclusion African Americans faced on Detroit's labour-market (and on those of other cities) and to Ford's efforts to reduce labour-turnover. In effect, employing African American workers reduced the turnover-rate. As one scholar has noted: "Black nonfoundry workers have the lowest quit rates.... Next come the black foundry workers and the white non-foundry workers, who appear to value their jobs about equally. Finally valuing their jobs least of all were the white foundry workers."[52]

Generally speaking, however, US industrial capital and the US trade-unions succeeded, throughout the 1920s and 1930s, in staying the attempts of African Americans to end discrimination and find industrial employment in the North and West of the country.[53] On the whole, the automobile sector preferred to recruit its assembly-line workers from the Mediterranean. Migrant-workers were recruited in Malta and South-Western Europe, a region not noted, until then, as a source of trans-Atlantic migration; only the most arduous tasks were given to African Americans. *During the 1920s, the selective recruitment of assembly-line workers extended as far as the Northern coast of the Mediterranean, from Portugal to Greece and Malta, where the British government signed an agreement with the United States stating that unemployed workers would be made available to*

---

48. Meier and Rudwick 1979, p. 10.
49. Foote, Whatley and Wright 2003, p. 500.
50. Cited in Denby 1978, p. 35.
51. Maloney and Whatley 1995, p. 468.
52. Foote, Whatley and Wright 2003, p. 518.
53. For example, Philadelphia's main industries refused (with rare exceptions) to employ African-American workers until the late 1930s. Licht 1992.

Detroit's automobile-industry. The Maghreb, the Fertile Crescent and Turkey still lay beyond the recruitment-area.

During the 'Red scare' that followed the Russian Revolution of 1917, the US political elite drastically restricted European emigration. The new immigration-policy produced a more stable labour-force even as the cost of training workers rose.[54] By the late 1920s, the newly restrictive immigration-policy had altered some of the population's demographic features; in addition, the first years of the Great Depression reduced occupational mobility. An examination of the changes in the composition of the labour-force would also need to take account of the fact that European immigrants tended to settle close to where their friends and family-members lived and worked. Moreover, 'the slower rates of migration from Europe were compensated for by increases in non-European immigration, particularly from Canada and Mexico, and by migration from the domestic agricultural to the industrial sector'.[55] The turnover-rates for industrial workers sank from 123.4 percent in 1920 to 37.1 percent in 1928. Generally speaking, workers in large firms were more likely to quit their jobs than workers in small firms; the Detroit of 1928 was characterised by a 'progressive increase in the quit rate from small firms under 200 employees to the large firms over 1000 employees'. Turnover-rates were high in Michigan's urban centres but low in smaller cities where workers were more isolated and less free to choose their place of work. Turnover-rates were also higher in the automobile-sector and in sectors related to it, as well as in the metal- and paper-industries.[56] Yet overall, the high turnover-rates typical of many of the United States' industrial labour-markets during the first two decades of the twentieth century were declining.[57] This decline was related to that in the number of workers quitting their jobs, such actions being crucial for overall labour-turnover. Obviously, workers tend to quit their jobs because they expect to find better ones.

Prior to industrial unionism's breakthrough during the 1930s, upward mobility within single firms remained a prerogative of managers and foremen. During the 1930s, one of labour's crucial demands, advanced throughout large industry, was that for seniority, which provided (among other things) a guarantee against the traditional discrimination of African Americans and other groups. Industrial unionism was forged in the white heat of the Great Depression and the New Deal, when immigration from Europe had dwindled almost to nothing. In other words, industrial unionism triumphed in a social context where the game of playing immigrants out against autochtonous (and particularly African-American)

---

54. Owen 1995.
55. Owen 1995, p. 834.
56. Blackett 1928, pp. 13, 16, 21.
57. The average labour turnover-rate began to rise again during the period following the war of 1939–45. Between 1950 and 1970, US industrial turnover-rates oscillated between 47 and 64 percent. Owen 1995, p. 822.

workers had been suspended.[58] When immigrant and autochotonous workers converged again, US union-activity contrasted markedly with the growing regimentation of the labour-force evident in the dictatorial régimes of Germany, Japan, Italy and the Soviet Union. (A similar contrast had existed, during the preceding years, between the regimentation of the labour-force in these dictatorial régimes and union-activity in France, Britain, the Scandinavian countries, Australia and New Zealand.)

This bifurcation of labour-policy was reversed only partly after the war of 1939–45. In continental Europe, Nazism placed left-wing political opponents in concentration-camps and engaged in a policy of discrimination, violence and expulsion towards Jews. Meanwhile, the military campaigns of Japanese imperialism involved the forced migration and enslavement of significant sections of the enemy-population. Towards the end of 1941, Nazism passed from expulsion to the so-called 'final solution', that is, to a policy of extermination through work enacted under the most inhuman conditions and on an industrial scale. This policy was unlike anything ever seen in human history; its victims were socialists, communists, Jews, homosexuals, Sinti, Romanies and other discriminated groups. Europe's other fascist régimes became active accomplices.

The migratory movements enforced by Japanese imperialism in Northeast Asia primarily affected Koreans and Manchurians. Forced migration continued from 1938 until 1945. Meanwhile, in Stalin's Soviet Union, wage-labour was largely replaced by various levels of forced migration and forced labour – a degradation of labour that would be reduced only after the death of Stalin in 1953.[59]

What kind of forced labour did these regimentation-measures aim at? Generally speaking, they aimed at dirty, dangerous and difficult serial work in industry – work that has prompted the working class to vote with its feet whenever it was able to. Forced labour – labour that does not allow workers to vote with their feet – is the key common feature of the dictatorial régimes of the period. As for forced migrants, they were coerced mainly because they were the ones who had to perform insalubrious work.

5. From the greenery of sugar-plantations to the greenery of well-engineered factory-complexes

Anticolonial struggles followed different trajectories, but they all persisted, from the victory of the Haitian slaves and the Indian Sepoy Revolt to Ethiopian resistance to fascism and beyond. The period ranging from the late 1930s and the

---

58. African Americans began demanding 'good jobs', more emphatically following the war of 1939–45. See Cartosio 1992.
59. van der Linden 1995.

war of 1939–45 to the three decades following 1945 was characterised by the intensification and proliferation of these struggles. By the late 1940s, the various anticolonial campaigns had moved to the centre of the international scene. The gates of migration were mostly half-closed, although they were opened selectively in the United States, Canada, Australia and the industrialised countries of central Europe, which had taken up the task of postwar reconstruction and faced manpower-shortages. Only a select group of minorities were allowed to emigrate from the Soviet bloc, although trusted cadres enjoyed a certain internal mobility.

In the industrial countries, Keynes's downward rigidity of money-wages had been corrected by policies of inflation implemented under the New Deal and, more importantly, after 1945. But these policies had been undercut by the extension of labour-recruitment pools. In the United States, employers had been constrained by the war-effort and the presence of African Americans in the new industrial union, the CIO, to accept the employment of African Americans in the federally funded military-industry. To be sure, African-American workers paid for their inclusion by performing the most strenuous and insalubrious work. During the postwar period, the industrial countries proved capable of absorbing the 30 million refugees produced by the war of 1939–45. While the process was long and convoluted, one can say that most refugees – those who avoided the pitfalls of repatriation and local vendettas – were able to turn their backs on the experience of war. The dislocation of various Asian populations was a considerably more tortuous affair, as Japanese invasions had disrupted traditional migration-routes.

US internal migration from the rural South to the industrial North and West proved an irreversible process, especially in the case of African Americans; it provided the basis for the campaigns against racist segregation. *When the anti-segregation campaigns began during the mid-1950s, their demands seemed no more than a weak echo of the ongoing anticolonial struggles in Africa, Asia and on the Antilles.* Unlike the period between 1945 and 1949, independence seemed within reach not only for the more populous countries (those hardest for the colonialists to control, such as the Philippines, India, Indonesia and Pakistan), but also for countries with smaller populations. While the natives of these countries continued to be denied their independence by force of arms, they were themselves taking up arms and fighting, against the odds, to overthrow the colonial order.

The decisive turning point was the Battle of Dien Bien Phu (May 1954), which saw the Viet Minh triumph over the French military. Only a few months later, the Algerians took up arms against their French occupiers in a war that would continue until French withdrawal from Algeria in 1962. *Populations that had demanded rights from the colonial powers without ever obtaining them could now no longer be treated as mere manpower-reserves; national independence entailed a public-education system and the right to a passport that allowed individuals to travel as citizens properly speaking, rather than as colonial subjects.* Eventually, natives of the Maghreb living in France would achieve these rights also.

Meanwhile, in the United States, what had seemed like a distant echo of the anticolonial struggles during the 1950s transformed and spread; the 1960s brought an unstoppable series of explosive desegregation-campaigns. The movement drove the US government to approve a new immigration-law, the Immigration and Nationality Act of 1965, which corrected the old system of annual immigration-quotas – fixed for whites only – by extending it to Africans and to the natives of many Asian countries.

It was thanks to this less discriminatory international climate that many a racist taboo was abandoned in Europe also. *The tables had turned: most migrants were of extra-European origin again. They arrived from Latin America, Asia and Africa, not from within Europe, and they no longer arrived in chains, even though they continued to be victims of discrimination.* The countries of the European common-market were forced by the anticolonial struggles, and by Algerian independence (1962) in particular, to abandon their policy of recruiting one generation after another of young immigrant-workers without allowing the workers' families to follow. The policy had seemed viable with regard to the Maghreb and African and Asian migrants in general, but this was now no longer the case. However, the oil-crisis of 1973–4 led to new restrictions on immigration throughout the countries of the common-market (the later European Economic Community), facilitating the introduction of new selective entry policies in the richer countries even as the countries of Southern Europe became a kind of waiting room for aspiring immigrants from Asia, Africa and Latin America.

The last fifty years have been characterised by the asymmetric development of migratory movements on the one hand and foreign direct investment on the other. Until the late 1950s, foreign investment commonly took the form of portfolio-investment. But from the mid-1950s onward, foreign direct investment by increasingly multinational corporations began to become prevalent – a tendency predicted and debated within Europe's socialist Left since the beginning of the twentieth century. Multinationals successfully sidestepped customs-barriers, in particular when accessing the more dynamic foreign markets, and they began to emancipate themselves from the most 'dangerous' working class, that of the United States, by establishing export-processing zones abroad. Countries striving for economic independence from Europe and North America followed the examples of Argentina and Brazil and opted for the strategy of import-substituting investments (ISI). This was the case in the larger countries that had successfully emancipated themselves from colonialism following the war of 1939–45. Some of these countries

(China and India in particular) succeeded in replacing imports with national products, but many others failed or gave up early on because they lacked the necessary
(demographic and capital-) resources. In some cases, such failure was reflected
in – and could in fact be measured by – the development of out-migration; this
is especially true for out-migration from many African and some Asian countries
(for example Egypt and the Philippines). The ranks of the migrants were swelled
by refugees fleeing the wars in Southeast Asia and Africa.

In certain cases, the transition from plantations to export-processing zones
(EPZs) was remarkably smooth. The trade-minister of the Fiji Islands spoke for
many when he expressed his 'hope [...] that one day instead of seeing the greenery of sugar cane fields, we see the greenery of well-engineered factory com-
plexes'.[60] The reality is that the workers of the Fiji Islands and other countries
are trapped in economic sectors that suffer from a paucity of investment and are
anything but 'well-engineered', such as the textile-industry. They are also denied
the right to organise at the workplace. By contrast, firms are granted multi-year
tax-breaks as the old principles of colonialism and export-dependence are reas-
serted beneath the thin technocratic varnish of the EPZs (and with the consent
of local bourgeoisies).

The oil-crisis of 1973 slowed international migration during the very years that
saw discriminatory practices become a feature both of immigration-policy and of
national-employment systems. The mid-1960s had seen some of the international
barriers of discrimination being torn down along with domestic barriers – South
African apartheid, which lasted until the early 1990s, being the notable exception.
Foreign direct investment in countries where institutionalised dictatorship and
industrial autocracy mutually supported one other became a viable alternative to
international migration. Such foreign direct investment represents an attempt by
industrial capital to emancipate itself from its domestic 'troublemakers'. After 1973,
the distinction between those migrants who enjoy the right to let their families
join them and settle permanently in their new home and those whose migration
is temporary and circular becomes ever more marked, the most significant and
best-known case of temporary circular migration being that of migrant-workers
in the oil-producing countries of the Persian Gulf. In fact, the 1973 'oil-shock'
provided the Gulf monarchies with an opportunity to extend their system of
selective and temporary immigration, recruiting workers from throughout Asia
and imposing upon them wages and working conditions that are determined
not by any 'free' labour-market but by wage-levels in the workers' countries
of origin.[61] Workers are denied the right to settle permanently, the argument
being that such settlement would be harmful to societies structured according

---

60. Quoted in Robertson 1993, p. 31.
61. Gambino 2003.

to ethnic and religious origins; alternatively, the threat to established relations of domination and subordination is invoked.

6. Areas for exploiting the life-sphere

The decline of colonialism coincides with the proliferation of productive enclaves sometimes reminiscent of those established in the colonies and in the so-called trading ports of Southern China between the crisis of slavery in the mid-nineteenth century and the war of 1939–45. Differently from the colonial area, these enclaves can be accessed not just by the dominant colonial power and its allies, but receive foreign direct investment (FDI) from a variety of countries (in addition to investment by local companies). The special areas where such investment is concentrated are characterised by multiple suspensions of national law and have been appropriately defined as states of exception.[62] In a pioneer study, a keen observer of East-Asian development noted early on that 'the proliferation of free trade zones represents in perhaps its purest form the new industrial face of contemporary imperialism'.[63]

A key tendency displayed by these productive enclaves consists in the proliferation of export-processing zones (EPZs) within them; in 1975, there already existed 79 such EPZs in 25 countries. EPZs are socially sterile zones where the rules of the local society are bent to suit the interests of investors – artificial islands where the absence of all life that does not coincide with the alienation of labour-power is accompanied by a discipline dictated by the rigid timetable of international shipping agreements. By 1997, the number of countries with EPZs had risen to 93; throughout these 93 countries, 22.5 million workers were employed in 845 EPZs. The turn of the century heralded further expansion, and in 2006, 66 million workers were employed in 3,500 EPZs located in 130 countries.[64] The majority of these tens of millions of workers are migrants arriving from other regions of the same country. In fact, the forced industrialisation associated with EPZs induces an excessive internal migration, with more people migrating than can be employed. Proletarian existences already precarious are rendered more so by the resulting devaluation of labour-power.

EPZs are geared primarily to the production of finished or semi-finished goods for export, usually under a labour-régime involving restrictions on trade-union activity. Work tasks are often repetitive and require no particular qualification; the work-pace is externally determined. The workers are often young women of rural origin. In the 1980s, the average period of employment – the time during

---

62. Finardi and Moroni 2001.
63. Selden 1975, p. 26.
64. International Labour Office 2007.

which workers were employed by a particular multinational corporation in a particular EPZ – was about five years.[65] Even then, EPZs revealed themselves as machines for sucking young workers dry, exploiting them for a few years before releasing them into small-scale production, domestic work or the underbrush of Asian and Latin American metropolitan areas.

In the case of Mexico's EPZs, the maelstrom is markedly more turbulent than elsewhere in the country. During the 1980s, the average duration of employment in the EPZs was five years, as compared to fifteen years elsewhere in Mexican industry.[66] Mexico's maquila-centred industrial scheme, developed in 1966, led to the opening of some 3,600 production-plants by the year 2000; they employed 1.3 million workers, most of them women. (About 62 percent of all maquila-workers work in Mexico's Northern border-region.) Maquila workers are employed primarily in the production of electronic goods (close to 440,000 workers), automobile-components (240,000 workers) and in the textile-industry (281,000 workers).[67]

During its early years, industrial development in Mexico's Northern border-region had little impact on internal migration, but this state of affairs changed in the course of the years, with the maquilas increasingly attracting manpower from distant regions. During the early 1980s, the labour-force employed in the maquilas of the Northern border-region already consisted overwhelmingly of Mexican migrants; they made up some 70 percent of the labour-force and arrived mainly from urban or semi-urban, but not from rural areas.[68] Workers quit their jobs very frequently.[69] In Ciudad Juarez, the turnover-rate was already high during the 1980s; in Tijuana, annual turnover-rates of 100 percent or more are not uncommon.[70] Firms are sometimes overwhelmed by such turnover-rates, with one firm closing shop after another, in a kind of chain-reaction: 'only 37% of the 67 maquilas surveyed in 1994 were still operating in 2004. Only 27% of the plants owned by Mexican nationals survived *versus* 46% of the TNC subsidiaries.

---

65. International Labour Office 1998, pp. 58–61.

66. Williams and Passe-Smith 1989, p. 7; Peña 2000.

67. Following a period of stagnation and decline between 2001 and 2003, the Mexican maquila-industry grew again in 2006, returning to the levels of development it had known in the year 2000. The industry generates about 100 billion USD worth of exports and accounts for almost half of the state's export-related fiscal income. Kohout 2009, p. 137; Sargent and Matthews 2006; Loess, Miller and Yoskowitz 2008, p. 260.

68. Fernàndez-Kelly 1983, p. 210.

69. Clearly, women frequently retain these jobs because they lack better opportunities on the labour-market. Research on Seoul, Kuala Lumpur, Bangkok and Manila has shown that women's turnover-rate is lower than men's. See Bai and Woo 1995. The situation is similar in the EPZs of Mexico and other countries. On the situation of young women in China's EPZs see: Pun 2005; Pun and Li 2008.

70. According to some estimates, the annual turnover-rate in Mexico's maquilas lies somewhere between 120 and 150 percent. Stoddard 1987, p. 46; Peña 2000, p. 124.

Relatively few maquilas producing apparel (23%), furniture (0%), or leather (0%) were still active, while 60% of the electronics and 68% of the auto part producers remained'.[71]

Once Mexico's northern border-region had become saturated with industry, labour-supply slumped. At that point, it became advantageous for firms 'to bring the jobs to the workers and not to try to get the workers to come to the jobs'.[72] The maquila-centred industrial-development programme was thus extended to Mexico's interior. This move was no solution, however, to the problem of turnover in the Northern border-region. Moreover, multinationals who opted to operate in the country's interior paid for lower turnover-rates with the disadvantage of being further removed geographically from their headquarters in the United States.

Various explanations have been offered for the high turnover-rates in Mexico's maquilas. Some have argued that the low wages result in lower purchasing power, thereby forcing part of the labour-force to search for employment elsewhere or emigrate to the United States. Others have pointed to the distance between the workplaces and workers' places of residence, which constrains workers to spend considerable time away from home. It has also been argued that the rapid work-paces in the maquila produce an army of discontented workers who, being poorly unionised, choose to vote with their feet.[73] When Chinese competition forced about 800 firms to close shop between 2001 and 2003, leading to about 300,000 layoffs, it turned out the monthly labour-turnover rate in those firms was almost three times as high as the one in the firms that survived (16.6 percent as opposed to 6.1 percent).[74]

Maquila-operators concede various benefits to workers in an attempt to lower turnover-rates, providing transportation, meal-vouchers and the like. Employers also agree on wage-levels in order to avoid competing with one another and so as to slow workers' inter-firm mobility. The hourly wages US multinationals pay Mexican workers amount to a mere 30 percent of US wages.[75] Then again, there are cases in which firms deliberately keep the turnover-rate high.[76] As one scholar has noted: '[In] some cases it may be financially profitable for a company to have a rapidly changing work force rather than to adjust its affairs in such a

---

71. Sargent and Matthews 2006, p. 1071.
72. Sklair 1989, pp. 97, 148.
73. Sklair 1989, pp. 217–8; Hutchinson, Villalobos and Beruvides 1997, p. 3203.
74. Sargent and Matthews 2006.
75. Tully 1999.
76. In the EPZs of the Philippines, 'high employee turnover, as a cost reducing practice, is often encouraged [...]. Thus, export-oriented industrialization can also lead to greater levels of rural-to-urban migration and a concomitant rise in urban unemployment'. Tyner 2003, pp. 70–1.

way as to attract a stable personnel'.[77] Some observers have also pointed out that Mexico's maquila-programme was initially implemented in order to develop a peripheral region of the country and prevent emigration to the United States.[78] In fact, what needs to be emphasised with regard to the relationship between maquilas and migration from Mexico to the United States are the processes of proletarianisation and the industrial apprenticeship the Mexican labour-force undergoes *before*[79] setting foot in the United States.[80]

While only a minority of the 12 million Mexicans residing in the United States in 2008 has experienced the enforced and insalubrious work-pace of Mexican EPZ production, chances are that such migrants will not succeed in avoiding the snare of repetitive work within the United States. During the first years of the twenty-first century, the emergence of new Hispanic migrant-destinations along the Southern US border coincides with the relocation of the meat-processing industry to the rural Midwest (Colorado, Kansas, Nebraska, Oklahoma and Texas). The process can be traced back to the 1970s, when the meat-processing industry began recruiting Southeast-Asian and Latin-American workers. In the year 2000, the US meat-processing industry employed about 500,000 workers; 60 percent of them worked in rural locations. The meat-processing industry's presence in rural areas is attractive to undocumented workers, who make up at least 25 percent of all workers within the industry.[81] While employers are loath to reveal their actual labour turnover-rates, estimates range from 60 to 100 percent or higher.[82] Until the late 1990s, US employers benefited from the availability of large numbers of Mexican workers thanks to the fact that the country's Southern border was effectively half-open to immigrants. Turnover-rates were driven up by the employers themselves in an effort to avoid having to provide social-insurance benefits, as well as to undermine union-activity.[83] But the desirability of high turnover-rates to employers has its limits.

One immense labour-pool that proved irresistible to US industry was that beyond the Pacific. The first experiments with industrial enclaves were undertaken in parallel with the repression of left-wing parties and trade-unions in Hong Kong, the Republic of Korea and Taiwan after the Korean War, during which Japan's *de facto* EPZs contributed largely to supplying materials to the US military. In Taiwan the right to strike and other union-rights were abolished by

---

77. Blackett 1928, p. 1.
78. Seligson and Williams 1981; Sklair 1989; Stoddard 1987.
79. It should however be noted that northward migration from Mexico predates the maquila-programme and that many workers have already undertaken *la migra* to the United States before they become maquila-workers.
80. Sassen 1996.
81. Kandel and Parrado 2005, pp. 457–9; Stanley 2005.
82. Grey 1999; Whittaker 2006.
83. Grey 1999, p. 18.

the Kuomintang as early as 1947, whereas in the case of the other three Asian Tigers, the elimination of militant unionists occurred later. In Singapore, the decolonisation process (1963) was the turning point. In Hong Kong, the elimination of militant unionists occurred during the 1960s and with the aid of Beijing. In the Republic of Korea, union-power was broken following the 1968–9 strikes against US employers.[84] *As has rightly been pointed out, the repression of the labour-movement went hand in hand with the establishment of an export-oriented economic system.*[85]

East-Asian experimentation with production-enclaves has been intensified and extended during the two closing decades of the twentieth century, and even more so during the first years of the twenty-first century, following the People's Republic of China's decision to welcome investment by foreign industrial capital. In 2002, China's EPZs employed about 30 million workers; by 2006, the number had risen to 40 million. Firms producing in Chinese EPZs account for about half of all the country's exports and some 75 percent of exports to the United States.[86] In an unprecedented development, more than 100 million Chinese workers have moved from rural to urban areas (and in particular to the urban agglomerations of China's Southern coast): the vastest internal migration in the history of modern industry.[87] The new division of labour brought about by China's so-called market reforms has entailed the entry of tens of millions of young women into serial factory-labour; typically aged between 16 and 29 and with a rural background, these women tend not to work in the factory for more than five to eight years. Their return to the countryside accords both with the principles of the patriarchal family and with those of an industrial efficiency in need of unspent neuromuscular systems.

Rachel Murphy notes that, '[t]o the consternation of the state, there are even more potential migrants; officials estimate that an additional 130 million rural people lack sufficient land or employment to guarantee their livelihoods'.[88]

As for what was originally the European Coal and Steel Community and went on to become first the European Economic Community and then the European Union, its founding countries have struck upon their very own maquilas following the fall of the Berlin Wall in 1989. The countries of Central and Eastern Europe had been integrated with the Soviet Union for close to fifty years, under a system that proffered a fiction of social equality. The cleavage of 1989 saw these

---

84. Deyo, Haggard and Koo 1987.
85. Fröbel, Heinrichs and Kreye 1980.
86. International Labor Office 2003 and 2007.
87. For discussion of the various estimates, see Murphy 2002, p. 1; Pun 2005, pp. 54–5. China's census for the year 2000 puts the so-called 'floating population' at 120 million people (*People's Daily*, 27 January 2001).
88. Murphy 2002, p. 1.

countries shift their economic centre of gravity towards the European Union, into which they have become integrated in a dependent position.

The restructuring process undergone by the productive base of the economies of Eastern Europe sheds new light on the transformations taking place within the European Union. What we are seeing is the establishment of a system of production and employment based on the ongoing interaction of autochtonous and Western employers on the one hand, and the local and foreign labour-force on the other. The decision to relocate production is intimately linked to the interest that firms have in recruiting a tolerably qualified and relatively cheap labour-force in areas close to the one of the world's most important consumer-markets, that of the European Union. Eastern Europe's favourable political climate and the prospect of economic stabilisation that comes with the entry of some Eastern European countries into both the European Union and the eurozone provide further incentives for investment.

What has emerged in the countries of Central and Eastern Europe is a new kind of maquila. These new maquilas are utilised by several firms simultaneously. And they are differentiated from one another in the sense that countries such as Poland, the Czech Republic, Slovenia and Hungary provide low- to medium-wage manufacturing services, whereas manufacturing in Bulgaria and Romania (and, in the medium term, in Moldovia and Ukraine) is supposed to remain strictly low-wage.[89] At the same time, the second group of countries already disposes of a non-sedentary labour-force whose movements sometimes correspond and sometimes contrast with the contingent requirements of the productive apparatus of some EU countries. The EU's attempt to reduce the differences and overcome the barriers between the countries of Western and those of Central and Eastern Europe aims at a convergence of employment-practices and prepares the ground for a closer coordination and exchange of experiences between the various countries. This tendency becomes all the more important given the growing presence of transnational corporations.

In general, since the 1990s the productive processes related to Central Europe's international market have accorded with schemes developed by the medium-sized and large firms of the EU. Within factories, the pace of production has intensified; this is especially the case in factories run by foreign capital. What we are seeing is a standardisation of productive rhythms[90] that is constantly fine-tuned, imposes clearly defined deadlines and tends towards 'closing the pores of the workday'. Local or foreign capitals encounter greater resistance to the imposition of the new work-methods in older factories, whereas in the new, so-called 'greenfield' factories (those located in rural areas), the absence of viable

89. Ellingstad 1997.
90. Rinehart 1999.

employment-alternatives promotes a kind of 'social truce' between workers and managers, at least for a few years.

Employment in the new factories is characterised by a high labour-turnover rate which constrains firms to extend their recruitment-area both socially and geographically. Up until the end of 2007, firms operating in the area around Bratislava – known as the 'Detroit' of Eastern Europe – were forced by man-power-shortages and high turnover-rates to recruit workers from areas up to 100 kilometres away (including areas outside the country), providing special bus-transportation for workers.[91] In their efforts to address the shortage of labour-power, business-organisations did not so much look to wage-increases as call for manpower-imports to be facilitated further. In effect, foreign direct investment in Eastern Europe increases the mobility of the labour-force and may attract seg-ments of neighbouring countries' working classes. This is the case in the Czech Republic and Poland; similar developments are to be expected in other coun-tries, such as Hungary and Romania. Once they have emigrated, however, many workers choose to set off again, this time to the countries of Western Europe, where wages are higher.[92] Throughout the 1990s, the annual turnover-rates for Polish, Bulgarian and Romanian workers ranged from 30 to 40 percent; average turnover-rates were lower, during the same period, in countries where economic restructuring did not proceed as fast, such as Slovenia.[93] Absenteeism, labour-turnover and migration are the principal instruments used by the labour-force of the various Eastern European countries in its effort to defend itself against the extended command of multinational capital.

Externally determined work-paces and repetitive work are to be found not only in Western-European industry but also and in fact especially in Eastern Europe's new areas of foreign direct investment. In the case of Western Europe, repetitive tasks lead to high turnover-rates, such that employers resort to immigrant-labour and extend the area from which manpower is recruited. In the case of Eastern Europe, externally determined work-paces and relatively low wages induce emi-gration to Western Europe, but also immigration from countries where wages and working conditions are even worse. On the one hand, workers who already have jobs are driven to emigrate, to the extent that wage-differentials between their country and other EU countries are substantial. On the other hand, the extension of labour-recruitment areas leads to social breakdown and the develop-ment of market-relations inducing a flow of emigrants who do not pass through

---

91. Perry and Power 2007.

92. The Czech Republic and Poland dispose of a relatively stable pool of migrant-workers; migratory processes have also begun, albeit on a much smaller scale, in Roma-nia and Bulgaria.

93. Nesporova 2002.

relocated production-sites to work there or do so only in a marginal and temporary way. Work-régimes under which workers are replaced rapidly and which require a constant extension of recruitment-areas are associated with two interrelated processes, one of which is geared to foreign direct investment, the other to migration. Labour-turnover has a catalytic effect on the mobility of both capital and migrants, resulting in a sort of spiral.

7. Individuality and collective action

Modernity has seen the mobilisation and displacement of labour-power occur under a wide spectrum of modalities:[94] from the various forms of perpetual slavery and temporary servitude to bilateral agreements between states, from recruitment undertaken by state-institutions to nationally and internationally active private recruitment-agencies. The adoption of one system rather than another is linked to institutional variables, as is the specific form assumed by each system.[95]

As long as capital has not succeeded in eliminating alternative, non-capitalist ways of life within a given territory, it is forced to go in search of labour-power. Once it has imposed its dominion, it calls the shots and exercises its power of attraction on individuals constrained to sell segments of their own life one day at a time in order to survive. Probing beyond the relatively discrete ways in which migrant-labour is recruited today, one finds excessive work-loads, work-paces and levels of health-risk, unpredictable periods of employment and work-schedules that preclude any sort of social activity. Moreover, as the pace of transportation and communication picks up, the geographical contours of labour-markets become ever more blurred. Attention should be paid not only to the institutions upholding a given system of employment but also to the forms of subsistence that escape such institutions; they tend to constitute social environments on whose basis individuals can renegotiate their conditions of existence.

What has proven socially and politically decisive is the message conveyed by those who resist the vortex of a productive process that sees capital striving to maximally de-subjectivise the labour-force, turning it into a mere carrier of the capacity for work: from the fugitive-slave in the Americas to all those whose struggle against the dictates of capital-accumulation has taken in the form of migration. Those typically considered 'normal' or 'economic' migrants are quite capable of 'shaking the tree' and upsetting the social conditions in which non-migrants exist. *Today as in the era of the fugitive-slaves, the strongest expression of*

---

94. Moulier-Boutang 1998.
95. Hoerder 2002; Massey and Taylor (eds.) 2004.

individuality coincides with the most powerful manifestation of collective action. It is within this nexus that the possibility of overthrowing the barriers of discrimination is situated.

The segmentation of the individual, his reduction to a mere bearer of labour-power whose various 'natural and [...] acquired capacities' can be repeatedly exploited[96] is a process that can be traced back to the dawn of capitalism. It continues to this day and will not, it seems, stop *ex proprio motu. If the living individual was and continues to be so vulnerable, there is no capitalist reason not to seize upon the entire life-sphere and place it under the command of the most varied and heterogeneous catalytic forces, resorting to each and every branch of knowledge in order to eliminate industrial production's so-called periods of dead time.* Those who prophesy the end of work and foresee a post-industrial future seem unwilling to listen to a simple question. Can serial work ever be overcome within the narrow bounds of accumulation?

---

96. Marx 1976, pp. 469–70.

Workerism: An Inside View: From the Mass-Worker to Self-Employed Labour

Sergio Bologna

The first generation of Italian 'workerists' studied and elaborated on Marx's writings between the early sixties and the mid-seventies. It could not have been any other way. Our approach to the writings of Marx did not follow any existing model. Individuals set about exploring certain parts of Marx's *oeuvre* – Mario Tronti, for example, devoted himself to *Capital* Volume II in his essays for the first issues of *Quaderni Rossi*, later re-published as *Workers and Capital*.[1] Once broadly received within the political space that was defined as workerism, the fixed reference-points established by such readings and interpretations came to constitute a sort of common ground. They were transformed into a series of 'mental prototypes' and underwent the well-known process of vulgarisation described by Geiger in his writings on intellectual labour.[2] They became slogans, eventually finding their way into the politico-ideological discourse that provided the 'workerist' group with its identity and public image. Then, a new research-effort would be undertaken, again on the initiative taken by an individual, continuing where the last exploration had left off. Thus we proceeded in fits and starts, by accumulation, re-launches and reprisals, but without any prior plan or programme, without a strategy. The body of work produced by the first generation of workerists and devoted to Marx's

---

1. *Quaderni Rossi* ('Red Notebooks'): workerist journal published between 1961 and 1965 (translator's note).
2. Bologna 1998.

writings is not very substantial, it consists of only a few texts. And yet that work has left an indelible mark; the path beaten by it remains difficult to avoid even today. What is the reason for this incisiveness? Why have a few pages left a mark so deep as to constitute the basis of a system of thought? I am convinced that the answer lies in the fact that the explorations undertaken by Panzieri, Tronti, Negri, Grillo and De Caro were embedded within a collective labour that was itself of a different nature. Each significant theoretical finding had to be exposed to the reality of the times and the various levels of collective inquiry [*conricerca*]. The reality of collective labour that the workerist patrol took on in direct contact with the world of factory-production aimed at penetrating the various levels that make up the system of productive relations: the sequential organisation of the productive cycle and the hierarchical mechanisms spontaneously produced by it, the disciplinary techniques and techniques of integration elaborated in various ways, the development of new technologies and processing systems, the reactions to the labour-force's spontaneous behaviour, the interpersonal dynamics on the shop-floor, the systems of communication employed by workers during their shift, the transmission of knowledge from older to younger workers, the gradual emergence of a culture of conflict, the internal division of the labour-force, the use of work-breaks, the systems of payment and their differential application, the presence of the union and of forms of political propaganda, risk-awareness and the methods used to safeguard one's physical integrity and health, the relationship to political militants outside the factory, work pace-control and the piecework-system, the workplace itself and so on. One could easily continue cataloguing the various levels on which 'factory-work' articulates itself. What distinguished the 'workerists' neatly from the political personnel of a left-wing party was their perfect awareness of factory-work's *complexity*. It is easy to speak of 'class-struggle' or 'industrial labour'; even from a purely analytical point of view, but inherent in these two expressions is a plethora of problems that the ideological language normally used by a socialist or communist party and echoed by its militants is incapable even of evoking. Hence the workerists benefited from an intellectual superiority that resulted from their awareness of how the reality of the factory, its mechanisms and social dynamics, are considerably more difficult to understand than even the most complicated and obscure Marxian text. The workerists had set themselves the task of exploring, one by one, the various levels on which factory-production articulates itself, thereby acquiring a degree of competence that would allow them to enter into a dialogue with workers, to speak their language, without imposing precepts, exhortations or slogans from above. Only the workers themselves – the most politically prepared and combative among them – disposed of a superior knowledge, with the exception of some PCI and CGIL militants from working-class backgrounds who had been laid off due to their participation in struggles conducted some years back.[3] The tacit knowledge of these 'grassroots political militants', as Danilo Montaldi calls them in his writings, was what the workerists were trying to 'grasp' – the irreplaceable legacy of a knowledge that was never formalised and impossible to transmit except through direct participation in factory- and worker-affairs. In my view, this was the decisive and defining aspect. The workerist interpretation of Marx derived its strength and validity from constant confrontation with the reality of the factory. Theory had to provide the mental frame capable of encompassing what went on in a world that was so difficult to approach, 'the world of factory production'. Without this active labour of constant confrontation with the everyday dynamics of production, nothing could justify the theory's existence. Intellectuals or knowledge-workers such as we all were, find it difficult to admit that theory has no intrinsic value, but rather that it represents an instrumental value. Intellectuals view theoretical production, or writing, as an end in itself, as an abstract value. It takes a certain violation of one's own nature, of one's professional code, to formally recognise that theoretical production is either a commodity or an instrument for action. Before considering the readings and interpretations of Marxian texts produced by exponents of first-generation Italian workerism, before examining the workerist Marx of the sixties and seventies, we need to clarify the role that theory and abstract thinking played within the workerist groups.

(1) It is worth starting from the context within which a young militant received his political and cultural education during the early 1960s. The Italian Communist Party was a powerful party, rooted in society and composed of thousands and thousands of militants who visited the local branches, participated in the life of the party and distributed its publications. The Party daily, *L'Unità*, was the most widely read Italian daily paper (thanks in part to the militants who sold it). The party was a giant machine, based on voluntary work, whose economic prowess derived from the organisations associated with it, and in particular from its powerful Cooperative League. The Party's prestige resulted first and foremost from its anti-fascist past; it was the party that had contributed most to the *Resistenza* and carried on the legacy of the socialist movement. In the intellectual world – the world of literature, cinema, painting, publishing, the graphic arts, design and journalism, the Italian Communist Party enjoyed considerable prestige; in some cases, it was absolutely hegemonic. Then there was the Socialist Party, which had

---

3. PCI: *Partito comunista italiano*, Italian Communist Party; CGIL: *Confederazione generale italiana del lavoro*, Italian trade-union federation (founded in 1944) (translator's note).

not broken with Marxist positions and tendencies; in fact, being the party in which various leftist currents and differences of opinion were tolerated, it had become the organisation within which the most explicitly anti-Stalinist positions – such as those of Lelio Basso, who elaborated on Rosa Luxemburg's work – could be formulated. As a result, all those who sought to renew Marxism and found the Communist Party's discipline and censorship intolerable ended up in the Socialist Party. People like Panzieri or Toni Negri were Socialist Party leaders and militants. The trade union federation CGIL, then the most powerful labour-organisation in Italy, was a common branch to both the Socialist and Communist Parties. In the factories of northern Italy, the CGIL had suffered a period of intense repression following the Christian Democrat Party's 1948 electoral victory. Thanks in part to financial aid from the United States, Italian capitalism had rebuilt the major centres of production in the North and had begun industrialising the South. State-owned industry was essential to this action; underpinned by a banking system controlled directly by the government, it allowed Italy to gain a foothold in economic sectors it had hitherto been excluded from (such as the energy-sector). The immediate postwar period's concluding cycle of proletarian struggles came to an end during the four years that followed the Christian Democrat electoral victory of 1948. The CGIL and the Italian Communist Party expended the last of their revolutionary energy. Union militants were subjected to systematic repression, a development facilitated by the CGIL's break with both the CISL (the Catholic trade union federation associated with the Christian Democrats) and the UIL (a trade union federation representing the right wing of the socialist spectrum). Many militants chose the path of emigration; in fact, emigration acted as a safety-valve in that it removed workers rendered supernumerary by their expulsion from the countryside. Most left Italy for South America and Australia, never to return, but many were absorbed by the factories of Germany, Belgium and France, where they went through the tough school of advanced production and participated in trade-union activities. Some returned to Italy during the late sixties and joined the most experienced and combative sections of the Italian working class. Repression, layoffs and mass emigration created a caesura of sorts, disrupting the continuity of memory and the transmission of tacit knowledge. Even within the Italian Communist Party, the culture of class-antagonism was gradually displaced by institutional issues, the problems associated with leadership, tactics of alliance and the effort to build a relationship both with the middle classes and with capital's most 'reformist' wing. Marx and Lenin were no longer the order of the day, Gramsci was reinterpreted along anti-Stalinist and reformist lines, and even the *Resistenza* was increasingly remembered as a patriotic, inter-class struggle. The break with the spirit of the *Resistenza* and the immediate postwar period became ever more marked, and the education received by the Party's young recruits was increasingly oriented towards parliamentary struggle and the administration of public bodies. The working class, the factory and the world of production receded ever further into the distance. Those readings and interpretations of Marx that were produced were the work of philosophers, of isolated intellectuals like Della Volpe. Given this climate of breaking with the past, a book such as *Militanti politici di base* by Danilo Montali amounted to a revelation.[4] Born in Cremona, Montaldi boasted a long history as a Communist Party militant, but he had also been in contact with the various currents of *Bordighista* internationalism and disposed of a vast network of contacts with revolutionary and workerist Marxist groups all over the world, from the United States to France. He was, for example, well acquainted with the development of *Socialisme ou Barbarie*. And yet, while Montaldi was perfectly familiar with Marx's writings and their interpretations as elaborated by revolutionary groups in the West, his decisive contribution to the education of those young men who would later join the editorial collective of *Quaderni Rossi*, and in particular to the education of Romano Alquati (also a native of Cremona), was to pass on the lost memory of values cherished during the *Resistenza* and the immediate postwar period. His book *Militanti politici di base* valorises the legacy of political and practical knowledge left by the worker- and peasant-militants who dominated the political scene during the decade 1943–53. The book is a collection of exemplary lives and models for life, and it was to exercise a profound influence on the young people who devoted themselves to politics within the void created by the caesura of defeat. The book reconstituted a tradition, reconnecting with a past that some would have preferred to have forgotten or to consider unrepeatable. But there was another reason why the book was important: Montaldi was born in Cremona, on the banks of the river Po, in an area dominated by capitalist agricultural enterprises. The fertile Po valley had been the site of memorable land-worker struggles that displayed peculiar affinities and similarities with factory-struggles, and can in fact be considered part and parcel of the same; they were linked to the struggles of factory-workers by a sort of continuum. Montaldi was one of the first to deconstruct, with great success, the Italian Communist Party's peasant-ideology. He considered rural capitalism to be a mature form of the organisation of the forces of production. The labour-force consisted of wage-workers who were not interested in owning land and did not want to become 'freeholders', but strove rather for better working conditions, just as factory-workers did. The Italian Communist Party's peasant-ideology was based on the image of the Sicilian *cafone*: a desperate, illiterate individual oppressed by the Mafia and the Church, who hopes one

---

4. Montaldi 1971.

day to obtain a small piece of land – the *cafone* is a *sem terra*. However, since the first decade of the twentieth century onward, Northern Italy's agriculture had been characterised by forms of intensive cultivation that relied on wage-workers for their manpower. The union-struggles conducted by these wage-workers had long represented the vanguard of working-class struggle in Italy, both in terms of the nature of their strikes and in terms of the demands formulated. Yet Montaldi's influence cannot be explained solely in terms of his book on grass-roots political militants; it was through another book, which inquired into the transformation of the urban reality, that he attracted the attention of a broader audience. It was the end of the 1950s. One of the driving forces behind the economic boom of the time was a rampant real-estate market that had produced dormitory neighbourhoods on the edges of the North's major cities, neighbourhoods destined for the factory-workers and the mass of people who had abandoned the countryside in order to live in the city, where they encountered conditions worse than those they had left behind. This 'real-estate fever' had also destroyed entire sections of the historic city-centres in order to make way for buildings demarcated for the lower and middle class-strata of the bourgeoisie. The protagonists of Montaldi's book *Autobiografie della leggera* are not political militants;[5] they are characters from the urban undergrowth: the prostitute, the petty thief and the sub-proletarian living with the newly employed workers of the metallurgical factories. The setting is that of poorly and hastily constructed buildings in neighbourhoods lacking basic services, shops and sewer-networks. Understanding the factory, understanding the city – this was the setting for this study of Marx. Following Montaldi's example, others began publishing additional book-length inquiries into the new urban realities; Goffredo Fofi's *Immigrati a Torino* is one such work. It was on the basis of these on-site inquiries, these direct testimonies, that the theory of the factory-city developed. In other words, Montaldi made an original contribution to Italian sociological thought, as has been well demonstrated by a relatively recent collection of essays on the Montaldian figure of the militant.[6] The *Quaderni Rossi* would go on to produce some of Italy's best known sociologists, such as Massimo Paci, Giovanni Mottura, Bianca Beccalli and Vittorio Rieser. As I see it, as I remember it, the *Bildungsjahre* of the group of young people who gravitated towards the *Quaderni Rossi* in 1961–2 were characterised first and foremost by a desire to understand the profound transformation that both productive facilities and the urban environment were undergoing; the need to master a theoretical-systematic framework by which to interpret what was happening in accordance with a Marxian logic came second. Marx was read collectively, together with comrades who reported on

---

5. Montaldi 1961.
6. Fiameni 2006. See also *Parole Chiave*, no. 38 (2007) and Montaldi 1994.

their encounters with FIAT workers, and an effort was made to establish a correspondence between the workers' stories and the pages of the first volume of *Capital*. But everything was still in an embryonic stage, almost in its infancy. Then came the qualitative leap, the historic turning point, an event that convinced everyone that workers' struggles would be the primary force for change during the years to come. This was the event that prompted our decision to devote ourselves entirely to becoming an integral part of the actual workers' movement: the strikes of the Milanese metalworkers in 1960. After years of silence and fear, years characterised by a divided trade-union movement, and for the first time since the caesura of 1950–3, we witnessed a struggle whose unity, compactness and combativeness were truly impressive. Milan's electromechanical sector boasted about 70,000 workers at the time; Tecnomasio Brown Boveri, General Electric, Siemens, Face Standard, Telettra, Ercole Marelli, Magneti Marelli, Riva Calzoni, Franco Tosi, Osram, Geloso and Autelco were only some of the major factories. During the 1960 strike, which continued for months and ended with a partial victory, the most sophisticated forms of struggle were employed – forms that would be generalised after the Hot Autumn.[7] It was a demonstration of maturity that left not just the employers dumbfounded, but the Communist Party as well. A comrade who was then a leader of the communist youth movement and later went on to become one of the most representative exponents of the feminist movement stated that the 1960 strike marks the moment when 'Milan recognised the workers as its citizens'. How was this demonstration of maturity possible, given the years of silence that preceded it? It was possible because the knowledge acquired by those grassroots political militants who had conducted the struggles of the immediate postwar period had been successfully passed on. Many of these militants had begun working for the union after being laid off; they had become trade-union functionaries. At the time, a trade-union functionary barely earned enough to live; the grassroots unionist of the period was not a bureaucrat sitting in his office but someone who stood outside the factory-gate at every shift change – as emerges from the testimonies gathered for the documentary film *Oltre il Ponte* and the small number of publications dedicated to the memorable struggle of 1960. Many other workers had not been laid off, but were working in the toughest factory-departments, where the health risks were the greatest. They were banished to the so-called *reparti confino*, relatively isolated departments reserved for unruly or troublesome workers. These were highly experienced people, 'grassroots-political militants' who preserved the memory of every struggle from 1943 onward. They knew the factory like the back of their hand because they never lost the habit of observing

---

7. 'Hot Autumn' [*autunno caldo*]: major Italian strike cycle (summer and autumn 1969) (translator's note).

every minor change introduced by the factory's management. Two or three of them were enough to get things rolling as soon as the attitude towards the boss began turn hostile. They were generally specialised workers, highly qualified and well-placed within the factory's hierarchy; younger workers looked up to them with respect and even with a certain awe. They were not mass-workers. In this sense, the 1960 strike marks both the beginning and the end of a cycle. Its protagonist was not the assembly-line worker (repetitive tasks were still performed almost exclusively by women), but rather the toolmaker, the fitter and turner, the worker who knows his machine inside out, who is the best, the most competent, who feels himself to be part of an elite and is a communist for that very reason: a worker who has a strong sense of discipline, who is very wary of spontaneity. His mentality is far removed from that of a typical workerist, who puts great stock in spontaneity and has an anarchist and libertarian streak. The strike was led by the Milanese FIOM branch, the Federation of Milanese Metalworkers, whose functionaries refused to let themselves be restrained by the bewilderment, fear and uncertainty expressed within CGIL and the Italian Communist Party. The Federation of Young Communists [*Federazione dei giovani comunisti*, FGCI] supported the strike and sent its militants to the factory-gates – against the Party's advice. The *Quaderni Rossi* failed to fully grasp the complexity of the 1960 strike. In fact, certain aspects of this fundamental episode in Italian labour-history still await proper exploration; this is especially true of the relationship between FIOM's Milanese leadership and the Rome-based leadership of the Italian Communist Party and CGIL.

(2) During the *Bildungsjahre*, the fundamental Marxian text was, of course, *Capital* Volume I, with its analysis of the production process; the other central text was Engels's book on the condition of the working class in England.[8] These two texts were sufficient for an understanding of the factory and the principles on which the direct extraction of surplus-value is based. But the workerists also needed to come to terms with the two dominant cultures within the Italian left: (a) the tendency represented by the Italian Communist Party, whose exponents devoted all of their energy to general issues of governance, public administration, foreign policy, economic policy, urban policy, the *mezzogiorno* and relations with the Church and the world of Catholicism; (b) the tendency represented by the anti-capitalist currents of the Left, who devoted all their energy to issues associated with Imperialism and Third World liberation-movements. Within the first of these two political cultures, the workerists were considered a 'unionist' minority, a movement that dealt only with factory-issues and was therefore incapable of confronting the real, 'political' problems of the day; within

---

8. Engels 1975–2004b.

the second political culture, the Western working class was seen as having been co-opted by capitalism. It was considered incapable of moving beyond economic demands – a class that aspired only to becoming a new petty bourgeoisie. The exponents of both tendencies refused, albeit for divergent reasons, to recognise the workerists as a 'political' movement. The workerists were seen as taking too narrow, too corporatist a perspective; they were considered incapable of grasping and affronting the great challenges of society – democracy and socialism. The reformists within the Italian Communist Party viewed the workerists with diffidence and suspicion; the anti-imperialists pitied them for lacking a 'general' perspective. They were not altogether wrong. A Marxism based solely on the first volume of *Capital*, the *Communist Manifesto* and an interpretation of the 'Fragment on Machines' (see Panzieri's essay in the first issue of the *Quaderni Rossi*) does not allow for a comprehensive understanding of capitalism's mechanisms of domination; these readings were insufficient. However, a turning point was reached with the publication of Tronti's first essay on 'social capital', based predominantly on an interpretation of *Capital* Volume II. This was the first exposition of hypotheses which would later be presented in *Workers and Capital*. The effect of these hypotheses on militants and their meaning within the history of Italian (and European) heterodox Marxism continue to be a subject of debate. In his analysis of social capital, Tronti showed that capitalist society – including its economic, urban, health and cultural policies – is modelled on the factory-system and ultimately geared to the extraction of surplus-value. This meant that whoever started from the factory already disposed of the true 'general perspective' and went right to the heart of politics, discerning the state's genuine foundation. Workerism was therefore not a sectoralist or 'unionist' movement; it represented the reconstitution of an up-to-date system of revolutionary thought in the West. *Workers and Capital* became workerism's fundamental text, the central reference-point in any militant's education. It is also interesting to note that workerism's method of theoretical elaboration requires the hypothesis formulated to be collectively verified and validated. Tronti published *Workers and Capital* in 1966, but the book's fundamental hypotheses were already presented in the *Quaderni Rossi* in 1962, and they were the object of discussion and interpretation for the entire period from 1962 until the founding of *Classe operaia* in 1964 and beyond.[9] Similarly, my hypotheses on the mass-worker, published in the 1972 volume *Operai e Stato*,[10] were first presented during an internal seminar held in Venice in 1967; the term 'mass-worker' is used throughout the publications and leaflets we produced in 1968 and 1969. And while *Militanti politici di*

---

9. *Classe Operaia* ['Working Class']: workerist journal published between 1964 and 1967 (translator's note).
10. Bologna *et al.* 1972.

base was published in 1971, the book's hypotheses were already circulating during the late 1950s. It's important to realise that the theoretical works we are dealing with circulated only within small groups of friends and militants associated with a particular individual (such as Montaldi) or journal (such as the *Quaderni Rossi*). They were pamphlets with a circulation no more significant than that of the *samisdat*; it could take several years for the ideas expressed in them to give rise to a movement or public debate and the large left-wing publishers of the time – Giulio Einaudi, Giangiacomo Feltrinelli – were certainly not inclined to publish no-name authors. In Italy, niche-publishers specialising in a certain type of antagonist literature emerged only after 1968; before then, only the major commercial publishers and those controlled by the Communist and Socialist Parties existed. Many of our sympathisers worked for commercial publishers – Einaudi in Turin and Feltrinelli in Milan were the most important, followed by *La Nuova Italia* in Florence – and some of us collaborated with them in various ways, as translators or copy-editors. Danilo Montaldi had been one of Feltrinelli's more important collaborators, and I myself occasionally worked for Feltrinelli on a freelance basis (almost all of us were precariously employed knowledge-workers). Raniero Panzieri had been one of Einaudi's most high-ranking editors before the publishing house asked him to leave. At the time, occasional or full-time work for a publishing company was one of the few income-opportunities available to an independent intellectual, the other being a teaching position at a school or university.

(3) One year after the publication of *Workers and Capital*, *La Nuova Italia* published the first Italian edition of Marx's *Grundrisse*, translated and edited by Enzo Grillo, who frequented the Rome-based editorial collectives of the *Quaderni Rossi* and *Classe Operaia*. This was, then, another decisive workerist contribution to the study of Marx in Italy. In the years that followed, the theoretical work produced in the ambit of Italian workerism made abundant use of the *Grundrisse*, a work that lends itself very well to non-orthodox interpretations and offers a wealth of extremely precious stimuli to anyone wishing to renew Marxist thought. Associated with this is the risk of arbitrary interpretations that lead into blind alleys and betray the spirit of Marx's text, but this is a constant risk for every exegesis. Just as *Capital* Volume I provided the workerists with instruments allowing them to understand concrete-labour, so the *Grundrisse* were immensely important in the understanding of the essence of *abstract labour*. Reading *Capital* Volume I, one begins to understand Fordism; reading the *Grundrisse*, one begins to understand Postfordism. We are on the brink of the movements of 1968. The first-generation workerists had split and formed two opposing fronts, even though they maintained friendly relations. One part of the movement decided to re-enter the Communist Party, while the other chose to

follow the path of the new extra-parliamentary groups. Theoretical work was abandoned. We were completely absorbed by the new cycle of struggles begun by the Pirelli workers in Milan, the ENI workers in San Donato Milanese and the petrochemical workers in Porto Marghera, a cycle that spread to Turin with the strikes at FIAT during the summer of 1969 and then exploded all over Italy. We resumed theoretical work a few years later in the form of Feltrinelli's *Materiali Marxisti* book-series, a project conceived by Toni Negri. Negri's contribution to the workerist reading of Marx goes back to the early 1960s. He had focused, in particular, on aspects related to state-theory. Negri was one of the few workerists to have a background in legal theory (most comrades in the workerist group had received a humanist or sociological education), and this allowed him to confront aspects of Marxist theory related to the problematic of institutions. He has continued developing these reflections even Forty years later, in *Insurgencies*, *Empire* and other works.[11] This line of research led him to become increasingly interested in problems related to the *government of the crisis*. In the Fordist era, whenever the state faced pressure from the working class, finding itself in a situation characterised by the immanence of social conflict and the crisis of control, it was constrained to preserve the conditions of capitalist accumulation through an articulation of political measures and disciplinary techniques. It became a crisis-state, not in the sense intended by outdated theories of capitalism's 'collapse', but rather in the sense that it had to continually adjust its systems of control to an unstable, dynamic situation. Workerists have always been sceptical of theories that assume capitalism will eventually 'collapse' as a result of its internal contradictions, errors or excesses. They have tended to view such accounts less as theories than as banal placebos ingested, like aspirin tablets, by small sects of self-proclaimed revolutionaries who never venture outside their stuffy rooms to face reality. Toni Negri's theoretical work was mainly devoted to those economic theories that were also the theories of institutions, theories of the state; in the period following 1968, he focused especially on Keynes. This labour of theoretical reflection became particularly fruitful and incisive during the 1970s, when it was conducted within the University of Padua's Institute of Political Science. There, Negri gathered a substantial following of students and militants such as Luciano Ferrari Bravo, Ferruccio Gambino, Guido Bianchini, Sandro Serafini and Alisa del Re. With the exception of Gambino, who went into exile for three years, they were all arrested during the *blitz* of 7 April 1979 and spent considerable time behind bars, incarcerated in high-security prisons built to detain *mafiosi* and terrorists. Never before had academics become the object of similarly severe and targeted punitive measures, not even under fascism. One

---

11. Negri 1999; Hardt and Negri 2000.

of the Paduans's most original and memorable theoretical contributions was their profile of a paradigmatic social figure, the *multinational worker*. Ferruccio Gambino still teaches in Padua today, and his work, like that of his students, still focuses on *migrants*, on those millions of people who leave their country of origin in search of a living wage. The efforts undertaken by the first generation of workerists to elaborate a theoretical framework and an historical exegesis of Marx's writings reached their conclusion during the mid-1970s, when the editorial collective of the journal *Primo Maggio* devoted itself to the themes of money and finance, taking up some of the questions I had addressed in my essay on Marx as a correspondent for the *New York Daily Tribune*.[12] The starting point for this reflection was a reading of the *Capital* Volume III. The work done by the editorial collective of *Primo Maggio* (Lapo Berti, Marcello Messori, Franco Gori, Mario Zanzani, Christian Marazzi, Andrea Battinelli and myself) is especially useful for understanding the dynamics that led to Postfordism and the financialisation of the economy, whose outcome – the most severe economic crisis since 1929 – the world is now facing. One of the key features of *Primo Maggio*'s approach is its holistic conception of the accumulation-process, according to which the error of viewing the 'real' economy as somehow separate and separable from the financial economy is avoided. In orthodox Marxism, by contrast, the 'real' economy and the financial economy are seen as two separate sectors, one productive, the other speculative; while a social function is attributed to the first sector, the second is considered purely parasitic (the entrepreneur is good, the banker bad). Within workerism's theoretical framework, these two sectors are understood as being interrelated and mutually dependent: profit contributes to interest and vice versa. It is no accident that the key essay produced by *Primo Maggio*'s working group on money bears the title 'Money as Capital'.[13] It was by this militant reading of the Volume III that the cycle of theoretical elaboration and interpretation of *Capital* – begun with a reading of Volume I in 1960 and continued by Mario Tronti's analysis of Volume II – was brought to a close. What began in an off-the-cuff manner, without any prior plan, became, within the arc of fifteen years (1960–75), a self-contained cycle of theoretical exploration.

(4) We must now consider the period during which the workerists (or those left over from the workerist movement, depending on whether or not one considers the movement's trajectory to have continued beyond the 1960s) altered their approach to reading and interpreting Marx. They abandoned an approach that had consisted in remaining as faithful as possible to Marx's texts while simultaneously striving to formulate an innovative interpretation maximally

---

12. Bologna 1973a (extended version in: Bologna, Carpignano and Negri 1974); Berti and Collettivo di Primo Maggio (eds.) 1978.

13. Berti 1974.

coherent with workerist practice, the quotidian experience of militancy and neo-capitalism's changing reality as revealed by daily observation and sociological analysis. The workerists now began reading Marx more 'freely', allowing themselves to be influenced by various philosophical currents of the time, and in particular by the theories of Foucault. During this period, the prevailing urge was to go 'beyond Marx' (a phrase used in the title of one of Toni Negri's books).[14] The beginning of this period can be dated precisely – 1977. Once again, the arrival at new theoretical positions was the product not of abstract thinking but of concrete experiences, and they reflected developments quite unlike the preceding cycle of struggles. In a break with the first part of this essay, I will not speak, in what follows, of the theoretical work done by other members of first-generation workerism. Nor will I speak of the work done by later generations. (I believe one can now speak of a fourth generation of workerists.) I will speak only of my own work and the intellectual path I have followed since 1977. The reason for this choice is that there has no longer been a direct and ongoing exchange between the first-generation comrades since 1973–5. Each of us has followed a different path, and while our trajectories have sometimes run parallel, they have more often diverged. It is only in recent years that there has been a degree of rapprochement, thanks to militants and students who belong to the most recent generation of workerists; these militants and students have sought to draw up a balance-sheet of the workerist experience and begin sketching the movement's history. We met again, for the first time in 30 or 40 years, in order to satisfy the curiosity of the most recent generation, in order to answer its questions. The first thing to be said concerning my own personal experience between 1977 and today is that it has not been a solitary but often (not always) a shared one, enriched by the discussions, contributions and ideas of various groups of comrades affiliated with journals (*Primo Maggio, Sapere, Altre ragioni, 1999*) or politico-cultural projects (the *Libera Università di Milano e del suo Hinterland* [LUMHI], the Foundation for Social History in Hamburg, the *Centro Studi Franco Fortini* at Siena University). I frequented places where meetings were held and networks were created (Primo Moroni's *Libreria Calusca*, the *Casa del Popolo* in Lodi, the *Libreria delle Donne* in Milan), participated in social movements and kept in touch with groups of workers who continued to defend their work and those rights conquered during the 1970s. The starting point was the movement of 1977: a movement born neither in the factory nor at university. Although it involved both, it was a movement with service-workers, members of tertiary society and young precarious and casual workers as its vanguard. It was a movement of young people who rejected wage-work, who preferred to retain control of their

---

14. Negri 1979a, 1998, 1996b.

life and time, and did not suffer from a sense of inferiority *vis-à-vis* the working class. Their attitude towards the factory was one of diffidence; they did not want to get too close. They faced new problems, problems that had never even existed for their colleagues in 1968, first and foremost that of drugs. They were pacifists and non-violent at heart, opposed to both the Red Brigades and the *Autonomia Operaia* movement.[15] They considered the Italian Communist Party a control structure and the trade-union federation CGIL an instrument for cooperating with the bosses. They were libertarians and individualists, anti-Marxists and anti-Leninists. In a sense, they foreshadowed the fall of the Berlin Wall. They were not interested in tradition; they lived in Year Zero. They scorned the 'militancy' of the extra-parliamentary groups; to them, these groups were merely aping traditional political parties. They saw themselves as full-blown citizens of the 'society of the spectacle', living in a world of virtual representations: the world of the media, of the languages, of television and music, of symbolic languages. It was a movement that emphasised the individual and highlighted subjective factors. The slogan 'The personal is political', coined by the first generation of feminists, was very popular within the movement of 1977; the ethical radicalism expressed by it went hand in hand with a preference for cynical statements. The ethic of the Marxist militant was considered a mask, donned perhaps to conceal ambiguous forms of personal conduct; the 'comrades' were seen as people who didn't 'walk the talk'. There was a strong temptation, within the institutional and Leninist Left, to consider this movement an anarchic-fascist one; many Communist Party militants and veterans of 1968 were repulsed or viewed the movement with disdain. The attitude taken by the armed groups was no less disdainful, but they understood that the sense of radicalism pervading the movement could make it an excellent recruiting ground (what could be more radical than armed struggle on urban terrain?). The phenomenon of 1977 left observers at a loss: it could not be understood using the old rationality of Marxist-Leninist categories; it did not fit into the framework of Western political thought. The movement had no leaders, no fixed reference-points for others to engage with; it was entirely post-Fordist – we just did not know it yet. The *Autonomia* movement, partly influenced by Toni Negri, made every effort to gain a foothold within the 1977 movement and impose its paradigms, but in this it was outdone by the armed groups. Nevertheless, *Autonomia* had familiarised itself, thanks to Toni Negri, with the philosophy of Foucault and with France's *nouveaux philosophes* (Gilles Deleuze in particular), and this allowed it to develop an accurate understanding of certain characteristics displayed by the 1977 movement, while

---

15. The Red Brigades were an urban guerrilla-group founded in Milan in 1970s; *Autonomia Operaia* was a loose network of autonomous groups active from the mid-1970s onwards, and best represented in Rome, Turin and Padua (translator's note).

crafting analytical instruments appropriate to the period that followed. Within the editorial collective of *Primo Maggio*, I acted as editor-in-chief between 1973 and 1980 (when Cesare Bermani took over), the 1977 movement provoked uncertainty and disunity. We decided to render our disagreements public, exposing our doubts and uncertainties to open debate. While some comrades within the editorial collective had quite obviously been influenced by Foucault, I chose a different approach, evident in my essay 'The Tribe of Moles'. The essay was first published as the editorial to the seventh issue of *Primo Maggio*, and triggered a controversy we chose to document in a volume published as part of Feltrinelli's *Opuscoli marxisti* series.[16] The hypothesis advanced by the comrades most influenced by Foucault was that the subjectivism and individualism evident in the 1977 movement represented the form of insubordination most appropriate to the 'microphysics of power': capitalist domination was no longer based on a disciplinary system, that of the factory, but rather, it was articulated in an extremely complex manner, employing multiple control models that penetrated people's individual lives and their affective and emotional dispositions. Consequently, the drive to 'liberate' the subject – and to liberate it from every totalising ideology, including those of Marxism and communism – represented the most authentic and appropriate form of rebellion. My own thoughts on this issue led me to take an entirely different position. Rather than choosing Foucault as my starting point, I began with the transformations undergone by the mode of production. *Primo Maggio* had continued to conduct inquiries, collaborating with groups of workers from various sectors of the economy not directly linked to the factory (the transport-sector, public administration). These inquiries had allowed us to grasp certain profound changes in the mode of production while establishing contact with varieties of working-class culture that differed from those typical of automobile- or chemical-workers. We realised production was being fragmented and decentralised, broken up into smaller productive units. Many former workers were becoming craftsmen and then small entrepreneurs. Outsourced work was on the rise again. The large factories had begun a period of radical restructuring that would perhaps lead to mass layoffs. Italy's *cassa integrazione* offered a temporary solution.[17] Workers were expelled from the factories without being

---

16. Bologna 1978.

17. The *cassa integrazione* (or *cassa integrazione guadagni*) is a state-administered fund established in 1947 to soften the social impact of economic restructuring. Under the *cassa integrazione* system, workers continue to be paid the greater part of their wage even after their position has been made redundant; workers in this situation continue to be formally employed, although they no longer work. The reduced wages are paid from the state-administered fund, not by the employer. In theory, this is a temporary arrangement (employers are expected to find new tasks for their workers once the process of restructuring has been completed); in practice, workers may continue to be paid from the state-fund for a decade or longer (translator's note).

laid off. It was a way of subsidising employers and finding a compromise with the workers, whose wages were reduced but who did not lose their claim to social insurance, health-insurance and a pension. The monolithic compactness of the Fordist factory was in the process of disintegrating into a myriad of productive units linked to one another in various ways. The assembly line itself was replaced with 'assembly-islands' and entire segments of the productive cycle were rendered automatic: the factory was changing both inside and out. Workers' struggles had not stopped short of the tertiary sector; entire sections of the public administration – where strikes were uncommon and employees were divided into small corporate groups, with most of the employees coming from the petty bourgeoisie – were on the move just as the factory-workers had been a few years earlier. *Primo Maggio*'s work with transport-workers was especially interesting from a political point of view; we worked mainly with dockworkers at first, but later also with warehouse-workers, truck-drivers, Alitalia hostesses and railway-workers. These were sectors with a long and glorious tradition of struggles, both in Europe and in the United States, although the tradition had been forgotten. Within the profound transformation of the mode of production, and with the first symptoms of the transition from a Fordist to a post-Fordist society becoming apparent, I felt that I could begin to understand the changes in the idea of work, or in the (non-)work-ethic of the younger generations. The process of bringing our analytical instruments up to date therefore had to be focused, in my view, on the new meanings that 'work' was assuming and might still assume. I did not believe that the time had come to abandon the workerist approach altogether or devote oneself to a critique of Marx's thinking that questioned the validity of the law of value. It seemed to me the extra-parliamentary political movement produced by the struggles of 1968 had forgotten the importance of closely observing the process of production. Instead, it was dedicating itself to questions of power and government, thereby repeating the very process of involution that the Communist and Socialist Parties had undergone, but with the additional handicap of being only a fragile and presumptuous minority, one with pretensions of leading the masses. Analysis of the new economic crises, and in particular of the 1973 energy-crisis, was another important milestone in my intellectual career. Here, I learned a great deal from my collaboration with the editorial collective of a journal devoted to the critique of science, *Sapere*. Previously, I had worked exclusively with people who had received a humanist (sociological or legal) education. *Sapere*'s editorial collective consisted almost exclusively of people with a techno-scientific background. It was a journal unlike any other, not only because it attacked the way science was being turned into the handmaid of capital. *Sapere* was an important reference point for the anti-nuclear and the anti-psychiatry movements, but also because the editorial collective included workers and engineers from the chemical industry who were organising the most advanced struggles against insalubrious working conditions and the permanent risk of chemical accidents. The 1977 movement helped me to understand that the new generations wanted greater liberty and autonomy and greater control over their lives. They were prepared to accept either self-employment or precarious and unpredictable employment conditions, as long as they were freed from obligations. But I still believed the transition to Postfordism was incomplete, so much so that one needed – especially in Italy – to remain grounded in traditional forms of struggle associated with the factory. Moreover, I believed the transition to Postfordism would not be a painless one. Worker subordination had been going on for too long; it had eroded factory discipline, and within the workers' movement, there had emerged a new generation of militants for whom peaceful acceptance of capitalist control was unthinkable. Something traumatic needed to happen, especially to rein in the so-called 'armed struggle': urban guerrillagroups whose activities had reached an impressive scale (an attack every three hours, according to one magistrate), but which seemed not to have any strategy whatsoever, nor to be prepared to enter into a dialogue with Italy's social movements (in fact, the guerrilla-groups increasingly seemed to be imposing themselves on the social movements and suffocating them). The traumatic event arrived in the form of a wave of arrests on 7 April 1979, which saw comrades and colleagues being incarcerated and was only the beginning of an unprecedented campaign of repression. The arrests coincided with a wave of layoffs and the expulsion of militant workers from the factories. I was suspended from my teaching duties in February 1982 and stayed abroad for three years in order to avoid the fate of my colleagues from Padua's Institute of Political Science. For all of us, for our families and children, this was a time when simply keeping one's head above water took precedence over anything else. Many of us were constrained to find a new livelihood. The network of international contacts we had built from the 1960s onward proved useful in this respect. While there was no formal organisation to stand up for us and protect us, we had the benefit of a very solid and reliable network of friends. The solidarity shown to us was truly extraordinary; beyond allowing us to overcome that difficult period, it introduced us to new realities and experiences, providing us with intellectual stimuli that have allowed us to continue our theoretical work to this day. Some who chose the path of emigration have not returned and continue to live far from Italy. Many others have died, partly as a result of the physical and psychological strain of years spent in prison – among them some first-generation workerists such as Luciano Ferrari Bravo and Guido Bianchini.

(5) For me, the final phase of theoretical elaboration and critical social analysis began with the campaign of repression in the early 1980s, and in particular with

my expulsion from the civil service and from the university-system, an expulsion that assumed a definitive character following my decision not to protest against it: I protested neither when I was suspended, nor two years later, when the ministry of education declared, *sua sponte*, that the faculty's decision had been unjustified. If I had asked to be reinstated at that point, I would very likely have been able to continue teaching, much like colleagues of mine who were arrested on 7 April. But that was not the choice I made, and so I had to begin a new life, earning a living as a self-employed or freelance worker – putting to use the knowledge I had accumulated during my work in the freight-services sector with *Primo Maggio*. This new situation allowed me to reflect further on themes I had barely touched on in 1977, in particular self-employed labour and the exodus from wage-labour, whose context – in Italy and elsewhere – was now that of mature Postfordism. After five or six years of self-employment, I was in a position to communicate the results of my reflections, thereby extending workerism's gallery of paradigmatic social figures (the grassroots-political militant, the mass-worker, the multinational worker, the social worker) through a new figure, that of the 'second-generation self-employed worker'. I remained faithful to workerism's standard procedure: I began by publishing my hypotheses in a 1992 issue of the journal *Altre Ragioni* (of which I was a co-founder); having exposed my hypotheses to evaluation and discussion by a large number of people, I allowed my thinking to mature by reflecting on the contributions of others and considering phenomena that initially I had neglected. Ten years went by before my 'Ten Hypotheses' were included in a volume edited by myself and Andrea Fumagalli and published by Feltrinelli. Hence we can say that one of the defining features of theoretical work done within the workerist tradition is the prolonged gestation period of every new idea. What may appear to be a very slow process is actually characterised by a wealth of suggestions and contributions; while the intellectual product to emerge from the process bears the name of a single author, it is in fact the product of a collective effort, of the 'general intellect'. This means that when a theoretical work is presented in its definitive form, it inevitably produces dynamics of aggregation; it is never simply the product of an intellectual effort, but a political gesture that demands transformative action – an innovation within the world of thought *and* within the social fabric. My 'Ten Hypotheses on Second-Generation Self-Employed Labour' were written to demonstrate just how radically Postfordism has changed our way of working.[18] They focus on the figure of the freelance worker because that figure, while not representing the majority of workers, is the furthest removed from the way work was performed under Fordism (be it blue- or white-collar work). The most far-reaching

---

18. Bologna 1997.

changes concern space and time. The freelance worker has no workplace; thanks to his laptop and the Internet, he can work anywhere. This means that he is not part of a community that meets in the same place (the office) every day, with everyone arriving and leaving at the same time. He is an isolated individual. His employment-contract makes no mention of working times and involves no commitment to being physically present. Nor does it involve a relationship of formal dependence *vis-à-vis* the employer (or rather client). The freelancer's autonomy may turn out to be a trap; while he is economically dependent on his client, this dependency is not formalised and he is unable to disobey. He is on his own and cannot go on strike; strikes are by definition a form of collective action. The freelancer's condition is therefore one of social powerlessness, although it is masked by the fact that his income appears to be higher than that of a dependent worker performing the same tasks. This is only an appearance because we are speaking of his pre-tax income, and income-taxes may be as high as 50 percent, so that the freelancer has no immediate perception of his actual income. The payment he receives is not a wage, meaning it is not intended to reproduce his labour-power; it is a compensation entirely unrelated to his needs and often paid with considerable delay, long after the work has been completed. The freelancer's condition of social inferiority becomes even more striking when we consider his lack of welfare rights. He has no claim to health-insurance, unemployment-benefits or a pension. What exactly do we mean when we speak of the 'second-generation' self-employed worker? We are essentially referring to someone who needs to be distinguished from small business-owners and farmers, as well as from notaries, lawyers, doctors, architects, professional journalists and all other liberal professionals, who often have the support of guilds and chambers, insurance-schemes and other forms of protection. The second-generation freelancer is living proof of the political shortsightedness and opportunism displayed by Europe's trade-unions, who have stubbornly persisted in defending only the prerogatives of regularly employed dependent workers, thereby leaving unprotected the new types of workers proper to post-Fordism (precarious workers and self-employed workers). Self-employed workers have even been denied the status of 'workers' by their designation as 'micro-companies' and 'one-man businesses'; they have been identified as entrepreneurs rather than as workers. The phenomenon of 'new' self-employed labour was first observed during the late 1970s and reflects three transformations:

(a) Companies are in search of more flexible forms of organisation and begin to outsource certain activities or purchase them on the market.

(b) Faced with budget-restrictions, the public authorities act in much the same way.

(c) Changes in lifestyle and the development of new forms of mass-consumption give rise to new personal services that either did not exist before or existed in a different form.

These three processes are substantially accelerated by the spread of new information-technologies that transform the way people work and communicate while allowing for the substitution of property-based forms of organisation by 'networks'. When I began writing my 'Ten Hypotheses', Marxism offered me no historical or theoretical reference-points whatsoever. There was not a single passage in *Capital*, the *Theories of Surplus Value*, the *Grundrisse* or any other text that I could make use of. I was truly 'beyond Marxism': capitalism's technological revolution (its development of new information-technologies) had ushered in a new era and there was no point in violating Marx's thought for the sake of establishing some sort of connection to what he had written. Marx is a historical personality; his ability to anticipate capitalism's dynamics has its limits. To deny these limits is tantamount to treating Marx as a prophet, as the founder not of a revolutionary movement, but of a religion. The absence of Marxian reference-points did not strike me as being a problem. It was enough for me to remain faithful to the workerist methodology and its cognitive procedures. This time, I also had the advantage of not having to enter a world of work that was not my own (that of blue-collar workers); this time, I was already within a certain world of work; it was my own and some of its nuances could not be described by anyone but myself. I nevertheless made an effort to search for possible reference-points in twentieth-century sociology, finding them in the work of Weimar Germany's Austro-Marxist and Catholic sociologists of language. The 'Ten Hypotheses' were published in 1997. At the time, I was unaware that a website called 'Working Today' had been set up two years earlier by a New York lawyer specialising in labour-law who was also the grandchild of a trade-unionist associated with the Garment-Union during the 1920s. On her website, this woman decried freelancers' living and working conditions and invited those affected to contribute to her blog by recounting their experiences and reflecting on the possibility of setting up a union. Eventually, the Freelancers' Union was formed; its members now number several thousand and it has become a powerful New York lobby-group, one the city's administration must reckon with. In my view, the success of this initiative owes much to the ability of the union's founders to tap into and articulate the American middle class's profound sense of unease ('Welcome to the Middle Class, Poverty!' is one of the union's slogans). As former Secretary of Labour Robert Reich has observed, the American middle class has lost much of its power and social prestige; its income-situation has never been worse since the Great Depression. In my view, Barack Obama's electoral victory can be explained in terms of this crisis of the middle class. Barbara Ehrenreich, a journalist associated with the feminist and pacifist movements and author of inquiry-books on the impoverishment of white-collar America, has set up a website (www.unitedprofessionals.org) that further promotes the tendency towards unionisation within the middle classes. This is an extremely interesting phenomenon, because it shows that when the middle classes face an economic crisis, they are capable of responding in a way that amounts to discovering the value of solidarity while simultaneously expressing rage and delusion *vis-à-vis* the 'American dream'. Unfortunately, the European Left, including its radical currents, has not understood this aspect of the problem and continues to reason according to the old scheme 'crisis of the middle classes – fascism' (in fact, this sort of thinking is particularly evident in the European Left's radical currents). The same failure to understand what is happening can also be seen in American Marxism, especially in the academic Marxism of tenured professors who teach Marx at university the way one teaches future priests the gospel. Aside from the interest displayed by the old and new generations of workerists – an interest prompted perhaps by sentimental motives rather than by genuine conviction – and aside from my friends at the *Centro Franco Fortini* and a few former Communist Party functionaries who now find themselves politically marginalised, my 'Ten Hypotheses' were received, within what remains of Italy's Left, with scepticism and indifference. They were met with respect and attention within some sections of the feminist movement; women are well represented within the field of the new self-employed labour. Academics responded very strongly. There was a positive reaction from lawyers specialised in labour-law, who are aware of the urgency of legal reforms by which to offer some protection to the new post-Fordist workers, whereas the lobby of labour-sociologists reacted quite negatively, including those sociologists who claim a workerist lineage. My most satisfying experience came several years later, when I learned that an association of self-employed workers had been set up in Milan (on the initiative of a woman, once again); the founders of this association had discovered in my hypotheses a theoretical foundation that corresponded perfectly to their need for unionisation and self-protection. The association is called ACTA (*Associazione Consulenti Terziario Avanzato*, Advanced Tertiary Sector Counselling Association); none of its founding members had ever met me or knew anything about my political and intellectual history. The association currently boasts about a thousand members, mostly from Milan; I myself have become a member of the executive-board. We are working to extend our network of contacts while pressuring members of parliament and other political representatives to approve legal reforms that will provide self-employed workers with the same welfare, health-care and pension benefits as dependent workers. The more visible our actions become, the more we are approached by members of the so-called 'creative class': people working in the fields of design, the graphic arts and publishing. These workers are part of Milan's vast media-sector, which comprises roughly a thousand full-time workers and even more occasional, precarious and self-employed workers. The practical challenges now emerging within the crisis produced by neo-liberalism and the unrestrained financialisation of the economy are enormous, involving the entire field of *cognitive capitalism*, or of the knowledge-economy. The revolution brought about by the introduction of new network- and information-technologies is perhaps the greatest revolution within the capitalist mode of production since the invention of the combustion engine. It has transformed the way firms are organised, turning them more and more into 'network-' firms, and it has transformed the way we work, dramatically increasing labour-productivity. But it has also created new possibilities for communication and collective organisation, new ways of passing on information without having to go through political, trade-union, cultural or media-institutions. We must learn to make the most of these spaces of freedom, defending them against those who would see them eliminated. The ideology of neoliberal Postfordism fosters the myth of the 'knowledge-worker', but we know that it is precisely the most well-trained and educated workers whose levels of exploitation are the highest. Most people who leave university with a degree are constrained to accept working conditions worse than a factory-worker's; those who succeed in practicing a profession related to their degree are very few in number. Self-employed workers are part of this group, but they are exposed to numerous risks and bereft of protection. Italy's workerists succeeded in confronting mature Fordism with the aid of adequate analytical and theoretical instruments, and they were able to make a contribution to the labour-revolts of the 1970s. The practical political work of defending post-Fordist labour and securing its autonomy is potentially more far-reaching, but those left over from Europe's socialist and communist left are proving themselves incapable of confronting this challenge, and the same holds true for what remains of Europe's radical Left. It's not enough to go 'beyond Marx'. We need to go 'beyond the Left'. Its historical cycle has come to a close and it has become an obstacle to the liberation of post-Fordist labour. In the preface to my book *Ceti medi senza futuro? Scritti sul lavoro e altro*,[19] I declared myself politically 'stateless' and explained that I am quite content with this status. I have remained faithful to certain principles of workerist methodology, especially the importance of paying attention to capitalism's transformations and innovations so as to better be able to protect workers. In the 1950s, Montaldi explored Italy's urban peripheries and the new forms of pros-

---

19. Bologna 2007.

titution; in much the same spirit, my daughter and I have produced a documentary-film on a Milanese neighbourhood's transformation from a neighbourhood of factories characterised by a high concentration of blue-collar residents to a fashion- and design-district, from a neighbourhood of council-housing to one of lofts. I wanted to take a look at how the so-called creative class actually lives and works while at the same time evoking, through interviews with old comrades, the great 1960 strike of the Milanese metalworkers. While the trajectory traced by workerism during the 1960s and 1970s can never be repeated, I remain convinced that the method by which the workerists approached capitalism's perennially shifting reality, the conceptual apparatus they developed in order to interpret that reality, and their ability to identify its weak points could all help coming Generations better to defend their freedom, both against open enemies and against false friends.

April 2009

Workers and Working Classes in Contemporary India: A Note on Analytic Frames and Political Formations

Subir Sinha

Introduction

To talk of workers and their politics in India today is both necessary and, in light of the positions in recent social and political theory, also difficult. The wide-ranging changes in Indian political economy over the past three decades have transformed the world of work, and have created new categories of workers. The Indian workforce is now far more differentiated, mobile, informalised and precarious than in the 1970s. Working-class politics in India, which has tradition-ally been associated with corporatist-clientilist forma-tions of unions, political parties and states, have also changed correspondingly: not only has there been an explosion in the number of self-proclaimed 'indepen-dent' unions, but also of unions in new sectors, and, significant for our purposes, of groups that claim rights based in part on their self-definition as 'workers' but that have few of the attributes of the paradigmatic working class. These movements have argued that they are oppressed and exploited, and have made demands for a full agenda of rights, some of them familiar as idioms of claim-making, and some new and novel constructions of rights, articulated for the first time by them. These exciting changes have happened at a time when the two frameworks associated with the produc-tion of theory of such social groups, subaltern studies (SS) and forms of class-analysis claiming to be Marx-ist, carry with them assumptions and support political projects that seem neither appropriate nor adequate to explain this rise of new workers and their movements.

The historiography of working-class politics in India stands at an interesting crossroads. One the one hand, votaries of class-analysis, explicitly invoking 'classical' Marxism, rue the decline of class-analysis in the study of Indian politics, and blame it on the rise of 'culturalist' approaches, in turn rooting their ascendancy in the specific dynamics of the American academy. They call for a 'return' to class-analysis.[1] On the other hand, postcolonial theorists and subaltern-studies scholars, argue that the transition from Fordism to Postfordism – or more accurately its vernacularised Indian form – and the subsequent erosion of the stability of factory-work as the basis of producing workers as classes signals the need to abandon 'class' as an analytic category altogether.

This chapter argues that the ontology of work in contemporary India requires a move well beyond the apparatus both of 'classical Marxism' and of canonical subaltern-studies. It draws on new workers' movements in India to show the limits of both of these approaches and identifies some points in the current intersections between Marxian analysis, postcolonial/subaltern theory and the emergent social categories to argue for a more expansive and fluid framework for analysing the politics of new workers in India. Particularly, it takes the conditions produced by neoliberalism, the transnational circulation of discourses, and the forging of contingent and indeterminate solidarities as the basis for sketching out new directions in thinking about work, workers and working-class politics.

The chapter is structured in the following ways. In the next section, I sketch out the issues in contention between orthodox class-analytic Marxism and canonical subaltern-studies, and identify some salient limits they have in describing the politics of their chief protagonists, workers and subalterns respectively. I then describe some contemporary movements to workers/subalterns in India to illustrate a) how non-proletarians appropriate the language of class, b) the problem of becoming workers in political-fields dominated discourses of cultural/racial supremacy; and c) the refusal to become proletarian. On this basis I illustrate my critique of orthodox class-analytic Marxism and canonical subaltern-studies. Finally, I want to sketch out some pathways out of what I believe is an impasse in theorising the working subaltern in contemporary India.

The working class in contention

Even though subaltern-studies as a historiographical project claimed a rootedness in the broader Marxist tradition, it also marked its disagreements with that

---

1. Herring and Agrawala 2006; Chibber 2006a, 2006b; Fernandes and Heller 2006.

tradition from the outset, particularly that the conditions of the arrival of capitalism under colonial rule and the failures of universalistic liberalism on the terrain of colonised India. From this early enunciation of the colonial difference, the vantage-point from which to approach the subcontinental experience with imperialism and modernity, the focus shifted to critiques of orthodox Marxism and its own universalistic assumptions and categories.

From the late 1980s and more decisively subsequently, the debates between these two approaches became both acrimonious and recriminatory. Subalternists accused Marxists' formulations on mediation and hegemony of being authoritarian, while Marxists accused subalternists of capitulating to culturalism and identity-politics that bore some resemblance to the neo-fascist forces of Hindu majoritarianism. I do not intend to regurgitate these debates.[2] In this section, I only review some of the more recent moves in each framework towards analysing contemporary politics in India, partly where subalternists declare the end of class as an analytical category and posit new forms of subjectivities, and Marxists claim the necessity to resuscitate it as a tool to analyse contemporary politics in India.

New directions in subaltern-studies

That class was an inadequate category for analysing Indian politics is implicit in the categorisation of 'elite/subaltern' with which Ranajit Guha prefaces the subaltern-studies (SS) project.[3] Guha locates his studies in the period between 1757, the inauguration of rule by the East India Company over India, and 1857, after which time the 'pure conditions' of subalternity were, according to him, irretrievably altered. These conditions include a 'split domain of politics' between subaltern and elite spheres which share a relation of mutual unintelligibility and hostility, the 'fragmentary' nature of subaltern experiences, and forms of subaltern solidarity based on community, contiguity and consanguinity. In other words, subalterneity was defined both by relations of domination and by spheres of autonomy and alterity.

The conditions in which 'classes' form, such as capitalism and discourses of classes, were both barely present in India during this period, and so 'subalterns' as a loose, contextual category was appropriate. What is a problem however, is that attributes that were appropriate to a particular time and place have been attributed both a timelessness and a universality in attempts to talk about subalterns in the present.

---

2. These debates are well encapsulated in Ahmad 1992 and Ludden (ed.) 2002 on the Marxist side, and in Spivak 1988 and Chakrabarty 2002 from the subalternist one.

3. Guha 1983a.

For example, Dipesh Chakrabarty, the leading theorist of the SS project, contends that 'peasants *do not* leave behind their own documents' and that the 'archives of peasant insurgencies *are produced* by the counterinsurgency measures of the ruling classes and their armies and police forces'.[4] This unproblematised continuity is at odds not only with Guha's implicit admission that subalterneity changed after 1857. It is, more importantly, at odds also with one of the more obvious features of contemporary 'peasant' movements, that is their production of copious documentary material. It would be no exaggeration to say that all 'peasant movements' in India over the past four decades or so have produced their own critique of structures of domination including the state, programmes of transformation, and movement-autobiographies. As a result, the very idea of an archive is now qualitatively different than in the period of the pure conditions: the state is hardly the only or even the most authoritative producer of archives. Indeed, in the Indian context, visual records of movements have proliferated since the inception of the documentary-film movement dating back to the late-1970s, and even more so since the subsequent eruption of computer- and Internet-usage by movement-activists. Additionally, the academy itself is deeply implicated in producing an alternative archive of subalterneity and subaltern movements.

This elision between subaltern pasts and present is compounded further by Chakrabarty's quaint and anachronistic reading of Gramsci, which he marshals to defend his conceptualisation of the subaltern subject as one whose history is episodic and fragmented, and who is incapable of imagining or thinking the state. For Chakrabarty, once subalterns can think the state, they transcend the condition of subalterneity.[5] Surprising for someone who insists on the *spatial* specificity of Europe, Chakrabarty does not attend to the *temporal* specificity of southern Italy *in the early twentieth century* in his reading of Gramsci. His framework therefore forecloses the possibility of using the subaltern concept to analyse movements of the rural poor in India today that both produce far-reaching critiques of the state and propose equally wide-ranging changes in state-policy. The fact of nationally coordinated and transnationally linked movements of fishers and forest-dwellers in India would imply, in this view, either that these populations are no longer subaltern, or that the conditions of subalterneity have changed considerably and outgrown the approach.

Chakrabarty thinks of 'subaltern' and 'modern' as mutually exclusive and unintelligible categories, and this underpins his very conceptualisation of the political field. For him, the field of contemporary Indian politics is set by 'the modernity that is the legacy of colonial rule'. Colonial modernity, which in his

---

4. Chakrabarty 2002, pp. 15–16. Note the present tense. Emphasis added.
5. Chakrabarty 2002, pp. 34–5.

formulation accounts for the Indian experience of modernity in its entirety, 'was fundamentally concerned with domination'.[6] This highly idiosyncratic view of 'the modern' creates several problems in analysing contemporary movements of the working subaltern.

What if subalterns decide to enrol the help of the modern in their struggles against tyranny, as is pervasive in social-movement writings? Chakrabarty antici- pates this question by rejecting modernity because it was rooted in 'a certain type of colonizing drive'. As such, to side with the project of modernity left one, according to him, with no *locus standi* from which to erect a critique of impe- rialism: 'if it is true that Enlightenment rationalism requires as its vehicle the modern state and its accompanying institutions – the institutions of governmen- tality in Foucault's terms – and this entails a certain kind of colonizing violence anyway... then one cannot uncritically welcome this violence and at the same time maintain a critique of European imperialism in India'.[7]

The problems are with his equation between state and modernity, with his understanding of 'governmentality', and a condemnation of modernity and ratio- nalism because of their original link with imperialism, as if their histories are entirely contained within the history of imperialism. That capitalism and power are separate categories, as Chakrabarty insists, is now common sense (except in some version of Marxism and Liberalism), as are his views that there will be no replication of the history of capital worldwide. I will also endorse his point that 'the genealogy of the peasant as citizen in contemporary political modernity' in locations such as India is unlikely to unfold along the same trajectory as in 'the west', and that it has not gone through the iteration of peasants becoming workers before becoming citizens.[8] However, the insistence on Indian specific- ity is both limiting and exaggerated. It will not do, it seems to me, to argue, as Chakrabarty has done, that the Calcutta working class was not a working class because it maintained links with the countryside: this was, of course, true also of the paradigmatic European working classes. 'Pure' classes, actually, only exist in the imaginations of some Marxists and some SS scholars. As Joyce and Sted- man Jones have both shown, the 'working class' in Europe was never pure in that sense.[9]

In an electoral democracy such as India's, where something like forty percent of the population is categorised as 'below poverty line' and more than seventy percent is still rural, all political parties seek constituencies among the rural poor. Aimed at occupying state-power, these parties articulate hegemonic elite projects

6. Chakrabarty 2002, pp. 54–5.
7. Chakrabarty 2002, p. 32.
8. Chakrabarty 2002, p. 19.
9. Joyce 1995; Jones 1995.

in which the numerical support of the poor is necessary, but their position is subordinate. This has induced political entrepreneurship, and all political parties now field 'representatives' from subaltern groups in elections. Their welfare and rights are included, in some form, in the electoral platforms of these parties. This web of institutions of elected, representational democracy has now expanded with the seventy-third amendment to the constitution in 1993, which creates new institutions, gives them wider powers and guarantees representation to subaltern-groups: women, tribals, dalits, and so on. It is, of course, far from the case that abstract concepts of solidarity, such as democracy (the people), citizenship (the rights conferred on the people by the nation-state) are structured around subaltern experiences of the world. But at the same time it complicates formulations, such as those of Chakrabarty, who argues for a possible democracy that is based on subaltern principles, and who criticises all forms of 'mediation' and solidarity as essentially threatening to the alterity and purity of subaltern-practices.

Another attempt to update the SS approach to talk about contemporary subalterns is Chatterjee's recent writings on civil and political society, and 'the politics of the governed'.[10] Persisting with the formulation of the 'split domain of politics' between elites and subalterns, Chatterjee argues that 'civil society', constituted on the basis of popular sovereignty and equal rights, is inhabited by western educated, west-emulating minorities, who believe in the rule of law, and who take a pedagogical stand towards the poor. Political society for Chatterjee stands for those associational forms and modes of collective action that connect 'populations of "the governed" to governmental agencies pursuing multiple policies of security and welfare'.[11]

Chatterjee rejects 'civil society' as a category through which to approach the politics of the new subalterns, as it is a *'closed* association of modern elite groups, *sequestered* from the wider popular life of communities, *walled up* within enclaves of civic freedoms and rational law'.[12] Those who occupy this domain are the agents of the 'universal ideal of civic nationalism based on individual freedoms and equal rights'. The political terrain, for him, is no longer divisible between 'rulers and the ruled' but 'those who govern and those who are governed'. This managerialisation of politics, he argues, is because of the elevation of population-categories as the basis for structuring politics: both the pastoral functions of the state concerned with the 'well-being of the population', and the demands by 'the governed' for the extension of welfare to cover them. The 'governed' occupy a different and oppositional domain which Chatterjee labels 'political society', and they pursue 'particular demands of cultural identity, which

---

10. Chatterjee 2004.
11. Chatterjee 2004, p. 37.
12. Chatterjee 2004, p. 4 (my emphasis).

call for differential treatment . . . on the grounds of vulnerability or backwardness or historical injustice'.[13]

Political society, for Chatterjee, emerged out of nationalist politics, but acquired a distinct form from the 1980s for two reasons. First, the idea that the performance of governments should be measured on the discharge of its 'pastoral functions' to secure the well-being of people who are not members of civil society proper has become generalised. Second, the widening of the arena of political mobilisation has become based on exclusively electoral considerations, rather than a meaningful expansion of participation of the governed in matters of state.[14] This has created a new governmentalised régime whose 'mode of reasoning is not deliberative openness but rather an instrumental notion of costs and benefits. Its apparatus is not the republican assembly but an elaborate network of surveillance through which information is collected on every aspect of the life of the population that is to be looked after'.[15] Chatterjee does not elaborate on how these idioms of claim-making are now constitutive of state-power in contemporary India. His project to identify and analyse 'politics spawned by governmentality' lacks a consideration of how 'governmentality' itself is spawned by politics.[16]

As incomplete citizens lying external to the domain of civil society, Chatterjee's 'governed' 'transgress the strict lines of legality in struggling to live and work'.[17] The denizens of political society have resisted efforts by 'modernizers' to make citizens out of them, he argues. Civil society either attempts to incorporate 'natural leaders' of groups that make up political society in the distribution of benefits and enforcing law and order, or they take the project of Enlightenment through the thicket of negotiation with political society. Agents of civil society realise that the claims made by these groups are justified, but they are not rights.

Chatterjee's identification of civil society as an elite and limited sphere is one I endorse. However, four problems remain with his characterisation of the politics of the governed. First, he sees the governed as merely a more contemporary version of the nineteenth-century subaltern, carrying with them vestiges of the characteristics outlined in Guha's foundational text of SS, *Elementary Aspects of Peasant Insurgency in Colonial India*.[18] For example, he still sees solidarity among the governed as rooted in community, consanguinity and contiguity, now thought of as affiliations of caste and place of origins of the migrant poor. Second, he still maintains violence and illegality as the primary mode of the actions

---

13. Chatterjee 2004, p. 4.
14. Chatterjee 2004, p. 47.
15. Chatterjee 2004, p. 34.
16. See Sinha 2008.
17. Chatterjee 2004, p. 40.
18. Guha 1983.

of the governed, particularly with respect to property-laws. Third, he locates their politics within the twin matrices of electoral democracy and redistributive state-programmes: social movements that challenge developmental models do not figure within his schema. And finally, while it does make analytical sense to think of civil and political society as non-identical, the fact that this boundary is always breached by social movements, who increasingly use the law and policy in favour of those they represent and act as translational agents between these two domains, poses an unresolved analytical problem for Chatterjee.

Fundamentally, these problems for the subaltern approach get compounded with respect to studying movement-politics in India today. For one, as in Chakrabarty's conception of 'the modern' and Chatterjee's of 'civil society', they actually replicate the presumptions of the very Eurocentrism that their project seeks to de-centre by tying them causally to the history of colonialism and imperialism. True, these are the forces that constituted 'India' as a political and economic entity and mediated its relation to the 'international'. But by the late-nineteenth century, transnational circuits of solidarity had developed between those opposing colonialism and imperialism in India and in 'the West'.[19] These contacts were between the elite of the Indian anti-colonial and anti-imperialist movements, and it would be accurate to categorise them as belonging to the domain of 'civil society' as Chatterjee has sketched out. However, from the 1960s onwards, movements of subalterns and 'the governed' – the denizens of 'political society' – too have been implicated in these networks, and are constitutive of such formations.[20] I agree with Spivak that there is politics *within* solidarity, with dominant agents attempting, but failing, to fully incorporate the object of their solidarity, and the latter maintaining an irreducible outside-ness to it.[21] However, as I shall argue later, the uni-directional exercise of power underpinning Spivak's positioning of 'dominant feminism' and 'the new subaltern' is a limiting way to think about power in transnational solidarity-networks. After all, organisations of Indian fish-workers, forest-workers, sex-workers and so on are also active agents in the construction and transformation of such circuitry.

Additionally, while a critique of capitalism certainly informed the formulations of Ranajit Guha,[22] SS has given up any concern with capitalism in favour of exploring the incompleteness of the projects of liberalism and nationalism, and the exteriority and alterity of subalterns – or, lately, 'the governed' – in relation to them. Of the major theorists associated with the SS project, it is Spivak who maintains an explicit but truncated affiliation with canonical Marxism, even as

---

19. See Gandhi 2006; Sinha 2008.
20. Dash 2008.
21. Spivak 2000.
22. See especially Guha 1989.

she posits alterity and fragmentariness as the essential markers of contemporary subalterneity. Spivak retains Marxism for its analysis of exploitation, but argues that post-Fordism has 'taken away the organizational stability of the factory floor and thus taken away the possibility of class consciousness', to the extent that class 'cannot produce an account of subalterneity',[23] a position insisting on locating the very possibility of class within a certain moment in the history of capitalism, not unlike those held by less ambiguously Marxist positions, such as Bernstein.[24] Still, for her the contemporary subaltern is the 'paradigmatic victim' of the 'international division of labour'. Subalterns cannot represent themselves and cannot organise, because, once they are able to, they are no longer subaltern.

Spivak marks an advance from Chakarabarty in that she recognises that while, historically, subalterns were 'those who were cut off from the lines that produced the colonial mindset', they are 'no longer cut off from lines of access to the centre'.[25] She argues that the constituent elements of the centre try to colonise the cultures and knowledge of subalterns under new intellectual property-rights régimes, and to bring them under the rule of finance-capital through 'credit baiting', by turning them into new subjects of the neo-liberal logic of micro-credit. Equally, international civil society, including what she calls the 'international feminist dominant', with its gender- and election-training programmes, wants to bring the new subaltern 'under one rule of law, one civil society, administered by the women of the international divided [sic] dominant'.[26] All of them use 'the subaltern will for globalization as a justification for policy'.[27]

That a plethora of agendas today, ranging from empire to revolution, justify themselves on the needs and desires of subalterns, is, of course true. But as I will show, the interactions between subaltern movements and 'the centre' is a rather different one than the insistence on alterity between the subaltern local and the hegemonic centre that Spivak posits. Work on transnational solidarity-networks indicates the ability of movements of subalterns to move beyond the status of 'pawns in the hands of veteran mainstream players'.[28] Batliwala studies the Slum Dwellers' International as a 'transnational grassroots movement'.[29]

Spivak raises the issue of mediations between subaltern and hegemonic domains of politics: of insurgent scholars who resist the incorporation of subalterns within hegemonic practices, of NGOs that make an effort to link the subalterns' 'indigenous democratic structure' to parliamentary democracy, and

---

23. Spivak 2000, p. 325.
24. Bernstein 2006.
25. Spivak 2000, p. 319.
26. Spivak 2000, p. 322.
27. Spivak 2000, p. 326.
28. Keck and Sikkink, 1998; Khagram *et al.* 2002.
29. Batliwala 2002.

of non-Eurocentric social movements who are pushing globalisation towards a subaltern-front. For his part, Chakrabarty argues that new social movements of subalterns have challenged notions of 'democracy' and 'bring into the sphere of the political *their own ideas* of well-being, justice', and so on.[30] For him the project of subaltern-studies aims 'to teach the oppressed of today how to be the democratic subject of tomorrow'.[31] The only form of mediation and solidarity that is permissible is one that pushes democracy towards a subaltern horizon, that makes a new democracy based on the episodic and fragmentary life-experiences of subalterns, not one which assimilates them into external political projects: indeed, this is Chakrabarty's point of departure from Gramsci. His ideal subaltern would be one who does not seek justice and citizenship from the state. For him, the emphasis of mediation must be on those moments of subaltern-practice that help construct such an agent.

The insistence on 'alterity', whose maintenance is the function of mediation, raises more questions than it answers. Admittedly, there remains a necessary chasm between subalterns and those in solidarity with them. As noted above, today's subaltern-movements engage a multi-level, often transnational, circuitry of solidarity. This circuitry itself has multiple histories: feminist, environmentalist, human rights, socialism, and movements for human dignity, for example, have for decades connected and constituted 'the local' and 'the global'. There is, therefore, an already existing set of discourses of rights and practices of solidarity that are not generated *by* subalterns, but *on their behalf.* This raises fundamental questions: a) what discourses of solidarity and political projects aim to encompass subalterns? b) what is the effect of these discourses and practices on projects of constituting collective subaltern-subjects? And c) what are the limits placed by the fields of the political and the economic on both the formation of new political collectivities and the terms on which they enter and create networks of solidarity?

The uncritical extension of the conditions of nineteenth-century subalterneity to the present, the subsumption of the entirety of Indian encounters and experiences of modernity within colonial and imperialist violence, the insistence on alterity and rejection of external mediation, the emphasis on vestigial rather than transactional forms of subalterneity, and their maintenance of an untenable duality between 'India' and 'the West' render SS approaches anachronistic in forging an analytical framework to study contemporary movements of subalterns.

---

30. Chakrabarty 2002, p. xx; emphasis added.
31. Chakrabarty 2002, p. 33.

The decline of class thesis

Despite the explicit though critical affiliation expressed in early SS writings to Marxism, it is from that political and theoretical position that some of the most trenchant critiques of SS have been directed. There is a history of this engagement that, again, is beyond the scope of this essay to fully reproduce.[32] Indeed, some of the positions of Chakrabarty, Chatterjee and Spivak outlined above have been formulated in response to criticisms from Marxists, and to that extent I shall selectively invoke some key points in the debate.

A key concern for Marxists has been the substitution of 'class' with 'community' in SS writings, pervasively in the work of Chatterjee. Indeed, they argued, even if one accepted Chatterjee's formulation that 'community' was the natural form of subaltern-organisation and authority, and also his argument that capitalism and colonial modernity were inimical to community, what became of such a formation and how it was reconstituted into *classes* over time needed analysis.[33] That 'subaltern' was an inadequate category in the face of rapid transitions towards a class-society has been a source of constant Marxist critique of SS.

The question of mediation has also received considerable attention from Marxists. If subaltern-consciousness were fragmented, as Gramsci and the SS approach have asserted, then, instead of celebrating the fragment and departing from Gramsci's formulation, they suggest external leadership to overcome this 'historical limitation' of the subaltern in the form of 'leadership' from 'independent class and mass organisations and a centralised revolutionary party', which was Gramsci's political project.[34] Others pointed out that the notion of 'autonomy' needed to be problematised: what were the empirical references of such a domain, why was it valorised in its own right, and whether the objective conditions of autonomy changed over time. After all, there was a history of mediation between subaltern- and elite domains, by nationalists and communists among others, and while they were never able fully to absorb within their projects the full experiences of subalterneity, they nevertheless transformed subalterneity and brought it into contact with a whole host of externally generated possibilities of liberation. If subalterneity was a marker of voicelessness and exploitation, how could SS maintain an uncritical and even protective stance towards it while simultaneously mounting a critique of the structures and processes of domination? This, of course, is the reverse of the SS critique of Marxist positions on modernity outlined above.

---

32. See essays by Alam 1983; Singh *et al.* 1984, Dasgupta, 1986; and especially Sarkar 1997.
33. Alam 1983.
34. Alam 1983, p. 45.

It is important to note that involved in this conflict between Marxists and subalternists is a battle over Antonio Gramsci. Orthodox Marxists realise, correctly in my opinion, the danger posed to some of their held beliefs by the ideas of Gramsci and the questions they inspire us to ask. They have identified his examination and re-formulation of the question of 'culture', its role both in the construction of hegemony and its medium-term maintenance, and thus the identification of the cultural field as a key site for the future of the socialist project as posing some severe problems, as well as the possible connections his work provides with those of Foucault. This connection is made explicitly in Laclau and Mouffe's 1985 volume *Hegemony and Socialist Strategy*,[35] whose suggestion on the material effects of discourses has also been a target of attack.

Following Anderson's unfair and ill-informed attack on Gramsci in the 1970s, some Marxists writing about India have also denigrated his body of work along the lines that they were so fragmentary and written in such conditions that it would be bad academic and political practice to assign them any coherence. Part of the denigration of Gramscians has been precisely that they can justify any position whatsoever by reference to one or another of Gramsci's notes.[36]

Another tack has been to argue that Gramsci's formulations of 'subaltern' and 'dominant' social groups referred actually to workers and capitalists, and were necessary masks for communist terminology given that he was in prison. Both Byers and Chibber have made these arguments, and so, interestingly, has Gayatri Spivak, the author paradigmatic of 'postmodern Marxism' in the Indian context.[37] This re-formulation of Gramsci have been part of a strategy to contain the 'Gramsci effect' within the safe confines of conventional Marxism. However, recent scholarship on Gramsci renders these judgements unsafe. Marcus Green, after a close reading of many of Gramsci's untranslated writings, for example, points out that Gramsci's usage of 'subaltern' and 'dominant' social groups far exceeds those suggested in conventional readings.[38] Johnson also provides justifications for using Gramscian categories such as 'hegemony' to understand new forms of politics in the age of contemporary neoliberalism, including those of movements and networks.[39] Another new direction in recent Gramsci-inspired work, such as that of Andrew Morton, aims to recoup a materialist understanding of the subaltern.[40]

---

35. Laclau and Mouffe 1985.
36. Harman 2007.
37. Byers 1995; Chibber 2006b; Spivak 1988.
38. Green 2002.
39. Johnson 2007.
40. Morton 2007.

A number of scholars have recently commented on the decline of class in the analysis of Indian politics.[41] Chibber has argued that this is because of a) the elevation of the American academy as the prime site for the production of globally authoritative knowledge about India; b) the history of identity-politics in the US which was then institutionalised in the academy (in the form of ethnic studies and the like); and c) the incentive structure within the academy that militates against class-analysis and rewards identity-politics. For this, he has particularly blamed 'postcolonialism' and 'poststructuralism' and has called for a return to the nostrums of 'classical political economy'.

This account of the decline of class puts the reasons for such decline external to the practices of class-analysis and -politics themselves, even though it is not entirely inaccurate in the picture it paints. Perhaps events – the emergence of new political subjects, of new social movements and new political parties – have exceeded what can be explained through the tool-box of conventional Marxist class-analysis. For example, Brass has chosen to label all new farmers' movements and environmental movements in India accurately as 'populist', but then problematically as providing the ground for fascism.[42] More significantly, the insistence by Herring and Agrawala that class and caste are somehow entirely overlapping categories, and that class-analysis therefore produces an adequate account of caste dynamics, has little bearing to the actual dynamics of caste-politics in contemporary India.[43] De Neve and Harriss-White and Prakash show both the advances made by dalits as entrepreneurs as well as the limits enforced on them.[44] Lerche explores the power wielded by dalits in India today, as well as their experiences with transnational solidarity-networks.[45]

While, as I have argued, subalternist scholars offer a thin account of the politics of mediation and leadership involving subalterns, Marxist attempts to offer the 'centralised revolutionary party' performing 'vanguard-functions' as the privileged agent of mediation does not do it any justice either. Based on his reading of how the mainstream Communist parties accommodated organisations of the working poor into their ruling coalition, Heller refers to such formations as 'social movement parties', parties that mediate between subaltern-organisations and state-structures.[46] Such attempts to bring back class-analysis do not make much new headway in talking about the contemporary movements of the working subaltern. Particularly, their readings of hegemony and mediation points to a pre-commitment to the CPI-M. While the party Left was no doubt in positions

41. Chibber 2006b; Herring and Agrawala 2006; Heller 2005; among others.
42. Brass 1995a, p. 15.
43. Herring and Agrawala 2006.
44. De Neve 2005 and Harriss-White and Prakash 2009.
45. Lerche 2008.
46. Heller 2005.

of leadership to a whole range of movements until the 1980s, the political terrain has shifted dramatically since then, and new movements have either formed outside the organisational and discursive formations of the party-left, or, increasingly, in opposition to it. Particularly as the Marxist parties have now come to enjoy longevity in government, as in Bengal, and have committed themselves explicitly to 'productivism' and 'the Chinese model', including forced evictions from agricultural land for the construction of factories and a commitment to Special Economic Zones, they have themselves become the targets of opposition from new movements.

While the larger majority of new movements in India today are opposed to neoliberal economic reforms, party-affiliated Marxists have adopted a very ambiguous position with respect to it. For example, party-managers have recently voiced their opposition to workers' right to strike, arguing that this creates conditions of capital-flight in extreme conditions and reduces business-confidence. They have been inimical to all unions not affiliated with their own parties, such that their only commitment to the rights of workers are to those rights that they have themselves articulated. In Nandigram and Singur in Bengal, not only has the party used state-agencies and private armies to evict farmers from lands to be handed over to Indian capitalists to manufacture cars, it has labelled all opponents of its policies 'Maoist' and simulataneously 'Hindu fascist' and thus deserving of such state-violence. An understanding of class-dynamics has been lacking in the policies of compensating evicted farmers: no count was made of those agricultural workers who worked these lands, nor efforts to compensate them.

Votaries of a return to Marxist class-analysis now openly support rapid transitions to capitalism. The official Indian-Marxist position opposes to neoliberalism, but it sees Chinese-style capitalism and the unfettered 'development of productive forces' as the best way forward for a transition to socialism. The 'centralised revolutionary party' is now an active agent of efficient capitalist growth, reflecting the way in which Warrenite orthodoxy now is generalised through the grafting of the 'Chinese model'. Indeed, as Sandbrook *et al.* state, capitalism is a pre-requisite for the survival of social democracy (of the sort Heller labels the CPI-M in India) and the strategy they suggest to the party left, facing the dilemmas unleashed by globalisation, is to 'pragmatically strive to reconcile liberty, equity, and community with the demands of a market economy'.[47] Because of this commitment to productivism and keenness to attract foreign and domestic capital-investment, the party Left now finds itself an opponent of movements opposing large dams and disengaged from movements against evictions of tribal

---

47. Sandbrook *et al.* 2007.

populations from sites like Niyamgiri in Orissa state, or of rural populations to make way for SEZs. The struggles of the victims of 'accumulation by dispossession' (David Harvey) and of those refusing proletarianisation, some of the key social movements in contemporary India, are thus outside of the domain of politics of the party-left. Its aversion to 'identity-politics', which it sees as anathema to class-politics, has also kept the left out of positions of centrality in movements of tribals and dalits, and from movements for human dignity.

The political field in India and globally has seen an increase in associational formations, often, and wrongly, bracketed under the term 'civil society'. Marxist parties in India have been quite suspicious of these formations for a variety of reasons. As Ray's study of feminism in Kolkata has shown, wherever such parties have been hegemonic, they have inhibited the formation of independent associations and organisations.[48] The democratic reforms they carried out in the field of local government have stopped well short of democratising civil society.

Civil society is not, as Harriss has rightly argued, a neutral terrain: it is constituted by and constitutive of social relations, including class-relations. However, just as uncritical celebration of civil society is problematic, so is its rejection.[49] Herring and Agrawal, and Harriss have argued that NGOs depoliticise development, and that they weaken the social basis for party-recruitment by their palliative and ameliorative actions.[50] And the party-left in India is particularly severe on NGOs that are recipients of 'foreign funding' which they believe is the thin end of the wedge for the forces of imperialism to colonise social space in India. It was for this reason that it was wary of the World Social Forum in India, even as it geared up to take 'leadership' of it. In the case of some population-groups, for reasons I shall elaborate below, NGOs for better or worse are among the few agencies for whom it is possible to perform mediation and welfare-functions.

Leaving for the moment the discordance between welcoming 'foreign direct investment' in the economic domain, while blocking funds from the domain of the social, there is the more important question, from the viewpoint of workers' rights, of using the lens of 'imperialism' as an adequate one to comprehend global, international and transnational dynamics. As Nigam has shown, the party-left rejected the opportunities for improvements in the life-conditions of Indian workers afforded by the call of OECD countries and their trade-unions for labour-standards, retreating in an outmoded position calling for a return of nation-state sovereignty.[51] The adequacy of the national frame to resolve issues of workers' rights expressed in this position is seriously in doubt in a time of

---

48. Ray 1999.
49. Harriss 2006.
50. Herring and Agrawala 2006, and Harriss 2006.
51. Nigam 2006.

transnational flows of capital, transnational forms of governance, and transnational network-formations of solidarity.

It is at such a time of a growing disconnect between working-class analysis and politics, presaged by Carter,[52] that the calls for a renewal of class-analysis are being made, and perhaps as with any other conceptual framework faced with the crisis of the real, a more orthodox position is being invoked than is warranted by the self-critiques of Marxism over the past three decades. The efflorescence of new movements, including those based on 'identity', and the subsequent pluralisation of the political field, far from being seen as a positive change, is seen as a key reason for the increased and apparently inappropriate interest in 'culture' and the demise of Marxism and class-analysis.

The call for a return to class-analysis by Marxists is also a partial one: while some good studies have emerged on the power of capitalists in relation to the developmental state[53] and on the rise of new middle-classes,[54] the category of 'working class' has been left relatively untouched, as if it has a retained a stability while all else in the political landscape has undergone radical transformation. While Porter and others have talked about the inadequacy of the bourgeois/proletarian binary in describing relations of production, the cue taken from this in the Indian context is to investigate the 'middle-class' and its role in the entrenchment of capitalism in conditions of neoliberalism.[55] What is often missed in these calls for returns to class-analysis is that class is seen as an 'economic' category, as if the 'economic' is an already constituted domain, autonomous from politics and culture. This continued and insisted-upon separation of culture and identity from questions of class poses challenges to the Marxist framework in approaching contemporary movements.

Illustrations: contemporary workers and their movements

Movements calling themselves workers' movements have, as I have said, become prominent in the Indian political field, well beyond organised industrial workers or agricultural workers understood in the 'traditional' sense. In those two sectors, workers' politics has long been incorporated within union-party-state structures, as had some fractions of 'informal workers' in states like Kerala. However, most of the new movements have remained outside of the mainstream unions, including those affiliated with the party-left: this has famously been the case with the

---

52. Carter 1995.
53. Chibber 2006a.
54. Fernandes and Heller 2006.
55. For example, Fernandes and Heller 2006.

National Fishworkers' Federation and the Chhatisgarh Mukti Morcha.[56] At the same time, these movements do not display the features of subaltern-politics in its original or updated versions either. In this section, I review the forest-workers' movement and the context of migrant-work to highlight how some of the limitations I have identified in these two frameworks operate in these cases.

The forest-workers' movements

The movements for forest-rights have often been categorised as 'tribal' or even 'environmental'. However, the questions of work and labour have been important constituents of these movements. This is not surprising, since the formation of the forestry-sector in the nineteenth century implied a reorganisation of relations between state, forests and populations, and introduced new forms of work. Forest-contracts, in which tracts were auctioned for a specified time period, brought contract-workers. As many forest-areas also were sites of rebellions, contractors often brought in workers from other parts. For example, in Uttarakhand, forest contract-workers came from the plains and from Nepal, a tendency that lasted over much of the twentieth century as well. Because the colonial state made demands on the forced labour of hill-dwellers, issues of labour-rights fused with those of rights to forests in the early part of the twentieth century, and both were the points of intersection between the politics of forest-regions and the emerging nationalist movement. No politics of forest-workers independent of the forest- and national-questions emerged during this period.

It was with the movement for the formation of forest labour-cooperatives in the 1950s and 1960s that a specifically forest-workers' politics emerged, closely allied with movements for regional autonomy and forest-rights. For a while, the unity between these and other strands, including feminism, student-politics, movements for democratisation, statehood, and so on was stabilised under the rubric of 'the Chipko movement'. The resolution of the demands of that movement, its legacy and its exhaustion by the 1980s on the one hand, and the creation of new conditions of access and use of forests at the same time by accelerated growth and decentralisation of the polity on the other, changed the direction of movements of forest-rights. It was in this milieu that the movement of forest-workers began.

The movement of 'forest-workers' signals to a new form of workers' politics, as it reconceptualises the very category of 'worker'. On its website, it claims to represent 150 million people dependent on forest-resources, the National Forum of Forest People and Forest Workers (NFFPFW) is a confederation of

---

56. See Baviskar *et al.* 2006 and Chandhoke 2003.

90 organisations from all over the country. Its primary adversary is the state that, in continuity with its colonial lineages, 'owns' 95 percent of forests covering 23 percent of Indian territory, and it aims to force their redistribution on those who depend on forests for their livelihoods. Forestry as a sector so far has seen an absence of corporations and multinationals, and the access of national capitalists too is tenuous. The chief adversary is the state, whose formal power is often welded together with the relations between state-agents and big landlords, the timber-mafia, and forest-contractors.

In keeping with Chatterjee's formulation of political society, the NFFPFW invokes the language of 'deprivation' and 'historical injustices'. However, rather than this being a threat to democracy, as he predicts for political society, the forest-workers' movement campaigns to 'force the government to bring democracy process to forestry', and to embed forest-dwellers and workers in the wider processes of politics and policy-making.

The forest-workers' movement exhibits an interesting hybridity, and exceeds the conceptualisation of new movements. While Day rejects the very category of 'hegemony' in arguing that movements are not concerned with state-power,[57] the NFFPFW resolutely aims to affect state-policy and -practice. Chatterjee's insistence that the politics of the governed is based partly on particularistic identities is borne out: forest-dwellers' movements often invoke tribal and indigenous identities. However, they do not claim an exteriority of such identities to developmental modernity. Rather, they wish to use 'community' and 'indigenous' knowledges to create new development-policy. Lest this appear to endorse Chakrabarty's call for 'creating development based on subaltern experiences', note that such forms of knowledge have been constitutive of international development for at least two decades now.

Part of the forest-workers' movement resembles the movements for land-reforms of the 1960s, more than the contemporary movements of the landless, even though 'land-capture' is an increasingly deployed strategy. Since ownership of forests is overwhelmingly vested in the state, forest-dwellers' use of forest land and forest produce is a point of conflict. Chatterjee argues that the politics of 'the governed' often are located in the zone outside the law. It is more accurately the case that the forest use-practices of indigenous populations are rendered illegal by state-ownership of forests. Unlike his argument that the claims of the governed, while legitimate, are still not understandable in the formal vocabulary of 'rights', the NFFDFW's campaign is precisely to create a charter of rights for forest-dwellers. Indeed, a chief campaign of the NFFDFW is to push through the Forest Rights Bill through the Indian parliament.

---

57. Day 2005.

Movements for forest-rights have mostly been called 'environmental', as in the paradigmatic case of the Chipko movement. However, the demands of the NFFDFW cannot that easily be assimilated within that category. While environmentalists have supported the evacuation of nearly 500,000 people living inside national parks and wildlife-sanctuaries, the forest-workers' movement has resolutely opposed forced resettlement, and has asserted the prior rights of forest-dwellers over demands for conservation.

Recall that the revised subalternist position is that the insurgent scholar in solidarity with subalterns will provide an ethical mediation between subaltern-politics and the external world. For Marxists, such mediation is – or ought to be – provided by the mass political party. However, the NFFDFW, like the preceding Chipko movement, has its own intellectuals, those who are not themselves forest-dwellers and -workers, but who have renounced other vocations to act on their behalf. While subalternists would like subaltern-movements to exist as fragments, and Marxists would like to see them as part of an alliance under the leadership of the mass political party, the NFFDFW has built alliances with the agricultural workers' movement, the informal sector workers' trade-union, and human rights and civil society groups, as well as movements of 'the poorest of poor', nationally and transnationally.

Both subalternist and Marxist class-analysis have ultimately been constrained by seeing the 'nation' as the ultimate stage of politics. As such, neither is well placed to explain the transnational solidarity networks in which the movements of forest-workers is located. The NFFDFW engaged in the WSF in Mumbai in 2005 in which they made links with forest movements from Latin America and Southeast Asia.[58] While the contexts are substantially different from those in India, the one important element that emerged from these encounters was the salience of 'identity-politics', particularly the politics of indigeneity, to which forest-rights movements in these other locations have engaged.

Marxist votaries of a return to class-analysis have often positioned themselves in opposition to 'identity-politics'.[59] Leaving aside for now the question of why 'class' is not considered an 'identity' in their manifestoes, I would point out that movements such as the NFFDFW represent 'the poorest of the poor', a category that it itself ethnically and culturally identified. For a variety of historical reasons, India's 'tribal' populations are the ones whose domicile and livelihoods are most closely connected to forests.[60] Questions of access and rights to forests, forest-lands and forest-produce are thus inevitably tied with multiple discourses: those of rights to livelihoods and environmental sustainability, as well as of tribal

---

58. Dash 2008.
59. Chibber 2006a; Herring and Agrawala 2006, Harriss 2006 among others.
60. See Guha 1999 for a detailed account.

rights and Indian federalism. These articulate the 'forest-worker' as a class in a different way to both subalternists and Marxists. The insistence on 'workers' in the appellation they give themselves suggests that while the fate of Fordism and the factory in our time has undermined the paradigmatic way in which the working class has been imagined, social groups that do not resemble such working classes in the least find it meaningful to enter the field of politics as workers. At the same time, given that 'the economy' is always already a political, social and cultural formation, such movements find it necessary to expand beyond the boundaries of the orthodox notion of class. The equivalence of 'dweller' and 'worker' in the very name of the NFFDFW signals the multiple locations and discursive formations that constitute this form of politics.

Those struggling to become working class: Bihari migrant-workers

If the examples of the fish-workers and forest-workers demonstrate both the continued relevance of 'workers' as a political and organisational category and its limits in ways that defy both subalternist and Marxist formulations, another category of workers find it hard even to be recognised as workers. The much-touted 9 percent growth-rate in India over the past decade has expressed itself, among other things, in massive construction of infrastructure and real estate in the regions where growth has been concentrated. The construction-sector is one of the largest employers in contemporary India, and is made up predominantly of migrant-labourers. These labourers come largely from parts of India that have low growth, or where large development-projects or annual disasters such as floods have evicted substantial populations. However, though work is the primary reason why Bihari workers have migrated in such large and increasing numbers, it is the case that the worker-identity and working-class consciousness of these groups holds far less valence than their Bihariness.

Bihar, one of the poorest and most ridiculed states in India, is the source of the largest number of migrant-labourers within India. Migration of labourers from Bihar to other parts of the world has had a long history, and has been well documented. However, excepting the study of the Calcutta working class by Dipesh Chakravarty, who has now repudiated this work,[61] and by Jan Breman[62] there is little analysis of the this significant outflow of labour and their conversion into 'workers'. Over the 1990s, 2.2 million Biharis of a total population of 80 million migrated out. Figures for significant earlier migration to Punjab and western UP states, the epicentres of capitalist agriculture in North India, are not

---

61. Chakrabarty 1989.
62. Breman 2003.

available, though Lerche reports jobbers picking up Bihari workers from railway-stations in Delhi, and also that they formed the bulk of the workers in brick-kilns in these states.[63]

The factors leading poor rural Biharis to migrate deviate substantially from the classic narrative of enclosures. The Ministry of Labour's survey of migrant-workers mentions 'inadequate employment opportunities', 'natural disasters' and 'displacement by development projects' as the three major 'push factors', though poverty- and caste-based violence are also significant factors. Prakash Jha's 1985 film, *Damul*, portrays the forms of direct violence unleashed on the families of workers migrating to Punjab by – for lack of a better word – feudal landlords. Used to free access to unfree labour from subordinate castes, and threatened by the wage-bill implications of such movement, they formed private armies of the upper castes such as the Sunlight Sena and the Lohit Sena to retain armed control over such labour. 'Massacres' such as those in Belchchi and elsewhere in the 1980s in North and Central Bihar were instances where the violence was made exemplary by its scale, brutality, and the impunity with which it was carried out.

On the other end of their migration, the work in the Green Revolution farms also was conducted under various contexts of violence. These migrants from poor regions of backward states traversed the simultaneity between 'feudal' Bihar and 'capitalist' Punjab. Pushed out by poverty enforced by feudal discipline, they landed in places where another logic of the Indian political-economic formation was playing out: a secessionist movement based on ethnic and linguistic exclusiveness: the Khalistan movement. In other words, the over-arching ethnic frame of this movement made it difficult for these migrants to be recognised as workers: they could only be recognised – and targeted – as contaminants on a pure land.

Bihari workers constitute a significant proportion of the labour-force of Punjab's agriculture and industry. They have often been the target of 'ethnic violence'. In the 1980s, Sikh separatists attacked Bihari labourers working on the Satluj Yamuna Link canal-project. In 1988, 30 Bihar agricultural workers were massacred in Majat village in Ropar district, followed by the killings of 19 Bihari migrants in Lakhowal village in Ludhiana district. Migrant-work is caught in other logics, not only those of production-relations: Sikh militants wanted to maintain the demographic purity of Punjab, on which their claims to separate nationhood were based.

Even though, in the 1990s, the incidence of targeted violence among migrant-workers decreased, and there were no massacres of such magnitude, the conditions

---

63. Lerche 1999.

of migrants opened them up to newer forms of violence. When Dalbir Singh, the serial killer who preyed on the children of migrant-workers in Jalandhar's industrial area, was arrested, and his photographs were widely displayed on television, the parents claimed to have informed the police about him previously. But the lack of political representation of migrant-workers in Punjab, language-barriers, and perceived cultural inferiority all prevented the police from taking any action until much later.

Resurgent regional nationalism in Punjab has again unleashed violence on migrant-workers. Earlier in 2008, bombs rocked the Shingar movie-theatre in the centre of the Ludhiana's famous hosiery-industry where thousands of migrants work. Punjab Police has said that the Ludhiana multiplex-blast could be the result of collaboration between jihadi groups and local Khalistani outfits like Babbar Khalsa International.

Over the 1990s, as India's economic reforms created regionally concentrated bubbles in construction, agro-processing and domestic work, migrations took on a complex and subcontintental form, with migrations from low to high growth-areas. Migrant-workers particularly became important in these sectors. In cities like Mumbai, migrant workers made up the bulk of the population of the slums, which house 60 percent of residents. New industries such as the wineries of Nashik, and the new industrial activities in 'tier-2 cities', recipients of recent finances from new linkages with cosmopolitan capital, also attracted migrant populations.

There has been a centrally conflictual dynamic at the centre of these migration-processes: while capital from Maharashtra, Punjab, Delhi and other locations attracted migrants, and in fact could not function without it in many sectors, formations of cultural politics also repelled and kept migrant-workers excluded. Traditional working-class organisations, themselves partly culturally constituted, have not had the flexibility to organise them, nor the communication-skills. Besides, the advent of neoliberalism in Mumbai was preceded by the destruction of strong trade-unions.[64] Targeted violence on migrant-workers in Mumbai and the rest of Maharasthra meted out by the regional supremacist Maharashtra Navnirman Sena is an ongoing phenomenon. Ridiculed as having cultural attributes of untrustworthiness, sloth, uncouth habits, inferior gods and so on, Bihari workers were attacked with impunity, causing the mass return of terrified migrants in overloaded trains back to their villages. These migrants are new workers and unconnected to pre-existing forms and discourses of workers' organisations and rights. They are loosely organised on the basis of village- and family-affiliations, and are organised by populist parties that are rooted in their

---

64. Sherlock 1996.

locations of origin, but have now established significant presence also in the new locations: witness the Samajwadi Party in Mumbai.

It is interesting that capitalists have been at the forefront of efforts to bring 'ethnic peace' in Maharashtra, as wages have escalated three-fold. Punjabi manufacturers from cities such as Ludhiana, where, over the last decade, UP-Bihari languages such as Bhojpuri are now spoken by up to 30 percent of the population, have made a bid for those migrants fleeing Maharashtra.

Another major context for the migration of Bihari workers is the construction-industry. Real-estate development by governmental agencies and private agencies have both exploded in the last two decades, with housing, mega-malls, commercial centres etc leading the way. Bihari workers have been heavily employed in the construction of flyovers, underground rail-systems and the like. Migration in the construction-sector often is area specific, in that labour-supply chains might extend from one building site in Delhi to a particular sub-district of Bihar because primarily of the history of such sourcing in relation to a contractor.

In many respects, Bihari migrant-workers straddle two worlds of production and labour in contemporary India, encapsulating within themselves, seasonally, both the position of the agricultural landless labourer or peasantry, and that of 'informal' and 'unorganised' sector-worker. This figure thus poses different challenges for both the Marxist and the SS approaches.

There are several aspects of migrant-workers' experiences that resonate with the formulations of the SS approaches. Groups of workers from the same village or from proximate villages, often distantly related to recruiting agents migrate, work and reside following principles of community, contiguity and consanguinity. However, the mediation between their worlds and that of the broader political process is undertaken in large part by NGOs, independent unions, non-Marxist left-populist political parties, and some agencies of the state. International agencies such as the ILO have collaborated with the Indian Ministry of Labour to provide social-security provision and welfare-coverage of some sort to these workers. While wages and work-conditions are two important issues for mobilising migrant-workers, their lack of identity-papers, and the challenges posed by their movement to their status of voters, has been a barrier to mainstream-left unions and parties. Lately, given that they have been labelled *a priori* suspects in the rising tide of 'crime' in the new metropolis, migrant-workers have formed regionalised associations, called for identity-cards, and developed links with the police and political parties. In other words, they have called for the 'institutions of surveillance' as means of protection, and as a basis for political participation. At the same time, they have taken all aspects of their world, not only that which is connected with work, as the basis for their nascent organisations.

Because the marks of their caste, linguistic and regional origins form the basis for their negative cultural identification, it is ethnic and caste-based political parties that have been most involved with the political organisation of Bihari migrants. In some cities, now there are regional associations of migrant-workers, but on the whole, the Bihari migrant-worker, by the very act of migration, defies the modes and logics of class-based political organisation, and thus of conventional class-analysis. That their relative size and spread create more 'collective-action' problems for workers relative to capitalists in becoming conscious of being a class-in-itself in order to take class-for-itself action has long been recognised, both in liberal political theory[65] and in analytical Marxism.[66] Carter has pointed out how 'relations in production' between workers and engineers/managers create further tension within the category of the working class.[67] Here, I have argued that migration provides another kind of barrier, not limited to self-interest or contradictions within the factory-floor, but one having to do with sedimented processes of identification and the cultural and social fields on which the immediate sites of work are situated. The question is not about a 'return' to class-analysis, but to think of class as a category which is not given *a priori* and whose constitution takes into account the shifting contours of an unstable and fluid socio-cultural terrain.

Social movements, bare life and sovereign power

What of the new categories and analytical directions initiated to comprehend the new movements? Trivedi attempts to import Agamben's notions of 'bare life' and 'sovereign power' to talk about anti-dam movements in India.[68] He argues that it is the abandonment by the state of distinct population groups that opens the space for movement-activists, but that activists' actions such as enumerating the displaced as a basis for rights-claims 'is actually what makes totalitarian states possible'. For Trivedi, the problem is that movements and sovereign power share the same terrain of contemporary politics, which he reads as a convergence between democracy and totalitarianism. But the non-similarity between the context of which Agamben is writing – Jews stripped of citizenship-rights sent to concentration-camps by a fascist state – and the one in contemporary India – population-groups claiming the appellation of 'workers' as a way to become and expand the category of 'citizen' in a democracy – is too important for this analogy to work all the way through.

It would also be difficult to accept that because movements claim rights from states and use state-categories in doing so, they work inexorably towards the

---

65. Olson 1971.
66. Elster 1985.
67. Carter 1995.
68. Trivedi 2005.

convergence between totalitarianism and democracy. This seems to suggest, *pace* the subalternists, that resistance to sovereign power must come from – and create – a political terrain that shares nothing with the terrain of sovereign power embodied in the state. But what constitutes sovereign power in the context of the Indian state? I have argued elsewhere that the discursive link between 'state-power' and 'the poor' in India is a primary ground for the production of sovereignty.[69] Precisely because movements such as those of forest-workers demand both rights that are already guaranteed by state-power but do not yet cover them, and the recognition of new rights claims by sovereign power, they are not heading towards a convergence with totalitarianism but rather towards a democratisation of democracy, and to create new connections between the constitution of sovereign power and the population over which it is exercised. To paraphrase Nilsen, movements return to the apparently accomplished forms of sovereign power embodied in the state and begin to build it afresh.[70] As Chakrabarty points out, the interesting difference that Indian democracy poses with western models (the basis of Agamben's theorisation) is that here sovereignty was constructed after, rather than prior to, the institutionalisation of political equality through universal adult-franchise.[71]

Trivedi's argument would appear to be more pertinent to the case of Bihari migrant-workers who have been attacked with impunity in various locations in India, and whose very act of migration – the transgression of the territorial/residential underpinning of citizenship – attenuates their rights and renders them bare to violence. But it is noteworthy that the ethnic violence is waged on them not by holders of state-power as much as by those social actors who aim to create ethnically pure societies. Indeed, activist-demands for equality for migrant-workers despite ethnic differences precisely seek the expansion of sovereign power. This is hardly totalitarian: indeed, it locates a certain totalitarian tendency within *society* and aims to direct state-power to protect migrant-workers from it.

The subaltern-worker: neither subaltern, nor the working class

It would appear that rapid and far-reaching changes felt in India have rendered both canonical subaltern-studies and orthodox Marxism inadequate as analytical frameworks. For subaltern-studies, the formation of powerful political parties of dalits and tribals – the original subalterns, as it were – many in positions of state-power in the provinces and in New Delhi, has indicated that those who were

---

69. Sinha 2008; See Amrit 2009 for a similar argument about 'hunger'.
70. Nilsen 2008, p. 324.
71. Chakrabarty 2007, p. 51.

subalterns under the conditions of colonial capital have moved well beyond that position, and that subalterneity is a changing category. That groups within these categories are still victims of social, political and economic practices is not in doubt. However, it remains the case that attributes of mutual unintelligibility, of the separation between civil and political society, and so on, are no longer obvious. Either one would have to concede that subalterneity is a receding horizon, and that one day there will be no subalterns of the sort visualised by SS approaches, or that there is a constant production of new subalterns as the world around them gets restructured. In this context, the rejection of 'the economic' in the constitution of subalterneity produces an analytical impasse.

It is a fact, as Spivak and Bernstein have separately argued, that the stability of fordism and of production-systems of the Fordist age, are now in the decline, and that we cannot think of class in the same way as before. But one reason not to extend this formulation to mean that class should be rejected as a category altogether is that those who are new entrants to the political field – forest-workers, fish-workers, migrant-workers, and so on – still consider the self-appellation of 'worker' as politically meaningful. By labelling themselves as workers, they hope to tap into the discourses of workers' rights and solidarity that already is an established idiom of claim-making and for demanding rights. At the same time, by also deploying discourses of caste, ethnic and regional oppression, they create possible points of intersection with myriad other national and transnational discursive flows. Enunciating a 'class-identity' in the narrow sense is important but not sufficient.

These two stories, one of the much looser and dispersed use of the appellation of the worker, and the other of the difficulty of migrant-workers to articulate themselves as 'workers', encourage us to rethink class, particularly working class, as a category in contemporary India. Rapid economic changes that have exacerbated regional inequalities have created new poles of population-flows. Stable relations of domination, as well as stable forms of solidarity, both of which are highlighted in canonical subaltern-studies, have been shaken to their foundations, even as new contexts of domination and solidarity have been created. Migrant-workers oscillate between these polar positions, and any rethinking of class as well as of subalterns thus has to address these realities. Also, insofar as new workers come from subordinate castes, backward regions or tribal areas, these identities are fused with their identity as workers. Employers, and older residents of the cities to which they move, deal with them as a complex entity encapsulating a whole range of negative attributes, each one of them becoming sites for the exercise of domination and exclusion. Witness the fact that for movements of migrant-workers, domestic workers and agricultural and forest-workers, the notion of 'dignity' is a key component of their agenda. At the same time, because there are already circulating discourses of claims to rights based on these identities, they also provide possible points of insertion into newly forming circuits of solidarity. For orthodox Marxists, this would imply that they either scale back their notion of 'class' so that is not 'economic' in the last instance, or to broaden their concept of the 'economic' itself.

This calls for subjecting the very notion of 'the economy' to substantial reworking. Both canonical subaltern-studies and orthodox-Marxist analysis are guilty of treating 'the economy' as a natural domain, whose separation from other domains of 'the cultural', the 'social' and so on is self-evident; the chief difference between the two being that one rejects the economic as the determinant of subalterneity while the other elevates it as the key to explaining the social. But the fact that we refer to an 'Indian' or a 'national' economy itself is indicative of the fact that the economy, even in its broadest sense, is a cultural and political construct. In a society with myriad crosscutting social categories, it is self-evident that 'economic' agents are simultaneously also cultural actors. And the further one descends down the social ordering of production, the more likely it is that the 'economic' and one's location within it, are perceived in 'culturalist' terms.

The only way in which the category of the subaltern retains meaning in contemporary India is to see how broad changes under the rubric of 'neoliberalism' have changed the conditions of oppression and domination; sticking with the original conditions, or merely updating it as Chakrabarty and Chatterjee have done, does not allow for understanding the massive changes taking place in the world of work. At the same time, the orthodox-Marxist fear of identity, culture and discourse as factors that contribute to the weakening of class, as I have shown, renders it antiquated and inadequate to understand new movements for rights, and problems faced by new categories of workers. If class, particularly 'working class' has to have relevance and meaning, it must address the whole set of factors that produce subordination, that is to see the worker as embodying a range of identities that are not only not reducible to the economic, but more accurately, which allow us to unravel the cultural underpinnings of the economy.

Revolutionary Subjectivity, the Limit to Capital
Detlef Hartmann

> Human anatomy contains a key to the anatomy
> of the ape.
>
> Karl Marx

Do we want to continue applying the concepts of yes-
teryear to the mature struggles of our century? As the
postmodern cycle of struggle takes off, management-
strategists are reaching for the so-called 'intangibles',
that is for people's immaterial resources. They are
reaching for love, desire and freedom, for people's
wishes, hopes and creativity, and they are seeking to
convert them all into sources of productivity and value.
They are also facing unheard of forms of self-assertion
and resistance. Political economy is strategically
'subjectivising' its self-conception. The capitalist is
yielding to the entrepreneur, the valorisation of the
status quo is being replaced by its innovative transformation, capital-equipment is losing importance vis-
à-vis innovative potential and it is no longer a firm's
material capital that requires assessment but rather
the energetic and creative potential of its innovative
forces. Firms no longer merely purchase 'labour-power'.
Nor do they 'borrow' it. They evaluate and remunerate subjective potentials: the capacity and willingness
to subordinate oneself and disclose one's innermost
secrets, to get involved and engage in self-organisation,
self-rationalisation, self-optimisation, without stop-
ping short of family- and social relations. The theorists of occupational science have announced that

'class struggle... has been relocated to the hearts and minds of workers them-selves'.[1] And the statement is apposite.

Few have warned as insistently as Marx against using concepts and categories ahistorically, as if they existed 'as such' or '*sans phrase*'. He repeatedly stressed the inherent historicity of even the most fundamental categories of social analy-sis: in his early writings, in *Capital*, in the introduction to the *Grundrisse*, in the *Results of the Direct Production Process*. In the 'most modern form of existence of bourgeois society – in the United States..., for the first time, the point of departure of modern economics, namely the abstraction of the category "labour", "labour as such", labour pure and simple, becomes true in practice.... Human anatomy contains a key to the anatomy of the ape.... The bourgeois economy thus supplies the key to the ancient, etc.'[2]

In other words, history – the history of class-struggles – is what causes con-cepts to acquire and lose their specific meaning. Struggles and their specific logic blast apart the conceptual world of each *ancien régime*. They require us to develop new epistemological frameworks adequate to the experiences gathered in struggle. Even basic concepts such as 'property', 'money' and 'credit' cannot be separated from the history of struggles. And this is all the more true of the category 'labour'.

It is patently absurd, then, to respond to our present situation and its emer-gent cycle of struggles by falling back, *sans phrase*, on Marx's concepts. Attempts to verify or falsify these concepts, to renew them eclectically or employ them selectively, are thoroughly nonsensical. 'Empiricism' *qua* scientifically refined, rule-governed method of data-collection, *qua* toolkit for representing social 'real-ity' and establishing movement- and labour-typologies is equally unviable. For there is a historical dimension to the self-conceptualisations of science too. There is no such thing as objective empirical data, no such thing as a neutrally describ-able situation. The Archimedean point from which such descriptions might be formulated simply does not exist.

All we have are the experiences gathered in emergent struggles. These experi-ences are what compel us to re-conceptualise struggle, developing new descrip-tions and new concepts. We cannot accomplish this task as academic observers; universities, research-institutes and so on are almost always the custodians of methods and concepts appertaining to an obsolete cycle of struggle. Still, even bourgeois science is searching for ways to latch onto the new management's combat-strategies and has begun working with the notion of an innovative process of knowledge-creation that involves successfully accessing immaterial resources, as we will see below. In light of this, the present essay should be

---

1. Voß and Pongratz 2002, p. 152.
2. Marx 1973, pp. 104–5.

considered a tentative undertaking. In it, I take my own experiential knowledge of the new cycle's struggles as the starting point for an investigation of today's global fields of conflict. In the section that follows, I recount a number of exemplary experiences gathered in contemporary struggles. I then reflect on how these experiences can help us gain an understanding of wider conflicts, including the contemporary crisis, which I analyse in the final section of the essay. It is, after all, capital's current innovation-offensive (and not some age-old accumulation *sans phrase*) that has just entered its first major crisis.

The virus of self-rationalisation

The strike conducted by the Gate Gourmet employees at Düsseldorf airport in 2006 and 2007 provides an especially suitable starting point for exploring some of the key aspects of today's antagonism.[3] This small but tenacious labour-struggle, which lasted half a year, saw knowledge-society's vanguard-strategists confront a multinational labour-force within a globally active corporation that had, moreover, just been bought by a particularly aggressive hedge-fund. Gate Gourmet is the world's second largest airline catering firm, present at all major airports. Originally owned by Swissair, it was purchased in 2002 by TPG, then the world's second-largest private-equity firm. Hoping to increase the revenue generated by the firm, TPG commissioned McKinsey to find ways of rationalising Gate Gourmet. McKinsey is one of the world's leading consulting firms. Specialised in process-enhancement, it has consulted and continues to consult numerous small businesses and about a hundred of Germany's largest firms, including DaimlerChrysler, EADS, Deutsche Post, Bertelsmann – and Gate Gourmet. McKinsey also consults universities, hospital-firms, kindergartens, city-councils and national governments. Professor Jürgen Kluge, the long-standing director of McKinsey's German branch, is an advisor to Chancellor Merkel and came close to being given a ministerial position; in 2006, Merkel invited Kluge to join an advisory commission that includes the CEOs of several other major corporations (such as Zetsche, Hambrecht). Kluge played a key role in developing the cluster dynamic I discuss later in this essay.

McKinsey represents a new type of socio-economic actor, one specific to the knowledge-society's take-off phase, the initial offensive. The firm deals in innovation- and rationalisation-strategies, selling them as commodities and competing with other major consulting firms such as Boston Consulting, A.D. Kearney, Bain & Company and Accenture. With 85 branch-offices in 44 countries (and eight such offices in the major cities of Germany alone), McKinsey is the

---

3. Flying Pickets (eds.) 2007.

largest of these firms. The strategy-packs it deals in are immaterial commodities, hybrid products that combine software-development with the 'subjectivation' of the capitalist offensive outlined above. These commodities are productive and strategic use-values in one. They are use-values in the struggle against the social 'objects' of valorisation. And they are use-values in the strategic organisation of 'class-struggle'. Competition on this 'market' renders the development and homogenisation of strategy an enormously dynamic process.

McKinsey operates on the front-line of post-Fordism's political economy. Gate Gourmet's striking workers succeeded in exposing a number of the firm's strategic principles. McKinsey thinks of itself as a capitalist agency of 'creative destruction'. It is on the basis of this self-conception that the firm pursues the transformation and destruction of the social, its subordination to the dictates of innovative entrepreneurship, self-entrepreneurship and self-flexibilisation as they present themselves in the transition to the 'knowledge-society'. McKinsey explicitly references Joseph Schumpeter, the twentieth century's most important exponent of capitalist political economy (besides Keynes). Schumpeter placed the innovative entrepreneur, whom he viewed as the barbaric destroyer of the old and creator of the new, at the centre of his theory.[4] He understood innovations as the dynamic core and driving force of long-term cycles. Innovations are not simply inventions or technological improvements; they are new products and procedures that impact, destroy and transform society against the resistance of everything old-established. For the period prior to the First World-War, Schumpeter cites the electrical industry, particularly the innovative forces of AEG, and Taylorism. The imperatives of adjustment thrust destructively into the fabric of society may intensify to the point of 'creative destruction'. For '[this] system [capitalism, D.H.] cannot do without the *ultima ratio* of the complete destruction of those existences which are irretrievably associated with the hopelessly unadapted'.[5] While Schumpeter referred to the major waves of economic adjustment as 'Kondratievs', he did not think of them as expressing the rigid mechanics often associated with the concept of 'long waves'. Rather, he viewed them as the historical expression of innovative forces that do not move in any pre-determined direction. We should recall that Schumpeter did not close his eyes to the resistance provoked by the innovations of the Fordist cycle. He spoke openly of the 'fundamental anticapitalist hostility' continuously engendered by capitalist entrepreneurship. He viewed the world economic crisis as an expression of such hostility, which puts paid to capital's cyclical expectations.[6]

---

4. For a more in-depth account, see Hartmann 2008.
5. Schumpeter 1934, p. 253.
6. Schumpeter 1939, Volume One, pp. 398ff.; Volume Two, pp. 695ff. See also Schumpeter 1950, pp. 81ff. and 143ff.

A neo-Schumpeterian wave, announced by US management-theorist Peter Drucker and Herbert Giersch, Andreas Predöhl's German successor at the Kiel Institute for the World Economy, has now succeeded the Keynesian era (without Keynesian strategies being abandoned altogether). The concept of the 'heroic entrepreneur', which alluded originally to Nietzsche's 'will to power', has been depersonalised and generalised into a notion of innovative energetics. In Germany, the most aggressive and best informed proponents of this model are associated with Jochen Röpke's 'Marburg school'. But the same model underlies Richard Florida's concept of the 'creative class'[7] and Manuel Castells's account of the IT sector's vanguard-actors. The neo-Schumpeterian turn is an expression of the basic, strategic subjectivation of political economy, which can also be seen in the work of Paul Romer (who refers explicitly to Schumpeter) and Elhanan Helpman – and more generally in the new conceptual strategies developed in Chicago. Or, for that matter, in the writings of Daniel Kahneman, Amos Tversky, Colin Camerer and George Loewenstein, as well as in Baruch Lev's firm-value calculations. Capitalism's front-line firms and strategists no longer look to 'capital' for their driving forces; they have turned instead to the innovative energies of entrepreneurship. They are using notions such as 'self-entrepreneurship' and the 'intrapreneur' to drive their destructive and innovative imperatives into the remotest corners of the firm and into all areas of society, but also into Asia, Africa and Latin America. The book *Creative Destruction*, penned by McKinsey theorists, outlines the guiding principles behind these transformative projects.[8]

Like the leading strategists and practitioners of knowledge-management,[9] McKinsey works with a concept of 'knowledge' that comprises tacit knowledge and the emotional aspects of subjective potential. In their *Knowledge Unplugged*, Jürgen Kluge, Wolfram Stein and Thomas Licht have compiled how-to tips from forty firms: advice on how subjective potential can be accessed by capital, turning it into a productive resource and eliminating its potential for resistance. This attempt to access and valorise human subjectivity aims at all conscious and unconscious aspects of the firm's 'hearts and minds', right down to the social relations of the employees: mental models, spontaneity, creativity, aggression, leadership and passion, empathy and patterns of sociability, motivation, wishes, love, desire, forms of communication and interaction and so on. 'Knowledge' as it was formerly conceptualised (as knowledge of objects) is only one aspect among many, and even this aspect is being seen in new ways. At bottom, what

---

7. Florida 2002.
8. Foster and Kaplan 2001a. A short version is Foster and Kaplan 2001b.
9. For an overview, see Nonaka (ed.) 2005.

we are dealing with is an attempt to break what Marx called 'that obstinate yet elastic natural barrier', man.[10]

> In addressing knowledge management problems, the inherent subjectivity of knowledge can be like sand in the gearbox. On first inspection, everything looks fine, but still the machinery is not working quite right. If the machine must be used anyway, the results will be spotty at best, but most people will choose to abandon the machine altogether. Likewise, grains of subjectivity can spoil an otherwise 'well-designed initiative'. Successful firms, we are told, have found ways of removing such 'grains' from the 'gearbox'.[11]

McKinsey conceives of the epistemo-strategic offensive as a struggle against the antagonism of human 'subjectivity', an antagonism that may express itself as open resistance, as an unwillingness to subordinate oneself or as knowledge hoarding. Those familiar with the beginnings of Taylorism will recognise in this a fundamental conflict that is now playing out on a new level. Productivity's immaterial resources can no longer be tapped using the methods of Taylorism and their underlying notions of systematicity and hierarchy. The incorporation of command in the apparently objective serial structure of conditional or if-then processes (assembly-lines, conveyor-belts) may have succeeded in concentrating command on the management-level. But it allowed for only a limited dynamic and exposed the apparently neutral command-structures to the 'informal' antagonism of an ever more threatening subjectivity. This command-structure, which McKinsey and others refer to as 'push', entered a major crisis in the 1960s and 1970s; it was contested in all areas of society where it had been implemented. If immaterial resources are to be made sources of value and dynamism, then the subject needs to be forced to actively subordinate its freedom, its desire for autonomy and the full range of its tacit knowledge to valorisation. Self-organisation, self-entrepreneurship, self-engagement, self-rationalisation and self-optimisation are the strategic keystones of this new approach. It is plain to see, and hardly needs to be pointed out, that this approach requires inherited ways of life and forms of social security to be broken up by means of 'deregulation', 'precarisation' and the systematic production of fear and insecurity, all of which amounts to the *ancien régime* being exposed to a comprehensive process of creative destruction. McKinsey calls the new strategy of complex and compulsory self-engagement 'pull'.

From a sociological point of view, it may seem like we are dealing with ideal types. But the push/pull distinction needs primarily to be understood as the guiding notion behind a cannily conducted practical project: McKinsey has

---

10. Marx 1976, p. 527.
11. Kluge, Stein and Licht 2001, pp. 71–2.

learned from first-hand experience of class-struggle that it must implement its strategy via a long-term process of 'learning by doing' that involves permanently confronting antagonistic subjectivity and the 'repellent yet elastic natural barrier'. Conflictuality and 'productive friction' are part and parcel of the approach employed by McKinsey and other consulting firms. Obviously, 'Toyotism', with its institutionalised imperative of constant self-improvement, is only one early expression of this complex strategy.

McKinsey's strategy for Gate Gourmet reflected the consulting firm's first-hand experiences with the 'elastic natural barrier' and its various forms of resistance and obstruction. McKinsey had been gathering such experiences for several years and had a good idea of what to expect. Its strategists view subjectivity as 'socially embedded'. 'Teamwork' in 'assembly-islands' was a decisive testing ground for the productive integration of subjective resources and the possibilities associated with it.[12] That teamwork and assembly-islands were a social laboratory designed to impact upon the overall firm-environment in a shock-like manner was evident from the fact that the teams were observed and controlled very closely by consulting firms like McKinsey, as well as by specialists from all sorts of research-institutes and trade-unions. These projects were a form of 'fieldwork'. And it was not long before new forms of antagonism and resistance were observed, ranging from open refusal to the more covert boycotting of cooperation-requirements: knowledge hoarding, sometimes systematically and cooperatively organised (with knowledge being withheld not only from the firm's management but also from unreliable colleagues); social loafing; adherence to an internal equality-principle that thwarted the informal hierarchies associated with team-representatives; the refusal to communicate experiences to field-workers and consultants (a refusal grounded in the knowledge that these field-workers and consultants would immediately record what they were told in their 'field journals' and use it against the team workers); exclusion of colleagues judged overly cooperative and so on.[13]

The experiences gathered with obstruction and resistance and the consequences drawn from these experiences were reflected in a statement by Roland Springer, Daimler-Chrysler's expert on occupational science and process-enhancement and a McKinsey consultant guided by a vision of 'creative destruction':

---

12. See Hartmann 2008 and the literature cited there.
13. See Minssen 1999, p. 177; Kühl 2001, p. 185. On social loafing, see Shepperd 2001, pp. 1ff.; Harkins 2001, pp. 135ff.; Oelsnitz and Busch 2008. The strategists of occupational science are keeping at it, as Michael Schuman of Göttingen's Sociological Research Institute (SOFI) and his colleagues (Schuman *et al.* 2006) demonstrate. Cf. Hartmann 2008, pp. 32ff. for further details and references.

> Intrapreneurship as practised today is characterised by a double move-
> ment. Binding targets and comprehensive performance evaluation go hand
> in hand with increased freedom of choice and greater responsibility. One
> might speak of the spread of a guided and closely controlled form of personal
> responsibility.[14]

All this was reflected in the strategies Gate Gourmet's workers were confronted
with prior to going on strike. There ensued a confrontation between the class-
subjectivity of these workers and the entire complex arsenal of the knowledge-
society offensive. Assembly-lines were disassembled at Gate Gourmet as they
were elsewhere, but the leeway granted workers in the fields of performance
and self-rationalisation was restricted to an extreme degree, with binding targets and comprehensive performance-evaluation conditioning workers' activities. The workers' isolation and their subordination to the constraints of mutual
competition were used to destroy inherited forms of collectivity, preparing
workers for the 'team' and its specific forms of evaluation (and self-evaluation).
The soft skills deployed by McKinsey's consultants in their dealings with the
social object of their strategies faithfully implemented the guiding principles of
change-management.[15] The agents of change-management acted affably. They
dressed casually and asked workers to address them using German's informal
'you' [du]. They asked not to be addressed by their doctoral titles. And they said
they wanted everyone to think about possible improvements together.

They started with the fun part: visits to the kart-racing circuit. The workers
felt they were being evaluated already, with the McKinsey consultants looking
to gain a first-hand impression of their assertiveness, aggression and enthusiasm.
The kart-teams were picked in such a way as to always make two thoroughly
unalike employees form a pair. Over-performers were made to cooperate with
average employees. The next step consisted in playfully assessing the workers'
capacities for self-rationalisation. Everyone was given a plastic car consisting of
22 parts. Six people were given the task of assembling 12 cars as quickly as possible, under the direction and advice of McKinsey's consultants. The name of the
game: do-it-yourself rationalisation and standardisation. This stage of 'change-
management' is part of McKinsey's standard repertoire. McKinsey put EADS
workers through a similar exercise. They were given toy-planes and asked to
assemble them at top speed. In this way, their pro-activeness was sucked up into
the rationalisation-offensive. In the case of McKinsey, this aim was achieved, at
least initially. As one Gate Gourmet worker reported self-derisively:

---

14. Springer 1999, p. 95.
15. Foster and Kaplan 2001a, pp. 270ff.

> Believe it or not, we often talked about this during the strike: I can't get this
> virus out of my system. When I'm boiling coffee at home, I'm already thinking
> of how to avoid unnecessary motions. What can I pick up now so I won't have
> to walk back and forth more than twice?

The time-limits set during the exercise were relatively generous – for a reason,
no doubt. When the exercise was over, the workers noted with a mixture of irony
and pride that they had in fact worked faster than required.

After this playful kick-off, things began to get serious. Isolated workers' motions
were analysed using optical instruments and then reduced to a strictly defined
optimum. Breaking collective work-processes up into individual ones was a key
aspect of the rationalisation-offensive. 'We need to make sure they have nowhere
to hide', write the authors of the official McKinsey account of the conflicts at
EADS. In the case of Gate Gourmet, images were drawn up specifying precisely
how airplane-meals ought to be prepared. Surveilling individual workers from
above was then no longer a problem. The instructions for other tasks were not
always as detailed and strict. But they were all performed under the pressure
of set times, with charts reminding workers of time-limits and maintaining the
constraints of self-rationalisation and self-optimisation. The time-limits were
calculated on the basis of the time required to perform the actual work-tasks, so
that resting periods and toilet-breaks were out of the question. Workers' social
relations were controlled by means of so-called 'review-meetings'. There, discussions were not limited to productivity levels at work, but also to private factors
influencing workers' performance (lifestyle, illness and such like).

Going on strike was the workers' way of pulling the rip-cord. The strike was
not simply about wages, but also about something the workers called 'human
dignity' on their strike-banners. During the strike, the workers established
contact with workers striking at another Gate Gourmet location, the one at
London's Heathrow Airport. The Düsseldorf workers visited those in London and
vice versa. The workers attempted to familiarise themselves with other settings
where McKinsey was active (hospitals, for example). It was by striking that the
workers asserted their claim to human dignity, rebuilding their social relations
as a form of protection and counterpower, and reconstituting their individual
and collective self. Supporters from other areas of society – members of the
unemployed people's movement, students – got involved in the strike and were
able to relate quickly to the workers. They did so on a personal level, not on that
of slogans and ideologies. Self-assertion against socially generalised constraints
and imperatives of self-subordination provided the common ground.

The strike's significance is not to be found in its outcome alone. The concessions won by the workers were moderate. Gate Gourmet had announced a 10
percent wage-reduction. After the strike, it conceded 1 percent wage-increases

for 2006 and 2007, a one-off payment of 156 euros per worker, a guarantee that there would be no layoffs until 2009, a curb on the flexibilisation of working hours and the temporary introduction of a 40-hour week. However, the wages of new employees were also lowered to by 15 percent. No overarching solidarity with workers elsewhere was achieved. The trade-union was partly responsible for preventing the solidarity of workers employed in other German Gate Gourmet branches. The energies unleashed during the strike were not sufficient for maintaining and extending solidarity with workers at Heathrow and other Gate Gourmet locations. Not only were relations to those struggling at other workplaces, at universities or as unemployed persons not intensified or extended, but those relations that were established tended to dissolve again. What was especially distressing was the fact that, while the Gate Gourmet workers were on strike, a similar rationalisation offensive was being conducted within Lufthansa's catering-service and at the Opel factory in Bochum; in both cases, embarrassing compromises were the outcome. The rationalisation-offensive in Bochum displayed all the characteristics of the Gate Gourmet strike. But in Bochum, nothing like the counterknowledge Gate Gourmet's workers developed in response to McKinsey's rationalisation-offensive was ever made public. This rendered the dilemma inherent to these struggles more than clear. Thanks to consulting firms such as McKinsey, capital disposes of a strategic space within which competing single capitals – 'hostile brothers', in Marx's words – can cooperate by permanently discussing, optimising and extending the strategies of struggle by which they assail their social object. Of course, such cooperation is no guarantee for success. The subject's self-will remains an obstacle to be reckoned with, and that is precisely why struggle occurs. But on the side of resistant subjectivity, strategic commonality and the unification of the various battle-fronts are to be found, at best, only in a nascent state, despite the fact that the various struggles being fought out are structurally identical. 'Model Germany' – the long-standing practice of teaching, rewarding and learning self-restraint – still functions effectively, as can be seen in the fact that most people are still concerned primarily with feathering their own nest.

The significance and radiance of the strike at Gate Gourmet lies elsewhere. The stamina and tenaciousness of the striking workers exposed certain paradigmatic aspects of future struggles. Discussions and debates with supporters from other areas of social struggle were an occasion for thematising the specific characteristics of the capitalist valorisation-offensive. There emerged a form of 'counterknowledge' or 'scientificity from below' that is reminiscent of other eras of struggle. It is reminiscent of the IWW's subversive knowledge, of Italian workerism's early initiatives, and of the conflicts seen during the early 1970s strike by Ford's workers in Cologne I can think of no German strike that saw the techniques of 'change-management' and the pressure to rationalise and optimise oneself – two key aspects of the current move away from Fordist social strategies, which have gone into crisis – being articulated with comparable precision and by the struggling subject itself. The strike showed in an exemplary and historically specific way that the direct production-process and work constitute central areas of struggle. In doing so, it has shattered the cloud-screen function of orthodox Marxism's cherished theoretical fetish, 'labour-power'. Central aspects of the Postfordist features of 'work-organisation' and their ideological terminology were exposed as a form of social engineering and an attack on subjectivity *qua* economic resource, a superation of Taylorist techniques rendered blunt by labour-struggles and an extension of the forms of assailment by means of pressures towards target-oriented and closely controlled self-rationalisation, communicative self-disclosure, self-optimisation and self-subordination. The workers, their supporters and I myself remember a public discussion on 9 March 2006 as one of the high points in the articulation of counterknowledge.[16] Experiences of struggle gathered during the strike and intellectually acquired counterknowledge merged surprisingly with experiences gathered in other areas of struggle. The discussion was also a high point in the sense that this counterknowledge had already found its own language: in the many conversations held in and around the strike-tent, during direct actions or in interviews. This was an aspect of the irreducible historicity mentioned above, the manifestation of what Walter Benjamin (writing in a different historical context) expressed in his statement that '[not] man or men but the struggling, oppressed class itself is the depository of historical knowledge'.[17] Working-class subjectivity, the locus of (active) cognition, asserted itself against the arrogance of a left-wing intellectuality that operates with notions of 'subalternity'. This point is especially important to me. For science, even where it expresses itself in the form of left-wing intellectuality, treats this subjectivity as the object of cognition, as a 'remainder' or, at best, a 'milieu'. And Marx himself rarely ventured beyond the liminal point of the 'repellent yet elastic natural barrier'. This subjectivity does not articulate itself in writing. It is hard to get a grip on it conceptually and it does not achieve the stasis of intellectual constructs, because it is on the move. But it contrasts sharply with the poverty of civilising hubris in all its inventive, technological and philosophical forms, revealing itself as the space of the generative powers that move world history forward and determine the world-process.

From the perspective of antagonism, this altercation with a leading strategic firm also helped expose the forms of 'subjectivation' proper to the political

16. Flying Pickets (eds.) 2007, pp. 203–14, 215–23.
17. Benjamin 1968, p. 260.

economy of post-Fordism as described above. In confronting McKinsey's consultants, the workers confronted the vanguard-specimen of the new 'creative class'. Casual and equipped with a masterly will not 'to power' but to the reappropriation of social space, doted with the energetic attitude of creative destroyers, the leading representatives of the 'creative class' consign the functional elites of the Taylorist era (whom Loren Baritz and others have described as 'servants of power') to the history-books.

Inquisition at the employment-office: the self-education of the 'reserve-army'

We now dispose of all the necessary prerequisites for understanding the central social techniques and strategies by which the subjective resources of the unemployed are administered under the principles formulated in the German government's 'agenda 2010' platform and the new 'Hartz' laws, techniques and strategies that are driven into the social body by the country's employment-offices. The following remarks are informed by my involvement in the *Agenturschluss* campaign that developed out of opposition to these measures. The motto of the new employment-policy, *'Fördern und Fordern'* ['promote and demand'], is directly oriented to the strategic imperatives of self-subordination and self-integration just discussed. Under penalty of immiseration, the socially isolated unemployed must subordinate themselves to tailor-made procedures of total communicative self-exposure known as 'profiling' and 'case-management'. The Hartz report to the German government, produced with the collaboration of people who represent the command-deck of German politics and the German economy (H.E. Schleyer, W. Tiefensee, H. Schartau and such like) and published under the title *Moderne Dienstleistungen am Arbeitsmarkt* ['Modern services on the labour-market'], explicitly calls this a 'paradigm-shift', a break with the labour-market strategies of the old Fordist régime.[18] McKinsey contributed significantly to this 'paradigm-shift'. The report very much bears the marks of a 'creative destruction' of pre-existing structures undertaken in the transition to new social strategies. What is at issue is the destruction of existing social milieus, attitudes and mental models. Thus, the section on 'The principle of promoting and demanding as it applies to case-management' (and in particular case-management as practised by the Cologne employment-office) contains the statement: 'Demanding means ... breaking up the culture of specific milieus'.[19]

---

18. The following remarks summarise the third chapter of Hartmann and Geppert 2008, and Gerald Geppert's report, also in Hartmann and Geppert 2008. Details and sources can be found there.

19. Bertelsmann Stiftung *et al.* (eds.) 2002, p. 104.

> The possibility cannot be excluded that the person seeking help has settled into and come to terms with their situation. This means that a good [employment] offer is often not enough to incite people to give up the way of life they have grown accustomed to. More often still, the offers themselves are not particularly inviting. A measure of pressure and coercion may well have the effect of stimulating people and instigating development.... This attitude requires sociopolitical pressure from above.[20]

In a situation in which s/he fears for his or her livelihood, the 'customer' being put through the 'profiling' procedure is forced to open him- or herself up entirely and leave nothing untold. S/he is made to report on his or her self-opinion, wishes, hopes for the future, private circumstances, loves, children, habits – his or her whole life. Non-compliance is punished by the withdrawal of unemployment-benefits. These pressures to disclose and confess are the basis for the 'target-agreement' or 'integration-contract' then drawn up in 'cooperation' with the case-manager. The 'target-agreement' serves as a benchmark for the self-optimisation efforts of the 'customer'. We can easily recognise in this procedure the operative elements we have encountered at Gate Gourmet: social isolation and a self-rationalisation structured by performance-targets. While one shouldn't trivialise certain historical events, it is difficult not to feel reminded of the Inquisition's coercive structure of self-subordination and compulsory confession. And there is a genuine relationship, as shown by Foucault in his history of coerced confession and self-optimisation, from antiquity to modern psychiatry (via the Christian pastorate and Puritan self-rationalisation). The pressures of self-subordination and self-optimisation have now been refined by means of a complex arsenal of social-psychological and psychiatric services. The involvement of McKinsey and other strategic firms (such as the Bertelsmann Foundation) shows how social strategies developed in the immediate process of production are extended to other areas of society – an extension analogous to the one observed during the preceding Taylorist era.

Much as in the case of Gate Gourmet, forms of resistance articulate themselves in the form of 'counterknowledge'. Experiences and direct actions on the front-lines of resistance to the new social techniques and their forms of social destruction display an analytic precision and a degree of practical knowledge that go far beyond sociological and managerial scientificity, exposing the core and the microstrategic dynamics of the offensive in detail. The counter-sociability that confronts the offensive can no longer be described in the now antiquated terminology of 'solidarity'. It creates new social relations, spaces of shelter and forms of mutual aid that immunise themselves against the new social techniques

---

20. Ministerium 2003, p. 40.

and develop into spaces of 'counterknowledge'. Its flexibility and lack of static stability express its process-character, which is on a par with the new historical level of conflict. This flexibility and lack of stability are no shortcoming. They result from the fact that social self-production takes the form of struggle.

Life is work and work is life

Our discussion of the Gate Gourmet strike and the employment-offices has shown that the diktat of self-subordination and self-rationalisation strives to get a grasp on the entirety of each individual's biographical background. The management-term 'work-life balance' expresses the ambition to convert this background into a resource for production and domination. The offensive is being conducted in such key areas as manpower administration, social work ('empowerment') on the varied front-lines of social case-management and the psychopolitical reaction to people's ostensibly 'pathological' resistance to the pressures of self-optimisation: 'burnout'. A few remarks on the latter. The literature on burnout is vast. The more thorough studies situate the menace to the authenticity and autonomy of people's individual sense of meaning – an expression of man's irreducible claim to self-realisation – at the core of the contemporary burnout-crisis.[21] Thus burnout is understood to be the Postfordist counterpart to 'neurasthenia' as it was diagnosed and discussed during the Fordist take-off.[22] On the level of the individual firm, the burnout-crisis leads to massive profit-losses; the losses produced on the macroeconomic level are in the billions. Hence a large number of service-firms has begun to try and tackle the problem. Their goal is to further radicalise the offensive and the total mobilisation of all aspects of life ('work-life-balance-coaching'). An exemplary statement from the one 'coaching' firm's programme: 'Given that emotional exhaustion is the key element of burnout, the first step consists in developing the right self-perception. If we think of our life as an 'inner enterprise', then the issue becomes that of optimally linking our abilities, skills, talents and potentials to the possibilities life offers, thereby generating the greatest possible (life) profit'.[23] The therapy's ingredients: meditation, Qigong, yoga and the various strategies of target-agreement and benchmarking *qua* 'contract with oneself', applied in accordance with the 'management by objectives' model familiar from the world of production and the employment-office. Post-Fordism's

---

21. Ehrenberg 2004; Hillert and Marwitz 2006. For additional bibliographical references, see Hartmann 2008, pp. 54ff.

22. Ehrenberg 2004, pp. 9, 12, 268 et passim; Hillert and Marwitz 2006, pp. 36, 91, 203, 217.

23. Schröder 2006, pp. 75, 82, 87, 95 and passim.

cognitive offensive is an attack and not an ideal-typical model; the psychopolitical engagement with the 'self' of the 'natural barrier' is ever in flux.

In practice, then, the opposition by which the 'self' responds to the offensive is perforce recognised. The same cannot be said for the boot-licking propaganda produced by occupational and political scientists. In it, contrariety and antagonism are elided, as in the following passage from Jurczyk and Voß:

> Employment shouldn't dominate a person's life; it should be part of a deliberate and flexible overall arrangement that is governed by its own individual logic. The classic alternative 'work in order to live' vs. 'live in order to work' loses its pertinence. The goal becomes that of achieving a dynamic combination of 'living and working'.[24]

In the words of Hardt and Negri: 'Labor and value have become biopolitical in the sense that living and producing tend to be indistinguishable. Insofar as life tends to be completely invested by acts of production and reproduction, social life itself becomes a productive machine'.[25] Or: 'Here too, there is no longer any outside. That is what we mean by biopolitics. The distinction between production and life disappears.... Instead of a resistant outside, we now have a productive inside. The concept of resistance is no longer suited to the development of an alternative'.[26]

Totalising the offensive

So far, we have examined various aspects of a comprehensive sociotechnical offensive, starting from experiences gathered in struggle. The offensive is being conducted under various labels. Occupational scientists speak of 'subjectivation' or 'subjectivising economisation'. They refer to 'immaterial resources' or 'immaterial labour'. Sometimes they abuse Foucault's approach and use the term governmentality'. The offensive represents the material core of what is sometimes called (in a very superficial manner) 'neoliberalism'. For while the liberties of entrepreneurial management always aim at providing the market with value from dimensions hitherto untapped, the ways in which they reach out for such values do not themselves correspond to the market-paradigm. It is by means of aggressive strategies that resources hidden deep within the subject are first

---

24. Jurczyk and Voß 1995.
25. Hardt and Negri 2004, p. 148. This is the reason why Germany's capitalist occupational scientists have recognised Hardt and Negri as their own and taken up their concepts. See for example Pongratz and Voß 2003, p. 219; Schönberger and Springer 2003, p. 13 (preface). See also Hartmann 2008, footnote 27 for further bibliographical references.
26. Interview with *die Tageszeitung* (Berlin), 18 March 2002.

valorised for the market. These strategies are not static but premised on new forms of coercion and violence, as well as on a 'learning by doing' approach that looks for insight and refinement within the process of antagonism itself. One could say the approach consists in learning from the sociotechnical war, such that the strategies are an instrument of valorisation and a martial laboratory in one. Foucault already emphasised critically that the concept of 'subjectivation' obscures this state of affairs, since what is at issue are strategies for operationalising and objectifying subjectivity along the shifting border to resistant subjectivity itself.[27] The same is true of the concept of 'immaterial production'. It mystifies the social technique of employing coercive measures to translate 'the immaterial' into the material form assumed by operative techniques of self-disclosure, expropriating it through its conversion into productive 'knowledge'. This is why the 'knowledge-society' is neither a regulated status quo nor an established relation of power, but an offensive that aims at appropriating subjectivity in the form of 'knowledge'.

This offensive is fundamental and geared to opening up new sources of value the world over ('globalisation'). And it has only just begun. Since it aims at increasing overall social productivity in all social dimensions, it operates in many areas simultaneously[28] – at universities, for example, where organisational and academic reforms break apart inherited structures by means of 'clusters of excellence' and student-curricula are closely controlled through modularisation, segmented target-orientation, benchmarking and self-evaluation. The same is true of schools; witness the 'portfolio' approach. In healthcare, informationally controlled self-responsibility becomes the vehicle of rationalisation. Aggressive gendering strives to open up and imbibe the productivity of women's 'affective labour'. Cluster-strategies mark a move away from the Fordist politics of business-locations; compulsory self-optimisation is used to dynamise the productivity of entire regions and place them under the diktat of the new entrepreneurship's energetic potentials. Clusters are the regional power-cores of global reorganisation: Silicon Valley, Austin (Texas), Cambridge, Nice, Wolfsburg. The 'Europe of clusters' is the guiding concept behind a new grab for global power. In fact, even the militarisation of the metropoles is undertaken in accordance with the new management-strategies; murderous energies and the willingness to sacrifice one's own life are considered 'immaterial resources' to be tapped. Destroying the social structures of entire societies and enforcing self-entrepreneurship and

---

27. Foucault 2001a and 2001b.
28. Here, I must refer the reader to my remarks in Hartmann 2008, pp. 91ff. In this case also, my experiences in political work groups such as an 'Anti-Bertelsmann Initiative', student groups and 'Bundeswehr Wegtreten' have proven valuable sources of insight.

self-economisation are also central aspects of the guiding strategies behind the imperial assault on those countries in Asia, Africa and Latin America that have been reduced to 'failed states' by means of wars of varying intensity (and sometimes by metropolitan support for warlords).

Technological and management-innovations: the core of the global offensive

Of course, there is a techno-innovative aspect to the new pressures of self-integration, namely what used to be called 'key industries': information- and communication-technologies. From the neo-Schumpeterian point of view, these technologies are not 'inventions', much less neutral, readily available use-values. Innovations are the centrepieces of a self-globalising offensive that aims at the transformation and forcible adjustment of all of society, a historical process of creative destruction. Talk of 'revolution in the forces of production', common on both the left and the right, elides the violent character of this process. Thus Manuel Castells has characterised IT innovations as forms of 'power' and 'violence' within the process of creative destruction. Their strategy consists in penetrating every dimension of society: 'Technology is neither good nor bad, nor is it neutral. It is indeed a force, probably more than ever under the current technological paradigm that penetrates the core of life and mind'.[29] Castells views this force as being socially embodied in aggressive entrepreneurial pioneers. As innovative elite formations, they make themselves the hegemonic agents of an asymmetrical globalisation-process, subordinating first their immediate environment and then world-society by means of comprehensive technological interventions. It is on this basis that they then strive to generate new wealth. On the rise of the new Internet-giants, Castells writes: 'Internet entrepreneurs are, at the same time, artists and prophets and greedy.... This techno-meritocracy was enlisted on a mission of world domination (or counter-domination) by the power of knowledge...'.[30] Castells analyses this technological rise to power and world-conquest from the familiar penetration strategies of 'supply chain management' as they play out in the organisation of supply-industries and distribution- and information-chains (with the practice of knowledge-acquisition reaching all the way into the private sphere) to the software-supported programmes of self-activation and self-flexibilisation at the workplace and their concomitant control-mechanisms ('total quality management'). Obviously, the grab for subjective resources would have been impossible and would never even have been

---

29. Castells 1996, p. 65.
30. Castells 2002, pp. 59ff.

attempted were it not for the new IT technologies. Their software, learning pro-grammes, control programmes and open-source architectures are designed to guide subjects closely and lead them to where they begin valorising their own selves. As such, these technologies reproduce the character of Fordist manage-ment and its technologies on a higher level.[31] Even more than during the Fordist era, this hybrid, combined assault exposes socio- and psychotechnical violence as coerced self-instrumentalisation. Like Castells, the newest approaches in IT theory, action-science and cognitive science have abandoned the notion that technology is a neutral invention or use-value. Technology is not discovered or invented by entrepreneurial innovators but developed by them in the context of their confrontation with subjectivity and its sociability, as part of an effort to transform this subjectivity and sociability into 'labour' and dominate it. I might point out in passing that a redefinition of the concept of technology, based on the Greek notions of *techne* and *poiesis* (including *autopoiesis*), has been ongoing for some time now.[32]

The process-character of the innovation-offensive, evident not just in the service-sector but also in industry, can be seen in the typical project-type, char-acterised by a modular 'rolling out', a global investment-process that proceeds step by step, module by module. It is no longer investment in material assets that is central, nor the 'division of labour' within the multinational factory, but the dynamic of a process in which the various parameters of the social and 'subjec-tive' milieu, and of course local value-levels ('the market') are explored step by step, in accordance with the principle of 'learning by doing'.[33]

I cannot discuss in detail the ways in which the pressure of increased produc-tivity and the energies and strategies from the metropolitan cores and clusters are transferred into peripheral spaces, thereby altering production- and labour-differentials. The fact that these energies and strategies originate in the met-ropolitan cores is not in doubt. The metropolitan left-wing intelligentsia's fear that capital might withdraw into a worldwide network of cathedrals of power,

---

31. See Hartmann 1987. The book's first edition (1981) was originally to be titled *Zur Gewalt der formalen Logik* ['On the Violence of Formal Logic'], since its theme was the genesis of the logical structure of Fordist organisational and systems-science, including the beginnings of cybernetics, in the context of class-struggle. As important as these reflections may still be today, their own historical context is that of the conflicts and con-frontations of the 1970s, during the transition to postmodern antagonism. While I already thematised the architectures of polyvalent logics and the paradigm of self-organisation developed by Jantsch and Prigogine, the context remains that of a transition that has since been completed.

32. I am preparing a manuscript on this subject (working title: 'Aristoteles, Foucault und die Sklaven der Wissensgesellschaft').

33. See Abele, Näher and Kluge (eds.) 2006, in particular chapter seven (on the exam-ple of Mercedes-Benz). Cf. also TI chief designer A. Goren, *Frankfurter Allgemeine Zei-tung*, 1 March 2008.

surrounded and supported by a globally homogeneous sea of poverty, have proved absurd. But the transfer of social and technological adjustment-imperatives – and of an investment-pressure that constantly operates, crisis-like, on the edge of over-accumulation – is ever in search of pathways to transnational penetration. This occurs via the dictates of supranational institutions and negotiation-rounds, via wars of varying intensity (by which the process of creative destruction is taken to societies declared backward),[34] via the playing off of national competition or via arrangements with ambitious new generations of peripheral entrepreneurs ('compradors', as they used to be called) who strive to shatter the old régime. Notions of pure capital-export, the international division of labour or a cascade of dependent development belong to a bygone era. New transnational production- and labour-differentials are being reorganised from the clusters of knowledge-society; they are being adjusted to its needs, from the hegemonic merging of firms and universities to the Taylorist regimen of Chinese and Indian migrant-workers only just forced under the factory-yoke, all the way to mobilised peasants and new forms of slave-labour. It is the dynamic of this reorganisation that is now being stalled in a state of crisis – blocked by social resistance the world over.

The Chinese revolts

What follows is an exemplary sketch of the way metropolitan valorisation-pressures are being transferred to China, where they face new forms of social-revolutionary subjectivity, in particular that of peasant-workers. The important role China plays within the dynamic of the global offensive makes it appropriate to provide a general account and characterisation of the social conflicts in this country. No account of the global offensive would be complete without reference to these social conflicts; vice versa, one cannot properly understand the social conflicts in China without taking into account the global offensive.

The reforms initiated under Deng Xiaoping have seized on the shock and aggression of creative destruction and extended it into China. The points of entry included the country's SEZs and new centres of growth such as Nanjing, Shanghai, Chongqing and the Hong Kong/Peal River Delta/Shenzhen complex. This strategy, which was further intensified in the context of the 1997 Asian financial crisis, transformed the centres of growth into energetic clusters where the innovative

---

34. The purpose of the war in Iraq and Afghanistan. See Hartmann and Vogelskamp 2003 and also Hartmann 2009.

aggression of new super-rich entrepreneurs[35] merged with a new 'creative class' and gained access to a multi-segmented reservoir of workers: workers given the boot by state-owned enteprises, migrant-workers driven from the countryside by fiscal pressure, 800 million super-exploited peasants, the labour-slaves of China's prison camps. This raging offensive is far from having been completed, and it has just entered its first crisis. It expresses a dynamic evident at the beginning of the Taylorist/Fordist cycle, when innovative impulses from the metropoles of the period (the USA, Germany and England) were transferred to Russia, but it does so on a new level. While would-be prophets are already talking of the American, Japanese and European metropoles falling behind the new colossus, the facts tell a different story. These would-be prophets are obviously unfamiliar with both the dynamic profile of historical cycles and the Russian experience. Then as now, the dynamic centres of growth operate within a 'sea of underdevelopment', as we used to say: 800 million peasants, 200 million migrant-workers and a working class privileged under Mao and employed in state-owned enterprises that still number several thousand (formerly 60,000).

Multinational corporations – such as Hitachi, VW and BASF, chain-stores (such as, Wal-Mart) who outsource production for metropolitan low-end markets to a swathe of factories – are still at the centre of what analysts call an 'evolving global supply-chain', a supply-chain anchored in China's development-locations. Since 2006, 60 percent of Chinese exports have been commanded by foreign firms, especially exports of new high-tech products. US corporations benefit most, but so do European and Japanese corporations. Thanks to their cheap imports, they are in a position to control wages and the rate of inflation. (This was a decisive element in the downward pressure on wages evident in the USA and Europe during recent years, an element that ensured the metropolitan population and working class profited *nolens volens* from the Chinese situation.) China's rising share of the world-market is not the key issue. 'In a globalised world, bilateral trade figures are irrelevant', as Dong Tao, a UBS Hong Kong economist, puts it.[36]

As for the 'mentalities' of the school- and university-graduates flooding the labour-market year after year, they are still a long way from having been flexibilised to the degree required under post-Fordism: 'They know their books, but the traditional, drill-like methods of ex-cathedra teaching hardly prepare them for the real world. . . . They are incapable of teamwork'.[37] This is evident in the typi-

---

35. The new entrepreneurs display all the characteristics of their American and European predecessors, as Sull 2005 has vividly described.

36. On all these points, see Barboza 2006. See also 'Duell der Giganten', *Der Spiegel*, Vol. 59 (2005), No. 32.

37. 'Immer nur lächeln', *Der Spiegel*, Vol. 60 (2006), No. 19.

cal blockades faced by the project of implanting postmodern clusters in China and making them serve as relay-points for the dynamic of innovation. These blockades are especially evident in Shanghai, the preferred location for the 'outsourcing' of high-tech sector-investments (particularly IT-related investments). In contrast with the scare-story about production-relocations by which multinational corporations in Europe, Japan and the USA attempt to enforce wage-cuts, entrepreneurs in search of qualified, 'high-potential' Chinese workers are faced with obstacles related to issues of qualification, mentality and wage-levels. Attitudes informed by traditional egalitarian notions on how workers ought to be treated and by the socialist or Taylorist command-structure combine with the refusal to accept low wages and make investment a risky business. The 'immaterial' qualities of postmodern self-activation and self-initiative, indispensable for the establishment of innovation-clusters, have developed only rudimentarily and lack dynamism. They are hardly sufficient for breaking up the traditional management-culture. Moreover, engineers dissatisfied with their wages simply scram, taking their experiences and patents with them.[38] In the spring of 2005, the government was forced to admit there were 88 vacancies for every experienced laboratory-assistant and 16 for every factory-technician.[39]

Given the ways in which the offensive is being extended into China, this discrepancy has not yet reached the point of posing a critical problem for valorisation. In most factories, value is produced by Taylorist methods of subordination. This socio-technical differential or broad spectrum of labour-forms (including forms of forced labour) is another typical feature of every cycle.

The offensive is ineluctably confronted with a growing hostility that ranges from open revolt to covert resistance. Manifest struggles are evident in every class-segment, from the workers and peasant-workers to the workers in state-owned enterprises right up to the rudimentarily trained grey- and white-collar workers. The peasant-workers, also called migrant-workers, are the most radical segment (as they were in Russia prior to the First World-War). Living in the cities without resident-permits, they are exposed to a ruthless régime of rapid work-paces, low wages and wage-arrears (a form of deliberate value pilfering). I will limit myself to only a few remarks on this issue. Massive tax-hikes (with head-taxes levied even on children and the elderly and the total tax-burden sometimes many times as high as the yearly income), fees and low fixed-prices for agricultural products all force peasants to migrate – although the peasants are also driven by hopes of escaping the patriarchal relations that characterise rural China. In January of 1999, reports directed the world's attention to the clash between 1,000 policemen and soldiers and 3,000 peasants in a village in

---

38. Ross 2006, pp. 14ff. and 117ff., 193–6.
39. Fuller 2005.

Changsha Province (central China), as well as to the roughly contemporaneous struggles in Hunan and Sichuan, the successful siege of Liaoyang's city-council by more than 1,000 steelworkers and the bloody street-fights in the villages of Shandong Province, triggered by a rise in the price of water and restrictions on irrigation.[40] As early as 1988, the Party leadership in Beijing reported more than 10,000 incidents involving security-forces; in 2000, human-rights groups in Hong Kong announced they had counted more than 110,000 incidents and riotous assemblies during the preceding 12 months.[41] The persecution of 'Falun Gong' is not to be explained by the group's sectarian character. Rather, its moral code appealed to many who felt their socialist hopes had been betrayed by a reprobate ruling class, who were no longer willing to tolerate the growing divide between the conspicuous wealth and corruption of China's *nouveaux riches* and the country's growing host of beggars, or those who had been deprived of guaranteed employment and the 'iron rice-bowl'. Thanks in part to its self-organised character, Falun Gong evoked memories of the secret societies involved in the great uprisings of the nineteenth and early twentieth centuries.[42] The number of uprisings in contemporary China is rising at an impressive rate, the composition of the insurgent-groups is changing and new forms of cooperation with left-wing intellectuals and veteran-fighters are beginning to emerge.[43] Even according to the whitewashed official statistics, the year 2008 brought 87,000 large public protests (normally, only protests involving more than 3,000 people are included in this category).[44]

Increased repression and surveillance (involving the use of security- and surveillance-technologies overwhelmingly imported from the USA) and the deployment of paramilitary forces and anti-terrorist units are one response to these developments.[45] The response was combined with announcements to the effect that the economic pressures would be mitigated and efforts made to construct a 'harmonious society' and a 'new socialist agriculture'.[46] Following the onset of the world economic crisis, these statements were developed into a broad programme based on massive deficit spending. The Chinese government is also attempting, in an almost classic manner, to invite the declining and newly emerging middle-classes and student-elites to participate in a new nationalism – with some success. The politics of tension – between China and Taiwan, Japan, the USA (over

---

40. *Neue Zürcher Zeitung*, 18 May 2000; *Frankfurter Allgemeine Zeitung*, 21 July 2000.
41. Thielbeer 2000a.
42. Seiwert 2001; Thielbeer 2000a and 2000b; Schmidt 2000.
43. Cody 2005; J. Watts in *The Guardian*, 12 and 15 April 2005.
44. Kolonko 2007.
45. *Washington Post*, 9 November 2006; *New York Times*, 11 September 2007; *The Guardian*, 9 and 12 December 2005 (paramilitary interventions).
46. *Frankfurter Allgemeine Zeitung*, 8 October 2005; *The Guardian*, 15 March 2006; *Der Spiegel*, vol. 63 (2009), no. 29.

the issue of armaments) and, more recently, the Tibetan and Uyghur minorities – is being newly orchestrated.[47]

These struggles, this resistance and defiance are situated within the overarching context of transnational valorisation. They are characterised by their confrontation with the Postfordist strategies of multinational corporations seeking to transfer their valorisation-imperatives and social techniques from the hegemonic industrial clusters into China. John Hagel and John Seely Brown propagate such a penetration of Chinese society and describe its effects on the social ecologies of Chongqing, the largest and fastest growing Chinese megacity.[48] It is from the clusters that the imperative of producing new exploitation-differentials originates. While such differentials feature advanced forms of postmodern labour-power entrepreneurship at one end, they also include Taylorist methods, the extraction of value from peasant-labour, forced labour and forms of enslavement. The differentials are dynamic. They are geared to transformation, not to the stasis of firmly and permanently constituted forms of exploitation. The subjectivity of self-affirmation and resistance fans out in much the same way, constituting a transnational spectrum. This will become more apparent once the efforts to develop the coercive pressures of Postfordist self-activation intensify.[49]

Just how inadequate nineteenth-century notions of class and subsumption are when it comes to understanding today's full-fledged antagonism and the way it plays out on the global front-lines of a globally diversified antagonism can be seen in the work of Pun Ngai. She examines the processes of self-constitution (or simply 'constitution', as it used to be called) of a new social-revolutionary subjectivity, that of the *dagongmei* [young women who migrate from the Chinese countryside to work in the country's industrial zones]. Her observations are partly based on her own experiences working in an electronics-factory in Shenzhen.[50] Much as I have described the metropolitan front-lines (using the Gate Gourmet strike as an example), she describes the tactics, strategies and experiences workers develop and gather as they constitute and affirm a 'self' in the course of their confrontation 'with the entire technology of power'. A decisive aspect of this process of self-constitution consists in the interiorising of conflict ('inner splitting of self'). Critically invoking E.P. Thompson, Pun Ngai describes how memory and the invocation of traditional ways of life in the village and family are transformed into techniques of self-protection and self-affirmation,

47. *The Guardian*, 15 April 2005, 27 February 2007 and 5 March 2007; *Frankfurter Allgemeine Zeitung*, 22 October 2005; Calder 2006; see also Seifert 2008.
48. Hagel and Brown 2005.
49. For examples and strategic visions, see Hagel and Brown 2005.
50. Ngai 1999; Ngai 2005; Ngai and Li 2008.

techniques for crafting a counter-sociability premised on the amicable and familial alliance of peasant-workers from different places of origin. Confronted with the technologically equipped pressures of discipline and self-discipline, the *dagongmei* transform their social relations of origins into relations of mutual protection, aid and trust while simultaneously abolishing the patriarchal pressures of rural society. The pioneers on this liberating path to the city show their sisters and cousins where they can find shelter and what they need to do, crafting networks of mutual aid in and between dormitories and factories. These family-relations, in which the 'oldest sister' – a trailblazer with more experience than the others – assumes a central role, are far more flexible than they appear at first glance, as they may integrate women with a similar background and interlock with other networks to form larger complexes.

The networks can be dissolved, reorganised, extended or transformed, making them extremely elastic and capable of development. They are little to do with 'ethnicity' and 'kinship' in the ethnological sense. Categories derived from ethnological concepts merely reflect the codifications of bourgeois scientificity. They cannot do justice to the historical dynamic of social antagonism.[51] Pun Ngai calls these strategies and techniques of self-invention, developed in confrontation with capitalist encroachment, 'life tactics from below'. The social dimension is not the only one she describes. She pursues these 'life techniques' all the way into the dimensions of dreaming and screaming, the scream being understood as 'a realization of... being in the world'.[52] Key passages in her book describe antagonism in much the same way as I have described it in the examples given at the beginning of this essay: 'As a worker-subject dagongmei is a subject over which the process of subjectivation [in the capitalist sense, as described above; D.H.] fights with the process of subject making and the struggle for a return to the actor'.[53] It is a process of 'inventing' the social-revolutionary self within conflict. The social-revolutionary self articulates itself within the subject via an 'inner splitting of self'.[54] This process of social self-production and self-invention is understood to be the source and space of an approaching 'social revolution from below'.[55] Pun Ngai unsparingly exposes the socialist régime that has emerged from the Chinese Revolution as an extension and transformation of patriarchal techniques of power mystified by a rhetoric of class. She

---

51. Ngai 2005, pp. 54ff. – see also pp. 8ff. Ngai's account implies that even as intelligent a concept as that of 'thick description' (see Geertz 1973a, pp. 3–30) remains indebted to bourgeois notions on the object of research (notions akin to the methodology of 'participatory observation'), despite the fact that Geertz comes close to an antagonistic outlook. See also Ong 1987, pp. 2ff.

52. Ngai 2005, pp. 185ff.

53. Ngai 2005, p. 15.

54. Ngai 2005, p. 195.

55. Ngai 2005, p. 19.

understands the concept of 'class' to reflect a questionable strategic reductionism to the extent that it reifies and abstracts from actual antagonism as it plays out in the fields of labour, subordination and self-assertion.[56] Generalisation of her observations on the *dagongmei* allows her to take the *dagongzai* [male peasant-workers] into account as well; her materialist approach entails that antagonism is a fundamental conflict that plays out, process-like, in other Asian and African 'nations' too. In fact, there is a wealth of reports on the same conflictuality as it plays out in other regions of Africa, Asia and Latin America (although its cultural trappings may vary).[57] Aihwa Ong has gone further than Pun Ngai in emphasising the spiritual character of self-assertion and self-invention, which articulates itself in the form of spirits of resistance and vengeance.[58] Yet today, in the era of the subjectivation of violence, the spiritual aspect has become a more contested territory than it was in past centuries. Mike Davis has drawn attention to the phenomenon of Pentecostalism,[59] a movement increasingly shaped by American fundamentalists from the Puritan tradition. Combining the promise of a better life with the propaganda of ethical lifestyle-optimisation, they are conducting a veritable offensive of capitalist and 'civilising' renewal. They invoke the historical waves of American 'awakening' and the fundamental spiritual conflicts associated with the birth of capitalism, conflicts that reached their apex in the British sects of the seventeenth century. Yet in their invocation of the past, they have use only for the 'Protestant ethic' and its guiding principles, which are concerned with the capitalist self-disciplining of the 'subaltern' classes. The complex articulations of a self-affirmation opposed to this ethic, and of social revolution, are elided, both in historical reconstruction and in present-day activities. It is the very concept of the 'subaltern' that effects this elision. Ching Kwan Lee appositely replaces Gayatri Spivak's well-known question 'Can the subaltern speak?'[60] with the alternative question: 'Can we hear the subaltern when it speaks?'[61]

We now dispose of a sufficient number of reports, including some by migrants, in which 'subalterns' from other regions speak to us and affirm their social-revolutionary ideas, life-tactics, sociability and moral economy. They derive their importance by virtue of being situated within a worldwide arc of tension. The confrontation between their varied existential strategies, their quest for income and self-liberation and the pressures of self-subordination and self-rationalisation is now playing out on a new historical level. This conflictuality transcends the self-conception of a 'world' in which one still believed it possible to

---

56. Ngai 2005, pp. 10ff., 27ff.
57. See Ong 1987, or Fardon 1987. See also Kondo 1990.
58. Ong 1987, Chapter Nine, especially pp. 201ff.
59. Davis 2006.
60. Spivak 1988.
61. Lee 1998, p. 34.

conceptualise not only things but also classes and the relations between them. This process sees new figures, new concepts and new methodological approaches emerging in all dimensions of action. They are 'emerging' historically, and at the same time, they are providing us with a new key to the anatomies of the old figures, concepts and approaches. Picking up on this essay's opening remarks, we can say that it is from the mature stage of this process that we must craft a new relationship to the history of struggles and to the notions, concepts and methods that came with them.

The offensive takes shape within the crisis of Fordism

One thing emerges clearly from the dynamic's current stage, in which the capitalist offensive seeks to develop overarching organisational strategies. The aggression and the fundamental and paradigmatic significance of these strategies is reaching a degree of intensity that makes the offensive comparable, in terms of the theory of historical cycles, to the Taylorist/Fordist offensive that began more than a century ago. And just as the Taylorist/Fordist offensive sought to escape the crisis that inherited forms of labour-subordination had entered (forms Marx was still familiar with), so the diktat of self-subordination seeks to escape the crisis of Taylorism/Fordism. The latter cannot be reduced to individual aspects. It was a comprehensive crisis that challenged capital's social command in all areas of the factory-society. The crisis was driven by claims to income and self-realisation that included the youth's revolt against the pressures of patriarchal discipline in the post-Nazi nuclear family and the reappropriation of public space against the coercive régime of functionalist programming and behaviour-control evident in housing estates, shopping centres and pedestrian-zones, but also the mass-strikes and the politicisation of wage-claims and micropolitical forms of struggle by which workers articulated their resistance to oppressive Taylorist forms of rationalisation and the dictates of productivity associated with them. At the same time, the revolution of expectations in the peripheries of Asia, Africa and Latin America challenged Fordist strategies of development that have been appositely described as 'bloody Taylorism'. The response to the crisis rose to the challenge and replicated earlier historical initiatives on a new scale. If subjectivity rejected Fordist command, then the encroachment of subjectivity needed to be reorganised. Confronted with claims to autonomy and self-realisation, the capitalist response took its cue from precisely these claims. It was through coerced self-activation – 'pull' – that access to the 'self' was now sought. Threatened with existential ruin, the self was to be constrained to fundamentally alter its mentality and proactively disclose, subordinate, mobilise and rationalise itself, in an entrepreneurial spirit, as a 'self-entrepreneur' or 'labour-power entrepreneur', thereby overcoming the historically palpable obstacle of 'self-will'. The emancipatory dawn of self-realisation became the cornerstone of new pressures of self-subordination, premised on notions of the self as an immaterial resource of value.

Political economy

Painful as it may be, the political economy of capital has long since moved far beyond Marxist orthodoxy and most left-wing concepts. In principle, it too can merely follow in the footsteps of the actual strategies of valorising violence and must limit itself to conceptualising them. For no political economy is ever the basis of capitalist development. In what follows, I will address some aspects of this problem.

With the notion of entepreneurship *qua* agent of destruction and innovation, political economy takes account of the energetic character of accumulation; it recognises that accumulation is part of a larger social process. The entrepreneur is no longer simply the 'capitalist' or owner and profiteer of existing means of production. Entrepreneurship qualitatively embodies the aggression of capitalist valorisation-strategies, right up to the 'will to victory' displayed by the entrepreneur's team-formations.[62] The leading spin doctor of the new economic theories, Moses Abramovitz, sees entrepreneurship at work in the innovative productivity of war *qua* 'ground-clearing experience opening the way for new men, new organizations, and new modes of operation and trade better fitted to technological potential'.[63] In Germany, the energetic character of innovative entrepreneurship is emphasised especially strongly by Jochen Röpke.[64] In his view, the concept of capital is transforming into 'capability' or 'potential'. Hence capital is no longer taken to consist in material assets; rather, it embodies a firm's immaterial potentials,[65] which require new valuation- and measuring techniques.[66] The notion of capital as object is dissolving its ontology in favour of notions of capital's intentional character,[67] categories of causation are yielding to categories of action and self-conceptions premised on a patriarchal habitus are being replaced

---

62. Oelsnitz and Busch 2008.
63. Abramowitz 1986, p. 389. See also Abramovitz 1993 (on immaterial resources in general).
64. See Transforming Knowledge 2003, pp. 21–5.
65. On the fundamental issues, see Abramovitz 1993, pp. 236ff. For a comprehensive overview, see the conference-papers and -discussions documented in Corrado Haltiwanger and Sichel (eds.) 2005.
66. Lev and Radhakrishnan 2003.
67. Cf. Röpke 2004.

by others premised on aggressive and dynamic gendering.[68] As for 'financial capital', it too has long since breached the barriers posed by older forms of investment. Myths of 'casino-capitalism' are a long way from the truth. Venture-capitalists, private-equity firms and hedge-funds are cooperating seamlessly with 'productive' and consulting firms. Beyond obsolete notions of 'ideology' and the 'superstructure', the cultivation of community-spirit and even religiousness is part and parcel of company-resources as they are administered in accordance with strategies of 'corporate governance' and company-ethics.[69]

Scientificity

When old scientific strategies transform and new ones emerge, they do not do so *qua* 'superstructure' determined by a putatively 'material' base, but rather as strands of a unidirectional and corresponding dynamic of knowledge and action (they 'co-evolve', as the jargon of postmodernism puts it). Cognitive science's basic notions of emergence, autopoiesis (or self-organisation) and intentionality join the entrepreneurial and innovative dynamic in breaking up the inherited and mostly static paradigms of Fordism: system, structure, function, causality (understood according to the deductive and nomological model of Hempel and his followers, a model that prevailed until the 1960s). Concerning my understanding of the relationship between social antagonism and 'scientific' paradigms or 'scientific' methodologies, I must refer the reader to ongoing research-projects[70] devoted to the articulation of social and scientific empowerment.

Occupational science

Entrepreneurs work with a clear perception of their confrontation with resistant subjectivity in the field of labour. The concepts with which occupational scientists operate are also formulated from the perspective of entrepreneurs, but they elide the offensive character of entepreneurial activity; often, they do not even consider entrepreneurs' antagonists or their perspective. In other words, occupational science is conceptually eliminatory. This is true of the vast literature on the 'subjectivation' of work. The rare admission that 'class struggle ... has

---

68. McCrimmon 2008; Breuer 2007. Tellingly, both authors work as directors of a coaching firm.

69. Ulrike Berger's essays on this topic are still worth reading. See Berger 1993, and also Krell 1993.

70. Hartmann, 'Aristoteles, Foucault und die Sklaven der Wissensgesellschaft' (working title). Some preliminary thoughts can be found in: Hartmann 2008. See also Hartmann 2006.

been relocated to the hearts and minds of workers themselves', with the goal consisting in tendentially 'total access',[71] prompts no change of perspective; nor does Ursula Holtgrewe's refreshingly candid admission that what is at stake is a 'perspective on subjectivity' that understands subjectivity to consist in 'proactive subordination'.[72] At best, subjectivity is granted the status of an object of subordination, but it is not recognised as a front-line actor confronting the strategies of subjectivation. In this way, established subject-object schemes of social and scientific empowerment are translated into aggressive forms of 'othering', in a martial gesture by which everything other is declared hostile. This strategy begins to assume eliminatory connotations when subjectivity is denied the status even of an 'outside', as occurs in the fantasies of imbibement associated with concepts such as 'Empire', 'biopower' and 'governmentality'.[73]

Social revolution and knowledge

The confrontation between the strategies of subjectivation and social-revolutionary subjectivity, which plays out in all areas of society and affects the very foundations of scientificity, has not only dissolved the Cartesian framework hitherto proper to the self-conception of the bourgeois sciences; it is also forcing the left to move beyond the old dichotomies of 'theory' on the one hand and 'practice' on the other. There is no Archimedean point to be found outside the context of struggle, no point from which the world or reality *qua* object could be contemplated, interpreted, analysed and understood. The subjects of analysis are all part of the process; they encounter one another in knowledge and counterknowledge. Cognition is impossible except as active cognition; it is closely bound to struggles. The experience of revolutionary subjectivity will remain a closed book to you for as long as you do not participate in these struggles. Access to subjectivity is bound to the confrontations occurring on the various front-lines where subjectivation and subjectivity meet. Other front-lines and horizons of global antagonism can be understood only from within the context of such experience. The notion that the condition of the world might be understood from some privileged observation-point or even from within the discursive fabric of a left-wing 'scientific community' is given the lie by the insurmountable conflictuality of the process itself. It is from the specific front-lines of one's own experiences that

---

71. Voß and Pongratz 2002, p. 152.
72. Holtgrewe 2003.
73. The concept of governmentality reflects such eliminatory tendencies not just in the work of Hardt and Negri, but also in that of Ulrich Bröckling. Contradiction and negation are denied every ontological status and the 'refusal to play along' becomes the fall from grace *par excellence*. See Hartmann 2006, pp. 152ff.; Hartmann 2008, pp. 103ff.

access to other front-lines needs to be sought – regionally, supraregionally and globally. There is no other way for the circulating experiences of struggle and the specific horizons of counterknowledge to confront strategies of subjectivation that are being organised globally. There is no other way for a globally dispersed subjectivity to realise itself in opposition to these strategies, developing its own specific forms and common language.

Beyond Marx?

Returning to this essay's opening remarks, we can say that it is from the mature stage of the process described that we need to develop a new relationship to past struggles and the notions, concepts and methods that emerged from them. Objectivist notions of value's mechanical self-valorisation have been exposed once again, and more clearly than ever before, as the ideology of self-professed socialist elites. Entrepreneurs extract value on the battle-site of work and in the context of a confrontation with subjectivity that occurs in all areas of society. Struggles are what determines the rate of surplus-value, the rate of profit and their crisis – and this is as true of the current recession as of any other (see below). In doing so, these struggles have conclusively revealed the 'use-values' of machineries, procedures and management-methods to be aspects of this conflict – instruments of struggle. It is not from labour-power's character as a commodity that social conflicts need to be analysed, but rather from work, the forms of sub-jugation and the ways in which they are renewed and refined within the context of a social engineering that leaves no area of society unaffected. Commodities and the commodity-form of social actors are one product of these strategies, but not their foundation. This is also true of labour-power's character as a commod-ity (its specific productivity).

It is useless to hold this against Marx today, from the point of view of struggles that have matured. It is not that Marx, in his day, was beyond Smith, or that we are now beyond Marx; what was, and continues to be 'beyond', are the struggles. And beyond which Marx? How could we object to someone who was himself involved in the struggles of the *Vormärz* and began his investigation of capital-ism by searching for the foundation of all economic categories in subordination and alienation as they occur *within the act of production and within produc-tive activity itself,* not vice versa?[74] Marx's theory remained open to the social-revolutionary subjectivity of the peasant-workers from the Eifel and Bergen regions, who shaped Cologne during the *Vormärz* period. To an extent, it did so even during those periods when objectivist-mechanistic and economistic

---

74. Marx 1975–2004i, p. 274 et passim.

approaches became dominant: in the passages on the ambivalence of science and technology in the *Grundrisse*, in the *Results of the Direct Production Process*[75] or in figures of thought such as that of the 'counteracting influences', which allow attention to focus not on the regularity of the 'tendency of the rate of profit to fall' but on such loci of struggle as the intensification of technological violence at the workplace or the assaults on peripheral societies.

Today, with the benefit of more than a hundred years of critical-methodological reflection on how objectivity is systematically generated by abstraction from subjectivity, we are better equipped to deal with Marx's methodical manoeuvres. If labour presents itself, from the perspective of capital, as 'subject', 'absolute poverty' and 'actual . . . non-value', whose objectivity can only be one 'coincident with [the person's] immediate corporeality',[76] then this is precisely what constitutes the 'law of value' *qua* law and the pseudo-validity of the calculations derived from it. Calculations are possible only for those who are no longer counting on class-subjectivity. Methodically generated figures of thought such as that of the emptiness and nudity of the 'class', the myths of the subjective residuum and of non-value – they all operate from the perspective of capitalist valorisation and fail to cross the line into the domain of struggling subjectivity, which appears only in a nebulous form, as a milieu to be accessed and tapped into. Struggling subjectivity's historically decisive significance as the source not only of value, but also of autonomous social creativity, liberation and cognition is rendered invisible and eliminated. It is the methodology of this inversion that allows the cadres of orthodox Marxism and their intelligentsia to write themselves a blank cheque legitimating their historic self-empowerment. We must not forget that real socialism's hour of birth, those first months of 1918 during which Russia caught up with the globalisation of Taylorism, marked the beginning of a ruthless war on the country's peasants and peasant-workers, who represented the most radical element in the social revolution not only of Russia but also of its neighbouring countries.[77] Value does not valorise itself. The law of value needs to be enforced against social-revolutionary subjectivity, against the 'self' of the class, and this is generally achieved through brute force.

Against Tronti and his reductive insistence that labour-power remains the crucial reference-point in all struggles,[78] we allowed ourselves to be inspired by the approaches developed in the *Quaderni Rossi* (first and foremost that of Alquati), where this ideological veil was lifted and attempts were made to understand the field of work itself as a field of struggle. We sought out living non-value in the

75. Hartmann 1987.
76. Marx 1975–2004j, p. 222.
77. Anonymous 1993, pp. 9ff. See also: Ebbinghaus 1978.
78. Hartmann 1987, p. 31.

struggles of workers, feminists and anti-racists, in struggles against the social violence of urban planning, schools and psychiatric institutions and in imperial strategies of devalorisation and annihilation.[79]

Looking back at these efforts today, from the perspective of the mature conflicts described in this essay, the investigations we produced reveal themselves as engaging with fundamental changes in the strategies of valorisation. Parts of the resistant intelligentsia discovered in these changes an opportunity to transform themselves into protagonists of the new, subjectivating strategies of violence: first by advocating 'first-person politics' and then as the innovative general managers of business-enterprises emerging from within social movements, as experts on a new type of creativity and ideologues of a new 'Empire' and 'immaterial labour'. We were quick to diagnose this transformation of the left-wing intelligentsia, by which notions of 'self-realisation' lost their original subversive character as they were integrated into the innovative process of capitalist subjectivation; we were already able to glean the general tendency in early 'alternative' strategic approaches, criticised by us as attempts to access 'mental reserves' and place 'love and leisure time in the service of productivity'.[80] These too were insights gained from personal experiences in social struggles, experiences that have developed, via various intermediary stages,[81] right up to the current stage of confrontation.

Written from within this history of experiences of 'action and cognition', the present essay is not concerned, primarily, with making a case for renewing categories and concepts in light of how struggles have developed. Rather, I would want it to be read as an exhortation to do justice to the radicality of actual struggles by critically engaging with a capitalism that is taking its socio-technical arsenal into new organisational dimensions. Such a critical engagement would need to take its cue from the many front-lines we are facing in order to craft from them a combined project of self-affirmation, self-realisation and self-liberation, in opposition to the pressures of self-subordination. This cannot be achieved without palpable efforts to establish a relationship to the struggles and forms of struggle evident in Asia, Africa and Latin America, where income-struggles are asserting themselves as part of the formation of a new social-revolutionary subjectivity and against the dynamic of the valorisation-offensive. We need to appreciate that those struggling are newly creating, within the context of the

---

79. See the exemplary investigations in Autonomie 1979 (on the new prisons) and Autononomie 1980 (on the second destruction of Germany by means of urban and regional planning), and Autonomie 1982 (on 'anti-imperialism in the 1980s').

80. I am quoting two chapter headings from Hartmann 1987, pp. 110ff., 133ff.

81. Materialien 1993; Hartmann 1994.

struggles they are involved in, their very own 'life-tactics', 'moral-economy' and sociability, but also their status as 'cognitive subjects'.

The concept of the 'multitude' is not suited to this undertaking; its origins and strategic rationale have spoilt it for good. Much like the vision of 'one big union' that emerged within the struggles of the IWW, the image of a 'many-headed Hydra' that Linebaugh and Rediker have used to reconstruct the movements of Puritan sects and uprooted peasants from the seventeenth century onward provides us with a better guiding notion. But we should remember that it was the progressive pioneers from the Puritan sects who emerged as a new middle class – 'the middle sort of people' – from the conflicts of their day, becoming a hegemonic force for religiously motivated discipline, the agents of the 'Protestant ethic'. Max Weber and Eduard Bernstein, intellectual exponents of an aggressive reformist entry into the emerging Taylorist cycle, invoked the authority of these forces. If we were to treat social-revolutionary subjectivity as 'subaltern' or as the object of ethnological and sociological investigations, as an audience to preach 'sustainable development' to, or a set of people to grant 'global rights', then we too would make ourselves pioneers of the new capitalist offensive and its project of a Postfordist subsumption of the entire world. The sinister traits progressivism and reformism displayed in an analogous situation 100 years ago are an object lesson in the barbarities this would involve. The history of the social revolution is still unwritten. But given the current crisis, the dangers are not to be over-looked.

The crisis: prelude to a new wave of 'creative destruction'?

After all that has been said, there is only one analysis of the contemporary crisis open to us. It represents a sticking point for the historical offensive described above, whose strategies of creative destruction have been stalled. What follows is a brief and summary sketch of what this entails.[82]

It was not for nothing that Obama made Christina Romer, one of the leading experts on the Great Depression, chair of his Council of Economic Advisers. 'The recession follows in the footsteps of the Great Depression', wrote Martin Wolf, another member of the Council, in an article for the 16 June 2009 issue of the *Financial Times* – a broadly shared view. Research conducted by US economic historians during the past 20 years has revealed the parallels between the innovation-offensives prior to 1929 and the current recession: new elites

---

82. The following remarks summarise a talk I gave at the 2009 'Bundeskoordination Internationalismus' (BUKO) conference in Lüneburg, Germany. See also the papers documented online at <www.materialien.org>: Detlef Hartmann, 'Globale Krise und soziale Revolution' (working title). On the issue of military strategies, see Hartmann 2009.

aggressively advancing dynamic transformation in the key industries associated with new technologies (electrical equipment then, information-technologies today) and managers assailing labour-power (by Taylorism then and by the accessing of immaterial resources today) in order to effect enormous productivity gains (in the automobile-sector and its suppliers then, and in knowledge-clusters and user-industries today), these developments being accompanied by the development of new financial instruments and the euphoria of a 'new era'. Both periods were characterised by fundamental innovations: 'general-purpose technologies' designed to penetrate not just specific economic sectors, but national economies as a whole and indeed the entire globe.

What did that mean then, and what does it mean today? And why was the offensive stalled? Economic penetration is no easy matter. The matter-of-fact, neutral terminology of accumulation, investment and labour-power mystifies the fact that not things, but human beings are at stake. They are not violent *sans phrase*, but in a historically specific form. Workers must be mobilised to surrender circumstances they have become habituated to; they must be trained, adapted, beaten into shape. Society, life-habits, forms of autonomy, notions of justice, solidarity and moral economy, gender-structures, -cultures and -mentalities all need to be transformed – or 'creatively destroyed' – to allow for new consumption and the optimisation of distribution. Taylorised mass-work, mass-consumption and mass-culture, their command-structures and state-institutions could not be established from one day to the next. The strategies for imposing them met with resistance from the outset, especially the resistance of migrant-workers in the new American and European industrial districts and neighbourhoods. The same was true in Russia, where the unrest of mobilised peasant-workers and pressured peasants simmered at a level of intensity just short of social revolution, and it was true in Mexico, where the revolutionary Zapatista movement and Pancho Villa's guerillas stood up to the pressure for change from the USA and to Yankee settlers. It was also true in the colonies, where indigenous societies opposed the valorisation-strategies of a 'scientific colonialism' that reflected the rationality of the metropoles.[83] These were all blockades to the project of a complex, globally staggered penetration – persistence, self-assertion, resistance and manifest struggles.

The spectrum of these blockades and the forms in which they articulated themselves changed in the course of the more than thirty-year period that the conflict lasted – a period sometimes referred to as '30 years of crisis' or '30 years of war'. Capital faced 'fundamental hostility' (Schumpeter) during the 1930s. It took two World-Wars – essentially wars of rationalisation and transformation –

---

83. See NN 2009, pp. 9ff. for further bibliographical references.

in order to take the formation of Fordist mass-society into the stage of Cold War in 1945. From the point of view of capital, instruments developed within the war-economy, trade-union cooperation, the mixed economy, the IMF and the World Bank guaranteed satisfactory prospects for a globally staggered penetration of national economies and global-command over investments. Recent research in economic history has conclusively refuted the vulgar Keynesian view that the world economic crisis was overcome primarily by deficit spending on welfare- and armaments-programmes. In the 1930s and even during the Second World-War, Keynes himself repeatedly expressed his belief in the efficacy of the war-economy's specific forms of macroeconomic management.

In 1929, macroeconomic management still had some way to go. The net value produced by the valorisation of labour – which is all that 'markets' and 'effective demand' are – failed to keep step with the enormous productivity of the economy's Taylorised sectors. This was true in the USA and in Germany, the country that had proceeded furthest in catching up with US economic development, and it was all the more true in Eastern and Southeastern Europe, where German investors operated. The dynamic was stalled. Capital had not yet developed the instruments it required to overcome the blockade; its financial régime, based on the gold-standard, was not even able to generate enough fictitious value to alleviate the problem. In 1928, the new financial instruments associated with investment-trusts and forms of consumer-credit developed on the crest of 'new-era' euphoria were barely sufficient for creating a last consumption- and speculation-bubble, following which the surge came to an end for lack of sustenance. The investment-boom collapsed into overinvestment; its dynamic stagnated.

Just like today, in the so-called financial crisis. The word has spread by now that the origins of the crisis are not to be found on the level of finance, but on that of the 'real economy'. Nor is the solution to be found in finance. Billion-dollar deficit-spending programmes will do no more than buy precious time in which to build up backup-lines and develop strategies of reorganisation. The left-wing mantra of 'overaccumulation' or (as the case may be) 'underconsumption' provides no more than a description of symptoms, couched in concepts *sans phrase*. It makes no reference to the strategic offensive's qualitative driving forces as discussed in this essay: forces that are seeking to shape history from within the Postfordist renewal. Capital will look to the intensification and consolidation of these forces for its further development, although it will also likely reconstitute its profitability by means of a devalorisation of labour and social security, affected, in part, by means of inflation. Obama has picked up on these trends. As people say in the USA, Obama is catering to the IT sector just as Bush catered to the oil-industry; in fact, Obama has turned to the leading IT corporations for advice from the time of his presidential candidacy onward. Energy, the environment, urban planning, social-control, immigration-control and health are the most important sectors for which Obama is propagating IT-driven rationalisation, which he hopes will reduce current expenses by several billion dollars.

What benefit does Obama and what benefit do we draw from comparisons to the Great Depression, if not that of an object lesson? The Great Depression is more important than earlier crises, because its origin and solution reveal capitalism in its most advanced stage of development – and we are still a long way from fully understanding the Great Depression. Will capitalism strive for a similarly murderous solution this time? We have not yet investigated the current crisis thoroughly enough to answer this question confidently. But it is clear that such a murderous solution is anything but out of the question; witness the tough approach Obama has taken to the war in Afghanistan and its extension into Pakistan – a war that follows the logic of 'creatively destroying' stagnant sociability that Dirk Vogelskamp and I already analysed as an anti-crisis strategy in our 2003 book on Iraq.[84] This is the context within which we must remember that between two and three billion people – two billion in China and India alone – are surviving by means of semi-subsistence agriculture, not counting lagers and slum-cities. Has the capitalist trajectory of 'creative destruction' ever respected their lives? In an interview that was both touching and disturbing, Eric Hobsbawm has warned of a new wave of 'creative destruction' analogous to the Second World-War.[85]

Whoever is thinking of contributing reformistically or in any other way to ending the crisis needs to know these things. First and foremost, s/he needs to face up to the violence proper to strategies of innovation and progress. Elision by means of *sans phrase* concepts amounts to participation. The revolutionary left must aim to contribute to the ways in which the offensive is being stalled the world over, acting from its specific location and on the basis of its specific counterknowledge. And since war is part and parcel of the logic of valorisation, the left's efforts must be first and foremost anti-militarist.

---

84. Hartmann and Vogelskamp 2003, pp. 13ff., 31ff. See also Hartmann 2009.
85. *Der Stern*, 17 May 2009.

Housewifisation – Globalisation – Subsistence-Perspective[1]

Maria Mies

Some may ask how the concepts of 'housewifisation', 'globalisation' and 'subsistence' relate to another and whether they are still topical after 35 years. How is reflection on the meaning of these theoretical concepts relevant to answering the questions women – and men – are struggling with in central Europe today? These are legitimate questions. In what follows, I will attempt to answer them. I will begin by formulating some hypotheses:

(1) Not only were the concepts of housewifisation, globalisation and subsistence the right key concepts for feminists seeking to criticise a worldwide, capitalist-patriarchal economic system, but they prove to be more apposite than ever when used to explain the consequences of this economic system, which also affect women and men in the industrialised nations.

(2) Established left-wing theories have proven insufficient both for adequately explaining a globally active capitalism and for opening up a perspective that safeguards the future of nature and of *everyone* on this planet, a future based on ecological and cultural diversity, self-organisation, democracy and a 'good life', meaning the satisfaction of needs and a pacified

---

1. This article is the revised version of a previously unpublished manuscript written around the turn of the millennium (editors' note).

conviviality within the limits of what our planet can provide. This is part of what the concept of the subsistence-perspective means.

(3) Those who demonstrated in Seattle have understood that the WTO is the institution that symbolises a global economic system that is hostile to nature, human beings and women. They have also understood that the WTO is the institution where political rules are established that give large transnational corporations (TNCs), globally operating patriarchal capital, full power not just over nations, provinces and municipalities, but over all aspects of life: food, health, education, culture and life itself are subjugated to commodity-production and the insatiable profit-motive.

(4) People from every country and culture are resisting this new totalitarianism: consumers and peasants, environmentalists and workers, young and elderly people, women and men. In doing so, they are not merely pursuing their own narrow interests; they are demanding an economy that sacrifices neither human beings nor nature to the logic of accumulation. 'People and the planet before profit' was one of the slogans I read in Seattle.[2]

(5) Seattle marks a turning point, a watershed,[3] demonstrating that thousands of people from every country in the world have lost their faith in the principles of neoliberal capitalism – which are destructive of nature, women and human beings – and have already begun replacing them with principles we hold to be fundamental to a subsistence-perspective. Vandana Shiva summarised these principles as follows:

> The centralized, undemocratic rules and structures of the WTO that are establishing global corporate rule based on monopolies and monocultures need to give way to an earth democracy supported by decentralisation and diversity. The rights of all species and the rights of all people must come before the rights of corporations to make limitless profits through limitless destruction.[4]

I want to elaborate on these hypotheses by recounting the genesis of the subsistence-approach as it was developed by Veronika Bennholdt-Thomsen, Claudia von Werlhof and myself in the late 1970s. Forgetful times like ours render such retrospection necessary. I will engage in it even at the risk of reiterating familiar notions (or rather notions that have *not yet* been forgotten).

---

2. Mies 2000.
3. Shiva (no date).
4. Shiva (no date).

The beginnings

In 1978 and 1979, Cologne's University of Applied Science hosted conferences on the topic of 'Underdevelopment and Subsistence-Production'. Much of the preparatory work was done by Hans Dieter Evers, Veronika Bennholdt-Thomsen, Claudia von Werlhof, Georg Elwert and others then working within the university's research-programme on development-sociology. At the time, I was a professor of sociology in the university's department of social pedagogy. I was invited to several of the conferences because I had spent several years living, working and doing research in a developing country (India), like Veronika Bennholdt-Thomsen, Claudia von Werlhof and my other colleagues in Bielefeld.[5]

These conferences marked the first steps towards formulating what would later be called the 'Bielefeld' or 'subsistence-' approach. I have always preferred the second moniker, since I contributed to developing the 'subsistence-approach' but always lived and worked in Cologne, not in Bielefeld.

At the time, the development-sociologists in Bielefeld were concerned primarily with resolving the theoretical conundrum of what name to give to the mode of production by which the majority of the people in this world continue to secure their 'reproduction' even today. It was the time of the left-wing debate on 'modes of production'. Marxists with first-hand experience of the situation in developing nations were especially concerned with this issue. These nations had not been industrialised or 'developed'. Most of the people living there were not 'free wage-workers' in the classic Marxist sense. They were peasants, share-croppers, artisans, small traders, casual workers, prostitutes, beggars and other types of 'subsistence-producers', both in the country and in the city. Some called their mode of production 'pre-capitalist', Maoists called it 'feudal' and still others characterised the diversity of this 'production for survival' as 'heteronomous'. But all were agreed that what people were doing within this mode of production was *not production in the classic-Marxist sense*. These people were not producing commodities, exchange-value and surplus-value; they were *re*-producing their own life. What was at issue, then, was subsistence. We struggled to find a terminology adequate to this mode of production. Hamza Alavi suggested we should speak of a 'colonial mode of production', arguing that the economy we were dealing with was a product of colonisation. I replied that one could just as well speak of a 'household mode of production', seeing as housewives in both industrialised and developing nations were engaging in a similar form of subsistence-reproduction. Being a feminist, I tried to introduce the issue of housework into the debate. The international women's movement had already

---

5. I completed my dissertation on Indian women in 1972 and researched the situation of rural Indian women in 1978 and 1979. See Mies 1982, 1986a.

been hotly debating the role of housework under capitalism for several years.[6] My female friends and I had been trying for as long to understand the theoretical and structural links between housework and the work of peasants in developing nations. As feminists, we were no longer prepared to follow the example of left-wing and liberal economists by ignoring women's work. We recognised that this work, just like that of peasants in Mexico and India, had been forgotten, and that it was a necessary condition for the functioning of the capitalist system. The feminist debate on housework and authors such as Mariarosa Dalla Costa and Silvia Federici had taught us that housework contributes to surplus-value, making it *productive* and not merely *re-productive*, for it is women who produce the commodity labour-power.[7] We recognised that subsistence-farmers played a similar role to ensure the functioning of capitalism. We tested our hypothesis on the importance of subsistence-production for capital-accumulation by means of further empirical research in India, Mexico and Venezuela.[8]

Our male colleagues in Bielefeld chose not to join us in our theoretical endeavour of integrating women's work into the analysis of subsistence- 'reproduction'. They eventually dropped the subsistence-approach, which came to be known as the 'Bielefeld approach'. Neither of the two women who had contributed significantly to the development of this approach was given tenure at Bielefeld University. They were in fact attacked and marginalised, precisely because of their role in developing the subsistence-approach. That is one reason why I feel it is wrong to continue calling the approach the 'Bielefeld approach'.

Rosa Luxemburg's 'The Accumulation of Capital' and the search for a new economics

We however continued our search for a convincing theoretical explanation of the 'blind-spots in the critique of political economy'.[9] In doing so, we 'discovered' Rosa Luxemburg and in particular her main work, *The Accumulation of Capital*. As *feminists*, we were looking for answers Marx, Engels and other male theorists of the left did not provide us with. The most important questions we were trying to answer were the following: (1) the women's question, and in particular the question of why housework has no value both in capitalist and in Marxist theory and practice; (2) the colonial question, or the question of why the nations of Asia, Africa and South America continue to be economic colonies of the imperialist metropoles of Europe, North America and Japan even after politi-

---

6. James 1985; Cox and Federici 1975; Bock and Duden 1977.
7. Dalla Costa and James 1972; Cox and Federici 1975.
8. Bennholdt-Thomsen 1982; Mies 1982; Werlhof 1985.
9. Werlhof 1998.

cal decolonisation; and (3) the nature- or ecology-question. How could women and foreign people be liberated given that they are treated merely as exploitable natural resources, just like outer nature? What is the relationship between the exploitation of these 'three colonies' in both the capitalist and the socialist industrialised nations? What is the relationship to nature that underpins both the capitalist and the socialist paradigm of progress?[10]

Rosa Luxemburg did not raise these questions as such. She was not a feminist. While she was a friend of Clara Zetkin, the founder and leader of Germany's proletarian women's movement, she did not think much of Clara's efforts to mobilise proletarian women. The Social-Democratic Party of Germany felt Clara Zetkin and the socialist women's movement ought to focus on strengthening the nuclear-family, maternity-protection, children and other 'women's issues'. But the women's movement was to have no voice within the party. 'That was the reason', according to Richard J. Evans, 'why a devoted revolutionary such as Rosa Luxemburg did not concern herself with the women's movement'.[11] She wanted to be in 'real' politics, and then as now, 'real' politics was the domain of men. Rosa Luxemburg criticised Clara Zetkin for concerning herself with 'just' the women's question. She once wrote to Leo Jogiches:

> Clara is good as ever, but she lets herself be distracted somehow. She remains caught up in women's issues and does not concern herself with general issues. So I am *all alone*.[12]

Rosa Luxemburg agreed, then, that women's issues were not *general* causes. At the very least, she saw no relationship between the women's question and what she called general questions, such as colonialism, the brutally violent treatment of so-called primitive peoples at the hands of the capitalist powers, militarism and the preparations for war. Nor was she upset by 'proletarian anti-feminism'. She overheard the chauvinist remarks made by many of her male comrades, such as Kautsky's statement that 'comrade Luxemburg confuses everything' because of her allegedly inferior capacity for rational thinking.[13] As for August Bebel, the author of a weighty theoretical work on *Women and Socialism*, he had this to say about Clara Zetkin and Rosa Luxemburg in a 1910 letter to Kautsky:

> Women are something of a riddle. Once their penchants, passions or conceits are somehow at issue, once they are disregarded or offended, even the most intelligent of them loses her temper and becomes hostile to the point of

---

10. Bennholdt-Thomsen, Mies and Werlhof 1998.
11. Evans 1979, p. 319.
12. Quoted in Evans 1979, p. 320.
13. Neusüß 1992, pp. 127–9.

> senselessness. Love and hate are ever in close proximity. Regulating reason is
> absent.[14]

Sounds familiar, doesn't it? It still does. Women are just emotional. They lack
'regulating reason', which is to be found only in the brains of men. But Rosa
Luxemburg wanted to be in real, general politics; she did not want to be left
standing in a corner. That is why she constantly took issue with the Social
Democratic Party's male thinkers and their faith in science and the possibility
of planning revolution in a rational, logical way, with military precision, as our
friend Christel Neusüß, who passed away in 1988, wrote. When her comrades
mocked her 'hysterical materialism', she simply overheard them. Like many
women in left-wing organisations up unto this day, she swallowed her dismay
at the treatment of women such as herself and her rage at her male comrades
because she believed in the importance of their common 'general cause'. To her,
the women's question was something that needed to be appended to this general
cause: a marginal problem.

As feminists, we had little to learn from Rosa Luxemburg. But because we,
like the entire new women's movement in its early stages, never thought of the
theoretical and practical solution to the women's question as a marginal issue to
be appended to other, general-theoretical models, we resolved to get to the heart
of the matter. And the fundamental fact, we soon realised, is that humans need
to exist in a material-corporeal form before they can make and produce history.[15]
This being-there does not just happen. Women – mothers – are the ones who
create human beings, and this act of creation is not merely an unconscious act
of nature: it is work.[16] Women have to perform an infinite amount of work to
turn a child into an adult who can then go on to stand in front of a factory-gate
or -office and sell 'their labour-power', a labour-power largely produced not by
themselves, but by their mother.[17] How is it, we and many other feminists asked,
that all this work, the work of mothers and housewives, has no value under capitalism? Why is the work that goes into producing a car valuable, while the work
that produces a human being is without value? Why is the production of commodities called production while the work of a housewife and mother is called
reproduction?

Looking for answers to these sorts of questions in Marx's writings, we soon
found he used the same concept of work as bourgeois national economists, and
in particular Adam Smith. *Production* was the manufacturing of commodities
or exchange-values for the purpose of obtaining surplus-value. The only work

---

14. Evans 1979, p. 52.
15. Marx and Engels 1975–2004a.
16. Bennholdt-Thomsen, Mies and Werlhof 1998, pp. 67–70.
17. Salleh 1997.

considered *productive* is work that serves this purpose. What women do is *reproduction*, and in particular the reproduction of labour-power. The production of commodities/surplus-value clearly ranks higher than so-called reproduction, because it is only the production of commodities/surplus-value that creates 'value', that is, capital. Thus, while capital requires ever new live, healthy, stalwart, well-nourished, clean and sexually satisfied human beings whose labour-power it can extract, the work performed in order to create such human beings is considered a mere repetition. Worse, it is considered a quasi-natural process, one that occurs all by itself, like the cycle of spring, summer, autumn and winter. And we are told nothing new ever comes of this repetition or reproduction. The new – ever new automobile-models, generations of computers, cloned sheep, genetically modified foods and the like – results only from production that aims at surplus-value. But we in no way objected to what was called reproduction, and I in fact insisted that it was genuine production: the production of life, or of subsistence, which is, contrary to the production of commodities, for the purpose of maximising profit. That is why I stopped using the term 'subsistence *reproduction*' and spoke instead of 'subsistence-*production*'.[18]

But simply noting that housework – and in particular the work of mothers – has no value within the capitalist economy was not enough. It was enough to simply ascribe this fact to the malice of men or interpret it (as some attempted to) as a residuum of feudalism. Why does capital require this unpaid, unpayable, 'valueless' work?

It was here that Rosa Luxemburg's *Accumulation of Capital* proved useful to us. Luxemburg wrote her main work, a study of economics, at a time when she was engaging, both theoretically and politically, with imperialism and fighting imperial Germany's warmongering. The book was first published in 1913. In it, Luxemburg criticised Marx for having argued, in *Capital* Volume II, that the 'expanded reproduction of capital', or the infinite process of capital-accumulation (now known as 'growth'), occurs only by virtue of capital's exploitation of the wage-working class. According to Marx, developed capitalism requires neither additional, extra-economic violence nor additional territories (such as colonies) for exploitation. Nor does it require nature. The wages the capitalist pays his workers never contain the full surplus-value they have created, but only as much as they need for the reproduction of their labour-power, and this is why, according to Marx, every production-cycle ends with a surplus that can be reinvested.

Yet Rosa Luxemburg shows that if capital is to maintain its perpetual accumulation, it requires additional means of production and raw materials, additional workers and additional markets, all of which are absent in its original territories

---

18. Mies 1983.

and can no longer be produced there. Rosa Luxemburg speaks of 'non-capitalist modes of production' that capitalism requires even in its most developed form, if it is to continue growing or accumulating.

'Yet, as we have seen, capitalism in its full maturity also depends in all respects on non-capitalist strata and social organizations existing side by side with it'.[19]

The first of these 'non-capitalist' societies and strata were the peasants of England and Europe, the African slaves (both male and female) deported to the Caribbean and the USA and all the colonies subjugated by Western capital all over the world. Rosa Luxemburg also points out that the exploitation and depredation of these 'non-capitalist' territories and societies does not occur through the 'civil' capital-wage relation that requires no 'extra-economic violence' (that is how Marx defined capitalist exploitation), but rather through direct and extremely brutal violence, through conquest, war, piracy and arbitrary appropriation. Marx believed such direct violence belonged to the genesis, the birth-pangs and the prehistory of actual capitalism: to the period he called 'primitive accumulation'. But Rosa Luxemburg demonstrated that this violence is necessary throughout the history of capitalism: 'The development of capitalism has been possible only through constant expansion into new domains of production and new nations. But the global drive to expand leads to a collision between capital and pre-capitalist forms of society, resulting in violence, war, revolution: in brief, catastrophes from start to finish, the vital element of capitalism'.[20]

This means capital-accumulation requires *'ongoing primitive accumulation'* and its methods, namely *violence*, if it is to continue at all. But Rosa Luxemburg derived another insight from her analysis: from first to last, capitalism aims at the depredation of the entire world, or, as Wallerstein says, it is a 'world system'.

> Capital needs the means of production and the labour power of the whole globe for untrammelled accumulation; it cannot manage without the natural resources and the labour power of all territories. [...] Yet if the countries of those branches of production are predominantly non-capitalist, capital will endeavour to establish domination over these countries and societies. And in fact, primitive conditions allow of a greater drive and of far more ruthless measures than could be tolerated under purely capitalist social conditions.[21]

Rereading this passage, I thought immediately of the nations of Southeast Asia: until the autumn of 1997, 'Asian tigers' such as South Korea, Thailand and Malaysia boasted growth-rates that made capitalism's core-states turn green with envy. But I was also reminded of the violence there, directed largely against young

19. Luxemburg 2003, p. 345.
20. Luxemburg 1972.
21. Luxemburg 2003, p. 346.

women within and without the free production-zones (FPZs) of Bangladesh, Hong Kong, Thailand, India and the entire region, a violence I had witnessed first-hand in November of 1997. Violence, and especially violence against women, practised in areas that I continue to refer to as economic colonies, is the secret of accumulation, which cannot be fully understood as long as reference is made only to wage-labour that is orderly, legally protected, unionised and usually male. Violence is an economic factor, as Rosa Luxemburg already understood. Violence is not simply a consequence of male sadism, as some feminists believe, nor was Marx right to consider it natural, a 'birth-pang' by which capitalism was born amidst blood and tears. Marx abuses this childbirth-metaphor to explain the original violence of capitalism. Christel Neusüß makes reference to Rosa Luxemburg in order to criticise his view:

> Later, once it's been properly established, it won't need violence anymore. It will work productively – peacefully, somewhat to the detriment of labour-power, it's true, but without anything resembling the murderous escapades of the conquistadors. This is the point at which our comrade [Luxemburg, M. M.] strictly refuses to believe Marx. He's wrong, it's plain to see. Violence is booming the world over. Enormous arsenals have been built over time, one colonial war follows another and entire African tribes have been liquidated *en passant*. [...] The hour of birth can't possibly last this long, four hundred years, still oozing blood and filth even though socialism is supposed to be around the corner! No, our old comrade must have been systematically mistaken.[22]

Women: the last colony, or, the housewifisation of work

I have already pointed out that Rosa Luxemburg did not reflect on the situation of women. But her analysis of capital-accumulation helped us, my friends and me, to gain a better understanding of the status of housework under capitalism. This work, like that of peasants, the colonies or other 'non-capitalist milieus' (as Rosa calls them), is available 'free of charge' like nature; unprotected by labour-law and contracts and available around the clock, it represents the cheapest and politically most efficient way of *reproducing* labour-power available to capital. Moreover, and as I discovered in my research on Indian lacemakers, *outwork* is also the cheapest and most efficient form of *production-work*.[23]

We extended Rosa Luxemburg's analysis to women's work, and in particular to housework under capitalism. It is these workers – along with nature, the colonies, subsistence-farmers and the many people working in the so-called

---

22. Neusüß 1988, p. 298.
23. Mies 1982.

informal sector the world over – who form the basis of what is called the economy: the articulation of capital and wage-labour. The *housewifisation of work* was and continues to be the trick by which capital keeps women's work devalued, unorganised and atomised, free to access it all times and to reject it whenever it pleases – at no cost. If we consider the economy from the point of view of women and women's work and take housework into account, we find that 50 percent of the world's population performs 65 percent of productive work but receives less than 10 percent of all wage-income worldwide.[24] This is possible because housework, including the work of mothers, is declared non-work and thus rendered invisible. This rendering invisible of what is vital and life-sustaining – women, nature, oppressed peoples, classes and tribes – is part and parcel of a patriarchal economy that has reached its apogee under capitalism. But actually existing socialism also failed to do away with it. As I was able to show in 1988, socialist accumulation also presupposes colonisation and the housewifisation of work.

Housewifisation

The redefinition of capitalism's sexual division of labour and the definition of the woman as housewife are not the result of a congenital male misogyny but a structural necessity for the process of capital-accumulation. Housework remains unremunerated and is therefore ignored in the calculation of the gross national product. It is not even defined as work, but rather considered an expression of female anatomy or 'love'. It is temporally unlimited and apparently abundantly available, like sunlight and air, like a natural resource or (as the economists say) a 'free good' that men and capitalists can simply appropriate. But according to feminism's analysis, it is precisely this unremunerated housework, in combination with the subsistence work of peasants, particularly in the Third World, whose exploitation constitutes the secret of ongoing capital-accumulation.[25] Without this 'housewifisation' of women, which now occurs on an international scale, the North could not maintain its productivity gains and economic growth.[26]

I coined the term 'housewifisation' in 1978–9, in the context of my research on lacemakers in Narsapur, southern India. Scottish missionaries brought the lace-making industry to this area in the nineteenth century and taught poor rural women to produce lace in their homes; this lace was then sold in Europe, the USA and Australia. The women earned a fraction of the minimum-wage

---

24. Salleh 1997, p. 77.
25. Dalla Costa and James 1972; Cox and Federici 1975; Bock and Duden 1977; Werlhof 1998; Bennholdt-Thomsen 1983; Mies 1986b; Waring 1989.
26. Bennholdt-Thomsen, Mies and Werlhof 1998.

normally paid rural workers (0.58 rupees). The exploitation of these women, who worked according to the putting-out system and received piece-wages, worked because the exporters, who had gone on to become millionaires, treated the women as housewives who might as well put the time they were assumed to spend sitting around at home to productive use. Thus housewifisation means not just that labour-power is reproduced free of charge thanks to private housework; to the extent that it takes the form of outwork or similar, typically female working relationships, it also represents the cheapest form of production-work.[27]

Yet this housewifisation of women is not called into question even when women are economically active or earn the entire family-income, as is increasingly often the case. Women's wages are lower than men's almost everywhere in the world; in Germany, they amount to only sixty to seventy percent of men's wages.

One of the justifications offered for this wage-difference is that women's income is merely a supplement to the income of the male breadwinner. Women are often not given secure jobs because their employers believe they will return to the hearth when they become pregnant or the economy goes into crisis. The categories of 'part-time work' and 'low wage groups' were invented primarily for housewives. They are the first to be sacked during an economic recession. Their chances of promotion are drastically lower than men's, even in academic work. There are hardly any women in the higher echelons of management or university.

Analysis of housewifisation remains incomplete, however, for as long as it is not related to colonisation or – to use the current term – the international division of labour. Housewifisation and colonisation are not just two processes that occurred during the same historical period, the eighteenth and nineteenth centuries. They are also substantially related to one another. Without the conquest of colonies and the exploitation of their resources and human labour, the European class of entrepreneurs would not have been able to begin its industrial revolution. Scientists would hardly have found any capitalists interested in their inventions. The middle class of salaried workers would hardly have had the money to pay for a 'non-working housewife' and servants. And workers would have continued leading a miserable proletarian existence. Colonialism was the material foundation for the increase in the productivity of human labour that made industrial expansion possible in the first place. Today's international division of labour rests on the same exploitative structures. Without them, the abundance of commodities and the relatively high standard of living that even the working class of the industrialised nations enjoys would be impossible to maintain.[28]

---

27. Mies 1982.
28. Mies 1986b. On 'housewifisation', see Mies 1997, pp. 207–10.

International housewifisation

But it has now become clear that the invention of the 'housewife' was/is more than just the best method to keep the reproductive costs of labour-power as low as possible; she is also the best possible worker for commodity-production. This first became clear in the Third World, to which central sectors of production were outsourced from the West during the mid-1970s, such as electronics, textiles and toys. The wages of the women working in these sectors amount to a tenth of the corresponding wages in the industrialised nations. The fact that the nations affected are known as 'low-wage countries' is strongly linked to the recruitment of young, female workers. These women are usually not unionised, they are often laid off when they marry or have children and their working conditions are exploitative. The classic form of 'housewifed' production work to be found on the world-market is, however, outwork, which allows women to combine domestic and family-work with the production of goods for the world-market. These women enjoy no employment protection and work in complete isolation. They receive the lowest wages and often work the longest hours. Female workers are also employed on the housewife-model in other branches of production, such as agriculture, retail and services.[29]

This can also be seen in the many development-projects conceived of for women in the Third World. Most of them fall into the category of 'income generating activities'. They generally start from the assumptions that women are married and that they are housewives whose livelihood is earned by a male 'breadwinner'. Their income is then considered supplementary to the man's. That is why their work is not defined as work but as 'activity' – such that it can be exempted from the stipulations of labour-law.

This strategy of 'international housewifisation' did not change substantially when the World Bank introduced a new terminology. In 1988, talk of 'integrating women into development' was replaced by talk of 'investment in women'. Women producing for domestic markets and for the world market were called 'entrepreneurs'. The World Bank had understood that poor women who must sustain their families work much more reliably than men: they are much more productive. Barbara Herz, the World Bank's Advisor on Women, writes:

> As a general proposal, it makes sense to grant women the same broad range of economic options as other entrepreneurs, so that they can weigh market potential against their family responsibilities instead of assuming they must continue with a certain activity. Culture may limit the range and pace of such expansion, *but the economic benefits of deregulation should be clear.*[30]

---

29. Werlhof 1985; Mies 1986a.
30. Herz 1988, p. 2 (my emphasis).

It is interesting to note that the use of the term 'entrepreneur' does not involve women being freed from their family-responsibilities, differently from male entrepreneurs. The concept of 'deregulation' is also revealing. It implies that these small producers, traders, peasants etc. have no claim to union-rights or social labour-protection. They are considered 'self-employed'. Thus the housewife becomes an entrepreneur as well. But what is at issue is still the exploitation of the cheapest source of labour-power for the purpose of world-market production.

The globalisation of the economy and the persistence of housewifisation

The relevance of this analysis today

What we wrote on the relationship between the exploitation of 'housewifed' female labour-power and capital-accumulation 30 years ago is revealing its full pertinence today, in the age of so-called economic globalisation. One could even say that in the globalised economy, this form of exploitation has become the model for the exploitation of labour in general. Today, the 'standard employment-relationship' is no longer a relationship between capital and a (male) 'free wage-worker' but one that involves 'flexible', 'atypical', 'Third-World-ified' and 'unprotected' – in brief: 'housewifed' – male and female workers. It's no wonder entrepreneurs no openly sing praises to the 'publicly unharnessed, global(ised) and applied housewife'.[31] Claudia von Werlhof quotes Christian Lutz, editor of the Swiss manager's magazine *Impuls*, welcoming the end of free wage-labour and demanding that workers acquire the skills of women and housewives in an article titled '*Die Zukunft der Arbeit ist weiblich*' ('The Future of Work is Female'). According to Lutz, the 'megatrend' now encompassing all 'valorisation-networks' requires 'proactive behaviour, ideas, a willingness to assume responsibility and social skills', all of which he claims are more likely to be found in women than in men. 'The worker of the future is female'.[32]

Thus capital is openly admitting what Claudia von Werlhof already described as the future of workers in 1983: the housewifisation of male as well as female workers. In her essay, 'The Proletarian is Dead: Long Live the Housewife!', von Werlhof showed that male, unionised workers remunerated according to the regular pay-scale no longer represented the best possible source of labour-power for capital, having ceded this status to the housewife. In contrast to that of the

---

31. Werlhof 1999, p. 81.
32. Christian Lutz, quoted in Werlhof 1999.

proletarian, the housewife's labour-power is flexible, available around the clock, cheap, and reliable; it also does not become a burden for entrepreneurs in times of crisis. Von Werlhof predicted that men too would become 'housewifed' in this way.[33]

In 1983–4, this strategy was still discussed under the heading 'flexibilisation of work'. It was praised as a necessary result of the rationalisation of work brought about by means of microelectronics and computers. Trade-unions responded to the strategy by demanding a reduction of the workday without any change in wages. But even this strategy was unable to stop the crisis of work, which was caused not just by new technologies but also by the globalisation of the economy. Former German Economics Minister Günther Rexrodt openly suggested creating a 'low-wage sector' within the German economy in order to stop German capital outsourcing to 'low-wage countries'. Following the collapse of the Soviet bloc, the list of such 'low-wage countries' included not just the nations of the 'Third World', but also all of Eastern Europe, including East Germany. These are the new colonies of capital.

It comes as no surprise, after the above, that Rexrodt envisioned Germany's new 'low-wage sector' as one employing mainly women. After all, Rexrodt argued, women are wonderfully qualified for such a sector. What he did not say, but what emerged from the free-trade agreements of the WTO, is that the entire world, including the wealthy industrialised nations, is to become a single free-trade zone. In it, TNCs plan to create the kind of employment- and environmental conditions currently familiar from Asia and Mexico (see below). The concept 'globalisation of the economy' refers to opening the world's economic spaces up to the capitalist market-economy. Capitalism has tended to function as a world-system from its colonial beginnings, as shown by Marx, Luxemburg and Immanuel Wallerstein. But today's talk of globalisation refers to processes promoted by institutions such as the General Agreement on Tariffs and Trade (GATT), the World Bank, the International Monetary Fund (IMF) and the US Department of Agriculture since the late 1980s. Negotiations over GATT were concluded with the creation of the World Trade Organisation (WTO) in 1995.

We can distinguish three phases of globalisation:

(1) The colonial phase, which lasted until the end of World War II and was replaced by developmental colonialism.

(2) The phase of the so-called international division of labour, which began in the early 1970s and is characterised by the outsourcing of entire branches of production – textiles, electronics, toys – from the traditional industrial centres to so-called low-wage countries (South Korea, Philippines, Malaysia, Mexico).

---

33. Werlhof 1998.

(3) The current phase, characterised by the worldwide abolition of protec-
tionist trade-barriers, promotion of free trade and the expansion of commodity-
production and commodity-consumption to all areas of reality. The worldwide
assertion of free trade by means of GATT and the WTO was originally to be
followed by the lifting of all barriers to investment. This was the aim of the
Multilateral Agreement on Investment (MAI). In December of 1998, a worldwide
protest-movement helped prevent its implementation.

What was said above concerning international housewifisation is especially
relevant to analysis of the second phase of globalisation, characterised by the
creation of world-market factories, free production-zones (FPZs) in Asia and
'maquilas' in Mexico. The fact that wages in these FPZs and world-market factories were and continue to be so low can be traced back not only to the fact
that about 80 percent of the workforce consists of young, usually unmarried,
women, but also to the fact that these women are defined as 'housewives'. They
are employed because of their housewifely qualifications: their 'dexterous fin-
gers', docility, diligence and sewing skills – not to forget the fact that they can
be laid off once they marry, which allows employers to undercut all claims to
maternity-leave and employment-protection. Moreover, trade-unions were not
allowed inside these factories. Profits could be exported in their entirety. Since
most of the female workers came from poor rural families, did not know their
rights and had no experience of labour-struggles, they were willing to accept
working and living conditions that were often inhuman, workdays of up to
12 hours, an inhuman work-pace, sexual harassment and security- and health-
risks that are legally punishable in the traditional industrialised nations. For
example, workers in South Korea were locked inside the factory until they had
produced a fixed quantity of goods. When people spoke of South Korea, Thailand, Singapore and Malaysia as successful 'new tigers', they overlooked the fact
that the economic miracle undergone by these nations rested largely on the brutal exploitation of women defined as housewives.

The ideological hegemony of neoliberalism

Asian 'free' production-zones (FPZs) and Mexican *maquilas* might be described as
laboratories for testing the neoliberal economic theory that has rapidly achieved
worldwide hegemony in the course of globalisation.

As an ideological and theoretical construct, neoliberalism was first developed
by the economists and social scientists of the so-called Chicago School.[34] Centres of neoliberal theory included the London School of Economics and later the

---

34. The term 'neoliberalism' was already used as early as 1945. It was coined in the
context of the founding of the Mont Pèlerin Society. See Walpen 2004.

Universities of Chicago and London, as well as institutions such as the Mont Pélerin Society, where the think-tanks of neoliberal theory met. Superating the theories of John Maynard Keynes was and continues to be neoliberalism's explicit aim. Keynes provided the theoretical foundations for the economies of the US New Deal (Fordism), National Socialism and the welfare-states and mixed economies of postwar Europe and many Third World nations. Neoliberals refer to the doctrines of Adam Smith (1723–90) and David Ricardo (1772–1823) in order to reject every form of state-intervention in the economy. They envision a market that develops purely in accordance with the laws of supply and demand, with unfettered international competition eventually creating a 'level playing field' for all 'global players'. A central assumption is that it is ultimately to everyone's benefit for the economy to be determined not by principles such as self-sufficiency or the protection of domestic firms and jobs (protectionism), but by the search for comparative cost-advantages.

According to Bernhard Walpen, this faith in the absolute power of the market is not based on empirical, scientific insights but on the generalisation of 'market theory's simplistic cost/benefit calculus, which is applied to human behaviour in its entirety'.[35] This generalisation of the cost/benefit calculus rests on a view of humans (or rather of men) that considers personal gain as the economy's only driving force. According to Adam Smith, the universal pursuit of egoism will bring about the greatest possible gain for everyone, 'as if by an invisible hand'.

If this faith in the absolute power of the 'free' market was able to achieve such hegemonic diffusion, this was not due to the plausibility or scientific value of the doctrine, but rather to various practico-political interventions. To begin with, neoliberal think-tanks made sure the decisive positions at universities, research-facilities and within the state were given to neoliberals.[36] Then, following the 1973 military coup in Chile, they seized the opportunity to transform neoliberal economic theory into political practice. This was done in the context of Pinochet's dictatorship. In the 1980s, Margaret Thatcher and Ronald Reagan restructured the economies of the UK and the USA in accordance with the neoliberal model.

In Third World nations, the structural-adjustment programmes (SAPs) developed by the World Bank and the International Monetary Fund were already being used to promote neoliberal economic policy. The free-trade zones of these nations already operated in accordance with neoliberal principles. All in all, neoliberalism's breakthrough was not a result of its superior theoretical arguments or the practical successes of the 'free market' but of dictatorial, top-down interventions. These interventions rested on three pillars: globalisation, liberalisation

---

35. Walpen 1996, p. 3.
36. Walpen 2004; George 1999; Clarke 1997.

and privatisation ('GLP policy'). Until the late 1980s, this GLP policy was limited to a few nations. Since the fall of the Berlin wall, the implementation of GATT (1994) and the creation of the WTO, neoliberal economic policy has been written into international treaties and is considered the only way forward.

Today, we are witnessing not only the factual globalisation of this ideology, with all the barriers that nations erected to protect their economies being torn down, but also a worldwide increase in violence, especially violence against women, children and other vulnerable groups. This violence is on the increase not only in the territories of the Third World (and especially within FPZs),[37] but also in the capitalist centres, which think of themselves as 'civil society'. As we have seen, this violence is part of ongoing primitive accumulation.

The best way to represent such an economy is by the image of an *iceberg*. Normally we only consider the part of the iceberg that is above water, capital and wage-labour, to constitute the economy. All unwaged labour – especially that of housewives, but also that of subsistence producers and all other colonies, including nature's production – is below the surface. All costs capital refuses to pay are relegated to this invisible economy or 'externalised'. Nor have workers and their representatives (trade-unions) fought to render this economy visible. To date, they have never called for it to be taken into account in calculations of the costs associated with, for example, the gross national product. For their share of economic wealth also rests on the exploitation of the 'underwater economy'. Within the iceberg model of the dominant economy, the term 'economy' is reserved for the visible part that is above water, namely the growth economy, which is limited to producing and trading in commodities for the purpose of accumulating ever more money and capital. The satisfaction of human needs is merely a side effect of this accumulation of money and capital. The part of the economy that is 'above water' is the only one to appear in the national economic calculus (gross national product or gross domestic product, the total goods and services produced during one year and expressed in monetary terms).[38]

But what appears 'above water' is far from being the entire capitalist economy; it is only the visible part. Yet the *visible* economy is supported and subsidised by the *invisible* economy. Generally speaking, all activities performed within the 'invisible economy' have been 'naturalised'. They are alleged not to contribute to capital-accumulation. Instead, they are said to have no other purpose than producing and maintaining one's own life, one's own subsistence. Thus, as Claudia von Werlhof argues, everything that capital wishes to dispose of free of charge is 'declared' to be part of nature. The lower strata subsidise the visible economy.

---

37. Mies 1999.
38. Waring 1989.

That is why we refer to them as colonies. Without this colonial foundation, capitalism would not exist.

Globalisation exposes reality

The effects of globalisation are not the ones expected by all those who have hitherto been given short shrift. Instead of improving their lot by means of 'catch-up development', more and more male and female wage-workers are losing their jobs in the visible economy and descending into the invisible economy. Secure employment becomes casual employment, factory-work becomes outwork, unionised and legally protected employment becomes housewifed employment. Nor is there any 'trickle-down effect', as dominant economic theory would have us believe: wealth is not spreading from the top of the pyramid to those given short shrift at its base. In fact, precisely the opposite is the case. More and more wealth is being accumulated at the tip of the 'iceberg'. It is extracted from the various strata of the 'underwater' economy, where it is then *lacking*. As early as 1996, a United Nations Development Project report noted that global growth has led to the wealthy 20 percent of the world's population increasing their share of global wealth from 70 to 85 percent within thirty years, even as the share of the poorest 20 percent was reduced from 2.3 to 1.4 percent. The growing gap between wealthy and poor nations, classes and sexes is not disavowed. Some even doubt that economic growth can close the gap, but no one is willing to admit that the gap is a necessary, structural consequence of permanent growth in a limited world. There can be no equality for all under global capitalist patriarchy. Even the World Bank admits this, albeit indirectly, when it states that inequalities in wages, income and wealth are a necessary corollary of the 'transition' from a socialist to a capitalist economy.[39]

Poverty and inequality are on the rise within wealthy societies as well. In the USA, the minimum-wage has become a mere pittance. An average hourly wage of 5.15 US dollars now buys 19 percent less than it did in 1979. Moreover, the average worker now has to spend an annual 148 hours more at work in order to earn this wage. By contrast, the income of top managers has increased many times over. In 1980, the average top manager earned 42 times more than the average worker; in 1997, he earned 326 times as much as a factory-worker.[40] The situation in Germany is beginning to resemble that in the USA. According to a study by Caritas published in 1999,[41] there exists an enormous gap between

---

39. The Economist 1996, p. 36.
40. Montague 1999, pp. 4–6.
41. Caritas is the German branch of the Roman Catholic Church's international relief-agency, equivalent to Catholic Relief Services (CRS) in the USA (translator's note).

the uppermost 20 percent of the German population, who earn a third of the national income, and the bottom 10 percent, who earn only 4.1 percent. This social inequality is even more pronounced in East Germany.[42]

Globalisation without a 'human face'

During the second phase of globalisation, people were still able to cherish the illusion that the export-ortiented industrialisation of the Third World would benefit not only consumers in wealthy nations, but also poor nations, such that everyone would eventually achieve Sweden's level of economic development. But the neoliberal restructuring of the world-economy we have been witnessing since the 1990s makes it impossible to maintain this belief. Christa Wichterich has poignantly described the negative consequences of globalisation for women in the Third World.[43]

The present third phase of globalisation involves the continuation and extension of processes that began during the second phase, but also their qualitative intensification. For example, GATT and the WTO entail that the strategy of out-sourcing production to low-wage countries is being extended to virtually the entire world. Moreover, it is no longer only labour-intensive, high-wage industries that are being outsourced, but also environmentally harmful heavy industry (the steel-industry, shipbuilding, the auto-industry, coal mining, and such like). In addition to this, and thanks to the new communications-technologies, entire large parts of the service-sector can now be outsourced to low-wage countries. A number of airlines have already moved their accounting departments to India, and Indian software-firms are successfully competing with firms in the USA and Europe.

The consequences of this global restructuring for the traditional industrial-ised nations go beyond the loss of women's jobs. It is now male workers (long-term employees) who are laid off when firms outsource production. In the USA, this development was already evident during the early 1990s. In Germany, it has become noticeable since the turn of the millennium, although it began much earlier. All industrialised nations thought globalising the economy and opening up markets was a good idea; at the very least, they thought these developments were inevitable. The governments of these nations agreed to GATT without exception. There were no protests except in some poor nations and by peasants, such as in India. Everyone seemed to believe that so-called free trade would also entail greater liberty for individuals. And yet it should have been as clear as day how capitalist free trade works. Capital always goes where wages are lowest, where there are no sanctions for exploiting the environment and where effective

---

42. *Frankfurter Rundschau*, 22 October 1999.
43. Wichterich 1998.

trade-unions that can enforce labour-regulations are absent (as in China). The dogma of *comparative cost-advantage*, central to neoliberal economic policy, is applied primarily to the advantageous labour-costs in low-wage countries. According to Pam Woodall, the hourly wages of production-workers were as follows in 1994:[44]

Germany	25	USD
USA	16	USD
Poland	1.40	USD
Mexico	2.40	USD
India, China, Indonesia	0.50	USD

In fact, this is how Pam Woodall describes the Third World's comparative cost-advantage within global free trade: 'The benefit of international trade consists in countries exploiting their comparative cost advantages, not trying to be 'equal'. And a large part of the comparative cost advantages of the Third World resides, in one way or another, in the fact that they are poor, and especially in their cheap labor and greater tolerance of environmental pollution'.[45]

A central aspect of comparative advantage that Pam Woodall does not mention is the fact that the cheapest of all cheap labour is women's labour, namely the labour of women who have been 'construed' as housewives. This already became clear during the second phase of globalisation, but it has become far more evident during the third phase, for global restructuring now affects all nations, all economic sectors (including agriculture) and all employment-relations – including those of women in the export-oriented textile-, electronics-, toy- and shoe-industries. These workers once hoped to achieve some approximation of humane working conditions – the 'core labour-standards' as defined by the International Labour Organisation (ILO) – by means of labour-struggles. But they have now seen the TNCs they worked for simply leaving their country and moving to where labour is cheaper still, from South Korea to Bangladesh or China. Or they have found that these TNCs will simply hire cheaper workers from China, as in Hong Kong. However, housewifisation and globalisation still constitute the main strategy for reducing the costs of female labour.

In 1995, the Committee for Asian Women (CAW) published an informative analysis of the consequences of global restructuring for female workers in Asia's industrial centres, focusing especially on the export-processing zones (EPZs) of the Philippines, South Korea, Hong Kong and Singapore. The authors describe an increase in sexist discrimination: men receive stable jobs while women are

---

44. Woodall 1994.
45. Woodall 1994, p. 42.

given only part-time and unprotected work. They also demonstrate that married women are excluded from the formal labour-market, as managers are keen to avoid the costs associated with maternity-leave and related benefits. The going argument is that married women are saddled with too many family-duties and cannot concentrate on their work.[46]

By no means does this entail that married women are 'supported' by their husbands and no longer need to work directly for capital. The pressure exerted on female workers by the transfer of EPZs to even cheaper nations has led to further 'casualisation' of women's work.[47] In other words, stable employment has become precarious employment, protected labour has become unprotected labour, full-time jobs have become part-time jobs and full-time workers have become part-time workers. Factory-work has also been converted to outwork, performed by laid off married women alongside their domestic work and child-care. Some women are also constrained to perform service-work of one sort or another for a few hours at a time. Seventy percent of the women who lost their jobs in industry became casual workers in the service-sector. Entrepreneurs are consciously restructuring employment-relations in accordance with a sexist or patriarchal strategy:

> Working processes are divided up in such a way that they can be paid by the hour, since the work is perceived as *women's work*. Married women can be paid lower wages, as they are perceived to be dependent on their husband. The rapid causalization of work is gender-specific.[48]

And where are these causal workers employed? They work for McDonalds, Spaghetti House, Maxim, in supermarkets, as cleaning ladies, domestic servants or office-workers.

The overall analysis provided by the authors of *Silk and Steel* reveals not just the tendential housewifisation of work associated with globalisation, but also, and more importantly, that this strategy has led to a general deterioration in the working and living conditions of women. Moreover, men feel less and less responsible for their families and may leave their wives and children behind. From capital's point of view, housewifisation represents the best strategy for realising comparative cost-advantages under the conditions of globalisation. For women, housewifisation amounts to a catastrophe.

---

46. Committee for Asian Women (ed.) 1995, p. 31.
47. Casualisation: English in original (translator's note).
48. Chan *et al.* 1995, p. 54.

What does this mean for us?

Our problem is that we cannot understand the processes now unfolding here for as long as we believe that capital employs a different strategy to reduce labour-costs *here* than it does in low-wage countries. The so-called '400 euro jobs' introduced in Germany are also based on the concept of the housewifisation of work.

The old counterstrategies are no longer sufficient

Faced with the new globalisation and liberalisation of the world-market and the 'deregulation' and 'flexibilisation' (or 'housewifisation') of labour described above, traditional trade-union strategy proves insufficient. For women, it has in fact always been insufficient. Not only is it based on the patriarchal-capitalist separation of 'gainful employment' and unremunerated domestic work; it also rests on the assumption that Western industrial society, with its specific patterns of production and consumption, represents a model that ought to be generalised in the course of 'catch-up development'. On this assumption, all putatively 'backward' societies, classes, races, peoples and women are to be gradually raised to the level of the wealthy classes in wealthy nations. Women are to be placed on an 'equal footing' with privileged men.

Yet a strategy that calls only for *redistribution* of the economic cake (from the top down or in such a way as to give women a greater share), without asking how the cake came about in the first place, what its ingredients are, and which areas of our reality need to be colonised for it to be baked, belies an illusionary view of reality.

Given the new worldwide strategy of patriarchal capital, women and men can no longer content themselves with demanding more legally protected wage-work on the basis of economic growth. In a globalised capitalist economy, the demands and rights of some workers can always be undercut by employing cheaper labour in other nations and regions. Typically, the providers of this cheap labour are women, and they are not protected from direct violence either. We need to think about an entirely different economic model. We need an economy that does steal one person's bread so that others may eat cake. Such an economy can no longer be based on permanent growth, that is, on the colonisation of women, nature and foreign peoples.[49]

An economy and a society that are not growth-oriented, non-colonial and non-patriarchal would have to be built upon the principles of subsistence and regionality. More is at issue than the limits of our planet: the principle of

---

49. Mies 1986b.

self-provision, another concept of the 'good life', a critique of consumerism, respect for natural cycles and the crafting of new relations between human beings and nature, men and women, the city and the country, as well as between different peoples, races and ethnicities.[50] In order to make all this real, the first thing we need is a new perspective on reality. We call this perspective the *subsistence-perspective.*[51]

The subsistence-perspective: from critique to perspective

We chose the term 'subsistence-perspective' in order to criticise the Marxist labour-theory of value and the dominant concept of work from a feminist point of view. Later we also used the term to explain our vision of a different economy and society, one congenial to women, nature and human beings. When we speak of 'subsistence', we express our rejection of all colonised conditions, but we also celebrate self-regenerating, creative and autonomous life, of which we are a conscious part.

It is subsistence that is fundamentally opposed to capital, not wage-labour.

For capital, it is a question of transforming all autonomous life into commodities and inserting it into a commodity-relation. Life against the commodity, the commodity against money. Those thus expropriated of their life and their autonomous production of life are left to do what they can to get their hands on at least some of the money. That is what the whole struggle turns on. We surrender our life-strength, and all we have to show for it afterwards is a little money. We have always insisted that the process 'life in exchange for money' is irreversible. Money engenders no new life. Life arises only from life. We must act to reappropriate our lives. That is what subsistence means. To begin with, it means regaining control over the means of subsistence: land, water, air, food and knowledge. In order to realise the subsistence-perspective, we need to create different, living relationships to other people, so that we might produce our life in common. Subsistence-relations between human beings and between human beings and nature need to be reconjoined. Capital has been waging war on subsistence for more than two hundred years.

The former president of the World Bank, Robert McNamara, once formulated the actual goal of capitalism very clearly: 'to draw peasants away from subsistence and into commercial production'. Peasants are to be transformed into market-producers: people who produce not for themselves but for the market. The process continues to this day, without interruption. Now our bodies – one

---

50. Bennholdt-Thomsen, Mies and Werlhof 1998; Mies and Shiva 1993.
51. Bennholdt-Thomsen and Mies 1997.

last part of nature that we have treated in a subsistent manner until now – are being divided into components to be sold and patented by means of genetic engineering. Our last scrap of autonomy over life is being sold neck and crop. To me, autonomy over life is only another way of saying subsistence. I still define 'subsistence-production' the way I did in 1983:

> Subsistence production or life production encompasses all work performed during the creation and maintenance of immediate life, to the extent that such work is directed towards no other purpose. As such, the concept of subsistence production is diametrically opposed to that of commodity or surplus value production. The purpose of subsistence production is life. The purpose of commodity production is money that produces ever more money (the accumulation of capital), with life accruing only as a kind of side effect. It is a typical feature of the capitalist industrial system that it declares everything it wishes to exploit free of charge to be nature or a natural resource. This includes women's housework and the work of peasants in the nations of the Third World. But it also includes the productivity of nature in its entirety.[52]

An alternative definition has been formulated by Erika Märke. According to her, 'subsistence' denotes the property of being self-reliant, of existing by virtue of oneself. Märke lists the following characteristics of subsistence: being self-reliant in the sense of being independent (autonomy), being content with oneself in the sense of not striving for expansion and persisting in oneself in the sense of maintaining one's cultural identity.[53] All of these specifications are central to our positive concept of subsistence. We need all of these qualities, especially when it is a question of formulating a new perspective for society. 'Subsistence' denotes a rejection of every form of colonialism, expansionism and dependence. If we want to be serious about regaining autonomy over our lives, then we have no other choice. The wage-worker can never be independent.

Is there no German word that expresses what we mean by subsistence? There is none. 'Self-reliance' [*Selbstversorgung*] is far too narrow and far too economistic; 'subsistence' opens up a whole new horizon and implies much more. The word expresses everything we expect from a changed social orientation, namely liberty, happiness and self-determination within the bounds of the 'realm of necessity' – not in some otherworldy sphere, but here on Earth. By this, we also express the fact that we retain materialism and are not idealists.[54] The concept of subsistence is awkward. People need to ask questions, they need to think things out. Today everyone is talking about sustainability. But no one stops to

---

52. Mies 1983.
53. Märke 1986.
54. Salleh 1997.

think what it means. We want to prevent 'subsistence' from becoming another such plastic word, stripped of all meaning.

The second point to be made is that 'subsistence' is no purely anthropocentric concept. It expresses our continuity with nature, with animals and other natural beings. This means directing one's attention in a fully conscious manner to the material foundations we want to hold on to – even though those foundations are depreciated. After all, subsistence is considered the very last thing to strive for – 'mere' survival. But what we want to express is precisely the opposite: that happiness or freedom are not to be found beyond subsistence, but within the bounds of our quotidian attendance to such things as food, living space and sociability – in other words, within immanence. The notion of subsistence starts from the assumption that happiness is not to be sought beyond the 'realm of necessity', as Marx imagined. Nor is happiness advanced by a steady reduction of work. In our modern world, such a reduction of work would mean utilising ever more machines and technology, as if happiness could be provided by commodity-producing industry, by an even greater quantity of consumer goods. But that is not how happiness is achieved. It can only be achieved by focusing once more on subsistence and creative cooperation both with nature and with other human beings. Moreover, our race to superate the 'realm of necessity' involves us destroying the ecological foundations on which all life depends, including our own. One final reason why we retain the term 'subsistence' is that it can be understood the world over. The subsistence-perspective is not a provincial point of view. We are not focusing merely on our little village or our little Germany; we always keep the entire world in view. That is why we have never limited ourselves to working with the German women's movement; we insist on retaining a feminist internationalism.

I do not know whether Rosa Luxemburg would have agreed with what we call the subsistence perspective. Much like Marx, she developed no detailed vision of what an alternative, socialist or communist economy might look like. Yet unlike Marx, she did not consider the destruction of 'natural economies' a necessary sacrifice, necessary for the development of the forces of production and the liberation of humanity from the realm of necessity. Rosa Luxemburg did not believe in a straightforward causal relationship between the development of the forces of production and revolution, as did the revisionist Social Democrats of her day. Comrade Bernstein and others believed the 'civilised peoples' of Europe needed to force the 'savages' to develop their forces of production: 'We will condemn and combat certain methods of subordinating the savages, but not the fact that savages are in fact subordinated and the rights of the of superior culture asserted'.[55]

---

55. Eduard Bernstein, quoted in Mamozai 1982, p. 212.

Rosa Luxemburg did not tire of criticising the crimes European colonial powers committed against 'primitive societies', because these societies were not only conquered but also robbed of their means of existence. In other words, they were colonised, but their populations were not turned into 'free wage-workers' like those in the 'civilised' nations. In Christel Neusüß's view, Rosa Luxemburg's ideas about a good, proper economy need to be reconstructed from the point of view of 'primitive' peoples. Their ideal is not that of an infinitely ascending hierarchy of productive advances. Like subsistence-farmers (and women, Neusüß adds), they give *consumption, freedom, dignity* and the *preservation of the life-cycle* pride of place within their economies. This explains why Rosa's comrades accused her of romanticising and idealising the 'savages'.[56] Rosa saw clearly that the capitalist world-system can produce only immiseration, enslavement and proletarisation:

> The self-growth of capital appears as the alpha and omega, the end in itself and the meaning of all production. Yet the idiocy of such social relations emerges only to the extent that capitalist production matures and becomes worldwide production. It is here, on the scale of the world economy, that the absurdity of the capitalist economy finds its appropriate expression in the image of an entire humanity suffering terribly and groaning under the yoke of blind social power that is its own creation: capital. [...] It is a distinguishing feature of the capitalist mode of production that human consumption, which was an end in every earlier economic system, becomes a mere means to accumulate capital.[57]

Rosa Luxemburg recognised the centrality of 'consumption' or the everyday production of life – what we call subsistence-production. Nevertheless, she followed all other exponents of scientific socialism in pinning her hopes for a socialist future on the development of the forces of production, which she supposed would 'turn the rebellion of the international proletariat into a necessity': 'At a certain stage of development there will be no other way out than the application of socialist principles. The aim of socialism is not accumulation but the satisfaction of tolling humanity's wants by developing the productive forces of the entire globe'.[58]

This is where Rosa Luxemburg was wrong. Today, capitalism clearly exists in a worldwide form. But neither has it produced a homogeneous mass of immiserised proletarians, nor has it led to expectations of proletarian world-revolution being fulfilled. What Rosa and many other socialists overlooked is the fact that the exploitation of capital's colonies (including nature and women) has not only advanced the accumulation of capital (that is to say, enlarged the tip of the

---

56. Neusüß 1992, pp. 309–10.
57. Luxemburg 1925, p. 289.
58. Luxemburg 2003, p. 447.

iceberg) but also proven advantageous to free wage-workers in the industrialised or 'civilised' nations. They have risen from the proletarian misery of early capitalism and achieved a standard of living that hardly differs from that of the so-called middle classes, and they were able to do so *because of* the exploitation of the colonies.

This improvement in wage-workers' living conditions led to an illusion about the future prospects of underdeveloped societies (the name given to our colonies today), namely that catch-up development would allow them to advance to the point where they are on a par with European welfare-states. I have criticised this illusion for some time.[59] The collapse of actually existing socialism and the progress of neoliberal globalisation have caused it to shatter before our eyes. The future doesn't hold the generalisation of the welfare-state and the extension of the Western lifestyle to all people on Earth. On the contrary, more and more people are being forced below the surface of the iceberg-economy, in wealthy as well as in poor nations. They are being housewifed, deregulated, marginalised. They lose the status of 'free' wage-workers as they become 'Third-World-ised', as people in the USA are already saying. The result of this politics is the same everywhere: a growing gap between rich and poor.

Given this backdrop, that of an openly aggressive, globalised capital that has used the WTO and international agreements to try and obliterate all previous, national attempts to tame capitalism, how can one conceive of a transition to anything resembling socialism? What would a socialism based on the interests of women and the majority of producers in the South, but also on nature as the foundation of our livelihood, look like? I agree with Arno Peters that globalisation has put an end to the age of national economies maintained by national politics (including the politics of war, colonisation and family-planning). But I fail to see how today's global 'Rambo' capitalism could possibly be tamed or even defeated by something resembling a world-government or 'global governance', even of the socialist variety.[60] Even economic blocs like NAFTA or the EU have proven impossible to control socially and ecologically. They are simply too big.

In my view, there is only one viable alternative to global capitalism: communities must regain control of their local and regional conditions of existence (land, forests, resources, labour-power, biodiversity, culture and knowledge). Veronika Bennholdt-Thomsen and I have formulated such a perspective in our book *Die Subsistenzperspektive. Eine Kuh für Hillary*.[61] In fact, people are already rediscovering subsistence in manifold ways – not just in the Third World, but in

---

59. Mies 1986b.
60. Peters 1996.
61. Bennholdt-Thomsen and Mies 1997.

Europe as well.[62] Subsistence-production is the order of the day in the former Soviet Union and Cuba. I remember reading an enthusiastic report on Cuba's new subsistence-economy by Donella H. Meadows. Cuba's new subsistence-economy became necessary with the collapse of the international socialist market, on which Cuba had become dependent. Meadows reports on tractors being replaced by oxes as every available piece of land is used for food-production, including urban land. Cuba's many scientists have begun questioning old peasants and craftsmen in order to retrieve and develop lost subsistence-skills. The subsistence perspective has become a vital issue to Cuba, at least to the extent that the island-nation does not want to surrender to US capital.[63]

What interests us is whether this subsistence-orientation is perceived as a temporary necessity, a form of crisis-management such as might be adopted in wartime, or as something more far-reaching. Do the people of Cuba still hope that they will eventually achieve the US standard of living or do they perceive their autonomous, self-organised subsistence-economy as the germ of a socialist future? That would entail calling scientific socialism's utopia into question. Meadows reported nothing of the kind in her article.

Globalisation from below

In conclusion, I would like to address the objection inevitably provoked by the subsistence-perspective, namely that subsistence may work well for small, regional or local communities but remains too trifling an approach to unhinge the global system. The subsistence-perspective, we are told, can never provide the foundation for a new internationalism.

I strongly disagree. Not only do I believe that regional, autonomous economies are the *only* possible foundation for a new internationalism; I also believe that such an internationalism already exists, and in many forms. Witness the international movements against neoliberal free trade, GATT, the WTO, MAI and the WTO's Millennium Round. An unusually large number of women are involved in these movements and campaigns: ecofeminists, pacifists, pensioners, housewives, workers. But men are also involved. They have joined Rosa Luxemburg and us in understanding that the only purpose of life is *life*, not the accumulation of capital. These movements and campaigns demonstrate that national, cultural and religious differences need not be obstacles but can actually express the wealth and diversity of international networks. In this sense, the name Vandana Shiva chose for the network she created in 1996 is paradigmatic: 'Diverse Women for

---

62. Grober 1998; Bennholdt-Thomsen, Holzer and Müller (eds.) 1999; Scherhorn *et al.* 1999.

63. Meadows 1997.

Diversity'. We have witnessed this new, diverse internationalism on many occasions. It is unlike the international solidarity of the past, typically propagated by centralised organisations, mechanical in character and premised on the fiction that the workers of the world are all the same in that they have nothing to lose but their chains. A male craft-worker employed in a German Mercedes plant has more to lose – as does his female colleague.

I also want to respond to critics of the subsistence-perspective by pointing out the wealth of theoretical and practical initiatives within which people the world over are searching for alternatives to the dominant paradigm. They may not all use the term 'subsistence', but they are heading in the same general direction. Most cherish the following principles:

- regionalisation (localisation) instead of globalisation;
- self-provision (self-reliance) instead of market-dependence;
- agriculture before industry;
- rejoining of production and consumption;
- organic agriculture instead of agribusiness;
- food-sovereignty instead of industrial food provided by TNCs;
- democracy from below (grassroots-democracy);
- new forms of international, democratic, ecological and social cooperation instead of a 'world domestic policy';
- no patenting of life.[64]

These principles are not the ideas of exclusive minorities, as shown by the mass protests in Seattle in December of 1999. Fifty thousand people or more took to the streets to protest not just against the WTO, but against globalisation as such. They summed up their resistance and their vision of the future in the following slogans:

- self-reliance
- self-organisation
- solidarity.

---

64. Bennholdt-Thomsen, Holzer and Müller (eds.) 1999; Bennholdt-Thomsen and Mies 1997; Grober 1998; Shiva (no date).

Notes on Elder-Care Work and the Limits of Marxism
Silvia Federici

Introduction

'Care work', especially elder-care, has in recent years
come to the centre of public attention in the countries
of the OECD in response to a number of trends that
have put many traditional forms of assistance into crisis. First among them have been the growth, in relative
and absolute terms, of the old-age population, as well
as the increase in life-expectancy,[1] that have not been
matched, however, by a growth of services catering to
the old. There has also been the expansion of women's
waged employment that has reduced their contribution to the reproduction of their families.[2] To these
factors we must add the continuing process of urbanisation and the gentrification of working-class neighbourhoods, that have destroyed the support-networks
and forms of mutual aid on which older people living
alone could once rely, as neighbours would bring them
food, make their beds, come for a chat. As a result
of these trends, it is now recognised that for a large
number of the elderly, the positive effects of a longer
life-span have been voided or clouded by the prospect
of loneliness, social exclusion, and increased vulnerability to physical and psychological abuse. With this
in mind, I present some reflections on the question of
elder-care in contemporary social policy, especially in
the USA, to then ask what action can be taken on this

---

1. Kotlikoff and Burns 2004.
2. Folbre 2006, p. 350.

terrain and why the question of elder-care is absent in the literature of the Marxist Left.

My main objective here is to call for a redistribution of the social wealth in the direction of elder-care, and the construction of collective forms of reproduction, enabling older people to be provided for, when no longer self-sufficient, and not at the cost of their providers' lives.

For this to occur, however, the struggle over elder-care must be politicised and placed on the agenda of social-justice movements. A cultural revolution is also necessary in the concept of old age, against its degraded representations (on the one hand) as a fiscal burden on the state and, on the other hand, an 'optional' stage in life that we can 'cure', 'overcome', and even prevent, if we only adopt the right medical technology and the 'life-enhancing' devices disgorged by the market.[3] At stake in the politicisation of elder-care are not only the destinies of older people and the unsustainability of movements failing to address such a crucial issue in our lives, but the possibility of generational and class-solidarity, which have been for years the targets of a relentless campaign, portraying the provisions which workers have won for their old age as an 'economic time-bomb', and a heavy mortgage on the future of the young.

The crisis of elder-care in the global era

The present crisis of elder-care, in some respects, is nothing new. Elder-care in capitalist society has always been in a state of crisis, both because of the devaluation of reproductive work in capitalism, and because the elderly, far from being treasured as depositories of the collective memory and experience, as they were in many pre-capitalist societies, are seen as no longer productive. In other words, elder-care suffers from a double devaluation. Like all reproductive work, it is not recognised as work, but unlike the reproduction of Labour-power, whose product has a recognised value, it is deemed to absorb value but not to produce it. Thus, funds designated for elder-care have traditionally been disbursed with a stinginess reminiscent of the nineteenth-century Poor Laws, and the task of caring for the old, when no longer self-sufficient, has been left to the families and kin, with little external support, on the assumption that women would naturally take on the task, as part of their domestic work.

---

3. Joyce and Mamo 2006. As Joyce and Mamo point out, driven by the quest for profit and an ideology privileging youth, a broad campaign has been underway targeting the elderly as consumers, promising to 'regenerate' their bodies and delay aging if they use the appropriate pharmaceutical products and technologies. In this context, old age becomes almost a sin, a predicament we bring on ourselves, by failing to take advantage of the latest rejuvenating products.

It has taken a long struggle to force capital to reproduce not just labour-power 'in use', but the class a whole, with the provision of assistance also for those who are no longer part of the labour-market. However, even the Keynesian state fell short of this goal. Witness the case of the social-security legislation of the New Deal, enacted in 1940 and considered 'one of the achievements of our century',[4] which only partly responded to the problems faced by the old, tying social insurance to the years of waged employment and providing elder-care only to those in a state of absolute poverty.

The triumph of neoliberalism has worsened this situation. In some countries of the OECD steps have been taken, in the 1990s, to increase the funding of home-based care, and to provide counselling and services to the care-givers.[5] Efforts were also made to enable caregivers to 'reconcile' waged work and care-work, giving them the right to demand flexible work-schedules.[6] But the dismantling of the 'welfare-state' and the neo-liberal insistence that reproduction is the workers' responsibility, have triggered a countertendency that is still gaining momentum and in the present crisis will undoubtedly accelerate.

The demise of welfare-provisions for the elderly has been especially severe in the US, where it has reached such a point that workers are often impoverished in the effort to care for a disabled parent. One policy, in particular, has created great hardship. This has been the transfer of much hospital-care to the home, a move motivated by purely financial concerns and carried out with little consideration of the structures required to replace the services hospitals used to provide.[7] As described by Nona Glazer, this development have not only increased the amount of care-work that family members, mostly women, must do.[8] It has also shifted

---

4. Costa 1998, p. 1.

5. OECD Health Project 2005; Benería 2008, pp. 2–3, 5.

6. Benería (Beneria 2008) cites as an example a law passed in Spain in 1999, mandating employers to provide 'different forms of temporary leaves to facilitate care work' (p. 5), followed by a more extensive one in 2006–7 'funding a portion of the expenses individuals household spend on care'. (*Ibid.*) In Scotland, the Community Care and Health Act of 2002 'introduced free personal care for the elderly' and also redefined caregivers as 'co-workers receiving resources rather than consumers [...] obliged to pay for services'. (Carmichael *et al.* 2008, p. 7). In England and Wales, where it is reckoned that 5.2 million people provide informal care, from April 2007 caregivers for adults were given the right to demand flexible work-schedules (*Ibid.*).

7. According to various surveys, as a consequence of these cuts, '20 to 50 million family members in the US provide care that has traditionally been performed by nurses and social workers. Family care givers supply about 80% of the care for ill or disabled relatives and the need for their services will only rise as the population ages and modern medicine improves its ability to prolongs lives [...]'? With more terminally ill people choosing to remain at home until their final days, family-members or friends now serve as informal caregivers for nearly three-fourths of sick or disabled older adults living in the community during their years of life, according to a report in the Archives of Internal Medicine of January 2007 (Brody 2008).

8. Glazer 1993.

to the home 'life threatening', and 'dangerous' operations, that only registered nurses and hospitals in the past would have been expected to perform.[9] At the same time, subsidised home care workers have seen their workload double while their visits' lengths have increasingly been cut,[10] thus being forced to reduce their jobs 'to household maintenance and bodily care'.[11] Federally financed nursing homes have also been 'Taylorised', 'using time-and-motion studies to decide how many patients their workers can be expected to serve'.[12]

The 'globalisation' of elder care, in the 1980s and 1990s, has not remedied this situation. The new international division of reproductive work that globalisation has promoted, has shifted a large amount of care-work on the shoulders of immigrant women.[13] As is generally recognised, this development has been very advantageous for governments, as it has saved them billions of dollars they would otherwise have had to pay to create services catering to the elderly. It has also enabled middle-class women to pursue their careers, and has allowed many elderly, who wished to maintain their independence, to remain in their homes without going bankrupt. But by no means can this be considered a 'solution' to elder care. Besides conferring a new legitimacy to the neo-liberal doctrine that governments have no responsibility for social reproduction, this policy is condemned by the living and working conditions of the paid care-workers, which reflect all the contradictions and inequities characterising the process of social reproduction in our time.

It is because of the destructive impact of 'economic liberalisation' and 'structural adjustment' in their countries of origins that thousands of women from Africa, Asia, the Caribbean Island, and the former socialist world, migrate to the more affluent regions of Europe, the Middle East and the US, to serve as nannies, domestics, and caregivers for the elderly. To do this they must leave behind their own families, including children and ageing parents, and recruit relatives or hire other women with less power and resources than themselves to replace the work they can no longer provide.[14] Taking the case of Italy as an example, it is calculated that three out of four 'badanti' (as care-workers for the elderly are called) have children of their own, but only 15 percent have their families with them.[15] This means that the majority suffer a great deal of anxiety, confronting the fact

---

9. As a consequence of this 'transfer', the home has been turned into a medical factory, where dialyses are performed and housewives and aides must learn to insert catheters, and treat wounds. A whole new sort of medical equipment has been manufactured for home-use. Glazer 1993, pp. 154ff.

10. Glazer 1993, pp. 166–7, 173–4.

11. Boris and Klein 2007, p. 180.

12. Glazer 1993, p. 174.

13. Federici 1999, pp. 57–8; Pyle 2006a, pp. 283–9.

14. Pyle 2006a, p. 289; Hochschild and Ehrenreich 2002.

15. Di Vico 2004.

that their own families must go without the same care they now give to people across the globe. Arlie Hochschild has spoken, in this context, of a 'global transfer of care and emotions', and of the formation of a 'global care-chain'.[16] But the chain often breaks down, immigrant women become estranged from their children, stipulated arrangements fall apart, relatives die during their absence.

Equally importantly, because of the devaluation of reproductive work and the fact that they are immigrants, often undocumented, and women of colour, paid care-workers are vulnerable to a great deal of abuse: long hours of work, no paid vacations, or other benefits, exposure to racist behaviour and sexual assault. So low is the pay of home care-workers in the US that nearly half must rely on food-stamps and other forms of public assistance to make ends meet.[17] Indeed, as Domestic Workers United – the main domestic-/care-workers' organisation in New York, promoter of a Domestic Workers Bill of Rights has put it, care-workers live and work in 'the shadow of slavery'.[18]

It is also important to stress that most elderly people and families cannot afford to hire care-workers or pay for services matching their real need. This is particularly true of elderly people with disabilities who require day-long care. According to statistics of the CNEL (Consiglio Nazionale Economia e Lavoro) of 2003, in Italy only 2.8 percent of the elderly receive non-family assistance at home; in France it is twice as many, in Germany three times as many. But the number is still low.[19] A large number of elderly live alone, facing hardships that are all the more devastating the more invisible they are. In the 'hot summer' of 2003, thousands of elderly people died throughout Europe of dehydration, lack of food and medicines, or just the unbearable heat. So many died in Paris that the authorities had to stack their bodies in refrigerated public spaces until their families came to reclaim them.

When family-members care for the old, the tasks falls mostly on the shoulders of women,[20] who for months, or at times years, live on the verge of nervous and physical exhaustion, consumed by the work and the responsibility of having to provide care, and often perform procedures for which they are usually unprepared. Many have jobs outside the home, though they have to abandon them when the care-work escalates. Particularly stressed are the 'sandwich generation' who are simultaneously raising children and caring for their parents.[21] The crisis

---

16. Hochschild and Ehrenreich 2002, pp. 26–7.
17. *New York Times*, January 28, 2009.
18. The Domestic Workers Bill of Rights was signed by the New York Governor on August 31, 2010.
19. Di Vico 2004.
20. However, in the US the number of men caring for elderly parents has been steadily increasing. Belluck 2009.
21. Beckford 2009.

of care-work has reached such a point that in low-income, single-parent families in the US, teenagers and children, some no more than 11 years old, take care of their elders, also administering therapies and injections. As the *New York Times* has reported, a study conducted nationwide in 2005 revealed that '3% of households with children ages 8 to 18 included child caregivers'.[22]

The alternative, for those who cannot afford to buy into some form of 'assisted care', are publicly funded nursing homes, which, however, are more like prisons than hostels for the old. Typically, because of lack of staff and funds, these institutions provide minimal care. At best, they let their residents lie in bed for hours without anyone at hand to change their positions, adjust their pillows, massage their legs, tend to their bed-sores, or simply talk to them, so that they can maintain their sense of identity and still feel alive. At worst, nursing homes are places where old people are drugged, tied to their beds, left to lie in their excrements and subjected to all kind of physical and psychological abuses. This much has emerged from a series of reports, including one recently published by the US Government in 2008, which speaks of a history of abuse, neglect, and violation of safety- and health-standards in 94 percent of nursing homes.[23] The situation is not more encouraging in other countries. In Italy, the country that, besides the US, I have most researched, reports of abuses in nursing homes are frequent.

Elder-care, the unions, and the Left

The problems I have described are so common and pressing that we would imagine that elder-care would top the agenda of the social-justice movements and labour unions internationally. This, however, is not the case. When not working in institutions, as it is the case with nurses and aides, care-workers have been ignored by labour-unions, even the most combative like COSATU in South Africa.[24]

Unions negotiate pensions, the conditions of retirement, and healthcare. But there is little discussion in their programmes of the support-systems required by people ageing, and by care-workers, whether or not they work for pay. Until recently, in the US labour-unions did not even try to organise care-workers, much less unpaid house-workers. Thus, to this day, care-workers working for individuals or families are excluded from the Fair Labor Standards Act, New Deal legislation that guarantees 'access to minimum wages, overtime, bargaining rights and

---

22. Belluck 2009. Other countries where children have become care-workers include Britain and Australia, which often recognise their right to participate in 'patient-care discussions' and ask for compensations for their work (*Ibid.*).

23. *New York Times*, August 30, 2008.

24. Ally 2005, p. 3.

other workplace protections'.[25] And the US is not an isolated case. According to an ILO survey of 2004, 'cross-national unionization rates in the domestic service sector are barely 1%'.[26] Pensions are not available to all workers either, but only to those who have worked for wages, and certainly not to unpaid family-caregivers. As reproductive work is not recognised as work, and pension-systems compute benefits on the basis of the years spent in waged employment, women who have been fulltime housewives can obtain a pension only through a wage-earning husband, and have no social security if they divorce.

Labour-organisations have not challenged these inequities, nor have social movements and the Marxist Left, who, with few exceptions, also seem to have written the elderly off the struggle, judging by the absence of any reference to elder-care in contemporary Marxist analyses. The responsibility for this state of affairs can be in part traced back to Marx. Elder-care is not a theme that we find in his works, although the question of old age had been on the revolutionary political agenda since the eighteenth century, and mutual-aid societies and utopian visions of recreated communities abounded in his time.[27]

Marx was concerned with understanding the mechanics of capitalist production and the manifold ways in which the class-struggle challenges it and reshapes its form. Security in old age and elder-care did not enter this discussion. Old age was a rarity among the factory-workers and miners of his time, whose life expectancy, if his contemporaries' reports are to be believed on average did not surpass twenty years at best.[28] Most important, Marx did not recognise the centrality of reproductive work, neither for capital-accumulation nor for the construction of the new communist society. Although both he and Engels described the abysmal conditions in which the working class in England lived and worked, he almost naturalised the process of reproduction, never envisaging how reproductive work could be reorganised in a different, non-exploitative society or in the very course of the struggle. For instance, he discussed 'cooperation' only in

---

25. Boris and Klein 2007, p. 182.

26. Ally 2005, p. 1.

27. Blackburn 2002, pp. 32, 39–41. As Robin Blackburn points out, it was at the time of the French Revolution that the first proposals for paying pensions to people in old age and want appeared. Tom Paine discussed the issue in the second part of *Rights of Man* (1792), so did his friend Condorcet who offered a plan that was to cover all citizens. On the footsteps of these proposals, 'The National Convention declared that 10 Fructidor was to be the date of the *Fête de la Vieillesse* and that there should be old people homes established in every department [...]. The Convention adopted the principle of a civic pension for the aged in June 1794, just a few months after the abolition of slavery...' (Blackburn 2002, pp. 40–1) These proposals, and others promoted by British radicals like William Godwin, stirred Malthus's bitter reply in the *Essay on Population* (1779), where he advocated the termination of all forms of social assistance. Marx did not bring his voice to the debate, not, at least in defence of pensions and elder-care.

28. Marx 1976; Seccombe 1993, pp. 75–7.

the process of commodity-production, overlooking the qualitatively different forms of proletarian cooperation in the process of reproduction which Kropotkin later called 'mutual aid'.[29] Typical of the limits of Marx's perspective is his utopian vision in the famous 'Fragment on the Machines' in the *Grundrisse* (1857–8), where he projects a world in which machines do all the work and human beings only tend to them, functioning as their supervisors. This picture, in fact, ignores that, even in advanced capitalist countries, much of the socially necessary labour consists of reproductive activities, and that this work has proven irreducible to mechanisation.

Only minimally can the needs, desires, possibilities of older people, or people outside the waged workplace be addressed by incorporating technologies into the work by which they are reproduced. The automation of elder-care is a path already well travelled. As Nancy Folbre (the leading feminist economist and student of elder-care in the US) has shown, Japanese industries are quite advanced in the attempt to technologise it, as they are generally in the production of interactive robots. Nursebots giving people baths or 'walking [them] for exercise', and 'companion robots' (robotic dogs, teddy-bears) are already available on the market, although at prohibitive costs.[30] We also know that televisions and personal computers have become surrogate *'badanti'* for many elders. Electronically commanded wheelchairs enhance the mobility of those who are sufficiently in charge of their movements to master their commands.

These scientific and technological developments can highly benefit older people, if they are made affordable to them. The circulation of knowledge they provide certainly places a great wealth at their disposal. But this cannot replace the labour of care-workers, especially in the case of elders living alone and/or suffering from illnesses and disabilities. As Folbre points out, robotic partners can even increase people's loneliness and isolation.[31] Nor can automation address the predicaments – fears, anxieties, loss of identity and sense of one's dignity – that people experience as they age and become dependent on others for the satisfaction of even their most basic needs.

It is not technological innovation that is needed to address the question of elder-care, but a change in social relations, whereby the valorisation of capital no longer commands social activity and reproduction has become a collective process. This, however, will not be possible within a Marxist framework, short of a major rethinking of the question of work of the type that feminists began in the 1970s as part of a political discussion of housework and the root of gender-

---

29. For Kropotkin's concept of mutual aid see in particular the last two chapters of the homonymous work. (Kropotkin 1998.)
30. Folbre 2006, p. 356.
31. Folbre 2006, p. 356.

based discrimination. Feminists rejected the centrality Marxism has historically assigned to waged industrial work and commodity-production as the crucial sites for social transformation, and they criticised its neglect of the reproduction of human beings and labour-power.[32] The feminist movement's lesson has been that not only is reproduction the pillar of the 'social factory', but changing the conditions under which we reproduce ourselves is an essential part of our ability to create 'self-reproducing movements'.[33] For ignoring that the 'personal' is the 'political' greatly undermines the strength of our struggle.

On this matter, contemporary Marxists are not ahead of Marx. Taking the Autonomist-Marxist theory of 'affective' and 'immaterial labour' as an example, we see that it still sidesteps the rich problematic the feminist analysis of reproductive work in capitalism uncovered. This theory argues that with the informatisation of production, the distinction between production and reproduction becomes totally blurred, as work becomes the production of states of being, 'affects', 'immaterial' rather than physical objects.[34] The examples given of the ideal-type 'affective labourers' are the fast-food female workers who must flip hamburgers at McDonald's with a smile, or the stewardesses who must sell a sense of security to the people to whom she attends. But such examples are deceptive, for much of reproductive work, as exemplified by care for the elderly, demands a complete engagement with the persons to be reproduced, which can hardly be conceived as 'immaterial'. Moreover, such examples continue to ignore women's unpaid reproductive work as a crucial form of exploitation, and do not problematise the reproduction of everyday life in the anti-capitalist movements and the 'new commons' these are trying to produce.

It is, important, however, to clarify that the concept of 'care-work' is also to some extent 'reductive'. The term entered the common usage in the 1980s and 1990s, in conjunction with the emergence of a new division of labour within reproductive work, separating the physical from the emotional aspects of this work. Paid care-workers hold onto this distinction, striving to specify and limit the jobs that can be expected of them from their employers, and to insist that the work they provide is skilled labour. But the distinction is untenable, and care-workers are the first to recognise it. Among the hardships they face are, in fact, the emotional traumas caused by their possible attachment to the people they

---

32. This is particularly true of the feminists in the Wages For Housework Movement, such as Mariarosa dalla Costa, Selma James and others, the author included.

33. The concept of 'self-reproducing movements' has become a rallying cry for a number of US-based collectives, who refuse the traditional separation – so typical of leftist politics – between political work and the daily reproduction of our lives. For an elaboration of this concept, see the collection of articles published by the collective Team Colors (Hughes *et al.* 2010), and *Rolling Thunder* 2008.

34. Hardt and Negri 2004, pp. 108–11.

serve [children, elders], which continuously enters into conflict with the constraints the 'market' places on their work. What differentiates the reproduction of human beings from the reproduction of commodities – despite their apparent merging due to the marketisation of important aspects of reproductive work, is the holistic character of many of the tasks involved. Indeed, to the extent that a separation is introduced, that is, to the extent that elderly people (or for that matter children) are fed, washed, combed, massaged, given medicines, without any consideration for their emotional, 'affective' response and general state of being, we enter a world of radical alienation.

Women, ageing and elder-care in the perspective of feminist economists

The revolutionary character of the feminist theories of reproduction partly lay in their recognition of this difference, as well as the many ways in which capitalism has exploited it. The feminists did not only bring reproduction to the centre of the class-struggle, uncovering its central function in the reproduction of the workforce. They also shifted the focus of anti-capitalist struggle from commodity-production to the production of human beings, from the factory to the home, the neighbourhood, the territory, reconnecting with the long history of radical reconstruction of 'everyday life', making the creation of a new type of subjectivity the priority of political organising. The theory of 'affective labour' ignores this problematic, and the complexity involved in the reproduction of life. It also suggests that all forms of work in 'post-industrial' capitalism are becoming homogenised, so that the divisions in the work-force created on the basis of age, gender and race would no longer be relevant to anti-capitalist politics. Yet, a brief look at the organisation of elder-care, as presently constituted, dispels this illusion.

As feminist economists have argued, the crisis of elder-care, whether considered from the viewpoint of the elders or their providers, is essentially a gender-question. Although increasingly commodified, most care-work is still done by women, and in the form of unpaid labor, which does not entitle them to any pension. Thus, paradoxically, the more women care for others, the less care they can receive in return, because they devote less time to waged labour than men, and many social insurance plans are calculated on the years of waged work done. Paid caregivers too, as we have seen, are affected by the devaluation of reproductive work, forming an 'underclass' that still must fight to be socially recognised as workers. In sum, because of the devaluation of reproductive work, practically everywhere women face old age with fewer resources than men, measured in terms of family-support, monetary incomes, and assets. Thus, in the US, where pensions and social security are calculated on years of employment, women are the largest group of the elderly who are poor and the largest number of residents of low-income nursing homes, the *lagers* of our time, precisely because they spend so much of their lives outside of the waged workforce, in activities not recognised as work.

Since science and technology cannot resolve this problem, what is required is a transformation in the social/sexual division of labour and above all the recognition of reproductive work as work, entitling those performing it to a compensation, so that family-members providing care are not penalised for their work. The recognition and valorisation of reproductive work is also crucial to overcome the divisions which the present situation sows among care-workers, which pit, on one side, the family-members trying to minimise their expenses, and, on the other, the hired caregivers facing the demoralising consequences of working at the edge of poverty and devaluation.

Feminist economists working on this issue have articulated possible alternatives to the present systems. In *Warm Hands in a Cold Age*,[35] Nancy Folbre discusses what reforms are needed to give security to the ageing population, especially elderly women, by taking an international perspective, and evaluating which countries are in the lead in this respect. At the top, she places the Scandinavian countries that provide almost universal systems of insurance. At the bottom are the US and England, where elderly assistance is tied to employment history. But in both cases there is a problem in the way policies are configured, which confirms an unequal sexual division of labour and the traditional expectations concerning women's role in the family and society. This is one crucial area where change must occur.

Folbre also calls for a redistribution of resources, rechanneling public money from the military-industrial complex and other destructive enterprises to the care of people in old age. She acknowledges that this may seem 'unrealistic', equivalent to calling for a revolution. But she insists that it should be placed on 'our agenda', for the future of every worker is at stake, and a society blind to the tremendous suffering that awaits so many people once they age, as is the case with the US today, is a society bound for self-destruction.

There is no sign, however, that this blindness may soon be dissipated. Faced with the growing economic crisis, policy-makers are turning their eyes away from it, everywhere striving to cut social spending and bring state-pensions and social-security systems, including subsidies to care-work, under the axe. The dominant refrain is an obsessive complaint that a more vital and energetic elderly population, stubbornly insisting on living on, is making even the provision of state-funded pensions unsustainable. It was possibly thinking of the millions of Americans determined on living past eighty. In his memoirs, Alan Greenspan confessed that he was frightened when he realised that the Clinton

---

35. Folbre, Shaw and Stark (eds.) 2007.

Administration had actually accumulated a financial surplus![36] Even before the crisis, for years policy-makers have been orchestrating a generational war, incessantly warning that the expansion of the 65+ population would bankrupt the present social-security system, leaving a heavy mortgage on the shoulders of the younger generations. It is now to be feared that, as the crisis deepens, the assault on assistance to old age and elder-care, whether in the form of a hyper-inflation decimating fixed incomes, or a partial privatisation of social-security systems, or the rising of the retirement-age, will accelerate. What is certain is that no one is arguing for an increase in government funding of elder-care.[37]

It is urgent, then, that social-justice movements, including Marxist scholars and activists, intervene on this terrain to prevent a triage solution to the crisis at the expense of the old, and to formulate initiatives capable of bringing together the different social subjects who are implicated in the question of elder-care: care-workers, families of the elders, and first the elders themselves – now often in an antagonistic relation. We are already seeing examples of such an alliance in the struggle over elder-care, where nurses and patients, paid care-workers and families of their clients are coming together to jointly confront the state, aware that when the relations of reproduction become antagonistic, both producers and reproduced pay the price. Meanwhile, the 'commoning' of reproductive/care-work is also under way.

Communal forms of living based upon 'solidarity-contracts' are presently being created in some Italian cities by elders, who in order to avoid being institutionalised, pool together their efforts and resources, when they cannot count on their families or hire a care-worker. In the US, 'communities of care' are being formed by the younger generations, socialising, collectivising the experience of illness, pain, grieving and 'care-work'. In this process, they are beginning to reclaim and redefine what is means to be ill, to age, to die. These efforts need to be expanded. They are essential to a reorganisation of our everyday life and the creation of non-exploitative social relations. For the seeds of the new world are not to be planted 'online', but in the cooperation we can develop to transform the lives of people who are on wheelchairs and in hospital-beds, which presently constitutes the most hidden but most prevalent form of torture in our society.

---

36. Greenspan 2007.
37. Watson and Mears 1999, p. 193.

Part Two

Cornelius Castoriadis's Break With Marxism
Jean-Louis Prat

In every country in the world a huge tribe of party-hacks and sleek little professors are busy 'proving' that Socialism means no more than a planned state-capitalism with the grab-motive left intact. But fortunately there also exists a vision of Socialism quite different from this. The thing that attracts ordinary men to Socialism and makes them willing to risk their skins for it, the 'mystique' of Socialism, is the idea of equality; to the vast majority of people Socialism means a classless society, or it means nothing at all.

George Orwell, *Homage to Catalonia*

Compared to the debates within the Trotskyist movement, the analysis presented in Cornelius Castoriadis's *Relations of Production in Russia* was an achievement. It would go on to provide a starting point for other analyses that would newly question the foundations of historical materialism, Marx's economic theory and the special importance Marx accords the relations of production for the analysis of society as a whole. The Russian Revolution, which had taken place in a country where capitalism was still in an embryonic stage, hardly illustrated the dialectical scenario of the bourgeoisie producing its own grave-diggers. And the example of China would soon make it clear that:

the constitution of a totalitarian bureaucracy is not necessarily the product of a development that is organic to a society. It is not a matter of the development of the forces of production giving rise to new relations of production, the new relations of production engendering a new class and the new class then seizing political power. [...] China's industrialisation is the result of the bureaucracy's rise to power, not vice versa.[1]

Such facts, and many others, were received with indifference by the majority of Marxists, who explained the role sometimes played by political or ideological factors in terms of the interaction of base and superstructure and held that the economic base ultimately retains its determining role. Whatever the detours by which the realisation of historical necessity occurs, it continues to be defined by the economic contradictions proper to a mode of production in which social relations oppose or obstruct the development of the forces of production. By virtue of this scholastic-sounding argument, Marxist theory evades all experimental verification. It can no longer be *falsified*, as Popper would say. No matter what happens, the events will always be compatible with the theory, which will never be at a loss to explain both the victories of the proletariat and those of the bourgeoisie. It will even be able to account for the apathy of the masses, when they withdraw from the political stage in order to integrate themselves in consumer-society and pursue happiness within the private sphere.

Marxist economics

Thus, if the theory is still to be discussed at all, this can only be done upon the terrain it has withdrawn to, that of the critique of political economy. It is this critique that provides Marxist theory with the basis for its negative verdict on the bourgeoisie. According to Marx, the bourgeoisie is condemned to disappear, albeit not for the ethical reasons invoked by Proudhonist socialism, which holds that 'property is theft' and that accumulation condemns itself as predatory or unjust – an absurd view, according to Marx, since moral criteria are themselves products of the historical development of the society in which they are applied; they will not allow one to leap over and transcend their own epoch. Capitalist society is not doomed because we consider it damnable, but rather for objective reasons: its dynamic is burdened with contradictions that express themselves, ultimately, in the tendency of the rate of profit to fall.

The examination of this hypothesis led gradually to a dismantling of the entire Marxist system; the inconsistency of the system's conclusions necessitated a critique that ended up calling into question the premises. In effect, the hypothesis rests on the notion that technological progress tends to modify the organic composition of capital, decreasing the share of variable capital from which labour-

---

1. Castoriadis 2005, p. 134.

power is remunerated and increasing the share of constant capital, or of the capital that is invested into raw materials and equipment, with the equipment's expected life-span being taken into account. It is in order to increase productivity that capital makes use of the most efficient technology, thereby modifying the relationship between the physical volume of the means of production and the number of workers operating them: the number of workers decreases by comparison to the amount of machinery. The machines become ever more efficient and ever more complex, allowing the workers to produce a greater quantity of finished products in less and less time. 'But in Marx's formula there is neither physical volume of produced means of production, nor number of men. [...] The obvious fact that more and more machines are handled by fewer and fewer men does not allow us to infer, without further consideration, that annual depreciation in value terms is constantly increasing as against the annual wage bill, also expressed in value terms'.[2]

From the fact that technological progress perpetually increases the physical mass of constant capital, it does not follow that the value represented by constant capital also increases:

> since that value equals physical mass multiplied by unit value, and the latter diminishes as the productivity of labour increases (there being no reason to assume that the productivity of labour increases more slowly in the sector producing means of production than elsewhere in the economy). When the quantity of machines, raw materials, etc. increases relatively to the number of workers, this does not mean that the value of constant capital must increase relatively to that of variable capital. [...] On the other hand, Marx asserts that the rate of exploitation (s/v) increases over time. How do we know that this increase is not sufficient to compensate for a possible rise in organic composition, or even to overcompensate for it, in which case we would be dealing not with a tendency of the rate of profit to fall, but with its tendency to rise?[3]

Finally, even granting that the rate of profit does in fact tend to fall, does it necessarily follow from this that capitalist production collapses and yields to new social relations? What would result would be a deceleration of growth, and one that socialism would be powerless to arrest:

> The reasons Marx gives for the tendency of the rate of profit to fall in capitalist society are technical reasons; they are nothing to do with the social structure of capitalism. They boil down to the fact that, whatever the number of workers, there will always be a greater number of machines, raw materials, etc. Since

---

2. Cardan 1979, p. 208.
3. Castoriadis 2005, p. 50.

we do not want to say that socialist society will be characterised by reverse technological development (Marx and the Marxists will in any case never be heard making such a claim), this factor will always be in place; in fact, it will be exacerbated insofar as the other factor, which acts as a counterbalance under capitalism, namely the increase in the rate of exploitation, will have disappeared in socialist society. Does this mean, then, that socialist society will be characterised by a fall in the rate of surplus production (we will no longer be able to speak of profit)? And what would that entail?[4]

Class-struggle or historical determinism?

More radically, Castoriadis rejects the idea that a socialist revolution can be charted in advance like a natural process, such as the one described in the preface to *Capital*, where Marx 'pictures the movement of society as a natural concatenation of historical phenomena, governed by laws that are not just independent of the volition, consciousness and intentions of men, but actually determine them'. This amounts to the claim that men never act except in the manner of actors who must stick to the role the dramaturge has chosen for them. What becomes of the class-struggle in the analyses of *Capital*, where the value of a commodity – and first and foremost that of labour-power – is necessarily defined by its cost of production and cannot be altered by the struggles of men? Labour-power is sold under conditions that allow the employer to pay the best possible price for it – meaning, the lowest – because, differently from other commodities, it cannot be stocked or held in reserve; it has no value except if sold in the briefest of time periods. Wages are determined, according to Marx, by the *labour-time* that is *socially necessary* for producing the means of subsistence consumed by the worker. Notwithstanding his abandonment of the iron law of wages, the author of *Capital* continues to conceptualise economic laws as physical laws that operate independently of historical circumstances, the class-struggle and the pace of technological development. His basic axiom, the law of value, is already rendered problematic by the *ongoing revolution of the mode of production*, which causes the production-costs of one and the same commodity, produced at the same moment by firms selling their products on the same market, to vary ever more widely. Is the labour-time socially required for the production of this commodity the amount of time the most efficient firm requires to produce it? It would be if that firm controlled the entire market. But what if other firms retain their own market-shares? Must one then equate socially necessary labour-time with the time required by the firm producing with the most backward technology,

---

4. Castoriadis 2005, p. 51.

since society has a use for what that firm produces? Or should one calculate an average, and will one be able to if technology continues to develop? 'But this average time period is an empty abstraction [...]. There is no real or logical reason for the value of a product to be determined by the result of a mathematical calculation that no one performs or could perform'.[5]

Commodity-values and struggles over the value of labour-power

As far as labour-power is concerned, Castoriadis emphasises that it has: neither a predefined use value nor a predefined exchange value. It has no predefined use value: the capitalist who purchases a ton of coal knows how many calories he can obtain from it at the given level of technological development, but when he purchases an hour of labour, he does not know what degree of performance he will be able to obtain from it. Now, Marx always proceeds from the postulate that, just as the capitalist will extract from the coal the maximum number of calories the technology of his day allows him to extract (the coal being passive), he will also be able to obtain from the worker the maximum performance allowed for by the development of technology (the type and speed of the machinery, etc.), the worker being necessarily passive as well. But this is false. Marx virtually never speaks of the embittered struggle over the exertion of labour power that occurs every day within industry [...]. Marx abstracts from this struggle. The rest of *Capital* depends on this 'analysis' of how the exchange value of the commodity labour power is determined, and so the entire edifice is built on sand. The entire theory is conditioned by this 'forgetting' of the class-struggle. One needs to reread the end of *Wages, Price and Profit* to see that, even when he admits workers' struggles may have an effect on wage-levels, Marx considers this influence to be conjunctural and 'cyclical', unable to alter the fundamental, long-term distribution of the product as regulated by the law of value'.[6]

Need one point out that this critique of Marx is nothing to do with the resurgence of neoclassical liberalism, that 'incredible ideological regression' Castoriadis denounced in one of the last texts published before his death? In that text, Castoriadis calls into question what he refers to as the 'rationality' (in quotation marks) of capitalism.

He recalls 'things that were taken, with good reason, to have been achieved conclusively, such as the devastating critique of academic political economy elaborated, between 1930 and 1965, by the Cambridge school (Sraffa, Robinson, Kahn,

---

5. Castoriadis 1978, p. 336.
6. Castoriadis 2005, pp. 46–8.

Keynes, Kalecki, Shackle, Kaldor, Pasinetti, etc.)', a critique which, he observes, 'is not discussed or refuted but simply passed over in silence or forgotten, while naive and improbable inventions like "supply-side economics" or "monetarism" are all the rage, neoliberalism's praise-singers present their aberrations as if they were common sense, the absolute freedom of capital movements ravages entire sectors of production in virtually every country and the world economy turns into a planetary casino'.[7]

What Castoriadis reproaches Marx for is his affinity to the project of an economic science modelled on the natural sciences and his abandonment of the idea of a *critique* of political economy: 'In economics, there are links, repetitions, "local" and partial regularities, general tendencies; there is such a thing as the intelligibility of economic phenomena, as long as one never forgets that if one is to understand anything, one has to re-immerse the economic in the socio-historical. But what does not exist is a political economy based on the model of the physico-mathematical sciences'. What Castoriadis rejects is the integral determinism of a theory that eliminates human initiative and the class-struggle, a theory that believes it can combine the 'locally regular' concatenations it observes into 'an exhaustive and permanent system of invariant relations'.[8]

Editorial Note: This chapter is a translation of Jean Louis Prat, *Introduction à Castoriadis*, Paris: La Découverte, 2007, Chapter III. Published with permission.

7. Castoriadis 1999a, pp. 65–6.
8. Castoriadis 2005, p. 53.

A Theory of Defeat:
Marx and the Evidence of the Nineteenth Century
Ahlrich Meyer

The following engagement with Marx's critique of
political economy has two implicit social-historical
assumptions, which can only be alluded to, here. I
assume, first, that the concept of the working class
employed by Marx was not suitable for the breadth
and heterogeneity of the proletarian class-composition
of the middle of the nineteenth century – just as,
incidentally, it was also never suitable for the class-
relations in revolutionary Russia or at the time of the
tricontinental liberation-movements in the twentieth
century. Second, it appears to me to be evident that
Marx's theory was not able to take up the virulence
of the anti-capitalist struggles and the massive social
challenges from below, as they appeared above all
in the European subsistence-revolts up until 1848. I
intend to show in these pages that this is no historically contingent deficit but regards, rather, the status
of the theory itself.

At is well known, before the wage-labour relation
could be generalised, the subsistence-basis, external to
capital, for large parts of the population of Europe was
destroyed from the middle of the eighteenth century.
Control over the reproduction and the first means of life
thus became the centre of struggles between the lower
classes and capital. The determination of grain-prices
according to market-laws, like all other commodity-
prices, was a precondition for making labour-power
itself marketable and for subjecting it to exploitation
in the value-form. The transformation of means of life

into commodities confronted the pauperised masses at the same time with the transformation of their own conditions of existence into conditions of capital. In a cycle of revolts that lasted for almost 100 years, they had to learn that their survival was no longer to be secured through the processing of external nature and was also no longer valid as an authoritative norm originating out of village communal habits and apportioned by the authorities, but rather represented a market-dependent variable. The passed down 'moral economy' of the lower strata (E.P. Thompson)[1] took on the form of a modern antagonism. Leading these struggles were mostly women, 'rebellious *femmes*',[2] who took over control on the market, over the costs of life and prices and over the circulation of grain and export. The made the subsistence-question a public affair, by positing for the first time the praxis of social appropriation of goods in the commodity-form against the violent expropriation and separation of the producers from the means of production.

The resistance against a mode of reproduction determined by capital united a broad spectrum of social layers and classes. It can be summarised under the concept of 'mass poverty'.[3] This mass poverty was not simply 'pre-industrial', as has been said; its roots were not predominantly in the late-feudal social constitution and in its periodic agrarian crises; but it was also not limited to the misery of the workers in the early factories. It was in the first instance absolute 'overpopulation', disproportional in relation to the social organisation of capital at the historical level then current, and the result of a directed policy of impoverishment of broad sections of the population as a precondition and lever for the accumulation of capital as well as for the industrial take-off. At the same time, it embodied the anomian effects of the process of industrialisation as well as the expectations and the uprising of people who had been set free from feudal society. Mass poverty was above all working poverty, the form of existence of a class that was bound to labour and for which labour now only meant lack of property. This class of the labouring poor consisted of beggars and vagabonds searching for work, day-workers in the country, impoverished farmers and share-croppers, weavers of the proto-industrial cottage-industry, domestic servants and city-handymen, seasonal migratory workers, railroad-construction workers, proletarianised craftworkers, the manufacturing and factory-proletariat and, last

---

1. Thompson 1971.
2. Perrot 1979.
3. The concept comes from the German *Vormärz*. It was taken up by the post-Nazi West German social historiography of the 1950s and 1960s, with the intention of explaining pauperism in the epoch of early industrialisation in Europe on the basis of pre-industrial causes – ultimately, from the growth in population. The industrial-capitalist integration of the 'workers', mediated by the social state, thus appeared as a tactical overcoming of mass poverty. An exemplary case is Conze 1954; Abel 1972.

but not least, those that Marx named the 'lumpenproletariat', the *classes dangereuses*[4] – men, women and children, in their totality an extensively mobilised class on a labour-market, which for the first time, due to the migration-processes, also took on a European dimension.[5]

The extent to and continuity with which the subsistence-question, the 'struggle of the people for the prime necessities of life' (Marx),[6] determined the 'epoch of revolutions' in Europe as an anti-capitalist current – the epoch of the bourgeois revolution of the late eighteenth century through to the implementation of industrialism in the middle of the nineteenth century – has been given too little attention in social-historical research.[7] In the discussion of the New Left, this decisive phase of European social history became contemporary again only against the background of the IMF riots of the 1980s, in which the pauperised masses of three continents attacked the global dictate of hunger and exploitation.[8] All the revolutionary upheavals in France – 1789, 1830, 1848 – were either accompanied by food-crises and -unrest, or came shortly after such unrest. The great French Revolution began with a peasant-uprising against the liberalised grain-market and against the capitalisation of agriculture in feudal garb.[9] Between 1789 and 1795 the revolution was pervaded by a chain of urban riots that were fundamentally food-revolts carried out by the *Sans-culottes*.[10] Even the actions of the Luddites[11] were aimed in the first instance against the implementation of agricultural techniques that robbed the poor of work and the right to the scraps of the harvest. The early workers' movement of the nineteenth century, and still even the mostly 'political' movement of Chartism of the late 1830s in England, formulated its claims as a 'bread and butter' question. All strikes and wage-struggles of the 'hungry 40s' had this character. For a long time, a customary standard, originating out of a socially defined extent of needs and not determined by the market, was included in the wage-demands of the workers.[12] The movements of 1846–7 were mass revolts against the last great 'hunger-pact' on European soil, against an industrial revolution with hunger, which alone in Ireland cost a million people their lives. In France as in Germany they flowed, in

---

4. See Chevalier 1958.
5. Compare Grandjonc 1975.
6. Marx mentions the subsistence-revolts before 1848 in a single passage, in his text on *The Class Struggles in France, 1848 to 1850*. (Marx 1975–2004k).
7. The most important presentations are: Rudé 1964; Thompson 1971; Tilly, Tilly and Tilly 1975.
8. See the last issue of the journal *Autonomie/Neue Folge*, 14 (1985); Meyer 1999.
9. Lefebvre 1970.
10. Mathiez 1973; Rudé 1959.
11. Hobsbawm and Rudé 1969.
12. Hobsbawm 1964b.

different class-constellations, into the 1848 revolution.[13] The translation of these social movements into reformism and into the political project of a bourgeois-democratic revolution has made us forget that in 1848 communism was on the order of the day in Europe, if we understand by communism the basic demand of the masses for the guarantee of the right of existence.

I

The development of classical political economy until its critique by Marx can be represented, in relation to the question of the wage, in the following broad brushstrokes: Adam Smith, on the basis of a concept of social labour that originated in the division of labour and period of manufacture, posed in 1776 for the first time a determination of rules for the exchange of commodities (the so-called labour-theory of value). It took the quantity of labour objectified in the commodities as its point of departure. However, he immediately fell into contradiction with this definition when he treated not simple commodity-exchange, but rather, the exchange between capital and labour-power, that is, the problem of profit and wages. What was valid as law in the exchange of objectified quantities of labour (commodities) appeared to him not incorrectly to be ruptured in the exchange between objectified labour and living labour. The worker clearly did not obtain in return in this act of exchange, Smith thought, the opposite value of his labour-product as wage, as he was accustomed to as craftsman and commodity-producer.[14] Since Smith found no theoretical solution for this contradiction, but instead tried to explain it historically with what he called 'previous accumulation' and capital's mediating role between acts of simple commodity-exchange. He doubted the validity of the law of value in general and switched to other different explanations. He wondered if the value of labour was not itself a fixed measure, which inversely regulated all other commodities and which for its part was established by the maintenance of the worker, measured according to an amount of corn.[15] This was an explanation that was not able to solve the

---

13. Meyer 1992. For an exemplary study on the role of the lower classes in the 1848 revolution in Germany, see Hachtmann 1997. It should, however, not be overlooked that in Germany the transition from social protest to anti-semitic pogrom was then imminent. According to recent historical studies, in the context of the revolution of 1848–9 there were riots directed against Jews in numerous places in Baden, Württemberg, Bavaria, Hesse, Upper Silesia and elsewhere.

14. Smith 1776, Book 1, Chapters 5, 6, 8. The concept of quantity of labour is already determined by Smith temporally; the concept of value of political economy, also taken over by Marx, thus reflects the implementation of a time-régime in the underclasses, which for the first time made the comparison of labour-times possible. See Thompson 1967.

15. Smith 1776, Book 1, Chapter 5.

theoretical contradiction. But it contained the historical truth that what Smith undifferentiatedly named the 'value of labour' (the value of labour-power in distinction from the objectified quantity of labour) was not ruled by the law of value in a twofold way: the wage paid by capital not only did not correspond to the expended quantity of labour, but the wage was not in any way measurable in terms of commodity and value; rather, it was established on the basis of the corn-standard. The inner theoretical contradiction in the political economy of Smith between objectified and living labour, between product and wage, the theoretical uncertainties in the determination of value by social labour or by the fixed standard of corn, thus reflect the class-contradiction posited by previous accumulation and form to a certain extent the breakthrough-point of the problem of the reproduction of labour as a class.

David Ricardo then objected to Smith – and he could also do this at the beginning of the nineteenth century – that the value of labour (the compensation of the worker) in no way influenced the value of the commodities in its determination by the quantity of labour contained in it. He insisted, rather, that the wage varied depending upon the market and upon how the value of all commodities was determined on average by the quantity of labour necessary for production. Ricardo says without any irony: 'If the rewards of the labourer were always in proportion to what he produced, the quantity of labour bestowed on a commodity, and the quantity of labour which that commodity would purchase, would be equal [...] but they are not equal'.[16]

He further writes in the *Principles of Political Economy and Taxation* (1817) about the wage: 'The natural price of labour is that price which is necessary to enable the labourers, one with another, to subsist and to perpetuate their race, without either increase or diminution [...] The natural price of labour, therefore, depends on the price of the food, necessaries, and conveniences required for the support of the labourer and his family'.[17]

This definition incorporated labour-power itself as commodity in the general validity of the law of value, by elevating the quantity of labour necessary for the production of food and the necessities of the worker in the commodity form to the measure for the costs of the reproduction of living labour. This was, however, only a pseudo-solution that it no way cast off the contradiction contained in the law of value. As a legacy of classical political economy, this pseudo-solution, the application of the law of value to the commodity of labour-power and the determination of the wage by the costs of reproduction, was substantially taken over by Marx in his theory of wages.

---

16. Ricardo 1951, Chapter 1, section 1, p. 14.
17. Ricardo 1951, Chapter 5, p. 93.

Until the middle of the nineteenth century, the history of economic doctrines mirrors precisely the socio-historical development that was summarised at the beginning. The theory of wage-labour is directly derived from the subjection of the poor and working classes to a new form of subsistence. That is clearest in Turgot, the economist and finance-minister of the *ancien régime*, who was responsible for the liberalisation of the grain-market in France in 1774 and who in this perspective sketched out a wage-theory. 'The mere workman, who depends only on his hands and his industry', Turgot wrote in his *Réflexions sur la formation et la distribution des richesses* in 1766, 'has nothing that he is able to dispose of to others than his labour. [...] In every species of labour it must, and, in effect, it does happen, that the wages of the workman is confined merrily to what is necessary to procure him a subsistence' [*que le salaire de l'ouvrier se borne à ce qui lui est nécessaire pour lui procurer sa subsistance*].[18]

It does not change anything substantial that Turgot establishes this regularity upon the competition of the workers amongst themselves, due to which his formulation was later shortened to an 'iron-wage law'. Rather, it expresses the historical process that Ricardo and Marx conclusively adhered to in political economy: the loss of the precapitalist basis of reproduction of the labouring classes (the market-dependence of grain and of labour); and the assertion of the capitalist population-law, according to which the production and reproduction of labour-power itself proceeds according to the rules of the commodity-economy (the subsumption of pauperism under the population-law).

The remainder of the needs of the working class, which was not to be accommodated in the simple determination of the value of the commodity labour-power by its costs of reproduction, was, indeed, still noted by Marx; however, in the critique of political economy generally it was treated as a *quantité negligeable*. In *Capital*, it is only incidentally noted that, in opposition to other commodities, the value-determination of labour-power contained 'an historical and moral element'. What is meant here are the traditional living standards, historical tradition and social custom.[19]

The early socialist theoreticians who immediately connected onto classical political economy (the so-called Ricardian socialists William Thompson and Thomas Hodgskin, amongst others) sought precisely to stay firm to this moral element of the wage – of course, already in the context of the labour-theory of value, which was bound to be unsuccessful theoretically, but was historically founded. They turned the contradiction in the law of value between the objectified product of labour or between labour as the measure of all values, on the one hand, and labour-income, on the other hand, against the law of value itself from

18. Turgot 1859, § 6, p. 247; translation modified.
19. Marx 1976, p. 275.

the standpoint of the working class. They demanded that the wage of the worker should fundamentally be measured according to the labour-product, that the worker had the 'right to the full labour income' or should obtain a just share of the product as wage. Expressed in Marx's terms: they claimed the use-value that labour-power had for capital, against its exchange-value. This 'egalitarian application' of the labour-theory of value to the wage – the 'application of morality to economics' (Engels)[20] – began from the critical view that the production of wealth was irresolvably irredeemably bound up with the production of poverty in capitalism, that living labour was just as much the source of social wealth as it was the source of impoverishment of the class bound to it. The Ricardian socialists therefore provided for the first time a wage-theory on the basis of the value-creating power of labour, which in this form was of even greater significance for the struggling self-consciousness of the early working class because the wage was still understood comprehensively and morally as the right to the produced wealth. But that was at the same time a worker-ideology that no longer allowed any legitimation for a right to existence outside of wage-labour.

II

Marx and Engels initially began from this early socialist view in the 1840s. According to this view, the greatest opposition to the abstraction of the law of value was the empirical fact of the poverty of the worker (his 'alienation' [*Entfremdung*], as Marx said in the *Paris Manuscripts*). In the early writings, and above all in the Introduction to the 'Critique of Hegel's Philosophy of Right' of 1843–4, which is among Marx's most revolutionary texts, the critique of religion and philosophy – as critique of the abstraction of a highest being – was directly translated into a critique of political economy, which demanded the practical cancellation of private property (of capital) and thus of all the laws set to work behind the backs of social subjects. This critique ended with a 'categorical imperative', '*to overthrow all relations* in which man is a debased, enslaved, forsaken, despicable being'.[21] It cannot be denied that the role of intelligence, as Marx saw it founded in this connection of critique and overthrow, was tailored to his own political claims; but it was also contrary to the poverty of the German intellectuals of the *Vormärz*. The concept of the proletariat that Marx used here was more derived from the Feuerbachian concept of human species-being (the quintessence of all social properties of the human) than from the actually existing waged working class. But this philosophically coloured concept left enough room for the breadth

---

20. Engels 1975–2004c, p. 281.
21. Marx 1975–2004l, p. 182.

and dynamic of the social process. Precisely because of this, it did not yet link the perspective of proletarian emancipation and liberation to the development of capital. It required a long and difficult theoretical process, a thorough-going transformation of the function of theory itself, which was still not complete in 1848, and dramatic political experiences of the defeat of the proletariat and the communist movement, before Marx had worked himself up to the recognition of the scientific character of the labour-theory of value and understood the economic categories of a Ricardo as abstractions of real relations.[22] By this stage, he also accepted as scientifically necessary and honest Ricardo's conception that the history of the development of the productive forces is its own end, regardless of the victims with which it was bought and 'although at first the development of the capacities of the *human* species takes place at the cost of the majority of human individuals and whole human classes'.[23] The pathos of a theory of revolution gave way to the prosaic anatomy of bourgeois civil society.

As an anatomy of bourgeois civil society, the critique of political economy in its definitive version contains not only an analysis of the commodity (analysis of exchange on the basis of the value-substance in social labour); rather, it also includes an analysis of the production-process and of labour. This analysis, in its differentiation of living labour-power's exchange-value and use-value, of necessary and surplus-labour, ruptures the contradiction of the law of value. [24] The problem of the value inequivalence between labour's wage and labour's product, which classical political economy had named without being able to explain it, is thus resolved in the following way: the wage is defined by Marx initially within the sphere of circulation as a form of exchange in which the commodity-character of labour-power is historically presupposed and is rendered in a value-form through the payment of maintenance-costs. This exchange act has, however, as we have said, presuppositions outside of itself: on the one hand, 'previous accumulation', the separation of labour and means of production or life; on the other hand, the presupposition of the capitalist production-process, which reproduces this separation in a law-like way. Stated briefly, the existence of living labour

---

22. 'To put the cost of manufacture of hats and the cost of maintenance of men on the same plane is to turn men into hats', Marx wrote in 1847 in the *Poverty of Philosophy*. This cynicism, however, lies in the facts, in the economic relations that Ricardo had uncovered. Marx 1975–2004m, p. 125.

23. Marx 1975–2004n, p. 348.

24. In the methodical transition of the critique of political economy from the sphere of exchange to the analysis of the production-process, however, the category of value itself changes: at first, value, just as in Smith, is founded in the socialisation of labour in simple commodity-exchange; then, however, as abstract labour, in the internal labour-organisation – in that which Marx calls the relation of necessary and surplus labour within the valorisation-process.

as 'non-value'[25] is presupposed, as something valueless when taken on its own and a source of value only in contact with the means of production *qua* capital. The contradiction of classical political economy is thus resolved by observing the foundational production-process under the aspect of the creation of value and by acknowledging that living labour in its expenditure has the particular quality of adding more value to the product than the value that it itself requires for its maintenance. Its use-value for capital is higher than its own exchange-value, Marx says. The labour-wage remains as circulation- and distribution- form (revenue) on a level where it is uninteresting for the critique of political economy. Wages are by definition no theme of value-creation. On the other hand, the value of labour-power – following its definition as commodity-quantum for the reproduction of workers – migrates, so to speak, into the production-process of capital. The reproduction-costs of labour become an organic component-part of capital.[26] Within the production-process, these reproduction-costs represent the part of the working day necessary for the worker, while in contrast, capital, with the appropriation of all expended labour in the value-product of the whole working day, has at its disposal surplus-labour for free. This relation of necessary and surplus-labour and its particular form of organisation, the form of production of surplus-value and of the exploitation of labour, are explained as the real contradiction of political economy.

The translation of the reproduction-problematic of the class into the interior of capital simultaneously witnesses the objectification of the class-contradiction. This contradiction now only appears inside capital itself, as a relation of constant capital (means of production/dead labour/accumulated surplus-value) and variable capital (costs of reproduction of living labour/wages). Every single capitalist commodity-product reflects the difference between the maintenance-costs of the labour-power that has gone into it, the constant capital applied to production and carried over into value-commensurate forms and the newly created surplus-value. In its turn, it is this total relation, this so-called 'organic composition' of capital in its growth and with the profit-rate calculated on this basis, to which ultimately Marx's pseudo-dialectic of the development of productive forces connects: the presupposition for both the liquidation of capital's own foundations in living labour as well as for the transformation of accumulated surplus-labour into non-labour time (disposable time) as condition of communism is sought in the laws of the movement and accumulation of capital itself.

At any rate, the critique of political economy and the theory of surplus-value leave the breakthrough-points of a subjective class-antagonism open. The struggle of the workers against machinery, against the capitalist labour-organisation

---

25. Marx 1973, pp. 295f.
26. Marx speaks of 'variable capital', by which he means the living source of value.

and the struggles over the normal working day are subsumption included in the dialectic of necessary labour and surplus-labour, just as the different forms of surplus-value (absolute and relative surplus-value) correspond to different historical answers and levels of labour to capital. Marx's wage-theory nevertheless does not go beyond the determination of reproduction-costs developed by classical political economy. This determination, taken in itself, is extremely narrow, insofar as it limits the class-reproduction to a quantity of commodities for the maintenance of the workers. Once it has been located in the sphere of circulation – as said – the wage-determination for the critique of political economy is essentially settled. Labour-wages do, indeed, affect profit and in the broadest sense the conditions of realisation of capital; they are a domain of trade-unions, which hold the price of labour-power to the level of its value. In the critique of political economy, however, the wage and the reproduction of the class are transformed into a moment of the reproduction of capital.

III

The critique of political economy of Marx is Janus-faced. Its scientific-critical side is to have uncovered the contradiction of political economy since Smith as a contradiction in the production-process of capital and to have represented the reproduction of labour-power *qua* class as occurring within capital – as its processing contradiction. In the critique of political economy – and this is its historical truth – the destruction of the precapitalist basis of the reproduction of the class and its transformation into abstract labour-power is conceptualised. From the moment when class-reproduction occurred in the commodity-form and was predominantly the result of wage-labour, it was in reality no longer a case of arguing in political economy about the corn-standard, the subsistence-economy or other allocations of reproduction, but rather, about the value of labour-power. The critique of political economy thus reflects the fact that the subsistence-question and class-reproduction in the course of the nineteenth century was factually taken up into capital; first, with the reproduction of the labour-power of the single worker, then – via the trade-union wage-dynamic and in the direction of social policy – the reproduction of the family and so forth.

The other side of the critique of political economy is that it anticipates and codifies this process. If anything compels us to the revision of Marxism, then it is the social history of the early nineteenth century. In his critique of political economy, Marx reduced the revolutionary social question that was thrown up with the subsistence-revolts before 1848 to the concept of the value of labour-power and the costs of reproduction. The mass poverty of the *Vormärz* was bound to labour, without wage-labour being a sufficient criterion of its class-status in relation to capital. The orientation of Marx's class-concept to the subsumption of labour is a one-sided reduction in which the demand for guarantees of existence is no longer reflected. The immediate material relations of the masses were not to be referred to the capitalist development of the means of production as condition for its appropriation. The contradiction that the oppressed position of the proletariat heralded at the same time the overthrow of the previous world-order was not taken up into the dialectic of necessary labour and surplus-labour.

In brief: Marx's critique of political economy doesn't really go beyond the problematic of bourgeois political economy. It takes the real subsumption of the working class for granted, instead of taking up the revolutionary content of the movements before 1848. Marxism theorises the abstraction of labour-capacity and derives from it the sketch of an industrial working class whose historical mission is supposed to consist in confrontation with capital. In the end, the revolutionary subject disappears into the pseudo-antagonism of the development of productive forces and of productive relations. On this point, Marxism represents a left variant of bourgeois answers and of the expropriation of the social movements on the stage of 1848 – it formulates only the defeat of a generation of class-struggles.

Marx tried – we will still have to come back to this – to interpret the defeat of the proletariat in the revolution of 1848 as the definitive defeat of the illusion according to which the proletariat could set forward its own class-interest within the bourgeois revolution, beside the bourgeoisie. However, he drew from this the conclusion that the cause of the defeat was to be sought in the lacking sociological development of class opposition, in the weakness of the early working class. Thus, on this basis, the critique of political economy is from the outset conceived on the basis of the development of the capitalist mode of production and of the modern means of production as 'means of revolutionary emancipation', that is, on the basis of the elaboration of a distinct industrial working class by capital itself.[27]

In terms of its consequences for class- and revolutionary theory, Marxism binds the social movements of the first half of the nineteenth century via the stage of the bourgeois revolution to the development and modernity of capital. The proletarian revolution becomes an imitation of the bourgeois revolution. The contradiction between the relations of production and the productive forces, which is supposed to give the overthrow its objective foundation, is oriented on the period of transformation from feudalism to capitalism. In its transfer, it lacks the medium in which the proletariat (like the revolutionary bourgeoisie) could develop itself as an historical subject, constituting itself as a class and developing

---

27. Marx 1975–2004k, p. 56.

the social and economic dynamic which would be antagonistic against the capitalist relations of production. In its position, there instead appears the worker-
and party-organisation as structural pendent of the development of technical
productive force; factory and party come together in their aspects of modernity,
organisational logic and discipline. The dimension of a social revolution of the
proletariat is ultimately reduced – and here also Marxism reflects the model of
the bourgeois revolution – to the question of the conquest of political power and
the installation of a dictatorship.

IV

The critique of political economy is, according to its own self-understanding, not
a theory of revolution. At any rate, the constitution of the revolutionary subject
has no systematic place in it. A social and economic dynamic that would be
unmediated with capital is not developed. There is no longer any economy of
the lower classes outside of the economy of capital – that Marxism announces
this and that it relocates the revolutionary contradiction in the development
of the capitalist mode of production itself is, as said, in favour of the transformation-process itself that gripped the Western European societies around the
middle of the nineteenth century. In Marxism's favour is the fact that the historical and material preconditions of a 'moral economy' had largely fallen away
by the time of its emergence, that all precapitalist modes of subsistence and
reproduction, when not destroyed, had been incorporated inside capital. On the
other hand, every objectification of the class-contradiction, as is undertaken in
Marxism, every perspective of an objective antagonism within capital – right
up to 'breakdown-theory' – has historical experience against it. The social revolution has been overdue since the nineteenth century. With the integration of
class-reproduction into capital there thus remains an empty place that signals
the imperative for the overthrow of the capitalist system.

Within the critique of political economy, that is, with its own conceptuality,
this empty space cannot be resolved. In fact, the contradiction of necessary labour
and surplus-labour in Marx is no pendant in the wage-theory. Marx methodically
distinguishes rigorously between value-theory and the theory of surplus-value,
on the one hand, and wage-theory, on the other. Thus there is a lack of a dialectic
on the side of the class as subject, a contradictoriness that would be bound to the
reproduction of the class.[28] The critique of political economy can only be held

---

28. If this strikes us as a deficiency, then it is only because we have the Keynesian
integration of demand into the capital-dynamic behind us, because the reproduction not
only of capital but even more of the class within capital via income- and population-
policy belongs to the classical instruments of the economy mediated by the state. Capital

if one takes it up one-sidedly as science: that is, as critical analysis of bourgeois society and at the same time as bourgeois thought-form; and if one, on the other hand, is willing to accept the fact that it defines the class in its sociality and revolutionary subjectivity only in negative terms – as 'non-value'.

How problematic the connection of political economy and theory of revolution in Marx is, between the laws of motion of capital and class-constitution, will be highlighted in the following with passages from the preparatory work for *Capital*.

The *Grundrisse* and the economic manuscripts of 1861–3 (first published in the new MEGA² in 1976) give a categorical definition of labour as commodity ('labour-capacity'; Marx says later: labour-power) and as class. It is first 'non-value', the purely subjective existence of labour as absolute poverty, excluded from means of labour and life. The worker:

> is as such, according to its concept, pauper, as the 'personification and bearer of his capacity isolated from his objectivity'. Second, labour is the 'living source of value', but it is this only insofar as it is taken up into capital, as it is use-value for capital. Third: the use-value of labour for the worker is its exchange-value, 'a *predetermined* amount of commodities', which is as little its own product as it is its own value. Sismondi says that the workers exchange their labour for grain, which they consume, while their labour 'has become capital for its master'.[29]

Marx defines the value of living labour-capacity on the model of already objectified dead labour. Thus begins the vicious circle. He carries over the definition of commodity-value without ado to the exchange-value of the commodity labour-power ('the cost of production, the amount of objectified labour, by means of which the labouring capacity of the worker has been produced').[30] In the process, he holds firm to the proposition that on this level of exchange between labour and capital (as wage) there reigns equivalence. He thus assumes a working class that is reproduced completely within capital and whose mere reproduction is not productive. The secret of the capitalist mode of production, the creation of value, consists in the consumption of the use-value of labour-power by capital – but that, for all intents and purposes, does not have anything to do with the working class anymore. With this application of the law of value to the value of labour-power, Marx bypasses, as said, only apparently the actual difficulty of the classical political economy of Smith: namely, the difficulty of unifying the

---

has subsumed class-reproduction just as extensively as labour, and nothing is changed if parts of this reproduction since the end of Keynesianism have once more been made unpaid.

29. *MEGA²*, II/3.1, p. 35; Marx 1973, pp. 304f.
30. Marx 1973, pp. 304f.

determination of value by the labour-quantum (quantity of labour) with the exchange of labour in living form, with value treated as resolved in the 'value of labour' and in profit or rent. The determination of the value of labour-capacity remains only an inessentially modified version of the wage-law, as it was presented by Anne-Robert-Jacques Turgot and David Ricardo. Marx also adheres to the 'minimum of the salary or average labour-wage'.[31] There are only a few moments through which a dynamic comes into the wage-law: the determination of the value of labour-power from a moral and historical perspective of class; the competition for the wage in the working class; the rise of labour-productivity that has an impact as a lessening of necessary labour-time; and finally the trade-union function of conforming the wage as price to the value of labour-power, or to push it beyond such value, in which case the wage becomes a dimension of struggle. But here it is only a case of modifications to a law, according to which the value of labour-power is measured according to the maintenance-costs of the working population; or it is merely a case of the function of regulating the price of the commodity labour-power in the context of economic growth.[32]

The lack of understanding regarding the social demands of the masses and their anti-capitalist dynamic that characterises Marx's theory in the period of 1848 is reflected in the deficiency of the economic categories. A social-historical concept of class-reproduction that was not itself an immanent component part of capitalist reproduction, but rather, was in immediate opposition to capital, does not appear in the critique of political economy. There is also lacking any reflection on the fact that capital always exploits, and not only in its primary accumulation-phase, preconditions not made and maintained by itself almost as a natural foundation: the subsistence-economy, the family-economy, forms of only formally subsumed labour and so forth.[33] Value-theory, applied to labour-power, defines reproduction only as a movement in capital and no longer as a moving antagonistic side from below. The leaving out of that side of reproduction has the consequence that Marx nowhere develops a concept of class as subject and of social power against capital. He initially uses a philosophical but then – as counterpart to the economic category of class as labour-power – a

31. *MEGA*[2], II/3.1, pp. 37f.

32. The reproduction-schemas in *Capital* Volume II present the reproduction of the working classes – with the movement of the wage from department 1/means of production – as mere mediation of the maintenance of constant capital of department 2/means of consumption or of the reverse transformation of the variable capital of department 1 into money-capital. The only thing that this movement does not allow to appear tautologically is that the maintenance of the working class forms the precondition for the expanded reproduction of total capital.

33. The preconditions are of course not only those that go under, or are tendentially subsumed to capital. Rather, they are regularly created anew by capital in global unevenness; capital always reverts back to labour-power that it does not reproduce itself.

political class concept, which is bourgeois through and through, and in which class-formation becomes an organisation-question. In this context, reproduction-costs and wages appear as a trade-union business of the maintenance of the existence of the working class, so that it remains capable of forming itself as a political force. Just as it is a consequence of the critique of political economy that the class-constitution remains completely subordinated to the capitalist indus-trial development-process and that the possibility of the proletarian revolution is made dependent on the state of capitalist development, so it is only logical when Marxism ultimately can grasp the revolution as a political act, not really as a social revolution. The break is always only political: politically, labour-power becomes the working class, but it becomes so for Marx only then when all sub-jects are labour-power.

In the critique of political economy the class is circumscribed, as it is to be comprehended from the inner of capital, with the concept of 'non-value'. We must understand that Marx – incidentally, exactly like Hegel – articulates with this a moment of liberation, that is, the historical progress that 'the worker is ... formally posited as a person who is something for himself apart from his labour, and who alienates his life-expression only as a means towards his own life'.[34] In Marx's dialectic of progress, poverty and freedom are indissolubly bound together. The person, the formal subject of rights of bourgeois society, is consti-tuted in the division of subjective existence and value (value-objectivity), and this division – with primary accumulation and the sublation of feudalism com-pleted – is the condition of 'free labour', for it is not the person of the worker that is sold, but rather, the temporary disposition over the worker's labour-capacity. But this definition of 'non-value' too, however much it may keep open the field of subjectivity outside of labour (it is the 'kingdom of freedom' that begins with the shortening of the working day, as Marx says) remains still a categorical deter-mination in relation to capital. It is more than merely an echo of Hegel's philoso-phy when Marx describes the labourer as pauper, 'as the personification of his capacity isolated from his objectivity'.[35] The concepts of proletariat and poverty not only do not correspond to the empirical poverty of the working classes, but are rather completely detached from their social-historical location. The class becomes an economic category; the speculative concept of the proletariat that Marx had taken in his early writings from Feuerbach's critique of religion is filled – since reality does not comply with it – with general determinations of politi-cal economy, namely – disposition over one's own capacity to labour as com-modity, non-ownership of the conditions of realisation of labour. The historical relation of this class-concept is now only that of the general capital-relation and

---

34. Marx 1973, p. 292.
35. *MEGA*[2], II/3.1, p. 35; compare Hegel 1970b, § 244.

its preconditions, which must be fulfilled in order for labour-power to appear as commodity.

V

Which historical reasons could justify the fact that Marx always sees the wage as located within narrow limits? That he even excludes any possibility of the regulation of the immanent crisis-tendency of the capitalist mode of production via the wage-dynamic?[36] The critique of political economy assumes the presence of a working class that can no longer orient and claim its 'self-value' in the subsistence-economy, in the social right of the old society. In other words: it assumes the destruction of the revolutionary challenges and social movements of the early nineteenth century just as it assumes the despotic programme of industrialism. The transformation of the orientation of social demands from the traditional right to existence and from the corn-standard to a wage-determination on the basis of capitalist development is assumed in the critique of political economy, but it is not theoretically considered. Already the early socialist wage-theories, which are valid as 'egalitarian application of the labour-theory of value' (in which the wage is supposed to be determined on the basis of the value of the labour-product), suggest this transformation – for the first time, wages and productivity were linked to workers' demand. Marx now has nothing more in front of him than the limited wage within capital. He sets out from the fact that family-reproduction in the middle of the nineteenth century was largely destroyed by capital – female and child-labour – and that the wage-struggles of the first worker-generation were largely aimed at the mere maintenance of existence. He neither describes the traditional wage-problematic in the form in which it is still to be found behind Smith's confusion between value and the corn-price, and which was only levelled by Ricardo, comprehended as being in a state of dissolution, nor does he note – which was just as decisive for the course of the wage-struggles of the nineteenth century – that process in which within determinate segments of the working class a new formation of the wage occurred, which was not dictated exclusively by the side of capital: the process of implementation of the male wage as family-wage through the trade-unionisation of labour-power,

---

36. Thus in *Capital* Volume III, in the section on the law of the tendency of the rate of profit to fall, where Marx indeed founds the general possibility of capitalist crisis in the falling apart of immediate surplus-value production and realisation. At the same time, however, he speaks of the limited power of the consumption of society as if it were that of a natural law ('[...] the power of consumption within a given framework of antagonistic conditions of distribution, which reduce the consumption of the vast majority of society to a minimum level, only capable of varying within more or less narrow limits'). Marx 1981, p. 352.

the stabilisation of the wage-levels of national labour-elites compared to newly subsumed labour, migration-labour and so forth.

Additionally, there is the following: already in the run-up to the revolution of 1848 the subsistence-question and the social conflictuality bound up with it was overlaid by politics as a masculine form of the public sphere and an agitation for the universal right to vote. The further development of capitalism was indissolubly entwined with the recent stabilisation of patriarchal structures in the proletariat. To the extent, that is, that capital advanced from the indiscriminate exhaustion of a pre-found generation of women, children and men to the ordered valorisation and reproduction of labour-power within itself; to the extent which labour-organisations developed and masculine wage-standards were won, a patriarchal worker-ideology[37] found its material basis, which ultimately repressed women back into the family. The index of this development is that the epoch of the subsistence-unrest in Europe came to an end. The historical limit of these struggles was reached around the middle of the century. A new model of political representation, the developed industrial and labour trade-unionism brought a type of class-confrontation to an end. It had been a form of class-confrontation in which women had been predominantly present and whose historical meaning and 'modernity' lay in resistance against the determination by capital of a mode of reproduction of the underclasses.

That the critique of political economy does not reflect on this historical turning point of the middle of the nineteenth century and the defeat connected with it as its own presupposition, does not represent any deficit, but rather, constitutes its affirmative character. Connected to this is a theory of history which – precisely where it is formulated as a theory of capitalist crisis – draws its ideas of progress and liberation from the dynamic of capital itself, which elevates the tendency towards destruction immanently dwelling within capital into the hope of the proletariat – and, indeed, in a process that goes on over generations. The materialist conception of history, the central points of which Marx and Engels had already worked out in 1845–6, and which were cast in the 'Preface' to the *Contribution to the Critique of Political Economy* of 1859 in that mechanical schema according to which history progresses as the contradiction of forces of production and relations of production – this conception of history was once again proposed in the *Capital* Volume III and ultimately justified as the 'automatic subject' of history on the basis of self-valorising value.[38] Whatever versions the contradiction assumes – between the historical progress of the working of nature and the inner composition of capital, between the limitless expansion of production and the limited capitalist distribution- and consumption-relations, as

---

37. Rancière and Vauday 1975.
38. Marx 1976, p. 255.

contradictory law of the development of productive forces, fall of the profit-rate and expansion of surplus-value masses or of total capital – Marx draws out of one side of this contradiction, out of the limitless development of the productive forces of social labour, the historical legitimation of the capitalist mode of production in its entirety and at the same time the objective guarantee – the material preconditions – of a 'higher form of production'.[39]

It thus makes little sense to refer back to the humanism of Marx's early writings or their revolutionary aspects, according to the style of the old discussion of Marxism. *Capital* is not a theory of revolution, but rather, a pitiless analysis of the capitalist mode of production in which the exploitation of labour-power is represented but in which the subjective side – the proletariat as revolutionary subject – is only present as a figure. Here there is also an insight. There are more than epistemological reasons (which we would need to look for in the development of Marx's work) for the fact that a revolutionary class in *Capital* is no longer present. This class comes forward in the real history of the second half of the nineteenth century only in the activity of the Paris Commune. Just as the other great revolutionary thinkers of the epoch, above all Blanqui, turned to cosmology and sought the guarantees for – or despaired of – the revolution in the orbits of the heavens, so Marx oriented himself according to the objective laws of capital.

VI

The affirmative character of Marx's theory, however, goes further. Why does Marx apply the idea of communism, which socially and historically contains nothing other than an equal distribution of goods and the guarantee of the right of existence,[40] not only to labour, to the association of producers (the utopia of the renewal of community with industrial means that had been formulated in early socialism and communism)? Rather, why does he raise a development of human capacities in the measure of production for the sake of production[41] to a precondition of communism? Behind this there is less the critique of the old communism as an equality of poverty, but rather, the establishment as seemingly self-evident of the thought of development as seemingly self-evident: Marx follows a paradigm of historical development that explains the subsumption of the subject as labour-power to be historically necessary and accepts its 'educative process' by capital – dulling down of its subjective particularities. Thus even

39. Marx 1981, p. 368.
40. Meyer 1999, pp. 199f.; Meyer 1977, pp. 223ff.
41. Marx 1975–20040, p. 348.

the lack of homogeneity and social breadth of the early proletariat appears as immaturity. Not only in Engels, Kautsky or in the Social Democracy of the nineteenth century but rather already in Marx, this thought of development, which was less oriented on Hegel than on Darwin, turns into the deterministic idea of an objectively necessary transition from one social formation to another, from capitalism to communism. Ultimately, it leads to positing technical-industrial development and proletarian emancipation as one and the same process. The fact that Marxism in its later phases, up until Bolshevism, appears as organisation-theory and development-ideology has its origin precisely here.

The political programme of Marxism is also affected by this conception of history, which initially – in the *Manifesto of the Communist Party* – assumes the immediate transformation of the bourgeois revolution into the proletarian revolution, thus already propagating the one as the necessary precondition of the other. Later, however, in its revision after the defeat of 1848, this led to a stage-ist model in which the proletariat only accepts, to a certain extent, the inheritance of the bourgeois era after a long process of formation. 'Bourgeois' and 'proletarian' revolution are pulled apart into distinct historical events, between which there is a consequential relationship. This, in its turn, gives the measure that has its real meaning less in the treatment of history than in the practical treatment of the question of class- and party-coalitions, namely, that social layers and classes in their struggles are committed to an epochal goal corresponding to each case. Ultimately, however, the political theory and revolution-theory of Marx and Engels, as they formulated it around 1848, arose from the attempt at legitimising a factional standpoint within the early labour-movement and the extension of the revolutionary process in the history of formation of the industrial working class.

Marx and Engels always assumed that the proletariat had to have an interest in the revolutionary movement of the bourgeoisie and in their direct political domination. The precondition of the constitution of the proletariat into a class and political party is its deployment for the political goals of the bourgeoisie, in which the workers' movement remains in the first instance only of a secondary significance. The proletariat and the bourgeoisie develop hand in hand. The bourgeois revolution is the condition of the proletarian revolution, because it clarifies the tenuous front-lines between the two classes and because the proletariat can appropriate the political educative elements and bourgeois freedoms, and turn them into weapons against the bourgeoisie. For communists in Germany, the *Manifesto of the Communist Party* therefore developed the tactic of not acting independently in the imminent bourgeois revolution, but rather of fighting together with the revolutionary bourgeoisie against the late feudal-absolutist system, while at the same time elaborating among the workers the opposition

278 • Ahlrich Meyer

contained in this alliance, since 'the German bourgeois revolution [...] will be
but the prelude to an immediately following proletarian revolution'.[42]

However, in Germany the workers' party had fallen under the leadership of
the petty-bourgeois democrats and had been 'exploited and taken in tow by the
bourgeoisie'; in France, the attempt of the proletariat 'to set its interests alongside those of the bourgeoisie' ended with the June defeat of 1848. From these
experiences, Marx and Engels, in the 1850 'Address to the Central Council of the
League of Communists', drew conclusions from this and demanded the organisational independence of the workers' party – in the context of a long, as they
said, revolutionary development and 'revolution in permanence'.[43] In the course
of the 1850s, in the analysis of the connection between the economic crisis of
1847 and the revolutions of 1848, Marx and Engels then became convinced that
one could no longer talk about a new revolution and 'that the state of economic
development on the Continent [...] was not, by a long way, ripe for the elimination of capitalist production'.[44] At the same time, when the League of Communists split in 1850 – over the question of the position of the German proletariat
in the next revolution, of the necessity of bourgeois domination in Germany
and of the presuppositions of a proletarian transformation – Marx and Engels,
against the Willich-Schapper faction, raised the charge of making human will
the driving force of the revolution, instead of real social relations.[45] Directed to
the workers, Marx and Engels – who already before 1848 had not concealed their
disappointment with the existing class in the form of the Parisian craftsmen-
workers – referred to the 'rudimentary development of the German proletariat' and declared: 'You will have to go through 15, 20, 50 years of civil wars and
national struggles not only to bring about a change in society but also to change
yourselves, and prepare yourselves for the exercise of political power'.[46]

Thus they definitively dissolved the initially postulated, close historical connection between the bourgeois and proletarian revolutions. In its place, from
1850 onwards in the critique of political economy, there appeared the deduction of the possibility of a transformation of capitalism from the economic cycle
of prosperity and crisis.[47] In the place of a theory of proletarian revolution, of
how it would come out of the bourgeois revolution as its immediate prelude and

---

42. Marx and Engels 1975–2004b, pp. 519f. In France, they say succinctly, 'the Communists ally themselves with the Social-Democrats'.
43. Marx and Engels 1975–2004c, pp. 277f.
44. Engels 1875–2004d, p. 512.
45. Marx 1975–2004p, p. 403. Fundamentally, in this they repeat a critique of Weitling's
social-revolutionary concepts that Schapper himself had made in the London 'Bund der
Gerechten'; see Bund der Kommunisten 1970, pp. 214f.; Meyer 1999, pp. 238f.
46. Marx 1975–2004p, p. 403.
47. First in the 'Revue' of 1850 – Marx and Engels 1975–2004d, pp. 490f.; compare
Engels 1975–2004d, pp. 510f.

could go further given the existing social wealth (the *Communist Manifesto* still assumed this condition as given), there appears schematism, according to which capitalist development of the productive forces of modern large-scale industry should form the condition and the driving force of a proletarian revolution. Only once again, in the writings on the Paris Commune,[48] does Marx again see the direct action of the proletariat. In its classical from, however, the form in which it was received by the social-democratic workers' movement, Marxism elevated the priority of the 'industrial revolution' for the working class into a programme, and, as Karl Korsch argued, conjured communism away, out of the contemporary movement.

Translated by Peter Thomas

---

48. Marx 1975–2004q, pp. 307–59.

Poverty, Labour, Development:
Towards a Critique of Marx's Conceptualisations
Max Henninger

The capitalist world-economy has manoeuvred itself
into a crisis that heralds far-reaching transformations.
The rapid immiseration of entire societies, evident in
large parts of Africa since the 1970s and in the former
Soviet republics since the 1990s, will doubtless continue
to shape political developments. A drastic lowering of
underclass reproductive standards is to be reckoned
with the world over. The process will no doubt play
out in a highly graduated manner. In the metropoles,
it threatens to go hand in hand with the enforcement
of new types of unfree und unremunerated labour; in
the periphery, it will likely be accompanied by major
famines. New international resource-wars may not yet
be in sight, but those warning of their advent are sec-
onded by historical experience: until this day, every
crisis of comparable magnitude has ended in major
outbreaks of military violence. Meanwhile, the political hopes by which the anti-globalisation movement
was able to sustain itself for a number of years have
yielded to a diffuse anxiety that resists articulation in
programmes and demands but transitions rapidly into
open hostility towards the state and its increasingly
militarised security-forces, as evidenced by the growing frequency of youth-revolts in the poorer neighbourhoods of European cities.

Parts of the intelligentsia have been prompted by the
crisis to engage anew with the work of Karl Marx and
his followers. This is by no means as natural a development as some would have it. There is no such thing as

a Marxist monopoly on the explanation of economic crises; professed non-Marxists explicitly place the 'necessary periodicity' of crises at the centre of their theoretical models.[1] Moreover, Marx's perspective on the social and political consequences of economic collapse is far too narrow to still be adequate today. This is partly related to his characterisation of the industrial proletariat as the prime agent of communism's emancipatory project, a characterisation that entails structural neglect of the non-industrial underclasses. Marxian theory also evinces a relationship to the industrialisation-process that is by no means only that of a ruthless critic. While the emergence of industrial capitalism, illustrated by reference to England in *Capital*, elicits many a critical remark from Marx, his view of this development remains essentially affirmative. Marx tells us capitalism creates labour that is 'superfluous from the point of view [...] of mere subsistence', to the point where 'natural need' is replaced by 'historically produced need'.[2] He argues that the *'most extreme form of estrangement'* promotes 'full development of human control over the forces of nature'.[3] And he insists that the 'total, universal development of the productive powers of the individual' – ostensibly the hallmark of communist society – requires this 'necessary transitional stage'.[4] Marx's view betrays a faith in the emancipatory potential of capitalist development that we should rid ourselves of – those of us, that is, who have not already been prompted to do so by the experiences of the twentieth century.

It was only once, towards the end of his life, that Marx self-critically revised his predictions concerning industrialisation, the crisis-wracked collapse of capitalism and the transition to communism – and even then, he did so only grudgingly and half-heartedly. He and Engels noted in the preface to the second Russian edition of the *Communist Manifesto* (1882) that 'Russia's present communal land-ownership may serve as the point of departure for a communist development' even without the processes of expropriation described, in *Capital*, under the heading of 'primitive accumulation' – albeit only on the condition that 'the Russian revolution becomes the signal for proletarian revolution in the West'.[5] This remark was the fruit of Marx's engagement with an issue whose full import was to become apparent only after his death: the prospects for social revolution in pre-industrial or only partly industrialised societies.[6] In a brief letter to Marx, the Russian revolutionary Vera Zasulich had pointed out the economic and social peculiarities of her country and cautiously questioned the historical necessity

---

1. Schumpeter 1934, p. 216.
2. Marx 1975–2004j, pp. 250f.
3. Marx 1975–2004j, pp. 411, 439.
4. Marx 1975–2004j, p. 439 (emphasis in original).
5. Marx and Engels 1983, p. 139 (translation modified).
6. Wolf 1969.

of primitive accumulation and industrialisation.[7] Marx's reply, which he spent several weeks drafting, was even shorter than Zasulich's original letter, and it must have seemed quite unsatisfactory, as he himself will have known. Marx assured Zasulich that, in writing the chapter on primitive accumulation, he had been thinking only of Western Europe, and that the process described in that chapter ought by no means to be understood as one all other countries would necessarily have to suffer through.[8] And yet in *Capital*, Marx had suggested quite strongly that the pertinence of the English case was universal.[9] Nor can there be any doubt the Marx of *Capital* would not have exempted primitive accumulation and industrialisation from those 'natural phases of its development' that a society can 'neither clear by bold leaps, nor by legal enactment'.[10] As we know, Marx was no longer able to systematically correct the predictions he had formulated on the basis of his earlier position.

Today, more than two centuries after the industrial revolution in England, and sixty years after US president Truman praised industrialisation as the royal way to prosperity and peace for Africa, Asia and Latin America, thereby inaugurating the golden age of international development-policy, some five billion people out of a world-population of 6.75 billion live in countries that continue to be considered underdeveloped. Out of these five billion, 1.4 billion live in conditions that meet the definition of poverty currently employed by development-experts, meaning they dispose of less than 1.25 USD purchasing power per day. No one can plausibly argue that their reproduction corresponds to the model developed by Marx on the basis of industrial England. The labour-conditions in these countries cannot be adequately described using the category of doubly-free wage-labour.[11] Moreover, if the process by which 'capitalistic production takes possession of agriculture' should be completed the world over during the coming decades,[12] the majority of the world's peasants (whose total number, 2.8 billion, still corresponds to more than a third of the world's population) would be rendered economically superfluous, that is, unemployable both within and without agriculture.[13] More than a billion people from the other, urban half of the world's population already find themselves in this position today. The informal proletariat of the world's slums survives in other ways than those posited in political economy and its critique; researchers have spoken of this proletariat

---

7. Geierhos 1977, pp. 170–91, 256–62. See also Shanin (ed.) 1983.
8. Marx 1975–2004g, p. 71.
9. Marx 1976, pp. 90f.
10. Marx 1976, p. 92.
11. van der Linden 2005; van der Linden 2008, pp. 17–37.
12. Marx 1976, p. 849, note 7.
13. Amin 2004.

posing a veritable 'wage puzzle'.[14] In what follows, I examine Marx's concepts of poverty, labour and development in order to do show that his analytical instruments are inadequate to these global realities.

I

How does Marx define the three concepts mentioned? Poverty is understood by him mainly in terms of the absence of property. (It also has a metaphorical meaning, that of limited needs and capacities, to which I return below.) A person's propertylessness can be understood as their inability to autonomously handle objects that are exterior, separable from them (an inability that is not naturally given, but rather posited legally and enforced by the threat of violence or by actual violence). Two subsets of such objects are of particular interest to Marx: the means of production (instruments of labour, raw materials) and the means of subsistence (prime necessities of life). The separation of individuals from their means of production and subsistence (in historically concrete terms: their separation from the land) was violently enforced in the course of primitive accumulation and constitutes the historical foundation of both pre-industrial pauperism and the capitalist mode of production.[15] Those who do not dispose of their own means of production can nevertheless put someone else's means of production to use, through work, but they will normally do so at the bidding and under the command of the owner. Those who do not dispose of their own means of subsistence and lack the possibility of producing them autonomously (because they lack the requisite means of production), will be constrained, given what are considered normal conditions under capitalism, to purchase means of subsistence on the market in order to survive. The coincidence of both cases of propertylessness with social relations under which alienating the right to dispose of one's labour-power constitutes a way of securing an income (and hence a way of purchasing the means of subsistence) characterises the proletarian: 'Labour as *absolute poverty*: [...] as a complete exclusion of objective wealth'.[16] The proletarian is a 'virtual pauper'.[17] Once he loses his income (the wage), he falls 'outside the conditions of reproduction of [his] existence' and can survive only 'by the charity of others'[18] or by theft – thereby becoming a lumpenproletarian.

Marx's comments on the lumpenproletariat are largely derisive, much as he rejected as quixotic Wilhelm Weitling's proposal to make the generalisation of

---

14. Davis 2006, p. 156.
15. Marx 1975–2004j, pp. 389ff., 399, 418–22; Marx1975–2004r, p. 202; Marx 1976, pp. 873–940.
16. Marx 1975–2004j, p. 222.
17. Marx 1975–2004j, p. 522.
18. Marx 1975–2004j, p. 528.

theft the basis of a social-revolutionary strategy.[19] Marx is less interested in poverty *per se* than in the poverty of those who work productively (for the owners of the means of production, in return for a wage and with capital-accumulation as the result), or whose separation from the means of production is revoked temporarily and heteronomously.[20] In other words, Marx conceptualises poverty from the perspective of labour. Poverty appears as a prerequisite or property of labour. It is, of course, the latter concept that takes centre stage in the theory presented by Marx in *Capital*.

According to the most general definition provided by Marx, labour is simply 'the use of labour-power', the employment of a capacity inherent to man (the 'bearer' of labour-power); moreover, it is 'first of all, a process between man and nature, a process by which man, through his own actions, mediates, regulates and controls the metabolism between himself and Nature', setting in motion 'the natural forces which belong to his own body' and thereby acting 'upon external nature and [changing] it'.[21] *Qua* activity, labour has a measurable duration, which is to say, it can be quantified. This is the basis of the axiom known as the law of value, according to which the value of the labour-products circulating on the market is determined by the average quantities of labour required for their production.[22] The law of value is an axiom in the sense that Marx never proves its validity, relying instead on its common-sense character and on the authority of the pertinent statements by Smith and Ricardo.[23] Marx treats the law of value as an *a priori* principle upon which to build the rest of his argument.

As is well known, Marx considers it an essential characteristic of capitalist societies that human labour-power appears in them as a commodity that can be bought and sold like other commodities. According to Marx, the labour-power employed under capitalism is owned by its bearer; in fact, in what Marx posited as the standard case, that of the proletarian, it is all the bearer owns. In Marx, the proletarian is doubly free: 'free' of his or her own means of production and subsistence and free to take his labour-power to market. It is no longer any secret that the 'doubly free wage-labourer' represents a gross simplification of both the historic and the current property- and labour-relations under capitalism, failing to do justice, among other things, to unfree labour's compatibility with capital-valorisation.

If, as Marx assumes, labour-power is as much a commodity as its products, then the general characteristics of commodities must apply to it, from which

---

19. Marx 1976, p. 797; Bund der Kommunisten 1970, pp. 221, 224, 303ff. See also Meyer 1977, pp. 157–222.
20. Marx 1975–2004j, pp. 230f.; Marx 1976, pp. 643–4.
21. Marx 1976, p. 283.
22. Marx 1975–2004j, p. 531; Marx 1976, p. 129.
23. Smith 1937, p. 30; Ricardo 1951, pp. 55f.

it follows that labour-power must also have a value determined by the average quantities of labour required for its production. Marx equates this value with that of the means of subsistence required for labour-power's maintenance.[24] This highly problematic equation – the truncations and elisions associated with it have been identified by the feminist critique of the 1970s and 1980s; I return to them below – allows Marx to point out that the exchange occurring between wage-labourers and capitalists is *de facto* an asymmetrical exchange despite being formally just. The value of labour-power has been justly remunerated when the value expressed in the wage corresponds to that of the commodities required for the worker's maintenance, yet the labour-power expended during the agreed working period will normally produce not just an equivalent of its own value, but also a surplus. The working day thus falls into two parts: one during which necessary labour (labour required for producing a product whose value is equivalent to that of labour-power) and one during which additional, surplus-labour is performed.[25] Wherever surplus-labour is performed, exploitation in the Marxian sense occurs. It is by reference to surplus-value, and hence to exploitation, that Marx formulates his account of the origins of profit.

Thus everything turns on commodity-producing wage-labour as performed by propertyless proletarians. Marx's remarks on how this form of labour emerges and develops fall within the rubric of his general concept of development. The first thing to say about this concept is that it turns on what Marx calls the development of the forces of production. 'Development of the forces of production' is not, as sometimes assumed, synonymous with 'development of the means of production'. In his general definition of labour, the central part of which was quoted above, Marx remarks in passing that man 'acts upon external nature and changes it, and in this way simultaneously changes his own nature'.[26] When Marx speaks of development of the forces of production, he is never referring only to the development of outer nature (to which the means of production belong), but always also to the development of human (or inner) nature as addressed in his definition of labour; he is always also referring, in other words, to the extension of human needs and capacities. Considered from the perspective of the communist society predicted by Marx, the development of the means of production is in fact no more than the reified expression of a more fundamental development of the human forces of production. In the *Grundrisse*, Marx formulates this notion by pointing out the restricted character of the economic concept of wealth: 'In fact, however, if the narrow bourgeois form is peeled off, what is wealth if not the

---

24. Marx 1976, pp. 272–7.
25. Marx 1975–2004j, pp. 244–51, 433; Marx 1976, pp. 299–300.
26. Marx 1976, p. 283.

universality of the individual's needs, capacities, enjoyments, productive forces, etc. [...]?'[27]

According to Marx, the 'absolute unfolding of man's creative abilities' addressed by this concept of development, the 'development of all human powers as such',[28] remains negligible until the capitalist mode of production has been imposed through violent expropriation. Of precapitalist economic orders based on communal ownership and agriculture, Marx says: 'Considerable developments are possible here within a particular sphere. Individuals may appear great. But free and full development, either of the individual or of society, is inconceivable here, since such a development stands in contradiction to the original relation'.[29] By contrast, the 'historical mission' of capitalism consists in 'constantly [whipping] on' the 'productive forces of labour'.[30] This mission is 'fulfilled when, on the one hand, needs are developed to the point where surplus labour beyond what is necessary has itself become a general need and arises from the individual needs themselves; and on the other, when, by the strict discipline of capital to which successive generations have been subjected, general industriousness has been developed as the universal asset of the new generation'.[31]

Capitalism marks a terminal stage in Marx's theory of history, as this last quotation makes clear. 'The exchange of living labour for objectified labour, that is, the positing of social labour in the form of the antithesis of capital and wage labour, is the ultimate development of the *value relationship* of production based on value'.[32] In a much discussed passage of the *Grundrisse*, Marx relates this terminal character of capitalism to progress in the natural sciences as reflected in the development of modern machinery, arguing that such progress entails a tremendous increase in the productivity of labour and a corresponding decrease in necessary labour. By its employment of machinery, capital becomes 'instrumental, *malgré lui*, in creating the means of social disposable time, of reducing labour time for the whole of society to a declining minimum, and of thus setting free the time of all [members of society] for their own development'.[33] To the extent that the exploitation or enforcement of surplus-labour continues, 'the relation of capital becomes a barrier to the development of the productive forces of labour. Once this point has been reached, capital, wage-labour, enters into the same relation to the development of social wealth and the productive forces as the

---

27. Marx 1975–2004j, p. 411.
28. Marx 1975–2004j, pp. 411f.
29. Marx 1975–2004j, p. 411. See also *Capital* Volume III, Marx 1981, p. 930.
30. Marx 1975–2004j, p. 250.
31. *Ibid.*
32. Marx 1975–2004r, p. 90 (emphasis in original).
33. Marx 1975–2004r, p. 94.

guild system, serfdom and slavery did, and is, as a fetter, necessarily cast off'.[34] This historical prediction, written with an eye to the (re-)appropriation of the means of production by the producers, is also formulated in a passage in *Capital* Volume III, albeit without reference to progress in the natural sciences. In *Capital* Volume III, Marx speaks of a 'conflict [...] between the material development of production and its social form' and of 'the contradiction and antithesis between, on the one hand, the relations of distribution [...] and, on the other hand, the productive forces', and he insists: 'Once a certain level of maturity is attained, the particular historical form is shed and makes way for a higher form'.[35]

Marx's historical prognosis clearly still impresses readers today. Yet it also very much bears the mark of the context within which it was formulated. Marx's fascination with the triumph of capitalism and the first world economic crisis, which appeared to herald the collapse of the entire mode of production,[36] is particularly evident in the *Grundrisse*. No less remarkable is the inevitability Marx attributes to the process described by him. The capitalist 'fetter' is 'necessarily cast off' – and much the same necessity is attributed to the processes of expropriation that precede the development of industrial capitalism. It has rightly been pointed out that such notions of historical necessity can easily foster a paralysing *Zwangsoptimismus* or compulsory optimism.[37] Most importantly, Marx's comments on the transition from one mode of production to the next remain astoundingly abstract. The chapter on primitive accumulation is a rare exception; the more characteristic passages compensate for their lack of precision with lapidarity ('Up to a certain point, reproduction. Then this turns into dissolution').[38] In particular, Marx has very little to say, in concrete terms, about how the transition to communism is to be enacted. On this point, it is hard not to concur with Hans-Jürgen Krahl, who remarked that the 'question concerning the genesis of the revolution' is largely elided in 'Marxian theory's reflection on class-struggles'.[39] Ahlrich Meyer has also pointed out that 'the critique of political economy is, according to its own self-understanding, not a theory of revolution. At any rate, the constitution of revolutionary subjectivity has no systematic place in it'.[40]

Three other features of Marx's concept of development should not be overlooked. Firstly, the development of 'society's productive power' does not cease with the superation of capitalism; on the contrary, it will 'develop [...] rapidly'

---

34. Marx 1975–2004r, p. 133.
35. Marx 1981, p. 1024.
36. Rosenberg 1974.
37. Lucas 1983, pp. 89–101.
38. Marx 1975–2004j, p. 419.
39. Krahl 1971, pp. 390f.
40. Meyer 1999, p. 121.

following the transition to communism.[41] According to Marx, mature capitalism's internal 'contradiction' consists precisely in the fact that 'the growth of the productive forces can no longer be tied to the appropriation of alien surplus labour'.[42] Secondly, Marx's notions of human development under communism (such as through use of newly-gained free time for artistic activity) are quite obsessive and nothing to do with the hedonist utopias formulated, for example, by the situationists on the basis of their interpretation of Marx. Charles Fourier's concept of *travail attractif*, or of the identity of labour and pleasure under communism, was held by Marx to be a 'childishly naive conception'; according to Marx, '[r]eally free work, e.g. the composition of music, is also the most damnably difficult, demanding the most intensive effort'.[43] Thirdly and finally, it is worth noting that the at best paradoxical notion that primitive accumulation – an act of violence that needs to be understood, in part, as a violation of inner nature – should represent the point of departure for the eventual unfolding of this very inner nature. In a work that builds on Edward P. Thompson's history of the underclasses in early industrial England, Michael Vester has emphasised primitive accumulation's traumatic character: 'More significant than the separation of people from nature or their land was the violence done to human nature. This violence took the form of unrestricted capitalist exploitation, a technologically determined separation of work and life, illness, poverty and a compulsion to work that consumed people's life-time in an undignified manner'.[44] No one ought really to have been surprised that the workers of the early industrial period struggled against a capitalist modernisation imposed in this manner. And yet the fact has long caused difficulties for socialist historians, who have tended to judge it by reference to Marx's comments on the Luddites,[45] thereby adopting Marx's characteristic faith in progress.[46]

The most important results of this section can be summarised as follows. The concept of poverty remains marginal in Marx, at least to the extent that it does not converge with that of labour; where it does not abstract from specifically capitalist conditions, the concept of labour refers to doubly free wage-labour, which is defined as the object of exploitation on the basis of a concept of value adopted from Smith and Ricardo; the concept of development refers to a transformation of both outer and inner nature that is supposed, firstly, to occur over a period of several generations, secondly, to be possible only under capitalism and

---

41. Marx 1975–2004r, p. 94.
42. *Ibid.*
43. Marx 1975–2004j, p. 530.
44. Vester 1970, p. 102.
45. Marx 1976, p. 554. See also Thompson 1963, pp. 604–59; Hobsbawm 1964a, pp. 5–22; Rudé 1964, pp. 79–92.
46. Henkel and Taubert 1979, pp. 9–30.

thirdly, to necessitate the transition to a new and egalitarian mode of production characterised, among other things, by the absence of wage-labour.

II

Evaluation of the Marxian concept of poverty should start from the fact that poverty was an overwhelmingly rural phenomenon in Marx's day and continues to be so today. The World Bank's development-strategists currently operate on the assumption that three-quarters of the world's poor live in rural areas, with most working there as well.[47] To be sure, the criterion for poverty on which this estimate is based (per capita income) has been criticised repeatedly,[48] and with good reason: it ignores the fact that people may secure their subsistence in ways that are non-monetary or only partially monetary (mediated by the circulation of commodities). The most important instance is peasant-, mostly family-based production of the prime necessities of life not just for the market, but also for the needs of the producers. It has faced considerable challenges during the twentieth century, including premeditated attempts to systematically eradicate it. The peasant-economy has nevertheless proven far more resilient than assumed by many observers, Marx included.

A groundbreaking contribution to our understanding of the peasantry was provided by Russian economist Alexander Chayanov.[49] Chayanov's evaluation of tsarist statistics on the Russian peasant-communes, whose members still made up roughly eighty percent of the population in the 1920s, led him to formulate a theory of what he called the 'self-exploitation' of labour-power within wage-free household-economies. The theory's central claim is that within such household-economies, the 'degree of self-exploitation of labor' is determined by the 'relationship between the measure of demand satisfaction and the measure of the burden of labor'.[50] Striving to meet its demand with as little effort as possible ('In meeting its demands, the peasant family strives to do this most easily'),[51] the household-economy eschews additional labour-effort whenever it judges such effort to be harder to bear than renunciation of its economic effect. This model, premised both on the physically demanding character of agricultural labour and on the fact of peasant self-employment, allowed Chayanov to explain what family-based agriculture has repeatedly been reproached for in twentieth-century

---

47. World Bank 2007. For a critique of this world-development report – the first on agricultural issues published by the World Bank since 1982 – see Paasch 2007.
48. Heim and Schaz 1996, pp. 125–6; Reddy 2007, pp. 269–79.
49. Chayanov 1966b; Chayanov 1966a. See also Thorner 1966; Kerblay 1971, pp. 150–60.
50. Chayanov 1966b, p. 81.
51. Chayanov 1966b, p. 108.

discourses of population and development: its low savings-rate, which prevents capital-formation and acts as an impediment to both capitalist and socialist development. Early Soviet debates saw peasants being accused of sabotaging the régime's policy of industrialisation, and in the Chinese press of the 1970s the peasants were 'eating up socialism'.

Almost a century has passed since Chayanov observed that 'significant blocs of peasant family labor units are interspersed in capitalist world economy'.[52] The observation still holds true today. This makes Chayanov's analyses of the 'very complicated conglomerations' that develop on the basis of such 'co-existence' highly topical.[53] Chayanov's model is rendered especially valuable by the fact that it does not limit itself to describing a pure subsistence-economy, that is, one in which money and commodities do not feature. The model's explanatory power is greatest where it takes commodity- and land-prices, taxes and the demand for seasonal wage-labour into account – where it no longer treats the subsistence-economy as a wholly extra-capitalist phenomenon, but explores the ways in which wage-free household-economies may be articulated with the capitalist economy. One especially interesting phenomenon discussed by Chayanov is that of hunger-rent: the seemingly paradoxical fact that the peasant-household will be willing to pay – and hence work – more, the less land it owns and the poorer it is.[54] As Chayanov demonstrates, high taxes are another instrument by which the peasant-household can be constrained to work ever harder even as its level of subsistence is lowered – a function typically performed by head-taxes in colonial régimes.[55] Heavy taxation of the rural population was also encouraged in the Soviet Union, as in Evgeni Preobrazhensky's programme of 'primitive-socialist accumulation'.[56] The rural revolts that have repeatedly shaken the capitalist periphery in times of war and crisis, and which presented a formidable obstacle to Soviet policies of modernisation, can be explained by reference to such methods of extracting greater quantities of labour from rural populations.[57] The age of such revolts may not yet be over; this, in any case, is suggested by the present situation in rural China.[58]

The ways in which peasant self-employment may be articulated with industrial wage-labour in developing countries were analysed by Marxist anthropologist Claude Meillassoux in a study of West African circular migration that was

---

52. Chayanov 1966a, p. 27.

53. Chayanov 1966a.

54. Microcredits provided to peasants and other self-employed workers at unusually high interest-rates are nothing but an up-to-date, generalised implementation of the hunger-rent principle.

55. Senghaas-Knobloch 1979, pp. 125–31.

56. Preobrazhensky 1971, pp. 219–26.

57. Scott 1976. On the Soviet Union, see Merl 1993.

58. Chen and Wu 2006.

first published in the mid-1970s (and much discussed at the time).[59] Meillassoux began from a simple observation: wages that do not correspond to the
value of labour-power in that they allow for no more than simple reproduction
(the reproduction of labour-power during the period of employment) are routinely paid both in developing and in industrialised countries. Using the French
minimum-wage as his example, Meillassoux pointed out that such wages are
supplemented, in metropolitan societies, by unemployment-benefits, family-
assistance and other transfer-payments associated with the welfare-state (Meillassoux referred to such transfer-payments as 'indirect wages'): 'Once workers
have been fully deprived of the means of production, the minimum-wage must
be supplemented by an indirect wage if the extinction of the working class is
to be prevented'.[60] In peripheral societies, capital relies instead on the peasant-
economy, which provides it with fully grown workers and into which these workers can be dismissed again after a few years of employment.[61] Articulated with
the capitalist sector in this way, the peasant-economy will tend to dissolve, being
constrained to continuously contribute to the reproduction of workers whose
labour is employed elsewhere. Yet given the benefits it provides for capital, the
peasant-economy may be artificially maintained or newly instituted – under
state-control, as in South Africa's 'homelands'. Thus capital preserves for itself
a sector of society where 'the labour force is able to reproduce itself, albeit only
on the level of subsistence'.[62] Meillassoux's meticulous attempts to analyse such
processes in terms of the Marxian theory of value and his insistence that the
peasant-economy constitutes a mode of production unto itself (an insistence
that makes him a genuine successor of Chayanov) have occasionally provoked
criticism.[63] Yet his theory undeniably has the merit of testing Marx's all too
simple wage-concept against the conditions under which the poor actually
reproduce themselves. In doing so, Meillassoux has set the course for a possible
correction of Marx's position.

The articulation of the peasant-economy with wage-labour that Meillassoux
described was not the declared aim of the modernisation-strategies enforced
in the capitalist periphery during the 1950s, but it was very much their result.
Efforts to transfer workers permanently from the 'traditional' agricultural to the
'modern' industrial sector were only partly successful, as had to be acknowledged in debates on the so-called 'dualism' of peripheral capitalist economies

---

59. Meillassoux 2005, 1982.
60. Meillassoux 1982, p. 25.
61. Meillassoux 2005, pp. 150–7. See also Elwert and Wong 1979; Senghaas-Knobloch
1979, pp. 16–20. An early reference to the problem examined by Meillassoux can be found
in Mitrany 1951, p. 111.
62. Meillassoux 2005, p. 177.
63. Moulier Boutang 1998, pp. 264f.

conducted during the 1960s.[64] While the measures adopted to rationalise agriculture (the 'Green Revolution') led to an erosion of the peasant-economy and to labour-redundancy within the agricultural sector, these developments did not go hand in hand with the emergence of an urban industrial proletariat of the European or North American type. Instead, there emerged a new survival economy, largely located in the expanding slums of the period: the so-called 'informal sector', which was neither 'traditional' nor 'modern' in the sense intended.[65] As a residual category meant to encompass a range of income-strategies that do not fall under the rubric of registered gainful employment, from small commodity-production and labour-intensive repair-work to garbage-disposal, prostitution and organ trading, the concept of the informal sector always was, and continues to be, quite vague. Some scholars have begun using it to analyse off-the-books labour in metropolitan economies, which has led to claims that the informal economy cannot be equated with poverty.[66] The debates such statements seem intended to provoke would be little more than terminological quarrels. In any case, the history of the concept refers us to the emergence of new forms of poverty within the capitalist periphery. These new forms of poverty were an embarrassment to the modernisation-theorists of the day; they also call into question Marx's claim that capitalist development goes hand-in-hand with the growing hegemony of doubly-free wage-labour. It might be added that the population-control measures by which the development-strategists of the World Bank and the United Nations have attempted to decimate peripheral pauperism from the 1960s onward, and the policy of tolerated famine revived under Nixon in the 1970s ('food-power') are more reminiscent of what Marx says about the emergence of industrial capitalism than of what he described as its mature form, a form that ostensibly requires the use of extra-economic force 'only in exceptional cases'.[67]

III

Marx's tendency consistently to relate labour and poverty to one another reflects an apposite observation: under capitalism, poverty appears primarily as labouring poverty; in other words, labour is performed primarily out of fear of immiseration (a fear that may be mediated to a greater or lesser degree) and under circumstances that cannot but constantly reproduce this fear. That was the case

---

64. Senghaas-Knobloch 1979, pp. 8off.
65. Senghaas-Knobloch 1979, pp. 155–90. See also International Labour Office 1972, pp. 5f., 51–72, 503–8; Sethuraman 1976, pp. 69–81.
66. Portes, Castells and Benton (eds.) 1989, p. 12.
67. Marx 1976, p. 899.

in Marx's age and continues to be the case today. Separating the two concepts is justifiable only to the extent that it allows for a more nuanced understanding of the various forms that labouring poverty assumes. Marx is not to be criticised for placing labour-issues at the centre of his theory, but rather for systematically reducing labour to doubly-free wage-labour and refusing to see in the various forms of unfree and self-employed labour anything other than contingent exceptions to the rule or moribund residues of pre-capitalist relations. The processes of proletarisation Marx sees at work in the early history of capitalism continue to this day. At times they remain stalled for several generations and at times they are reversed.[68] Neither case has ever represented a serious impediment to the efficient functioning of capitalism.

During the past quarter of a century, capitalist development has played out in a form corresponding roughly to Marx's predictions in some parts of the world (Southeast Asia), but this has gone hand in hand with contrary developments elsewhere (Africa and Latin America). Nevertheless, dependency-theory's claim that the structure of the world-market prevents African, Asian and Latin American countries from replicating the industrialisation-processes undergone by Europe and North America has clearly been refuted by the economic advances of the 'Asian Tigers'.[69] The economic take-off experienced by South Korea, Taiwan, Hong Kong and Singapore has since been dwarfed by China's. Today, the Pearl River Delta alone boasts more industrial workers than the entire United States. China's rapid economic development has occurred in the context of far-reaching social changes. Jump-started by reforms introduced by the post-Maoist régime in the late 1970s, these changes have lastingly reconfigured China's class-structure.

At the risk of imposing overly rigid categories on an exceptionally dynamic social process, one can distinguish between three working classes within contemporary China. First, there are the peasants or *nongmin*, who number more than seven-hundred million and have returned to the Chayanov economy since the dissolution of the 'people's communes' in the early 1980s; their ongoing disputes with the local authorities are frequently prompted by tax-issues. Second, there are the state-employed workers or *gongren*, who were guaranteed an 'iron-ricebowl' (lifelong employment and the social benefits associated with it) under Mao, fifty million of whom have however been forced into precarious employment or unemployment since the beginning of the reform-era. Third, there are the peasant-workers or *mingong*, who number more than one hundred million.

---

68. There is only one passage in Marx that sees him discussing the reversal of proletarisation at greater length: his remarks on Edward Gibbon Wakefield's theory of colonisation. But Marx is not prepared to treat such a reversal as anything other than an intermezzo. See Marx 1976, pp. 932–40.

69. Hauck 1990.

Under the 'household-registration' or *hukou* system that has been in place since 1956, the *nongmin* are considered rural residents and granted urban residence-permits on a temporary basis only; in fact, they migrate constantly between rural and urban areas in order to supplement the incomes of their peasant-households with wages from urban employment, but also to escape the strictures of rural life and win new liberties for themselves in China's urban conglomerations. The so-called 'working sisters' [*dagongmei*] represent a subgroup of the *mingong*: they are female workers, employed in free production-zones, whose informally organised strikes and demonstrations for improved working conditions, higher wages and the implementation of Chinese labour-law have rightly attracted considerable attention in recent years.[70]

The *dagongmei* are especially relevant to the issues raised in this essay in that they remind us of an important constant in the history of industrial-capitalist development. The creation of industrial enclaves in some Asian, African and Latin American countries, discussed in terms of a 'new international division of labour' during the 1970s and 1980s,[71] already rested largely on the poorly remunerated labour of young unmarried women from rural areas.[72] The share of female workers employed in the free production-zones and world-market factories of the time was estimated at more than seventy percent,[73] an estimate that later turned out to understate the actual figure by ten percent.[74] It should be recalled that industrial labour represents only a fraction of the aggregate-labour performed by women in the course of industrialisation-processes. Prostitution, remunerated housework and the small crafts and trades of the informal sector are often to be found in the immediate proximity of world-market factories. Most female factory-workers move into these and similar forms of employment around the age of twenty-five, when they are not made to perform unremunerated reproductive labour within the family. In the case of the *dagongmei*, these tendencies – the temporary character of female industrial labour and the early transition of women-workers into other forms of labour, some unremunerated – are reinforced by the current economic crisis and the layoffs it has prompted.

As is widely known, the industrial overexploitation of female labour-power and the parallel relegation of unremunerated reproductive labour to women[75] were already constitutive features of European industrialisation. Marx never

---

70. Ngai and Wanwei 2008. Sisterhoods of migrant women-workers are not an altogether new phenomenon. See Honig 1984. (I would like to thank Marcel van der Linden for drawing my attention to this article.)
71. Fröbel, Heinrichs and Kreye 1977, 1984.
72. Lenz 1980.
73. Fröbel, Heinrichs and Kreye 1977, p. 529.
74. Klemp 1993, p. 298.
75. Hausen 1976; Duden 1977.

succeeded in doing justice to the issue of remunerated and unremunerated women's labour – an issue that should not overhastily be reduced to the more general one of remunerated and unremunerated labour *tout court*. In his discussion of the 'labour of women and children',[76] a labour supposed by him to commence only with the rise of machinofacture, he never reflects on the fact that what he takes as his starting point, namely a proletarian family whose male adult-member works in industry and receives a family-wage while the other family-members, and in particular the mother, occupy themselves with raising the children and tending to the household, was itself a historical product and tended, moreover, to be the exception in the pre-machinofacture period. In chapter 15 of *Capital* Volume I, the proletarian woman appears as a mere unremunerated houseworker even prior to the introduction of machines in the factory; her's is the domain of 'independent labour at home, within customary limits, for the family itself'.[77] Marx's account renders invisible the manifold forms of remunerated labour which underclass-women have historically been compelled to perform both within and without the household. The question concerning the genesis of unremunerated housework *qua* distinctly female domain opposed to and supplementary to male wage-labour is never raised.[78] In some passages, Marx's perspective is fully that of bourgeois reform-movements; he misjudges the realities of underclass-life in especially disappointing ways when he insists, for example, that the 'employment of the mothers away from their homes' results in the 'neglect and maltreatment' of children, or that female employment results in an 'unnatural estrangement between mother and child' that may even culminate in 'intentional starving and poisoning of the children'.[79] While such remarks may have been informed by accurate observations on certain aspects of early industrial pauperism, they also betray Marx's failure to recognise that there was in the pre-industrial underclasses no culture of childcare and childraising *qua* distinct domain of familial reproduction.[80] The point is important because it shows Marx misjudged or indeed failed to problematise not just the history of remunerated women's labour in proto-industrial Europe,[81] but also an important aspect of industrial-capitalist development, namely the inculcation of a certain reproductive behaviour in the underclasses. Rather than predating machinofacture and being eroded by it, the forms of motherly care and domesticity Marx has in mind in the passages quoted were first introduced into underclass-culture in a lengthy process that began in the ninetheenth century, lasted well into the

---

76. Marx 1976, p. 517.
77. Marx 1976, p. 517.
78. Bock and Duden 1977, pp. 118–99.
79. Marx 1976, p. 521.
80. Bock and Duden 1977, pp. 133ff.; Shorter 1975.
81. Medick 1977, pp. 132–8.

twentieth century and intensified, tellingly, with every further advance in industrialisation.[82]

The articulation of socially acknowledged male wage-labour with a 'natural', meaning negligible female domestic labour was rightly identified, in 1970s feminism, as the 'blind spot' of every theory focused on the relationship between wage-labour and capital.[83] Such theories follow Marx in overlooking the fact that in the case wrongly posited by him as normal (the man performs wage-labour and the woman domestic labour), the man's wage does not simply secure the reproduction of his family in addition to his own. Rather, one of the housewife's key services consists in creating the conditions under which it will be possible for the family to maintain itself using the male breadwinner's wage. (She does this by comparing prices, administering savings and engaging in supplementary productive and repair-work.) Marx does in fact recognise that the services and material goods the housewife provides free of charge do not need to be purchased on the market, so that the housewife effectively reduces the expenses required for labour-power's maintenance.[84] But he does not pursue the point. And that is precisely why he fails to anticipate that industrial development would go on to involve unremunerated female reproductive labour being promoted and institutionalised in multiple ways – not by coincidence, but because it proved functional to capital. Differently from the reproductive services that have been and continue to be left to peasant-households in peripheral societies, the metropolitan variety of domestic work is 'fully tailored to the reproduction of present and future labour power and entirely configured by capital'.[85]

Both the metropolitan and the peripheral version of unremunerated reproductive activity have been changing for some time now. New models are being experimented with. Occasionally a transfer of reproductive models from the periphery to the metropoles is proposed,[86] a phenomenon familiar from earlier crises. What is striking and begs analysis is the regularity with which authors from a range of fields – from social work and urban sociology to development-studies – fall back on women as the guarantors of successful familial and social reproduction, and this at a time when the extent to which international industrial production relies on female labour-power can no longer be denied.

---

82. Bauer 1985.
83. Werlhof 1978.
84. Marx 1976, p. 518, note 39.
85. Bauer 1985, p. 149.
86. Dahm and Scherhorn 2008. For a critique of this book, see Henninger 2010.

IV

The Marxian concept of development is given the lie by history as it has actually played out. The suspicion that it might prove untenable goes some way towards explaining the 'crisis of Marxism' that set in shortly after the death of Engels, a crisis that produced not only Eduard Bernstein's revisionism, Rudolf Hilferding's theory of 'organised capitalism' and Rosa Luxemburg's attempt to combine the theory of capitalism's collapse with an analysis of imperialism, but also currents whose reception of Sorelian syndicalism eventually led them to endorse programmes of what Enrico Corradini called 'socialismo nazionale'.[87] These complex theoretical developments cannot be discussed here; I will limit myself to a few remarks on Luxemburg's correction of certain Marxian assumptions. As is widely known, the theory Luxemburg presented in her 1913 book, The Accumulation of Capital, was harshly criticised by Lenin and other Marxists. It is hard to avoid the impression that the attacks on Luxemburg were motivated by something more than the desire to establish the truth. What seems also to have been involved is the need to repress a theoretical approach that focuses on a fact flatly denied in Marx (a fact that must, however, have been glaringly evident to Luxemburg's more attentive contemporaries), namely that capitalism is constrained to continuously open up for itself, through violent processes of expropriation ('primitive accumulation'), societies that have not yet been fully integrated into the world-economy's valorisation-chains. Luxemburg's comments on the 'disintegration of non-capitalist formations' and the 'transition to commodity economy' are more than clear: capital 'employs force as a permanent weapon, not only at its genesis, but further on down to the present day'.[88] By contrast, Marx relegated primitive accumulation to the 'antediluvian conditions of capital; to its *historical presuppositions*, which, precisely as such *historical* presuppositions, have vanished and therefore belong to the *history of its formation* but by no means to its *contemporary* history'.[89]

Luxemburg's theory of imperialism provided her internationalism with a solid theoretical foundation, rendering unthinkable the sort of bellicose diatribe that Marx and Engels occasionally engaged in (and to which I return below). There is little in Marx to match the pathbreaking analyses of European colonial policy Luxemburg published in her 1913 book.[90] And Luxemburg's characterisation of the 'final phase of capitalism' as a 'period of catastrophe' is worlds apart from

---

87. Sternhell, Sznajder and Ashéri 1989, pp. 34ff., 292–318. Franz Neumann has sketched out the links between this ideology and that of Nazism. See Neumann 1944, pp. 193–9.

88. Luxemburg 2003, p. 351.

89. Marx 1975–2004j, p. 387.

90. Luxemburg 2003, Chapters 27–9.

Marx's account of capitalism's decline:[91] Marx spoke of the 'expropriation of a few usurpers by the mass of the people', insisting that capitalism's genesis needed to be seen as 'an incomparably more protracted, violent and difficult process'.[92]

As for Luxemburg's failed attempt to revise Marx's reproduction-schemes, it is as irrelevant to analysis of present-day capitalism as the reproduction-schemes themselves. What requires attention today is Luxemburg's argument that the epochal processes of destruction Marx attributed to the formative period of capitalism persist over and beyond this period. When Marx says of an Irish famine that it 'and its consequences have been deliberately exploited both by the individual landlords and by the English Parliament through legislation so as to accomplish the agricultural revolution by force and to thin down the population of Ireland to the proportion satisfactory to the landlords',[93] he addresses a phenomenon whose relevance to the experiences of the twentieth century – and perhaps also to those of the coming decades – is far greater than it ought to be given the overall structure of Marx's theory. In the same passage, Marx refers to the formidable migratory movements prompted by the capitalist transformation of Ireland into an 'English sheepwalk and cattle pasture'.[94] In doing so, he touches upon a key aspect of capitalist modernisation in nineteenth-century Europe, namely the emigration of a quarter of the European population. And crucially, he addresses a phenomenon that has lost none of its significance more than a century later, even if the migratory routes have changed and those on the run from the havoc wrought by the capitalist process no longer aspire to agricultural self-employment in pre-industrial North America[95] but to the functioning infrastructure, the income-opportunities and the social-security systems of the metropoles.

Yet it is not just the persistence of ostensibly pre- or early capitalist phenomena that renders Marx's entire theoretical narrative doubtful; the explanations he proposes for these phenomena are also unsatisfactory. The theory of 'relative surplus-population', which Marx illustrates by reference to Ireland, and which sees him addressing a problem coeval with political economy,[96] invokes changes in the composition of capital and the fluctuations of a mature capitalist market when it would have been more appropriate to look beyond mature capitalism's immanent laws of movement. Marx's rebuttal of the Malthusian

---

91. Luxemburg 2003, p. 427.
92. Marx 1976, p. 930.
93. Marx 1976, p. 869, note 41.
94. Marx 1976, p. 869.
95. Marx 1976, pp. 935–6.
96. It is telling that the first chair of political economy, established at Hertfordshire's East India Company College in 1805, was held by the man whose name is associated more than any other with pessimistic theories of 'overpopulation', Thomas Robert Malthus.

position, according to which pauperism is a consequence of the 'constant tendency in all animated life to increase beyond the nourishment prepared for it',[97] is nothing but a more elaborately argued variant of Ricardo's remark that 'overpopulation' ought to be defined by reference not to the 'means of subsistence' but to the 'means of employment'.[98] Marx criticises Malthus for attempting to explain 'overpopulation' 'not by saying that part of the working population has been rendered relatively superfluous, but by referring to its excessive growth'.[99] The becoming 'relatively superfluous' of part of the population results, in Marx's view, from changes in the organic composition of capital that cause the absolute growth of capital to be accompanied by a relative decline in the demand for labour.[100] 'The working population therefore produces both the accumulation of capital and the means by which it is itself made relatively superfluous'.[101]

It is hard not to sympathise with Marx when he refuses to accept a universally valid 'law of population' and insists the emergence of an economically supernumerary population – or of a group of people that can be employed only intermittently and is thereby condemned to poverty – needs to be explained in terms of the given economic order. Yet closer scrutiny reveals the flaws inherent to Marx's critique of Malthus. The critique acknowledges no social relations other than those of mature capitalism. It presupposes ongoing industrial production and its expansion (in terms of both capital-stock and productivity) as well as a working class available for 'attraction' and 'repulsion'.[102] Marx's account has provoked the justified criticism that it fails to explain pre-industrial pauperism, which is something other than an industrial working class, and which was precisely the phenomenon that Malthus was addressing (however inadequately). Ahlrich Meyer has emphasised 'that the origins of pre-industrial pauperism cannot be explained in terms of the teleology of capital, that is, by reference to capital's future manpower requirements'.[103] Arguments that invoke 'industrial demand for labour' to account for the antecedent 'production of a pool of potential workers in the form of the poor' stipulate an absurd reverse causality and explain nothing.[104] And yet it is precisely this sort of teleological approach that underpins Marx's remarks on the emergence of a relative surplus-population. One consequence is that questions concerning the possible relationship between the dissolution of traditional peasant- and craft-economies and absolute population-

97. Malthus 1992, p. 14.
98. Ricardo 1951, pp. 397f.; Marx 1975–2004j, p. 526.
99. Marx 1976, p. 787.
100. Marx 1976, pp. 783–4.
101. Marx 1976, p. 783.
102. Marx 1976, p. 781.
103. Meyer 1999, p. 99.
104. Meyer 1999, p. 99.

growth remain unaddressed. Marx has next to nothing to say about the fact that the population of England and Wales doubled between 1800 und 1850.[105] The so-called 'demo-economic paradox' – the pre-industrial phenomenon of consistent population-growth within a context of fluctuating economic development – can in fact not be explained using Marxian categories. It is telling that, when Hans Medick succeeded in formulating a convincing socio-historical explanation for such absolute population-growth, he relied on Chayanov more than on Marx.[106] Medick focused on developments prior to industrialisation: the dissolution of the traditional peasant-economy and the transition to a family-based craft-economy (the so-called 'proto-industrial family-economy'), pointing out that these developments involved changes in the reproductive behaviour of the rural underclasses. The proto-industrial family-economy was characterised, according to Medick, by the 'need to maximally employ familial labour-power'; it favoured early marriage and intense procreation, as children were an important source of labour-power by which families could hope to increase their productive capacities and escape poverty.[107] Medick emphasises that this tendency towards 'early marriage and intense generative reproduction' was not significantly correlated with developments on the labour-market.[108]

Contemporary discourses of 'overpopulation' (such as references to Africa's 'youth-bulge') are of course a staple ingredient of the threatening scenarios invoked by the political class of the European metropoles to justify its immigration- and security-policies. Medick's hypothesis concerning the relationship between unfettered generative reproduction and poverty should no doubt be approached critically, given that it lends itself to being instrumentalised for such rhetoric. The fact remains that Marx's approach appears hopelessly simplistic by comparison to Medick's. Much like the reproduction-schemes in *Capital* Volume II, Marx's theory of relative surplus-population effaces the possibility of autonomous underclass-behaviour and recognises no other logic but that of capital-valorisation.

This is a general problem with Marx's theory, and one that is nowhere more evident than in the abstractness of the stadial model implicit in Marx's concept of development. I will conclude by illustrating this point by reference to the issue of civil and interstate wars. That no account of the capitalist process would be

---

105. Vester 1970, p. 72; Marx 1976, p. 764. Comparable rates of population-growth were registered in other European countries, with Russia's population increasing from thirty-five and a half million to sixty-eight and a half million and Prussia's from eight and half million to sixteen and a half million between 1800 and 1850. See Hachtmann 2002, pp. 27f.

106. Medick 1977, pp. 97–101.

107. Medick 1977, p. 125.

108. *Ibid.*

complete without reference to military aggression is a point that hardly needs to be laboured. What is striking is that Marx's theory largely elides the extent to which mature capitalism relies on such aggression. To be sure, Marx's discussion of capitalism is rife with military metaphors,[109] and his economic manuscripts do contain scattered remarks on the distinct role played by war and the military in the emergence of specifically capitalist relations of production.[110] But these remarks are not developed in the theory presented in *Capital*. Marx's observations on Bonapartism remain similarly extraneous to that theory.[111] And while they have turned out to be impressively accurate, the elder Engels's worried premonitions of the coming world-war cannot plausibly be described as anything more than a marginal note,[112] tardily appended to a historical model that fails to devote the requisite attention to the interrelatedness of military and economic development. Luxemburg's theory of imperialism no doubt represents a tremendous step forward in this regard, but the concepts provided by it are also ultimately inadequate to the task of analysing the present modalities and consequences of war. Luxemburg focuses on the military aggression of mature capitalist states as directed against non-capitalist societies. When mature capitalist economies are militarily dismembered and their assets redistributed by means of pilferage and blackmail, with foreign currencies or relief-supplies replacing the national currency as a means of exchange before legally guaranteed property-relations are reintroduced on the basis of such largely informal transfers of value,[113] this represents a process of transformation that cannot be adequately analysed by means of Luxemburg's or any other classic theory of imperialism.

There is no ruling out the possibility that conflicts of this kind will resurge within Europe. Should that occur, then discourses of ethnicity will likely be involved. If anyone believes they can counter such threats by means of Marxist rhetoric, they would be well advised to study the statements made by Marx and Engels during the revolutionary years of 1848–9.[114] At the time, Marx called for a German war of aggression against Russia. Such a war, he argued, would constitute 'a war of revolutionary Germany, a war by which she could cleanse herself of her past sins, could take courage, defeat her own autocrats, spread civilisation by the sacrifice of her own sons as becomes a people that is shaking off the chains of long, indolent slavery and make herself free within her borders by bringing liberation to those outside'.[115] Engels went one better by engaging in racist diatribes

---

109. See, e.g. Marx 1976, pp. 443, 562.
110. Marx 1975–2004j, p. 45.
111. Marx 1975–2004s, pp. 99–197.
112. Engels 1975–2004e, pp. 367–94.
113. Kaldor 1999.
114. For a comprehensive discussion, see Thörner 2008, pp. 69–94.
115. Marx 1975–2004t, p. 212.

about the Southern Slavs, whom he described as 'residual fragments of peoples' [*Völkerabfälle*].[116] According to Engels, the Southern Slavs could not but become 'fanatical standard-bearers of counter-revolution and remain so until their complete extirpation or loss of their national character, just as their whole existence in general is itself a protest against a great historical revolution'.[117] Engels concluded: 'The next world war will result in the disappearance from the face of the earth not only of reactionary classes and dynasties, but also of entire reactionary peoples. And that, too, is a step forward'.[118] Marx never objected to these remarks by Engels.[119] They contrast sharply with earlier and later statements by both him and Engels, but they were never revoked.

In 1848–9, Marx's stadial model of history became a hierarchy of more or less developed 'peoples', with 'the mighty bulwark of European reaction – Russia' at the bottom.[120] Like Moses Hess before him,[121] Marx repeatedly ranked the nations of Europe according to their progress along the path of capitalist modernisation. His remarks on Germany's backwardness in the *Introduction* to the *Contribution to the Critique of Hegel's Philosophy of Law* ('If I negate the German state of affairs in 1843, then, according to the French computation of time, I am hardly in the year 1789, and still less in the focus of the present') are merely one of the less unsavoury examples.[122] Whenever a stadial model of history such Marx's is applied to an empirically given multiplicity of political, social and economic relations, bellicose positions such as those just cited are only a small step away. This alone ought to warn against adopting the Marxian concept of development.

V

The conclusion that imposes itself is that any critique of capitalism that does not want to see Marx's '*categorical imperative to overthrow all relations* in which man is a debased, enslaved, forsaken, despicable being'[123] relegated to the history of

---

116. Engels 1975–2004f, p. 234. The English translation of *Völkerabfälle* fails to capture the venomous racism of the original German. The word *Abfall* (of which '*Abfälle*' is the plural) might be more faithfully translated as 'refuse' or 'offal'. As Klaus Thörner has pointed out, Engels was echoing a similar statement by Hegel on the Bulgarians, Serbs and Albanians: Thörner 2008, p. 89.

117. Engels 1975–2004f, p. 234.

118. Engels 1975–2004f, p. 238.

119. In fact, Marx allowed a number of articles on South East Europe published under his name to be penned by Engels. See Marx and Engels 1956, p. 597, editorial note 200.

120. Engels 1975–2004g, p. 126.

121. Hess 1961a, pp. 150–63.

122. Marx 1975–2004l, p. 176.

123. Marx 1975–2004l, p. 182 (emphasis in original).

unrealised utopias ought to distance itself from Marx's own theory on several key points. In order to do justice to the current state of our knowledge and to the historical experiences garnered thus far, such a critique ought to display: firstly, a concept of poverty that is something more than the residual category 'lumpenproletariat'; secondly, a concept of labour considerably wider than that of doubly-free wage-labour, capable of accounting, among other things, for the manifold forms of unremunerated labour to be found in both metropolitan and peripheral societies; and thirdly, a critical concept of development that fully relinquishes Marx's stadial model of history and emphasises the unprecedentedly destructive character of capitalist modernisation. Last but not least, such a critique ought to rid itself utterly of the illusion that the devastations suffered thus far and those still to be expected can in some sense be understood as the prelude to a historically guaranteed 'realm of freedom' capable of justifying or compensating its own prehistory.[124]

What this conclusion should not make us forget is that the prime challenge posed by the intensification of the twenty-first century's first world economic crisis will not be that of fine-tuning our concepts. Such fine-tuning is in any case justified only to the extent that it sharpens our awareness of global capitalism's complexity and allows us to determine our own position within the global capitalist order more accurately. Desperate attempts to rescue Marx's theorems can only render this task more arduous. Banking on the possibility that reality may yet align itself with the Marxian model would amount to reasserting a concept of revolution that fails to do justice to the composition of the world's underclasses and rests on a teleological and reductive account of the dynamics of the capitalist process. To date, every event subsequently declared a 'revolution' has played out as a conjunction of highly diverse revolts, thereby giving the lie to such concepts.

March 2009

---

124. Marx 1981, p. 958.

What is Sold on the Labour-Market?[*]
Thomas Kuczynski

The question formulated in the title has already been answered for the great majority of those who accept as correct the basic concept of Marx's labour-theory of value – the commodity of labour-power. It is sold by wage-workers and bought by capitalists. Marx establishes it in the following way in *Capital* Volume I:

> On the surface of bourgeois society the worker's wage appears as the price of labour, as a certain quantity of money that is paid for a certain quantity of labour. Thus people speak of the value of labour, and call its expression in money its necessary or natural price. [...] It is not labour which directly confronts the possessor of money on the commodity-market, but rather the worker. What the worker is selling is his labour-power. [...] In the expression 'value of labour', the concept of value is not only completely extinguished, but inverted, so that it becomes its contrary.[1]

I myself held this answer to be among the so-called fundamental truths of Marxism which distinguished themselves above all due to the fact that they seemed to be so self-evident as never to be placed in question. What, however, does it mean, 'to sell one's labour-power'? More generally: what does it mean, anyway, to sell a commodity?

[*] Originally published in German as 'Was wird auf dem Arbeitsmarkt verkauft?', in Wolf, Eicker-Wolf and Reiner (eds.) 1999, pp. 207–24. *Translated by Peter Thomas.*
1. Marx 1976, pp. 675–7.

Whoever has sold a commodity does not own it anymore. The book-seller no longer owns the book which he sells, in exactly the same way that the articles of clothing sold by the tailoress no longer belong to her, and so on, throughout the entire world of commodities. Regaining commodities that have been sold would be possible for those who have sold them only if they bought them back. Conversely, those who have bought commodities have at any time the possibility of reselling those commodities – perhaps at a loss, but that is of course another question.

With the commodity discovered by Marx – namely, labour-power – this must be different in any relationship. Those who have bought labour-power certainly have the possibility of disposing of the commodity – of dismissing workers – but they clearly do not have the possibility, except in certain special cases, of reselling the commodity of labour-power. Conversely, those who have sold their labour-power – at least theoretically – can always regain it and have it once more at their disposal, indeed, without buying it back. They thus appear to be in the truly fairy-tale situation of being able to have their cake and eat it at the same time – to sell labour-power and nevertheless to have it again later at their disposal.

After this, nothing is simpler than to abandon the concept of *commodity of labour-power* and with that simultaneously to document a very limited knowledge about the real world of commodities – that 'immense collection of commodities', as which 'the wealth of societies in which the capitalist mode of production prevails, appears'.[2]

In her in other respects extremely stimulating text, *Die Arbeitskraft – eine Ware?*, Ingeborg Dummer argues:

> Only under the one condition that the owner of labour-power and the owner of the means of production enter into an immediate exchange-relation does labour-power gain the character of a commodity, does it appear as a commodity. However, it is not a commodity. As a particular product of human labour [...], as a form of value, labour-power is ranged alongside other value-forms (commodity as consumer-goods, means of production and services, as well as money or capital).[3]

However, an *immediate* exchange-relation would be a relation in which the two owners immediately exchanged their property, that is, an immediate exchange-relation would be the case when, after the completed exchange, the original owner of labour-power were the owner of the means of production and the

---

2. Marx 1976, p. 125.
3. Dummer 1997, p. 25.

original owner of the means of the production were the owner of labour-power. Yet it is precisely this that is clearly not the case.[4]

In order to move a little closer to the answer to the question which I posed at the beginning, I would like to take a little distance from it for the time being, momentarily turning my attention to another market-segment in order to pose the question: what is sold on the housing market?[5] Whoever answers this question with 'houses' is certainly not entirely incorrect. Their answer, however, registers only a small fraction of what is actually sold on the housing market, for the majority of people in Germany are simply not in a position to buy a house. What do they do on the housing market? They rent a house.

Now, they are certainly – in fact, for both sides – two very different procedures, to rent a house or to buy a house. However, are not the rented – or, as the case may be, leased – houses integral parts of the 'immense accumulation of commodities'? Insofar as the owner of a house leases that house, he *sells* to the renter the temporally limited rights of use of the house, and the renter can – in the context of the valid renters' rights and the conditions agreed in the rental agreement – do and let be done whatever she wants with the house that she has rented. This situation regularly leads her in everyday life to speak of 'her' house: at the end of the working day she returns to 'her' house, invites guests to 'her' house, renovates 'her' house and so on; it wouldn't even occur to her in her dreams to demand that the house's owner should have the external windows painted or the heating repaired in his house. She asks, rather, that he employ tradesmen to do that in 'her' house. However, at the latest on the day when she receives notice of the next increase in rent or even that her rental of the house has been cancelled, it once more become clear to her to whom 'her' house belongs.

It is thus the rights of use – the temporally limited rights to use the house – which the owner of the house sells to the renter for a determinate period of time and for a determinate recompense, namely rent. We recognise that the owner has actually sold the rights of use which originally belonged to him for this period of time by the fact that he himself may not use the house during this period of time; he is not allowed even to enter the house without the consent of the renter.

---

4. Moreover, in her remark, added in parentheses, Dummer gives the impression that money and capital would not be commodities. They are not only commodities, but they are commodities of a specific type (the *differentia specifica* of a thing, as is well known, changes nothing in its *genus proximum*).

5. In order to avoid misunderstandings, I should establish here from the outset that I draw on the housing market sometimes and only for didactical reasons as an appropriate object of comparison, but that I in no way claim an identity of the labour- and housing market. The view of Artur Mülberger cited by Engels in *The Housing Question* – 'What the *wage worker* is in relation to the *capitalist*, the *renter* is in relation to the *house owner*' – is not mine; cf. Engels 1975–2004h, p. 319 (emphasis in original).

At the end or cancellation of the contract, however, the house belongs to him once again outright. He does not need to buy it back, for he had not sold it.

Even though, therefore, the majority of people in Germany are not in a position to buy housing, they use housing. The individual users may do that not because they have bought a house, but because they have bought the temporally limited rights of use of a house. The fact that there is a serious difference between the thing itself, and the right to use it, is an experience of everyday life which does not need to be treated any further here.

All the more pressing seems to me to be the question of whether we should not also distinguish on the labour-market between the thing itself and the right to use it. Marx by all means sees the problem but, in my view, does not give a consistent solution to it. In the second section of *Capital* Volume I, the section that deals with the transformation of money into capital, he notes:

> [...] labour-power can appear on the market as a commodity only if, and in so far as, its possessor, the individual whose labour-power it is, offers it for sale, or sells it, as a commodity. In order that its possessor may sell it as a commodity, he must have it at his disposal, he must be the free proprietor of his own labour-capacity, hence of his person. He and the owner of money meet in the market, and enter into relations with each other on a footing of equality as owners of commodities, with the sole difference, that one is a buyer, the other a seller; both are therefore equal in the eyes of the law. For this relation to continue, the proprietor of labour-power must always sell it for a limited period only, for if he were to sell it in a lump, once and for all, he would be selling himself, converting himself from a free man into a slave, from an owner of a commodity into a commodity. He must constantly treat his labour-power as his own property, his own commodity, and he can do this only by placing it at the disposal of the buyer, i.e. handing it over to the buyer for him to consume, for a definite period of time, temporarily. In this way he manages both to alienate [*Veräussern*] his labour-power and to avoid renouncing his rights of ownership over it.[6]

Whether or not we sell [*verkaufen*] or sell [*veräussern*] is in my view essentially the same thing in this case; to claim otherwise would be quibbling. If the commodity remains the property of the seller, then a sale of the commodity has not taken place. For the owner has actually only placed it at the disposal of its user for a temporary, determinate period of time. The owner of the commodity labour-power has not sold the labour-power, but rather, merely the right to use it, cancellable at any time.

---

6. Marx 1976, p. 271.

In this context, at least the following should be noted: in the *Communist Manifesto*, wages are not only treated as the price of labour – that is well known – but it is also established that 'These labourers, who must sell themselves piecemeal, are a commodity, like every other article of commerce'.[7]

That, if at all, either labour or the labourer must be sold – in reality, however, neither of them are – does not need to be commented on in more detail here. However, it seems to be worth reconsidering if 'to sell piecemeal' does not mean, in its intention, the same as the previously cited phrase, 'placing it at the disposal of the buyer temporarily, ceded to his use, for a definite period of time'. *Piecemeal* would then be understood not literally but in the metaphorical sense, as related to a piece of time, a period of time. At any rate, this is the way that Engels appears to have seen the thing, connected however with a comment which is extraordinarily interesting for our discussion. In *The Housing Question*, he notes that 'in the case of commodities with a long period of wear, the possibility arises of selling their use value piecemeal and each time for a definite period, that is to say, to let it out'.[8] Unfortunately, this definition, that *leasing* is tantamount *to selling something piecemeal for a determinate time*, did not prompt Engels to considerations on the problem of the concept of the *sale of the commodity labour-power*.

If the differentiation between selling and leasing appears to be mere juridical sophistry, we should consider questions which can in the first instance once more be formulated in relation to the housing market: why can so many people in this country not buy a house, but merely the rights of use for a house? Why is it therefore so desirable to buy a house and not only the rights of use for a house? Why is it then so much more lucrative to buy a house and thereafter to sell the rights of use (which can be cancelled at any time) for that house to others (in other words: to lease one's own house)? Reference to the injustices of the free unsocial market-economy is certainly correct, but unfortunately does not explain anything. Rather, we should ask whether and in what way entirely real economic relations are reflected in supposedly juridical sophistries.

Before I go into this question concretely, however, I must pose another: to be able to work is a quality of humans. We can learn it and have it at our disposal. We can lose it – for example, though sickness or disability – temporarily or permanently, but in these cases nobody has it at their disposal any more as a quality of this concrete individual. One has lost this quality, not in the sense that another individual can find it and appropriate it. The quality of being able to work is therefore not detachable from the concrete individual. An individual can thus sell [*veräußern*] it just as little as it can be bought from him.

---

7. Marx and Engels 1975–2004b, p. 490.
8. Engels 1975–2004h, p. 374; translation modified; *MEGA*², I/24, pp. 65f.

Generally, it is to be established that we can indeed distinguish determinate qualities and behavioural patterns in a thing or in a person, but we cannot separate them: whoever wants to enjoy the greenery of trees in their own garden must buy trees – greenery in itself cannot be bought. Whoever wants to enjoy a comfortable bed must buy a bed – comfortableness in itself without the thing that affords such comfort is nowhere to be found. The thing [*Sache*] and its behaviour [*Verhalten*] are simply not to be separated from each other, and the German language expresses this beautifully in the bureaucratic-philosophical concept of a state of affairs [*Sachverhalt*].[9] Just as little as we can buy the greenery of trees without the trees can the owner of money buy the quality of the individual of being able to labour without buying the individual. The buying and selling of individuals, however, is exactly what Marx claims to see as impossible in the buying and selling of the commodity of labour-power – and rightly so, because this transaction does not belong to the capitalist mode of production but to that of antiquity, namely, in the form of slavery.

But perhaps the quality of being able to labour is something other than labour-power and as a result the arguments that have been presented here are in truth an equivocation, the foisting of another conceptuality in order to reach the desired result? Let us read Marx, for example, in the following passage:

> We mean by labour-power, or labour-capacity, the aggregate of those mental and physical capabilities existing in the physical form, the living personality, of a human being, capabilities which he sets in motion whenever he produces a use-value of any kind.[10]

The sentence shows, in my opinion, that the concept of *labour-power* used by Marx fundamentally aims at nothing more than at the quality of being able to labour. That labour-science today correctly distinguishes between knowledge, capabilities and skills, and that we therefore do well more generally to speak of qualities or behaviour does not change anything. Even more astonishing is the fact that Marx regarded a sale of 'the aggregate of those mental and physical capabilities existing in the physical form, the living personality of a human being' as a really possible transaction in capitalist reality at all.

But is it then at least the case that the employer pays those who sell the rights of use for their labour-power on the labour-market, the use 'of those mental and physical capabilities existing in [...] the living personality of a human being'? Not at all. The graduated lawyer, for example, unable to find work in her profession

9. This interpretation occurs in outline in Wittgenstein 1966; see especially proposition 2.01 and 2.031.
10. Marx 1976, p. 270.

and so working as a taxi-driver, is certainly not paid according to her physical and intellectual capacities by the transportation-company which employs them. Why should it do so? The transportation-company gains nothing at all from her legal training, the knowledge, capabilities and skills which she has acquired there, and pays her for the use of the knowledge, capabilities and skills which it has at its disposal after signing the work-contract, in the sense that they are utilised for its goals. Both must come together: availability and utilisability – what is not available cannot be utilised, but not everything which is available is also utilisable. The former miner, after retraining now a worker on the assembly-line for Ford in Cologne, is paid by the firm for the use of the knowledge, capabilities and skills which are utilised by the firm on the assembly line. Everything of which he was capable as a miner 'naturally' does not count anymore, which is supposed to mean: in this society it counts for nothing, for he does not receive a single penny for that. The craftswoman who upgrades herself to an engineer by evening study-classes will not be paid for her newly acquired knowledge and skills so long as they are not utilised by the company.

With these examples, the problems contained in our initial question are not solved, of course; however, they are perhaps clearer and thus we are now better able to formulate them. The conceptual distinction between the knowledge, capabilities and skills which a human has at their disposal and those which are utilised by a business seems to me to be indispensable. In this regard, I would like to remark that Marx – for reasons which I have not discovered up until now – employed the term *labour-capacity* [*Arbeitsvermögen*] in the *Grundrisse* and in the manuscript *Zur Kritik der politischen Ökonomie* of 1861–3; in the economic manuscripts of 1864–5, he goes over to using, in parallel with this, the term *labour-power* [*Arbeitskraft*] as well; and finally, in *Capital*, he almost exclusively uses the term *labour-power*. A phrase like the above cited 'labour-power, or labour-capacity' – in which the *or*, according to the logic of the passage, means an inclusive *vel* and not an exclusive *aut* – is rarely pronounced. In reality, however, there is not only a large difference between the capacity, the real possibility, to do something and the doing itself – that is the distinction Marx makes in *Capital* between capacity for labour and labour.[11] We should also distinguish between the capacity for labour itself and that part of it which is effective in the labour-process as labour-power, in this sense not only real possibility but reality [*Wirklichkeit*] in the narrow sense of the concept.

What the business pays their employees for is, in the first instance and very generally, a fee for the temporally limited sale of the right to use their labour-power. Which ability to labour this labour-force has at its disposal besides that

---

11. Cf. Marx 1976, p. 277.

is of no interest so long as it is not usable profitably for the business, that is, so long as it cannot be utilised. For the business, it is never a case of the capacity for labour, but always one of labour-power, the part of the capacity for labour which the business is able to utilise. The price that the business pays to its employees for the temporally limited sale of the right to use their labour-power is wages. (That wages in other fields of activity or business are named a salary [*Gehalt*] or honorarium should not interest us here). Wages are a price, thus the monetary expression of a value. Which value? Whoever answers this question with 'the value of the commodity of labour-power' is completely mistaken.

In order to clarify the problem, let us look once again at the housing market. The price of a house, apart from all the factors which modify it, is the monetary expression of its value. We pay this price when we buy the house, and it is then our own house. Hereafter it is immediately obvious that the rent, understood as the price for the right to use a house, must be something other than the price of the house itself: nobody would have the idea of paying a rental price month after month which was exactly as high as the price which is paid once off upon the purchase of one's own house. The rental price is quite clearly different from the sale-price, even if both are associated in determinate ways which cannot be analysed further here. Clearly, however, things are even stranger in the case of the commodity labour-power, for it is unable to be sold in capitalist society and can therefore as a result not have a sale-price. Nevertheless, its owner demands fair payment for the right to use it. But what is that is this context – a 'fair payment'?

Let us begin from a statement in *Capital*, namely, one we encounter in the section on wages, which establishes that 'the value of a commodity is determined not by the quantity of labour actually objectified in it, but by the quantity of living labour necessary to produce it'.[12] That corrects – unfortunately, only implicitly – the definition which we find in the second section: 'In so far as it has value, it represents no more than a definite quantity of the average social labour objectified in it'.[13] The difference between the two statements will become even clearer to us if we examine a third on the basis of their consistency. It says: 'The value of labour-power is determined, as in the case of every other commodity, by the labour-time necessary for the production, and consequently also the reproduction, of this specific article'.[14] Considering this sentence more exactly, we must ask ourselves, first, if then the necessary labour-time for the production of labour-power can be equated without further ado with the labour-time

---

12. Marx 1976, pp. 676–7.
13. Marx 1976, p. 274.
14. *Ibid.*

necessary for its reproduction and, secondly, whose reproduction is being considered here.

It is undoubtedly not only and in the first instance a case of the reproduction of the concrete individual, whose labour-power is utilised by the business. For the capacity for labour, and thus also that essential part of it which can be utilised by the business, is, indeed, a quality of an individual; but which individual that concretely is, is completely a matter of indifference for the business. It must simply worry about having at its disposal tomorrow once more a labour-power equally able to be utilised, whereupon *tomorrow* means – from the point of view of the business (thought by itself to exist forever) – the *entire future*. Already, therefore, the simple reproduction of the commodity labour-power – and only this should be treated here – includes numerous elements.

In the first instance, the business must pay labour-power so much that it can work again on the next day, since the reproduction of muscle-, brain- and nerve-power spent in the labour-process occurs outside of it, that is, in the consumption-process. Expressed in money, that is the so-called minimum-wage which allows the individual to buy that mass of commodities 'which have to be supplied every day to the bearer of labour-power', as Marx expresses it, 'so that he can renew his life-process'.[15] The minimum-wage is, however, not the monetary expression of 'the ultimate or minimum limit of the value of labour-power' referred to by Marx in this context, for also here it is a case only of the value of the labour-power used in the production-process.

But with the so defined minimum-wage, the simple reproduction of the commodity labour-power is at best secured for the next day, not for eternity. Marx remarked on this question:

> The owner of labour-power is mortal. If then his appearance in the market is to be continuous, and the continuous transformation of money into capital assumes this, the seller of labour-power must perpetuate himself, 'in the way that every living individual perpetuates himself, by procreation'. The labour-power withdrawn from the market by wear and tear, and by death, must be continually replaced by, at the very least, an equal amount of fresh labour-power. Hence the sum of means of subsistence necessary for the production [rather, reproduction – T.K.] of labour-power must include the means necessary for the worker's replacements, i.e., his children, in order that this race of peculiar commodity-owners may perpetuate its presence on the market.[16]

---

15. Marx 1976, p. 276.
16. Marx 1976, p. 275. Marx referenced the citation in his text in a footnote with merely the word: 'Petty'. The citation itself is not verified even in the apparatus for *MEGA*², II/6.

Rightly declining Marx's patriarchal mode of speaking, we must nevertheless state that in reality the costs of that socially necessary labour of reproduction, which is to be achieved in the circle of the family and thus outside of the business, are already contained in the wages paid by the business itself.[17] This is not an expression of its generosity, but rather a simple calculation of the economic egotism which must secure means for its reproduction and in fact also does this.

By means of both of the elements treated up to now, the mere survival of the individual or their offspring in the future is secured. But it is a matter only of the reproduction of its physiological foundations, that is, of the merely formal capacity for labour. The real capacity for labour – the knowledge, abilities and skills of the respective individuals – is certainly not reproduced at all with that. The real capacity for labour applies to the capacity for labour which is effective as labour-power, that is, that part of the capacity for labour which is effective in the labour-process as labour-power.

If we now take labour-time which is socially necessary in order to equip the individual with the knowledge, abilities and skills which the individual brings into the production-process as labour-power and which are utilised there, it is still to be asked if it is not an essential determining element of that which Marx names the value of the commodity of labour-power. He himself said in this regard:

> All labour of a higher, or more complicated, character than average labour is expenditure of labour-power of a more costly kind, labour-power whose production has cost more time and labour than unskilled or simple labour-power, and which therefore has a higher value. This power being of higher value, it

---

17. It would thus contradict the entire free-market logic to pay this reproduction-labour again in the form of 'housewives' wages'. Apart from this elementary fact, the realisation of this demand would subjugate the living together of humans even more strongly than previously to the laws of the free market. The notion that paid domestic labour enjoys another recognition from that of unpaid domestic labour makes, in reality, the commercial usability of labour the sole criterion of its social recognition. Taken to its logical extreme, it implies that only those women who are paid for sex by their men (husbands, lovers, friends etc) would be fully recognised by them. With that, admittedly, the statement which we encounter in the *Communist Manifesto* would be confirmed in a very peculiar way: 'The bourgeoisie' – and obviously not only it – 'has torn away from the family its sentimental veil, and has reduced the family relation to a mere money relation' (Marx and Engels 1975–2004b, p. 487; cf. the version which Engels quotes in his essay *Refugee Literature*, and which corrects the original text, in *MEGA*[2], I/24, p. 376; Engels 1975–2004i, p. 17). The whole endeavour therefore adds up to an eternalisation of the servile free-market money-relations; servitude would therefore be moderated ('humanised'), but not abolished.

expresses itself in labour of a higher sort, and therefore becomes objectified during an equal amount of time, in proportionally higher values.[18]

But the matter does not ever remain like this. The phrase Marx himself coined applies to this view of his: 'In fact, this way out is even more absurd because the value of a commodity is determined not by the quantity of labour actually objectified in it, but by the quantity of living labour necessary to produce it'.[19] This question is thus in no way to be answered simply with 'yes', particularly because the concrete individual's own abilities, skills and knowledge are reproduced above all in the production-process itself.[20] If this reproduction does not occur, the individual gradually loses his capacity for labour, he unlearns the type of work which he once knew and in this sense becomes de-qualified.

This process on the side of the subjective means of production is completely comparable with that on the side of the objective means of production – if they remain unused, they are not utilised, and that is pure loss for their respective owners. Regarding that aspect, Marx very instructively described it in *Capital* in the following way: 'Furnaces and workshops that stand idle by night, and absorb no living labour, are "a mere loss" to the capitalist. Hence, furnaces and work-shops constitute "lawful claims upon the night-labour" of the labour-powers'.[21] In another passage, in the *Theories of Surplus Value*, he remarked on the problem of the destruction of capital:

> Machinery which is not used is not capital. Labour which is not exploited is equivalent to lost production. Raw material which lies unused is no capital. Buildings (also newly built machinery) which are either unused or remain unfinished, commodities which rot in warehouses – all this is destruction of capital. All this means that the process of reproduction is checked and that the *existing* means of production are not really used as means of production, are not put into operation. Thus their use-value and their exchange-value go to the devil.[22]

The latter is also valid for the individual who has a determinate capacity for labour at his disposal but cannot let it be effective in the production-process. The graduated law-student working as a taxi-driver loses a once essential integral

---

18. Marx 1976, p. 305.
19. Marx 1976, pp. 676–7.
20. To be distinguished here is the expanded reproduction of the individual capacity for labour in the form of further training, for example, by studying new specialist literature, attending evening classes etc. A large share of the costs of this expanded reproduction is borne by the workers themselves. Nonetheless, it should once more be emphasised that here only the problems of simple reproduction will be treated.
21. Marx 1976, p. 425.
22. *MEGA*[2], II/3.3, p. 1119.

part of her capacity for labour just like the former miner who now works on the assembly-line at Ford. The costs of their training become mere loss due to not being used anymore, they are written off and are not utilised.

With that, however, we encounter a further problem: if simple reproduction of the capacity for labour takes place, to a significant degree, in its utilisation, that is, in labour itself – automatically, so to speak, inside the labour-processes – then the business does not at all need to pay the owner of the commodity labour-power for this side of reproduction, for the act of reproduction does not cost those working anything. However, the qualification, the ability to perform complicated labour, should represent a decisive element of the value of the commodity labour-power, it should correspondingly be reflected also in the wages which allow the individual to secure his reproduction. If, however, the ability to perform complicated labour is reproduced quasi-gratis, that is, in the labour-process itself, then nobody needs to pay and this essential ground of determination for the value of the commodity labour-power appears invalid.

We could naturally manage with the pretext that it is only through higher payment that the individual would be brought to performing complicated labour or – even more nobly formulated – to undertake higher responsibilities. This way of speaking means nothing else but saying that profit is the wages of the capitalist for the labour which he performs. Rather, we have to remember that the reproduction of the capacity for labour of individuals always includes the production of the capacity for labour of their offspring as well.

In this context, I would like at first to cite two statements from the *Communist Manifesto*, statements which nonetheless have not been seen in this context until now:

> The bourgeoisie has stripped of its halo every occupation hitherto honoured and looked up to with reverent awe. It has converted the physician, the lawyer, the priest, the poet, the man of science, into its paid wage labourers. [...] He [the worker] becomes an appendage of the machine, and it is only the most simple, most monotonous, and most easily acquired knack, that is required of him. Hence, the cost of production of a workman is restricted, almost entirely, to the means of subsistence that he requires for maintenance, and for the propagation of his race.[23]

These are of course sharp, climactic formulations from a political pamphlet, written with hate and passion, not the result of researches conducted *sine ira et studio* and then written up with carefully chosen words. Nevertheless, they permit the question of whether or not the costs which, for example, the intellectuals transformed into paid workers cause, are limited almost only to the food etc.

---

23. Marx and Engels 1975–2004b, p. 487.

which they require for their sustenance and for the continuation of their race, in which race here must surely be translated with the phrase 'social layer'.

That is by all means the case; nevertheless the costs of producing a university-professor are even today higher than those for the production of an assembly-line worker. By that I mean not only those training costs which today in Germany – still – are paid by the state. For it is certainly not the case that the means of reproduction of the commodity labour-power can be reduced to the individual costs for education and the raising of children. Generally, higher qualified labour-forces – as Dummer formulates it – 'actually also have greater needs of further education and culture which must be satisfied if the attained intellectual and cultural level is supposed to be maintained and further developed'.[24] It is, however, as I would like to add, not the intellectual and cultural level in itself but precisely that which – at least potentially or as accompanying general framework – is utilised for the reproduction of the business. How far this circle, if need be, can reach is shown in the experience of the North American farmer who played Mozart to his cows – they thanked him with an increase in the amount of milk they produced.

Precisely in the reproduction of the higher qualified labour-forces – intellectuals, managers, and so on – the whole socialisation of adolescents plays a large role. This however necessarily costs, just as the cultural environment does – to the point of that phenomenon which the famous doctor Rudolf Virchow has grasped in the classic saying that physicians bequeath their vocation also to their step-sons, and that, of course, has its social price too.

Under market-preconditions and in the sense of elementary cost-accounting in the establishment of socially necessary labour-time, it is, in fact, assumed that on the social average children go into professions which are allied to those of their parents. The means of reproduction inherent to the free unsocial market-economy thus grant not only a certain amount of social mobility but rather, equally, a certain amount of social immobility. Exceptions there only prove the rule – such individual cases in which the daughter of an assembly-line worker becomes a university-professor and the son of a bank-manager a social worker does not change anything in the social average. Therefore, as a rule, the one receives no additional wage for the relatively expensive production of a university-professor as the other receives no salary-deduction for the relatively cheap production of a social worker. On the contrary, the tax-relief due to children is for poor people much less than for the richer – reckoned in terms of cash, and that alone interests those concerned. Tax-legislation therefore, although in an understated way, gives expression to the fact that in this society the education of the children

---

24. Dummer 1997, p. 71.

of rich people costs more, on average, precisely because they are supposed to reproduce *their* parents.

Therefore, even though the capacity for labour, in so far as it is effective, is, on the one hand, immediately reproduced (that is, during the production-process and in the producing individual itself), on the other hand, for its 'eternalisation' it needs just as much the reproduction outside the immediate production-process. The labour-time necessary for this reproduction – no longer related to the individual, but to his social layer – determines to a considerable extent the reproduction value of the commodity labour-power. For the temporary use of labour-power, the business pays wages to those whose property it is and whose property it remains.

In this sense, the amount of wages is fundamentally determined in the same way as, for example, the rental price on the housing market: in this case also, the point of departure is the labour-time which is socially necessary for the reproduction of the house.[25] There is, therefore, treated in economic terms, also no difference in the case of labour-forces which in the literature are commonly not called wage-workers but rather mercenaries or hirelings, salaried employees or receivers of an honorarium. Their payment conforms fundamentally to the value of the labour-power being reproduced. That the price thus determined is subject to diverse variation on the market, changing according to supply and demand, subordinated to the general means of utilisation of capital and occasionally – very occasionally – is dependent upon the accomplished performance for its amount,[26] is a fate now shared by wages – *mutatis mutandis* – with the normal prices. Working out the grounds of determination for these variations is, however, a task for another day. On the one hand, it assumes the answer to our initial question but, on the other hand, goes far beyond it.

---

25. The point of departure is not the whole. On further aspects cf. Engels's *On the Housing Question*, particularly *MEGA*², I/24, 66; Engels 1975–2004h, p. 317f.

26. For a critique, see Dummer 1997, 30f., where the 'illusion of the principle of performance' is treated. See also, generally, Gikas 1985.

In And For Itself: Freedom.
On the Historical Tendency of a Renewed Critique of the Political Economy of Labour[1]

Sebastian Gerhardt

Marx's critique of political economy strove to explain the history of modern society, to discover the 'natural laws of its movement'.[2] Marx was convinced that bourgeois society's historical development and self-reflection in the form of political economy had established, in his own time, every prerequisite for its systematic exposition and critique. He tried to replace 'conflicting dogmas' with 'conflicting facts'[3] and to present a scientific theory of the economic foundations of modern social development that would equal the theories of natural science both in rigour and wealth of content. Not only that, his investigation of the prospects and limits of the capitalist dynamic was intended to simultaneously provide proletarian class-struggle with a scientifically grounded code of practice. To provide scientific grounds for the self-liberation of the working class, and hence for the abolition of class-society and the leap into the 'kingdom of freedom'[4] – that was the ambition behind Marx's programme: 'In place of the old bourgeois society, with its classes and class

---

1. Given the magnitude of the topic proposed by the editors, I have chosen a title that I hope puts this topic in more concrete terms. Nevertheless, the following paper is no more than an introduction – one that must make do without much of the material upon which it builds, and which has been published elsewhere (in the form of investigations devoted to other problems than the one discussed here). I am referring especially to the following essays by the author: Gerhardt 1997, 2002, 2003, 2005.

2. Marx 1976, p. 92.

3. Marx 1975–2004u, p. 127.

4. Engels 1975–2004j, p. 270.

antagonisms, we shall have an association, in which the free development of each is the condition for the free development of all'.[5]

The question of whether this goal could realistically be achieved was already raised during Marx's own life time. Marx no doubt underestimated the scientific difficulties involved, especially the methodological ones, just as he underestimated the scope of the research and presentation-issues that continued to emerge.[6] This was our good fortune, for Marx would hardly have found the strength to tackle ever new questions and problems had he not cherished the false hope that he would soon be able to complete his work.[7] This biographical aspect apart, we can say Marx's combination of scientific analysis and political intention raised more questions than anything else – questions that cannot be answered only on the basis of his writings, now published almost *in toto*.

Many felt Marx's extensive investigation of the ways in which capital's contradictions unfold was insufficient, and some even perceived it as a direct obstacle to the development of political and social resistance to the progress of capitalism. Karl Korsch felt Marx's critique of political economy was an expression of resignation prompted by the defeat of the revolution of 1848–9.[8] And how could a determinist exposition of capitalism's historical development mobilise people who were simultaneously expected to transform the very substance of this society? How could a path to the superation of bourgeois society be found starting from a perspective situated within that very society?[9] Thomas Kuczynski once suspected 'the Hegelian principle of self-abrogation [*Selbstaufhebung*] utilised by Marx' to have been 'positively "realised" only in literature – in the character of Baron Münchhausen, who pulled himself out of the swamp by his own hair'.[10] It is not just the practico-political project of the proletariat's self-abrogation, but also the theoretical project of the critique of political economy that must confront the question to what extent the elements of something new actually become 'generally apparent' within 'the old society'[11] – and how far these elements will get one.

Others have censured Marx's analysis of capital for not being scientific enough. They find that even *Capital* is shaped by political intention and philosophical prejudice – as in Marx's exposition of labour's 'dual character', which he described as 'crucial to an understanding of political economy', the point from

5. Marx and Engels 1975–2004b, p. 506. Engels would later, and somewhat less dramatically, put this as follows: 'It goes without saying that society cannot free itself unless every individual is freed' (Engels 1975–2004j, p. 279).
6. Gerhardt 2005.
7. See, for example, Einführung der Bearbeiter 1992 and 2003.
8. Korsch 1967, pp. 181–3.
9. Weinholz 1993.
10. Kuczynski 1996a, p. 6.
11. Engels 1975–2004j, p. 253.

which the entire theoretical system of bourgeois economy could be unhinged.[12] Friedrich Engels's remark that one can either be a 'man of science' or a 'party man', but not both, has repeatedly been turned against his and Marx's project. Cornelius Castoriadis combined both strands of criticism, denying both the scientific validity of Marx's analysis of capitalism and the possibility of combining that analysis with revolutionary practice.

An old saying warns against throwing out the baby with the bathwater. It may be too late, 140 years after the publication of *Capital* Volume I, to attribute childlike innocence to Marx's ideas. Nevertheless, I believe Marx's approach – the combination of causal explanation with freedom – is the capstone on which an up-to-date, genuine critique of the political economy of labour can be built.[13] Scientific literature may not be so different from poetry, of which Yury Tynyanov remarked:

> The teacher is generally assumed to prepare the admission of the student. In fact, the opposite is the case. [...] Years of hidden, underground fermentation are required before the fermenting element appears on the surface, not as an element but as an appearance. [...] It is the students who prepare the appearance of the teacher.[14]

More than just terminological difficulties

The aspiration behind Marx's project must clash from the outset with any view according to which cognition of significant parts of the real world principally represents a doubtful or even futile endeavour. Whenever such scepticism becomes more pronounced, as is the case today, there results 'the tendency to replace responsible commentary on the problem by an exposition of how the problem has been scientifically engaged with so far, completed with a catalogue of the various approaches and an inductive emphasis on the "view currently predominant", which is sometimes taken to also represent the "soundest" solution'.[15] In his classic 1928 work, *Marxism and the Philosophy of Language*, Valentin Voloshinov

---

12. Marx 1976, pp. 128, 131–2. Compare Steedman 1977.

13. In the words of Spinoza, 'Man does not form a State within a State'; he is no supernatural power (1678, Book III, Preface) – and this is precisely the point from which to develop a realistic, secularist concept of freedom. Lev S. Vygotsky began his 1926–7 study of the crisis of psychology and its historical significance with a quotation from the Bible: 'The stone the masons discarded as flawed is now the capstone!' (Psalms 118:22). And Vygotsky discovered this capstone 'in the interrelatedness of practice and philosophy' peculiar to psychology. See Wygotski 1985, pp. 57, 203. Vygotsky stresses the significance of a 'philosophy of practice' almost in passing (Wygotski 1985, p. 203).

14. Tynjanow 1982a, p. 52.

15. Voloshinov 1975, pp. 236–7.

defined this 'altered destiny of the word in modern bourgeois Europe' as a 'reification of the word, a degrading of the thematics of the word'.[16] Under such circumstances, Voloshinov continued, scientific debates become a mere exchange of opinions, 'and even these opinions do not foreground what is actually "believed", but *the way in which it is believed* (in an individual or typical manner)'.[17] Matterof-fact debate yields to the interpretation of statements and points of view. It is only against this background that Michael Brie's hope of 'changing the world by means of its interpretation'[18] makes any sense: the world to be changed is only a totality of texts. In the winter of 1994–5, a lecture-series on the eleventh of the *Theses on Feuerbach* was held at Berlin's Humboldt University, the foyer of which features that Marxian statement in golden letters. Interestingly, not one of the philosophers lecturing there found it strange that his occupation should be described as 'interpreting the world'. They apparently share the view insinuated in that characterisation, namely that the world is a curiously intricate text.[19] A view that begs the question: Who is the author? The simple fact that human knowledge is the product not of divine revelation, but of a specific form of labour, and that it therefore involves human subjectivity, is stood on its head and becomes the claim that there is no such thing as objective knowledge. Actual knowledge, which might curb freedom of interpretation, is reduced to a bashfully cultivated utopia or forthrightly denounced as a form of domination. Not one of the philosophers was prepared to argue as crudely as Spinoza, who compared the production of knowledge to that of material objects:

> The matter stands on the same footing as the making of material tools, which might be argued about in a similar way. For, in order to work iron, a hammer is needed, and the hammer cannot be forthcoming unless it has been made; but, in order to make it, there was need of another hammer and other tools, and so on to infinity. We might thus vainly endeavor to prove that men have no power of working iron. But as men at first made use of the instruments supplied by nature to accomplish very easy pieces of workmanship, laboriously and imperfectly, and then, when these were finished, wrought other things more difficult with less labour and greater perfection [. . .].[20]

But what are the instruments proper to the critique of political economy, and how are they to be employed? Can the premises of this critique be developed consistently? Is there room for the concepts of liberation and freedom within

16. Voloshinov 1975, pp. 236–7.
17. Ibid.
18. Brie 1993, p. 15.
19. Gerhardt (ed.) 1996. Marx's 'Theses on Feuerbach' can be found in Marx 1975–2004v, pp. 3–5.
20. Spinoza 1891a, pp. 11f.

such development? Or do these concepts represent a bourgeois, (perhaps) Hegelian residuum, one that shares with many an odd expression used by Marx in *Capital* the feature of serving mainly to confuse students of the critique of political economy? On this point, the *Communist Manifesto* strikes an appeasing note: 'But don't wrangle with us so long as you apply, to our intended abolition of bourgeois property, the standard of your bourgeois notions of freedom, culture, law, &c. Your very ideas are but the outgrowth of the conditions of your bourgeois production and bourgeois property, just as your jurisprudence is but the will of your class made into a law for all, a will, whose essential character and direction are determined by the economical conditions of existence of your class'.[21] This notion of a will 'whose essential character and direction are determined by the economical conditions of existence' follows the Enlightenment-materialists' social critique, whose wittiest protagonists Voltaire and Feuerbach both described human deliberation as a natural process, and the apparatus of deliberation (the head or the body, depending on whether a reductive or a holistic perspective is taken) as a natural product which cannot be controlled – precisely because it is a natural product.[22] Holbach asserts categorically that if, 'for a short time, each man was willing to examine his own peculiar actions, to search out their true motives, to discover their concatenation, he would remain convinced that the sentiment he has of his natural free-agency is a chimera that must speedily be destroyed by experience'.[23] The inflection given this figure of thought by the young Marx and Engels has often been quoted: 'It is not a question of what this or that proletarian, or even the whole proletariat, at the moment *regards* as its aim. It is a question of *what the proletariat is*, and what, in accordance with this *being*, it will historically be compelled to do'.[24]

Marxism's broad consensus on this issue can be seen in a work Lenin described as Karl Kautsky's final and best attack on opportunism: the 1909 pamphlet *Der Weg zur Macht* [*The Road to Power*]. There, Kautsky clearly rejects the notion of an automatic economic development that proceeds 'without the willing human personality' and argues that '[a]ll economic theory becomes mere mental gymnastics for those who do not proceed from the knowledge that the motive force of every economic event is the human will'. Kautsky continues: 'Certainly not a *free* will, not a will existing by itself [*Wollen an sich*], but a *predetermined* [*bestimmter*] will. It is, in the last analysis, the *will to live* which lies at the basis of all economics, which appeared with life as soon as it was gifted with movement and sensation'. Of organic life, Kautsky says: 'The conditions of life determine

21. Marx and Engels 1975–2004b, p. 501.
22. Voltaire 2010 (entry on 'Free-Will').
23. Mirabaud 1853, Part One, Chapter Eleven.
24. Marx and Engels 1975–2004e, p. 37.

the character of its volition, the nature of its acts and their results'.[25] Equal conditions of life – the famous class-position – ought therefore to produce equal volition. In just a few short sentences, the great Marxist dogmatist of the Second International described the square circle that came to be known as 'objective interests', fooling entire generations of Marxists. How broadly this position was accepted can be seen not only from the absence of avowedly left-wing polemics against formulations such as Kautsky's, but also from their reiteration in the work of such writers as Julian Borchardt or Herman Gorter.[26]

While various currents of the labour-movement struggled for liberation from coercion and oppression at all times and as a matter of course, and despite the pathos of individual freedom and equality shared, for example, by Thomas Paine and August Bebel, there always remained a certain distrust of the concept of 'freedom'. The ascendant bourgeoisie's pathos of liberty could be taken up and developed only up to a point; it encountered an obstacle in the working class's conditions of life, which were so very different from those of the bourgeoisie. 'Freedom is only a vain phantom', said Jacques Roux, 'when a class of men can starve another with impunity'.[27] Here, 'freedom' is understood as the key propaganda-term of the ruling class ('the free world'), one to be challenged daily by reference to the pressures imposed by dependent employment. The apotheosis of 'free will' presented itself as a cynical glorification of the powers that be. Moreover, the political freedoms eventually granted did not fulfil the expectations of the early proletarian revolutionaries. The 'battle of democracy' was not equivalent to 'raising the proletariat to the position of ruling class', as the *Communist Manifesto* had claimed. The tension between the reality of bourgeois freedom and the goal of social liberation remained unresolved.

In fact, bourgeois individualism poses a practical challenge to every form of resistance against the demands and impositions of state and capital, a problem Pierre Bourdieu already defined clearly several years ago:

> The atomistic [...] mode of production so dear to the liberal way of thinking favours the rulers, who benefit from *laisser faire* and are in a position to content themselves with individual (reproductive) strategies because the social order or structure works to their advantage. As for the ruled, their individual strategies, complaints and other forms of quotidian class struggle are not particularly efficient. For them, an efficient strategy has to be a collective strategy, and this in turn presupposes strategies for building and articulating a common opinion.

---

25. Kautsky 1909, p. 39.
26. Borchardt 1923; Gorter 1910.
27. Roux 1793.

Bourdieu stressed that the formulation of efficient strategies cannot be achieved via the constitution of a counter-elite: 'The political problem consists in understanding how to use the instruments required for controlling the anarchy of individual strategies and bringing about concerted action. How can the group exercise control over the opinion expressed by a speaker who speaks in their name and in their favour, but also in their place?'[28]

What could become of the *Manifesto*'s pathos during the class-conflicts of the twentieth century has been described, with some poetic license, by poet and communist Stephan Hermlin:

> One of the statements that had long seemed self-evident to me was the following: 'In place of the old bourgeois society, with its classes and class antagonisms, we shall have an association, in which the free development of all is the condition for the free development of each'. I don't know when I began reading the sentence as I have just quoted it. That is how I read it; it was formulated thus because that was how it corresponded to my worldview of the time. How great was my astonishment, indeed my fright, when I discovered years later that what the statement actually expresses is exactly the opposite: '[...] in which the free development of each is the condition for the free development of all'.[29]

And yet the original Marxian formulation does make reference to the problem of freedom's conditions, at least in terms of its linguistic construction, even if this problem is essentially dissolved into the notion of an overarching social relation.

The reality of individuals

The question of freedom's conditions repeatedly provoked the claim that there is no such thing as free will. Much as in Holbach, human will was reduced to its content and then broken down into the series of its conditions of existence, which were in turn broken down into the conditions of their existence, and so on – a procedure by which one could just as well demonstrate the non-existence of any individual or specifiable system, since these too have their conditions and prerequisites of existence. Yet even if a thing's various conditions can exist in near-total independence from one another, they must all be present for the specific result – the thing itself – to emerge. Thus the identity of the thing is posited, an identity that is distinct from the thing's conditions or closed off to its

---

28. Bourdieu 2003, p. 87. Compare the sceptical attitude towards organised forms of protest in Piven and Cloward 1977.

29. Hermlin 1995, p. 18.

prehistory, so to speak.[30] Digression into the infinite series of conditions merely betrays a lack of interest in the object requiring explanation, or a lack of control over one's own theoretical procedure. This objection was already formulated, in a less general form, by Lothar Kühne: 'Bourgeois materialism was unable to distinguish between the specific Being of human individuals and its conditions. [...] Since bourgeois materialism was only able, due to the class-related restrictedness of its mental horizon, to conceive of labour as the condition of human Being, but not as the essential mode of human self-activity, self-generation and history, its social theory could not but take on a naturalist character and remained predisposed to idealist conclusions'.[31]

It is also true, however, that bourgeois materialism contained considerable – and much feared – critical potential, despite its incompleteness and inconsistency. Not only did it reject certain circumstances as inhuman; its search for the underlying reasons also involved focusing on society's material conditions of existence. This is the aspect of bourgeois materialism that early socialism was able to build on. If people were shaped by the circumstances in which they lived, then inhuman behaviour needed to be explained by reference to inhuman conditions of existence. But this critique was unable to explain the genesis of said inhuman conditions. And it had nothing to say on the way out. For who was to alter the conditions in which people live? The people shaped by those very conditions? The vicious circle, which haunts critical social thought to this day, cannot be broken for as long as the powerlessness of individuals is posited in the

---

30. This is not the place to discuss the logical forms of identity and non-identity or the 'Hegelian "contradiction"' (Marx 1976, p. 744, n. 29) in Hegel and Marx. The following will have to suffice: Wolff 1981 already refuted the widespread notion that Hegel (or Marx) developed a specific, dialectical logic contrary to the laws of traditional formal logic. Yet Wolff remains undecided on the logical issues proper. The Hegelian formula for contradiction ('identity of identity and non-identity') can only be adequately understood if the formula for non-identity is correctly recognised to be 'x is not not-x'. As is well known, Hegel added to Kant's extension of the Table of Judgements by subsuming identical statements under the rubric of infinite judgement. Identity and non-identity correspond to the two forms of infinite judgement. Hegel recognised that such statements contain no claims about x, but only claims about the term 'x'. It is also clear that Hegel was both polemically alluding to the first two principles of Fichte's Doctrine of Science and rejecting the modern persuasion that avoiding antinomies requires one to discuss signs and propositions in a 'meta-language'. This belief has spread widely among philosophers following Alfred Tarski's (1935) essay on the concept of truth in formalised languages, even though Tarski's teacher, Stanislaw Lesniewski, and Aleksandr Zinovyev, demonstrated in their own work that coining names for signs and propositions does not lead to contradictions as long as certain well-founded 'grammatical' constraints are observed. In his classic work, Tarski explicitly pointed out his findings cannot be applied to Lesniewski's systems: Tarski 1935, p. 328, n. 56. But his remark played no role in the debates that followed. 'Philosophers of language' are poor readers.

31. Compare Kühne 1981, p. 88.

very premise of the entire, putatively materialist consideration – in the tendency to trace every issue back to the fashioning of the outer, 'material conditions of existence' or the individual's supposed natural disposition. In fact, this amounts to abstracting from human individuals, who are no less material. Thoroughgoing materialism begins from the reality of individual things as posited by Spinoza in a classic statement at the end of the first book of the *Ethics*: 'There is no cause from whose nature some effect does not follow'.[32] It is only when the reality of individuals, their individuality and their correlatedness are taken into account that the specifics of human individuality become accessible to rational analysis, and it is only then that the repercussions of action and its effects on individuals can be conceptualised, and with them self-determination, doubt, hesitation and the conflict of the passions within each single person. This new and necessary approach to the unbiased exploration of society is announced by two apparently simple sentences from the *German Ideology*. There, Marx and Engels state: 'The premises from which we begin are not arbitrary ones, not dogmas, but real premises from which abstraction can only be made in the imagination. They are the real individuals, their activity and the material conditions under which they live, both those which they find already existing and those produced by their activity'.[33]

Like all materialists before them, Marx and Engels emphasised the natural conditions necessary for human social existence. 'The position of the earth in our planetary system, the qualities of our planet, friendly to life, the living nature giving mankind a habitable environment – none of these are product of social labour. Nature is the insuperable precondition of man, who is himself a natural being. This is what makes possible his wonder and horror, living and loving, suffering and death'.[34] But as 'real individuals', human beings do not merely partake passively of nature, but also actively, by means of their activity. Indeed, the domination of nature by means of labour, thanks to which the missing means of daily subsistence are produced, is a basic precondition of human existence.[35] It occurs on fields and in factories, in kitchens and laundry-rooms, with each group of labourers handling its specific set of instruments in accordance with their specific forms of cooperation.[36] For even the shaping of outer nature is mediated

---

32. Spinoza 1678, 1P36. In explaining the will, Spinoza thus begins with the specific nature of the subject; in other words, the nature of the subject is not erroneously traced back to external factors, but considered to be proper to the subject itself. Compare 2P11; see also Hegel 1986, § 471.

33. Marx and Engels 1975–2004a, p. 31.

34. Kühne 1971, p. 5.

35. Marx 1976, pp. 283ff.; Marx 1978, p. 201; Marx 1981, pp. 958–9. Concerning this last passage, it should be noted that Marx's distinction between utility and ends in themselves refers to the chapter on teleology in Hegel's *Logic* and the passage on the notion that follows it. See Hegel 1970a, § 1593ff.

36. See Shaikh and Tonak 1994, pp. 20ff.

by other human beings. It is not only arbitrary external objects that are real, but also the active human being and other persons with different goals and different behaviour. Alongside the shaping of outer nature stands the way human beings shape each other through communication in all its forms, from mutual aid to struggle. By starting from the reality of individuals and proceeding to examine social relations, Marx and Engels accounted for a social objectivity that refuses to be reduced to external conditions, be they given or created, but consists rather in the 'mutual behaviour' of individuals.[37]

Labour and freedom

Marx assumed that rather than being characterised simply by the use of tools, labour involves the deliberate employment of those tools to achieve a certain end.[38] Emphasising that fabricated instruments of labour are 'an exclusively human characteristic'[39] does not amount to exempting these instruments from the larger social context of the relationship between man and outer nature. Marx prudently avoided adopting the definition of man as a 'tool-making animal'.[40] Human beings, and not their instruments, are what determines the 'various uses of things'.[41] An instrument's proper use follows from the end of the activity it is used for. The labour of producing the instrument is relevant only to the extent that it has produced certain properties, or in the case of the producer having added an informative instruction manual.[42] Still, one aspect of the labour-process is ignored in the

---

37. Marx and Engels 1975–2004a, p. 437.

38. Marx 1976, pp. 283ff.

39. Marx 1976, p. 284. On the findings of evolutionary biology, see Mayr 2006, pp. 297ff.

40. Marx 1976, p. 444, n. 7: 'The real meaning of Aristotle's definition is that man is by nature citizen of a town. This is quite as characteristic of classical antiquity as Franklin's definition of man as a tool-making animal is characteristic of Yankeedom'. Christel Neusüß (1988, p. 42) overlooked this remark in her fierce polemic against the 'brainchildren of the labour movement', where she comments only on an earlier, brief reference to Benjamin Franklin's definition of man.

41. 'Every useful thing is a whole composed of many properties; it can therefore be useful in various ways. The discovery of these ways and hence of the manifold uses of things is the work of history'. Marx 1976, p. 125. See also Marx 1976, p. 288.

42. An instrument's purposive employment cannot be deduced from the instrument itself, as suggested by Leontief's 'reification-appropriation approach' or the 'object meanings' of critical psychology. See Keiler 1997a. When Klaus Holzkamp claims that 'to the extent that they are use value reifications, world states of affairs differ from other states of affairs in that they express generalised human ends in an objective form perceptible by the senses', he formulates an understanding of use values that is certainly not Marxian: 'Therefore, whenever products enter as means of production into new labour processes, they lose their character of being products [...]. [...] [It] is by their imperfections that the means of production in any process bring to our attention their character of being products of past labour'. Marx 1976, p. 289.

comments Marx offers in *Capital* Volume I. For the ends that people pursue by means of their activity must first be determined by those very people.

In their polemic against Georg Lukács's view of labour, Peter Ruben and Camilla Warnke develop the notion that 'the system called "society" displays the feature of objective purposiveness or an objectively teleological character for the simple reason that society exists only if the conditions of its simple reproduction are met. Conservation is the basic objective telos'.[43] In effect, Ruben and Warnke pick up on a time-honoured Stoic notion, applying it not to the individual but to all of society. Yet if self-preservation is the overarching end that the actions of every individual and collective subject are directed toward, the question of how exactly this end is to be achieved remains open. The notion that everyone already knows what is good for them is not always realistic. And pointing to the needs of individuals is not sufficient for answering the question. Perceived deprivation – Hegel's definition of need – tells us nothing about its underlying reasons or possible remedies. This is why Hegel drew a precise distinction between need and interest, where the latter refers to our inclination towards the means by which we hope to end deprivation.[44]

Using the various ends of human activity, their content and their genesis as distinguishing criteria, Hegel was able to distinguish between several quite diverse forms of human freedom – forms he found historically realised in equally diverse combinations. Lev S. Vygotsky picked up on Hegel's reflections and developed the notion of a developmental history of the higher mental functions that would empirically reveal (linguistic) means of controlling one's own behaviour by means of a comprehensive analysis of human sign-usage, thereby laying the foundations for free will and showing the way to conscious self-transformation.[45] The differentiated concept of freedom this requires can be spelt out in Hegelian terms by distinguishing between freedom in itself, freedom for itself and freedom in and for itself.

(1) Freedom in itself consists in the realisation of a given (familiar or assumed) end. This is impossible without mastery of one's own behaviour, or of the individual's inner and intrinsic nature, such that the end continues to be pursued even when environmental influences change. Here we can already say that there can be no labour without self-determination. But self-determination is not enough. A will that shows no interest in its conditions of realisation owes its success only

---

43. Warnke and Ruben 1979, p. 30.
44. Hegel 1986, §§ 360, 475.
45. Vygotsky 1987b. See also the conclusion of Vygotsky 1987a, which needs to be read in light of Vygotsky's comprehensive study of will and emotion (compare Vygotsky 1999).

to good fortune, while its failure becomes a baleful fate. Its realisation is not free but merely a matter of chance. Success or failure results from a purposive action that requires consideration not only of the end pursued but also of one's own power and of the reality of the object. 'Hence it is only the will itself that stands in the way of attainment of its goal, for it separates itself from cognition [...]'.[46] Even here, the subject must become its own object of cognition; only in this way can it assess its own power and then gradually adjust reality to its end by a process of continual transformation. This procedure involves the determined end taking on a life of its own and becoming something absolute that the person must subordinate himself to.[47] The individual is free in its dealings with outer nature, but it is not free vis-à-vis its own ends. Even when a choice is made between various ends (freedom of choice), the ends themselves are not questioned, but merely evaluated.

What really puts these ends in question is the attempt to realise them. For the mere fact that someone disposes of the required instruments of labour does not guarantee that he will realise what Marx calls 'a purpose he is conscious of'.[48] By no means does production always yield 'a result [...] which had already been conceived by the worker at the beginning'.[49] Production is 'the unforeseeable' (Brecht),[50] and mastery over nature, tools and one's own behaviour is never absolute. Many a discovery owes itself to the failure of well-devised plans. And every new assembly-line proves to what extent apparently pre-calculated production-norms depend on the division of labour within the plant and the creative cooperation of its employees. Only the absence of necessary reserves transforms the uncertainty of production into a genuine danger: 'Consider the English saying: 'Tis an ill wind that blows no one any good!'[51]

(2) Freedom for itself starts from a subjective determination of ends or from the fact that an individual can devote himself to a number of possible – and

---

46. Hegel 1970a, § 1772.
47. See Marx 1976, pp. 284f.; *MECW*, vol. 35, pp. 188f. This was the position defended by Pirker 1949.
48. Marx 1976, p. 284.
49. Ibid.
50. Benjamin 1967, p. 168.
51. Brecht 1963, p. 98. Engelbert Stockhammer and Paul Ramskogler (2007) have recently taken it upon themselves to establish uncertainty and the 'distribution of uncertainty' as concepts to be used in class-analysis (alongside the concept of exploitation). Unfortunately, they have ignored the vast literature on the social history of the perception and use of time. Worse, they fail to challenge a common preconception that is itself socially determined, namely that uncertainty is inherently negative. In fact, this is not always true. Uncertainty may indicate the openness of a situation and a renunciation of control by which the new is rendered possible. It constitutes a response to a certain distribution of resources, one that engenders an 'entrepreneurial' love of risk in one set of people and prompts the other to search anxiously for certainty and security.

impossible – ends, which is why Hegel regularly speaks of 'arbitrariness' in this context. Recognition that each determinate end is nothing but the product of a specific subject may become the starting point for a critique of existing institutions and norms, even of an entire social order – just as critique can limit itself to questioning its individual place within the given order.

(3) Even when an agent recognises the path leading to his goal, disposes of the necessary means and has developed sufficient control over his own behaviour to be able to bring about the envisaged state of affairs, it remains an open question whether or not the realised end will actually satisfy (directly or indirectly) that agent's need. Sometimes it is only after a goal has been reached that the agent finds he derives little benefit from the desired result. The reason may consist in a false self-perception or in the fact that the agent has thoroughly transformed, in the course of realising his goal, both himself and his environment. A rationale-critique of ends is to be found in human self-cognition. It represents freedom in and for itself, the much sought-after 'unity of theory and practice'. This entails distinguishing human subjectivity from mere atomistic individuality as well as from abstract universality.[52] The first person to have formulated this insight in general terms seems to have been Hegel; his 'Absolute Idea' is nothing but a human being that becomes its own object of cognition (a person who examines or explores himself).[53] Concrete self-cognition always refers to specific human beings and the circumstances in which they live, which is why it always needs to be conceptualised in individual and historically concrete terms. It provides a rational pathway to the production of common ends, ends that do justice to the needs of the various persons involved.

Historically, the superation of natural determination has developed in contrary ways for different groups of human beings.[54] It is no accident that the limits of a freedom premised on the exploitation of others have long been thematised by the social sciences.[55] Genuine leeway for social development resulted from the emergence of plant-cultivation and animal-husbandry during the 'neolithic revolution' (Childe) – probably the first event in human history to bring about

---

52. Hegel 1970a, §§ 1778–9. On another widespread misunderstanding see, see Lothar Kühne (Kühne 1979, p. 811): 'Consistently applied, the anthropological concept of universality [Allseitigkeit] can synthesise contrary possibilities only in the manner of the criminal investigator who is himself a criminal'.

53. Hegel 1970a, §§ 1776–80. Unfortunately, the revolutionary Lenin mistook the word for the thing itself and was thus led astray: 'I am in general trying to read Hegel materialistically: Hegel is materialism which has been stood on its head (according to Engels) – that is to say, I cast aside for the most part God, the Absolute, the Pure Idea, etc.'. Lenin 1914, p. 86.

54. Engels 1975–2004j, pp. 166ff.

55. Spinoza 1678, 4P37. Cf. also the deduction in 4P73, the concluding proposition in Part IV of the Ethics (Spinoza 1678).

food-security and the possibility of a stable surplus-product. Yet those who decide over the use of the surplus-product decide over society's developmental options.[56] The living conditions of human beings increasingly became the product of social labour, whose (re-)production is far from coincident with, and in fact often excludes, the reproduction of natural conditions. Thus the reproduction of human society was no longer bound by the limits of pre-existing ecosystems. In fact, it began to transform these ecosystems irreversibly – and sometimes in unsustainable ways (a problem that already arose in antiquity).[57] If discovering 'the uses of things' is a 'historical act', then so is discovering which things and methods are best left alone.

Commanded labour and the labour of command: labour-power and entrepreneurial freedom

A realistic and differentiated concept of human freedom is immediately relevant to a rational critique of political economy insofar as private individuals encounter one another as free and equal persons on the market. Marx sharply criticised this freedom as mere appearance. But as he goes on to explain, the appearance is a necessary one. The 'doubly free' worker's factual dependence on wage-payments leaves his freedom of contract and the freedom of choice he disposes of qua consumer unaffected, just as it does not transform him into a machine that responds mechanically to orders. Like every other coercion, the coercion of wage-labour banks on the acquiescence of the coerced, their voluntary submission. The provision of labour-power is the subjective service of a subject that is free for itself, and it is no accident that Marx's discussion of this service includes a lengthy quotation from Hegel.[58]

The question of whether labour-power is a commodity at all has been raised many times. Is labour-power not a capacity rather than a thing? Peter Keiler cites the following as the first of four contradictions he has identified in Marx's concept: 'Principally, labour-power [...] qua commodity is 'an object outside us, a thing [...]'. Yet when we look more closely, [...] it is [...] the very opposite of a thing, [...] namely a property or complex of properties'.[59] In two footnotes, Keiler draws attention to various allusions to Hegel that inform the argument presented by Marx in *Capital*, and reminds the reader of the critique of Hegel Marx formulated in 1842, according to which predicates must not be transformed into subjects. In Keiler's view, Marx himself is guilty of transforming a quality

---

56. Okishio 1993.
57. Tjaden 1990.
58. Marx 1976, pp. 271–2, n. 3.
59. Keiler 1993.

into a thing, a predicate into a subject – such that Marx's critique of Hegel applies to Marx himself.

Yet the later Marx shed the philosophical ambitions of his Feuerbachian youth.[60] The Hegelian solution offered by the later Marx, in the form of a quotation, is the following: it is the subject itself that reifies its 'particular physical and mental skill' and its 'power to act' by distinguishing them from its own totality and making them the basis of considerations on their most profitable employment.[61] Labour-power's failure to become tangible or take the form of a discrete physical object is a feature it shares with many other commodities: 'The legal mind recognizes here at most a material difference, expressed in the legally equivalent formulae: "*Do ut des, do ut facias, facio ut des, facio ut facias*" '.[62] Like the jurists of antiquity,[63] Hegel and Marx will not let ontological prejudices stand in their way when it comes to considering any object of negotiation – such as the rights, the labour-capacity or the services of a person – as a thing. Incidentally, this un-ontological heedlessness of Hegel and Marx has an exact corollary in the un-ontological character of their mother-tongue.[64]

Unlike the precarious freedom of wage-labourers, the freedom of entrepreneurs has scarcely been put in doubt. Their right to determine the ends of production is more than mere juridical appearance; it is an everyday phenomenon not to be done away with even by the outer limits of the market or the material requirements of production. The freedom for themselves of these (few) ladies and (more numerous) gentlemen is beyond doubt. True, under the conditions of industrial fabrication, the product of labour is essentially a non-use value for

---

60. All logical systems, even those content to reproduce traditional syllogistics, must dispose of a rule-governed procedure for the so-called conversion of predicates into subjects. It is only in science, that is, when logic is no longer confused with ontology, that the subordination of human subjects to the objective products of their action can be rationally explained, since this subordination is in fact not a problem of logic.

61. Marx 1976, p. 272, n. 3.

62. Marx 1976, p. 681.

63. For an early example, see Gaius 1904, II, §§ 12ff. Hegel dwelt extensively on this problem in §§ 42 and 43 of his *Philosophy of Right* (Hegel 1970b).

64. Both of the German words typically used in this context, *Ding* [thing] and *Sache* (item) derive from the field of public dispute. Linguists trace *Sache* to the Old High German *sahda* [controversy, legal dispute, issue], while *Ding* has been traced back to the Old Germanic *thing*. Middle High German still featured the word *dinc*, which referred to public parley before the people's assembly. The basic meaning of *dingen* is therefore 'to negotiate', while *bedingen* meant only 'to stipulate the conditions of a contract' (a meaning still preserved in contemporary if somewhat antiquated expressions such as *ausbedingen*, 'to stipulate', and *dingfest machen*, 'to determine'). Historically, the abstraction that led to the notion of 'anything' [*ein beliebiges Ding*] – the notion of an arbitrary object of debate – occurred later. The subsequent, modified reference to sensible objects is derivative. All indications are drawn from: Wasserzieher 1971, although the *Großer Duden* 1985, the *Synonymwörterbuch* 1973 and *Wörter und Wendungen* 1962 draw attention to the same etymological complex.

the producer, and the social division of labour causes the dependence of economic subjects on the satisfaction of manifold needs to grow in step with the increasingly restricted and specialised character of individual products.[65] But the questions of how the needs of economic subjects are satisfied, of what products are brought to market at what price, and of how production ought to be organised, are decided by the owners of private property and their agents. The success or failure of their projects engenders the 'system of needs' that Marx describes as characterising the division of labour in bourgeois society – a process that requires no overarching plan.[66]

This is precisely the point from which a realistic, differentiated concept of human freedom becomes immediately relevant to the prospects of the critique of political economy. For it is only from the explanation of conscious ends that a concept of how ends might be collectively determined can be developed, and such a concept would need to serve as the basis of a free planned economy. There can be no alternative social division of labour without superation of the distinction between commanding and commanded labour. This goal was formulated in precise terms by the East German philosopher Lothar Kühne in 1970: 'Labour qua form assumed by the subjectivity of labourers does not merely require those labourers to relate consciously to the technical and economic conditions of production; it rests essentially on labourers relating consciously and creatively to the ends of production. This presupposes a critique of needs'.[67] 'It is only when the ends of production have been exposed, when the semblance of their being-in-itself has been shattered and ends are consciously determined, that the subjectivity of labour unfolds'.[68]

'For you have a goal in view...'

The statements just quoted were formulated shortly before the unsuccessful conclusion of an attempt to thoroughly modernise real socialism's moral economy. Rather than dwell on cybernetic optimisation models, Kühne took stock of a period of several decades characterised by the failure to revolutionise the

---

65. Marx 1981, pp. 958f.
66. In his *Philosophy of Right* (§§ 189–208), Hegel (Hegel 1970b) already analysed bourgeois society's division of labour under the rubric 'system of needs'. Marx picked up on the theme – Karl Marx, *Outlines of the Critique of Political Economy* (Marx 1975–2004w, pp. 451f.) – and developed it: in the 12th chapter of *Capital* Volume I, in the third part of Volume II and in the tenth chapter of Volume III. Ute Osterkamp (Osterkamp 1976, p. 33) is therefore mistaken in claiming that a 'consistent treatment of the problem of needs' exists 'only in the form of a programme' in Marx.
67. Kühne 1971, p. 5.
68. Kühne 1971, volume 2, p. 30.

relations of production. He was able to analyse the character of communist labour far more precisely than Marx and Engels – not because he was in a position to depict a model-reality but because the pitfalls of contradictory notions had become apparent.

New scientific and social ideas resemble new human beings in that they do not see the light of day fully grown or fully equipped to reveal their true nature in a consistently unambiguous manner. On the contrary, it is precisely where such ideas appear most systematic – like Pallas Athene, who was constrained to appear in full armour in order to survive – that they go on to reveal themselves as systematisations of ruptures and contradictions, the ruptures and contradictions of the New, which must always be incomplete. In the case of Marx, one can point to two sentences whose effect has long been that of conveying a confusing message. In his famous 'Introduction' to *A Contribution to the Critique of Political Economy*, Marx wrote: 'No social formation is ever destroyed before all the productive forces for which it is sufficient have been developed, and new superior relations of production never replace older ones before the material conditions for their existence have matured within the framework of the old society. Mankind thus inevitably sets itself only such tasks as it is able to solve, since closer examination will always show that the problem itself arises only when the material conditions for its solution are already present or at least in the course of formation'.[69]

It is hard to think of a text that was received more enthusiastically within the labour-movement. For while the labour-movement is constituted by 'doubly free' workers, these workers are commanded, subject to directives, excluded from the determination of economic ends and entrusted with only a limited degree of responsibility. By joining or perhaps even founding a political movement that aims at reshaping society, such persons fly in the face of every pertinent proverb ('cobbler, stick to your trade'). Through their political work, they place themselves in opposition not only to entrepreneurs, but also to a large number (often the majority) of their colleagues. For in effect they are demanding to have a say and even to participate in matters supposedly reserved for the bosses: the organisation of work and life. They leave the place assigned to them in society and 'meddle in other people's affairs'. Within bourgeois society, socialists and communists have never been a 'majority movement acting in the interest of the majority'. They have always been a political minority.

Along comes a scholar named Karl Marx, claiming that the very emergence of the social question constitutes proof of its possible resolution. That, 'properly

---

69. *Contribution to the Critique of Political Economy* – Marx 1975–2004c, p. 263.

examined', the workers' need for a solidary social order already points to the conditions for establishing such an order. And further that, notwithstanding its minoritarian character, the labour-movement has the entire historical process behind it. The conflictual relationship between politically active workers and their more quiescent colleagues was glossed over by reference to the 'historical necessity' of the transition to socialism. No philosophical work could have captured the optimism associated with this view better than one of Louis Fürnberg's most popular songs (whose popularity extended beyond the official communist movement): *'Du hast ja ein Ziel vor den Augen, / damit du in der Welt dich nicht irrst, / damit du weißt was du machen sollst, / damit du einmal besser leben wirst'.* ['For you have a goal in view / To prevent you from going astray / To make sure you know just what to do / To get a better life one day'].

Like other varieties of fatalism, the notion that the working class is doted with an objectively determined historical mission did not necessarily prevent workers from engaging in political activity. On the contrary, its effect could be highly mobilising. The problem lies elsewhere: in the suggestion that there would never be any disagreement over which political goals are desirable. This is why the concept of 'freedom' never found its proper place in attempts to formulate a Marxist theory of revolution. When disagreements did become apparent, divergent political positions were made out to result from divergent biographical circumstances: the contrary position was simply excommunicated as 'bourgeois'. There were no genuinely objective criteria available to justify such a decision – but no matter, as long as organisational unity was preserved. In Fürnberg's song, the verse just quoted is followed by two lines that any Marxist-Leninist philosopher would surely have identified as a prime example of 'subjective idealism': *'Denn die Welt braucht dich, genau wie du sie. / Die Welt kann ohne dich nicht sein'* ['For the world needs you just as you need it / The world cannot exist without you']. Thus every current had its own world, and the others were bourgeois, non-proletarian elements. Genuine solidarity was unthinkable under these circumstances, and the very real question of the character and origins of a labour-movement's subordination to the goal of integrating into bourgeois society remained unanswered.

On the reproduction of capital

Reason enough to return to the point of departure, the 'Introduction' to *A Contribution to the Critique of Political Economy*. Karl Hermann Tjaden has subjected the construct of the so-called 'forces of production', prominently developed within Marx's text, to a consistent and ultimately devastating critique.[70] Tjaden demonstrates that Marx's remarks on the 'forces of production' provide an inaccurate, reified view of the actual relationship between the productive power of labour and the social conditions of production. The distinction between subjective and objective conditions of production, closely observed by Marx elsewhere, is elided. As for the popular phrase 'dialectic of the forces of production and the relations of production', Tjaden would later comment: 'This combination is one of the most frequent abuses of the three terms'.[71]

An abuse that can be traced back to the work of Marx, notwithstanding the fact that the expression 'forces of production' is seldom used in *Capital* and never systematically introduced (unlike the concept of the productive power of labour).[72] The notion that the hand-mill produces feudalism goes back to Marx. He was convinced the economically determined development of technology would inevitably lead to the decline of capital. This is the idea behind the so-called law of the tendential fall in the rate of profit, which Marx was unable to prove despite making every effort to do so.[73] Caught up in calculations he was unable to verify personally, Marx missed the crux of the problem: you can't prove what is not true. And the claim that the rate of profit must fall in the course of capitalist development is not true. George Stamatis was the first to employ the requisite mathematical tools in his systematic analysis of Marx's law. He paid his respect to Marx for having precisely determined the conditions under which the rate of profit falls but was unable to rehabilitate the fall as a general law of capitalist development.[74] The rate of profit may fall, but it does not have to. The bracket supposed to combine two distinct elements of Marx's work – his description of the dynamic of capital, which 'revolutionises all conditions', and his conviction that the social formation known as capitalism is historically finite – was lost.

In his preparatory manuscripts for *Capital*, Marx in fact penned forceful analyses of the many circumstances under which the reproduction of capital remains possible. He starts from the definition of value itself, on whose content he remarks: 'Secondly, with regard to the foundation of the quantitative determination of value, namely the duration of that expenditure or the quantity of labour, this is quite palpably different from its quality. In all situations, the labour-time

70. Tjaden 1990.
71. Karl Hermann Tjaden in *junge Welt*, 26 August 2006.
72. 'By "productivity" of course, we always mean the productivity of concrete useful labour; in reality this determines only the degree of effectiveness of productive activity directed towards a given purpose within a given period of time'. Marx 1976, p. 137.
73. Gerhardt 2005.
74. Stamatis 1977.

it costs to produce the means of subsistence must necessarily concern mankind, although not to the same degree at different stages of development'.[75] This is why I believe quantifying value through vertically integrated labour-coefficients is not just a legitimate, but also a necessary instrument both in the exposition of Marx's theory and in empirical research.

The more than centennial debate on the transformation-problem has seen the very concept of a Marxian theory of value begin to be viewed as problematic even by that theory's defenders.[76] It seems the scientifically verified and widely accepted results produced by the discussion since the days of Mühlpfordt and Bortkiewicz are no help when it comes to discussing run-of-the-mill themes of capitalist production such as labour and exploitation, the working day, coopera-tion, the division of labour, machinery, wages, accumulation and unemployment. Years of debate have led to Marx's all too unilinear thinking on the relations between values and prices of production – the (in)famous equalities – being dismantled with considerable precision.

Yet the bold rejection of traditional fields of inquiry proposed, in Germany, by Michael Heinrich and other advocates of a 'monetary theory of value',[77] fails to escape the objective problems associated with Marx's legacy. While it is surely correct that any analysis of the capitalist economy that fails to take account of monetary mediation remains blind, it is no less true that a monetary value-theory that says nothing about the figuration of use-value and the employment of labour-power, nowhere intersects with empirical investigation and is unable to argue in quantitative terms remains empty. A scientific solution cannot consist simply in heroically taking sides by opting for an arbitrarily chosen position. The point is rather to arrive at new insights. Positions grounded in the labour-theory of value allow one to demonstrate that the use-value structure of production is determined by the parameters of the labour-process itself. The theory of value is neither superfluous nor a mystical arcanum accessible only to the initiated.[78] On the contrary, analysis of the value-form's development begins precisely from knowledge of why commodities expose, through the relations between them, a content entirely alien both to their own corporeality *and* to their producers.[79]

---

75. Marx 1976, p. 164. Cf. also Marx's letter to Ludwig Kugelmann in Hanover, 11 July 1868 (Marx 1975–2004x pp. 67–70).

76. Quaas and Quaas 1996.

77. Heinrich 1999.

78. Gerhardt 2003b.

79. The substance of value cannot be shown other than through exchange. Thus the rule of exchange appears as the property of a related thing, and money appears not as a medium for representing the general (or as a standardised measure), but rather as the general itself. 'All forms of society are subject to this distortion, in so far as they involve commodity production and monetary circulation'. Marx 1981, p. 965.

Marx began from these reflections and extrapolated elements of the theory of accumulation even within the framework of *Capital* Volume I; in Volume II he developed a first theory of the reproduction of social capital, that is, of the structure of the social division of labour; finally, he introduced the notion of the necessary formation of a general rate of profit.[80] Marx was aware that the theory of accumulation cannot be adequately discussed within the framework of the abstractions presented in *Capital* Volume I, for the expanded reproduction of capital presupposes the successful realisation of commodities on the market; the theory of accumulation needs therefore to take into account categories associated with the mature process of circulation (capitalism's 'surface'). Moreover, realisation on the market is an aspect of the struggle over distribution, or of the distribution-process, which determines key elements of capitalism (the real wage, the rate of accumulation, the distribution of investments and total labour) while simultaneously occluding the categories of the production-process (prices of production instead of value, fictitious capital and interest). Supply and demand are not autonomous forces. They merely reflect superficial notions of production and individual and productive consumption, processes that relate to one another in multiple ways and do not need to be linked together *ex post* through politics and forms of regulation. Not only do cutbacks in production negatively affect the prospects for income from labour and profit; they also make means available that can be used to curb losses. Economic crises are no superation of capitalism. They represent the violent restoration of a dynamic equilibrium – even if one needs, perhaps, to be a Marxist like Anwar Shaikh in order to understand this.[81]

Since Marx had understood that accumulation consists not in the amassment of wealth but in the reproduction of the capital relation, discussion of classes was moved to the book on capital and could find its systematically justified place nowhere but at the end of Volume III. Objective class-position is decided not by one's relationship to individual aspects of the abstract labour-process, which in fact has long featured several collective labourers as its agents, but by the ways in

---

80. Evidently, a distribution of proceeds, and hence of the means of accumulation, that follows the rule 'price = labour-value' as formulated in *Capital* Volume I would lead to (relative) overaccumulation in labour-intensive and insufficient investment in capital-intensive branches of the economy. The resulting discrepancy would entail limits on production even in labour-intensive branches once all reserves have been used up (due to lack of supplies). In the USA, the level of internal sourcing of gross investment has never sunk below eighty percent since 1960 (sometimes rising considerably higher); in the German Federal Republic, it has not sunk below sixty percent: van Treeck, Hein and Dünhaupt 2007. A greater or smaller proportional reduction presupposes a relatively unified growth-rate across all reproductive branches; this growth-rate is represented by the dual of a unified rate of profit in the production-price system. See Pasinetti 1977.

81. [https://sites.google.com/a/newschool.edu/anwar-shaikh/].

which one's social position is reproduced. The integrated theory of accumulation Marx strove to formulate would in fact have provided us with modern bourgeois society's law of movement. But the task lay far beyond the capacity of any single person.

The second half of the twentieth century saw Marxist economists such as Oskar Lange, Robert Goodwin, Anwar Shaikh, Gerard Dumenil and Dominique Levy use Marx's legacy to produce significant work on the dynamic of capitalist development. They have not only clarified many issues debated since Marx's day, but also realised much of what Marx himself could only aspire to. But there was one thing they have been unable to do, namely prove the economic necessity of capitalism's downfall from its supposed inability to continue developing the productive power of labour. Instead, it has become evident that both the 'economy of constant capital' and the exploitation of subjectivity, or of human labour-power, has been augmented to an unexpected degree under the conditions of capitalism.[82] During the twentieth century, capitalism has reproduced itself both extensively and intensively, in the centres as well as in the periphery. Its successes have taken many of its critics by surprise. Since the right-wing liberal offensive that began under Reagan and Thatcher, such critics have ceased discussing the contradictions of accumulation, refusing to speak of anything but the limits to growth.

Critique of the moral economy

In a parallel development, the question of the 'mature conditions' for emancipation from the movement of capital was put in doubt, partly as a result of the actual attempts to bring about such an emancipation undertaken in the periphery of the capitalist world-system. In the eventual failure of these attempts, one can choose to see proof that conditions had not yet matured enough, or that the Russian Revolution was faced with the purely bourgeois task of 'primitive accumulation' – an attitude somewhat reminiscent of a certain caricature of historical explanation that was viciously and appositely criticised, before the rise of Marxism, by the left-Hegelian Arnold Ruge: 'It is a miserable and despicable wisdom that consists only in one-sidedly detecting necessity once history has played itself out'.[83] After all, the Soviet camp that exited the world-stage in 1989–90 consisted of countries whose national economies had long been industrialised. In part, such sweeping rejections are a way of immunising one's own notions of a superior society, which one does not want, of course, to have

---

82. Lüthje 2001.
83. Ruge 1840, column 740.

anything in common with the horrors of Stalinism or the closed-mindedness of the late Soviet Union.

In any case, when Stalin canonised the political economy of socialism, what he declared to be the basic economic law was a conviction long cherished not only in the organised labour-movement, but also in the very moral economy of the working class, namely that under socialism, production ought no longer to aim at profit, but at satisfying the needs of society.[84] Not only does this postulate distance itself from the bourgeois production of wealth; it also starts from one of the results of bourgeois wealth-production: the fact that, once a certain degree of mastery over nature has been achieved, the end of production is no longer naturally and obviously given. On the one hand, the postulate implies a consensus on common ends ('needs of society'). On the other hand, it says nothing about the necessary interrelationship of particular labours. The simple fact that production for the individual can occur only to the extent that there is social cooperation is virtually stood on its head. The end of productive activity is supposed to already have been determined even before the economy has been inquired into.[85] The economy is considered no more than a means to a social end, and so the end appears as something external. All rhetoric of 'levers' derives from this approach.

But production is not *just* a means to the end that is consumption.[86] When the production of needs is ignored, they become a natural, premise of the labour-process that cannot be influenced.[87] If the needs articulated within society could be satisfied just like that, and all of them at the same time, that would amount to a veritable renaissance of Gottfried Leibniz's 'pre-stabilised harmony' (or, for that matter, Walter Ulbricht's coincidence of 'individual, workplace and social interests').[88] Well, in paradise, no one needs to work anyway. But until the Greek calends, the determination of social ends will have to involve engagement with real conflicts.

The problem with an instrumental definition of the economy is that workers' subjectivity is left aside when it comes to determining the ends of production; workers are reduced to consumers. Thus the basis for the production of common ends is lost, and good intentions stand in their own way by virtue of refusing to allow the existing system of needs to be criticised. The division between

---

84. The principle was first formulated as such in Stalin 1952.

85. Claus Krömke in Pirker *et al.* 1995, p. 49. The 'computer-socialism' advocated by W. Paul Cockshott and Allin Cottrell (Cockshott and Cottrell 1993) shares the limitations of this model.

86. Marx 1975–2004j, pp. 30–2.

87. Marx 1975–2004j, pp. 27ff.

88. Walter Ulbricht was the General Secretary of the German Democratic Republic's Socialist Unity Party from 1950 to 1971 (translator's note).

commanding and commanded labour, a historically inherited division appropriate to inherited conditions of life, is legitimated. The classic formulation of
the concomitant worker-self-perception is provided by the words of one of the
striking Polish dockers debating with Edward Gierek and Piotr Jaroszewicz in
Szczecin in 1971 (and can just as well be applied to the German Democratic
Republic): 'We'll work the best we can, and you'll govern the best you can'.[89]
The contrariety accepted thereby is not abrogated by (appositely) pointing to the
need for collaboration that follows from the nature of the economic-process.[90]
While 'everyone is in the same boat, some are on the lower deck and others
are at the helm'. What was intended to superate capitalism turned out to be a
strange variant of class-society, one that could no longer feel certain of its historical superiority.[91]

The consequent working-class passivity, evident when capitalism was reintroduced, did not result simply from workers' recognition that they were powerless
to arrest their society's decline. Rather, the fact that workers viewed themselves
as powerless was the consequence of a universally accepted 'enslaving subordination of the individual to the division of labor'[92] that is proper to all forms of
moral economy. Today's calls for 'social justice' reveal the extent to which the
present social division of labour is accepted; all that is being asked for is that its
results be more humane.

The simple truth will not do

In 1966, GDR writer Volker Braun thought the existence of 'antagonist contradictions' justified sticking to the 'simple truth' (Brecht), limiting oneself to 'representation from the point of view of one class' and assuming the existence of 'a
single solution' that merely needs to be demonstrated to the audience. He was
willing to make an exception only for socialism. His was a double error. 'Actually
existing' socialism was not free of 'antagonistic contradictions'. And the simple
truth will not do even where it is a question of social classes confronting one

---

89. Rote Fahnen über Polen 1972, p. 102. This is the German translation of an audio
recording of the discussion. A comprehensive account of the events can be found in
Adamczuk 1981.

90. Within the hierarchy of workplace-descriptions, ostensibly grounded in the means
of production, the exercise of a political function is mistaken for workplace-behaviour
and the social context of particular forms of labour is elided. The resulting representations reduce social oppositions to mere differences and do no more than illustrate the
world-view of technocrats. This is the worldview that serves Rudolf Bahro as the basis
for his neo-Leninist project. See Bahro 1990, pp. 191ff.

91. 'We were weak; sneezing was not allowed inside our house of cards'. The statement was made by Kurt Zeiseweis (Zeiseweis 1995).

92. Marx 1975–2004y, pp. 86f.

another in mutual hostility. Who is the class? Who decides which point of view is that of the class? Who pays for the solution? The mere existence of a common enemy is no guarantee of unanimity. Activists are fond of discussing the proposal of a political strike in Germany; they will even discuss changing the law and the constitution. But the very thought of solidarity strikes, by which the more powerful sections of the class might support the weaker ones, remains virtually unheard of and is rejected with reference to the country's present collective-bargaining law.

By contrast, the tendency of an up-to-date, genuine critique of the political economy of labour does not aim at offering advice on how to retreat from the great conflicts of the day, but rather at the formation of political subjectivity within the labouring class. Rather than sympathising with the actually existing powerlessness of the dependent employed and unemployed, it strives to explain this powerlessness, and with it the actually existing responsibility of individuals to devote their strength, however limited, to the crafting of a solidary alternative. Even today, consistent solidary resistance to capital will not be achieved unless people engage politically with the notion that they are the ones who will one day have to take over the whole joint and begin working quite differently from the way they do today. An up-to-date, genuine critique of the political economy of labour looks toward the common liberty of each and all, in and for itself. The means and methods will have to be appropriate to this end.

The 'Fragment on Machines' and the *Grundrisse*: The Workerist Reading in Question
Massimiliano Tomba and Riccardo Bellofiore

Faced with a highly concrete dilemma, the protagonists of Western films often cite a passage from the Old Testament. Torn from their proper context, words from the Book of Psalms or from Ezekiel nevertheless seem to fit naturally into the contingent situation in which they're pronounced. Philological care is inappropriate in the moment of peril, in the middle of a gunfight or some abusive act. The biblical citation is short-circuited with some urgent practical necessity. It was in this way that Karl Marx's 'Fragment on Machines' has been read and cited since the 1960s.

Thus wrote Paolo Virno in the first issue of *Luogo Comune* (1990), a journal that returned to the Marxian 'Fragment' in order to reflect politically on what was underway at Italy's universities. It was the heyday of the *Pantera*, a student-movement that had emerged in December 1989 in order to protest the privatisation-measures proposed by education-minister Ruberti. Virno continued: 'These pages [those of the "Fragment"], written almost breathlessly in 1858 and with pressing political tasks waiting to be attended to, have been cited many a time by those seeking rough-and-ready orientation in the face of unprecedented workers' strikes, mass absenteeism, the behaviour of the younger generations, the introduction of robots at [the Turinese FIAT plant] Mirafiori or the rise of office-computers. The story of the "Fragment" 's successive interpretations is a story of crises and new beginnings'.[1]

---

1. Virno 1990.

In what follows, we intend to read the history of these interpretations against the grain, while seeking simultaneously to promote an authentic confrontation with some of them. Our essay will also involve an incursion into the prehistory of said interpretations.

The story begins with the fourth issue of the *Quaderni Rossi*, published in 1964.[2] It was there that Renato Solmi published the first Italian translation of the 'Fragment on Machines'. Marx's manuscripts from 1857–8 were first published by the Moscow-based Institute of Marxism-Leninism, in two instalments (1939 and 1941) and under the title '*Grundrisse der Kritik der politischen Ökonomie (Rohentwurf)*' or 'Foundations of the Critique of Political Economy (Rough Draft)'. In 1953, the manuscripts were re-issued by Dietz, the Berlin-based publisher of the works of Marx and Engels.

Marx's piece on machines was enthusiastically received by Italian Marxists, who discovered in its pages the possibility of a new reading of Marx: the 'Fragment on Machines' was seen by them as containing that surplus of subjectivity by which the established interpretations of the Italian Communist Party's Stalinist orthodoxy could be subverted. In '*Plusvalore e pianificazione*' ['Surplus-Value and Planning'], an essay published in the same issue of the *Quaderni Rossi* as the 'Fragment on Machines', Raniero Panzieri discovered in Marx's notes from the *Grundrisse* 'a theory of how capital becomes "unsustainable" once it has reached its maximum level of development, once the 'giant' productive forces enter into conflict with the system's 'limited foundation' and the quantitative measurement of labour becomes patently absurd'.[3] Here we glean the basic coordinates of what will become Italian workerism's line of interpretation. Capitalism is viewed and analysed as having reached its 'maximum level of development', and it is seen as giving rise to a contradiction between the superabundant development of the machine-system and the system's limited foundation, a contradiction that renders absurd the 'quantitative measurement of labour'. Panzieri was not to be the one who would push this approach to its conclusion. Other workerists – Mario Tronti and Toni Negri – would develop his intuitions to the point of declaring the law of value defunct.

In order for them to be able to do this, the *Grundrisse* needed to be played off against *Capital*. But here too, it was Panzieri who led the way. 'In the fragment we have cited, one finds the model of a *direct* "transition" to communism – *against* numerous passages from *Capital* and the *Critique of the Gotha Programme*'.[4] This statement would be echoed by Mario Tronti, for whom the *Grundrisse* represented, in all its freshness, a book 'more advanced than the other two', viz. *Capital*

2. Wright 2002, pp. 32–62.
3. Panzieri 1994, p. 68.
4. *Ibid.*

and *A Contibution to the Critique of Political Economy*.[5] Thus began the story of an overestimation of the *Grundrisse*, which continues, via Toni Negri and Paolo Virno, right up to post-workerism, which reduces Marx to the scant pages of the 'Fragment on Machines'. Quotations from *Capital* are now few and far between in Italian post-workerist texts, as can be seen from *Empire* and *Multitude*, the works that have attracted the greatest attention internationally. Let us be clear! We do not intend to re-open the debate on whether *Capital* is to be preferred to the *Grundrisse* or vice versa. But we do feel it is useful to read Marx against the grain, to try to relate him to the present situation and make him function like an alarm-signal that warns of impending danger. Some steps in this direction will be taken towards the end of our essay.

Recounting the history of the 'Fragment''s Italian interpretations requires some consideration of their prehistory, or of what preceded the publication of the fourth issue of the *Quaderni Rossi* – a prehistory thoroughly rooted in the most consistent anti-Stalinist Marxism. The first to stress the importance of the 'Fragment' in Italy was Amadeo Bordiga,[6] who was made aware of it by Roger Dangeville, a member of the Internationalist Communist Party and editor of the first French edition of the *Grundrisse*, which was published by Editions Anthropos in 1967.[7] Perhaps one could identify some genealogical link or indirect familiarity linking Bordiga's writings to the editors of the *Quaderni Rossi* (via Danilo Montaldi or others).[8] But that question does not concern us here. We are more interested in demonstrating the theoretical and political tensions Bordiga emphasised in 1957.

Bordiga was interested in interpreting automation from a Marxist perspective. Automation had left 'bourgeois economists' no less dumbfounded than 'that gang of workers representing Russia's false socialism'.[9] It posed the problem of a drastic reduction of the industrial labour-force, a new unemployment and the foreseeable difficulties a large mass of men and women would encounter in their attempt to earn money and, most importantly, spend it to purchase the vast mass of commodities produced in half-empty automated factories. On the one hand, Bordiga meant to attack the epigones of the Soviet Union's slogan of 'full employment' and those social-democratic communists whose strove for the democratisation of capital. On the other hand, there were those 'half-baked communists' who, faced with the prospect of a 'totalitarian automated production', worried only that with it, the law according to which all value stems from the labour of

---

5. Tronti 1966, p. 210.
6. Bordiga 1957.
7. See Grilli 1982, p. 253.
8. Some analogies between Bordiga and Panzieri have been discussed in Rovatti 1975.
9. Bordiga 1976, p. 189.

wage-workers might become defunct. Bordiga's riposte: 'Good riddance to the laws of value, equal exchange and surplus-value – once they become defunct, so does the very form of bourgeois production'.[10] For Bordiga, it was a question of deducing the necessity of communism directly from the phenomena of capitalism. That was the general framework within which he worked. The analysis of certain passages from Bordiga's work – all of them were written in the white heat of his polemic against Soviet and progressivist Marxism – reveals the general thrust of his politics. Bordiga quotes from Marx's Grundrisse: 'The Science, which compels the inanimate limbs of the machinery to act as Automatons, in conformity with the machine's design, does not exists in the consciousness of the Worker, but rather acts upon him through the machine as an alien Power, as the Power of the machine itself'.[11] The various elements of the machine function like a single automaton because the purpose for which the machine was designed and built is that of being an automaton. It is precisely because of the means and ends with an eye to which machines are constructed that machines function like an automaton. This is the purpose of machine-construction, to simultaneously increase the power and the intensity of labour. Not only does this purpose not exist in the consciousness of the worker, but it in fact opposes itself to him as an alien force that wants to turn him into an automaton also.

What follows from this is not only that 'the entire system of automatic machinery constitutes a monster crushing an enslaved and unhappy humanity under its oppressive weight, a monster that dominates Marx's entire depiction of present-day society', but also that science is 'first and foremost technological superiority, or the monopoly of an exploitative minority'.[12] Bordiga attacks reformism's progressivist optimism, which perceives scientific and technological progress as one more step towards greater welfare. What Bordiga questions is not so much scientific progress in itself, but rather its class character, the fact that the production of greater welfare is at the same time the production of the misery of another class. Against the enthusiastic apologists of technological progress *tout court* – characterised by him, in his unmistakable prose, as the 'baleful advocates of dead labour' – he writes: 'Those who appropriate the capital produced by living labour (surplus-value) are not to be portrayed as human beings or as a class of human beings: they are the monster, objectified labour, fixed capital, the monopoly and stronghold of the *capital-form itself*, a beast devoid of a soul and

---

10. Bordiga 1976, p. 190.

11. Bordiga 1976, p. 193. In order to preserve Bordiga's style, we translate the passage from Bordiga's Italian translation into English. This is instead the same passage in MECW 29, p 83: 'The science that compels the inanimate limbs of the machinery, by their construction, to act purposefully, as an automaton, does not exist in the worker's consciousness, but rather acts upon him through the machine as an alien power, as the power of the machine itself.'

12. Bordiga 1976, pp. 193f.

even of life, but which devours and slays living labour, the labour of the living, and with it the living themselves'.[13]

Bordiga took aim at Russian Marxism and hit several variants of Stalinist Marxism. First and foremost, his critique addressed the Soviet ideology, which presented the growth of Russia's industrial output as the prefiguration of a steely socialism – when the conversion of surplus-labour not into disposable time but into surplus-value for the production of fixed capital is precisely what character-ises the capitalist mode of production: 'Fixed capital in the form of machines – what is called the instrumental-goods complex and praised as the royal way to swell the forces of production both in the East and the West – is the new monster suffocating humanity today. The praise it receives both in the East and the West is a true index of how dominant the capitalist mode of production has become'.[14] But Bordiga is not simply attacking the Russian ideology that passes off the development of the forces of production as socialism (an ideology also present in many professedly anti-Stalinist currents); he also attacks the notion that what makes the capitalist mode of production monstrous is the private appropriation of surplus-value by capitalists. It is fixed capital, which devours living labour, that is monstrous. 'The beast', writes Bordiga, 'is the firm, not the fact that it has a boss'.[15] Bordiga also attacks the anti-worker variants of real socialism: the vision of socialism as *self-management* or *workers' control* is rejected. It does not put paid to the despotism of the factory, which is due not the malice of single capitalists but to the laws of capital, and prolongs capital's valorisation-process. The degradation of living labour in the capitalist firm cannot be ended by replac-ing the firm's proprietor; it can only be ended by revolutionising the forms and conditions of work. For Bordiga, 'the antithesis between capitalism and socialism is neither to be found nor to be decided on the level of property or management, but only on that of production'.[16]

The apology of technological development offered useful support both to cap-italist accumulation in Russia and to social-democratic gradualism in the West; in both cases, capitalism was seen as something that could be harmonised with socialism. For Bordiga, Stalinism and Western social democracy constituted the danger at hand. And they in fact continued to stall the renewal of the revolution-ary working-class movement for several years longer.

Elements of this approach can be found in Panzieri and Italian workerism. In the *Quaderni Rossi*, Panzieri too would challenge the Marxist orthodoxy then dominant, an orthodoxy incapable of grasping the relationship between technology and class-domination. For Panzieri, what needed to be questioned

13. Bordiga 1976, p. 200.
14. Bordiga 1976, p. 211.
15. Bordiga 1957, p. 56.
16. Grilli 1982, p. 264.

was a notion of technological progress as something neutral, external to class-relations. In the first issue of the *Quaderni Rossi* (1961), Panzieri published *Sull'uso capitalistico delle macchine nel neocapitalismo* ('On the Capitalist Use of Machines Under Neo-Capitalism'), where he argued that 'capitalist use of machines is not [...] simply the distortion of or deviation from an 'objective' and intrinsically rational development; rather, it is what determines technological development'.[17] Panzieri arrives, then, at a notion of technological development as intrinsically capitalist: 'Technological development manifests itself as capitalist development'.[18] These reflections by Panzieri were still based on *Capital*, and not yet on the *Grundrisse*. If CGIL's theorists started,[19] in their exploration of capitalism's new organisation of labour, from the premise that the labour-process is intrinsically rational, Panzieri relied on the Marx of *Capital* to demonstrate the non-neutrality of science, which is subjugated by capital in order to increase 'the power of the "master"'.[20] For Panzieri, the automatic machine is precisely what Marx described it as, an 'instrument of torture'[21] to be analysed starting from the specific use-value of constant capital and the technology that sets it in motion, given that machines are designed, from the very outset, to maximise the subordination of living labour.

The critique of the 'stagnationism' inherent in traditional Marxism was supplemented by the discovery, in Marx, of a 'duality' of 'labour-power' and the 'working class' that had been lost in the Marxism of both the Second and the Third International, with their 'economistic' vision of the world of work as ineluctably characterised by 'passivity'. This was a theme that would be radicalised, after Panzieri, by Tronti. Panzieri began supplementing his emphasis on the non-neutrality of the forces of production and of machines with the concept of a 'plan of total capital'. Total capital, he argued, is in a position to plan not only the economy but society as well. From the outset, this was a powerful critique of the notion that socialism consists simply in ownership of the means of production plus planning. Workers' struggles increasingly replace the anarchy of the market as capitalist development's limiting factor, becoming the principal if not the only contradiction – not so much because labour is inevitably one of capital's integral 'elements', but rather because workers' struggles begin to take on political characteristics. Tronti proceded from here. His first step was to separate Marxism qua science of capital from Marxism qua revolutionary theory. As the science of capital, Marxism considers workers as 'labour-power', from the point of view of the theory of economic development, and labour-power is fully reduced to variable

---

17. Panzieri 1994a, p. 27.
18. Panzieri 1994a, p. 27.
19. CGIL: *Confederazione generale italiana del lavoro*, Italian trade-union federation (founded in 1944) (translator's note).
20. Marx 1976, p. 549.
21. Marx 1976, p. 548.

capital, or to work insofar as it is fully subaltern to capital. This is 'labour' as seen through the eyes of capital. As a revolutionary theory, Marxism considers workers as the 'working class', or to the extent that they refuse politically to be included within capital – Marxism as the theory of capital's political dissolution, a theory that considers capital from the point of view of the working class.

These reflections opened up new spaces for both research and political intervention: the non-neutrality of the rationalisation-process, the non-neutrality of science and technology could only be grasped from living labour's partisan point of view. The workers of Marghera – but not only they – would later initiate new reflections and political battles over insalubrious working conditions, starting from the fact that 'illnesses and disturbances contracted in the factory are directly linked to technological development'.[22] As we will go on to see, this political approach was abandoned in the 1970s, because a new approach, accompanied by a new reading of the 'Fragment', was then in the process of replacing the mass-worker with the social worker – a theory that 'would finally call the whole meaning of workerism into question'.[23] Notwithstanding the powerful elements of political innovation contributed by Negri, this transition was partly rooted in the history of workerism. In the second issue of the *Quaderni Rossi* (1962), Tronti had launched a fiery arrow: '*La fabbrica e la società*' ['The Factory and Society']. There, Tronti radicalised the approach proper to nascent workerism's heterodox Marxism by underlining the fact that the relations of production are power relations first and foremost. At the same time, as Steve Wright has observed, Tronti's essay 'bore within it a number of ambiguities and misconceptions soon to be transmitted to workerism itself. The most striking of these concerned the essay's central theme of the socialisation of labour under 'specifically' capitalist production, and the implications of this for the delineation of the modern working class'.[24] Tronti went so far as to maintain that labour-power potentially produces surplus-value even prior to the commencement of the labour-process, in so far as the amount of labour to be provided is stipulated on the labour-market, in the labour-contract. Value-production is thereby potentially constituted. The qualification 'potentially' would gradually be abandoned within workerist discourse, but the consequences were clear from the outset. Wage-struggles that cause wages to rise faster than productivity, and the refusal of labour within production, represent the practical transition from 'labour-power' to the 'working class'. As soon as the working class has constituted itself, conflict immediately becomes antagonism and revolutionary rupture. Capital responds by means of development, and development extends antagonism from the factory to society. The crisis is characterised, in an immediatist manner, as

---

22. Assemblea Autonoma di Marghera 1975, p. 65.
23. Wright 2002, p. 141.
24. Wright 2002, p. 40.

consequent to antagonism. At the same time, the crisis is negated, in so far as it is immediately transfigured into capitalist development. The opposite is also true: capitalist development is simultaneously the development of the working class, or of whichever antagonist subjectivity has been identified as dominant. Development and the crisis are ultimately one and the same. They result from the 'independence' achieved by the power of 'labour' when it comes to determining, through wage- or income-struggles, the amount of 'necessary labour'. Development and the crisis can also be traced back to the capacity for immediate value-production that social cooperation bestows on a 'living labour' soon to be characterised as on the verge of 'exodus' – at which point the premises of the 'post-workerist' *dispositif* will almost all be in place, and with them the theoretical and practical incapacity to tackle those elements of class-decomposition that result from periods of crisis and restructuring – an incapacity already evident in Negri's thinking during the 1970s.

In *Workers' Party Against Work* (1973), Negri started from two pre-*Capital* Marxian manuscripts (the *Grundrisse* and the *Results of the Direct Process of Production*) in order to address the changes undergone by class-conflict and capitalist accumulation during the phase of labour's real subsumption under capital. The law of value was definitively cast aside. New forms of insurgency such as the refusal of work by large numbers of young people served as the starting point for a new theoretical framework that turned the parts of the working day into two independent and mutually antagonistic variables.

It was at this point that Negri began extending the notion of productive labour, tending to make it coincide with wage-labour and what lies beyond. In this way, he began conceptualising 'the new social figure of a unified proletariat'.[25] This approach was then taken further one step at a time. In *Proletarians and the State* (1976), the transition from the mass-worker to the social worker is made explicit: the book's entire theoretical framework is constructed in such a way as to make room for a new revolutionary subjectivity, identified as existing on the edge of marginalisation.[26] This model would be replicated several times. The forms of conflictuality proper to whichever new subject is declared *hegemonic* serve as the starting point for an analysis of the capitalist *tendency* that displaces other worker-types into a residual position.

Negri needed to push *Marx beyond Marx*. In order to achieve this, he resorted once again to the *Grundrisse*. According to Negri, the work's farsightedness is greatest in the analysis developed in the 'Fragment on Machines', with its emphasis on capital's 'necessary tendency'[27] towards the subsumption of all of society.

---

25. Negri 1974b, p. 129.
26. Negri 1976, p. 65.
27. Negri 1998, p. 170.

Once this subsumption has occurred, according to Negri *'capitalist appropriation of society is complete'*.[28] Marx's claim that 'production based on exchange value breaks down' is enthusiastically taken up by Negri, according to whom what is at stake is an 'impossibility of measuring exploitation' by which 'the theory of value is rendered vacuous'.[29] Devoid of every element of commensuration, the 'theory of value' is transformed 'into command pure and simple, the pure and simple form of politics'.[30] Negri discovers in the crisis of the law of value the 'apex of Marx's inquiry' and assumes that the late 1970s mark the historic transition to a 'phase characterised by the crisis of the material functioning of the law of value'.[31] Whence this transition? It's simple: According to Negri, value is no longer measurable, such that 'the theory of surplus value, in its centrality, eliminates every scientific pretension to centralisation and domination conceptualised from within the theory of value'.[32] This is precisely where Negri identifies the superiority of the *Grundrisse*, which he sees as not (yet?) caught up in the analysis of value and therefore open to the 'action of revolutionary subjectivity', an action supposedly stalled by the categories developed and deployed in *Capital*.[33]

It would be more appropriate to say the 'catastrophism' inherent in the way the fall of the rate of profit that is presented in the 'Fragment on Machines' results not only from Marx's wish to give a political twist to his reflections, whose occasion was an economic crisis, but also, and more importantly, from the opacity of his categories, an opacity evident with regard to issues that are absolutely fundamental for understanding the relationship between absolute and relative surplus-value. Marx had not yet adequately defined the notion of value; in fact, his definition of this concept was elaborated only in the course of his writing the *Grundrisse*. The first chapter, which was supposed to deal with the notion of value, was never written. The beginning of the *Grundrisse* – 'II. Money' – refers the reader to a first and *as yet unwritten* chapter on value. It is therefore wrong to maintain that the 'Fragment' celebrates the breakdown of the law of value: Marx's thinking about value had not yet matured. The requisite theoretical work was undertaken by him in the manuscripts he produced during the 1870s. It is also relevant to the issues raised in the 'Fragment' that the Marx of the *Grundrisse* had not yet defined *socially necessary labour* as labour that becomes objectified, in a quantifiable manner, as exchange-value. When Marx speaks of necessary labour in the *Grundrisse*, he encounters problems that he attributes to Ricardo,

---

28. Negri 1998, p. 173.
29. Negri 1998, p. 178.
30. Negri 1998, p. 178.
31. Negri 1998, p. 29.
32. Negri 1998, p. 30.
33. Negri 1998, p. 22.

whose theory of value Marx had still occasionally considered correct in 1858,[34] but which he would definitively dismiss for its tendency to confuse *value* and *cost-prices* four years later,[35] that is, in the middle of compiling the notebooks that would become the *Economic Manuscript of 1861–3.*

In a piece on the 'Fragment' written during the late 1970s, Paolo Virno demonstrated that objectivistic readings of the 'catastrophism inherent in the declining rate of profit' prevent a more enriched understanding of living labour as non-capital. Virno analysed the modalities of socialisation engendered by machine-production, modalities that develop in step with the development of the machine-system. 'The explosive effect of the complete subsumption of the labour-process under capital consists in the enormous expansion of control-related tasks', such that the socialisation of labour occurs outside the immediate production-process.[36] Virno's conclusions were interesting because they rendered Marx's account more sophisticated and argued that the 'general intellect' does not coincide with fixed capital but rather articulates itself 'via the specific dislocation of living labour that occurs at production's neuralgic points'. Virno worked to develop an analytic of concrete labour and subjective behaviour premised not on the unity of the 'general intellect' and fixed capital but on the rift between them. If the living labour that exists within this rift becomes a labour of surveillance and coordination that cannot be straightforwardly traced back to labour-tasks in the factory, then the various forms of refusal evident in people's behaviour could be read as a crisis of the capital-relation that plays out in the field of subjectivity.

In 1990, theoretico-political analysis thought it had discovered the subject of its dreams: the *Pantera* movement with its combative high-school- and university-students was seen as a synecdoche on the basis of which one could explain contemporary relations of production. In a gesture typical of workerism, reference

---

34. Marx to Ferdinand Lassalle in Berlin, 11 March 1858: 'As you yourself will have discovered from your economic studies, Ricardo's exposition of profit conflicts with his (correct) definition of value [...]' (Marx 1975–2004z, p. 287). According to Vygodskij (1974, pp. 20f.), Marx was still moving 'upon the terrain of Ricardo's theory of value' when he wrote *The Poverty of Philosophy* (Marx 1975–2004m); what he had yet to develop was the 'concept of abstract labour as labour that creates value'. According to Vygodskij, Marx's great discovery, the theory of surplus-value, occurred in 1857–8 and presupposes the theory of value. Walter Tuchscheerer (Tuchscheerer 1968) also argues that the Marx of *The Poverty of Philosophy* subscribed to essentially Ricardian positions as far as the theory of value is concerned. He further argues that Marx developed his own theory of value during the 1850s, with the *Grundrisse* representing a 'provisional conclusion'. More recent studies speak of Marx's reflection on value as having taken place during the early 1860s; even more remarkably, Marx continued to work on value-issues even from one edition of *Capital* to the next.

35. See Marx's letter to Engels in Manchester, 2 August 1862: Marx 1975–2004aa, pp. 394–8.

36. Virno 1980, p. 48.

was made to the 'fundamental *tendency* of capitalist development'; if the '*tendential* preeminence of knowledge renders labour-time a miserable foundation',[37] then those who announced from the occupied lecture-halls that 'knowledge has assumed a central function as a force of production' could be identified as the new combative subjectivity on which the relationship between production and knowledge now hinged. Thus was the new and 'principal force of production' discovered, one that relegated 'specialised repetitive labour to a *residual position*'. In this way, the weakest aspects of the analysis developed by Marx in the 'Fragment' were taken up and short-circuited with the present: 'What is most conspicuous today is the full factual realisation of the *tendency* described by Marx'. Just like Negri, Virno considered the so-called law of value to have been 'blown apart and refuted by capitalist development itself'. This analysis is based on a stadial model of the modes of production. Negri would never renounce his own stadial model, in which the craft-worker is succeeded by the mass-worker proper to Fordist and Taylorist work-régimes, who then gives rise to the social worker, in whom 'the various threads of immaterial labor-power are being woven together'.[38] Negri is so convinced of having discovered the 'tendency', or perhaps of producing it, that he can draw up veritable conceptual equations: 'I'm convinced the metropolis is related to the multitude in just the way that the working class was related to the factory'.[39]

In Negri's view, the *Grundrisse* is an 'extraordinary theoretical anticipation of mature capitalist society'. In it, Marx supposedly tells us that 'capitalist development gives rise to a society in which industrial labour (as immediate labour) represents no more than a secondary element within the organisation of capitalism'. Once capital has subsumed society, 'productive labour becomes intellectual, cooperative, immaterial labour'. Negri draws a clear conclusion: 'We are living today in a society ever more characterised by the hegemony of immaterial labour'.[40] While, according to Negri, 'there are numerous different forms of labor that exist side by side', 'there is always one figure of labor that exerts hegemony over the others'.[41] According to this model, the industrial labour of the nineteenth and twentieth centuries has lost its hegemony; 'in its stead emerged "immaterial labor" [...]'.[42] The 'general intellect' becomes 'hegemonic within capitalist production', 'immaterial, cognitive labour becomes immediately productive' and the 'cognitariat' becomes 'the fundamental force of production that keeps the system

---

37. Virno 1990, p. 10.
38. Hardt and Negri 2000, pp. 409–10. The same stadial paradigm can be found in: Negri 2006b, pp. 91f.
39. Negri 2006b, p. 179.
40. Negri 1997, in: Negri 1998, pp. 7f.
41. Hardt and Negri 2004, p. 107.
42. Hardt and Negri 2004, p. 108.

functioning': the new hegemonic figure.[43] Constrained to respond somehow or
other to those critics who pointed out that 'immaterial labour' is relevant only to
a minority of the world's population, Negri and Hardt stated: 'Immaterial labor
constitutes a minority of global labor, and it is concentrated in some of the dominant regions of the globe. Our claim [...] is that immaterial labor has become
hegemonic in qualitative terms and has imposed a tendency on other forms of
labor and society itself'.[44] Negri and Hardt simply turn the question around.
Their reply to the criticism that immaterial labour is a minoritarian phenomenon, quantitatively relevant on no more than perhaps a fifth of the planet, is
that the predominance they mean is a *qualitative* and tendential one. Negri is
not particularly interested in the fact that immaterial labour is minoritarian and
linked to only a few areas of the Western metropoles; what interests him is that
immaterial labour represents a tendency.

Within this linear vision, the most developed sector precedes the more backward ones and prefigures their future: 'Immaterial labor [...] is today in the same
position that industrial labor was 150 years ago, when it accounted for only a
small fraction of global production and was concentrated in a small part of the
world but nonetheless exerted hegemony over all other forms of production. Just
as in that phase all forms of labor and society itself had to industrialize, today
labor and society have to informationalize, become intelligent, become communicative, become affective'.[45] The issue at stake here is certainly not that of
determining the quantitative extension of so-called immaterial labour. The point
is that Negri's model, which hinges on the notion of the tendency, is blind to
how different forms of surplus-value extraction intersect with one another. Such
intersection cannot be reduced to a linear scheme, just as it cannot be a question
of simply drawing up a catalogue of the forms assumed by surplus-value extraction, thereby continuing to treat those forms as thoroughly distinct from one
another. Capital's higher technical composition in some parts of the world does
not automatically give rise to a corresponding tendency. Rather, much as the
development of the textile-industry in England lead to the extension of slavery
in the Americas, capitalist development may produce, at one and the same time,
a massive expulsion of labour-power within the Western metropoles (by which
this labour-power is rendered precarious and underpaid) and a transfer of surplus-value to productive areas characterised by low wages, a low technical composition of capital and absolute exploitation. This is why the explosion of strikes
in the world's so-called peripheries, almost completely ignored in this part of the
world, speaks directly to the proletariat of the Western metropoles, and does so

---

43. Negri 2006b, pp. 135, 148.
44. Hardt and Negri 2004, p. 109.
45. Hardt and Negri 2004, p. 109.

not from a backward position but *on a par with the form currently assumed by capitalist production worldwide.*

Workerism criticised and distanced itself from the millenarian objectivism proper to theories of capitalism's imminent 'collapse', but it remained imbued with elements of a philosophy of history. Postmodernism seizes on the hypothesis according to which the distinction between centre and periphery has lost its relevance in order to turn it against the theory of value. But what would need to be shown is that 'peripheral' forms of exploitation can be found within the 'centre' and vice versa, precisely because of the law of value. It is a question of demonstrating that, because of inter-capitalist competition, an increase in the production of relative surplus-value entails an increase in the production of absolute surplus-value. This idea can already be found in the *Grundrisse*, but it is only in the *Economic Manuscript of 1861–3* that Marx begins to focus on the relationship between relative and absolute surplus-value: 'The fall [in the rate of profit] may also be checked by the creation of new branches of production in which more immediate labour is needed in proportion to capital, or in which the productive power of labour, that is, the productive power of capital, is not yet developed'.[46] By reading the *Grundrisse* against the grain, that is, starting from *Capital*, we can see how Marx focuses his attention on this second aspect, or on the countertendencies that result from the creation of new sites of production characterised by a high level of absolute surplus-value extraction and the intensification of work. These sites of production do not coexist with others, characterised by the production of relative surplus-value and high-tech equipment, in a sort of 'world exposition' of production-forms.[47] Instead, they are violently produced and reproduced in order to slow the decline of the rate of profit, thereby allowing the production of relative surplus-value to continue.

---

46. Marx 1975–2004c, p. 135.

47. Sandro Mezzadra (2008) analyses the juxtaposition of real and formal subsumption almost exclusively by reference to the *Grundrisse*. Mezzadra's entire analysis remains inconclusive and inadequate for two reasons. First, it does not go beyond the categories of the *Grundrisse*, thereby rendering itself incapable of doing justice to the problematic developed in *Capital*. Second, Mezzadra's analysis is incorrect because it does not properly grasp the relationship between the two forms of surplus-value. The question is in fact not that of the coexistence of different forms of exploitation, but that of *how* the production of relative surplus-value gives rise to the production of enormous amounts of absolute surplus-value. The different forms of exploitation are not juxtaposed in a sort of postmodern world-exposition. Rather, capital needs to continuously produce wage- and labour-intensity differentials by means of extra-economic violence. The value produced by the so-called cognitive labourer rests on the pedestal of enormous quantities of absolute surplus-value produced elsewhere. From this point of view, the claim, advanced by George Caffentzis (1999b), that 'the computer requires the sweatshop, and the cyborg's existence is premised on the slave', is in no way exaggerated. Post-workerism has become a Eurocentric conception of late capitalism, and this is no less true for those currents within it that flirt with postcolonial studies.

Today, we no longer need *that* reading of the *Grundrisse*. To be sure, *other* readings are possible. What we need *today* is an understanding of the forms of exploitation that measures up to the existence of the *Weltmarkt*, the world-market. Whoever really wants to go beyond the dualism of centre and periphery needs to also go beyond the *stadial model* according to which 'we are living today in a society ever more characterised by the hegemony of immaterial labour', a society once characterised by real subsumption and now declared to have entered the phase of 'total subsumption'.[48] One would need to interpret the reciprocal relationship between the different forms of exploitation without settling for a notion of the tendency on the basis of which other forms of labour can be considered *residual* or *secondary*.[49]

If one were to ask us about the relationship between this variant of workerism and the Marx of the *Grundrisse*, we could answer only by going beyond the 'Fragment on Machines' and examining the 'ambiguity' of the 1857–8 manuscripts on issues such as 'labour', 'development' and the 'crisis'.

The central question, both in the *Grundrisse* and in *Capital*, is the following: How is it possible for money to begin producing more money, or to 'transform' itself into capital? In *Capital*, Marx systematically employs the metaphor of the 'caterpillar' withdrawing into its 'chrysalis' in order to successfully transform itself into a 'butterfly'. (The same metaphor is also used once in the *Grundrisse*.) Of course, the answer to the question lies ultimately in the category of 'living labour', which crystallises into greater value than that of the capital advanced. The point is that while the Marx of the *Grundrisse* has already arrived at a clear distinction between labour-power and labour as such, or as an 'activity', he continues to express himself in a highly ambiguous manner. In 1857 and 1858, the expression 'living labour' (or 'labour' *tout court*) is frequently and deliberately used to refer to both aspects. This ambiguity then disappears almost entirely in *Capital*.

In the *Grundrisse*, Marx speaks somewhat hastily of an exchange between 'labour' and capital, an exchange in which 'labour' is ceded to capital and capital obtains 'labour'. When one reads these phrases against the grain, starting from *Capital*, the ambiguity disappears. For nothing else is meant than the dual nature of the social relation between capital and labour: a relation marked, on the one hand, by the wage-payer's 'purchase' of labour-power on the labour-market and, on the other hand, by the 'use' or exploitation of labour-power within the immediate production-process. Marx is referring to how the first moment, which is proper to the sphere of circulation, leads to the second, proper to the sphere of

---

48. On the notion of total subsumption, see the work of Carlo Vercellone.
49. Tomba 2007.

production: the (potentially conflictual) extraction of 'active' labour from the worker, an 'activity' which is 'fluid' or processual by its very nature. It is only in a figurative sense that the process can be described as an 'exchange', as Marx himself will repeat tirelessly as his thinking about the issue proceeds.

The thrust of Marx's reflection is clear, and if one wants to understand the *Grundrisse*, then one needs to read it 'against the grain'. It is then that one understands the emergence of a complex of concepts that requires the reader to distinguish clearly, whenever the word 'labour' is used, between the 'living labour capacity', which is 'labour' qua activity in a potential form, and the erogation of labour properly speaking. Both – labour-power and living labour – are inseparable from the formally 'free' worker as a socially determined human being. However, the ambiguity of the language used in the *Grundrisse* allows for an interpretation of living labour 'as subjectivity', whereby living labour is identified with either the ability to work, or with the worker, or with both, if it is not identified with non-activity, instead of with activity. In brief, what emerges from such an interpretation is a concept of 'living labour' that refers to everything except 'labour', thereby preparing the ground for the oxymoron 'exodus from living labour' – an interpretation to be found first in theoretical workerism and later in post-workerism.

The *Grundrisse* tells us that the 'labour' the commodity-producer performs for the sake of the general exchange of commodities (that is, the labour of the wage-worker commanded by capital) is 'objectless'. This property of being 'objectless' informs every dimension of 'labour', and perhaps this justifies, at least in part, the terminological ambiguity on the part of Marx that we have lamented. It informs the 'living labour-capacity' in the sense that the worker disposes of no property or no means of production and is therefore unable to procure for himself his means of subsistence other than by alienating his labour-power to the capitalist. Consequently, it also informs labour qua 'activity', or as the use of the 'living labour-capacity' by another. In so far as the worker's product is produced by means of an 'alien' activity, it does not belong to him. As a human being, the worker is 'naked subjectivity'. He emerges from the production-process just as he entered it. He is 'absolute poverty', no matter what his payment.

It is the 'ambiguity' of the *Grundrisse* that renders possible the error by which the distinction between labour qua 'activity' and labour qua 'labour-capacity' is collapsed, to the point where 'living labour' is equated with the mere subjectivity of the living human being. The result is the same when 'cooperation', a property of 'social' labour, is attributed first to living workers and then to each and every subject, prior to and regardless of its 'incorporation' into capital. Such notions are proper to the 'vulgar' reading of the 'Fragment on Machines' we have already discussed.

In the *Grundrisse*, the drive to extract surplus-value is identical with the drive to produce, in a kind of endless spiral, an 'extra quantum' of abstract wealth. Capital is identified with the universal tendency to extract, in an insatiable manner, the greatest possible amount of 'additional' labour over and beyond necessary labour. It is here that one finds capital's universality *in nuce*, the universality of a world of ever more developed needs and of a generalised laboriousness – capital's irresistible pulsion towards the creation of a 'world-market'. In its drive to maximise surplus-value, capital ends up reducing the relative magnitude of wages. In its 'pure' form, this tendency plays out by means of the methods used to extract relative surplus-value. But if this is how things are, and if valorisation proceeds thanks to demand, then how is the problem of realising the value contained in commodities to be solved? In the *Grundrisse*, Marx explains that in the case of absolute surplus-value extraction, and even more so in that of relative surplus-value extraction, the expansion of a single capital is unthinkable without the contemporaneous formation of other capitals. This means, obviously, that an expanding capital relies on the contemporaneous presence of other points where labour and exchange occur. The creation of value and surplus-value – or rather the extraction of value and surplus-value – cannot proceed in step with one another without a multiplication of the branches of production. To the 'quantitative' extension and to the 'qualitative' deepening of the division of labour on the market there must correspond, in order for supply to find somewhere a corresponding and adequate demand, the effective realisation of definite and precise quantitative relations between branches of production.

The *Grundrisse* tells us that these conditions of 'equilibrium' stand in a necessary relationship to the proportion between necessary and additional labour – that is, to the rate of surplus-value as it is determined within the immediate production-process. They depend, moreover, on how the surplus-value extracted is distributed across the spheres of consumption (surplus-value spent as revenue) and investment (surplus-value spent as capital). But while the conditions of equilibrium express a kind of 'internal necessity', such that they must be met if capital-accumulation is to proceed smoothly, it remains a matter of contingency whether or not they are met in reality. For Marx, the problem consists less in the 'contingency' of exchange-relations or the 'erratic' character of equilibrium-conditions as such than in the fact that the rate of surplus-value cannot but change constantly, precisely because capital is forced to constantly increase surplus-value. This means that the relation of equilibrium between different industries must also change constantly, both in material and in value-terms. The crisis of 'overproduction' results then, not merely because of the 'anarchy' of the market, but for reasons 'internal' to capital, related to the features of surplus-value production and to the emergence of a 'specifically' capitalist mode of production. The crisis goes from being merely 'possible' to becoming ever more 'probable' – and its deferral by means of credit will only render it all the more devastating.

We have here one of the most interesting approaches developed by Marx in the *Grundrisse*. The capitalist crisis can be traced back to a combination of exploding 'disproportions' on the one hand and the generalisation of these 'disproportions' on the other, where the generalisation of the 'disproportions' takes the form of excessive total supply on the market as a whole, caused by 'low mass-consumption'. As we have already indicated, the problem is that as one continues reading in the *Grundrisse*, one encounters another cause of the crisis, also internal to capital and more radical than the other, but reminiscent of theories of capitalism's 'collapse'. One the one hand, the exigencies of valorisation force capital to maximise the amount of labour it 'sucks up' or absorbs. But on the other hand, the methods it must employ in order to obtain ever more surplus-value, and in particular those associated with relative surplus-value extraction, lead inevitably to an explicit or implicit expulsion of workers from the immediate production-process. That is, they lead to those human subjects who alone can provide living labour, which is the only source of the new value crystallised in the products of each production-cycle, being evicted from capital's 'hidden abode of production'.

At first, capital can solve the problem by 'extending' and 'intensifying' labour-time within the single labour-process. Another solution consists in multiplying 'contemporaneous' working days. Properly considered, this solution is nothing but a corollary to the multiplication of the points of trade and production associated with the extraction of relative surplus-value – a multiplication that amounts, by its very nature, to the inclusion of new workers and the extraction of additional labour within the mill of valorisation. This second solution corresponds, then, to capital's tendency to create a 'world-market' and to the related tendency towards a general crisis of overproduction, in which capital is caught between the disproportions 'behind' and the falling rate of profit 'before' it. While not abandoning this finalistic outlook altogether, the Marx of *Capital* reconfigures it as a dialectic internal to the 'cycle' of tendency and countertendencies. The Marx of the *Grundrisse* seems more inclined to the notion that these processes lead, by virtue of a purely economic dynamic, to a mechanically conceived terminal point in the accumulation-process. His reasoning is essentially as follows: dead labour, or the labour objectified in the material elements of constant capital, can be augmented endlessly, but there are clear limits to the expansion of the 'social workday', given a specific working population. Even on the patently absurd assumption that workers live on air, or that variable capital is equal to zero, and that they work 24 hours a day, or that the time during which living labour is active is fully identical to the time during which surplus-labour is performed, the extraction of surplus-value would 'peak' and encompass the entire social work-day – but no more. While the rate of profit has an upper limit, the same is not true for the formula's denominator. It follows that if the extraction of relative surplus-value involves an increase in constant capital, the highest possible rate of profit will have to fall sooner or later, and with it the actual rate of profit. This reasoning is, however, fallacious. The specifically capitalist mode of production 'devalorises' the unit-value of individual commodities, and there is no necessary reason why an increase in the elements of constant capital, considered as use-values, should be accompanied by a corresponding increase in value-terms. Moreover, if the world-market includes sectors of production characterised by a low composition of capital and high rates of absolute surplus-value, these sectors will keep the average productivity of socially necessary labour low, thereby allowing for the production of relative surplus-value where the composition of capital is higher.

It is against this double backdrop, sketched out in those passages of the *Grundrisse* that deal with crisis-theory (the crisis of realisation and the fall of the average rate of profit) and bound up with Marx's reflections on the 'world-market', that the 'Fragment on Machines' and its specific vision of capitalism's 'collapse' need to be considered.

The introduction of machines and the 'general intellect' are important elements within Marx's theoretical analysis of the specifically capitalist mode of production. Machines are the 'body' of capital in its material constitution, which includes 'labour' within it. The means of production are no longer labour-instruments; on the contrary, it is labour which becomes an instrument for its instruments, in a clear case of 'real hypostasis', or of the substitution of the predicate for the subject. This inversion of the subject/predicate relationship is essential for producing the increase in social labour's productive power that is mystified as the 'productivity of capital', an increase that appears to be a natural property of 'things' qua things (means of production, money), the property of producing surplus-value and surplus-produce. This fetishism results, as is explained to us more fully in *Capital*, from the 'fetish character' of capital. The delimitation of valorisation-time constitutes an important scientific and political achievement for the political economy of the working class.[50] If the capacity to generate surplus-value were an intrinsic quality of capital, then capital would be nothing but an automaton, devoid of any exteriority[51] and without any limit. There would result the phantasmagoric image of an autonomised subject elevated to the rank of totality – the secular religion of fetishism with its

50. Political economy of the working class: English in original (translator's note).
51. Marx 1975–20040, p. 451.

trinity-formula.[52] Those who speak of the law of value having become defunct by virtue of a valorisation-process that has subsumed all human activity, such that communication and human relationality become productive in and of themselves, fall back into fetishism and obscure the conflict between living labour and dead labour within production. Just as in neoclassical economics, the formula M-C-M' is reduced to its outer terms, M-M', and capital appears as an 'automatic fetish'.[53] This fetishism also manifests itself in the rhetoric used, with the volatilisation of the real relations of production finding expression in celestial 'immaterial labours' performed by immaterial labourers. Everything remains within the sphere of circulation. No matter how subversive it declares itself to be, this political approach fails to consider the old and new forms of insalubrious work and focuses only on contractual forms and rights. When the demand for a basic income is formulated, the basic income is conceptualised as a right of which individuals should dispose in so far as they produce, qua individuals, value or wealth (the distinction is held to have become meaningless). In formulating this demand, the post-workerist approach finds itself rubbing shoulders with neoliberal political approaches – although the latter are more consistent in that they concede the 'basic income' only in return for the privatisation of social rights – and even with social liberalism, which holds that a wealth that can be produced only in the most inegalitarian fashion can nevertheless be distributed in a (more) egalitarian manner.

What does the 'Fragment on Machines' tell us? Science and the capitalist use of science enter into the machines, or into the 'body' of the production-process. 'Wealth' (use-values) becomes ever more dependent, both quantitatively and qualitatively, on use of the 'general intellect'. In this sense, capital as the ensemble of qualitatively and technologically specific objective and subjective factors becomes the only producer of use-values – to which corresponds the 'concrete' labour of a collective labourer organised and commanded by the various competing capitals. It is on this level, the *Grundrisse* tells us, that labour-time must cease, at a certain point, to be the measure of 'wealth', namely of concrete wealth. And this is declared to be another reason for the 'collapse' of production based on exchange-value. But in what sense? If this line of reasoning were applied to the production of 'value', it would not be convincing. Capital's use-value productivity does not alter the fact that capital valorises itself only by means of the 'activity' of workers, by 'living labour' insofar as it is 'abstract' or subject to quantitative measurement. Seen in this way, reducing the labour-time crystallised in the single commodity means no more than directly or indirectly reducing the labour-time remunerated by capital and required to reproduce the

---

52. Marx 1981, pp. 992f., 969.
53. MEGA² 3.4, p. 1454.

working class over time and on a certain level of 'subsistence'. By incessantly increasing use-value productivity, capital reduces the 'value of labour [-power]' and increases the amount of 'disposable' time beyond that required for subsistence. However, the Marx of *Capital* reminds us that capital will never allow this disposable time to translate into a reduction of the direct producers' labour-time. On the contrary, it will ensure that disposable time remains labour-time, which it will in fact extend and intensify. Machines and the 'general intellect' do not lead to a reduction in overall, 'macro' labour-time; they lead to the very opposite, to an increase in labour-time.

A different reading of the 'Fragment on Machines' is possible, however, if one relates what is said there to the problematic of the general commodity-overproduction crisis and the tendency to create the 'world-market'. The commodity, as we know, is the unity of 'use-value' and (exchange-) value. Capital, which produces commodities in order to produce money and more money, organises and commands a 'collective' labourer. This 'combined' labourer is, among other things, a technological body that bears the mark of capital. The material, quantitative aspect of this process cannot be separated from its 'formal determination' or qualitative aspect, the fact that the value of the product/commodity must under all circumstances be realised on the market, in the stage of circulation that concludes the valorisation-cycle. It is true that the potential reduction of labour-time entailed by the 'specifically' capitalist mode of production cannot be realised, due to capital's insatiable hunger for 'living' labour and surplus-labour. But it is precisely this tendency towards the maximisation of (surplus-) labour that leads, sooner or later, to the concretisation of a limit to capital engendered by capital itself – for this is precisely what the general crisis is, with regard to demand. As it expands, capital requires a greater market. The extension of the market requires the development of needs, which in turn implies the emergence of the 'social individual'. But the social individual emerges only to the extent that labour-time is actually reduced – to the extent, that is, that disposable labour-time is not converted entirely into additional labour-time, but rather into time disposable for activities other than labour. But this is precisely what capital, by its very nature, cannot consent to unless it is constrained to do so by conflict (and even then, there are strict limits to what it can allow). This is why the 'theft of alien labour-time' becomes a 'miserable foundation' for the development of the forces of production. The pertinence of the labour-theory of value to issues of exploitation is in no way affected.

What the *Grundrisse* calls 'labour as subjectivity' (workers) is included within capital because capital has purchased the workers' labour-power on the market. This labour-power, this 'labour-capacity', must 'set in motion' ever greater amounts of 'living labour' so that capital may obtain for itself and its immediately unproductive dependents absolutely and relatively increased quantities of surplus-value. But the 'fluidum' of living labour needs to be extracted from the bearers of labour-power, and the bearers of labour-power are the workers themselves, a socially determined subject capable of 'resistance'. It is impossible to 'employ' labour-power without putting the worker, a socially determined human being, to work. Capital is not interested in the worker but in labour, the source of value, but in order to obtain labour it must purchase labour-power, namely include and subordinate workers within the immediate process of production. It is precisely the Marx of the *Grundrisse* who writes that if capital could obtain labour without workers, that would be its *ne plus ultra*. While it is true that once it has purchased labour-power, capital becomes the 'owner' both of that labour-power and of its use, actual labour, it is no less true that living labour must always remain an activity performed by the worker – and this is the basis of the inevitable 'class-struggle within production'.

Which refers us back to a problem that contains the very essence of Marx's value-theory, a problem at once intuited and evaded by workerism. The problem is already posed in the *Grundrisse*, but in a preliminary and confused manner, at least as far as its exposition is concerned, and it becomes perfectly clear in *Capital*, to the point of constituting the true and hidden 'centre' and the driving force behind the dialectic of that work, from Volume I onward. This is the problem of the contradictory internal unity, within capital, of labour-power and living labour, a unity constituted by workers as a collective. Yet paradoxically, it is precisely the confused character of the *Grundrisse* that provides an opportunity for illustrating how this internal unity is at one and the same time a contradiction – something that became evident during the 'social' crisis that shook relations of production between the late 1960s and early 1970s. Briefly put, the ability of the 'mass-worker' to contribute crucially to disrupting the valorisation-process within the historically specific form then assumed by capital invites interpretations of this kind. But the opposite is also true. The struggles of the period drew attention to aspects of Marx's work that had remained latent and poorly understood. On the other hand, this sort of point of view also allows one to understand capital's response, which has shaped our present.

For what is today's financial globalisation? Manipulation of money's symbolic nature represents an essential aspect of the new forms of economic policy, which are nothing other than a mediated 'command' over labour. It is through them that 'precarisation' becomes generalised. At the same time, precarisation is the corollary of an unheard of 'centralisation without concentration'.[54] Capital unifies itself against a fragmented and dispersed labour-force, but its unification no

54. Bellofiore 2008, pp. 15–29.

longer goes hand in hand with technical 'concentration'. This is true in at least the following sense: 'Large-scale' production and the use of science within it, the capitalist development and use of machines and science – in brief, capital's 'specific' mode of production, which involves an extraction of relative surplus-value that entails an increase both in the volume and in the intensity of labour – no longer require the long-term development of the technical aspects of the productive unit from one industry to the next (the constant growth of the 'factory', the concentration of large numbers of workers in one place and their juridical and qualitative homogenisation). Capital's response to the 'social' crisis of the 1960s and 1970s consists precisely in this reversal: a dramatic 'decomposition' of 'labour' that resulted, at least in part, from the fear of large concentrations of workers, and that has become the basis of valorisation even as it engenders new crises and conflicts.

There can be no doubt about Tronti's lucidity in grasping, via his distinction between 'labour-power' and the 'working class', and against an inherited and in many ways ossified Marxism, the triangular relationship between labour-power, living labour and the worker upon which his entire discourse on Marx is based. Tronti's achievement can hardly be overestimated: nothing of the kind had been 'conceived of' in almost any variant of Marxism, and the notion would remain alien to most currents of Marxism even after it had been formulated, right up to today's Marx renaissance. And yet Tronti's intuition was immediately distorted. Labour qua 'labour-power' was reduced to something fully integrated into capital. As for labour qua 'working class', it refers to nothing but the workers themselves, albeit only to the extent that they demand higher wages or refuse labour qua activity. Instead of being 'within and against' capital, as Tronti was fond of saying, 'labour' is either within capital or against it. Negri will take up and radicalise Tronti's positions on all of these issues. And the *Grundrisse* can provide ample support to such an interpretation, thanks to its ambiguities. What emerges is a false, but not an impossible interpretation of the *Grundrisse*, one that combines the greatest possible objectivism with the greatest possible subjectivism. According to this point of view, once capital has purchased labour-capacity on the labour-market, it is as if it had already purchased living labour. There remains only one possibility for struggle, theoretically articulated around the alternative between (merely) distributive struggles and an exodus from labour that is (in actual fact) impossible. The contradiction between capital and labour is neutralised as it yields to the labour-market, the 'incompatibility' of wage-struggles and the wage as an 'independent variable': the worker's wage will soon be replaced by the social wage, then by the citizen's wage and finally by the basic income. The centrality of labour is there, but only in its negative form. This variant of workerism neglects the everyday forms of class-struggle within the labour-process, because in fact it discovers conflict only where workers are not working – only, that is, where they articulate their refusal of work within the production-process. The working class is fully present only in sabotage, in the refusal of work.

Here lies 'theoretical' workerism's original sin. A sin that will remain concealed for some time, thanks to first-generation workerism's wealth of concrete and positive experiences, but which will bear ever more poisonous fruits during the decades to come, particularly from the mid-1970s onwards.

Revolution from Above?
Money and Class-Composition in Italian *Operaismo*
Steve Wright

The Italian-Marxist school of *operaismo* [workerism] of the 1960s and 1970s is best known for its thematic of class-composition. Unlike those of their contemporaries who talked of false consciousness, class-alliances or socialism, the exponents of workerism sought to discover 'new laws for action'.[1] Most of all, they sought to identify the 'laws of development'[2] through which the economic input labour-power periodically constituted itself as the political subject working class, able to challenge the power of capital – and ultimately, the *operaisti* hoped, the continued reproduction of the capital-relation itself. In developing their discourse of class-composition, the Italian workerists were in the forefront of those in the West who, in exploring what Marx had once called 'the hidden abode of production', 'rediscovered the labor process as the contested terrain of managerial prerogatives and workers' resistance to exploitation'.[3]

Labour-power, Marx argued in *Capital* Volume I, is a 'peculiar' commodity.[4] It 'exists only in [the worker's] living body', and so is inseparable from his or her person. More than this, and unlike all other commodities, 'the determination of [its] value...contains a historical and moral element' that is subject to debate across time and space. It is unique in a further sense,

1. Tronti 1971, p. 15.
2. Tronti 1971, p. 89.
3. Arrighi 2007, p. 20.
4. Marx 1976, pp. 272, 274, 275, 301, 324; cf. Bellofiore 2004.

according to Marx, in that its 'specific use-value' lies in 'being a source not only of value, but of more value than it has itself'. Having discovered how to harness this last attribute of labour-power, capital could begin in earnest its drive towards the apparently endless accumulation of wealth; thanks to labour-power's other properties, capital can never presume *a priori* how the social working day will be divided between that surplus-labour which is its lifeblood on the one hand, and that necessary labour required on the other for its workers' own reproduction.

Money, which workers receive in exchange for their labour-power, is deemed an equally peculiar commodity by Marx. In a certain sense it is – to use an awful pun – the other side of the coin to labour-power, the representation of that abstract wealth (value) that is labour-power's 'specific use-value'. According to Marx, money plays a number of different roles within the capitalist system, a circumstance that can easily confuse the unwary observer (and indeed the reader of *Capital* itself, as more than a few commentators have noted).[5] The first part of *Capital* Volume I, which Marx[6] reworked significantly between the first and second editions,[7] presents money as variously a 'measure of value', a 'medium of circulation', and as an 'instrument of hoarding'. As a 'measure of value', money permits the exchange of commodities based upon the socially necessary labour-time required to produce them: this is the regulatory mechanism commonly known within Marxism as 'the law of value',[8] even if Marx himself did not often use that term. While money 'can, in certain functions, be replaced by mere symbols of itself', Marx is insistent that it is not itself 'a mere symbol'. On the contrary, like all other commodities, its value is a consequence of the socially necessary labour-time required to produce it. Finally, with the generalisation of commodity-exchange within social relations, commodity-money assumes pride of place, embodied in precious metals, since these 'are by nature fitted to perform the social function of a universal equivalent'.

The second part of *Capital* Volume I takes the discussion of money further, identifying the distinctive nature of 'money as capital' in the practice of 'buying in order to sell'.[9] In its guise as money in pursuit of 'the original sum advanced plus an increment', capital seeks to command labour-power to generate 'surplus-value which, for the capitalist, has all the charms of something created out of nothing'. Money thus plays a key role in the class-relationship of capital and labour – or as Augusto Graziani would later put it:

---

5. Compare Elson 1979a.
6. Marx 1976, pp. 185, 186, 183.
7. Arthur 2004.
8. Henninger 2007.
9. Marx 1976, pp. 248, 251, 325.

> The circulation of money therefore does not solely exercise the function of per-
> mitting easier commercial relations, but also serves the much more relevant
> function of putting the class of capitalists in relation to the class of workers.[10]

During its short existence as a distinct political tendency, Italian workerism had
much to say about labour-power and class-composition – but what about money
and class-composition? This chapter will examine critically the *operaista* debate
concerning the relationship between money and class-struggle, above all in a
period of dramatic social upheaval, economic crisis and 'stagflation'. After an
account of the discussion of money in the years before the oil crisis of 1974,
attention will be turned to the reflections to be found in and around the journal
Primo Maggio, which sought to understand money as a privileged tool through
which capital might outmanoeuvre the workplace-unrest of the period. How did
operaismo address this second 'peculiar' entity of the capitalist system, money?
What particular insights did it offer, and what limitations did it encounter in
its efforts to develop an understanding of money worthy of the conditions that
arose within the global cycle of struggles that is commonly abbreviated as '1968'?
Finally, in what way might this encounter a generation ago between the critique
of political economy and class-composition analysis remain relevant today?

First approximations

Intermittent discussion of money can be found during the early years of workerism's 'classical' phase – above all, in Maro Tronti's book *Operai e capitale* – but
generally only within two contexts where its character as a social relation comes
to the fore: the exchange between labour-power and capital, and the overall circuit of capital. Then again, the most novel argument in *Operai e capitale*, that the
secret to overcoming capital's rule lay in labour refusing its function as labour-
power, already carried implications for an understanding of money, or at least of
one of its key functions in capitalist society. '*How* the law [of value] asserts itself'
(with this phrase Tronti makes reference to Marx in 1868) was above all considered a political act, given capital's dependence upon labour as the measure of
its value: '*Labour is the measure of value because the working class is the condition
of capital*'.[11] If 'only labor through its own struggles can determine the value of
labor',[12] then any working-class offensive of sufficient magnitude against capitalist command could threaten to undermine both the accumulation-process and
the regulatory mechanism upon which commodity-exchange is premised.

---

10. Graziani 1983a p. 22.
11. Tronti 1971, pp. 224–5.
12. Baldi 1972, p. 14.

In the light of a new cycle of workplace-struggles that opened in 1968, money came to be seen by the workerists primarily through the prism of the wage, as an index of the relations of force between capital and a new class-composition led by the mass-worker, 'the human appendage to the assembly line'.[13] Antonio Negri had already made the case for this line of argument the year before, acknowledging the importance of Keynes's discovery of the 'downward rigidity' of wages, and thus the reality under modern capitalism of the wage as the 'ultimate independent variable'.[14] For all their differences on other matters, there was a strong convergence between Tronti's argument that 'For today's worker – correctly – hours, tempos, piecework, bonuses are the wage, pensions are the wage, power itself in the factory is the wage',[15] and the assertion of the workerist group Potere Operaio during the 'Hot Autumn' that '*More money and less work* was the slogan, the political objective of the strategy of refusal of work as the strategy of workers' power'.[16] Seeking to uncouple the link between income and productivity, the demand of '– work and + money' (as one leaflet distributed amongst FIAT workers put it in May of 1969)[17] struck at the heart of the valorisation-process by demanding wage-increases whilst simultaneously challenging capital's right to dispose as it saw fit of the labour-power it had purchased. In the words of the journal *La Classe* (the predecessor of the newspaper *Potere Operaio*), 'The refusal of work expresses itself "positively" in the struggle to appropriate an ever larger slice of social wealth: at this point, the struggle for the "social wage" (equal for all and linked to workers' material needs, rather than the productivity of the bosses) is a qualitatively, totally different thing to the negotiation of the wage as recompense for labour'.[18]

Last but far from least, this stance would appear to find some corroboration in the pronouncements offered by leading exponents of the Italian political class, such as the governor of the Bank of Italy, who could be heard arguing well into the 1970s that 'in recent years the surplus has disappeared. Industry distributed to its workers, in the form of wages, more than it produced'.[19]

The late 1960s would also see the first sustained workerist reflections upon the link between class-struggle and capitalist crisis. While little was said explicitly about money in Negri's essay 'Marx on Cycle and Crisis',[20] an original interpretation was offered instead of some of the most common (and, seemingly, mutually

---

13. Baldi 1972, p. 11.
14. Negri 1994, p. 44.
15. Tronti 1968, p. 508.
16. Potere Operaio 1969, p. 35.
17. Classe 1970, p. 214.
18. Classe 1980, p. 35.
19. Carli 1981, p. 206.
20. Negri 1988a, p. 66.

exclusive) Marxist approaches to crisis. Negri understood capital's cycle as 'the form of a power-relation between classes in struggle', and followed the *Grundrisse* in locating the touchstone of any proper analysis in 'the correct relation between necessary labour and surplus labour, on which, in the last analysis, everything rests'.[21] Indeed, it was argued, the periodic necessity of crisis for capital lay precisely in the requirement to establish a new relation between necessary labour and surplus-labour able to underpin a new cycle of accumulation. In this manner Negri extended the reading of Marx's critique of political economy begun in the essays collected in Tronti's *Operai e Capitale*, wherein 'the meaning and relevance of every concept' was to be determined by 'the immediate development of working-class struggle'.[22] Romano Alquati had already reread Marx's notion of organic composition of capital in terms of the composition of the working class:[23] soon it would be the turn of money to be reinterpreted in still greater depth from 'the working class point of view'.[24] But as will be seen, what such a reading of money actually entailed would prove rather different once the capitalist development of 'the thirty glorious years' had come to an end in the early 1970s.

Perhaps the most radical social critique developed within Potere Operaio after 1969 was that inspired by the encounter between *operaismo* and feminism. And yet, while the text *The Power of Women and the Subversion of the Community* led workerist politics into a distinctly new realm, that of the unwaged work to be found in the sphere of reproduction, the logic of its argument about money and power was still the same as that advanced by Potere Operaio during the 'Hot Autumn': 'If our wageless work is the basis of our powerlessness in relation both to men and to capital, as this book, and our daily experience, confirm, then wages for that work, which alone will make it possible for us to reject that work, must be our lever of power'.[25]

With their analysis largely falling on deaf or hostile ears, the workerist feminists would break away in June 1971 to form the group Lotta Femminista. For the militants who stayed in Potere Operaio, however, a more significant event that summer was likely to have been in August, when the US abandoned the Bretton Woods international monetary-system established after the Second World-War. Premised on fixed exchange-rates, with the US dollar as 'the key international currency', Bretton Woods had provided an important scaffolding for postwar accumulation in the West, even if it was subject in turn to instabilities within the American economy.[26] In the wake of President Nixon's 1971 decree that the

---

21. Marx 1973, p. 446.
22. Cleaver 2000, p. 30.
23. Alquati 1975.
24. Tronti 1971, p. 232.
25. Dalla Costa and James 1972.
26. Holloway 1996, p. 29.

US dollar no longer be convertible into gold, however, a new global régime of floating exchange-rates soon appeared that would shift the *operaista* analysis of money into a higher gear.

If Potere Operaio could not claim to have anticipated the end of Bretton Woods, the group was far from uncomfortable in the new climate of monetary uncertainty. A number of essays by Giario Daghini, in the pages of *Aut Aut*, continued the *operaista* discussion of the role played by money within the exchange between labour and capital, with the chief novelty being the attention now paid to Marx's arguments in the *Grundrisse*.[27] But it was to be Negri's programmatic text, 'Crisis of the Planner-State', written for Potere Operaio's 1971 conference, that would set out a line of argument with profound repercussions for *operaismo*'s understanding of money and class-composition. Like Daghini, Negri started with a review of the treatment of money in the *Grundrisse*, before arguing that the 'tendency' revealed in these notebooks through which socially necessary labour-time no longer provided the measure for capital's process of valorisation, had become actual, thanks to widespread rebellion in the workplace: 'In the massified struggles of the mass worker, work has been disconnected from the value of labour'.[28] As this disruption in the ratio between necessary and surplus-labour filtered through the broader cycle of accumulation, it generated inflationary effects that threatened to become permanent, forcing capital to invent new stratagems in order to ensure its continued reproduction. If, Negri argued, the end of Bretton Woods meant that states were no longer able to agree on the question of 'general equivalence', space had opened up for multinational corporations to replace them as centres of initiative. As for money itself, having abandoned its function as mediator in the marketplace, all that is left for it now was to play the role of money as capital, as pure command over the labour of others.[29]

The belief that such a role – what one wit called the 'production of commodities by means of command'[30] – would be far from easy was repeated in a series of articles in the workerist group's press. For example, in a passage first published in *Potere Operaio* under the title 'The American Working Class is on Our Side',[31] and later incorporated into a longer essay, Paolo Carpignano quoted *Fortune* magazine to the effect that 'the new rigidity in our economic structure . . . is not so much an increase in the relative power of unions as in the power of labor as a whole'.[32] Given this, it is all the more disappointing to discover that, despite

---

27. Daghini 1971, 1972.
28. Negri 2005a, p. 23, translation modified.
29. Negri 2005a, pp. 23, 24, 4.
30. Potere Operaio 1972b.
31. Potere Operaio 1972a.
32. Carpignano 1975, p. 23.

an evocative subtitle ('Well dug old mole!'), the only sustained discussion of the collapse of Bretton Woods by Potere Operaio offered no detailed account at all of the part played by class-struggle in proceedings, preferring instead to sketch in detail the implications of the US manoeuvring for inter-state rivalries.[33]

One consequence of Nixon's actions was the question-mark raised for certain aspects of Marx's own analysis of money, starting with the role of commodity-money itself. As the money-form, Marx had written in *A Contribution to the Critique of Political Economy*, gold is 'the material symbol of physical wealth', 'the compendium of social wealth', 'the god of commodities'.[34] But as Paul Mattick explained to the readers of *Radical America*:

> Based on gold, the dollar appears as commodity money, the symbol of a real asset, with a definite value, either in terms of production costs or in such terms as modified by supply and demand. Within the national frame money has long since ceased being commodity money but by necessity remains acceptable [...]. Without a gold backing, however, the dollar is just a claim on American resources which, if not immediately satisfied, may, in the course of further inflation, dwindle down to nothing.[35]

Reflecting on 'The Destruction of Money' some years later, Mattick argued that 'Even with the dollar no longer convertible, gold retains its function as commodity money. Other commodities could also serve the same function, however'.[36] In a series of essays published in *Quaderni Piacentini* from 1973–4, Sergio Bologna – a former leader of Potere Operaio who had broken with the group over its born-again Leninism – pondered just which 'particular commodity' might step into the breach should that become necessary. The obvious candidate, he suggested, was oil, both for its role as a symbol of US power, and for its ability to epitomise a new relationship between capital and labour, based upon a high organic composition of capital perhaps less vulnerable to the refusal of work than that found in the consumer-durable industries typically inhabited by the mass-worker.[37] After all, with the coupling of inflation and sluggish growth, the global economic-system was clearly in crisis, and as Marx had argued in the *Grundrisse*, in a passage earlier highlighted by Negri,[38] crisis entailed amongst other things a 'revolution in the forces of production [that] further alters these relations [that define a given organic composition of capital, and thus a given class composition – SW],

33. Potere Operaio 1971.
34. Marx 1975–2004c.
35. Mattick 1972, p. 12.
36. Mattick 1980, p. 78.
37. Bologna 1993b, p. 41.
38. Negri 1988a, p. 69.

changes these relations themselves, whose foundations [...] always remains the relation of necessary to surplus labour'.[39]

In a second essay, Bologna noted the growing importance of borrowing as a means to finance-accumulation within Italian industry, arguing that *'The power of banking capital and the accentuation of the crisis are almost the same thing'*.[40] While capital had responded to the first cycle of struggles led by Italy's mass-worker a decade before with deflation and a credit-squeeze, such tactics seemed ineffectual in the very different circumstances of the early 1970s, where work-place-militancy was buttressed by a tight labour-market.[41] Bologna proceeded to quote Marx again (this time from *Capital* Volume III), as to the key role that credit could play in imposing capital's command:

> credit offers the individual capitalist; or the person who can pass as a capi-talist, an absolute command over the capital and property of others, within certain limits, and, through this, command over other people's labour.[42]

Finally, in a paper focused on the politics of the 1974 oil-shock, which had further fed the West's inflationary spiral, Bologna returned to the possibility of oil as the new commodity-money (what Negri would dub 'an "ecological currency"').[43] If the end of Bretton Woods had meant a 'rupture of the barriers of value', Bologna concluded, capital was still unable to escape 'the law by which wealth must nonetheless find a material basis, a coupling with "production"', since any 'future world money' must ultimately 'allude to the relations between necessary labour and capital, to real relations of exploitation'.

All in all, considerable ambiguity had by this point begun to creep into the workerist understanding of value-relations, and of money as their expression. Reviewing these texts three decades later, it is not always possible to decipher the full meaning of their arguments. None of this is helped by the realisation that, with certain notable exceptions, the writings of the Italian workerists, with their clipped vocabulary and obscure allusions, can often be notoriously difficult to unpack.[44] As for individual *operaisti*, Negri for one had clearly begun to take the first strides down a path that, in proclaiming the crisis of 'the law of value', would ultimately depict money: 'less and less [as] a measure of value (a measure that was subverted and overturned, but nevertheless a measure) and increasingly

---

39. Marx 1973, p. 444.
40. Bologna 1973b, p. 83.
41. Graziani 1979, pp. 96ff.
42. Marx 1981, p. 570.
43. Bologna 1974b, pp. 10, 11; Negri 1974, p. 173.
44. For the reflections of translators on this score, see Mandarini 2003, p. 1; Bove *et al.* 2005, p. xxx.

[...as] an index of a symbolic relationship that organized the hierarchical, disciplinary, and repressive procedures of power'.[45]

What probably can be said with some confidence is that by early 1974, and for all their other many differences, the *operaisti* were largely agreed that if the so-called 'law of value' had not collapsed altogether, it was in the very least in serious crisis, due above all to capital's uncertainties at that point concerning its capacity to harness labour-power to its own ends. In other words, what Daniel Bell at the time dubbed the 'revolution of rising entitlements' had, in disrupting capital's ability to subordinate labour to its ceaseless pursuit of accumulation, somehow undermined money's capacity to perform a number of its traditional functions. As to what this might mean exactly for the 'contending classes', beyond programmatic talk of the 'maturity' of communism on the one hand, or capital's need for a dramatic and global overhaul on the other, could only be the subject of further investigation. And to be successful, that investigation must venture into new territory, beyond the 'singular myopia' that in the past had limited workerism's understanding of 'every process of restructuring *exclusively* to the terrain of labour processes'.[46] For without a more considered focus upon monetary phenomena such as inflation – 'privileged weapon against the refusal of work'[47] – the historic gains made in the years immediately past, and the possibility of moving beyond them to some new level of working-class power, might soon be whittled away.

Primo Maggio's exploration of money

The journal *Primo Maggio* (1973–88) addressed many aspects of class-composition and politics in its time, even if it may be best remembered today for its 1977 analysis of a new social movement that seemed to throw many traditional workerist precepts into confusion.[48] Starting from the premise that an understanding of past struggles could throw important light on contemporary social conflict, *Primo Maggio* examined the experiences of earlier mass-movements against capital's dominion, from the Industrial Workers of the World to European revolutionary syndicalism and the communist movement of the 1920s. By its fifth issue, *Primo Maggio* had begun to address itself explicitly to the current Italian situation, with essays on industrial restructuring as well as the politics of money. Indeed, for the rest of the decade the journal would largely set the terms of debate concerning money amongst the *operaisti*, influencing even those (such as

---

45. Negri 2005d, p. xlvii.
46. Negri 1974, p. 170.
47. Bologna 1974c, p. xvii.
48. Wright 2002, Chapter Nine.

Negri) who had by that point embarked upon a very different political trajectory to the one chosen by *Primo Maggio*'s editors.[49] In doing so, the journal-collective would insist that the role within a revolutionary movement of intellectuals such as themselves was to aid all efforts:

> to return to the class the techniques and knowledge expropriated from it [...] to prepare those logistical instruments which it is not yet able to deploy [*dotarsi*] [...] to extinguish themselves as producers of smoke and as party leaders.[50]

Issue number one of *Primo Maggio* appeared in September 1973, and contained the first half of Bologna's essay 'Money and Crisis: Marx as Correspondent of the *New York Daily Tribune*, 1856–57';[51] the whole essay would appear the following year as part of the Feltrinelli 'Materiali marxisti' series, together with chapters by Negri and Paolo Carpignano. Following a suggestive aside in Rosdolsky's classic work on the *Grundrisse*,[52] Bologna set out to explore the resonances between Marx's journalistic work (in particular, those articles concerning the unfolding monetary crisis in Europe) and the theoretical reflections in the *Rough Notebooks*, with particular attention to the development of a revolutionary political project: 'But in the relation between crisis and money form there is something more: political institutions are reinterpreted from the starting point of monetary organisation, the laws of value starting from a now mature stage of capitalist development'.[53]

Rather than being capitalism's 'death-knell', for Marx crisis presented opportunities to capital and labour alike. If for the former it offered 'an almost privileged terrain of organisation for power', it reminded the latter that 'development and crisis are indissolubly linked because they are unified in the same institutions ... The causes of crisis are intrinsically necessary to development'.[54] 'Money and Crisis' thus contained an extended account of the place of financial institutions within French capitalist development following the Bonapartist ascendancy, as well as the various socialist political projects concocted by Proudhon and others on the monetary front. As an *operaista*, Bologna was also curious about the composition of the French working class during the 1850s, leading him to register a number of points of affinity with the situation in the 1970s. For example, he notes that 'As in Italy 1973, the chronic lack of small change and

---

49. Bologna 1976, p. 39.
50. Berti 1978b, p. 9.
51. Bologna 1993a; 1993b.
52. Rosdolsky 1977, p. 7.
53. Bologna 1974a, p. 11.
54. Bologna 1993b, p. 39; translation modified.

coin led to an effective increase in prices, especially on articles of working-class consumption'.[55]

What was most striking, however, was Bologna's concern – expressed on several occasions in the essay – as to Marx's apparent lack of any detailed interest in working-class behaviour as part of the broader story of unfolding monetary crisis in the mid-1850s. While Marx was disparaging of those 'official revolutionists' who 'know nothing of the economical life of people', he himself had little to say on this front, emphasising instead the ways in which, after the failure of 1848, 'the upper classes' have unwittingly prepared the ground for a new social revolution. This is all the more surprising, according to Bologna, given that the sense of 'disproportionality' underlying Marx's reading of crisis was above all one between necessary and surplus-labour: 'Without a disproportionate expansion of credit there could be no expansion of industrial capacity; without a disproportionate growth in the organic composition of capital there could be no increase in the mass of profit; without a disproportionate growth of the sphere of exchange, no world market; without a disproportionate increase of surplus labour no control over necessary labour'.[56]

One of the central functions of 'Money and Crisis' was to begin to sketch out the concept of 'revolution from above', capital's response to the threat to its reproduction posed by living labour. Given the essay's Bonapartist setting, the attentive reader may presume that this term was an allusion to Marx's discussion of the state-form in *The Eighteenth Brumaire*. In part this was true, but for Bologna, revolution from above denoted much more than Bonapartism or all the assorted theories of the exceptional state (e.g. fascism) that have been constructed in its wake:

> The revolution from above, the transformation in the mechanisms of extraction of surplus value, exalts above all "the mania of getting rich without the pains of producing". The historical significance of monetary speculation resides precisely in the fact that it avoids a direct relationship with the working class; it resides in the devalorisation of labour.[57]

Exploring the nature of speculation meant addressing the relationship between the interest-rates set by lending institutions and the profit-rates of commercial concerns. In doing so, Bologna argued, Marx delineated the terrain within which a conscious 'revolution from above' might attempt to reshape class-relations through monetary policy: 'In denying the existence of a natural rate of interest, and in attributing the rate of interest to capitalist subjective command, to its

---

55. Bologna 1973a, p. 45, translation modified.
56. Bologna 1973a, p. 39, translation modified.
57. Bologna 1973a, p. 52, translation modified.

historical decisions (or at least to the historically-given level of the allocation between productive capital and interest-producing capital), Marx reaffirms the entirely political nature of monetary mechanisms. Only crisis succeeds in bringing the average rate close to the market rate of interest; then 'the market' opposes itself to the capitalist as a hostile force'.[58]

All the same, this attempt to sidestep the immediate process of production, and seek to transform the initial money outlaid into 'the original sum advanced plus an increment' within the sphere of circulation instead, could not be sustained indefinitely. While they might appear to 'smash' value relations, 'modern crises':

> derive not from a disfunctioning of the law of value but from the failed capitalist attempt to break it and to suppress it. So, if we start at the other end of things, the working-class refusal of work confirms the law of value in antagonistic terms and enters into contradiction with capitalist attempts to conceal it, to 'forget it'. It is capital 'recalled to its concept' which enters into crisis. And it responds by imposing new relations on the law of value, and a new organic composition on itself'.[59]

Other articles in the early issues of *Primo Maggio* continued with the theme of 'revolution from above'. For example, in his rereading of the rise to state-power of Italian Fascism, Marco Revelli addressed, as might be expected, the violent attacks upon autonomous class-organisation in city and countryside. 'No less violent', in his view, was the counterrevolution that 'the capitalist brain' unleashed in factories such as FIAT.[60] This, Revelli argued, had followed in the wake of the failed attempt to continue the wartime-policy of reducing the working class to a cluster of atomised labour-powers through 'the savage growth of inflation': an attempt that, if anything, fuelled a wage-offensive at the end of the war.[61] In an anticipation of his later contribution to the journal's debate around the movement of 1977, Revelli insisted here in placing the question of restructuring in the workplace in pride of place alongside monetary policy as a central component of the 'revolution from above', rather than leaving it as part of the broader backdrop. Elsewhere in *Primo Maggio*, in a piece on the early Comintern, Bologna noted the relevance of the German crisis of 1923.[62] There, in the face of rampant inflation, the most militant sections of the working class had been led by a communist movement lacking 'an offensive theory on wages', which limited in turn its choices for action. There too, Bologna noted, it had taken a massive

---

58. Bologna 1993b, p. 84.
59. Bologna 1993b, p. 84.
60. Revelli 1975, pp. 68, 65.
61. Revelli 1975, p. 72.
62. Bologna 1975, p. 92.

intervention from above in the form of the Dawes Plan to restore some temporary equilibrium to the relations between capital and labour, and to kickstart a new phase of economic development.

In 1974, in the wake of a controversial reorganisation in the journal's editorial membership, a *Primo Maggio* working group on money was formed. With more than half a dozen regular participants, it set out to explore the questions addressed in Bologna's work on money and crisis within the dramatic and unstable circumstances of the mid-1970s.[63] Although the number of articles arising from the reflections in and around this working group would prove somewhat modest, their significance lay in the questions they posed both for the *operaista* theoretical framework and the opportunities facing anti-capitalist practice. At their time of publication, the working group's papers prompted considerable interest within the Italian movement, being reprinted first as a Feltrinelli book and then again as a pamphlet. The first essay, penned by Lapo Berti, was one of the few texts presented as the outcome of a collective process; in a similar manner, the response to a letter from the Communist economist Claudio Napoleoni also appeared on behalf of *Primo Maggio*. As Bologna later recalled, the premise of the working group was not to establish (or reconstruct) an orthodoxy for others to cleave to, but rather to bring together 'individuals who each thought with their own heads, organised around "strong hypotheses" and shared methodologies', beginning with a reading of Marx filtered through workerist sensibilities themselves forced to confront scenarios unimaginable in the 1960s.[64]

Berti's essay, 'Money as Capital', addressed four problems: why a new politics of money was needed; the role of money and monetary institutions within the class-dynamics of the 1970s; the meaning of inflation; the relationship between the rate of profit and the rate of interest. It opened by conceding the provisional nature of its theses, since a discussion of such matters could only be tentative in the absence of 'a systematic theoretical framework able both to take account of the overall unfolding of the crisis, and to read its political conducting thread in such a way as to render it a term of reference for action'.[65]

Reiterating the workerist emphasis upon the role of money in subordinating labour within the production-process, Berti characterised the current difficulties facing monetary mechanisms on a world-scale as 'precisely a crisis of the functioning of capitalist command on the basis of hitherto given relations of force'.[66] Having set out these premises, Berti then moved on to criticise one of the central aspects of Marx's reading of money. In particular, Berti argued that

---

63. Bermani and Cartosio 1984, pp. 5–6.
64. Bologna 1993a, p. 18.
65. Berti 1974, p. 3.
66. Berti 1974, p. 5.

Marx's dependence upon the explanatory function of the category of commodity-money – which he described diplomatically as 'retaining a certain importance' – nonetheless 'no longer correspond[ed] *immediately* to the actual capitalist reality since the time of the First World War'.[67] Instead, Berti began to sketch out an alternative approach he believed was better suited to a global monetary system that operated in circumstances quite different to those found in Marx's time. Key to this new understanding was a reading of the role of both national monetary institutions and international firms in the post-Bretton Woods environment. In Berti's words, 'The creation of money, with all the consequences that this process entails in terms of the distribution of income and the economy's equilibrium, is now a process that depends, in a *theoretically* unlimited measure, upon the decisions of the [national] central bank'.[68]

From this perspective, central banks were seen as possessing some degree of flexibility in coaxing along economic growth within a national framework, juggling interest-rates and the money-supply within the parameters of fluctuating exchange-rates. In the medium to long term, however, the obstacles facing capital in resolving reasserting its authority over labour were considerable. If the central banks in Western nations such as Italy had come to assume a new strategic importance in terms of the cycle of accumulation, it must not be forgotten that the 'economic subjects that hold in their hand the levers of productive transformation' were first and foremost the multinational corporations, bodies that faced enormous challenges in 'representing themselves as bearers of the general interest: the indispensable (even if ideological) premise for the exercise of political power'. All told, it was by no means certain what form 'a new order of inter-capitalist power and therefore a new configuration of command' might assume, nor how soon it might actually come into being.[69] In the shorter term, inflation could help to tilt the existing relations of force, given its ability both to undermine labour's share of aggregate social wealth, and to shift wealth within the capitalist class itself from creditors to debtors; here Berti counselled a re-examination of Marx's discussion in *Capital* Volume III of the relationship between the rate of profit and the rate of interest. As to what other options lay ahead, Berti concluded by ruling out neither 'genuine war' nor 'the opening of a revolutionary process'.[70] In a more detailed examination of the policy of Italy's central bank, Berti once again concluded by insisting that the fundamental problem for Italian capital continued to be its inability to reassert command over labour within the

---

67. *Ibid.*
68. *Ibid.*
69. Berti 1974, pp. 11, 12.
70. Berti 1974, p. 11.

production-process.[71] As a result, the most important consequence of the central bank's loosening of credit-flows had been industry's borrowings to finance new arrangements in the workplace – the decentralisation of production, experiments in job-organisation, investments in new technology – intended to break up the compactness of class-composition forged during the 'Hot Autumn'.

Another article from a *Primo Maggio* working-group member that remains of interest was an essay by Franco Gori on the topic of public spending. Polemicising with a number of viewpoints, including that found in James O'Connor's influential 1973 book, *The Fiscal Crisis of the State*, Gori took as his starting point the increased pressures for social services that sectors of the population – both waged workers engaged in the immediate process of production, and unwaged proletarians located in the sphere of reproduction – were imposing upon the state. As a number of texts in *Primo Maggio* had begun to argue, looking above all to the American struggles documented by the likes of Frances Fox Piven and Richard Cloward (1972), more and more of those with nothing to sell but their ability to work were demanding not only improved public services, but more money from the state: not in the form of a wage, for which they obliged to provide labour in return, but as revenue. According to Gori, the importance of such conflict, which in the Italian case also encompassed the mass refusal to pay increased utility-costs, should not detract from a critical examination of the challenges that the continued fragmentation of these struggles posed for the process of recomposition.[72] For the greater part of the essay, therefore, Gori focused his attention upon the implications that this new context of increased pressures for public spending held for the state's function within capitalist society. In the Italian case, he argued, 'the structural nature of the contradiction between public spending and balance of payments assumes an irreversible character for a national system unable to control its own trade-deficit'.[73]

This problem in turn had to be situated with the broader challenge facing the state as it attempted to ensure a framework for continued accumulation. His conclusion was a drastic one, even if not inconsistent with the spirit of 'political' reading that workerism had long sought to bring to the critique of political economy:

> within the rupture of the general law of profit and the decline in the very foundations of the mechanism of accumulation, the extreme dilation of state functions creates the possibility of extending and ensuring [*far sopravivere*]

---

71. Berti 1974, p. 26.
72. Gori 1976, p. 58.
73. Gori 1976, p. 54.

the complex of capitalist relations of production, as pure relations of a social nature, beyond their effective economic validation.[74]

The last major text produced by a member of *Primo Maggio*'s working group on money first appeared in the second and final issue of the North American journal, *Zerowork*. Beginning with an account of the international setting, Christian Marazzi's essay 'Money in the World Crisis: The New Basis of Capitalist Power' turned its attention to the implications of the end of Bretton Woods for capital, state and labour at a national and local level. Much of the argument here was familiar. One of capital's most pressing issues was to rein in public spending, redirecting value towards 'productive' investment and away from the efforts of the working class – the unwaged in the lead – to 'convert wages to income through its refusal to function as labor power'.[75] This was the perspective from which regional fiscal crises such as in New York City could best be understood: a combination of 'the downward movement of weak currencies and the upward movement of interest rates' that flowed from the new international set up of floating exchange-rates compelled local authorities to slash social services.[76] In the process, the powers-that-be were obliged to move carefully, so as not to trigger off a frontal confrontation that they could not be sure of winning. If the exact contours of a new class-composition could not yet be discerned against this backdrop, Marazzi still saw some pointers in sectors seemingly far from the mass-worker that had led the previous wave of conflict, citing 'confrontations ranging from the uprisings of black youth in Soweto and London, to the food-price riots in Poland and Egypt, to the pitched battles between students and police in Italy and Britain'.[77]

There was a certain ambivalence about Marazzi's essay when it came to the matter of value-theory. Not all critics agree: for George Caffentzis, 'Money in the World Crisis' 'developed a corollary of the end of work theme: money is no more a part of the process of measuring work'; as such, it provided 'the focus of the official split' and subsequent demise of the *Zerowork* project.[78] Early in his article, Marazzi reiterated the dependence of Marx's own stance upon the unique role played by gold as commodity-money, before suggesting that after 1971:

> both domestic and international credit have been increasingly transformed into credit *ex nihilo*, into artificially created money which is no longer based on accumulated surplus value, but on *no existing value*. The requirement for 'artificial money' to act as a productive force beyond the value embodied in gold

74. Gori 1975, p. 48.
75. Marazzi 1977, p. 99.
76. Marazzi 1977, p. 107.
77. Marazzi 1977, p. 111.
78. Caffentzis 2001.

reserves is that it must become money as capital, that is, it must become credit which *commands* alien labor: money must become command. But precisely because this form of money as capital makes for both an extension and inten- sification of the basis of accumulation, gold comes to function increasingly marginally as the measure of value, which in turn comes to depend less and less on socially necessary labor time and increasingly on *imperial command.*[79]

Unlike Negri (or Berti for that matter), here command was presented not as something simply *arbitrary*, but rather as operating (or attempting to operate) as an extension and surrogate for gold in its role as measure of value, even as it pursued the task of encouraging labour-power to produce sufficient surplus- labour such that capital's 'original sum advanced plus an increment' could be recovered. At the same time, 'The risk is that short term transitional measures are already taking on the characteristics of a *highly volatile permanent emergency* for the capitalist system as a whole'.[80]

But this was only a risk: the implication remained that should command over labour finally be restored – in what Marazzi called 'the only long term way out of the crisis for capital'[81] – then a more 'traditional' role for money might likewise be restored.

How did critics of the time address the hypotheses set out by *Primo Maggio*? A thoughtful analyst of value-theory in his own right, Napoleoni questioned Berti's characterisation of his position on the place of unproductive labour within capitalism, as well as what he saw as Berti's confusion between a working-class refusal to produce surplus-value, and the difficulties in *realising* surplus-value in the form of profit within a period of crisis. Against this, Berti's response centred upon the political implications of Napoleoni's stance, which he criticised for its inability to break free of a reformist logic subordinate to capital.[82] A more sus- tained engagement with Berti's work came from Suzanne de Brunhoff, a French Marxist who had written widely on monetary policy and Marx's own views on the significance of money within a capitalist society. De Brunhoff defended a 'capital logic' approach against what she called the 'great temptation' held out by 'Money as Capital', with its claim 'to establish immediately a direct link between credit money and class struggle'[83] (and indeed, faint traces of workerist influence were apparent in at least one of her books from this period).[84] When Berti's framework was examined with more care, however, it proved quite unable, in

79. Marazzi 1977, p. 96.
80. Marazzi 1977, p. 100.
81. Marazzi 1977, p. 107.
82. Napoleoni *et al.* 1978.
83. De Brunhoff 1976a, p. 36.
84. De Brunhoff 1978.

De Brunhoff's opinion, of distinguishing between the quite different functions that money was called upon to assume in the current circumstance: to take one clamorous example, money could not be equated simplistically with credit. Agreeing that 'the effects of a class strategy upon what appear to be purely technical choices' could be discerned in the years immediately following the 'Hot Autumn', De Brunhoff went on to conclude that:

> the problem with Berti's analyis lies in his exaggeration of the central bank's capacity to intervene in credit flows and hence upon the entire economic conjuncture. There is a confusion between the instrumentalist character of monetary policy (outlined in a keynesian manner) and its degree of political viability in a given context. Therefore, Berti's treatment of inflation is excessively functionalist, both in terms of its objectives (the erosion of nominal wages) and its modes of operation (through an abundant supply of money by the central bank). Inflation, however, is a form of capitalist crisis, as well as a means of attempting to make workers bear the costs of the crisis. If the loosening of monetary and market-based constraints makes it possible to defer final settlements and thus dilute the crisis over time and space, it certainly does not eliminate these constraints.[85]

Why did the journal's debate concerning the politics of money fade away in the late 1970s? Part of the reason lay in the energy that *Primo Maggio* directed elsewhere, particularly to the so-called 'Movement of 1977'. This is not to say that the journal simply lost interest in the question of money: on the contrary, the emergence of a new cycle of social conflict in Italy raised fundamental questions about the threads binding class-composition and money.[86] Thus, in seeking to make sense of 'a strange movement of strange students'[87] intimately connected to struggles in the tertiary sector, the journal's editors began to debate the very utility of Marx's version of the critique of political economy. Bologna was quite sanguine on this front: in an influential analysis of the new movement as a 'tribe of moles', he acknowledged the 'crisis of the traditional-Marxist conceptual apparatus', including categories such as 'revenue', calling for the development of 'a yet-to-be discovered creative Marxism'.[88] Of even more interest for Bologna were the new possibilities of collective action and analysis that stemmed from the spread of industrial conflict from the world of the mass-worker into other moments within capital's cycle. For example, in the case of bank-workers,

---

85. De Brunhoff 1978, p. 93.
86. Bologna 1993, p. 17.
87. Lerner *et al.* 1978.
88. Bologna 1978 (ed.), p. 7.

who are often regarded as a privileged sector of the workforce because of their relatively high wages, [...] the interlock with overall class composition has also been facilitated by the large numbers of workers from the credit institutions and from the service sector in general who have enrolled in the Universities. The fact that they are employed by interest-producing capital has allowed bank workers to grasp the way in which capital is managing the crisis, and the function of money within the crisis.[89]

At the same time, Bologna appeared to hedge his bets regarding the explanatory worth of a framework based upon the analysis of value-relations. In a reflective piece written in September 1977 for the newspaper *Lotta Continua*, for example, he argued that

> notions of productivity and profit no longer make economic sense, and therefore are no longer useful for defining, for instance, a power-hierarchy between various capitalist states. Then we might say that the terms of exchange are defined instead by a series of measures that we can call monetary dictatorship – real 'acts of illegality' against the law of value [...] is profit still an economic notion? [...].[90]

Nonetheless, for all the references in the article to the *Grundrisse*'s theme of destroying the 'barriers of value', Bologna still seemed to hold that capital's present wriggling and squirming to break free from its dependence upon labour could only be a temporary measure, the prelude to some new determination of the

> correct' proportion between necessary and surplus-labour: 'On this terrain [outside the production process, capital] [...] can regain some margins of manoeuvre which later, with the completion of the crisis-cycle, can be recycled into direct command over labour inside the factories [...] New factories are being built: they await new workers.[91]

As discussion amongst the journal's editors unfolded, it became clear that Bologna's position was an intermediary one, with distinct camps to either side. For example, members of *Primo Maggio*'s collective in Turin continued to place the primary political emphasis upon the immediate process of production, and thus the strategic significance of workers employed there in launching a new offensive 'in and against capital'. Arguing that a new relationship between factory and society was unfolding, Marcello Messori and Marco Revelli conceded the importance of capital's efforts to use monetary policy as a weapon against labour, but insisted upon placing this within the broader context of restructuring

---

89. Bologna 1977b.
90. Bologna 1977a, pp. 117–18, 121.
91. Bologna 1977a, pp. 118, 122.

in the workplace.[92] Without being a celebration of the mass-worker, their analysis concluded that one of the most pressing problems was how the workers of the large factories could move beyond a defence of gains enshrined after the 'Hot Autumn' to engage with some of the themes and practices espoused by the Movement of 1977. What was noticeable by its absence in their framework was any angst concerning, or repudiation, of value-theory as a tool of analysis. Other editors, however, were increasingly of the view that, even when recast in workerist terms, Marx's central categories had become irrelevant for those attempting to understand both new social movements and the tyranny of capital that confronted them. According to Gori, the attempt to apply Marxism 'outside its field of coherent applicability' had produced nothing but an 'abstract formalism'.[93] In terms of class-analysis, the social subjects associated with the new movement could not be comprehended through the 'factoryist' spectacles that continued to distort the vision of the *operaisti*. Turning to *Primo Maggio*'s discussion of money, Gori held that this had been 'efficacious' so far as it went, but unfortunately it stopped too soon, being overtaken by the practices of the Italian state:

> The whole second part of the discourse – the disintegrative effect of inflationary policy on the wage logic of struggles, the transformation of public spending into direct control over revenue, the progressive determination of credit and fiscal instruments as operators external to terrain of factory-relations – remained either outside the schema, or was covered only by a subordinate part.[94]

As for Berti, his contribution to the debate likewise questioned the continued relevance of the established workerist *dispositif*, noting (but not elaborating upon) 'the exhaustion of the law of value as categorical node able to explain the movements of capitalist society'.[95] Finally, in a piece that presented itself as a contribution to the revival of the journal's working group, Marazzi traced part of the problem back to the *operaismo* of the 1960s, which in separating the qualitative aspects of the law of value from the quantitative, had hamstrung later efforts to unravel the novel situation of the 1970s.[96] To Marazzi's mind, even the category of

> revolution from above' had become an impediment, in so far as it failed to see that 'the *linearity* in the process of transformation-organic recomposition of capital [...] had been *broken* by the emergence of the clash in the social sphere, in circulation-reproduction.[97]

---

92. Messori and Revelli 1978, pp. 64–6.
93. Gori 1978, p. 122.
94. Gori 1978, p. 109.
95. Berti 1978a, p. 125.
96. Marazzi 1978c, pp. 77–8.
97. Marazzi 1978c, p. 79.

Given such doubts about Marx's conceptual apparatus in general and its work-erist variant in particular, many in the *Primo Maggio* working group on money chose instead to look for new lenses through which to read the nexus between money and power. Abandoning the ambivalence of 'Money in the World Crisis', Marazzi asserted that 'the enlargement of social productive labour to the sphere of circulation-reproduction brings to an end any categorical distinction between money as capital and revenue'.[98] Perhaps there were some affinities here with the logic of Negri, who had recently argued that the labour engaged in the sphere of circulation had also become productive of value[99] – but as always, Marazzi's path remained his own. Echoing Gori in another text, Marazzi complained that 'the provincialism of *operaismo* has become an elegant way of talking abstractly about concrete things', adding that 'faced with this *impasse*, Foucault seems to offer new material'.[100] While his gaze remained focused upon the relationship between money and class-composition, Marazzi continued to call for a renewed attention to the sphere of circulation, since it was there that 'the crisis of curren-cies [*monete*]' found 'its privileged place of manifestation':

> The problem that is posed with every greater urgency is no longer the return
> to a general equivalent, to a measure, in its function of the *production* of capi-
> tal, but rather the necessity of fixing a measure for the *re*-production of capital,
> for the re-production of the commodity-labour-power.[101]

On the other hand, such pessimism concerning the relevance of Marx's work for a contemporary understanding of money and crisis did not convince all inter-ested parties. For his part, Negri would offer a range of arguments about value-theory not inconsistent with the likes of Marazzi or Berti, while proclaiming that such views in fact facilitated the recovery of a 'Marx beyond Marx' for whom money was a '*tautology of power*'.[102] In polemicising with what it called *Primo Maggio*'s 'theory of the pure domination of money', one article in the journal *Collegamenti* sought to reinvigorate Marx's analysis of money by explicitly aban-doning its dependence upon the category commodity-money.[103] Writing in *Unità Proletaria*, Messori and Revelli took a course directly opposite to Gori, Marazzi and Berti, identifying one of the biggest failings of *operaismo* in its abandonment of the theory of value ('in the best of cases reduced to a coercive *law* of the capi-talist system's functioning'), which had in turn weakened the tendency's ability to read the relationship between the technical and political composition of the

---

98. Marazzi 1978a, p. 88.
99. Negri 2005c.
100. Marazzi 1978b, pp. 32, 33.
101. Marazzi 1978b, pp. 38, 39.
102. Negri 1979a, p. 46.
103. Del Monte 1980.

working class.[104] Lastly, in the pages of *Primo Maggio* itself, Guido De Masi called for a rebuttal of the various Postmarxisms, championing instead 'a restoration of the law of value, in strictly productive terms, that expresses vigour and political centrality to the working class'.[105]

After the deluge

The 1980s are remembered in the West as the heyday of Reagonomics and Thatcherite politics. Even before the election of President Reagan, however, a dramatic shift in the global politics of money could be detected, as 'the looseness of US monetary policies that had characterised the entire Cold War era gave way to an unprecedented tightness'.[106] Only a few years earlier, Marazzi had asserted that 'Monetarism and policies deriving from it presuppose a relation of class forces completely subordinated to money as capital. But such a relation cannot be assumed the present situation'.[107]

Now, however, as defeat relentlessly followed defeat for workers (or those in the West, at least, starting with Italy itself), it became increasingly obvious that all past assumptions were off, and that a new and markedly gloomier phase in class-relations was in the making.

Those who had participated in the workerist debates of the 1970s took various paths after 1980. With the 'Red Institute' in Padua all but destroyed through repression, Bologna sought refuge for a number of years in Germany, where he continued to focus upon transport-workers and new social movements. *Primo Maggio* maintained its work on working-class history and contemporary struggles against workplace-restructuring, but few of its pages were devoted any longer to that other fundamental plank of the 'revolution from above': monetary policy. One important exception was Riccardo Bellofiore's 1982 account of the push to scale back Italy's wage-indexation system, an essay of interest not only for its reflection upon the connections between inflation and accumulation, but also for the implications of various policy-decisions for an Italian working class that had become more and more balkanised since the mid-1970s.

While Berti maintained his interest for the question of money, this now occurred within milieux and viewed from perspectives increasingly distant from those outlined in 'Money as Capital'. Writing in 1981, he concluded that the critique of political economy was irredeemably cut adrift from real processes of social change:

---

104. Messori and Revelli 1980, p. 117.
105. De Masi 1979, p. 7.
106. Arrighi 1994, p. 314.
107. Marazzi 1977, pp. 109–10.

Marxism is no longer today what it was, perhaps for the last time in this tumultuous Italian decade and a half: the language spoken by subjects of transformation. It no longer produces movement, identification, fissions. It is only the ground-noise [*rumore di fondo*] of a defeat, the training ground of scribes who bury the green field of praxis beneath their irrelevant papers.[108]

More specifically, he argued, the grounding of Marx's understanding of capitalism in the notion of commodity-money led to an inability to understand contemporary phenomena such as permanent inflation.[109] Looking back a few years later upon the significance of *Primo Maggio*'s work, Berti held that the straitjacket of Marxism prevented the journal both from abandoning the immediate process of production as the central reference-point of its frame of analysis, and from engaging with relevant theoretical innovations offered by the likes of Foucault and Luhmann. As a consequence, the promise of the *operaista* work on money remained unfilled, with 'the germs of important theoretical and analytical developments' contained within it being left to languish undeveloped.[110] If at least one of Berti's papers from the 1980s addressed the matters of social movements and inflation side by side,[111] it would fall to Marazzi to provide the most sustained discussion of money and class-composition penned in that decade by a former editor of *Primo Maggio*.[112] The paper in question was an intriguing piece, full of fascinating allusions, but the reader cannot help but notice how the discussion of class-recomposition unfolds in evermore abstract terms within a framework where 'there is no longer substance, foundation, anything: only the will of the state (through monetary regulation) determines the direction of social transformations'.

From this point, where the themes raised within Italian *operaismo* concerning money were kept alive in some form, this would largely be the work of others based elsewhere. Now back in Switzerland, Marazzi continued to chart his distinctive course around the issue of money and finance.[113] In Britain, Werner Bonefeld and John Holloway explored the class-politics of money from an 'open-Marxist' perspective that shared certain affinities with workerism, while in the United States Harry Cleaver, a former editor of *Zerowork*, examined both the politics of international debt and the more general question of money as a means of class-domination.[114] The journal *Midnight Notes*, also based in North America, likewise devoted much of its attention in the early 1990s to the use of

---

108. Berti 1981b, p. 189.
109. Berti 1981a, p. 137.
110. Berti 1984, pp. 58, 57.
111. Berti, *et al.* 1983.
112. Marazzi 1986.
113. Marazzi 2002.
114. Bonefeld and John Holloway (eds.) 1996; Cleaver 1989, 1996.

structural-adjustment programmes and other tools for imposing monetary discipline upon the labour-power of the world's South.[115] There were, however, two notable exceptions to this geographical shift. One of these entailed the journal *Altreragioni*, where former editors of *Primo Maggio* were amongst those in the 1990s examining contemporary social issues alongside younger writers with a particular interest in monetary matters.[116] The second exception also involved a number of scholars who had earlier written for *Primo Maggio* on financial matters, who during the 1980s contributed to the development of a distinctly Italian reading of the monetary circuit, an approach that has become known in the English-speaking world through the writings of Augusto Graziani and Riccardo Bellofiore.[117] In particular, as part of this process, such writers would now explicitly follow through some of the most important implications for the critique of political economy alluded to in the discussions of the 1970s, developing their own case for a 'theory of value without commodity money'.[118]

Some brief reflections in conclusion

Surveying the European monetary crisis of 1856, Marx had characterised the precepts of 'European Old Society' as follows: 'In politics, adoration of the sword; in morality, general corruption and hypocritical return to exploded superstitions; in political economy, the mania of getting rich without the pains of producing'.[119] There is, on the face of it, much here that resonates with the global scene of one hundred and fifty years later. As Loren Goldner has recently argued, there is also much that resonates between the global scene of today and the circumstances of the 1970s.[120] Financial gloom and doom is a constant theme in the news (and there is even talk of the return of stagflation), the price of oil is again on the rise, the United States is once more mired in an unwinnable military conflict. For these reasons alone, surveying the debates of thirty years ago can be of considerable interest, especially when viewed via subsequent efforts to revolutionise the capital-relation from above through monetarist policies and ideologies. At the same time, there is much that has changed in the politics of money: in terms of financial markets, for instance, the picture has been complicated (if far from ameliorated) by the emergence of new processes such as securitisation, while the continued internationalisation of money-markets has restricted the ability of

---

115. Caffentzis 1999a; Federici 1990; Cleaver 1990.
116. Fumagalli 1993.
117. Graziani 1983a, 1983b; Bellofiore 1997, 2004.
118. Messori 1997; Bellofiore and Realfonzo 1997.
119. Marx 1975–2004bb, pp. 113–16.
120. Goldner 2008.

central banks to manoeuvre to the same degree as before. Perhaps the biggest difference with the 1970s, however, is the absence of any overt wave of class-conflict that might challenge the capital-relation from below, even if the increased global prominence assumed by the politics of food and debt raises the hope that some practical examples of the contemporary ties between money and class-composition will soon demonstrate once again 'the limits within which monetary reforms and transformations of circulation are able to give a new shape to the relations of production and to the social relations which rest on the latter'.[121]

How to assess the *operaista* discussion of money? The first thing that can be said is that the changed circumstances of the 1980s quickly rendered inoperable many of the premises informing the workerists' perspectives. Perhaps the 'crisis of the law of value' had indeed for a time stemmed from capital's inability to tame labour in the workplace; even if this was so, the restoration of order that followed the defeats in Italy and elsewhere soon put paid to such a line of argument. The spiralling growth of financial speculation in the meantime intimated that many agents of capital continue to seek to circumvent the sphere of production in hopes of 'begetting money from money'. And in doing so, perhaps they are consciously aiming '[to bet] on the future exploitation of labour'.[122] What seems rather less convincing, however, is that they are taking such action in flight from some insurgent protagonist in the workplace. In the text that frames the current collection of essays, Karl Heinz Roth has indicated in considerable detail just how complex the questions of class-composition and -recomposition have become today: the overall picture that emerges from his survey is a far from happy one, even if infused with possibilities no less than dangers.[123] What is striking in this context is that, faced with the defeat of the great cycles of struggles bound up with '1968', many of those former workerists who continue to insist that 'the law of the value' no longer functions have simply turned their backs upon the (diverse) majority of those with nothing to sell but their ability to work. While those upon whom they focus their attention instead may well part of the overall puzzle, this choice seems to confuse the defeat of a particular class-composition with the secular decline of the working class itself.

Roth has further called for the ' "de-substantialisation" and dynamisation of our thinking, going beyond Marx, about the position of labour inside the economic field of the capitalist social formation'.[124] Of course, the very premises upon which the workerists operated in the 1970s could have been fundamentally flawed to begin with. At the very least, certain of their assumptions about the process

---

121. Marx 1973, pp. 145–6.
122. Bonefeld & Holloway 1996a, pp. 213–14.
123. Roth 2007.
124. Roth 2007, p. 3.

of class-composition – for example, what Negri once called 'the fundamental thesis underlying the theory of workerism [...] that of a successive abstraction of labour parallel to its socialisation'[125] – may need to be re-examined if class-composition analysis is to remain a useful tool for social critique. As for the question of money, amongst those who still care about such things, there appears to be no general agreement as to what a Marxian theory of money within capitalist society would look like, even if the notion that 'that *money does not have to be a commodity in Marx's theory*'[126] seems to be slowly gaining ground.

To conclude: for all its flaws, the best efforts of the workerist project can teach us that any serious effort to undertake that task of examining 'the constitution of the global class of workers' today must address the question of money no less than that of the labour-process. In terms of how to go about this difficult undertaking, there is also much to learn from *Primo Maggio*'s insistence that critique must be a collective process if it is to serve the goals of social self-organisation and social equality. As for the prospects facing the critique of political economy, and whether its continued relevance demands the jettisoning of value-theory, the experience of Italian workerism offers a series of novel attempts to reread this facet of the Marxian tradition through an encounter with the reality of the present, even if many of the implications of that rereading have yet to be clarified.

Pondering the significance of the debate within *Primo Maggio* of the 1970s, Bologna could claim with some justified satisfaction that:

> we demonstrated that money mattered: in the formation of classes, in the constitution of the modern state, in the mechanisms through which crises unravelled. Without money and credit, there would be no capitalist economy. Money was (and is) a political factor of primary importance: knowing its secrets is indispensable for anyone seeking to develop a political culture.[127]

As always in the brief history of *operaismo*, there is much to be learned from the questions posed by its exponents, even when the answers provided would subsequently prove less than satisfactory. If we are to develop that 'political culture' of which Bologna wrote – one adequate to the challenges of today – no small part of our energy must be devoted to a collective understanding of the relationship between money and class-composition. In this respect, this is still much to be learned from reviewing critically at still greater length how, in their own time, the Italian workerists attempted to 'confront the Marxian (and Marxist) conception of the labor theory of value and labor history with [... contemporary] global relations'.[128]

---

125. Negri 1979b, p. 11.
126. Moseley 2005a, p. 14.
127. Bologna 1993a, p. 10.
128. Roth and Van der Linden 2007, p. 1.

Marxism after the Death of Gold
C. George Caffentzis

> On all occasions, the measures in which rents are collected ought to be the same throughout the diocese'. 'Let the measure applicable to the corn-rent, due the seigneurs and others, be settled in Brittany so as to be one only and the same'. 'And when the dues are paid, let that be by one measure throughout the kingdom, the measure of his Majesty.[1]
>
> From the *Cahiers de doléances* of 1789

> Railroad trains are the great educators and monitors of the people in teaching and maintaining exact time.[2]

'Slightly stretched' or broken?

The Marxist critique of political economy has been often criticised empirically. The 'laws' of the falling rate of profit and the increasing immiseration of the working class have been cited as central hypotheses of Marx's analysis of capitalism that have been falsified 'by the facts'. These criticisms, in turn, have been answered by Marxists in ways that have kept the criticisms from being fatal to Marx's critique, but they, in effect, have left the debate on the status of these 'laws' in a conceptual purgatory due to long-standing disagreements as to the meaning of terms like 'rate of profit' and 'immiseration' and how they should be measured.

---

1. Quoted in Kula 1986, p. 187.
2. William F. Allen, *Report on Standard Time* (1883), quoted in Galison 2003, p. 125.

It is therefore surprising that the 'Marx killers' have not latched onto a much more vulnerable aspect of Marx's critique of political economy: his account of the central role of gold in a capitalist world. Indeed, money provides an important test case for the viability of a Marxist 'research-programme'. For the options appear simple: Marx clearly argues that gold is necessary for the functioning of capitalism; but since Nixon's decision to 'shut the gold window' on 15 August 1971, gold has played a peripheral role at best in the managing of national or international transactions. The last thirty-seven years have seen many crises *in* capitalism without, however, a crisis *of* capitalism (to use Michael Lebowitz's distinction).[3] Capitalism is surviving without the working class's 'cross of gold' in the same way it survived the end of chattel-slavery. What might have seemed essential at one point in capitalist history has been shown to be a mere 'accident' in the case of chattel-slavery.[4] Does the same error apply to gold *as* money? That is, does the end of gold (and indeed of any precious metal) as *the* money-commodity constitute the crucial negative experimental test of Marxism? If so, the late Sir Karl Popper would have us say, 'Falsified! Onto a new theory!'

But we know since the work of W.V.O. Quine, Thomas Kuhn and Imre Lakatos in the 1960s that anomalies are not usually falsifications of a core theory (and that there are no *logically* 'crucial experiments', though there might be *historical* ones). Anomalies are often simply negative moments productive of revisions of a core theory in a research-programme. Is this the case with Marxism and the end of gold-money? Does the post-1971 story of gold force us to stretch or break with Marxism? As Frantz Fanon pointed out in the case of colonialism: 'Marxist analysis should always be slightly stretched every time we have to do with the colonial problem'.[5] Does the 'death of gold', like colonialism, require a 'slight stretching' of Marxist categories or a revolutionary break from them?

In order to answer this question, I will (a) examine Marx's notion of gold as the ultimate monetary commodity and (b) the consequence of the cutting of the tie of gold with the dollar in 1971 for Marxism and, finally, (c) show how a 'slight [class-struggle] stretch' of them can give us an adequate analysis both politically and theoretically.

---

3. Lebowitz 2003.

4. Though *chattel*-slavery is now a thing of the past or to be found only in the most marginal (either geographic or productive) areas, other forms of slavery are pervasive in contemporary capitalism; for a discussion of the issue of sexual slavery and 'trafficking', for example, see Federici 2006. Moreover, there is good reason to claim that capitalism has an inherent drive to slavery in general (independent of any if its particular form). See Dockès 1982.

5. Fanon 1963, p. 40.

'For the sake of simplicity': on Marx's theory of money. The notion of essence and appearance in Hegel's 'Logic' and measurement in nineteenth-century science

What role does gold play in the functioning of capitalism according to Marx? The answer is not simple, although he begins his chapter on money in *Capital* Volume I with the claim: 'Throughout this work I assume that gold is the money commodity, for the sake of simplicity'.[6] Marx's effort at achieving simplicity in exposition clearly did not achieve empirical universality, for at the time of the publication of *Capital* Volume I, very few nations were operating with a gold-standard, and therefore gold was not yet *the* money-commodity of the planet.[7] As Niall Ferguson notes: 'In 1868 [a year after the publication of *Capital* Volume I – CGC] only Britain and a number of its economic dependencies – Portugal, Egypt, Canada, Chile and Argentina – were on the gold-standard. France and the other members of the Latin Monetary Union [Belgium, Switzerland, Italy, the Papal States-CGC] as well as Russia, Persia and some Latin American states were on a bimetallic system while most of the rest of the world was on the silver standard'.[8]

Marx's 'simplicity' became a fact about 'world-money' in 1900 when (still with significant exceptions) the gold-standard became the global norm and World War I, of course, disrupted even that.

Gold 'as the money-commodity' was in 1867 not only marginal in what Marx called 'world-money', but its use in the form of coins was also marginal to 'domestic' monetary transactions among capitalists and between workers and capitalists. By 1867, gold-coins were literally banished to the hoards of banks, states, or wealthy individuals and only peered out of their shells in rare circumstances. Indeed, if we see money as having three different sources (and supporting institutions) – the fiat-source (state), the commodity-source (market), and the credit-source (banks) – then in Marx's time the commodity-aspect of money was relatively small and diminishing. Gold was becoming more of a spectre than communism in his time.

This slow 'demise' or demonetarisation of gold need not necessarily have perturbed a Marx who had thoroughly recorded the illusions generated by its

---

6. Marx 1976, p. 188.

7. Indeed, in 1867 the major economic power across the Atlantic still had a wartime state-issued 'greenback' paper-currency whose date of eventual convertibility to gold was a matter of intense speculation. It was only in 1875 that the gradual retirement of greenbacks began. Even though it proceeded slowly, the process unleashed a devastating deflation that stimulated a significant class-struggle over the form of money for a generation, marking the last time, perhaps, that money in general became a self-conscious political issue in the U.S. Malone and Rauch 1960, pp. 302–5.

8. Ferguson 2001, p. 329.

fetishistic power. Moreover, there were other kinds of money – credit-money as well as government-issued fiat-money – that increasingly dominated a monetary horizon apparently not in need of gold as *the* money-commodity or even any money-commodity at all. Marx, however, rejected the possibility of the demise of gold in a capitalist system and he was not alone.[9] Did Marx, the arch-defetishizer, get trapped by gold's fetishistic power? Let us consider why gold became something of conceptual '*idée fixe*' for Marx.

Throughout *Capital* (and the earlier *Contributions to a Critique of Political Economy*) Marx explored many aspects of money that explicitly were categorically detached from gold and indeed he recognised that this detachment was functional to their operation.[10] Though he wrote very little on national fiat-money (such as the US 'greenbacks' issued in the Civil War), he was especially interested in the relation between commodity-money (gold and silver) and credit-money (that is, the discussion of bills of exchange, securities, bank-notes and cheques in *Capital* Volume III comprises what Suzanne de Brunhoff has called Marx's 'monetary theory of credit'). One could understand his interest, since credit-money was crucial for *the circulation of commodities* in the 1860s (and, of course, is even more so down to the present day). In this function it proceeds according to the rules of a commodity-monetary system even though it has no direct relation to gold as the monetary-commodity.[11] Credit-money in Marx's time also became *an instrument of hoarding* as well, again even though it had no direct exchange-correlation to gold.

Credit-money thus satisfied two of the three major functions of money Marx noted in Chapter 3 of *Capital* Volume I: (i) the measure of value, (ii) the circulation of commodities, and (iii) an instrument of hoarding. The only function of money that credit-money could not fulfil is that of *the measure of value of commodities*. This 'two-thirds' monetary theory of credit indicates that Marx was conceptually ready to see a shift from a commodity-aspect of money to credit-money as the basic vehicle of the circulation of commodities... *up to a point*. Marx's hesitation here leads to questions like: What role does value-measurement play in capitalist society? Is it central to the operation of a monetary system? If so, why? Why can't credit-money measure the value of commodities?

---

9. Georg Simmel (1858–1918), even though two generations younger than Marx, was also convinced of the continuing usefulness of gold, silver or some other material substance to a modern monetary system. In his *Philosophy of Money* (1900), he wrote, in agreement with Marx: 'Thus, although money with no intrinsic value would be the best means of exchange in an ideal social order, until that point is reached the most satisfactory form of money may be that which is bound to a material substance' (Simmel 1978, p. 191).

10. Marx 1970.

11. De Brunhoff 1976a, p. 77.

Marx's initial answer to these questions, however, poses more questions than it initially answers. He starts off by proposing a definition of money as a measure of value: 'the necessary form of appearance of the measure of value which is immanent in commodities, namely labour-time'.[12] This complex sentence, laden with Hegelian jargon, needs some analysis. First, Marx claims that there are two measures of value: (i) labour-time and (ii) money. Second, labour-time is *immanent* in commodities while money is its *form of appearance*. Why are there two 'measures of value', the immanent as well as the apparent one? Why is the 'apparent measure', money, necessary?

The textual evidence shows that this is important territory for Marx (though extremely labyrinthine for the reader), since he returns to it again and again in the *Grundrisse*, in *Contributions to a Critique of Political Economy* as well as in *Capital*.[13] The immanence of the labour-time measure of value is exactly what the Hegelian jargon Marx uses would lead one to expect: labour-time is the *essence* of the commodity's value. It is what is 'hidden' in commodities. Similarly, continuing with the Hegelian jargon, essence must 'shine forth' in the form of appearance that, in the case of value, is necessarily money.[14] However, one can ask Hegel in general, 'why can't we remain at the level of essence and eschew appearance?', and Marx in particular, 'If labour-time is the measure of value, then why is money as a measure of value necessary at all?' Hegel's answer to the first question verges on the tautological: 'To show or to shine is the characteristic by which essence is distinguished from being – by which it is essence; and it is this show which, when it is developed, shows itself, and is Appearance'.[15] Marx's answer to the second question verges on the poetical: 'Although invisible, the value of iron, linen and corn exists in these very articles; it is signified through their equality with gold, even though this relation with gold exists only in their heads, so to speak. The guardian of the commodities must therefore lend them his tongue, or hang a ticket on them, in order to communicate their prices to the outside world'.[16]

Given these unsatisfactory responses, perhaps an example of immanent and apparent measures from another discipline that Marx was familiar with might be in order: the measures used for heat in nineteenth-century physics. One measure of a gas's heat is the average kinetic energy of the atoms that constitute it.

---

12. Marx 1976, p. 188.

13. Marx commented on the role of money as a measure of value versus labour-time in Marx 1973, pp. 153–85, and again in Marx 1970, pp. 64–86.

14. The discussion of essence and appearance in the 'Little Logic' can be found in Hegel 1892, pp. 207–41. For an excellent discussion of the impact of Marx's 'coquetting' with Hegel's *Logic* in part 1 of *Capital* Volume I, see Cleaver 2000.

15. Hegel 1892, p. 239.

16. Marx 1976, p. 189.

This measure is 'invisible' in two senses: (a) it is ideal, as any average inevitably is, and (b) gas-atoms are not directly observable. The average kinetic energy is the immanent measure of heat of a gas (in a Hegelian sense), but it cannot be directly measured (and even Maxwell's accounting demon would eventually collapse from trying).[17]

The other apparent measure of a gas's heat is that determined by thermometers (heat=thermo, meter=measure). There have been an enormous variety of methods and instruments used to measure heat throughout history, from the expansion of a gas that pushes a liquid, to the rising of alcohol or mercury in a glass-tube, to the bending of a bimetallic strip.[18] But all of them lead to observable, apparent results that 'shine forth' or 'communicate' (though not directly) the immanent measure. Changes in the average kinetic energy of a gas are reflected in the changes of the length of mercury in a glass-tube placed in the gas, but there is no identity between them. This independence can be seen in the development of the nineteenth-century theory of thermodynamics that was based on a non-atomic conception of heat-phenomena and the results of apparent, observable measurements. Many supporters of thermodynamics like Georg Helm and Ludwig Ostwald developed a phenomenological 'energetics' programme that rejected the atomistic 'reduction' of thermodynamics and questioned the epistemological status of an unobservable 'metaphysical' atomic stratum of reality.[19] They would therefore, in Hegelian terminology, be advocating for appearance and rejecting essence.

Marx rejected attempts by economists from both the left and right who advocated the elimination of either essence (the labour-time measure of value) or appearance (the money as gold-measure of value) in the theoretical discussions of capitalism in his time.[20] The tension between these two measures is crucial for the understanding of capitalism, according to Marx. The relationship between them is complex since they are neither polar opposites nor homologous. Let us examine the contradictions and the identities of these two measures.

---

17. von Baeyer 1998, pp. 145–55.
18. Whitelaw 2007, pp. 80–1.
19. Kragh 1999, pp. 7–9.
20. Those who wished to eliminate money as gold and use labor-time instead as a measure of value included early socialists like John Gray. Marx expounds and criticizes Gray's time-chit proposal in the *Grundrisse* (Marx 1976, pp. 153–65). For a discussion of the development of Gray's views on money and whether they degenerated into 'currency quackery' see Claeys 1987, pp. 125–9. Those who wished to eliminate the labour-time measure of value include many of the so-called 'vulgar economists' who 'only flounder around within the apparent framework of those [bourgeois] relations [of production], ceaselessly ruminate on the materials long since provided by scientific political economy, and seek there plausible explanations of the crudest phenomena for the domestic purposes of the bourgeoisie' (Marx 1976, p. 175).

The labour-time measure of value is quite similar to the atomic measure of heat in that it is invisible, immanent and notional. The value of a commodity is measured by the labour-time socially necessary to produce the commodity 'under the *normal* conditions of production, and with the *average* degree of skill and intensity *prevalent at the time'*. When a commodity shines before us, it tells us nothing about the value immanent within it that can be directly observed. Nor do the details of its particular history of production tell us of its value any more than the velocity of an individual atom in a gas tells us of the average kinetic energy of the whole ensemble of gas-atoms.

'Normal', 'average', 'prevalent' are words in the definition of the value-measure that indicate both a concrete story and an abstract and time-span dependent dimension. The application of these terms might not be as difficult to accomplish as the task of Maxwell's demon (who has to distinguish between 'slow' and 'fast' gas-atoms), but it is hard enough and certainly gives results that are both real and yet extremely untimely since the phrase 'prevalent at the time' is sensitive to the commodity being produced.[21] It is also in the nature of notions like 'normal' and 'average' to be *post factum*. There is a measure here in labour-time, but there is hardly measurement. Even though value exists and exerts a tremendous effect on the world of commodities (just as the average kinetic energy of a gas exists and exerts a tremendous effect on the world of gases), it is hardly the basis of a definitive equation like 'the value of x commodity y = 10 labour-hours', because in order to make such a statement one must investigate the whole branch of production devoted to commodity y and have agreement concerning the meaning of sensitive words in the phrase 'under the *normal* conditions of production, and with the *average* degree of skill and intensity *prevalent at the time'*.

The money-measure of value dramatically differs from the labour-time measure in that it is not based upon a review of entire branches of the economy and the making of delicate decisions concerning the 'normal' and 'average' in order to make a measuring statement like 'the value of x commodity y = 1/32 ounce of gold'. One simply observes what the commodity's *price* (the money form of its value) is in the publicly traded markets and from that one can infer a potentially infinite series of price equations. In other words, the apparent money measure of value allows one to conclude, 'the endless series [of price-equations] itself is now a socially given fact in the shape of the prices of the commodities'.[22] What would

---

21. For more on Maxwell's demon see Weiner 1965, pp. 58–9 and von Baeyer 1998. As for the issue of the variability of the time-framework, one must consider that the time involving the building of a luxury-liner or an office-tower is different from the time involved in the production of a t-shirt. It would be difficult or impossible to devise a universally agreed upon time frame for the labour-time measure of value. Marxist economists have often discussed the problematics of a Marxist statistics in cases like this.

22. Marx 1976, p. 189.

have required an elaborate investigative process to determine the immanent value of a commodity is short-circuited through the creation of the price-form through which this immanent value shines forth in its price, or, as Marx puts it, 'Price is the money name of the labour objectified in a commodity'.[23]

Though the apparent measure of value is not in contradiction with its immanent measure, it is not completely homologous either, as Marx delighted in pointing out.[24] The labour-time measure of value, though immanent and difficult to determine, has an important property of any good measure: changes in the measurement of X's quantity Q are due to changes in X and not in the measure of Q. This is true of the labour-time measure of value, since any changes in a commodity's value would be due to the changes in the commodity's production or in its branch of production (involving changes in 'normal', 'average' and 'prevalent' as noted above); labour-time being an invariable unit across branches of production, national economies and within historical periods. But this is not true of the money measure of value, for if the value of gold changes due to changes in its production, the price of many commodities will change, even though (in fact, because) there were no changes in their production or their branch of production. Consequently, whenever there is a change in a commodity's price, it is not clear whether it is arising from changes in the value of the money-commodity or changes due to the value of the commodity (or both). The measure can affect the measured (and vice versa, if the measured is an element in the production of gold). This would appear to be a major defect in the appearance or measure of value in this price-form, but instead of railing at the confusion of value the price-form creates, calling for 'reform', and demanding, as so many in the past have done, 'just balances, just weights', Marx calmly states that a confused and confusing measure is perfectly appropriate for a confused and confusing system: 'This is not a defect, but, on the contrary, it makes this form the adequate one for a mode of production whose laws can only assert themselves as blindly operating averages between constant irregularities'.[25]

In conclusion, Marx insisted on the centrality of the gold-measure of value because it is the way in which a crucial aspect of commodities could be expressed. Money as gold allows for the value of commodities to be expressed definitively and concisely, to shine forth as price, even though in doing so it can distort their absolute value. This is certainly important, especially since the labour-time measure of value, though essential, is entirely inapplicable by capitalists to do 'what bosses do'. Thus for Marx, without gold there would be no prices, and

---

23. Marx 1976, pp. 195–6.
24. Marx 1976, p. 196.
25. Marx 1976, p. 196. Much class-struggle throughout history has been over measurements. A good overview on these types of struggles can be found in Kula 1986.

what would capitalism be without prices? But why does Marx insist on the 'real thing' and not upon some imaginary unit of account or 'notional equivalent of gold' in order to arrive at prices?[26] As he insists, even though price-equations, for example, the value of two ounces of the commodity iron=1/36 of an ounce of gold, need not involve 'the tiniest particle of real gold', they must equate labour-times between gold and iron in actual exchanges.[27] He doggedly defended this insistence on *real gold* versus *imaginary gold* in an amazing variety of images and tropes utilising religious, biological, and philosophical references at the end of the section on 'Money' in *Capital* Volume I. The use of such a pyrotechnic display is a sure sign of Marx's ironic ire against gold-abolitionists and other sorts of monetary cranks and serves almost as a warning to those like Nixon who would venture to detach money from gold:

> In order, therefore, that a commodity may in practice operate effectively as exchange-value, it must divest itself of its natural physical body and become transformed from merely imaginary into real gold, although the act of transubstantiation may be more 'troublesome' for it than the transition from necessity to freedom for the Hegelian 'concept', the casting of his shell for a lobster, or the putting-off of old Adam for Saint Jerome [...]. If the owner of the iron were to go to the owner of some other earthy commodity, and were to refer him to the price of iron as proof that it was already money, his answer would be the terrestrial equivalent of the answer given by St Peter in heaven to Dante, when the latter recited the creed: 'Right well hath now been tested this coin's alloy and weight; but tell me if thou hast it in thy purse'. [...] Hard cash lurks within the ideal measure of value.[28]

'The act of transubstantiation', 'the transition from necessity to freedom for the Hegelian "concept"', the casting of a lobster's shell, 'the putting-off of old Adam for Saint Jerome', and St. Peter's question all point to the fact that 'Between the essence/And the descent/Falls the Shadow'.[29]

Since this passage expresses Marx's insistence on gold, it would be worthwhile reflecting on this surfeit of tropes and metaphors. Marx first describes the sale of a commodity for gold-money that makes it an exchange-value in practice a form of 'transubstantiation'. Transubstantiation is, of course, the transformation of the

---

26. I will not discuss Marx's critique of the Quantity Theory of Money (QTM) in this essay, though it provokes very important strategic issues concerning the proper defence against capital's post-1971 neoliberal attack on the wage. What should an anti-capitalist movement's attitude be toward inflation? Should the working class climb back up on the 'cross of gold'? For a good discussion of Marx's critique of the QTM see De Brunhoff 1976a, pp. 31–8 and Campbell 2005.

27. Marx 1976, p. 190.
28. Marx 1976, pp. 197–8.
29. Eliot 1962, p. 59.

bread and wine into the body and blood of Christ during the consecration in the Catholic and Eastern Orthodox masses. This transformation was not understood by the faithful of these religions in a metaphorical or symbolic sense. At some point in the mass, an *actual* miracle is supposed to take place and the *heavenly* body and blood of Christ is *really* infused into the earthly bread and wine. In Marx's trope, the exchange of a commodity with money is a transubstantiation simply because the commodity's value (which was purely imaginary or 'heavenly' before) becomes real in the money *qua* gold it is exchanged for.

The transubstantiation of the commodity is, according to Marx, more 'troublesome' than the three other transformations in logic, biology and religion he mentions. It is worth thinking through this series to understand why.

First, consider the philosophical one: the transition from necessity to freedom. Hegel argues that necessity and freedom *in the abstract are* mutually exclusive (hence there can be no transition from one to the other), but when we examine the *inner nature* of necessity we find 'the members, linked to one another, are not really foreign to each other, but only elements of one whole, each of them, in its connexion with the other, being, as it were, at home and combining with itself'.[30] Once this inner richness of necessity is recognised, it is 'transfigured into freedom – not the freedom that consists in abstract negation, but freedom concrete and positive'.[31]

The commodity-version of the transition from necessity to freedom is when a commodity fulfils its destiny as a commodity in being exchanged for money and verifies its actual price, 'concrete and positive'. In what sense is this transition more troublesome for a commodity than the Hegelian 'concept's' transition? Consider one of Hegel's examples of this transition: a criminal can only become free when s/he recognises his/her punishment 'is a [necessary] manifestation of his own act'. This recognition, however, comes from within.[32] But a commodity finds the commodity-equivalent of Spinoza's 'intellectual love of God' when it is exchanged for gold. But this transition is 'more troublesome' than the criminal's because it requires facing the possibility that it might not be sold at all, that is, it requires more than self-reflection, but a hazardous, potentially embarrassing relation to another.

The next transition is from the biological realm: the casting off or molting of the lobster's shell. Clearly it is a necessary action, since the lobster cannot grow without periodically casting off its shell, but it is a troublesome one, since it exposes the lobster to attack before it can grow a new shell.

---

30. Hegel 1892, p. 283.
31. *Ibid.*
32. *Ibid.*

When casting off its shell, the commodity becomes vulnerable in an even 'more troublesome' way, for it might discover that it is not able to grow its golden shell, and perpetually remains vulnerable to total annihilation.

The final transition in the series is 'the putting-off of old Adam for Saint Jerome' that refers to Jerome's (340–420 C.E.) self-confessed difficulty in discarding ('putting-off') his human tendency to sin ('old Adam', a variant of original sin). This was hard enough to do when he had to deal with the desires and temptations of his material flesh, but he also had to wrestle in his old age with 'the spiritual flesh', wrote Marx.[33] Jerome confessed in a letter to a disciple, Julia Eustochium, that after a life of world-renowned austerities he dreaded going before his maker because he thought that when the Judge of the Universe asked, 'Who art thou?', and he answered 'I am a Christian', the response was going to be 'Thou liest, thou art nought but a Ciceronian [that is, a clever and eloquent orator, a man of words, and dubious ones at that – CGC]'.[34] The implication of St. Jerome's thought is that it is difficult to *actually* be a Christian, though it is easy to *believe* or *imagine* that one is.

Making that transition from belief or imagination to reality is 'troublesome' enough, but the transition from being a commodity waiting to be sold for money and actually being sold may be even more troublesome because its 'imagined gold-shape', or price, gives no guarantee that it will be sold whatever the quality of its will, hence for the commodity's god, its owner, it is a Ciceronian indeed until it does.[35]

Marx uses these metamorphoses in logic, biology and religion to show the different dimensions of transition that are echoed in the exchange of a commodity for money as gold, that for all its 'troublesomeness', is necessary.

Finally, Marx uses Dante's border crossing into Paradise to once again point out that a price determined by an imaginary unit of account is a world apart from the price as determined by an actual exchange. As Dante's tale goes, passing the heavenly immigration-officer, St. Peter, was bound to be difficult, since after all, Dante was not dead. St. Peter put difficult questions to Dante to test his knowledge of Christian doctrine before he would let him through. When he proved to be an adept student of the creed, Marx noted that St. Peter asked: 'Now that you have thoroughly/examined both this coin's alloy and weight/tell me, do you have such in your purse?' Dante's response, one that Marx left unquoted, is, 'Yes I do, so bright and round/I have no doubt of its quality'.[36] The brightness

---

33. Marx 1976, p. 197.
34. *Ibid.*
35. The imaginary voice that dismissed Saint Jerome's pretensions knew what it was speaking about, for Jerome became known as 'the Christian Cicero' (Kelly 1975, p. 333)!
36. Dante 1984, p. 285. Marx's many references to Dante's *Divine Comedy* in *Capital* should not be surprising once it is recognised, as Sol Yurick, the novelist, has pointed out

shines forth its purity and its roundness the fact that it has not been clipped, that is, it is a coin of quality; but the most important point of the exchange is Dante's 'Yes, I do'.

After such a remarkable series of metaphorical reiterations of the point it should easy to agree with Marxist commentators like Claus Germer (although he arrives at this conclusion through a different path than I do): 'Examination of Marx's work shows that, without a doubt, he conceives of money in capitalism as a commodity'.[37] From this conclusion one is led to an overwhelming question: 'Can there be a capitalism without gold as commodity money?' It is somewhat equivalent to the question in the religious sphere, 'Can there be Christianity without Transubstantiation?' The answer to the latter is, of course, 'Yes'. After all, transubstantiation was one of the basic bones of contention in the Church's confrontation with medieval heresy and Protestantism. Wyclif, Hus, Luther, Calvin, Bucer and Melanchthon all rejected it (though for different theological and political reasons).[38] We shall consider the monetary version of this question, 'Can there be an anti-gold capitalist 'Protestantism'?', in a later section of this paper. In the next section we shall examine the desecrating moment when the 'transubstantiation of the commodity' definitively and universally was abolished at the hands of Richard Nixon on 15 August 1971.

The demonetisation of gold: a précis. Richard Nixon, the exemplary postmodernist. A class-analysis of the decision and its consequences. Was the demonetisation of gold the apotheosis of Keynesianism or its demise?

I remember quite clearly watching with comrades in a *Capital* study-group on Sunday 15 August 1971, the broadcast of Nixon's announcement that he had ordered the 'closing of the gold-window'. Given that we were reading for the previous few months passages like the following from *Capital*: 'money in the form of precious metal remains the foundation from which the credit system can *never* break free, by the very nature of the case',[39] we left each other that night with the thought that either capitalism or Marxism was coming to an end before our very eyes!

---

to me, that Beatrice was a banker's daughter and Dante's beloved (and hated) Florence was the centre of international banking in the fourteenth century. St. Peter's interest in what is in Dante's pocket is echoed by Kant in his critique of the ontological proof of the existence of God when he points out that a *taler* in imagination is quite different from a *taler* in one's pocket (Kant 2007, p. 504).

37. Germer 2005, p. 34.
38. Bainton, 1952, p. 48.
39. Marx 1981, p. 620.

The technical aspect of Nixon's decision is simple enough to describe. The U.S. government pledged to exchange for every $35 returned by foreign central banks one ounce of gold. This pledge of gold-convertibility was put into question in the long period, especially in the 1960s, when the US's balance of payments was consistently negative. More dollars were sitting in the accounts of foreign central banks than gold in the US Treasury's. As Tom Wicker describes the situation: 'This [gold convertibility] pledge was the guarantee of stability in international trade and finance; the dollar was backed by gold, and most other currencies were backed by the dollar. By 1971, however, the US had nowhere near enough gold at Fort Knox to redeem all the world's dollars at that price; and the supply it did have – $18 billion against $36 billion in potential dollar claims abroad – was shrinking, as occasional redemptions were demanded'.[40]

In fact, the rather heavy straw that broke the golden camel's back dropped during the week of 9 August 1971, when the British government demanded $3 billion in gold for the dollars in its vaults in London.[41]

Why did Nixon make a decision that would inevitably generate so much opposition in his own Republican Party ranks? After all, in 1896 the Republican Party, in response to William Jennings Bryan's 'Cross of Gold' campaign, declared for 'sound money' in its Electoral Platform: '[The Republican Party] caused the enactment of a law providing for the resumption of specie payments in 1879. Since then every dollar has been as good as gold. We are unalterably opposed to every measure calculated to debase our currency or impair the credit of our country'.[42]

Adherence to the gold-standard became the watchword of Nixon's predecessors in the twentieth century Republican Party. So it is not surprising that one Republican remarked in 1971 that, with the closing of the gold-window, 'American fascism arrived on August 15'.[43]

It was no accident that Nixon made this decision in conjunction with announcing a wage-price freeze, for these policies were closely connected. As he said at the time as an explanation for these decisions, 'now I am a Keynesian'.[44] This self-description meant that he recognised the power of the US working class to impose wage-settlements and resist unemployment (*the* class-problematic of Keynesianism). This level of autonomy had dire consequences on the 'normal' functioning of a gold-based monetary system.

---

40. Wicker 1991, p. 545.
41. Wicker 1991, p. 553.
42. Quoted in Fink 2001, p. 198.
43. Wicker 1991, p. 557.
44. Wicker 1991, p. 551.

In the so-called normal case, an increase in wages would lead to price-increases and a reduction in exports, to be followed by an outflow of gold from the central bank's coffers and a deflation in the money-supply. An increase in unemployment and a reduction of wages would result, leading to a lower price for exports. The concomitant increase in exports would lead to a positive balance of payments and a return of gold to the central bank's coffers.

Thus goes the 'normal' story. But with a 'rigid' working class that has the power to impose wage-increases, resist unemployment and widen the scope of the wage (including social-security pensions, welfare-payments, food-stamps), the unfolding of this story is blocked at every turn. Wage-increases might lead to increased prices and reduced exports, but instead of imposing a deflation caused by the shipping out of gold, the government would have to 'print' more money to support the wage-increases and stimulate investment to stop an increase in unemployment. This eventually leads to a gold-shortage and a crisis of the international standing of the currency. There need not be harm done to the national economy in these circumstances (in effect, the crisis would be transferred abroad), especially if the nation was at the peak of the panoply of states (and that could be said of the US in 1971!) The working-class struggle therefore forced the system to abandon and transcend its gold-backed currency.

In effect, the combination of a wage-price freeze and the closing of the gold-window (the 'New Economic Policy') was simultaneously a direct attack on and a recognition of the power of the US working class. The first responded to the capitalist class's need for direct governmental help in controlling wage-increases and a squeeze on its profitability. The second simply accepted the *fait accompli* of the class-struggle and anticipated the inevitable demise of gold-convertibility that was looming. Nixon, instead of thinking that he could defeat the power of the working class, decided the best path would be to blunt it and to defuse its impact. (It is often forgotten that the working class won its historically highest average real wage under the Nixon Administration in 1973, while the most direct financial assault on working-class power and wages – the Volker interest-rate increases – was under the Carter Administration in 1979).

Nixon, who loved to throw the 'long bomb', appreciated the fact that 'closing the gold-window' was a shocking act for most in his party (and many beyond). He taunted his Republican cronies by calling himself a 'Keynesian', and, if he had the vocabulary, he might have also enjoyed in taunting them even more by describing himself as the first 'postmodern' President. For if postmodernism has the rejection of representation as the defining element of symbol-systems, then he debunked the last monetary myth of reference: the dollar-gold convertibility enshrined in the Bretton Woods accords of 1944. 15 August 1971 was apparently the last act in the long, slow and intermittent saga of the elimination of referentiality from the monetary world.

Did Nixon understand the metaphysical role he played for his class in this saga? That is not clear. Did most workers understand the consequences of this decision for their class? Again, the evidence is unclear. From a working-class perspective, however, the delinking of the dollar and gold was the final rejection of the automaticity of the 'laws of capital' whose intent was to continually doom wage-struggle to a Sisyphus-like series of moves that led to the point it started from. There was no way out of the bad infinity that I described in the 'normal' sequence of events as long as the 'golden law' was operative. Nixon, in his fear of mass-unemployment, ironically was a 'handmaiden' of the working class's moment of autonomy (which, however, was very short-lived).[45] It did show that in the period of the late 1960s and early 1970s there was a significant breakdown in the apparent 'objectivity' of capitalism. Marx argued violence was necessary in forcing agricultural folk in the sixteenth and seventeenth century to accept 'the discipline necessary for the system of wage-labour', partially because the system was alien and made no sense to them, but: 'The advance of capitalist production develops a working class which by education, tradition and habit looks upon the requirements of that mode of production as self-evident natural laws. The organization of the capitalist process of production, once it is fully developed, breaks down all resistance'.[46]

Yet the working class of the most advanced capitalist nation was not willing to accept its fate as the dependent variable of the production-function and pronounced the 'self-evident natural laws' null and void through their actions. As I mentioned, on that hot Sunday night in Princeton on 15 August 1971, it seemed to my comrades and to me that Nixon was willing to go to the limits of the system in response to this refusal. Was the consequence, then, either the end of capitalism or the end of Marxism? We thought so then, for the very text we were studying that day, *Capital* Volume III, seemed to argue that capitalism requires a commodity-money measure of value because only a commodity that has a value can measure value (see the previous section). Nixon, therefore, challenged Marx by initiating the 'crucial experiment' and simply observing that capitalism did not collapse on 16 August 1971.

The demonetarisation of gold, it turns out, was not the equivalent of defetishising the commodity, and the end of the gold-standard was not the end of capitalism. Nixon's experiment showed that capitalism could survive without having

---

45. The Nixon Administration devised and pushed into Congress a basic-income proposal, euphemistically called the 'Family Assistance Plan', which was for many capitalist ideologues even more heretical than the end of gold convertibility of the dollar. It was defeated in the Senate by a coalition of left-wing Democrats and right-wing Republicans, according to the major participant observer of the campaign, Daniel Patrick Moynihan. For an informative account of the Nixon Administration's effort at a 'postmodern' delinking of work and income and its political defeat see Moynihan 1973.

46. Marx 1976, p. 899.

a monetary system based upon gold and that the major world-currencies could operate without a foundation of golden material substances. This gave capital a new flexibility in responding to class-struggle that was recognised and utilised in the later 1970s with the rise of effective neoliberal strategies to attack working-class struggles.

An alternative, 'slightly stretched' explanation. The notion of measurement in contemporary thought: the end of the 'shared substance' view of measurement (global versus local measurement). The critique of the notion of a necessary apparent measure. The underdetermination of measure makes it an object of struggle. The final determination of the money by labour-time and surplus-labour, hence the impact of class-struggle on the functioning of money. The history of proletarian struggles over the measure of value: a new scene.

Nixon's decision to 'close the gold-window' did not end capitalism on 16 August 1971. Since then some gold-bugs and other super rigorists of capitalism have continued to view the era after 1971 as a post-capitalist twilight-zone preceding some more or less horrific version of apocalypse. Other speculators point to the continuing shadowy presence of gold in the international financial scene and claim that this era is a transition back simply to a revived gold-standard. But after thirty-seven years there is now a widespread consensus that though there are some important differences between pre- and post-1971 capitalism, what we have had during this time is capitalism all the same.[47]

If the end of the gold-standard did not end capitalism, then did it end Marxism (as the members of my study group feared)? Surely Marxism faced some severe historical tests in the post-1971 period (especially the dissolution of the Soviet Union and the development of a strange capitalism in an even stranger China governed and guided by the world's largest Communist Party that presumably reveres Marx's name), but as a theory of capitalism it still has many adherents throughout the planet (myself included) for whom it is incontrovertible common sense and the foundation of their analysis of capitalism.

How is this possible? Marx argued that capitalism needed to have a money-commodity to function as the measure of value for commodities, but since 1971

---

47. The main difference has been often called the 'financialisation' of capitalism in the post-1971 era. There has been a dramatic increase in the volume of international money-market exchanges compared both to the past and relative to the post-1971 international commodity trade. As for the US, there has been a dramatic shift in the distribution of profits from manufacturing and agricultural sectors to the FIRE (Financial, Insurance, and Real Estate) sector.

there has been no such commodity-measure in action (that is, there are no direct commodity-gold money-transactions), even on the most general level (for example, as the measure of balance of payments) and even after many severe monetary crises. Is it not logically incoherent to continue to employ this theory and to even use it as a sort of socio-political 'common sense'? No, if there are good reasons to (1) reject Marx's *idée fixe*, and (2) to detach it from the rest of his theory that still is confirmed. In this section I will present these reasons.

Marx's determination to uphold a money-commodity measure of value is based upon philosophical and metrological presuppositions that I for one do not accept. The metrological presupposition Marx holds is: the measure of quantity Q must possess Q. He makes this point clearly in his elaborate analogy between two kinds of measurements – weight and value – in the chapter on commodities in *Capital* Volume I when comparing the weights of a sugar-loaf and a piece of iron (presumably on a scale) with the value of linen and a coat:

> [...] in order to express the sugar-loaf as a weight, we put it into a relation of weight with the iron. In this relation, the iron counts as a body represent-ing nothing but weight. [...] *If both objects [the sugar-loaf and the iron] lacked weight, they could not enter into this relation, hence the one could not serve to express the weight of the other.* [...] Just as the body of the iron, as a measure of weight, represents weight alone, in relation to the sugar-loaf, so, in our expres-sion of value, the body of the coat, represents value alone.[48]

This elaborate analogy is connected to the philosophical presupposition that essence has a unique and necessary appearance. For if the essence is inner and must shine forth to be measured, the measure must share in the essence. The apparent measure for an essence is necessarily determined by that essence. As a consequence, the relationship between the apparent measure and the essence is not contingent and open to revision or negotiation. As Hegel (in a rare philo-sophical joke) said, there is a necessary relation between an appearance and an essence: 'we have all reason to rejoice that the things which environ us are appearances and not steadfast and independent existences; since in that case we should soon perish of hunger, both bodily and mental'.[49]

Given these two presuppositions it is not surprising that Marx concluded that capitalism was bound to the money-commodity, gold, as long as there is need to measure value. Value is an essence of commodities that must be measured and re-measured, since commodities' values are different and continually changing. Value must have only one kind of measure, according to Marx's metrological presupposition, and its appearance (up to unit-changes) is unique and necessary,

---

48. Marx 1976, pp. 148–9 (my italics).
49. Hegel 1892, p. 241.

according to Marx's philosophical presupposition. QED. A corollary is that there is no point struggling around the existence of the gold-standard, since it is rooted in a logical necessity of the system. It will only end with the final expropriation of the expropriators. Marx thought that one of the most important functions of his theory was to indicate to working-class militants what can be changed within the system and what can only be changed with the end of the system.[50] For example, chattel-slavery was not an essential aspect of the system and could be abolished within capitalism, but the wage-system itself could only be abolished with the abolition of capitalism.

But Marx's conclusion and corollary are mistaken. Metrology has recognised that a measure of Q need not possess Q. Thus a gas's heat can be measured by the quality and quantity of light emitted by the gas. Similarly, the correlation of mechanical, chemical, electromagnetic, and heat-phenomena that were unearthed in the establishment of the conservation of energy principle (often called the 'First law of thermodynamics') immediately created a wide variety of cross-dimensional measures. Moreover, the development of quantum- and relativity-theories has shown us that measurement has a complexity and observation-dependency that the metrology of the nineteenth century was totally unfamiliar with.[51] Consequently, for every immanent quantity Q there can be a wide variety of measures, M_1, M_2, M_3 ... of Q with different relations to Q, and they need not possess the quantity Q. The only requirement is that the quantity measured by M_1, M_2, M_3 ... is invariant (across a given transformation).

Moreover, the relation between essence and appearance or between immanent properties and their apparent measures, the Hegelian 'mode of expression' that Marx 'coquetted with' in *Capital*, by no means necessitate each other.[52] Surely, in the almost two centuries after Hegel presented his dialectical logic, there have been many philosophical transformations and the essence/appearance distinction that Hegel makes so much of has been soundly rejected by most twentieth-century philosophical tendencies and schools from existentialism to logical positivism to pragmatism to postmodernism. Consequently, the relation between the surrogates for Hegel's essence and appearance that are recognised in contemporary philosophy has lost the character of necessity.

---

50. Here I refer to the distinction between reform and revolution in working-class politics. For example, Marx thought it very important to demonstrate to workers that the iron law of wages is not essential to the operation of capitalism, and it was perfectly possible for workers to use trade-unions to better their lot and weaken the capitalist class long before the working class was able to overthrow the capitalist system. In other words, working-class organisation can eschew the conspiratorial 'Blanquist' type organisation that had been a staple of proletarian politics in France since 1789.

51. Galison 2003.

52. Marx 1976, p. 103.

The rejection of Marx's metrological and philosophical 'presuppositions' leading to the necessity of a golden measure of value opens up a conception of capitalism that has many different kinds of measures of value that need not be commodities themselves. In a nutshell, monetary systems are as open to class-struggle as was chattel-slavery. This perspective allows us to see that the long history of measures of value is not only shaped by the changing requirements of the capitalist class's so-called rationality, but also by presences alien to capital whose own value-rationality pointed in directions antagonistic to it.

The working class in its broadest definition – those who are exploited by capitalism – has had its own history of measures of value that included 'ancient', 'primitive' and 'proletarian' measures of value that differed from the official gold- and silver-coinage as well as the world of bankers' promissory notes and governmental fiat-currency. Workers not only have an inverse relation to money than capitalists – operating by definition with C-M-C transactions rather than the M-C-M' ones – they have complex but different conceptions and measures of value from capitalists as well. There has been an explosion of interest in the relation of capitalism to this aspect of proletarian life called the 'unwaged-work' sector, 'the shadow economy', 'the general economy', 'the moral economy', and the 'informal economy'.[53] The extensive work on the gift-exchanges in anthropology is simply the earliest and most formalised of the efforts to study how indigenous measures of value conflicted with capitalist measures in many of the colonial areas.[54] Similarly, the long history of counterfeit currency, of autonomous token-currency, of the so-called underground 'informal-economy' methods of debit and credit within the most advanced capitalist regions, makes for a similar rich area of struggle.[55] Finally, the increasing abstractness, dematerialisation and velocity of money is a response to a class-struggle over the appropriate measures of value.[56]

In other words, Marx's theory can be 'slightly stretched' (by dropping his *idée fixe*, the necessity of gold as money as a measure of value in capitalism) to deal with the post-1971 era and to realise that the labour-time measure of value, though still operative, co-exists with a wide variety of other measures of value that included gold in the past, but no longer. Thus forms of credit or fiat-money can measure value, though with their own idiosyncrasies and their

---

53. See Dalla Costa and James 1972; Illich 1981; Bataille 1988; Thompson (ed.) 1991; and Latouche 1993 respectively, and Caffentzis 1999a for an overview.

54. For measure of value struggles in Africa, see Atkins 1993; Guyer (ed.) 1995 and 2004.

55. Caffentzis 1989 and 2000.

56. Silvia Federici, Peter Linebaugh, Massimo De Angelis and David Graeber have made important contributions in their recent work to the understanding of the history of class struggles over value and value's contradictory meanings within capitalism. See Federici 2004; Linebaugh 2008; De Angelis 2007; Graeber 2001.

different strategic strengths and weaknesses in the class-struggle. An interesting case of this is hyperinflation – a dramatic breakdown in the ability of money to measure the value of commodities – of the sort we have recently seen in the political struggles in Zimbabwe. It is only certain kinds of money that are subject to hyperinflation. For example, commodity-moneys are not prone to such a phenomenon. But the governmental decision to subvert the measure of value function of money is not necessarily a flaw in the measuring instrument. Indeed, hyperinflation arises from a government's political objective in the intra- and inter-class war (as it is in Zimbabwe).

This revision to the core of Marxism leaves it as an empirically consistent theory of capitalism and class-struggle while showing something new about capitalism's past before 15 August: there has always been a complex, multi-dimensional struggle about not just the quantity of money in the pay-packet, but also about what is money and how it measures value. This struggle appeared most overtly two times in US history: the struggle against the gold-standard in the late nineteenth century and in the wage-struggles of the late 1960s and early 1970s that led to the end of dollar-gold convertibility as I mentioned above. But these struggles were neither the first nor last of the class-struggles over the measure of value. Many other class-struggles in the past have been about measures of value, as there will be many others in the future. So with a doctrinal loss (the rejection of Marx's 'idée fixe'), this 'slight stretch' introduces a new set of observations, explanations, and possibilities.

This approach also shows that one is not forced to respond to Nixon's decision by rejecting the labour-time measure of value as so many Marx-influenced postmodern 'beyond Marx' thinkers have.[57] They see the post-1971 world as proof positive that capital has gone beyond work and labour, and it is not tied any longer to the necessity of enforcing a work-régime that will lead to the creation of surplus-value. Hence the putative value of commodities is more a control-mechanism than the creation of collective human labour meeting a capitalist system of exploitation.

Ironically, however, these postmodernists are crypto-gold-fetishists despite themselves, and are as committed to gold as the measure of value as Marx and the gold-bugs, though with a different conclusion. For I reconstruct their argument as:

---

57. The 'Marx-influenced postmodern thinkers' I am referring to are Christian Marazzi, Antonio Negri and Michael Hardt (though there are many others deserving the 'postmodern' label who have also written extensively about money's purported loss of referentiality, like the late Baudrillard, for example). For some orientation to this tendency see Marazzi 1977 and Hardt and Negri 2000.

Premise: gold, as Marx argues, is the only possible measure of value, but gold can no longer measure value;

Conclusion: there cannot be any measure of value;

Corollary: value is measureless!

But this reasoning is unsound because its premise is false. Gold is not the only possible measure of value and so its displacement is not fatal to the measurability of value.

The demonetarisation or 'demise' of gold leads neither to a transition from capitalism into a hyper-symbolic social system beyond work and exploitation nor to the end of Marxism as a study and practice of class-struggle. I conclude, then, *A luta continua!*

From the Mass-Worker to Cognitive Labour: Historical and Theoretical Considerations

Carlo Vercellone

The current transformation of the labour-capital relation is perhaps historically even more important than the one announced by Gramsci during the 1930s, in his notes on 'Americanism and Fordism'. In the following essay, we will attempt to reconstruct the essential characteristics of this 'great transformation', at the heart of which lies the transition from the class-composition of the mass-worker to that of immaterial and cognitive labour. The essay, divided into three sections, adopts an approach that directly combines theory and history. The first section aims at presenting the method and concepts on which a post-workerist analysis of capitalism's dynamic is based. It emphasises the conflicts over knowledge and power associated with the social organisation of production. We will also address some crucial theoretical and political implications concerning the historical significance of the law of value and its crisis. The second and third sections will be devoted to putting the crisis of Fordism and the transition to cognitive capitalism in historical perspective. We will look closely at the origin of cognitive capitalism, its meaning and the issues at stake. Finally, we will show how the ever more central role of rent-income deplaces the terms of the traditional antagonism based on the opposition between wages and company-profit – a deplacement that leads to the transition from a 'vampiric' to a 'parasitic' capitalism in which the *becoming-rent of profit* presents itself as the other face of the crisis of the law of value.

Knowledge, the law of value and the dynamic of the labour-capital relation

Since the crisis of Fordism, capitalism has entered into a period of major trans-formation that simultaneously affects the social organisation of production, the valorisation of capital and the modes of distribution of wages, rent and profit (which are nothing but the other face of the social relations of production). This development destabilises the measurement-criteria and the fundamental categories of political economy: labour, capital and value. At the origins of this transformation lie the growing importance of labour's cognitive and immaterial aspects and, more generally, the role of knowledge. It goes without saying that the key role played by knowledge within the dynamic of capitalism is not, in and of itself, a historic novelty. Thus the role played by knowledge within the antagonistic labour-capital relation and the logic of the law of value is already a central factor in Marx's analysis of capitalism's tendencies, based on the notions of formal subsumption, real subsumption and the 'general intellect'.

The question that poses itself, then, is the following: In what sense can one speak today of knowledge playing a new role, and what is the relationship between knowledge and the changes in class-composition? Our approach starts from this problematic and develops a critique of the political economy of apolo-getic theories of the 'knowledge-based economy'.[1] This critique operates on two levels: one conceptual, the other methodological.[2] On the one hand, the 'pallid' notion of the 'knowledge-based economy' is replaced with the concept of cogni-tive capitalism. This concept highlights the historical dimension and the conflict-ual relationship between the two terms from which it is composed. 'Capitalism' refers to the persistence, within the process of change, of certain fundamental invariants of the capitalist system, such as the driving role of profit and the cen-trality of the wage-relation, or more precisely of the various forms of dependent labour upon which the extraction of surplus-value rests. 'Cognitive' draws atten-tion to the new character of the labour, value-sources and property-forms on which the accumulation of capital is now based, as well as to the contradictions thereby engendered. Such contradictions manifest themselves much more on the level of the labour-capital relation than on that of the ever more pronounced antagonism between the social character of production and the private charac-ter of appropriation. As we will go on to see, these contradictions result from the fact that capitalist exploitation has assumed an essentially parasitic character: capitalism stands in a parasitic relation to the autonomy and power of social

---

1. Knowledge-based economy: English in original (translator's note).
2. For a critical review of theories of the knowledge-based economy, see Lebert and Vercellone 2004 and Vercellone 2008.

labour (both common and cognitive), which opposes itself to the narrow telos of capital-valorisation. Moreover, the attempt to transform knowledge into a form of capital and a fictive commodity engenders a paradoxical situation: the more the exchange-value of knowledge is artificially increased, the more its social use-value decreases, and this decrease results precisely from the privatisation and rarefaction of knowledge. In sum, the intensification of society's submission to the logic of commodification occurs in such a way as to contradict the law of labour-time value, and the objective and subjective conditions of the development of an economy based on knowledge and its diffusion (or, as Marx would have said, the creative faculties of society's agents) are negated.

On the methodological level, the cognitive-capitalism approach situates knowledge within the concrete historical dynamic proper to the conflictual relations of knowledge and power that shape the capitalist division of labour. To put this more clearly: it is important to remember how labour qua cognitive activity, labour as the indissociable unity of thought and action, is the specific characteristic and, in some ways, the very essence of man.[3] From this point of view, the crucial issue seems to us to be the following: if the cognitive dimension of labour is the very essence of human activity, then awareness of this fact can become an obstacle to capitalist control of the production-process, and thereby to the accumulation of capital. One begins to see, then, why the relations of power and knowledge associated with the organisation of production are essential to the antagonism between capital and labour. There are two basic reasons for their importance.

The first is that those who control and dictate the ways in which work is performed are also in a position to control the intensity and the quality of work. To the extent that the buying and selling of labour-power aims at the rendition of a quantity of time and not at the actual labour performed by wage-labourers, capitalists are faced with structural uncertainty. This is a central issue, already at the heart of the thinking of the first great theorists of the industrial revolution, such as Ure and Babbage. Their thinking would be taken up and systematised by Taylor, who was confronted with the power of the craft-worker's class-composition in the key industries of the second industrial revolution. Taylor recognised that knowledge is 'the most precious good' workers dispose of in their conflict with capital, and made this insight the crux of his analysis of the worker's 'idleness'. He deduced from his insight the necessity of expropriating the 'tacit knowledge' of workers in order to transform it, via time- and motion-studies, into a codified knowledge held by management and returned to workers in the form of strict work-pace and task-prescriptions. Taylor believed he had

---

3. See in particular Marx 1976, pp. 320–39.

thereby established the incontrovertible foundations of a 'scientific management of labour' that removes all uncertainty with regard to the performance of workers, thereby allowing capital to plan *ex ante* the law of surplus-value.

The second reason is that those who possess productive knowledge can aspire to manage production themselves; that is to say, they can determine not only how production is be organised, but also to what end it occurs. A large body of workerist historiography has demonstrated that the spread of Taylorist and Fordist methods of work-organisation cannot be explained purely by reference to their concordance with the logic of serial production. Rather, the spread of these methods was also and in fact primarily a result of the need to dissolve the class-composition of the craft-worker, who had begun to advance demands for self-management, in particular during the workers'-council movement between the two world-wars. Finally, the importance of the conflict over the control of the *intellectual powers of production* explains why the logic of the capitalist division of labour that emerged from the first industrial revolution turned on the attempt to strip labour of its cognitive dimension (at least to the extent that this is possible) in order to turn it into the very opposite of the cognitive: a mechanical and repetitive activity. Within this logic lie the origins of alienated labour, of labour *sans phrase* or abstract labour, measured in simple units of time and unqualified – the starting point for the tendency Marx characterised as the passage from the formal to the real subsumption of labour under capital.

In many ways, this tendency was historically realised in the Fordist model of economic growth. And yet its realisation can never be perfect. A new type of knowledge, situated on the most developed level of the technical and social division of labour, will always tend to emerge. Or rather, the dynamic of class-struggle will tend to create, within capitalism, ruptures and requirements resting on a different logic, one pointing in the direction of what Marx called the *dissolution* of capitalism qua the *form dominating production*. Within the historical conjuncture that inaugurated the crisis of Fordism, this dynamic played out in conflicts that led to the emergence of a *diffuse intellectuality*, especially via the (however partial) 'democratisation' of access to higher education. This was the beginning of a process of collective reappropriation of the *intellectual powers of production*, a process that represents a necessary prerequisite for overcoming the industrial capitalist division of labour. In our view, this renders topical those passages in the *Grundrisse* where Marx, after dealing with the phase of real subsumption, develops the hypothesis of the 'general intellect' and anticipates the rise of an economy based on the diffusion of knowledge, driven by knowledge and dominated by the productive power of intellectual and immaterial labour.[4]

---

4. Negri 1996a.

The law of labour-time value goes into crisis and the logic of real subsumption is called into question (at least as far as the labour-process is concerned) by the return of the cognitive dimension of labour.[5] Industrial capitalism, which made the mass-production of commodities and the continuous lowering of their unit-value the measure and the driving force of the development of social wealth, loses much of its progressive thrust. It should be noted that this critical development within contemporary capitalism – a development that some, including André Gorz,[6] have identified as a structural crisis of capitalism – does not entail that market-relations lose their grip on society. Nor does it entail that labour, and in particular the cognitive aspect of labour, ceases being central to the production of value and surplus-value. On the contrary, the blurring of the boundaries between labour and non-labour results in exploitation extending to social time in its entirety; the labour-capital relation undergoes a radical change, in accordance with a logic that holds a number of lessons for the analysis of capitalism's contemporary transformation – a point to which we will return.

In order to properly understand the hypothesis concerning the crisis of the law of value, it is important to clarify an essential point. It seems to us that many authors fail to distinguish clearly between what we call the law of surplus-value and a reductive notion of the law of value that considers immediate labour-time the measure of the value of commodities.[7] Why do we characterise this notion

5. It is important to distinguish between two aspects of the logic of real subsumption. The first concerns the organisation of the social-production process. Capital tends to expropriate the workers of their knowledge; technical and organisational development is oriented towards controlling the labour-force by progressively reducing labour to a simple appendix of the machine-system. The second aspect concerns capitalism's tendency to subordinate society and social relations in their entirety to the logic of the commodity. Under cognitive capitalism, these two aspects of real subsumption give rise to a historically new configuration. It is as if a formidable intensification of the subsumption of society and the mechanisms by which subjectivity is produced under the logic of the market went hand in hand with a crisis of the real subsumption of the labour-process under capital, due to the emergence of a diffuse intellectuality and the hegemony of cognitive labour.

6. Gorz 2003.

7. Two variants of the theory of value coexist within the Marxist tradition, as Negri 1992 has rightly emphasised. The first insists on the qualitative aspect of the exploitation upon which the labour-capital relation rests, an exploitation that presupposes the transformation of labour-power into a fictive commodity. This is what we call the theory of surplus-value. It views abstract labour as the substance and common source of value within a capitalist society characterised by the development of market-relations and wage-labour. A second variant of the theory of value insists on the quantitative problem of determining the magnitude of value. It considers labour-time the measure of a commodity's value. This is what we call the labour-time theory of value. In our view, the labour-time theory of value is more properly Ricardian than Marxian: just as in Ricardo, labour-value is traced back to a hypothetical stage of simple commodity-production in order to then explain capitalism on this basis. Marx (the Marx of *Capital* Volume I included) treats the law of labour-time value as a function of the law of surplus-value

as reductive? Because while measuring labour and the value of commodities in units of simple and abstract labour-time was no doubt central to economic growth and the 'rationalisation' of production under industrial capitalism, the practice cannot be elevated to the rank of a structural invariant of capitalism, *pace* the hypothesis defended by a certain current of Marxism. On the contrary, it is the law of surplus-value qua law of exploitation and antagonism that gave rise, at a certain stage in the history of capitalism, to the law of labour-time value, engendering it as a kind of side product and dependent variable. In effect, the origin and the historical meaning of the law of labour-time value are closely linked to the specific configuration of the labour-capital relation that emerged in the wake of the industrial revolution and in accordance with the logic of the real subsumption of the labour-process under capital. Understood in this way, the law of labour-time value reveals itself as the concrete expression of the disciplinarisation and abstraction of the very content of labour, an undertaking that made the clock and later the chronometer its preferred instruments for quantifying the economic value produced by labour, defining labour-tasks and augmenting labour-productivity. At the same time, and as far as socially necessary labour-time is concerned, the law of labour-time value assures the *a posteriori* regulation, through market-exchange, of the relations of competition linked to the decentralised activity of mutually independent productive units.

It is important to remember that the notion of labour as something that can be homogenised and measured – the expense of energy during a given period of time – became common currency in society and within management practice *before* the labour-theory of value was elaborated within the political economy of the classics. In sum, there is no justification for maintaining a genealogy of the law of value that refers back to a mythical society of independent simple commodity-producers, as in the interpretation of Engels. On the contrary, people's relationship to time and production was a radically different one before the industrial revolution; the pace of work was discontinuous and largely self-determined.[8] The relationship was inverted following the development of the capitalist firm: time became the measure of labour and the amount of time spent became the norm by which production and the remuneration of labour

---

(the law of exploitation); the law of labour-time value disposes of no autonomy whatsoever vis-à-vis the law of surplus-value. Marx's controversial choice to begin *Capital* Volume I with an analysis of the commodity has nothing to do with the hypothesis of a pre-capitalist society based on simple commodity-production; Marx's choice reflects the necessity of demonstrating how labour-power's transformation into a fictive commodity, the articulation of labour power's exchange-value with its use-value, contains the answer to the mystery surrounding the origin of profit. In sum, the law of labour-time value, qua law of equal exchange, is in no way fetishised by Marx; he does not treat it as a kind of structural invariant of capitalism's *modus operandi*.

8. Thompson 1967.

were evaluated. More generally, we can say that the historical significance of the industrial revolution consists, more than in a technological revolution, in a veritable *revolution of society's temporal régime*. The law of labour-time value presents itself, then, as the expression of a *biopower* that caused the clock to penetrate every sphere of life; all of social time was synchronised with and subordinated to the pace of the factory. This was one of the most important aspects of the establishment of disciplinary society. Since the crisis of Fordism and the renewed significance of the cognitive aspect of labour, disciplinary society is ceding to control society and the application of a new temporal régime.

What does this mean?

First, that the law of labour-time value is indissociable from the law of surplus-value, of which it represents an historically determined articulation. The law of surplus-value, which makes surplus-value the source of profit and rent, is therefore primary and autonomous from the law of labour-time value as a criterion for measuring labour and the development of relative commodity-prices.

Second, that the intensification of the law of surplus-value and the extension of the commodity-sphere (the two elements upon which the law of value qua social relation of exploitation rests) may enter into contradiction with the logic of labour-time value. The development of contemporary capitalism indicates that this is precisely what is happening, in a threefold sense:

(1) The exchange-value of a growing number of commodities is elevated artificially, by means of various institutional devices, despite the fact that the production-costs of these commodities, in terms of labour, are extremely low and even tend towards zero in some cases. Moreover, the domain of market-relations now covers goods such as knowledge and biological life, goods that are essentially common and cannot properly be reduced to commodities whose substance (and measure) is to be found in labour-time. In a sense, we can say that capital's attempt to maintain the logic of the commodity and of exchange-value is precisely what constrains it to try and rid itself of the law of labour-time value. This development marks the crisis of the law of labour-time value, but also, and more consequentially, the crisis of the very essence of the law of value qua social relation – a social relation that makes the logic of the commodity the touchstone for the development of use-value production and the satisfaction of needs.

(2) The growing significance of so-called immaterial capital also escapes measurement in terms of labour-time. Its value can only be the expression of a subjective evaluation, the profit-expectations of the financial markets for whom immaterial capital becomes a source of rent-income. More fundamentally still,

the very notion of immaterial capital is a symptom of the crisis undergone by the category of constant capital that emerged under industrial capitalism, where C (constant capital) presented itself as dead labour, labour crystallised in the form of machines and imposing its dominion on living labour. The crisis is confirmed by the controversy surrounding the origins of 'goodwill' (the growing gap between the market-value of firms and the value of their tangible assets): the 'intellectual capital' of a firm – constituted by the competence, experience, tacit knowledge and cooperative capacity of its labour-force – is said to be the immaterial asset upon which the additional value embodied in 'goodwill' depends most. In other words, it is not a question of capital at all (despite the conceptual stretch evident in such notions as 'intellectual capital' or 'human capital'), but rather of the quality of the labour-power, which is by definition a non-negotiable asset (slavery aside). That is why, as Halary has observed,[9] attempts to explain 'goodwill' or a firm's additional value by reference to that firm's non-specific immaterial assets (not by reference to patents) remain caught in a circle and fail to arrive at a satisfactory definition of the value of said immaterial assets. Why is the reasoning circular? Because the reply given to the question 'What does goodwill depend on?' is: 'The firm's human capital!' And the reply given to the question 'What determines the value of the firm's human capital?' is: 'Goodwill!' This means that the measure of capital and the basis of its power over society depend less and less on the dead labour and knowledge embodied in constant capital; they depend on a *social convention* whose principal material foundation is the power and violence of money.

(3) Finally, the renewed importance of the cognitive and intellectual aspect of labour means that the use of simple abstract labour-time as a measure for the value of commodities and criterion for the organisation of production in accordance with the norms of the clock and the chronometer is called into question in numerous productive activities. The labour measured in terms of the time certifiedly spent in the firm is often no more than a fraction of the actual social labour-time involved. Here begins the domain of what is beyond measure.

Our analysis allows us to clear up a number of misunderstandings that have frequently arisen with regard to one of the crucial issues at stake. When we speak of a crisis of the law of value based on labour-time and relate this phenomenon to the hegemony of cognitive labour and the 'becoming-rent of profit', we are not questioning the fact that labour remains the only source of surplus-value. Rather, we are emphasising that the mechanisms for appropriating surplus-value have changed radically vis-à-vis industrial capitalism and the period of the real

---

9. Halary 2004.

subsumption of labour under capital. This means that the law of surplus-value persists, but like an envelope that has been emptied of everything Marx considered, rightly or wrongly, to constitute the progressive functions of capital with regard to the organisation of work and the development of the forces of production, functions on the basis of which it was possible to develop a theoretically coherent distinction between the category of profit and the parasitic aspect of rent. (See 'Rent and Profit: Some Definitions'.)

Rent and profit: some definitions

The concept of rent displays considerable theoretical complexity. By considering *three closely related aspects* of rent, we can nevertheless appreciate the role it plays both within the reproduction of the relations of production and within capitalist relations of distribution.

First, we can characterise the genesis and essence of capitalist rent as resulting from a process by which the social conditions of production and reproduction are expropriated. The varying importance of rent within capitalism's dynamic results from what can be described, following Karl Polanyi, as the historical succession of periods of desocialisation, resocialisation and renewed desocialisation of the economy. The genesis of modern ground-rent coincides with the enclosure-movement: the first expropriation of the commons, which constituted a preliminary condition for the transformation of the soil and of labour-power into fictive commodities. A common logic governs these first enclosures, which concerned the soil, and the 'new enclosures', which aim at knowledge and biological life. This is also the logic governing both the destabilisation of welfare-institutions and the 'privatisation of money' that accompanies the rise of financial rent in the present historical conjuncture.

The second aspect concerns the relationship between rent and a scarcity that is sometimes natural but more often artifical. The logic at work here is that of a given resource's rarefaction, as in the case of a monopoly-position. Here, the existence of rent rests on property-forms and power-relations of a monopolistic type; these property-forms and power-relations make it possible to create scarcity and impose prices that are in no way justified by the corresponding production-costs. This is usually achieved by means of institutional devices, as can be seen today in the case of intellectual property-rights and their reinforcement.

The third and final aspect, capitalist (as opposed to feudal) rent, can be characterised as a *pure distributive relation* insofar as it no longer accomplish any function, or at any rate no normal function, within the production-process (see Marx, *Capital* Volume III). In sum, rent presents itself as a claim or right to property over material and immaterial resources that legitimates an *appropriation of value from a position outside of production.*

> The distinction between rent and profit is in many ways less clear than often assumed. To appreciate this, it is worth considering again the example of ground-rent. Ground-rent is the remuneration a landowner receives in return for ceding the right to use his land to another. According to the model we have inherited from the classics, rent can be understood as *that which remains when all who contribute to production have been remunerated.* We should note that if we accept this model, everything depends on how we define 'contribution to production' and 'those who contribute to production'. If one accepts the classic definition of profit as the remuneration of capital, consisting of a revenue that is proportional to the *capitals* employed in production, then – and Smith himself emphasises this – profit has nothing to do with compensation for the functions of coordinating and surveilling production the entrepreneur or company-manager may perform.
>
> On these premises, one could say that the remuneration of capital is also a form of rent, comparable to the remuneration of the landowner. After all, the owner of capital may content himself with providing the means of production without putting them to use himself. Two main arguments have been advanced in order to solve this aporia of classical theory, and to establish a clear distinction between rent and profit – two arguments that lose much of their validity under cognitive capitalism, for reasons analysed in this essay. According to the first argument, capital occupies a position internal to the production-process insofar as it represents a necessary condition for commanding and organising labour, as can be observed under the conditions proper to the real subsumption of labour under capital. According to the second argument, profit is distinct from rent insofar as it is essentially reinvested into production and plays a decisive role in the development of the forces of production and the struggle against scarcity.[10]

In order to demonstrate more clearly the heuristic value of our hypothesis, we will now venture some historical considerations on the dynamics that has taken us from the centrality of the mass-worker's class-composition to the hegemony of cognitive labour.

Fordism and the class-composition of the mass-worker

In many ways, the labour-capital relation proper to Fordism represents the full realisation of the logic of industrial capitalism and of the tendency known as the real subsumption of the labour-process under capital. The Fordist labour-capital

---

10. For a more detailed account of the categories wages, rent and profit, see Vercellone 2007.

relation engenders a dynamic that sees the opposition between knowledge and the collective worker developing in step with a form of distribution that turns on the antagonism between wages and company-profit. In this section, we will describe those features of the Fordist mode of regulation that were central to the conflictual dynamic of the mass-worker and the transformation-process that led to the rise of cognitive capitalism.

Knowledge, value and the labour-capital relation in the large Fordist firm

Fordism rests on a logic of accumulation whose driving force is the large firm specialised in the mass-production of durable goods. As far as the status of knowledge within the labour-capital relation is concerned, Fordism represents the full realisation of four basic tendencies proper to the capitalism that emerged from the first industrial revolution: a social polarisation of knowledge based on the separation of intellectual and manual labour; the hegemony of the knowledge embodied in fixed capital and managerial organisation of firms and of the forms of knowledge mobilised within the labour-process; the centrality of a material labour subject to Taylorist norms of surplus-value extraction; the strategic role of fixed capital, which represents the principal form both of property and of technological progress.

We can put this more precisely by saying that within the paradigm of mass-production, the labour-capital relation rests on two basic principles. The first principle concerns the hierarchy of two separate functional levels within the large Fordist firm's division of labour. On the one hand, there is the scientific management of labour in the factory-departments, which operates by means of prescribed tasks and fixed times and aims at stripping manufacturing activities of every intellectual dimension. The tendency to render the content of labour abstract is realised practically through the reduction of labour to a simple expense of energy during a given period of time. Labour's subjective factor is relegated to its objective factors. Labour is conceived of as a mechanical activity by which variable capital is assimilated into constant capital. The separation affected between labour and the subjectivity of the labourer results from a process whereby labour itself is objectified; labour is reduced to an ensemble of tasks that can be described and measured according to the norm of the chronometer.

On the other hand, there are the management-offices and the centres of Research and Development (R&D), where a minoritarian faction of the labour-force holds a monopoly on design-related labour and on the production of knowledge for the purpose of innovation.

The second principle concerns the measurement of value and the regulation of the exchange between capital and labour. In the large Fordist firm, and on the basis of the division of labour just described, the principle of measuring productivity in terms of output-volume becomes the main criterion of profitability. The planning of the law of surplus-value and its articulation with the law of labour-time value appear to achieve perfect coherence: time presents itself incontestably as the key criterion for the measurement of labour and economic efficiency. We should note that the validity of this criterion also rests on the fact that the creation of value occurs essentially in the sphere of immediate material production, where the labourer's activity consists principally in acting upon inanimate matter by means of tools and machines and in accordance with an energetic paradigm. This centrality of simple, unqualified material labour allows for a convergence of technical (physical) and economic (monetary) productivity-criteria as time becomes the 'general equivalent of performance and value creation'.[11]

The centrality of simple material labour also facilitates meeting the two central conditions that lie at the origin of the definition of the canonic wage-relation: (1) in return for their wages, the workers renounce every claim to ownership of the product of their labour, which is physically separated from them and appropriated by the employer; (2) under industrial capitalism, the wage effectively functions as the return-service for capital's purchase of a clearly defined segment of human time that is placed at the firm's disposal. Within the energetic paradigm, productive labour-time corresponds to the remunerated time spent within the factory in accordance with the modalities stipulated in the labour-contract.

We should note, finally, that this conception of productive labour corresponds to a social representation of time that turns on the cleavage between direct remunerated labour-time and all other social time, with the latter being considered unproductive. This cleavage is articulated on several levels:

(1) in the opposition between 'labour-time', a time of subordination, and 'so-called free time', which is formally beyond the control of the firm;
(2) in the opposition between wage-labour and the unremunerated labour of domestic 'reproduction', an opposition in which the inequalities between men and women are given a concrete form;
(3) in the opposition between the sphere of production and that of consumption, where Fordist consumer-goods, and in particular domestic goods, are essentially geared towards reducing the time and expense associated with the reproduction of labour-power;

---

11. Veltz 2000, p. 77.

(4) in the organisation of a ternary life-cycle (education, employment, retirement), each stage of which is clearly distinct from the others.

It was because all these conditions were met that mainstream economic theory could make them the basis of its conceptual models and of its distinction between *work* and *leisure*. As we shall see, the possibility of meeting these conditions is called into question by the renewed centrality of the immaterial and cognitive aspects of labour.

Wage, profit and rent in Fordist economic growth

According to French regulation-theory, the golden age of Fordist economic growth rested on a compromise between labour and capital whereby workers were guaranteed regular wage-increases (indexed to the basis of prices and productivity-gains) in return for their acceptance of the employers' monopoly over the organisation of work. This compromise is said to have allowed for a coherent articulation of the logic of mass-production with that of mass-consumption, with stable rules governing the partition of newly created value between wages and profits and between consumption and investment.

It needs to be said, however, that this account of how the Fordist wage-relation was regulated is an *a posteriori* rationalisation that misses the mark in several ways. For example, in both Italy and France, the long-term coupling of productivity-increases with wage-increases was not the product of an *ex-ante* compromise, but rather the *ex-post* result of a highly conflictual dynamic.

On the other hand, there can be no question, in our view, that the dynamic of economic growth proper to the Fordist and Keynesian model of development rested, like the distribution of revenue, on the centrality of the wage-profit relation and went hand in hand with a marginalisation of rent.

Four crucially important factors account for this marginalisation of rent during the golden age of Fordist growth:

– The power of property-owners was restricted by a range of institutional devices related to the regulation of financial markets, progressive taxation and control of the money-supply; these devices promoted inflation and extremely low, sometimes even negative real interest-rates.
– The development of welfare-institutions allowed for a socialisation of the conditions of labour-power's reproduction; a growing mass of revenues was kept exempt from the logic of capital-valorisation and from the power of finance (as in the case of the public pension-system).

- The large Fordist firm specialised in mass-production expresses the hegemony of an industrial capitalism that is directly implicated in the creation
  of surplus-value and corresponds to the golden age of managerial capitalism
  as described by Galbraith. By this we intend the power of a technostructure
  whose legitimacy derives essentially from its role in organising production and
  planning innovation (in its management-offices and R&D laboratories). Such
  a technostructure gives rise to a managerial logic that privileges the extension
  of the firm's productive capacity over the interests of shareholders and 'non-
  productive' modalities of capital-valorisation.
- Finally, and in accordance with a logic of accumulation and property cen-
  tered on fixed capital, the role of intellectual property-rights remains strictly
  limited.

In sum, we can say that under Fordism, the two theoretical conditions for a
clear distinction between rent and profit are met. Capital presents itself as an
internal element of and a necessary condition for the management and organisation of labour. Through mass-production and the productive reinvestment of the
greater part of profits, it plays a decisive role in the development of the forces
of production and the struggle against scarcity. Under such circumstances, the
distribution of revenue will turn on the opposition between company-profits
and a wage-dynamic that has largely been socialised but continues to be driven
primarily by conflicts within the large Fordist firm.

Rent seems to play only a secondary role. True, there is the expansion of
ground-rent in the wake of urbanisation, but the logic governing this process can
almost be described as diametrically opposed to the logic of profit – as can be
seen, for example, from a proposal advanced by Agnelli during the early 1970s.[12]
Agnelli spoke out in favour of a neo-Ricardian alliance between employers
and trade unions, both of whom he felt should take action against urban rent-
increases. The latter were to blame, in his view, for the inflationary wage-demands
advanced by workers during Italy's 'Hot Autumn'.[13]

The crisis of Fordism and the transition to cognitive capitalism:
its origins, its significance and what is at stake

The social crisis of Fordism represents a higher-level major crisis compared to
the other major crises that have punctuated the history of capitalism since the

---

12. Giovanni Agnelli (1921–2003): Italian industrialist and principal shareholder of
FIAT (translator's note).

13. 'Hot Autumn' [*autunno caldo*]: major Italian strike-cycle (summer and autumn
1969) (translator's note).

first industrial revolution. Its historic significance goes beyond the mere dissolution of the foundation of one of industrial capitalism's modes of development
(Fordism). Its character as a higher-level major crisis[14] results from the fact
that it was simultaneously a crisis of industrial capitalism as a *historic system of
accumulation*. It was the expression of a transformative dynamic that has led to
some of the most fundamental invariants of industrial capitalism being called
into question, while preparing the ground for a post-industrial, knowledge-based
economy. One of the main sources of this new great transformation of capitalism
is to be found in the reversal of one of industrial capitalism's long-term tendencies, namely the tendency towards the polarisation of knowledge.

In brief, knowledge and intellectual labour are no longer, 'like every other
employment, the principal or sole trade and occupation of a particular class of
citizens', as Adam Smith claimed in *The Wealth of Nations*. They are beginning
to disperse throughout society. And the forms in which knowledge is dispersed
throughout society increasingly manifest themselves within organisations and
inter-firm relationships.

The origins of this reversal lie in the conflicts that led, from the late 1960s
onward, to the (political) wage being declared an independent variable and to
the spread of behaviour that expressed a refusal of work, dissolving the social
foundations of the *scientific management of labour*. These conflicts also led to a
formidable extension of the *social wage* and of the collective services associated
with welfare,[15] an extension that went beyond the point at which such services
remain compatible with Fordist regulation of the wage-relation. The results were
an attenuation of the monetary pressure to enter into the wage-relation and a
process whereby the *intellectual powers of production* were reappropriated, in
particular thanks to the development of mass-scolarisation and a formidable
rise in the average level of education. Moreover, this phenomenon, which has
played a key role in the rise of so-called *intangible capital*, did not take the form
of a gradually unfolding long-term tendency. Historically considered, the process was rather extremely swift, driven by the social demand for a democratisation of access to knowledge. Knowledge was perceived both as a means to
improve one's social mobility and as the key to a self-fulfilment that broke with
the norms of the Fordist wage-relation and disciplinary society. It should also be
noted that one of the most striking features displayed by this phenomeon, the
spread of knowledge and the reversal of the division of labour, consisted in the
massive extension of women's access to secondary and higher education, with

---

14. The concept of higher-level major crises designates an intermediate phenomenon
situated between the phenomena described by the regulation school as crises of the
'mode of development' and crises of the 'mode of production'.

15. Welfare: English in original (translator's note).

women outnumbering men in many university-departments. This development was significantly correlated with the feminisation of wage-labour. What is more, relational and emotional skills associated with the reproductive work traditionally performed by women came to be seen, albeit in an ambiguous manner, as decisive to the new paradigm of cognitive labour.[16]

It was via this dynamic of antagonism that the mass-worker brought about the Fordist model's structural crisis while constructing, within capital, the elements of a *commons* and an ontological transformation of labour that *points* beyond the logic of capital. The working class negated itself (or at least its centrality) by constructing and giving way to the figure of the collective worker of the 'general intellect' and the class-composition of cognitive labour. It also created the subjective conditions and structural forms required for the emergence of an economy whose driving forces are knowledge and the diffusion of knowledge. This marks the beginning of a new historical phase in the labour-capital relation, a phase characterised by the constitution of a *diffuse intellectuality*.

Two crucial points need to be stressed if the genesis and the nature of the new capitalism are to be adequately described.

First, the essential factor within the emergence of a knowledge-based economy lies within the power of living labour. Both logically and historically, the establishment of a *knowledge-based economy* is prior and contrary to the genesis of *cognitive capitalism*. The latter is the product of a restructuring process by which capital attempts, in a parasitic manner, to absorb and subjugate to its own logic the collective conditions of knowledge-production, smothering the emancipatory potential contained within the society of the 'general intellect'. When using the concept of cognitive capitalism, we are referring to a system of accumulation in which the productive value of intellectual and immaterial labour takes priority; the centrality of capital-valorisation and certain property forms lead directly to the expropriation, in the form of rent, of the *common* and to the transformation of knowledge into a fictive commodity.

Second, and contrary to what is claimed by theories of the informational revolution, the most crucial aspects of the contemporary transformation of labour cannot be explained by means of a technological determinism based on the development of new information- and communication-technologies (ICTs). Such theories overlook two essential facts. First, ICTs cannot function properly without a *living knowledge* capable of putting them to work: information processing is governed by *knowledge*, without which information remains as sterile a resource as capital without labour. The principal creative force behind the

---

16. Monnier and Vercellone 2007, pp. 15–35.

ICT revolution cannot be traced back to a capital-induced dynamic of innovation. Second, the ICT revolution rests on the constitution of social networks for the cooperation of labour whose organisation represents an alternative to both the firm and the market as forms for coordinating production. This is the basis upon which ICTs reinforce the development of the immaterial aspect of labour while simultaneously promoting a process that leads to the distinction between labour-time and free time becoming increasingly blurred.

The principal features of the new labour-capital relation

The new significance of labour's cognitive aspect entails that the knowledge mobilised by capital is now hegemonic with regard to the knowledge embodied in fixed capital and in the managerial organisation of firms. The principal source of value now lies in the knowledge set in motion by living labour and not in material resources or material labour. Under the new capitalism, the work performed by a growing section of the population consists increasingly of processing information, producing knowledge and providing services based on the circulation of knowledge and the *production of man by man*. Routine productive activities and material labour, which consists in transforming matter with the aid of instruments and machines that are themselves material, become less important than the new paradigm of a labour that is simultaneously more intellectual, more immaterial and more communicative. Living labour now performs a large number of the central functions once performed by fixed capital. This means that knowledge is collectively shared to an ever greater degree, a fact that subverts the internal organisation of firms no less than their relations with the outside world. As we will see, the new configuration of the labour-capital relation entails that labour occurs within the firm but is also increasingly organised outside it.[17]

This development has two fundamental consequences. On the one hand, and as far as the individual firm is concerned, value-creating activity accords less and less with the criterion of the unity of time and space on which the regulation of collective time was based under Fordism. On the other hand, and concerning society as a whole, the production of wealth and knowledge increasingly occurs beyond the company-system and the market-sphere. Its reintegration into the logic of capital-valorisation is possible only in an indirect manner, or on the basis of a relation of exteriority to production that in many ways resembles the extraction of rent.

---

17. Negri 2006a.

This development entails profound changes for all Fordist-industrial conventions on the wage-relation, the notion of productive labour, the sources and the measure of value, the forms of property and the distribution of revenue. The scale of this transformation can be illustrated by reference to several stylised facts.

Knowledge and the changes in the labour-capital relation: reversal of the relationship between living labour and dead labour and between the factory and society

The first stylised fact concerns the historic dynamic by which the component of capital called intangible (R&D but also and especially education, training and health), which is essentially embodied in human beings,[18] now makes up a larger part of the overall capital-stock than material capital, becoming the crucial growth factor.[19] This tendency is directly linked to factors that explain the rise of a diffuse intellectuality; the latter accounts for the greater part of the increase in so-called intangible capital. To put this more precisely, we can say that this stylised fact has at least four major implications, which are obscured in an almost systematic way in economic literature.

The first implication is that, contrary to what is maintained by the majority of mainstream writers on the 'knowledge-based economy',[20] the social prerequisites and the veritable driving sectors of an economy based on knowledge are not to be found in privately owned R&D laboratories. The opposite is the case: they correspond to the collective production of *man for and by himself*, traditionally ensured by the public institutions of the welfare-state (health, education, public and academic research).[21] This aspect is systematically elided by OECD economists, and the pressure to privatise this collective production and/or subordinate it to the logic of the market is extraordinary. The reason for this gross elision lies in the vital importance of the biopolitical control and market-based colonisation of welfare-institutions for cognitive capitalism.[22] Not only do health, education, training and culture represent a growing part of overall production and demand, but it is also through them that ways of life are created. This is the terrain on

---

18. And which is often wrongly described as 'human capital'.
19. Kendrick 1994.
20. Knowledge-based economy: English in original (translator's note).
21. For a more in-depth analysis of the role of the welfare-state within capitalism's current transformation, see Monnier and Vercellone 2007.
22. Contrary to the prevailing ideological discourse that stigmatises welfare-related public services by pointing to their costs and their supposedly unproductive character, the goal for cognitive capitalism consists not so much in a reduction of total outlays as in their reintegration into the circuits of trade and finance.

which a major conflict is fought out between the neoliberal strategy of privatising the commons on the one hand, and the project of resocialising the economy via a democratic reappropriation of welfare-institutions on the other.

The second implication of the stylised fact is that labour now performs certain essential functions formerly performed by constant capital. This is true both with regard to the organisation of production and insofar as labour has become the key factor in the knowledge-related aspects of competitiveness and in the development of knowledge.[23] Picking up on (and redefining somewhat) a concept developed by Luigi Pasinetti,[24] we can say that under cognitive capitalism the collective worker of the 'general intellect' approaches the abstraction of a *pure-labour economy* in which the labour-force's capacity for learning and creativity replaces fixed capital as the key factor in accumulation.

The third implication is that the conditions for the constitution and reproduction of labour-power have become directly productive, such that the 'wealth of nations' now stems increasingly from a cooperation situated outside individual firms. It should be noted that this development renders obsolete those canonic versions of the theory of knowledge that attribute the production of knowledge to a specialised sector.[25] This sector, if one still wants to use the term, corresponds today to the whole of society. It follows that the very concept of productive labour needs now to be extended to all social time that contributes to economic and social production and reproduction.

Finally, the so-called complex services historically provided by the welfare-state now correspond to activities in which the cognitive, communicative and affective aspects of labour are dominant. These activities hold the potential for unprecedented forms of self-management, based on a co-production of services that directly implicates beneficiaries.

The cognitive division of labour, the working class and the destabilisation of the canonic terms of the wage-relation

The second stylised fact concerns the transition, evident in a number of productive activities, from a Taylorist to a cognitive division of labour. Under these circumstances, reducing the time necessary for the performance of work-tasks is no longer the key to efficiency. Instead, efficiency depends on the knowledge and versatility of a labour-force capable of maximising its ability to learn, innovate and adapt to continuously changing contexts. This development tends to

---

23. Marazzi 2007.
24. Pasinetti 1993.
25. The *locus classicus* for this model is an article by Arrow 1962.

dissolve the once-rigid distinction between conception and execution as the dynamic of innovation returns to the workshop from which industrial capitalism sought to banish it. At the same time, the criteria by which efficiency was evaluated under industrial capitalism are called into question: in a large number of cases, homogeneous time can no longer be utilised as the reference-point by which to describe and organise labour, just as it ceases to be a reliable measure of value and production-costs.[26]

It should be noted that the proliferation of tasks related to information processing and the production of knowledge goes beyond the paradigmatic fields of complex services and high-tech activities associated with the 'new economy'. It affects the economy in its entirety, including low-tech sectors – witness the rising degree of autonomy of which workers dispose across the economy.

To be sure, the tendency is not univocal. Within a single firm, certain phases of the production-process may be organised along cognitive principles while others, and in particular the more standardised tasks, may still be organised according to a Taylorist or neo-Taylorist logic.

Nevertheless, it remains the case that cognitive labour is central to the valorisation-process both in qualitative and in quantitative terms (at least as far as the OECD countries are concerned); it is the cognitive worker, therefore, who holds the power to break with capitalism's specific mechanisms of production.

The destabilisation of the canonic terms of the exchange between labour and capital

The third stylised fact concerns the manner in which the growing significance of labour's cognitive aspect induces a twofold destabilisation of the canonic terms governing the exchange between labour and capital.[27] In effect, within those knowledge-intensive activities in which the product assumes an eminently immaterial form, one of the most fundamental conditions of the wage-contract is being called into question, namely the workers' renunciation of all property-claims to the product of their labour (a renunciation compensated for by the wage). In activities such as scientific research or software-development, labour does not crystallise in a material product that can be separated from the worker. Instead, the product rests within the worker's brain and can therefore not be separated from his person. This helps explain the pressure firms exert to bring about a reformulation or tightening of intellectual property-rights; these efforts

---

26. Veltz 2000.
27. On these points, see also Vercellone (ed.) 2006; Negri and Vercellone 2008.

are simply an attempt to appropriate knowledge and block the mechanisms that allow it to circulate.

Moreover, the precise delimitation and synchronic unity of the time and place of work, fundamental to the Fordist wage-contract, are profoundly modified. As we have seen, under industrial capitalism's energetic paradigm, the wage is paid by capital in return for a clearly defined segment of human time, which the firm purchases and is then free to dispose of as it sees fit. The employer seeks to put this time to use as efficiently as possible, so that he may obtain from labour power's use-value the greatest possible quantity of surplus-labour. This obviously requires some degree of effort and ingenuity, as labour's interests are by definition diametrically opposed to those of capital. The principles of scientific management, which turned on the expropriation of workers' knowledge and entailed strict time- and motion-prescriptions, once represented an adequate solution to the problem. In the Fordist factory, effective labour-time, the productivity of the various tasks and the volume of production were in effect planned and hence known in advance by the engineers in the management-offices.

Yet everything changes once labour, having become increasingly immaterial and cognitive, refuses to be reduced to a simple expense of energy affected during a given period of time. Capital is forced to grant labour a growing degree of autonomy with regard to the organisation of production, even if this autonomy remains limited, with workers being given freedom to choose by which means certain goals are to be achieved, but no say in the determination of the goals themselves. The old dilemma of how labour ought to be controlled reappears in new forms. Not only has capital once more become dependent on the knowledge of its workers, but it must also achieve the mobilisation and active implication of the entirety of its workers' knowledge and life-time. By its very nature, cognitive labour presents itself as the complex articulation of an intellectual activity – that of reflecting, communicating and sharing and elaborating knowledge – affected as much beyond or outside the field of direct labour (the labour of production) as within it. Consequently, the traditional distinction between work and non-work becomes blurred. The dynamic by which this occurs is eminently contradictory. On the one hand, so-called free time can no longer be reduced to its cathartic function, that of reproducing labour-power's energetic potential. It begins to involve activities related to education, self-education and voluntary work, implicating communities of knowledge-sharing and knowledge-production that cut across the various fields of human activity. Each individual takes their knowledge with them when they transition from one social time-order to another, thereby increasing the individual and collective use-value of the labour-force. On the other hand, this dynamic gives rise to a conflict and to growing tension between labour's tendency to become autonomous and capital's attempt to subject all social time to its heteronomous logic of capital-valorisation.

The prescription of a certain subjectivity, characterised by the introjection of company-objectives, the obligation to achieve certain results, management by projects, pressure exerted by the client and the straightforward constraint associated with precarity are the principal means employed by capital in its attempt to solve this altogether new problem. Thus the precarisation of the wage-relation is also and in fact primarily an instrument by which capital attempts to bring about, and benefit from, the total implication/subordination of wage-workers, without recognising or paying any wages for the labour that does not correspond to and cannot be measured by the categories of the official labour-contract. These developments translate into an increase in the amount of work that goes unmeasured, work that can in fact scarcely be quantified by means of traditional measurement-criteria. This is one of the factors that ought to lead one to rethink entirely the notions of labour-time and the wage we have inherited from the Fordist era. And it is also one of the factors that can help us understand why the dequalification of the labour-force characteristic of Fordism appears to be yielding to a process of precarisation and *downward social mobility*, a process by which young people and women are particularly affected and which amounts to a downgrading of their remuneration and working conditions that flies in the face of the qualifications and skills they bring to the labour-process.

The crisis of the trinity-formula: the rent-economy and the privatisation of the commons

The transformations undergone by the mode of production are directly related to a major change in the mechanisms by which surplus-value is appropriated and revenue distributed. Understanding this requires an awareness of two major developments in particular.

The first of these developments concerns the flagrant mismatch between the increasingly social character of production and the ways in which wages are determined: the latter continue to be shaped by Fordist norms that make access to revenue dependent on employment. This mismatch has strongly contributed to the stagnation of real wages and the precarisation of living conditions. At the same time, and with regard to transfer-payments based on the objective rights that arise from being a citizen or member of society, we are witnessing a dramatic decline both in the sums paid out and in the number of beneficiaries. As a result, we are seeing the return of a purely residual welfare-state whose policies target only specific, stigmatised sectors of the population. The tendency towards very low welfare-payments, access to which is made dependent on a number of conditions, marks the transition from a *welfare-* to a *workfare-*state.

The second development concerns the renewed importance of rent. Rent presents itself as the main instrument both for appropriating surplus-value and for desocialising the commons. The significance and the role played by this return of rent can be analysed on two basic levels. On the one hand, and as far as the social organisation of production is concerned, the traditional distinction between rent and company-profit is becoming increasingly untenable. This *blurring* of the rent/profit-distinction can be seen, for example, in the way that powerful financial actors are remodelling company-governance criteria in such a way as to make the creation of shareholder-value the key criterion. It is as if the autonomisation of labour-cooperation were accompanied by a parallel autonomisation of capital in its most abstract, eminently flexible and mobile form: money-capital.

This represents another qualitative leap with regard to the historical process that led to a growing separation between the management and the ownership of capital. Why? The answer lies in the fact that the age of cognitive capitalism is characterised not only by the irreversible decline of the Weberian entrepreneur, that idyllic figure in whom the functions of capital-ownership and control over production were combined, but also, and more importantly, by the end of Galbraith's technostructure, whose legitimacy derived from its role in planning innovation and organising the labour-process. Both the Weberian entrepreneur and Galbraith's technostructure are yielding to a management whose principal function consists in coordinating operations that are essentially financial and speculative; we have already seen that the organisation of production is in fact increasingly left to wage-workers. This development can be observed both on the level of the individual firm – with regard to which one could speak of an absolute rent – and on that of the relationship betweens firms and society. To be competitive, firms increasingly rely on external rather than internal economies; in other words, what matters is their ability to appropriate the productive surpluses that result from the cognitive resources of a certain territory. This amounts to the realisation, on a historically unprecedented scale, of Alfred Marshall's definition of rent as an 'extra income' that results from the 'general progress of society' and needs therefore to be distinguished from other, more ordinary sources of profit.[28] Thus capital enjoys free of charge the benefits of society's collective knowledge, as if this knowledge were a gift of nature; this component of surplus-value is fully comparable to the differential ground rent received by the owner of land

---

28. Marshall 1920, Book v, Chapter Ten.

with greater than average fertility.[29] In brief, and as described by Marx, both profit and rent tend to present themselves increasingly as a *purely distributive relationship*: capital appropriates surplus-value *from outside*; in the majority of cases, it no longer performs any real, positive function within the organisation of production.

On the other hand, the current development of rent is the development of rent's *purest* functions, those that already underpinned the genesis of capitalism from the enclosures onwards.[30] Rent appears again as the product of a privatisation of the *commons*, an income made possible by an artificial scarcity of resources. This is the logic underlying both the rent based on real-estate speculation and the major role that the privatisation of money and public debt have played in the rise of financial rent and the destabilisation of welfare-state institutions since the early 1980s. An analogous logic governs the attempt to privatise knowledge and biological life by strengthening intellectual property-rights and keeping the prices of certain commodities artificially high, despite the fact that the reproduction-costs of these commodities are extremely low or even zero. There results an increasingly acute contradiction between the social character of production and the private character of appropriation. The situation contradicts the very principles by which the founding fathers of economic liberalism justified property as a weapon in the struggle against scarcity. It is now the creation of property that leads to scarcity. This is what Marx described as the strategy of forcibly maintaining the primacy of exchange-value against a wealth that depends on abundance and use-value, and hence on gratuitousness. We are dealing, then, with a major manifestation of the crisis of the law of value and of the antagonism between labour and capital as it presents itself in the era of the 'general intellect'.

These profound changes within the relationship between wages, rent and profit also underpin a politics that consists in segmenting today's class-composition and the labour-market in order to arrive at a markedly dual configuration.

In one sector, we find the privileged minority of workers employed in the most lucrative (and often most parasitic) activities associated with cognitive capitalism, such as financial services, patent-oriented research, specialist legal advice on the defence of intellectual property-rights, and such like. Those making up this sector of the *cognitariat* – one might call them capital-rent functionaries – enjoy full recognition and remuneration of their abilities. Their payment increasingly

---

29. As Marx points out in a striking passage in *Capital* Volume III that sketches out a theory of the becoming-rent of profit, such a situation eliminates 'the last pretext for confusing profit of enterprise with the wages of management', such that profit appears 'in practice as what it undeniably was in theory, mere surplus-value, value for which no equivalent was paid, realised unpaid labour' (Marx 1981, p. 514).

30. Enclosures: English in original (translator's note).

includes a share of financial bonuses. Moreover, these workers enjoy the benefit of private pension-funds and health-insurance.

In the other sector, we find a labour-force whose qualifications and skills are not recognised. As we have seen, workers within this majoritarian sector of cognitive labour are faced with the phenomenon of a severe 'downward social mobility'. They are left to perform not only the more precarious jobs within the new cognitive division of labour, but also the neo-Taylorist tasks associated with newly standardised service-work and the development of poorly remunerated personal services. In a genuine vicious circle, the dualism evident both on the labour-market and in the distribution of revenue reinforces the dismantling of the welfare-state's collective services. These collective services yield to an expanding sector of commodified personal services that is the foundation of modern-day servitude.

Conclusion: towards a process of class-recomposition

Finally, rent in its various forms (financial, real estate, patent-based, etc.) plays an ever more strategic role in the distribution of revenue and the social stratification of the population. This leads to a decomposition of what are usually called the middle classes and to the emergence of an 'hourglass-society' characterised by an extreme polarisation of wealth.

It seems that this devastating dynamic will continue to unfold by an almost ineluctable logic, unless – and this is the only reformist option we can imagine for the time being – capital is constrained to grant labour growing autonomy in the organisation of production and recognise that the principal source of value resides in the creativity, versatility and inventiveness of wage-workers, not in fixed capital or standardised work-tasks. To be sure, capital is already granting labour more autonomy, but only with regard to means; the ends for which labour is employed continue to be heteronomous, or determined by capital.

The political challenge consists, then, in stripping capital of this power to determine the ends of production and therefore to propose in an autonomous way new institutions of the commons. A democratic reappropriation of welfare-institutions that starts from the dynamic of association and self-management already traversing society would seem essential – both in terms of production- and consumption-norms – to the formulation of an alternative development-model. A model based on the primacy of non-market goods and on the *production of man for and by man*. To the extent that the production of the 'general intellect' involves *man himself becoming the most important form of fixed capital*, the production of man for and by man needs to be understood in terms of a logic of social cooperation situated beyond the law of value and the *trinity-formula* (wages, rent and profit). This is also the context within which the struggle for an unconditional or guaranteed social income is situated. Such an income needs to be understood as a primary income, resulting not from a policy of redistribution (like the French RMI)[31] but from recognition of the ever more collective character of value- and wealth-production.

More precisely, the proposal of a guaranteed social income qua primary income is based on a twofold re-examination and extension of the notion of productive labour:

– With regard to the concept of productive labour, understood within the dominant tradition of political economy as labour that creates profit and/or contributes to the creation of value, it needs to be noted that we are witnessing a major extension of labour-time over and above the official working day; this additional labour-time is directly or indirectly involved in the creation of the value appropriated by firms. As a social wage, the guaranteed social income would remunerate the increasingly collective character of a value-creating activity that extends across all social time, giving rise to an enormous quantity of work that is presently unrecognised and unremunerated.
– Productive labour can also be seen as the labour that produces use-values, creating a wealth that escapes the commodified logic of subordinated wage-labour. From this point of view, the issue becomes that of showing that labour can be unproductive for capital while still producing wealth, and that such labour needs to be remunerated (as is already the case with non-market public services).

It is worth stressing the simultaneously antagonistic and complementary relation these two contradictory forms of productive labour entertain under the development of cognitive capitalism. The expansion of free labour actually goes hand in hand with its subordination to value-producing social labour, and the reason lies in the very tendencies that are dissolving the distinction between work and non-work, or between the spheres of production and reproduction.

The guaranteed social income not only raises the issue of recognising productive labour's second aspect (use-value productivity) but also, and more importantly, that of emancipating productive labour from the sphere of value and surplus-value production. The guaranteed social income would restore and

---

31. The French RMI (*revenu minimum d'insertion*), introduced under the government of Michel Rocard in 1988, is a French form of social welfare aimed at working-age people without income.

reinforce the bargaining power of the entire labour-force while withdrawing from capital a portion of the value currently appropriated by means of rent. At the same time, the weakening of the monetary pressure to enter into the wage-relation would favour the development of labour-forms that have emancipated themselves from the logic of the market and of subordinated labour.

Editorial note: This chapter was written in 2007, before the beginning of the subprime crisis.

Results and Prospects
Karl Heinz Roth and Marcel van der Linden

In our introduction to this volume, we drew attention to five problem-areas that we feel stand in the way of our conceptualising the findings of global labour-history in terms of a Marxist critique of political economy: the subaltern and subordinate position of the working class within the analysis of the capitalist dynamic; the tendency toward a 'scientific' objectification and determination of class-contradictions that gives priority to the capital-relation; the privileged and exclusive position of the 'doubly-free wage-worker' within the global class of workers; methodological nationalism; the almost consistently eurocentric perspective. In this concluding chapter, we will formulate a positive interpretation of the findings of the preceding eighteen contributions to the themes of 'labour-history' and the 'concept of labour'. We wish to raise the question of how the gap between the historical evidence and theory might be superated. In order to frame our problem more precisely, we will start with five hypotheses that represent the result of the discussion between us, the editors. These hypotheses should not be read as evaluative criteria by which to assess the arguments and findings of our contributors. They are merely intended to point the way to a synoptic presentation of our contributors' positions.

Labour-history and the concept of labour: five hypotheses for the superation of the 'poverty of theory'

(1) Every critically and emancipatorily oriented conceptualisation of the political economy of labour has as its elementary presuppositions the historical reconstruction and the analysis of the current condition of the global multiverse of those classes, strata and social groups that are constrained, in order to exist, to make their living labour-capacity available to the owners of objectified labour, or of capital in all its manifestations. This multiverse has been and continues to be extraordinarily diverse. Before we grasp it conceptually, we need to make it visible in its social, economic, sexual, generational, ethnic and cultural heterogeneity. We also need to understand its specific dynamic of resistance, by means of which it recurrently seeks to avoid being subjected to and exploited by the structures of objectified labour. It is in this sense that labour-history and the empirical analysis of the current composition of the class of male and female workers – and of its forms of exploitation, experiences and ways of behaving – constitute the indispensable foundation of every critique of the political economy of labour.

(2) Starting from this premise, we may define the essential functions of the critique of the political economy of labour that we wish to develop. First, it needs to demonstrate, qualitatively and quantitatively, that, and how, the strata and social groups of the global multiverse are subjected to and exploited by the processes of capital's production and reproduction. Second, in doing so, it should operate on the assumption that these processes of subjection, valorisation and exploitation always involve a certain degree of friction: workers are never fully incorporated into the processes of valorisation; rather, they resist them on all levels and/or seek to evade them. This manifests itself in everyday conflicts over the degree to which workers are subordinated to the technology of capital (subsumption) and over the amount of effort they expend within the labour-process. It also manifests itself in major strike-movements that concern the distribution of the value-product, as well as in recurrent mass-uprisings, in which the contours of self-determined, alternative modes of production are glimpsed. We may thus consider the global class of workers a 'processual contradiction': on the one hand, it is subject to capitalist exploitation; on the other hand, it is always striving to divest itself of this relation of exploitation. From this perspective, we can think of the dynamic of capitalist development as an ongoing process of adjustment to the independent counter-dynamic of the multiverse of workers.

(3) From this empirical fact there results the urgent necessity of reconfiguring the labour-theory of value, the core element of every critique of the political economy of labour, in such a way as to take labouring subjects, the bearers of

living labour-power, seriously, rejecting the objectifying approach that treats them as mere appendages of the capitalist process of production and reproduction. In other words, it is a matter of getting beyond the static models of the labour-theory of value developed thus far, replacing them with a dynamic conception of labour-value that recognises the bearers of living labour-power as the equal-ranking adversaries of objectified labour.

(4) Consequently, every stringent dynamic labour-theory of value that seeks to do justice to the facticity of the historical and contemporary class-struggle, a struggle conducted on all levels of the processes of capitalist production and reproduction, is faced with the task of developing concepts, functions and proportions that express the fact that workers and capital are principally equal-ranking. The process of the accumulation of capital is simultaneously a process of the 'accumulation of the proletariat' (Linebaugh/Rediker); the outcome and the direction of this process are in no way predetermined. The categories of the critique of the political economy of labour need therefore to be open in every direction. They must not be constructed in such a way as to imply objectivistic automatic processes such as the 'infinite accumulation of capital' or the 'tendency of capitalism to collapse'; nor must they resolve themselves in a purely subjectivistic but equally automatic counter-process of self-liberation, by which the global multiverse of workers frees itself from the impositions of the capitalist world-economy. The task of a dynamic labour-theory of value is rather that of integrating the actions of the two antagonistic agents, living labour-power and objectified labour, into the structures, functions and proportions of value-production in such a way as to allow us to conceptualise every possible variant of socio-economic development as an effect of class-conflict. In doing so, we will also have to take account of the increasingly apparent destruction of the material foundations of the capitalist processes of production and reproduction – the damage done to the bio- and geospheres – as one factor that conditions the actions of the two agents.

(5) If, however, we should fail to develop a dynamic and non-determinist labour-theory of value, one that points to ways in which the exploited may liberate themselves, then the critique of political economy would be superfluous, even after having been developed into a critique of the political economy of labour (and natural resources). It would need to be replaced by a theory of revolution that does not take capitalist value-production as its starting point, but rather starts from the findings of labour-history and bases itself on the fact that nature and labour – qua self-determined, active life-process – are the only sources of social wealth by which to globally satisfy the needs that all persons share equally, and which constitute their fundamental right to existence.

Starting from these basic considerations on a broadened definition of the working class, and on the superation of the poverty of theory (Edward P. Thompson) via the redefinition of the relationship between labour-history and the critique of the political economy of labour, we wish to now summarise the findings of the contributions to this volume. This task is facilitated by the fact that all contributors have addressed the issue of how empirical evidence and theory interlink in the case of the global working class's past and present, although they have placed the emphasis differently and displayed varying degrees of approval or dissatisfaction.

The multiverse of workers considered from the perspective of labour-history

The synopsis of the contributions to this volume holds some surprises even for those who are familiar with the global social history of workers. Following the contributors to the first section, we can say that the new findings concern five essential aspects: first, temporal and geographical in scope; second, mobility; third, socio-economic diversification; fourth, the question of the coexistence or sequentiality of different labour-relations; fifth, the formation- and fragmentation-processes within proletarian class-development. The global working class constitutes itself not as a homogeneous entity but as a multiverse of strata and social groups whose learning processes, experiences, coalitions and actions are supported less by individual subjects than by families, communities, fraternities and sororities, benevolent societies and craft-associations, secret societies and action-groups. They form a diffuse social infrastructure that is decisive to the survival and formation of self-determined cultural norms. This infrastructure persists even when the large political and syndicalist associations that are periodically generated by it suffer shipwreck. It is nevertheless also subject to ongoing transformation, renewing itself constantly. This is precisely why it displays a degree of staying power that has allowed it to last through centuries of capitalist development. One need think only of the persistence of the peasant-family economies in the redistributive communes of Tsarist Russia, the indigenous regions of Latin America and contemporary China. Or one might reflect on the continuity of the decision-making processes that have been playing out within these peasant-families for centuries, prior to the departure to foreign lands – a continuity that Ferruccio Gambino and Devi Sacchetto have drawn attention to in their essay. Or one might attempt to understand the bitterness with which many auto-worker families in Detroit have recently commented on the decline of their once powerful industrial union, which their grandparents – the veterans of the late 1936, early 1937 sitdown-strike in Flint – once fought so vehemently for. Will the union's current decline and the brutal restructuring at General Motors, Chrysler and Ford be followed by a new beginning, and if so, will they live to see it?

The temporal dimensions spanned by this multiverse, which Peter Linebaugh and Marcus Rediker describe as the 'many-headed Hydra', are vast. They span more than half a millennium. Their beginnings lie in the mid-fifteenth century, when the agents of transcontinental long-distance trade discovered an additional source of revenue in the international division of labour and made use of a peculiar commodity – the slave-workers and indentured servants (Gambino and Sacchetto). This was the beginning of an extremely violent process of proletarisation. In Europe, the direct producers were separated from their means of subsistence and placed in workhouses and prisons, pressed into service in the navy or army or shipped overseas as indentured servants (Linebaugh/Rediker, Niklas Frykman, Peter Way). Meanwhile, in large parts of Asia and the two Americas, manufacture-like plantation-systems developed. They were not just the destination of the slave-shipments that had, by the middle of the nineteenth century, depopulated large parts of sub-Saharan Africa (Gambino/Sacchetto); they also served as a laboratory for the development of a sophisticated division of labour involving slaves, indentured servants, artisans and free workers. The experiences thus garnered were subsequently transferred to the European system of manufacture.

This primitive accumulation of the proletariat was the antagonistic corollary of the primitive accumulation of capital and of the genesis of the world-economy. By no means did it end with the industrialisation of capitalism that began in England, spreading through the trans-Atlantic region by the mid-nineteenth century. Rather, it meshed with these industrial-proletarisation processes. The Indian and Chinese coolies and indentured servants, the US ex-slaves released into the ghettos of unfree contract-labour and the worker-artisans of emergent industry were initially kept apart within the division of labour (Gambino/Sacchetto). Yet this changed during the second stage of the capitalist industrialisation-process, which gave rise to Taylorised mass-work (Sergio Bologna, Carlo Vercellone), and even more so after the Second World-War. In the end, the accumulation of the proletarian multiverse left no angle of the globe untouched, even as the multiverse was increasingly transformed into a reserve-army for the accumulation of capital. Today, almost five hundred and fifty years after the beginnings of the trans-Atlantic slave-trade, two hundred years after the first phase of industrialisation and sixty years after the proclamation of the US doctrine of development, more than a billion informal proletarians are penned up in slum-cities. Moreover, more than two-thirds of the peasants in the Global South are threatened with the loss of their land-rights and commons (Max Henninger).

The extraordinary mobility of the proletarian multiverse was – and continues to be – an essential feature of this more than five-hundred year genesis. It always consisted of two components: transportation-work and labour-migration. The exploitation of transportation-workers was what long-distance trade rested on; it also functioned as the basis for the international division of labour that began to take shape during the fifteenth century. Since then it has gone through a number of climaxes. The first occurred during the pre-industrial phase of capitalism, when the navy-sailors of the seventeenth and eighteenth centuries, who had typically been forcibly recruited, were used to protect the transoceanic trade-routes and imperialist expansion, although they also formed the core of the motley crew of slaves, indentured servants and artisans whose revolts preceded the European revolutions (Linebaugh/Rediker, Frykman). Today, these workers appear to us as the docile servants of standardised, networked international transportation-chains, and the massive strike-movements they organised from the 1970s until the early 1990s seem to have been forgotten – but who knows what the future will bring?

To this were added, from early modernity onward, the major continental and transcontinental waves of migrant-labour. Often migrant-workers first stepped onto the world stage in chains, as Gambino and Sacchetto emphasise. There followed, after four centuries, the migration-currents of fixed-term servitude, bilateral state-agreements and international mediating agencies. But all this did not add up to a one-way street leading to ever freer labour-relations: since the 1970s, ghettoised contract-labour has once more become dominant in the Gulf states, and the Chinese 'snake-heads' have long since re-established the structures of indentured servitude and fixed-term slavery, just like the human traffickers of Eastern Europe, in order to provide their clients with cheap and docile labour-power. Migrant-labour's functional position within the cycles of exploitation has not changed either: migrant-labour compensates for resident-workers's ongoing flight from difficult, unhealthy and poorly paid work (Gambino/Sacchetto). For this reason, it eventually becomes an integral component of the coming and going that employment's managers refer to as fluctuation.

Moreover, all contributors agree that the proletarian multiverse has been characterised, since its inception, by an extraordinary diversity and complexity. This many-headedness has changed in the course of capitalism's long cycles, but some of its components have persisted over the centuries. One essential constant has been and continues to be the reproductive work performed by women. It was long invisible because it had to performed without compensation (Maria Mies, Silvia Federici, Max Henninger); only during recent centuries has it in some cases begun to yield to poorly remunerated labour-relations (cf. Silvia Federici on the example of care-work). Other forms of labour have persisted throughout, such as the self-employed labour of peasants and artisans, although these forms have also changed radically in character, thanks to the emergence of network-capitalism's knowledge-workers (Sergio Bologna). What is astounding is the continuity displayed by the above-mentioned peasant-family economies (Mies, Henninger). In the trans-Atlantic region, the dual system of the peasant-family economy and of communal land-ownership began to fall victim to enclosure, the destruction of the commons and the state-terror of expropriation as early as the sixteenth century. But in Tsarist Russia and the Soviet Union, it persisted until the forced collectivisation of the early 1930s; in China, it has undergone a renaissance since the 1980s, and in parts of Asia, Africa and Latin America, it has withstood the shock waves of the 'Green Revolution', or of the industrialisation of agriculture, to this day.

In order to better understand these continuities within the changes undergone by the proletarian multiverse, we would require comparative temporal profiles of the multiverse's composition for the past centuries. On the basis of the contributions of British and US labour-historians, such 'time-windows' on class-composition could easily be compiled for the last two centuries prior to industrialisation; in them, we would re-encounter the workers of the colonial plantations and trans-Atlantic manufactures, the workshops of small artisans, the crews of navy- and merchant-vessels, military garrisons, serfs and the inmates of workhouses, prisons, orphanages and poor houses. In reconstructing a profile of the composition of the continental European proletariat around the middle of the nineteenth century, we can make reference to the opening remarks in Ahlrich Meyer's essay, which identifies seasonal workers in agriculture, impoverished peasants and sharefarmers, employment-seeking beggars and vagabonds, proto-industrial domestic producers, farmhands and servants, urban odd-job men, itinerant labourers, railway-workers, proletarianised artisans, manufacture- and factory-workers and the criminalised urban subproletariat as essential components of the class-composition and their common subsistence revolts. During the two subsequent phases of industrialisation, the industrial proletariat no doubt gained much importance, but it never achieved the ideal state of 'doubly-free wage-labour'; thanks to migrant- and peasant-labour, it remained largely non-sedentary, displayed a transcultural and transnational composition and retained its link to the class-structures of less developed rural areas. Nor did the stratum of industrial workers ever dominate social class-compositions, even if its most highly qualified segments temporarily achieved political hegemony in the form of the trade-union and political labour-movement. Outside the trans-Atlantic region, there still is a dominant class-composition that has never lost the heterogeneity of the nineteenth-century European proletariat, not even in the so-called newly industrialising countries.

Nor will this heterogeneous constellation change in the future. As the essays by Bologna, Federici, Vercellone, Gambino/Sacchetto, Mies, Henninger and Subir Sinha demonstrate, the multiverse of wage-dependent workers continues to diversify in every direction – downward, into new forms of indenture and non-contractual exploitation, and upward, all the way to the new segments of knowledge-workers, whom the council communists once simply referred to as 'intellectual workers', contrasting them to 'manual workers'. Moreover, the past decades have seen major concentrations of workers within large industry being either radically downsized or relocated to the new emergent economies. This development involves large numbers of retrenched factory-workers being forced to reinvent themselves as freelance craftsmen, offer their services as self-employed workers or revive forms of domestic production – albeit with a numerically controlled machine-tool in the basement, rather than a hand-loom.

The creativity of the proletarian-accumulation process is inexhaustible. The proletariat is constantly striving to defend its social existence and cultural identity against the working times, hazardous working conditions and other impositions of managers and regulatory authorities. No doubt the success of this endeavour is limited, as flight from the relation of exploitation rarely leads to subsistence-economics or more tolerable self-employed work; in most cases, it leads simply to unemployment. When we compare Henninger's figures on the extent of today's global pauperism with the structure of labour-markets in the 1850s as recorded by Marx, we find that the British reality of Marx's day, with its gradations within the reserve-army of labour – 'dangerous classes', pauperism, the stagnant unemployment of occasional workers, latent agricultural unemployment and temporary ('flowing'), crisis-induced unemployment – has imposed itself the world over and left its mark on the global multiverse. But this takes us back to the old question of whether mass-poverty ought really to be interpreted only as a result of capitalist development – as a 'relative surplus-population' and concomitant of the concentration of capital – or whether it does not display a dynamic of its own.

Of course, there are also issues related to labour-history and/or the current development of labour-relations that our contributors do not agree on, or at least consider from different angles. One such issue is raised, for example, by Subir Sinha when he reflects, from the perspective of the global South, on the growing discrepancy between actual class-processes and the instances of their politico-intellectual mediation. According to Sinha's analysis, India has also seen its class-relations undergo considerable transformation and differentiation during the past decades. Yet this fact does not serve as the starting point for class-theoretical reflections for him; it provides him with a basis upon which to critically engage both traditional Marxism's tendencies toward state-centralist cooptation and the culturalist conceptual alternatives developed by the Subaltern-Studies group, which considers the fragmentation of the Indian class irreversible. Yet Sinha does not stop at his diagnosis of these two dead ends; nor does he venture onto the 'third' level of an intellectual theory of formation. Instead, he examines the real developments undergone by the Indian part of the multiverse, discussing the self-organisation of fishermen and forest-workers and the situation of migrant-workers from the state of Bihar. He thus demonstrates the need to newly mediate economic and cultural categories.

The second controversy concerns the current transformation of labour-relations within the new high-tech sectors of capitalism. In his essay, Carlo Vercellone starts from the observation that the transformation-crisis of the Fordist era has led to the emergence of a new type of worker: the 'immaterial' or 'cognitive worker'. Vercellone argues that what we are seeing is the reappropriation of the 'scientific forces of production'. While principally inherent in living labour-power, these were expropriated during the Fordist era, when the labour-process was fragmented into a series of repetitive operations. The tendency imposing itself today is that of labour qua inseparable unity of thought and action moving to the heart of the processes of production. Vercellone also argues that this labour has now assumed, within the overall spectrum of labour-relations, the hegemonic position once held by mass-labour.

We will go on to discuss the theoretical implications of this approach below. Here, it will suffice to note that several contributors to this volume criticise this approach, which has become widely known as 'post-workerism'. At the end of their contribution, Gambino and Sacchetto emphasise that capital-accumulation continues to rely mainly on the exploitation of repetitive work, while Massimiliano Tomba and Riccardo Bellofiore point out that the capitalist world-system is always striving to combine different labour-relations so as to be able to exploit them simultaneously. Critical comments can also be found in the contributions by C. George Caffentzis, Detlef Hartmann and Silvia Federici. We can therefore assume that the notion of a certain type of worker occupying a hegemonic position within the global multiverse – a notion first formulated by Marx and Engels in 1847–8, in their remarks on the doubly-free wage-worker – is no longer very widely endorsed.

Deficits of the Marxian critique of political economy: the view of the contributors

This comment on the highly controversial issue of a 'hegemonic hierarchisation' both of the historical and of the contemporary global working class may serve to conclude our recapitulation of the contributions on labour-history. We turn now to labour-history's conceptualisation within the Marxian critique of political economy. For obvious reasons, the dispute surrounding the model of 'doubly-free wage-labour' is key to this. But our contributors' reflections on the interplay of labour-history and the concept of labour are much more broadly oriented. Some essays are largely or even entirely dominated by such reflections (this is especially true of the essays in Section II); elsewhere, they can be found only in brief passages, asides or even footnotes. In order to assist our readers in their engagement with this crucial theme of our edited volume, we will now sketch out the key issues: the sustainability of the concept of doubly-free wage-labour, the status of reproductive work, problems immanent to the labour-theory of value, the relationship between monetary theory and value-theory, engagement with different variants of Marxist orthodoxy and the attempt to systematically criticise Marx's approach by confronting it with the labour-relations of the past and the present.

Affirmative, reductionist and critical positions

Before we begin with this overview, we need however to draw attention to those contributions whose authors consider this way of posing the question irrelevant, either because they retain the Marxian approach or because they have principally situated themselves beyond the perspective of the critique of political economy. Gambino's and Sacchetto's essay could be interpreted as affirmative given the way the two authors refer to Marx's reproduction-schemes from *Capital* Volume II: migrant-labour's special importance is illustrated by reference to the increased turnover-rate of labour-power that has been objectified as circulating capital.

Carlo Vercellone assumes an instructive intermediate position. The fulcrum of his argument is constituted by the hypothesis that the labour-time-based 'law of value' is increasingly losing its significance, due to the transition from the Fordist régime of labour and accumulation to the 'immaterial' labour-relations of 'cognitive capitalism'. Vercellone argues that the 'crisis of the law of value' does not create a situation in which labour-power is no longer exploited for the purpose of extracting surplus-value; rather, the 'law of labour-time value' that governed the disciplinary society of Fordism is yielding to the superior 'law of surplus-value'. In support of this claim, Vercellone refers to an observation by Antonio Negri, according to which there have always been two models of the theory of value within the Marxist tradition. The first emphasises the qualitative aspect of the exchange-relation between capital and labour, treating the labour-power that has been transformed into a fictive commodity as abstract labour, the substance and source of value. Alongside this qualitative 'theory of surplus-value', there also exists a 'theory of labour-time value', which treats labour-time as the measure of a commodity's value, thereby limiting itself to the quantitative aspects of the theory of value. According to Vercellone, Marx always thought of the 'labour-time law of value' as a secondary function of the 'law of surplus-value', the crucial 'law of exploitation'. He also points out that the 'law of surplus-value' has the advantage of not being burdened with the mystificatory model-character of 'simple commodity-production'. In fact, the superiority of the 'law of surplus-value' and its character as capitalism's genuine structural invariant are conclusively demonstrated, according to Vercellone, by the current development of the capital-labour relation: production-times become virtually immeasurable, and the surplus-value embodied in the 'goodwill' of 'immaterial capital' is nothing other than the 'intellectual capital' of the workforce.

The prehistory of this approach, the reduction of the theory of value to the essentiality of 'abstract labour' qua 'substance of value', is critically discussed, in this volume, by Tomba and Bellofiore; we return to it below. There is certainly something fascinating about the attempt to refer back selectively to the ontological essentialism of the Marxian theory of value (considered redundant by many value-theorists), in order to justify the hegemonic role of knowledge-work (or 'immaterial' work) in capital's new high-tech sectors. Yet serious objections come to mind, and not just with regard to the degree of 'abstraction' from the complexity and breadth of real class-relations; said objections are also, and in fact primarily, of a methodological nature. What should however be borne in mind is that Vercellone, and the exponents of post-workerism he represents, are at pains to emphasise that if they are fully retaining the theory of surplus-value, they are doing so in order to be able to critically analyse – and develop alternatives to – the intensified exploitation of a largely precarious 'immaterial' labour as it occurs in the context of that labour's 'total subsumption' under capital.

Cornelius Castoriadis and Detlef Hartmann represent the antithesis to this affirmative and/or reductionist invocation of Marx. As Jean-Louis Prat explains, Castoriadis argued, from the 1950s onward, that human labour-power does not have a fixed use- and exchange-value that can be objectively determined. The capitalist who buys a ton of coal knows how much energy may be extracted from it assuming a particular state of technology; but if he or she buys labour-power for a month, it is fundamentally uncertain what the output of that labour-power will be. For labour-power is a human commodity that can oppose its use. For the same reason, labour-power does not have a fixed – scientifically calculable – price, since the height of the wage is not the result of invisible economic laws, but of the relationship of forces between capitalists and workers. What Castoriadis reproached Marx for was therefore that he kept the concept of class-struggle outside his critique of political economy. If one did include the concept of labour-power as a human commodity in the analysis, then all the laws Marx had formulated (labour-value, increase in the organic composition of capital, tendential decrease of the rate of profit) would turn out not to be laws at all, but the more or less accidental result of power-relations and -struggles. From this perspective, the historical process becomes unpredictable and 'open'.

Detlef Hartmann argues in favour of an entirely different perspective. Fundamental considerations lead him to call engagement with the Marxian critique of political economy into question. First, he begins from the observation that the current political economy of capital, an aggressive strategy of 'valorising resistant subjectivity', has left Marxist orthodoxy and indeed most of the left's theoretical approaches far behind, offering this as the reason for the long-standing focus of his own analyses. Second, since only 'revolutionary subjectivity' confronts capital's intensified subordination-strategies, the left's old theory-/practice-dichotomies have also become obsolete. Conceptualisations situated outside the 'context of struggle' are no longer possible and no longer able to access revolutionary subjectivity, since such access is bound up with 'experiencing the confrontations on the various battle-fronts'. Third, from this perspective, past notions of 'value's mechanical self-valorisation' have been exposed as the 'ideology of self-professed socialist elites'. There is no point, according to Hartmann, in reproaching Marx for the fact that the degree to which the rates of surplus-value and profit are prone to crisis is determined by 'struggle', or for the fact that it is not labour-power's character as a commodity that needs to be deciphered as the starting point of social confrontation, but the 'forms of subjugation' and the renewed socio-technological subordination of labour. Consequently, it is not we who are beyond Marx, but the 'mature struggles'. Today, after more than a hundred years of critical reflection on how 'objectivity is systematically generated by abstraction from subjectivity', we are better equipped to deal with Marx's methodological manoeuvres, just as we can move beyond Mario Tronti's 'reductive insistence that labour-power remains the crucial reference-point in all struggles'. We, the editors, view this argument as marking an important limit-point and as indicating the possible fault-lines of any attempt to conceptualise labour-history and -struggles. For this reason, we consider Hartmann's essay an indispensable contribution to the present volume. To what extent Hartmann's implicit rejection of our project *sans phrase* is justified is for the reader to decide. It is up to him or her to weigh Hartmann's system of thought and his language against the approach advocated by us, that of a heterodox and pluralist resumption of the discussion on the 'last things'.

Rejection of the hegemonic position of free wage-labour

But let us turn now to those contributors who are led by the findings of their historico-methodological inquiries to engage critically with 'doubly-free wage-labour' as the key concept within Marx's historical determinism and the labour-theory of value. They are united in their rejection of the 'paleo-Marxist postulate' (Linebaugh and Rediker) that the working class did not develop until the emergence of the factory-system during the 1830s. They also agree in noting that the factory-system and the segments of the working class associated with it have not gone on to become the globally dominant sphere of exploitation, and that they will not do so in the future either. Rather, they agree with Tomba and Bellofiore in recognising that on the level of the world-economy, capital has always combined the most diverse forms of surplus-value extraction, with the past decades seeing it intensify the related tendency to combine the most varied labour-relations. Given these premises, any attempt to subsume the ensemble of capitalist labour-relations under the dominant category 'doubly-free wage-labour' is necessarily moot.

This critical basic tendency is developed in various ways, or from the perspectives of different areas of study. Thus in his reflections on the interpretation of military service as a relation of work and exploitation reminiscent of indentured servitude, Peter Way points out that Marx's concept of primitive accumulation provides an extremely reductive account of the extraordinarily long – and ultimately still incomplete – process by which the direct producers are violently separated from their means of subsistence and production, this being the reason why the ongoing re-emergence of unfree labour escaped him. In fact, the 'triumph of wage-labour' never occurred, and between the two poles of slavery and free labour we find a 'maze of labour-relations and modulations of unfreedom', with a preponderance of relations of exploitation that are unfree, or based upon open or covert violence. Sergio Bologna also emphasises that Marx did not systematically think through the reciprocal transitions from the proletariat to the working class, arguing that there is therefore no point in doing violence to Marx's thought by trying to make it serviceable to comprehension of the labour-relations developing today. Similar comments can also be found in the essays of those contributors who have made an effort to systematically contextualise labour-history and the concept of labour (Meyer and Henninger).

The elision of reproductive work and its consequences

Another key theme is represented by the critique of the Marxian system's neglect of reproductive work. Silvia Federici emphasises that Marx wholly misperceived reproductive work's central position both within the accumulation of capital and within the building of a communist society; he treated the process of reproduction almost as if it were a 'natural process'. This lacuna is all the more astounding as there existed, in his day and age, numerous initiatives that took the process of proletarian reproduction in hand, creating networks of mutual aid that saved

major segments of the class from ruin. Instead of making reference to these experiences, Marx thought of the 'cooperation' between workers as a 'mere effect of
capital', discussing it only with an eye to the efficiency- and productivity-criteria
of the capitalist production-process. Due to his elision of the proletarian experiential horizons of solidary aid and mutual assistance, he was unable to reflect on
the question of what role reproductive work might play within the struggle for a
society not based on exploitation. Marx thought of the prospect of a communist
future purely as resulting from ever more developed capitalist cooperation, to
the point where workers do no more than supervise the machine-system. He
overlooked that even in developed capitalism, a large part of socially necessary
labour consists of reproductive work, which can only be automated to a limited
extent. But because of the extreme degree of alienation it entails, the automati-
sation of reproductive work is also out of the question when it comes to building
a society not based on exploitation.

Like Federici, Maria Mies also points out that reproductive work, performed
mainly by women, is largely absent from Marx's approach. By contrast, in the late
1970s the 'Bielefeld school' of feminism was able to show, according to Mies, that
women, the producers of labour-power, engage not just in reproductive, but also
in productive work and contribute to the creation of surplus-value. Mies argues
that their position within the capitalist system corresponds to that of peasants
in the global South; as subsistence-producers, peasants are equally indispensable
to capital-accumulation. However, the significance of women and the peasants
of the South within patriarchal capitalism is systematically 'overlooked'. What
is true of peasant subsistence-labour is, however, even more true of the creation
of human beings: it is not an unconscious act of nature but a conscious act on
the part of women, who have an overwhelming amount of work to perform
before the children have been raised and can sell their labour-power. Consequently, Mies argues, reproductive work qua reproduction of life and subsistence
is the real work, and stands opposed to value-creation for the purpose of maximising profit. At the same time, capital is only capable of accumulation because
it constantly appropriates non-capitalist forms of subsistence – as first demonstrated by Rosa Luxemburg in her critique of Marx. As a result, it has no choice
but to persistently prolong the process of primitive accumulation, imbibing raw
materials, means of production and workers from the colonies. This process
has been taken so far that today women represent the 'last colonies': capital
has recognised the extraordinary efficiency of female domestic work, and it has
begun to affect the 'housewifisation' of formerly socially protected metropolitan
labour-relations, transforming them into precarious forms of exploitation.

The feminist critique of Marx's model of the political economy of labour, represented here by Federici and Mies, is one that we owe much to; it points us far

beyond the rejection of the determinist approach of 'doubly-free wage-labour'. The feminist critique ought to be considered an integral component of every attempt to expand the concepts of labour and reproduction.

Conceptual deficits of Marx's labour-theory of value

The third main theme within the critical analysis is related to the key concepts of Marx's own system; Thomas Kuczynski and Sebastian Gerhardt question some of the 'fundamental truths of Marxism' (Kuczynski). Kuczynski corrects three essentials of the labour-theory of value. First, he demonstrates that what is normally sold on the labour-market is not labour-power but its employment for a determinate period of time. Since there is no change of owner, this transaction resembles the letting of an apartment; it is a typical relationship between leaser and lessor. Second, Kuczynski emphasises that in the normal case, capital never leases and valorises the living labour-capacity in its entirety; it only transforms those parts into labour-power that are profitable for it. Basic distinctions need therefore to be drawn between the subject, the living labour-capacity that is inextricably bound up with it (qua ensemble of socialised knowledge, skills and abilities) and the labour-power that is actually valorised and remunerated. Third, this observation entails that it is never the entire labour-capacity that is repro-duced within the direct production-process, but only the part that is valorised as labour-power. This means that major components of living labour-capacity need to be reproduced socially, that is, at no cost to capital. At first sight, these insights, achieved by means of a meticulous analysis of the Marxian approach's internal contradictions, seem like mere 'gradualist' corrections. But they are far from being only that; they establish important prerequisites for an expanded reformulation of the labour-theory of value that does justice to the realities of the exploitation-process. The demonstration that it is only on the markets for slaves, indentured servants and serfs that labour-power is sold (along with its bearers), while in every other case it is leased, allows one to situate the complex forms of (pseudo-) self-employed contract- and fee-work within the process of the provi-sion of labour-capacity, thereby methodologically liquidating the false monopoly position of 'doubly-free wage-labour'. Moreover, the distinction between living labour-capacity and labour-power provides a methodological link to the femi-nist discourse on women's usually underpaid reproductive work. And thirdly, the distinction allows us to grasp theoretically the phenomenon – very much in evi-dence today – of highly developed labour-capacity's devalorisation: the labour-capacity of a taxi-driving graduate knowledge-worker is remunerated only to a very limited extent, in addition to being systematically devalorised. The topical-ity and methodological significance of these critical insights is obvious, and so we have decided to include Kuczynski's essay in our volume in spite of it already having been published ten years ago, in a now hard-to-find anthology. Kuczynski had originally agreed to provide us with a summary of the inquiries undertaken by him for the verification and enhancement of the labour-theory of value, but this project took on a life of its own and began developing into a book-length manuscript that would have gone beyond the scope of our edited volume.

Sebastian Gerhardt's reflections on living labour-capacity's unnecessarily 'asymmetrical' position within the capitalist process of production and reproduction are equally stimulating. In Gerhardt's view, the asymmetry is due to Marx according to the worker only closely circumscribed possibilities for freedom. Even if the worker's labour-power is commodified and thereby reified and varlorised, it remains bound up with the subject, according to Gerhardt, and this subject, the worker, is equipped with the ability to decide freely. For this reason, there is always the possibility of linking the ends of labour with a concept of freedom that translates self-determined volition into action, following a critical examination of external circumstances ('freedom in and of itself' in Hegel's sense). Yet this is the very aspect, Gerhardt argues, that Marx neglected. He replaced it with a determinism that attributes the task of transforming social relations not to the proletarian subjects but to the development of the forces of production. Not only did this foster, within the labour-movement, a fatalistic faith in automatic progress; it also led Marx to axiomatically posit a 'law of the tendential fall of the profit-rate' qua objective limitation of the capitalist social formation. Within the actual accumulation of capital, such a law has never operated, according to Gerhardt; the 'law' has been refuted both practically and theoretically. Gerhardt's verdict is unambiguous: subjectivity qua potential freedom of action, 'in and of itself', needs to be reintegrated into the critique of political economy, and the critique of political economy can only reconquer this freedom by seizing upon the altogether different freedoms of 'commanding labour' and uniting it with 'commanded labour', thereby abolishing the hierarchies inherent in the capitalist process of production and reproduction.

The role of money in the labour-theory of value

The fourth main theme within the critical reflections on Marxian theory compiled in this volume may seem odd or at least 'marginal' at first blush, for what is monetary theory to do with the critique of the political economy of labour? That this first impression is misleading becomes clear as soon as we engage with the central propositions of the essays by C. George Caffentzis and Steve Wright. Caffentzis begins his essay by noting that the 'Marx killers' have failed, so far, to latch onto a serious problem faced by Marxian theory: the fact that the August

1971 dropping of the gold-standard refuted a core element of Marxian economics. Marx always assumed, Caffentzis argues, that money qua circulating credit-money can only function for as long as it is linked to gold qua 'world-money' and universal measure of value. Marx held that there was no other way to give expression to and actually measure the average labour-time required for the production of a commodity, this average labour-time being the immanent measure of value. It was precisely this axiomatic relationship that was eliminated in August 1971, when the Federal Reserve abandoned its guarantee to issue gold in return for dollars (at an exchange-rate of one fine ounce per 35 dollars), yet capitalism did not collapse the next day; there has been massive turbulence on currency-markets since, and there have been crises within the capitalist system, but there has been no crisis of the capitalist system itself. How is this to be explained? Caffentzis has an answer. He begins by pointing out that the day the gold-standard was abolished also saw the USA freezing wages and prices. This amounted to recognising the power of the working class to increase real wages, but it also meant that the struggle against working-class 'rigidity' was taken to a new level and rendered far more flexible. The highest historical increase in real wages (1973) was followed three years later – under the administration of Jimmy Carter, a Democrat – by the neoliberal counterattack, which consisted in raising interest-rates. To this 'slight stretching' of Marx's approach to monetary theory – its contextualisation and the reference to the class-struggles of the 1970s – Caffentzis adds a supplementary methodological consideration: it is quite possible to do without Marx's *idée fixe* that capitalism cannot exist without gold-money qua universal money-commodity, since the immanent measure of value (labour-time) remains in effect and can now be expressed in many other measures. Price represents only one of many possible variables; there are also the 'historical' and 'moral economic' standards of value the working class has used alongside credit-money. We should not, however, let these stimulating reflections lead us to assume that we can close the book on the debates about the role the precious metals, qua 'world-money' and universal money-commodity, play for the stabilisation of world-markets and the global financial architecture. These debates continue. They are being conducted behind the closed doors of international institutions, and they are increasingly being weighed against a proposal advanced by the governments of the leading emergent economies: that of creating, under the auspices of the International Monetary Fund and on the basis of an expanded currency-basket, an international deposit-currency.

Steve Wright's essay also starts by historically contextualising capitalist monetary policy by reference to labour-struggles, and he also takes the 1970s as his reference-point. Following the demonetarisation of gold, Italian workerists engaged in a lively debate on money and class-composition. This made sense, for insofar as capitalists use the circulation of money to engage with the working classes, money plays a key role within the class-relation between capital and labour. Understandably, the workerists looked at money through the prism of the wage, something they had learned to do, at the latest, during the labour-struggles of 1968. They considered the wage the decisive index both of the relations of power between the classes and of the new class-composition: not only was it characterised by downward rigidity, and not only did it function as an independent variable of capitalism, but it was also seen by them as an instrument within which the entirety of workplace and non-workplace labour-struggles coalesced, and which could be used to extricate the working class from capital's logic of productivity. In this sense, the wage was everything at once: working hours, work-pace, piecework and premium; in fact, it was the universal expression of counterpower, by means of which labour-power transformed itself, in Mario Tronti's words, into a 'power of attack'. The 'political wage' became the key slogan associated with this model: an increase in monetary income accompanied by a deliberate reduction and curtailment of work-performance, in the sense of a progressive refusal of work. This model struck a nerve: the workerists deconstructed the Marxian axiom of the 'law of the tendential fall of the relative wage', and they did so within a historical constellation that did in fact see relative wages[1] increase, both in the metropoles and in the newly industrialising countries, at a pace far beyond that of productivity increases. Ultimately, the workerists were simply replicating the workers' own refutation, within the social revolts, of a key proposition of Marx's political economy of labour.

To be sure, these goings-on were increasingly halted from the early 1970s onward – following the demonetarisation of money qua 'world-money', money-commodity and basis of the credit-system. The workerists perceived this turning point clearly. Wright discusses the debates conducted in the journal *Primo Maggio* from 1973 onward, exploring how militant theorists engaged with a crucial junction in the labour-struggles of the period and struggled to expand their range of theoretical instruments. As in Caffentzis's *ex post* analysis, the workerists struggled to get a theoretical grip on capitalist monetary policy and the counterattack conducted by means of it. Unfortunately, this debate was soon discontinued; it is nevertheless worth recalling its first partial results. First, it was recognised that interest-rates and the expansive or restrictive monetary policies of the central banks represent a regulatory framework that allows capitalists to

---

1. The relative wage is the share of overall value accrued during a production-period represented by real earnings from dependent labour. When compared to the overall profit earned during the same period (interest, dividend, rent and entrepreneurial profit), it can be used to calculate the monetary expression of the rate of surplus-value. This approach to the measure of relative wages goes back to Jürgen Kuczynski, who performed calculations of this kind for the US trade-union federation AFL. See Roesler 2007.

alter the class-composition on the level of the factory, restoring the conditions for enforcing the provision of labour-capacity: cheap credit and liquidity made it easier for capitalists to smash 'rigid' concentrations of workers in their mammoth factories; at the same time, given sufficient discipline, the deflationary tight-money policy favoured reconcentration and the renewal of the structures of exploitation. Second, the workerists understood that inflationary monetary and price-policies can be used to 'neutralise' high-wage constellations for as long as workers do not adopt countermeasures on the level of reproduction, by engaging in rent-, gas- and electricity-boycotts (as well as food-riots); by the same token, a tight-money policy and high interest-rates facilitate the attack on relative wages on the level of circulation, in addition to liberating entrepreneurial impulses toward the technological and organisational 'rationalisation' of production-processes. Wright is correct in emphasising that the workerist debate failed to shed light on many of the intermediate elements linking the monetary and credit-policies of the capitalist regulation-sphere with the effects of those policies on class-conflict within the sphere of production and reproduction. Nevertheless, the debates on the relationship between money and class-composition that were conducted, between 1973 and 1977, within *Primo Maggio*'s editorial collective (a collective coordinated by Sergio Bologna) deserve to be remembered.

The critique of orthodox Marxism and of post-workerism

In light of the massive and broadly articulated critique of Marx's understanding of labour-history and the concept of labour, it comes as no surprise that the contributors to this volume are anything but gentle in their treatment of orthodox Marxism and its offshoots within the contemporary left. We have already mentioned Linebaugh's and Rediker's ironic comment on the 'paleo-Marxist postulates' of most left-wing labour-historians. Castoriadis criticised not just the inappropriately essentialist and static character of 'abstract labour' and its failure to do justice to the dynamism and variety of real labour-relations; he also repeatedly pointed out the exceptional importance of technological innovations and their relationship to the constantly changing social composition of the working class. Federici laments the way both labour-organisations and the discourses of the Marxist left ignore the problem of elder-care, a key component of metropolitan reproductive work. Bologna invites us to go not just beyond Marx but also beyond the left, since in his view it has proven unable to understand today's transformation of labour-relations. Hartmann castigates the historic legacy bequeathed by 'self-proclaimed Marxist elites' and resolutely rejects all efforts to grasp the condition of the world 'from within the discursive fabric of a left-wing "scientific community"'. And Subir Sinha reports with quiet sarcasm on how India's communist parties are forcing the pace of capitalist development in the interest of an accelerated development of the forces of production – a transparent imitation of the dynamic of China's post-communist executive despotism in waiting.

What about post-workerism? Carlo Vercellone, whose essay is a presentation and defence of the genesis of this current, finds no supporters. We already pointed this out when discussing the linearity of hegemonic worker-types. But the critique goes further. Silvia Federici criticises the post-workerists for the failure of their concept of 'affective and immaterial labour' to do justice to feminist analyses of reproductive work under capitalism. She argues that the post-workerists have thoroughly blurred the distinction between production and reproduction and are suggesting that labour now produces nothing but special states ('affects') and immaterial objects. To classify smiling flight-attendants as 'affective workers' is to overlook that reproductive workers need to engage comprehensively with those they reproduce, so that the physical and the affective elements of their labour are rendered indistinguishable. More seriously, the post-workerists continue to ignore the still largely unremunerated reproductive work of women and its exploitative character, according to Federici.

Massimiliano Tomba and Riccardo Bellofiore address the prehistory of post-workerist notions of hegemonic 'immaterial' and 'affective' labour; their essay might even be read as a partial self-critique within Marxist heterodoxy. When, in 1964, the *Quaderni rossi* published a translation of the so-called 'Fragment on machines',[2] the document was enthusiastically received by the workerists. It seemed to provide the surplus of subjectivity that was absent elsewhere in Marx, a surplus the workerists needed in order to successfully fight back the orthodoxy of the Communist Party. This was the beginning of a lengthy and convoluted reception-history, one characterised mainly by serious misunderstandings. Within the context of this volume, we are especially interested in the variant of heretical exegesis that paved the way for post-workerism. Simplifying somewhat, we can say it began with Marx's prophecy that by making ever greater use of science, capitalist machinery will develop to such an extent that the labour-time required for the production of commodities tends toward zero; by broadly impacting on the development of society's forces of production, science will also give rise to the 'general intellect' required for the supervision and control of the increasingly automated production-process.

The prediction was – and continues to be – fascinating. Not only does it anticipate the crisis of the Fordist process of exploitation; it could also be used to interpret the resulting processes of fragmentation and the student-worker

---

2. Marx 1973, pp. 692–706.

revolts by which they were accompanied. All one needed to do was posit a 'crisis of the law of value' – a law Marx had not even formulated at the time he was writing the *Grundrisse*, at least not in a way that went beyond the paradigms of classical political economy – in order then to separate the concept of class from its value-theoretical labour-time determination. The steps leading from the mass-worker to the socialised worker (*operaio sociale*) and then on to the immaterial worker of the post-workerists' 'cognitively' transformed capitalism are retraced by Tomba and Bellofiore. Their essay is a gripping piece of heretical history, whose protagonists insist, to this day, on tracing their model back to Marx. We have pointed out the methodological reductionism this involves in our discussion of Vercellone's essay – part of whose importance lies in the fact that it presents the post-workerist workshop's methodological instruments in a logically stringent manner.

Elements of a comprehensive historico-methodological critique

At the end of this section, we wish to refer to two contributions whose authors have set themselves the task of questioning the status of labour within Marx's critique of political economy by confronting that critique with the proletarian multiverse's historical and contemporary contexts. Ahlrich Meyer begins by invoking socio- and theorico-historical findings about the composition of the proletarian lower classes and their 'logic of revolts' during the first half of the nineteenth century. He uses these insights to verify a hypothesis first formulated by Karl Korsch in 1929, namely that the working class's disappearance from the conceptual logic of Marx's political economy needs to be understood as a response to the historical defeat of 1848–9.[3] In fact, this conclusion becomes difficult to avoid once one recognises that neither the extraordinary heterogeneity of the period's class-composition nor the virulence of the anticapitalist struggles for subsistence and the right to existence are reflected in Marx's critique of political economy. Instead, Marx drew on classical bourgeois economics and occupied himself with the riddle bequeathed by it, namely that workers do not receive, in their wages, the full value of the quantity of labour that has been objectified in their products. Like others before him, Marx assumed that the value of labour-power is determined by the price of the means of subsistence required by the worker and his family. Like his predecessors Adam Smith and David Ricardo, he considered labour-power a commodity for which the 'law of value' holds true. In other words, he treated the quantity of labour required for the production of the means of subsistence and the reproduction of the worker as the standard

---

3. Korsch 1974.

by which to determine the worker's reproductive costs. This was a consequential pseudo-solution. It led to the subsistence of the poor and of workers being incorporated into capital. It also meant that while there remained a 'moral and historical' residuum that defied straightforward categorisation, this subsistence now remained within a closely circumscribed range, so that its price-form, the wage, was degraded to the status of a secondary variable, with Marx even going so far as to reject the Ricardian socialists' egalitarian interpretation of the labour-theory of value. Thus the working class vanished inside the capital-relation in multiple ways, and it was expected to remain thus 'concealed' until the blasting apart of the relations of production by the development of the forces of production, at which point the working class, unified by capital, would appropriate the means of production. According to Meyer, the pathos of revolution had become a sober analysis of the anatomy of bourgeois society, which had successfully subordinated the working class.

Working from these premises, Marx succeeded in superating the contradiction that had until then characterised the classical labour-theory of value: he separated the exchange-value of labour-power (its wage-function) from its use-value (adding new value to the product) and introduced the distinction between socially necessary labour and surplus-labour. By thus demonstrating that labour-power is the source of value and the creator of surplus-value, Marx became the last exponent of classical political economy. But the price to be paid for this solution was high. The entire problematic of the reproduction of the working class was transferred within capital; the class-contradiction was objectified and would henceforth appear only as the ratio of constant to variable capital (or to labour-power's reproduction-costs). While the subjective bearers of labour-power had not disappeared altogether, they remained bound up with the dialectic of necessary and surplus-labour, and the theory of wages did not get beyond classical political economy's concept of reproduction-costs, that is, it remained very limited. There was no longer anything in the objectified 'regularities' of political economy for the theory of revolution to latch onto. In this sense, Marxian political economy did more than merely theorise the proletarian defeat of 1848–9; it also extended that defeat into the future, because the constitution of the revolutionary subject no longer featured within it.

Supplementing Meyer, Max Henninger confronts three core elements of Marx's critique of political economy – poverty, labour, development – with the constitution of the proletarian multiverse of the present. In doing so, he demonstrates that the selected methodological and analytic parameters are largely deficient. First, Marx always defined poverty from the perspective of labour, or from the perspective of its industrial reserve-function; in his polemic against Malthus, he attributed the dynamic of poverty exclusively to the relative displacement of labour that results from the progress of capital-accumulation (relative surplus-population). But neither historical nor contemporary mass-poverty can be defined purely by reference to the preconditions of capital-accumulation, Henninger argues. An orienting survey of the logic of subsistence-production, the informal sector, population-control and endemic hunger reveals that far more complex forces are at work. The peasant subsistence-economy of the South and the welfare-transfers of the metropoles allow capitalism to keep a significant share of total reproduction-costs off the wage bill. Moreover, the agricultural labour-displacement resulting from the 'Green Revolution' has not given rise to an urban industrial proletariat, Henninger argues. The rising birth-rates evident during the transition from peasant subsistence-production to other forms of family-based small enterprise reveal an autonomy of reproductive behaviour that has been eliminated from the Marxian reproduction-schemes, as those schemes recognise human beings engaging in reproductive activity only as objects of the reproduction of capital.

Henninger arrives at a similarly negative conclusion in his discussion of the Marxian concept of labour. Contrary to Marx's axiomatic stipulations about doubly-free wage-labour, the processes of proletarianisation continue to this day, and this involves the constitution of more than one working class, as can be seen especially clearly in the case of China. At the centre of these developments lies the overexploitation of workers who are mostly female. This overexploitation is accompanied, in a constellation already evident during the industrialisation of Europe, by the allocation of unremunerated reproductive work. Ultimately, Henninger argues, it is the various forms of remunerated and unremunerated, domestic and extra-domestic women's work that dominate the world over, a fact that needs to inform every new attempt at conceptualising global labour, rather than continuing to be ignored.

Henninger's reflections on the Marxian concept of development are also note-worthy. They go beyond critical rejection of Marx's determinist tenet that the most developed national economies assign other countries their developmen-tal paths, exposing a number of other serious deficits. The Marxian concept of development was soon given the lie, according to Henninger, by the evidence of the historical processes. It was Rosa Luxemburg who refuted Marx's faith in progress, noted the violence of a perpetually renewed 'primitive accumulation' (the pillage of non-capitalist domains) and imagined the formation's terminal phase as a 'period of catastrophe'. In discussing these issues, Henninger draws attention to an important phenomenon that Marx and Luxemburg refer to only in passing: the appropriation of the economic and currency-potentials of fully developed capitalist economies by rival imperialist powers in the course of war, a development that goes far beyond colonialism's 'asymmetrical' policy of force. These reflections supplement Frykman's and Way's historical analyses of (forced) military labour 'from above' and should be taken into consideration in every attempt to enhance the critique of the political economy of labour.

Karl Marx and the problem of slave-labour

Before we turn to the synopsis of our contributors' proposals for a renewal of the political economy of labour or the development of an alternative concept of revolution, we wish to critically review the Marxian theory of value ourselves. We will do so by reference to the problem of slave-labour. We have already pointed out in our Introduction that the Marxian concept of class rests on exclusion. It is only the 'pure' doubly-free wage-workers who are able to create value; from a strategic perspective, all other parts of the world's working populations are secondary. We will use the problem of slave-labour to demonstrate just how problematic this perspective is.

As is well known, Marx engaged with issues related to slave-labour in many passages of his work. Marx was more aware of the contrast between 'free' wage-labour and slavery than most twenty-first-century Marxists. As an expert on European antiquity and as a contemporary to the American Civil War, Marx was very much aware of the slavery-problem.[4] *Capital* Volume I was published two years after the abolition of slavery in the United States in 1865 and 21 years before it was officially proclaimed in Brazil. Marx considered slavery a historically backward mode of exploitation that would soon be a thing of the past, as 'free' wage-labour embodied the capitalist future. He compared the two labour-forms in several writings. He certainly saw similarities between them – both produced a surplus-product and 'the wage-labourer, just like the slave, must have a master to make him work and govern him'.[5] At the same time, he distinguished some differences that overshadowed all the common experiences they shared. We will offer some brief critical comments on them and indicate our doubts.

First: wage-workers dispose of labour-capacity, viz. 'the aggregate of those mental and physical capabilities existing in the physical form, the living personality, of a human being, capabilities which he sets in motion whenever he produces a use-value of any kind'[6] – and this labour-capacity is the source of value; the capitalist purchases this labour-capacity as a commodity, because he expects it to provide him with a 'specific service', namely the creation of 'more

---

4. Backhaus 1974; Ste. Croix 1975; Lekas 1988; Reichardt 2004.
5. Marx 1981, p. 510.
6. Marx 1976, p. 270.

value than it has itself'.[7] The same is not true of the slave's labour-capacity. The slaveholder 'has paid cash for his slaves', and so 'the product of their labour represents the interest on the capital invested in their purchase'.[8] But since interest is nothing but a form of surplus-value, according to Marx,[9] it would seem that slaves would have to produce surplus-value. And it is a fact that the sugar-plantations on which slave-labour was employed yielded considerable profits, because the commodity of sugar embodied more value than the capital invested by the plantation-owner (ground-rent, amortisation of the slaves, amortisation of the sugar-cane press and so on). So is it really the case that only the wage-worker produces the equivalent of his/her own value plus 'an excess, a surplus-value'?[10] Or is the slave a 'source of value' as well?

Second: Marx states that labour-power can 'appear on the market as a commodity only if, and in so far as, its possessor, the individual whose labour-power it is, offers it for sale or sells it as a commodity. In order that its possessor may sell it as a commodity, he must have it at his disposal, he must be the free proprietor of his own labour-capacity, hence of his person'.[11] The future wage-worker and the money-owner 'meet in the market, and enter into relations with each other on a footing of equality as owners of commodities, with the sole difference that one is a buyer, the other a seller; both are therefore equal in the eyes of the law'.[12] In other words: labour-power should be offered for sale by the person who is the carrier and possessor of this labour-power and the person who sells the labour-power offers it exclusively. Why should that be so? Why can the labour-power not be sold by someone other than the carrier, as for example in the case of children who are made to perform wage-labour in a factory by their parents? Why can the person who offers (his or her own, or someone else's) labour-power for sale not sell it conditionally, together with means of production? And why can someone who does not own his own labour-power nevertheless sell this labour-power, as in the case of rented slaves, whose owners provide them to someone else for a fee?[13]

---

7. Marx 1976, p. 301.
8. Marx 1981, p. 762.
9. 'Rent, interest, and industrial profit are only different names for different parts of the surplus value of the commodity, or the unpaid labour enclosed in it, and they are equally derived from this source and from this source alone'. Marx 1975–2004e, p. 133.
10. Marx 1976, p. 317.
11. Marx 1976, p. 271.
12. Ibid.
13. Marx was quite aware of this practice of renting slaves, but he drew no theoretical conclusions from it. See for example: Marx 1981, p. 597: 'Under the slave system the worker does have a capital value, namely his purchase price. And if he is hired out, the hirer must first pay the interest on this purchase price and on top of this replace the capital's annual depreciation'.

Third: the wage-worker embodies variable capital:

> It both reproduces the equivalent of its own value and produces an excess, a surplus value, which may itself vary, and be more or less according to circumstances. This part of capital is continually being transformed from a constant into a variable magnitude. I therefore call it the variable part of capital, or more briefly, variable capital.[14]

'It is only because labour is presupposed in the form of wage-labour, and the means of production in the form of capital (that is, only as a result of this specific form of these two essential agents of production), that one part of the value (product) presents itself as surplus-value and this surplus-value presents itself as profit (rent), the gains of the capitalist, as additional available wealth belonging to him'.[15] To Marx, the slave is part of fixed capital and no different, economically, from livestock or machinery. 'The slave-owner buys his worker in the same way as he buys his horse'.[16] The slave's capital-value is his purchasing price, and this capital-value has to be amortised over time, just as with livestock and machinery.[17] But how justified is Marx in defining only wage-labour as variable capital, on the grounds that 'this part of capital' can 'be more or less'?[18] Is the same not true of commodity-producing slave-labour?

Fourth: when the wage worker produces a commodity, this commodity is 'a unity formed of use-value and value', for which reason 'the process of production must be a unity, composed of the labour process and the process of creating value [*Wertbildungsprozess*]'.[19] No one will doubt that slaves producing cane-sugar, tobacco or indigo are producing commodities, just like wage-workers. But if this is the case, then slaves also produce value. Marx denies this, since he considers slaves part of constant capital and holds that only variable capital creates value.

Fifth: the wage-worker always divests himself of his labour-power 'for a limited period only, for if he were to sell it in a lump, once and for all, he would be selling himself, converting himself from a free man into a slave, from an owner

---

14. Marx 1976, p. 317.
15. Marx 1981, p. 1021. This is why surplus-labour appears in two very different forms in these two cases. In the case of wage-labour, the wage-form eradicates 'every trace of the division of the working day into necessary labour and surplus labour, into paid labour and unpaid labour'. Marx 1976, p. 680. By contrast, in the case of slave-labour, 'even the part of the working day in which the slave is only replacing the value of his own means of subsistence, in which he therefore actually works for himself alone, appears as labour for his master. All his labour appears as unpaid labour'. Marx 1976, p. 680.
16. Marx 1976, p. 377; the *Grundrisse* contains a similar passage: Marx 1973, pp. 489–90.
17. Marx 1981, p. 597.
18. Marx 1976, p. 317.
19. Marx 1976, p. 293.

of a commodity into a commodity'.[20] Normally, one would refer to such a transaction (the 'sale' of a commodity in installments, without any change of owner) as a lease and not as a sale – an obvious idea that was already formulated much earlier.[21] The distinction between a lease and a sale may appear insignificant, but it is not. 'When a sales-contract is closed, the substance of the commodity becomes the property of the other party, whereas when a lease-contract is closed, the other party merely purchases the right to use the commodity; the seller only makes his commodity available temporarily, without relinquishing ownership of it', as Franz Oppenheimer has rightly noted.[22] When A sells B a commodity, B becomes the owner in lieu of A. But when A leases B a commodity, A remains the owner and B merely receives the right to use the commodity for a fixed term. The 'substance' of the commodity remains with A, whereas B receives its 'use and enjoyment'.[23] Thus, if wage-labour is the leasing of labour-power, the difference between a wage-worker and a slave does not consist in the 'definite period of time'[24] for which labour-power is made available, but in the fact that in one case, labour-power is leased, while in the other it is sold. Why do we not find this consideration in Marx? Presumably because it makes the process of value-creation appear in a different light. The substance of the value of labour-power is retained by the worker rather than being yielded to the capitalist. Engels held that lease-transactions are 'only a transfer of already *existing*, previously *produced* value, and the total sum of values possessed by the landlord and the tenant *together* remains the same after as it was before'.[25] Thus if wage-labour were a lease-relation as well, it could not create surplus-value.

Sixth: according to Marx, the rate of profit tends to decline because the social productivity of labour increases constantly: 'Since the mass of living labour applied continuously declines in relation to the mass of objectified labour that sets it in motion, that is, the productively consumed means of production, the

20. Marx 1976, p. 271.

21. Marx himself referred repeatedly to the analogy between rent and wage-labour. He did so most extensively in the *Theories of Surplus Value*, where he writes that the worker is paid for his commodity (his labour-capacity) only after he has finished working: 'It can also be seen that here it is the worker, not the capitalist, who does the advancing, just as in the case of the renting of a house, it is not the tenant but the landlord who advances use-value'. Marx 1975–20040, p. 302; see also Marx 1976, p. 279: 'The price of the labour-power is fixed by the contract, although it is not realized till later, like the rent of a house'. On this, see also Thomas Kuczynski's contribution to this volume.

22. Oppenheimer 1912, p. 120.

23. Differently from what Oppenheimer believed – '[...] only the labour-capacity that is intended for sale (e.g. that of the work ox, the slave) is a commodity, not that intended merely for lease' (Oppenheimer 1912, p. 121) – a lease-contract also operates according to the logic of the commodity; this is precisely why the leasing fee depends on the value of the leased commodity.

24. Marx 1976, p. 271.

25. Engels 1975–2004h, p. 320.

part of this living labour that is unpaid and objectified in surplus-value must also stand in an ever-decreasing ratio to the value of the total capital applied'.[26] The endpoint of this tendency would of course be a situation in which variable capital has been reduced to zero and total capital consists exclusively of constant capital. In such a situation, the collapse of capitalism would be a fact. But the odd thing is that there already existed such a terminal phase prior to the industrial revolution, namely on the plantations of the seventeenth and eighteenth centuries. These plantations employed slave-labour, so that according to Marx's premises, total capital consisted exclusively of constant capital. How are we to account for the economic dynamism of the plantations on this basis?

The example of slave-labour shows Marx did not provide a consistent justification for the privileged position productive wage-labour is given within his theory of value. There is much to suggest that slaves and wage-workers are structurally more similar than Marx and traditional Marxism suspected. The historical reality of capitalism has featured many hybrid and transitional forms between slavery and 'free' wage-labour. Moreover, slaves and wage-workers have repeatedly performed the same work in the same business-enterprise.[27] It is true, of course, that the slave's labour-capacity is the permanent property of the capitalist, whereas the wage-worker only makes his labour-capacity available to the capitalist for a limited time, even if he does so repeatedly. It remains unclear, however, why slaves should create no surplus-value while wage-workers do. The time has come to expand the theory of value in such a way as to recognise the productive labour of slaves and other unfree workers as an essential component of the capitalist economy.

The contributors' arguments for and against extending the critique of the political economy of labour

The critique of labour's status within Marx's historical and economic thought, which we have summarised in the two preceding sections, is impressive. Most of our contributors reject the construct of doubly-free wage-labour's primacy and the associated notion of a succession of hegemonic labour-relations. The elision of reproductive work this involves is judged by them to constitute a serious flaw. Some of the labour-theory of value's most elementary key concepts do not hold up to critical scrutiny and need to be rejected because they entail an objectification of the bearers of living labour-capacity. Orthodox Marxists have failed to eliminate these deficits, tending to aggravate them instead, and the same is true

---

26. Marx 1981, p. 319.

27. Such as on the coffee-plantations around São Paulo, or in a chemical factory in Baltimore. Hall and Stolcke 1983; Whitman 1993.

of the 'heretical' exegesis of certain fragments of Marx's work. It is quite clear that the defeat of the proletarian mass-uprisings of Marx's time was 'ratified' by him within economic theory. He also extended this defeat into the future, such that the realities of the contemporary multiverse cannot be grasped by means of his concepts of poverty, labour and development. But the same is true of the phenomenon of slave-labour, an extremely violent form of exploitation that is currently experiencing a renaissance – even if contemporary slavery tends not to be permanent.

Given these findings, does it even make sense to refer back to the last classic of political economy in order to attempt to develop the labour-theory of value into a dynamic critique of the political economy of labour, one that represents the antagonism of workers and capital in a balanced and 'open-ended' way? Most contributors to this volume do not think so. Cornelius Castoriadis already reached the conclusion that if one wants to remain a revolutionary, one needs to abandon Marxism. He called for a new, critical theory of society that does not identify the contradiction between the social form of production and private ownership of the means of production as the fundamental problem of capital-ist society, but rather situates that fundamental problem within the sphere of production itself. In every firm and in every office, Castoriadis stated, there is a permanent struggle between the managers, who want to make everyone work as hard and as well as possible, and the blue- and white-collar workers who are alienated from their work. Management faces a fundamental problem: it is impossible to formulate all-encompassing rules and regulations which prescribe all work tasks for all personnel. A minimum-space is always needed for impro-visation and individuality, since there is no such thing as total knowledge of all people and all situations. Therefore, a certain effort is also always required from the workers, an effort that goes further than the official requirements. Hence the paradoxical fact that the production-process stops in very short order as soon as everyone does exactly what they are supposed to do and acts according to management-rules. This is also the explanation for the possibility of 'working-to-rule'. While management is forced to appeal for the cooperation of the staff, it continually tries to limit this room for irregular activity. But management can never succeed in entirely reducing humans to robots.

Sergio Bologna also warns against treating Marx as a prophet and turning Marxism into a religion, arguing that it is only workerism's instruments of inquiry that have withstood the test of time and might therefore be used to promote a new association of knowledge-workers. Detlef Hartmann sees nothing worth picking up on either: it is only from the immediate experiences that revolution-ary subjectivity garners in its struggle against capital's most recent valorisation-strategies that new social-revolutionary prospects for asserting the right to existence can arise. Max Henninger's verdict is also negative: in his view, any perspective that is oriented toward liberation from oppression, subordination and exploitation needs to distance itself from key elements of Marx's theory. The illusion that history's devastations will necessarily be followed by a 'realm of freedom' has been lost forever, and it is equally illusionary, according to Henninger, to engage in 'desperate attempts to rescue Marx's theorems' in order to 'reassert a concept of revolution that fails to do justice to the composition of the world's underclasses and rests on a teleological and reductive account of the dynamics of the capitalist-process'. A similarly negative conclusion is reached by Ahlrich Meyer, although Meyer does implicitly indicate weaknesses of Marx's approach whose conceptual elimination – by linking the theory of wages to the theory of surplus-value, superating the asymmetric and static character of the concept of reproduction and making class-subjectivity a cornerstone of the critique of political economy – might allow for the development of a social-revolutionary perspective oriented toward a guaranteed right to existence and an egalitarian distribution of goods.

Silvia Federici and Maria Mies also hold that there is nothing in the Marxian system that one could pick up on. But like Castoriadis before them (albeit adopting a different procedure), they search for positive alternatives beyond Marx's obsolete concept of labour and his labour-theory of value. Federici indicates the strategic role of the reproduction-sphere, where workers – still, or once again – belong to themselves, locating it at the centre of the class-struggle. It is here, she argues, that the new subjectivity develops, this being the first objective of political organisation. By shifting the focus of the emancipatory perspective from commodity-production to the production of human beings and from the factory to the household and the city-quarter, the women's movement rendered possible an extension of the radical traditions of transforming everyday life. Maria Mies also subscribes to this approach, but she gives it a global dimension by relating it to peasant subsistence-production in the Global South. In doing so, she broadens the concept of subsistence, using it to refer not just to the economics of self-sufficiency, but also to the 'celebration of self-regenerating, creative and autonomous life', which advances the reconstruction of a 'different economy and society, one congenial to women, nature and human beings'. For it is not wage-labour but only subsistence in this broad sense that is opposed to capital, according to Mies, and capital is constantly striving to commercialise subsistence. This tendency gives subsistence-production its decisive frontline-position, establishing the antagonism between it and commodity and surplus-value production. Qua production of life, subsistence-production 'encompasses all work performed during the creation and maintenance of immediate life, to the extent that such work is directed towards no other purpose'. But it is not an anthropocentric concept, according to Mies; it expresses life's continuity with nature, its material foundation. Mies holds that the revolutionary process breaks with the development of labour's forces of production. The infinite progression of labour-productivity is done away with and the era of happiness begins: a happiness that is situated within necessity and replaces enslavement, immiseration and proletarianisation with freedom, dignity and the preservation of the cycle of life. Mies holds that in this way, the generalisation of wage-labour and the universalisation of the welfare-state can be transcended in favour of the emergence of new regional and autonomous economies, which would be linked by a new internationalism.

An altogether different approach is chosen by Carlo Vercellone, who also elaborates on the practical consequences of his analysis. In doing so, he likewise moves far beyond the core element of orthodox Marxism, namely the notion that the development of the forces of production results, more or less automatically, in the superation of the relations of production. He begins from the fact that the new labour-relations of 'cognitive capitalism' necessarily entail an extremely segmented and dualist recomposition of the working class, such that the overwhelming majority of workers is subject to constant downgrading and forced into precarious employment. Vercellone argues that in countering this destructive dynamic, one should start from capital's reluctant recognition that the value-creating potential of a labour that has become creative, polyvalent and innovative needs to be granted greater autonomy. This might serve as the basis for opposing to capital new structures of the 'common', democratically reconquering the institutions of the welfare-state and using the 'dynamic of association and self-management already traversing society' as the starting point for an alternative model of development. Since the production of the general intellect increasingly involves man becoming fixed capital, one can derive from this a logic that transcends the law of value, using it and the increasingly collective nature of value- and wealth-creation to struggle for the introduction of a 'guaranteed social income'. Such a social income would express both the antagonist and the complementary character of productive labour, according to Vercellone. Moreover, it would clear the way for a recomposition of the totality of workers, reduce the monetary pressure to enter into a wage-relation and point the way to the liberation of labour from the sphere of value and surplus-value production.

Understandably, such alternative models are foreign to those who believe the Marxian paradigm can and should be developed further in a critical manner. This position is taken by two contributors to this volume, Thomas Kuczynski and Sebastian Gerhardt. Kuczynski remains somewhat guarded; his first priority is that of eliminating false conceptual certainties and superating the internal contradictions of the Marxian approach. We noted above that our invitation to contribute to this volume has prompted him to attempt to systematise and expand his earlier considerations on the labour-theory of value, understood as the basis of every critique of the political economy of labour; we look forward to the results. By comparison, Sebastian Gerhardt goes one step further. He emphasises the urgency of reintroducing the subject into the system of the critique of political economy, whose value-theoretical foundation he does not question, although he feels it needs to be revised and enhanced. This step is essential, however, for there is no other way to superate the distinction between 'commanding' and 'commanded labour', without which the capitalist social formation cannot be overcome. Consequently, the rehabilitation of the proletarian subjects who employ their freedom in and of itself needs to be accompanied by a consistent revitalisation of workers' education. For capitalism will not superate itself, Gerhardt insists; its superation needs to be advanced via the cultivation of 'political subjectivity' within the working class. It is only when the class is aware that it will one day need to take over 'the whole joint' and begin working quite differently from today that it will be able to begin engaging in solidary resistance against capital. It is here that the dimensions of a critical renewal are situated, according to Gerhardt: 'An up-to-date, genuine critique of the political economy of labour looks toward the common liberty of each and all, in and for itself'.

Can the critique of the Marxian concept of labour be formulated positively? Contours of a dynamic labour-theory of value

The above summary of our contributors' critical reflections on the status of labour-history and the concept of labour within the Marxian system makes it seem quite doubtful whether that system can continue to serve as a reference-point for considerations on the development of a dynamic critique of the political economy of labour. Thus it comes as no surprise that most contributors who address this issue – Sergio Bologna, Silvia Federici, Detlef Hartmann, Max Henninger, Ahlrich Meyer, Maria Mies and Peter Way – explicitly or implicitly reject this option. Given the massiveness of the problems and in particular the deterministically objectifying approach of Marx's critique of political economy, this seems quite understandable. Nor would this precarious basic constellation change significantly if it were to emerge, after the completion of the Marx/Engels 'Gesamtausgabe', that the final years of Marx's life saw him not only doubting the stringency of his approach but also striving to make substantial corrections. We may expect just this to emerge: a careful reading of Marx's drafts for a reply to Vera Zasulich's query about the possibility of a socialist revolution without prior capitalist development[28] shows that Marx not only ended up endorsing

---

28. Marx 1975–2004a3, pp. 346–69.

the Social Revolutionaries' model of agrarian revolution but also began to question the applicability of his former determinist approach to other contexts. For example, his remark that the 'vandalism' of British rule aggravated the famines in India by destroying the country's subsistence-economy without bringing about capitalist development[29] is hardly compatible with the axiom that the most industrialised capitalist countries dictate to the lower-ranking national economies their future development. But even if it should emerge that Marx's engagement with the long depression of the 1870s and its effects on the socio-economic development of India, Russia and the United States prompted him to distance himself from the objectifying tendencies of his middle period and caused him to return, in a sense, to his social-revolutionary early period, this would make little difference to the issue that concerns us here.[30] Such a discovery would merely help accelerate a conceptual clearing out of the Marxian critique of political economy that has been overdue for more than a century, helping us to answer the question of whether we should renounce said critique altogether or whether we should boldly attempt to include workers, the bearers of living labour-capacity, within a dynamically expanded critique of political economy that recognises them as the equal antagonists of surplus-value-extracting objectified labour. In what follows, we will present some basic considerations that we feel such a synthesis cannot do without. In doing so, we are also attempting to give the present volume a forward-looking conclusion. We will make reference not only to the arguments presented by the five contributors who have endorsed an extension of the Marxian approach – C. George Caffentzis, Sebastian Gerhardt, Thomas Kuczynski, Massimiliano Tomba and Riccardo Bellofiore – but also to the critical insights of those contributors who believe such an extension to be a futile undertaking.

An emancipatory critique of the political economy of labour should start from two elementary premises: first, a definition of exploitation and of the totality of exploited classes; second, a conceptual clarification of what the production- and reproduction-process of a society without exploitation might look like. Starting from these two poles, it should then be possible to work out the main structural elements of a dynamic and open-ended critique of the political economy of labour.

Definition of exploitation

The term 'exploitation' should be defined as broadly as possible. It should refer to three interrelated processes: first, the violent expropriation of the direct

---

29. Marx 1975–2004cc, pp. 364–9.
30. Anderson 2010.

producers' means of subsistence and production; second, the conversion – sometimes more violent, sometimes less – of these expropriated persons and their propertyless descendants into people who are expected to offer their labour-capacity for sale and make it available for heteronomously determined purposes (schools, barracks, re-education camps); third, the process of labour-capacity actually being made available and valorised. A special case of exploitation is represented by humans being forced to make their labour-capacity available for the purpose of extracting a surplus-product, because they require the compensation given them in return to support themselves. All persons who find themselves within the embattled process of expropriation, disciplining and employment/valorisation of their labour-capacity, constitute the global proletariat, the multiverse of the exploited. Those among them who find themselves in the equally embattled process of the exploitation and valorisation of their labour-capacity constitute the working classes of the multiverse or the global working class. What should always be borne in mind when utilising or referring to this definition is that the concept of labour also refers to reproductive activities: there are remunerated and unremunerated relations of exploitation in the sphere of reproduction as well, as demonstrated some time ago by the feminist debate on exploitation within the family. This terrain is increasingly being 'discovered' and occupied by capital. The childcare-worker in a nursery and the care-workers in Taylorised senior citizens' homes are exploited no less than the shiftworkers in a steel-factory, and an unemployed surrogate mother who gives birth to a test-tube baby in return for financial compensation is also being exploited as a reproductive worker.

In parallel to this, we should also define the concept of 'exploitation' negatively. What might such a definition look like? Can we say, for example, that as a rule, only those people are exploited who do not exploit others? This is by no means clear: patriarchal peasant- and worker-families display internal structures of exploitation that are stabilised and reinforced by external factors (extreme poverty, the failure to take account of reproductive work when determining workers' remuneration). Yet aside from these internal structures of 'introjected' exploitation – whose relevance to any process of self-emancipation is considerable – we can draw a clear dividing line between the exploited and their exploiters: whoever is not active as an exploiter at one or more of exploitation's five socio-economic junctions (appropriation of the personality, the labour-capacity, the means of labour and subsistence, the products and the reproductive sphere of other people) does not belong to the classes and strata of the exploiters. Of course, one cannot conclude from this that they are themselves being exploited. The latter question can be decided only on the basis of our positive definition of the concept of exploitation.

A third step toward the concretisation and clarification of the interrelationship between exploitation and the concept of class consists, in our view, in classifying relations of exploitation in terms of how the exploiting classes gain access to the proletarian multiverse. Both historically and with reference to the present, we can distinguish between five levels, based on the area of social life on which access occurs. First, the exploiters can seize upon the exploited as a person, transforming him or her into a slave, indentured servant, serf, forced labourer or contract-worker. Second, they can limit themselves to seizing upon his or her labour-capacity, either purchasing it for a fixed term (leasing it) or binding it to themselves and valorising it by some other contractual agreement (such as fee-agreements). Third, they can decide either to make work-equipment and work-objects available to the exploited or to allow the exploited to retain this equipment and these objects (self-employed workers), using other unequal contracts to establish control over labour-capacity (contract-farming, exploitation of peasant-families by means of unequal trade-contracts, extortionate rates of interest and so on). Fourth, they can seize the labour-product, either in whole or in part, without paying for it. Fifth, they can proceed to place the reproduction-processes of the exploited under their control as well (company housing-estates and company-dwellings, regulations on generative reproduction and internal family-structures and so on). In most cases, the exploiters and their functionaries will combine several of these access-points, in addition to differentiating them from one another. The result is an extraordinary multiplicity and multifacetedness of the constellations of exploitation, so that the most varied constitutive forms of dependent labour coexist even within small firms and closely delimited local constellations, not to speak of the vast number of relations of exploitation that make up the global valorisation-chains of the present.

Labour as an active life-process for the satisfaction of the needs of an autonomous society

Before setting out to expand and enhance the critique of political economy, we should supplement our conventions on the concepts of exploitation and class by reaching an agreement on what a society might look like in which people produce and reproduce their own self-determined social existence by producing, consuming and renewing the requisite useful objects and social states (use-values) as freely associated individuals. In other words, we are assuming, both explicitly and implicitly, that the provision of labour-capacity and the products of labour to capital has ceased, or that the domination of living labour by objectified labour has come to an end. Starting from these basic assumptions, we should recall that nature and labour, qua active life-process of an autonomous society, are the two elementary prerequisites for the creation, consumption and reproduction of wealth. This insight into the twofold foundation of a social life-process that has been liberated from oppression, hierarchies and exploitation is of elementary importance, for there are natural limits to the process by which needs develop in an autonomous society that is oriented toward the right to existence. Consequently, we can distinguish, within the reproductive model of a society free of domination and exploitation, between four significant and interrelated levels of reproduction. First, there is the level of the social process of reproduction itself, a process that develops with the development of needs. Second, there is the level of the requisite consumption and reproduction-goods. The third level is that of the reproduction of the natural resources consumed and of the minimisation of the damage done to the bio- and geospheres by the three other levels. The fourth and last level is that of the reproduction of the means of production (work-equipment and work-objects) needed for the expanded repro-duction of the three other levels of reproduction and of the fourth level itself.[31] This model represents a radical reversal of the expanded capitalist reproduction-process, for it is not governed by the accumulation of labour as an end in itself, qua 'infinite' extraction of surplus-value and conversion of surplus-value into capital; instead, society's self-determined reproduction-process assumes a prom-inent role, and the other three divisions of reproduction provide the material foundations needed for it to function and prosper. This process is dominated by the development of needs, starting from the elementary needs of the right to existence, which all persons in the world have an equal claim to. In order to rea-lise these needs, all persons are active in a freely associated and self-determined manner, producing and renewing use-values. Within their active life-process, planning, direction and execution coincide, and the secondary levels of repro-duction, which concern society's metabolism with nature, are intended to serve nothing but the priorities of the satisfaction of needs as determined in direct democratic decision-making processes. Average labour-time will perhaps con-tinue to serve as the standard for the globally coordinated planning of an auton-omous world-society until the mass-poverty of the South has been overcome and the subsistence-economies have been restored and expanded. But it will have become irrelevant to individual and/or familial reproduction: while all will contribute to the building of an autonomous society according to their abilities and their free choice, their reproduction will in no way be determined or limited by the extent of their contribution. Rather, it will be based on the character of their individual, familial, communal and social needs.

---

31. Outlines of such an expanded model of reproduction can be found in Kuczynski 1996b and 2007.

Requirements for a critique of the political economy of labour

Having clarified these premises, which we consider indispensable, we wish now to sketch the most important markers of a dynamic critique of the political economy of labour. In other words, we are proceeding to the critical analysis of a state in which the exploited are confronted, by virtue of being the bearers of living labour-capacity, with the process by which labour-capacity is made available and valorised. We have already emphasised repeatedly that they only become involved in this process when and to the extent that they have no other way of reproducing their existence. They therefore consider their subjection to the physical and valorisation-oriented production- and reproduction-processes a lesser evil and are always striving to obtain the greatest possible share for the reproduction of their individual and/or familial and communal existence – at least for as long as they dispose of no reliable alternative. Nevertheless, the exploited always have the option, in principle, of actively curbing the extent of their exploitation by means of everyday resistance; they can refuse work at least periodically or escape the relation of exploitation through flight, breach of contract and/or open rebellion. Starting from Hartmann's finding that capital's aggressive subordination- and valorisation- strategies always produce and reproduce an antagonistic subjectivity, the dynamic labour-theory of value needs therefore to ensure that there is an analytic symmetry, on all levels, between the bearers of living labour-capacity and the functionaries of exploitation and valorisation. Simply put, it is a matter of revising the 'asymmetry' that the relationship between labour and capital began to assume in Marx's work during the late 1840s. But it would be unrealistic to respond to this asymmetry by an equally exclusive asymmetry of 'revolutionary subjectivity', for while the working class has indeed waged major struggles against the capitalist social formation, the process by which living labour-capacity is objectified into capital has nevertheless been renewed again and again, and the powers by which objectified labour dominates living labour have to this day not been substantively weakened.

We consider the first cornerstone of a dynamic critique of the political economy of labour to consist in the use-value of living labour-capacity. Marx offered a one-sided account of this use-value, formulated from the perspective of the capitalists' interest in it: to the capitalists, the use-value of living labour-capacity resides in the fact that during the process of value-creation, it produces new value, namely surplus-value. But the use-value of living labour-capacity exists, first and foremost, for the person with whom that labour-capacity is inextricably bound up. It simply consists in the satisfaction of those basic needs for which specific labour-products are required. This 'personal use' of the use-value of labour-capacity is diametrically opposed to the capitalist's valorisation-interests. Nor is it weakened or even eliminated by the exchange-acts and associated transactions that occur within the direct production-process, for living labour-capacity can never be separated from the subject employing it. By making this essentially banal and obvious correction, we ensure that labour is not objectified in the course of the production- and reproduction-process of capital.

Second, we hold that the concept of 'living labour-capacity' needs to be expanded. Labour-capacity is always also reproductive capacity. Its employment does not exhaust itself in the creation of useful objects and/or commodities under capitalist conditions of valorisation. Rather, it is also capable of repro-ducing itself, both individually and within its family- and social networks, for its bearer is the paragon, qua 'species-being', of a social mode of existence. Yet under capitalist conditions, this reproductive capacity can also be exploited, even if this often happens invisibly. The labour-capacity of freely associated indi-viduals expresses the totality of the vital activity they engage in to satisfy their ever developing needs, but the opposite is also true: labour-capacity is exposed to the expanding totality of the capitalist valorisation-effort.

On this basis, we believe it is also necessary to provide a more differentiated account of the process by which labour-capacity is subordinated to capital. Marx coined the term 'subsumption' to describe this, distinguishing between 'formal' and 'real' subsumption on the basis of capital's material development. He essen-tially identified 'formal subsumption' with the era of manufacture and 'real sub-sumption' with the period following the introduction of machines. By contrast, we propose a distinction between four phases of subsumption; in doing so, we are following a suggestion by the Bielefeld school of feminism.[32] In the case of marginal subsumption, peasant subsistence-economies, proto-industrial family-economies and the so-called shadow-economies of the South are integrated into the world-economy's exploitation-chains in a mediated way. Formal subsump-tion refers to the direct incorporation and combination of pre-existing modes of production into plantation-economies, manufactures and poorly mechanised sweatshops. Real subsumption should be understood to refer to the two major stages of capitalist industrialisation, which saw the introduction of large machin-ery-complexes in some centres and regions and the combination of those com-plexes with Taylorist procedures for the intensification of labour-performance. We should reserve the term 'absolute subsumption' for the most recent subordi-nation of knowledge-work under capitalism's automated and informational net-work-structures. In doing so, we should however heed Tomba and Bellofiore and keep in mind that all four forms of subsumption are bound up with one another in today's world-economy, with the technologically most advanced labour- and valorisation-processes building upon a broad pedestal of exploitation that is

---

32. As far as we are aware, the term 'marginal subsumption' was first introduced by Veronika Bennholdt-Thomsen: Bennholdt-Thomsen 1981, p. 45.

structured in accordance with the criteria of marginal, formal and real subsumption. What needs also to be borne in mind is that there is a large technological and labour-organisational gap between the forms of exploitation found in the sphere of production and those found in the sphere of reproduction, so that the forms of subsumption differ not just from one geographical region to the next, but also within single locations. We should describe this ensemble of forms of subsumption as total subsumption.

A significant problem-area for each and every critique of the political economy of labour is represented by military labour. Niklas Frykman and Peter Way have joined Peter Linebaugh and Marcus Rediker in emphatically drawing attention to the practice of military indenture during the period of the 'primitive accumulation of the proletariat' in the seventeenth and eighteenth centuries, and Max Henninger has supplemented their remarks by pointing out the economic role military violence plays within the process of capital-accumulation. The problem becomes even more serious when we consider that military indenture, a particularly disparaged form of bloodletting (Peter Way), is still part and parcel of proletarian processes of constitution today. Since the late nineteenth century, it has also forced itself upon the class of workers in a new and equally ugly form – that of labour in the armaments-industry. The multiverse of the lower classes is inextricably linked, by these two class-components, to the openly violent and destructive side of capital's reproduction, even though it has repeatedly engaged in staunch resistance to this abomination – as for example during the international working-class revolution of 1916–21.

But what does this mean for a critique of the political economy of labour that strives not just to abolish exploitation but also to eliminate all associated elements of domination, oppression and violence? The product of military labour cannot be consumed socially; rather, it represents a form of unproductive state-consumption. We are therefore dealing with a special challenge to the labour-theory of value: while military campaigns allow for the appropriation of foreign economic potentials as revenues of national economies, and while the requisite armaments-production generates profits and income, it is nevertheless a case of 'negative production'. As Marx said, it is 'exactly the same as if the nation were to drop a part of its capital into the ocean'.[33] In the context of this conclusion, we cannot elaborate on this parasitic aspect of the violent expansion of national economies and the associated armaments-complexes.[34] Yet it ought nevertheless to be clear that there can only be one way for the global multiverse of the exploited to respond: uncompromising rejection of labour in the armaments-industry and of military indenture in all its forms.

---

33. Marx 1973, p. 128.
34. For a more in-depth look at the problem, cf. Roth 2001, pp. 49ff.

There are plenty of other issues that the dynamically expanded critique of the political economy of labour still needs to confront, but in the present context, the example of military labour and of labour in the armaments-industry will suffice. In many other sectors, the problems still need to be properly posed and worked through. This is true, for example, of the dynamic labour-theory of value's correlation with the devalorisations of capital and labour-capacity that are intermittently brought about by technological innovation. It is also true of the relations between labour-values, reproduction-values and total surplus-value that are 'anticipated' within the ever more strongly expanding sphere of credit.[35] Yet what we ought not to forget when addressing these issues is that we require a dynamic critique of the political economy of labour. Exposing the dynamics and the overall violence of the capitalist social formation is only the secondary task of such a critique. Its first task is to establish junctures that promote the development of revolutionary subjectivity, and to indicate the fault-lines starting from which we may hope to superate a system that is constituted by the exploitation of man by man.

In conclusion, we wish to emphasise once more that we consider this sketch of a possible dynamic critique of the political economy of labour a thought-experiment. It is merely intended to show how the critique of the Marxian concept of labour presented in this volume might be given a positive direction. There will likely be no royal road to the working out of the essential intersections between the critique of the political economy of labour and a model of social revolution. It seems more likely that more than one road will lead to Rome. The considerations on a critical synthesis presented here may prove useful to just such an approach, supplementing alternative ideas for the assertion of a universal right to existence that is grounded in the sphere of reproduction.[36]

Concluding remarks

It has not been easy organising and presenting the 18 contributions to this extensive volume. We have tried to use the contributors' largely negative verdicts on

---

35. Krätke 2007 provides a good overview of the tasks still to be addressed by a critique of the political economy of labour that is adequate to the realities of class-conflict.

36. We would point out that, in principle, the theory of value can be separated analytically from the theory of exploitation. We may speak of exploitation whenever workers produce commodities (goods and services) that are worth more than the 'countervalue' they receive from their 'employer', in the form of wages, means of subsistence etc. The question of whether commodities derive their value from the labour of workers or from some other source can be discussed separately. Even if the value of the goods and services produced were determined by their colour, their weight or something else, workers could still justifiedly claim to be exploited. Cohen 1988a, p. 214.

the status of labour in Marx's historical and economic thought as a starting point from which to develop a proposal for the further development of the critique of the political economy of labour, a proposal that does justice to the composition of the global multiverse and its forms of resistance. The superation of Marx's determinism, and of the orthodoxy that determinism has given rise to, has been overdue for more than a century; the coming months and years will show whether our proposal will contribute to this superation or whether it will be remembered as one of the last expressions of a heresy that has become more or less obsolete. There is no reason to engage in displays of calculated optimism, especially in light of the development of the global crisis, which has, a few significant exceptions aside, so far been testament to a rather far-reaching passivity of the lower classes. But this could soon change, for the ruling elites have now begun to impose upon the lower classes the social costs of their deficit-financed bailouts and stimulus-programmes. Perhaps these compiled efforts to anticipate a social formation that has been liberated from oppression and exploitation will then bear fruits after all. And perhaps the hitherto fatal gap between the intellectual, vanguardist anticipation of 'revolutionary subjectivity' and the emancipatory action of the class of workers will then actually be closed. Like the editors, the authors who have contributed to this volume are knowledge-workers and thus tendentially a part of the multiverse's new composition. If they and the majority of our readers, who will likely also belong to the more or less precarious segments of knowledge-work, should no longer think of themselves as a hegemonic stratum but rather as equal partners and actors within this multilayered multiverse, they could exert a tremendous catalytic effect. A society free of violence, oppression, domination and exploitation would then be within reach.

Bibliography

A British Seaman 1829, *Life On Board a Man-of-War: Including a Full Account of the Battle of Navarino*, Glasgow: n.p.

A Captain in the Royal Navy 1804, *Observations and Instructions for the Use of the Commissioned, the Junior, and other Officers of the Royal Navy, on all the Material Points of Professional Duty*, London: P. Steel.

Abel, Werner 1972, *Massenarmut und Hungerkrisen im vorindustriellen Deutschland*, Göttingen.

Abele, Eberhard, Jürgen Näher and Ulrich Kluge (eds.) 2006, *Handbuch globale Produktion*, Munich: Hanser.

Abramowitz, Moses 1986, 'Catching Up, Forging Ahead, and Falling Behind', *Journal of Economic History*, 46, 2: 385–406.

—— 1993, 'The Search for the Sources of Growth: Areas of Ignorance, Old and New', *Journal of Economic History*, 53, 2: 217–43.

Acerra, Martine, José Merino, and Jean Meyer (eds.) 1985, *Les Marines de Guerre Européennes XVII–XVIIIᵉ Siècles*, Paris: Presses de l'Université de Paris-Sorbonne: 103–22.

——, Pousson, Jean-Pierre, Michel Vergé-Franceschi and André Zysberg (eds.) 1995, *État, Marine et Société: Hommage à Jean Meyer*, Paris: Presses de l'Université Paris-Sorbonne.

Adam, Paul (ed.) 1980, *Seamen in Society/ Gens de mer en société*, s.l.: Perthes.

Adamczuk, Lujan 1981, *Rewolta szczecinska. Analiza socjologiczno-historiczna*, Łódź, reprinted with documents in Marciniak and Modzelewski 1989.

Ahmad, Aijaz 1992, *In Theory: Classes, Nations, Literatures*, London: Verso.

Alam, Javeed 1983, 'Peasantry, Politics and Historiography: Critique of New Trend in Relation to Marxism', *Social Scientist*, 11, 2: 43–54.

Albrecht, Volger (ed.) 1997, *Lexikon der Internationalen Politik*, Munich: Oldenbourg.

Ally, Shireen 2005, 'Caring About Care Workers: Organizing in the Female Shadow of Globalisation', Mexico City: Center for Global Justice/Centro para la Justicia Global conference paper, at <www.globaljusticecenter.org/papers 2005/ally_eng.htm>.

Alquati, Romano 1975, 'Composizione organica del capitale e forza-lavoro alla Olivetti' (1962–3), in Romano Alquati, *Sulla FIAT e altri scritti*, Milan: Feltrinelli.

Amin, Samir 2004, 'Der kapitalistische Genozid', *Blätter für deutsche und internationale Politik*, 48, 7: 817–24.

Amrith, Sunil 2008, 'Food and Welfare in India, c.1900–1950', *Comparative Studies in Society and History*, 50, 4: 1010–35.

Anderson, Fred 2000, *Crucible of War: the Seven Years' War and the Fate of Empire in British North America, 1754–1766*, New York: Knopf.

Anderson, Kevin 2010, *Marx at the Margins: On Nationalism, Ethnicity and Non-Western Societies*, Chicago: University of Chicago Press.

Anderson, M.S. 1988, *War and Society in the Old Regime 1618–1789*, Leicester: Leicester University Press.

Anderson, Perry 1976–7, 'The Antinomies of Antonio Gramsci', *New Left Review*, I/100: 5–78.

Andrea Fumagalli 1993, 'L'economia italiana sotto il giogo di Maastricht', in Lapo Berti and Andrea Fumagalli, *L'antieuropa delle monete*, Rome: manifestolibri.

Anonymous 1993, 'Soziale Revolution und das Kommando der Akkumulation. Zur Aktualität der russischen Revolution', *Materialien für einen neuen Antiimperialismus*, 4.

Anton, Anatole, Milton Fisk and Nancy Holmstrom 2000, *Not For Sale: In Defense of Public Goods*, Boulder, CO: Westview Press.

Arbeitsgruppe Bielefelder Entwicklungssoziologen 1979, *Subsistenzproduktion und Akkumulation*, Saarbrücken: Breitenbach.

Arena, R. and N. Salvadori (eds.) 2004, *Money, Credit, and the Role of the State. Essays in Honour of Augusto Graziani*. Aldershot: Ashgate.

Arendt, Hannah 1958, *The Human Condition*, Chicago, University of Chicago Press.

—— (ed.) 1968, Walter Benjamin, *Illuminations*, translated by Harry Zohn, with an Introduction by Hannah Arendt, New York: Schocken Books.

Arrighi, Giovanni 1994, *The Long American Century*, London: Verso.

—— 2007, *Adam Smith in Beijing: Lineages of the Twenty-first Century*, London: Verso.

Arrow, Kenneth J. 1962, 'Economic welfare and the allocation of resources for invention', in Nelson (ed.) 1962.

Arruzza, Cincia (ed. 2008), *Pensare con Marx. Ripensare Marx*, Rome: Edizioni Alegre.

Arthur, Chris 2004, *The New Dialectic and Marx's Capital*, Chicago: Haymarket.

Asiegbu, J.U.J. 1969, *Slavery and the Politics of Liberation, 1787–1861: A Study of Liberated African Emigration and British Anti-Slavery Policy*, London: Longman.

Assemblea Autonoma di Marghera 1975, *Assenteismo: un terreno di lotta operaia*, Padua.

Atkins, Keletso E. 1993, *The Moon is Dead! Give Us Our Money! The Cultural Origins of an African Work Ethic, Natal, South Africa, 1843–1900*, Portsmouth, NH: Heinemann.

Autonomie 1975–85, *Autonomie – Materialien gegen die Fabrikgesellschaft/Neue Folge*.

Autonomie 1979, *Autonomie – Materialien gegen die Fabrikgesellschaft/Neue Folge*, 2.

Autonomie 1980, *Autonomie – Materialien gegen die Fabrikgesellschaft/Neue Folge*, 3.

Autonomie 1982, *Autonomie – Materialien gegen die Fabrikgesellschaft/Neue Folge*, 10.

Backhaus, Hans-Georg 1978, 'Materialien zur Rekonstruktion der Marxschen Werttheorie 3', *Gesellschaft. Beiträge zur Marxschen Theorie*, 11: 16–117.

Backhaus, Wilhelm 1974, *Marx, Engels und die Sklaverei. Zur ökonomischen Problematik der Unfreiheit*, Düsseldorf: Schwann.

Bahro, Rudolf Bahro 1990, *Die Alternative*, Cologne: Bund-Verlag.

Bai, Moo Ki [Pae, Mu-gi] and Woo Hyun Cho 1995, *Women's Wages and Employment in Korea*, Seoul: Seoul National University.

Bainton, Roland H. 1952, *The Reformation of the Sixteenth Century*, Boston: Beacon Press.

Baldi, Guido 1972, 'Theses on Mass Worker and Social Capital', *Radical America*: 6, 3, May–June.

Baran, Paul A. and Paul M. Sweezy 1966, *Monopoly Capital. An Essay on the American Economic and Social Order*, New York, Monthly Review Press.

Barboza, David 2006, 'Some Assembly Needed: China as Asia Factory', *New York Times*, 9 February.

Bartolovich, Crystal and Neil Lazarus (eds.) 2002, *Marxism, Modernity, and Postcolonial Studies*, Cambridge: Cambridge University Press.

Bataille, Georges 1988, *The Accursed Share*, New York: Zone Books.

Batliwala, Srilatha 2002, 'Grassroots Movements as Transnational Actors: Implications for Global Civil Society', *Voluntas: International Journal of Voluntary and Non-Profit Organisation*, 13, 4: 393–409.

Bauer, Ilona 1985, 'Frauenarbeit und kapitalistische Reproduktion', *Autonomie/Neue Folge*, 14: 147–99.

Bauer, Joanne (ed.) 2006, *Forging Environmentalism: Justice, Livelihood and Contested Environments*, New York: ME Sharpe.

Baugh, Daniel A. 1988, 'Great Britain's "Blue-Water" Policy, 1689–1815', *International History Review*, 10, 1: 33–58.

—— 1994, 'Maritime Strength and Atlantic Commerce: The uses of "a grand marine empire"', in Stone (ed.) 1994.

Baviskar, Amita, Subir Sinha and Kavita Philip 2006, 'Rethinking Indian Environmentalism: Industrial Pollution in Delhi and Fisheries in Kerala', in Bauer (ed.) 2006.

Beckford, Martin 2009, '"Sandwich Generation" Families Torn Between Demands of Children and Parents', *Daily Telegraph*, April 1.

Bellofiore, Riccardo 1982, 'Scala mobile: analisi del dibattito recente', *Primo Maggio* 17.

—— 1997, 'Guest Editor's Introduction', *International Journal of Political Economy*, 27: 2.

—— 2004, '"As if its body were by love possessed". Abstract Labour and the Monetary Circuit: a Macro-Social Reading of Marx's Labour Theory of Value', in R. Arena and N. Salvadori (eds.) 2004.

—— 2008, 'Centralizzazione senza concentrazione?', in Arruzza (ed.) 2008.

—— and Riccardo Realfonzo (1997) 'Finance and the Labor Theory of Value', *International Journal of Political Economy*, 27, 2: 97–118.

Belluck, Pam 2009, 'In Turnabout, More Children Take on Caregiver Role', *New York Times*, February 23.

Benería, Lourdes 2008, 'The Crisis of Care, International Migration, and Public Policy', *Feminist Economics*, 14, 3: 1–21.

Benjamin, Walter 1967, *Versuche über Brecht*, Frankfurt am Main: Suhrkamp.

—— 1968, 'Theses on the Philosophy of History', in Arendt (ed.) 1968.

Bennholdt-Thomsen, Veronika 1981, 'Subsistenzproduktion und erweiterte Reproduktion. Ein Beitrag zur Produktionsweisendiskussion', *Gesellschaft. Beiträge zur Marxschen Theorie*, 14: 30–51.

—— 1982, *Bauern in Mexiko. Zwischen Subsistenz und Warenproduktion*, Frankfurt on the Main: Campus.

—— 1983, *Auch in der Dritten Welt wird die Hausfrau geschaffen. Warum?*, Bonn: DGH.

Bennholdt-Thomsen, Veronika and Maria Mies 1997, *Die Subsistenzperspektive. Eine Kuh für Hillary*, Munich: Frauenoffensive.

Bennholdt-Thomsen, Veronika, Brigitte Holzer and Christa Müller (eds.) 1999, *Das Subsistenzhandbuch. Widerstandskulturen in Europa, Asien und Lateinamerika*, Vienna: Promedia.

Bennholdt-Thomsen, Veronika, Maria Mies and Claudia von Werlhof 1998, *Women: The Last Colony*, London: Zed Books.

Berg, Lars Otto 2000, 'The Swedish Navy', 1780–1820, in Fred Sandstedt (ed.) 2000.

Berger, Ulrike 1993, 'Organisationskultur und der Mythos der kulturellen Integration', in Müller-Jentsch (ed.) 1993.

Bergmann, Wili *et al.* (eds.) 1978, *Autonomie im Arbeiterkampf*, Munich: Trikont.

Berlin, Ira 1998, *Many Thousands Gone: The First Two Centuries of Slavery in North America*, Cambridge, MA: Harvard University Press.

Bermani, Cesare and Bruno Cartosio 1984, 'Dieci anni di "Primo Maggio"', *Primo Maggio*, 19–20: 22–5.

Bernstein, Barton J. (ed.) 1970, *Towards a New Past: Dissenting Essays in American History*, London: Chatto & Windus.

Bernstein, Henry 2006, 'Is there an Agrarian Question in the 21st Century?', *Canadian Journal of Development Studies*, 27, 4: 449–60.

Bertelsmann Stiftung *et al.* (eds.) 2002, *Handbuch Beratung und Integration*, Gütersloh: Bertelsmann.

Berti, Lapo 1974, 'Denaro come capitale', *Primo Maggio*, 2: 9–18; now in *Primo Maggio* (eds.) 1978.

—— 1976, 'Riposta a Suzanne de Brunhoff', *Primo Maggio*, 6, now in Primo Maggio (eds.) 1978.

—— 1978a, 'Astrattizzazione del lavoro', *Primo Maggio*, 9–10, now in Bologna (ed.) 1978.

—— 1978b, 'Al cuore dello stato e ritorno', *Primo Maggio*, 11.

—— 1980, 'Appunti per un dibattito possibile', *Collegamenti*, 8.

—— 1981a, 'Sul nesso moneta-potere – Primo approccio', in Lauricella *et al.* 1981.

—— 1981b, 'Sulla trasformazione sociale', *Unità Proletaria*, 3–4.

—— 1984, 'Dibattito su "Dieci anni di 'Primo Maggio'"', *Primo Maggio*, Spring.

Berti, Lapo and Primo Maggio (eds.) 1978.

Berti, Lapo and Andrea Fumagalli 1993, *L'antieuropa delle monete*, Rome: manifestolibri.

Berti, Lapo *et al.* 1983, *La Politica possibile*, Naples: Pironti.

Binder, Leonard 1986, 'The Natural History of Modernization Theory', *Comparative Studies in Society and History*, 28, 1: 3–33.

Bisschoff, Joachim and Klaus Steinitz (eds.) 2003, *Linke Wirtschaftspolitik. Bilanz, Perspektiven, Widersprüche*, Hamburg: VSA.

Blackburn, Robin 2002, *Banking on Death. Or, Investing in Life: The History and Future of the Pensions*, London: Verso.

Blackett, Olin Winthrop 1928, *Factory Labor Turnover in Michigan*, Ann Arbor: University of Michigan Press.

Blaut, James M. 1993, *The Colonizer's Model of the World: Geographical Diffusionism and Eurocentric History*, New York, Guilford Press.

—— 1999, 'Marxism and Eurocentric Diffusionism', in Chilcote (ed.) 1999.

Bock, Gisela and Barbara Duden 1977, 'Arbeit aus Liebe – Liebe als Arbeit. Zur Entstehung der Hausarbeit im Kapitalismus', in Gruppe Berliner Dozentinnen (eds.) 1976.

Bologna, Sergio 1973a, 'Moneta e crisi: Marx corrispondente della New York Daily Tribune, 1856–57', *Primo Maggio*, 1: 1–15. [English: 'Money and Crisis: Marx as Correspondent of the *New York Daily Tribune*, 1856–57', *Common Sense*, 13, June 1993].

—— 1973b, 'Questioni di metodo per l'analisi del piano chimico', *Quaderni Piacentini*, 48–9.

—— 1973c, 'Ancora sul piano chimico (II) Materiali per una discussione', *Quaderni Piacentini*, 50.

—— 1974a, 'Moneta e crisi: Marx corrispondente della "New York Daily Tribune", 1856–57', in Bologna, Carpignano and Negri 1974.

—— 1974b, 'Petrolio e mercato mondiale: cronistoria di una crisi', *Quaderni Piacentini*, 52.

—— 1974c, 'Introduzione' to N. Moszkowska, *Per la critica delle teorie moderne delle crisi*, Turin: Musolini editore.

—— 1975, 'Per la storia dell'Internazionale comunista', *Primo Maggio*, 5.

—— 1977a, 'An Overview', now in Red Notes (eds.) 1978.

—— 1977b, 'The Tribe of Moles', translated by Ed Emery, <http://libcom.org/library/tribe-of-moles-sergio-bologna>.

—— (ed.) 1978, *La tribù delle talpe*, Milan: Feltrinelli.

—— 1993a, 'La ricerca del gruppo di "Primo Maggio"', in Berti and Fumagalli 1993.

—— 1993b, 'Money and Crisis: Marx as Correspondent of the *New York Daily Tribune*, 1856–57 (Part 2)', now in *Common Sense*, 14.

—— 1997, 'Dieci tesi per uno statuto del lavoro autonomo', in Bologna and Fumagalli (eds.) 1997, 13–42.

—— 1998, 'Il ruolo e le caretteristiche sociologiche degli intellettuali come ceto in uno scritto di Theodor Geiger', in Centro Studi Franco Fortini 1998.

—— 2007, *Ceti medi senza futuro? Scritti, appunti sul lavoro e altro*, Rome, Derive/Approdi.

Bologna, Sergio *et al.* 1972, *Operai e Stato: Lotte operaie e riforme dello Stato capitalistico tra rivoluzione d'Ottobre e New Deal*, Milan: Feltrinelli.

Bologna, Sergio, Paolo Carpignano and Antonio Negri (eds.) 1974, *Crisi e organizzazione operaia*, Milan: Feltrinelli.

Bologna, Sergio and Andrea Fumagalli (eds.) 1997, *Il lavoro autonomo di seconda generazione. Scenari del postfordismo in Italia*, Milan: Feltrinelli: 13–42.

Bonefeld, Werner and John Holloway 1996a, 'Conclusion: Money and Class Struggle', in Bonefeld and Holloway (eds.) 1996.

—— (eds.) 1996, *Global Capital, National State, and the Politics of Money*, New York: St. Martin's Press.

Borchardt, Julian 1923, *Einführung in den wissenschaftlichen Sozialismus*, Berlin: E. Laub.

Bordiga, Amadeo 1957, 'I fondamenti del comunismo rivoluzionario marxista nella dottrina e nella storia della lotta proletaria internazionale', *il programma comunista*, 13–15.

—— 1976, *Economia marxista ed economia controrivoluzionaria*, Milan: Iskra Edizioni.

Boris, Eileen and Jennifer Klein 2007, 'We Were the Invisible Workforce: Unionizing Home Care', in Cobble (ed.) 2007.

Borring, Erik K. 1998, 'Livet Ombord: Danske Orlogstogter til Vestindien, 1755–1807', Ph.D. dissertation, University of Copenhagen.

Bourdieu, Pierre 2003, *Interventionen 1961–1980*, Hamburg: VSA.

Bove, Arianna *et al.* 2005, 'Translators' Note', in Negri 2005.

Boxer, C.R. 1973, *The Dutch Seaborne Empire, 1600–1800*, Harmondsworth: Penguin.

Brass, Tom 1995a, 'Introduction: The New Farmer Movements In India', in Tom Brass (ed.), 1995.

—— (ed.) 1995, *New Farmers' Movements in India*, London: Frank Cass.

Brass, Tom and Marcel van der Linden (eds.) 1995, *Free and Unfree Labour: The Debate Continues*, Bern: Peter Lang.

Brecht, Bertolt 1963, *Dialoge aus dem Messingkauf*, Frankfurt am Main: Suhrkamp.

Breman, Jan 2003, *The Labouring Poor in India: Patterns of Exploitation and Subordination*, Oxford: Oxford University Press.

Brendel, Cajo 2008, *Die Revolution ist keine Parteisache. Ausgewählte Schriften*, edited by Andreas Hollender, Christian Frings and Claire Merkord, Münster: Unrast.

Breuer, Hans-Jürgen 2007, 'Silberrücken in Chefsesseln', *Frankfurter Allgemeine Zeitung*, 12 November.

Brewer, John 1989, *The Sinews of Power: War, Money and the English State, 1688–1783*, London: Routledge.

Brie, Michael 1993, 'Von den Schwierigkeiten, über die DDR zu sprechen', in Brie and Klein 1993.

Brie, Michael and Dieter Klein, *Der Engel der Geschichte. Befreiende Erfahrungen einer Niederlage*, Berlin: Dietz, 1993.

Brody, Jane E. 2008, 'When Families Take Care of Their Own', *New York Times*, November 11.

Bröckling, Ulrich *et al.* (eds.) 2003, *Anthropologie der Arbeit*, Tübingen: Günter Narr.

Bromley, J.S. (ed.) 1976, *The Manning of the Royal Navy: Selected Public Pamphlets, 1693–1873*, Greenwich: Navy Records Society.

—— 1980, 'The British Navy and its Seamen: Notes for an unwritten history', in Paul Adam (ed.) 1980.

Bruijn, Jaap R. 1979, 'Seamen in Dutch Ports, c. 1700–1914', *Mariner's Mirror*, 65: 327–37.

—— 1993, *The Dutch Navy of the Seventeenth and Eighteenth Centuries*, Columbia, SC: University of South Carolina Press.

Bruijn, Jaap R. and Els S. van Eyck van Heslinga 1984, 'Seamen's Employment in the Netherlands (c. 1600 to c. 1800)', *Mariner's Mirror*, 70: 7–20.

Bund der Kommunisten 1970, *Der Bund der Kommunisten. Dokumente und Materialien*, volume 1, 1836–49, Berlin: Dietz.

Büsch, Otto *et al.* (eds.) 1975, *Die frühsozialistischen Bünde in der Geschichte der deutschen Arbeiterbewegung*, Berlin: Colloquium.

Byers, Terry 1995, 'Development Planning and the State in India', in Byers (ed.) 1995.

—— (ed.) 1995, *The State and Development Planning in India*, Oxford: Oxford University Press.

Cabantous, Alain 1980, 'Les gens de mer et la mort: l'exemple de l'amirauté de Dunkerque au XVIIIᵉ siècle', in Paul Adam (ed.), *Seamen in Society/Gens de mer en société*, s.l.: Perthes.

—— 1984, *La Vergue et les Fers: Mutins et déserteurs dans la marine de l'ancienne France (XVIIᵉ–XVIIIᵉ s.)*, Paris: Tallandier.

Caffentzis, C. George 1989, *Clipped Coins, Abused Words, and Civil Government*, Brooklyn: Autonomedia.

—— 1990, 'On Africa and Self-Reproducing Automata', *Midnight Notes*, 10.

—— 1999a, 'On the Notion of a Crisis of Social Reproduction', in Dalla Costa and Dalla Costa (eds.) 1999.

—— 1999b, 'The End of Work or the Renaissance of Slavery? A Critique of Rifkin and Negri', *Common Sense*, 24: 20–38.

—— 2000, *Exciting the Industry of Mankind: George Berkeley's Philosophy of Money*. Dordrecht: Kluwer.

—— 2001, 'TPTG's Conversation with George Caffentzis', <http://www.wildcat-www.de/en/material/tptg_caf.htm>.

Calasanti, Toni M. and Kathleen F. Slevin (eds.) 2006, *Age Matters. Realigning Feminist Thinking*, New York: Routledge.

Calder, Kent E. 2006, 'China's and Japan's Simmering Rivalry', *Foreign Affairs*, 85, 2: 129–39.

Campbell, Martha 2005, 'Marx's Explanation of Money's Functions: Overturning the Quantity Theory', in Moseley (ed.) 2005.

Canny, Nicholas 1987, 'Identity Formation in Ireland: The Emergence of the Anglo-Irish', in Canny and Padgen (eds.) 1987.

Canny, Nicholas and Anthony Pagden (eds.) 1987, *Colonial Identity in the Atlantic World, 1500–1800*, Princeton, NJ: Princeton University Press.

Cardan, Paul [Cornelius Castoriadis] 1965, *Modern Capitalism and Revolution*, London: Solidarity.

—— 1979, *Capitalisme moderne et révolution*, Paris: 10–12, english translation by Maurice Brinton, in Cardan 1965.

Carli, Guido 1981, 'Guido Carli with Eugenio Scalfari' (1977), in Furio Colombo (ed.) 1987.

Carmichael, Fiona, *et al.* 2008, 'Work Life Imbalance: Informal Care and Paid Employment', *Feminist Economics*, 14, 2: 3–35.

Carpignano, Paulo 1975, 'U.S. Class Composition in the Sixties', *Zerowork*, 1.

Carter, Bob 1995, 'A Growing Divide: Marxist Class Analysis and the Labour Process', *Capital and Class*, 55.

Cartosio, Bruno 1992, *Anni inquieti. Società, media e ideologie da Truman a Kennedy*, Rome: Editori Riuniti.

Castegnaro, Alessandro 2002, 'La Rivoluzione occulta dell'assistenza agli anziani: le aiutanti domiciliari', *Studi Zancan*, 2: 11–34.

Castellano, Luciano (ed.) 1980, *Aut. Op. La storia e i documenti: da Potere operaio all'Autonomia organizzata*, Rome: Savelli.

Castells, Manuel 1996, *The Rise of the Network Society*, Oxford: Polity Press.

—— 2002, *The Internet Galaxy*, Oxford: Oxford University Press.

Castoriadis, Cornelius 1978, *Les Carrefours du labyrinthe*, Paris: Seuil.

—— 1984, *Crossroads in the Labyrinth*, translated by Kate Soper and Martin H. Ryle, Brighton: The Harvester Press.

—— 1987, *The Imaginary Institution of Society*, translated by Kathleen Blamey, Cambridge: Polity Press.

—— 1988–93, *Political and Social Writings*, translated and edited by David Ames Curtis, Minneapolis: University of Minnesota Press.

—— 1991, *Philosophy, Politics, Autonomy*, edited by David Ames Curtis, Oxford: Oxford University Press.

—— 1997, *World in Fragments: Writings on Politics, Society, Psychoanalysis, and the Imagination*, edited and translated by David Ames Curtis, Stanford, CA: Stanford University Press.

—— 1999, La 'rationalité' du capitalisme, in: id., *Figures du pensable*, Paris: Seuil.

—— 1999a, La 'rationalité' du capitalisme, in Castoriadis 1999.

—— 2005, *Une société à la dérive*, Paris: Seuil.

—— 2007, *Figures of the Thinkable*, translated by Helen Arnold, Stanford, CA: Stanford University Press.

—— 2010, *A Society Adrift: Interviews and Debates, 1974–1997*, edited by Enrique Escobar, Myrto Gondicas, and Pascal Vernay; translated by Helen Arnold, New York: Fordham University Press.

—— 2011, *Postscript on Insignificance: Dialogues with Cornelius Castoriadis*, edited with an introduction by Gabriel Rockhill, translated by Gabriel Rockhill and John V. Garner, London and New York: Continuum.

Centro Studi Franco Fortini 1998, Annual review, Siena: Quodlibet.

Chakrabarty, Dipesh 1989, *Rethinking Working Class History: Bengal 1890–1940*, Princeton: Princeton University Press.

—— 2002, *Habitations of Modernity: Essays in the Wake of Subaltern Studies*, Princeton: Princeton University Press.

—— 2007, '"In the name of politics": Democracy and Power of the Multitude in India', in Dipesh Chakrabarty *et al.* (eds.) 2007.

—— *et al.* (eds.) 2007, *From the Colonial to the Postcolonial: India and Pakistan in Transition*, Oxford: Oxford University Press.

Chan, Anita Kit-wa *et al.* 1995, 'The Impact of Industrial Restructuring on Women Workers in Hong Kong', in Committee for Asian Women (ed.) 1995.

Chandhoke, Neera 2003, *The Conceits of Civil Society*, Oxford: Oxford University Press.

Chandler, Michael Alison 2007, 'When a Kid Becomes the Caregiver', *Washington Post*, August 25.

Chatterjee, Partha 2004, *The Politics of the Governed. Reflections on Popular Politics in Most of the World*, New Delhi: Permanent Black.

Chatterjee, Partha, and Jeganathan P. (eds.) 2000, *Subaltern Studies XI*, New Delhi: Permanent Black.

Chayanov, A.V. 1966, *The Theory of Peasant Economy*, Homewood: Irwin, 1966.

—— 1966a, 'On the Theory of Non-Capitalist Economic Systems', in Chayanov 1966.

—— 1966b, 'Peasant Farm Organization', in Chayanov 1996.

Chen, Guidi and Chuntao, Wu 2006, *Will the Boat Sink the Water?*, New York: Public Affairs.

Chevalier, Louis 1958, *Classes laborieuses et classes dangereuses à Paris, pendant la première moitié du XIXe siècle*, Paris: Plon.

Chibber, Vivek 2006a, *Locked in Place: State-building and Late Industrialisation in India*, Princeton: Princeton University Press.

—— 2006b, 'On the Decline of Class Analysis in South Asian Studies', *Critical Asian Studies*, 38, 4: 357–87.

Chilcote, Ronald (ed.) 1999, *The Political Economy of Imperialism: Critical Appraisals*, Boston, Lanham, MD: Rowman and Littlefield.

Childers, Spencer (ed.) 1908, *A Mariner of England: An Account of the Career of William Richardson from Cabin Boy in the Merchant Service to Warrant Officer in the Royal Navy, as told by himself*, London: J. Murray.

Christianson, Scott 1998, *With Liberty for Some: 500 Years of Imprisonment in America*, Boston: Northeastern University Press.

Christopher, Emma 2006, *Slave Ship Sailors and their Captive Cargoes, 1730–1807*, New York: Cambridge University Press.

Christopher, Emma, Cassandra Pybus, and Marcus Rediker (eds.) 2007, *Many Middle Passages: Forced Migration and the Making of the Modern World*, Berkeley: University of California Press.

Claeys, Gregory 1987, *Machinery, Money, and the Millennium. From Moral Economy to Socialism, 1815–1860*, Princeton: Princeton University Press.

Clarke, Tony 1997, *Silent Coup: Confronting the Big Business Takeover of Canada*, Toronto: James Lorimer.

Classe 1970, 'Le lotte alle FIAT. Documenti', *La Classe* 2.

—— 1980, 'Il rifiuto del lavoro', *La Classe*, 6, 4, now in Castellano (ed.) 1980.

Cleaver, Harry 1989, 'Close the IMF, Abolish Debt and End Development: a Class Analysis of the International Debt Crisis', *Capital and Class*, 39: 17–50.

—— 1990, 'Notes on the Origin of The Debt Crisis', *Midnight Notes*, 10: 18–22.

—— 1996, 'The Subversion of Money-as-Command in the Current Crisis', in Bonefeld and Holloway (eds.) 1996.

—— 2000, *Reading 'Capital' Politically*, Second Edition, San Francisco: AK Press.

Clifford, James 1992, 'Traveling Cultures', in Grossberg, Nelson and Treichler (eds.) 1992, 96–116.

Cobble, Dorothy Sue (ed.) 2007, *The Sex of Class. Women Transforming American Labor*, Ithaca: Cornell University Press.

Cockshott, W. Paul and Allin Cottrell 1993, *Towards a New Socialism*, Nottingham: Spokesman.

Cody, Edward 2005, 'In Chinese Uprisings, Peasants Find New Allies', *Washington Post*, 26 November.

Cohen, G.A. 1988, *History, Labour and Freedom. Themes from Marx*, Oxford: Oxford University Press.

Cohen, G.A. 1988a, 'The Labour Theory of Value and the Concept of Exploitation', in Cohen 1988.

Colletis, Gabriel and Bernard Paulré (eds.) 2008, *Les nouveaux horizons du capitalisme. Pouvoirs, valeurs et temps*, Paris: Economica.

Colley, Linda 1996, *Britons: Forging the Nation, 1707–1737*, London: Vintage.

Colombo, Furio (ed.) 1987, *In Italy: Postwar Political Life*, New York: Karz.

Committee for Asian Women (ed.) 1995, *Silk and Steel: Asian Women Workers Confront Challenges of Industrial Restructuring*, Hong Kong: CAW.

Conze, Werner 1954, 'Vom "Pöbel" zum "Proletariat". Sozialgeschichtliche Voraussetzungen für den Sozialismus in Deutschland', *Vierteljahrsschrift für Sozial- und Wirtschaftsgeschichte*, 41: 333–64; reprinted in Wehler (ed.) 1966.

—— (ed.) 1976, *Sozialgeschichte der Familie in der Neuzeit Europas*, Stuttgart: Klett.

Cormack, William S. 1995, *Revolution and Political Conflict in the French Navy, 1789–1794*, Cambridge: Cambridge University Press.

Corrado, Carol, John Haltiwanger and Daniel Sichel (eds.) 2005, *Measuring Capital in the New Economy*, Chicago: University of Chicago Press.

Corvisier, André 1979, *Armies and Societies in Europe, 1474–1789*, translated by Abigail T. Siddall, Indiannapolis: Indiana University Press.

Costa, Dora L. 1998, *The Evolution of Retirement. An American Economic History. 1880–1990*, Chicago: The University of Chicago Press.

Cowell, Alan 1994, 'Affluent Europe's Plight: Graying', *New York Times*, September 8.

Cox, Nicole and Silvia Federici 1975, *Counterplanning from the Kitchen: Wages for Housework – A Perspective on Capital and the Left*, New York: New York Wages for Housework Committee/Falling Wall Press.

Crentz, Helmut *et al.* 1999, *Zukunftsfähige Gesellschaft*, Vienna: INWO International.

Curin, Philip D. 1969, *The Atlantic Slave Trade: A Census*, Madison: University of Wisconsin Press.

Daghini, Giario 1971, 'Sul "valore del lavoro"', *Aut Aut*, 123–4.

—— 1972, 'Genesi e funzione della forma denaro in Marx', *Aut Aut*, 128.

Dahm, Daniel and Gerhard Scherhorn 2008, *Urbane Subsistenz. Die zweite Quelle des Wohlstands*, Munich: Econ.

Dalla Costa, Mariarosa and Giovanna F. Dalla Costa (eds.) 1999, *Women, Development and Labor of Reproduction. Struggles and Movements*, Trenton, NJ: Africa World Press.

Dalla Costa, Mariarosa and Selma James 1972, *The Power of Women and the Subversion of the Community*. Bristol: Falling Wall Press. Also <http://libcom.org/library/power-women-subversion-community-della-costa-selma-james>.

Dann, John C. (ed.) 1988, *The Nagle Journal: A Diary of the Life of Jacob Nagle, Sailor, from the Year 1775 to 1841*, New York: Weidenfeld and Nicolson.

Dante 1984, *Dante's Paradise*, translated by Mark Musa, Bloomington: Indiana University Press.

Dasgupta, Ranajit 1986, 'Significance of Non-Subaltern Mediation', *Indian Historical Review*, 12, 1–2: 383–90.

Dash, Mamata 2008, 'The World Social Forum Through the Eyes of Movement Groups in India', paper presented at the CACIM Workshop on the WSF Process in India, New Delhi September 1–2.

Davids, Karel 1997, 'Maritime Labour in the Netherlands, 1570–1870', in van Royen, Bruijn and Jan Lucassen (eds.) 1997.

Davies, Matt and Magnus Ryner (eds.) 2006, *Poverty and the Production of World Politics: Unprotected Workers in the Global Political Economy*. New York: Palgrave-Macmillan.

Davis, David Brion 2001, 'Slavery – White, Black, Muslim, Christian', *New York Review of Books*, 48.

Davis, Joshua 1811, *A Narrative of Joshua Davis, an American Citizen, who was Pressed and Served On Board Six Ships of the British Navy*, Boston: B. True.

Davis, Mike 2006, *Planet of Slums*, London and New York: Verso.

Day, Richard J.F. 2005, *Gramsci is Dead: Anarchist Currents in the Newest Social Movements*, London: Pluto Press.

De Angelis, Massimo 2007, *The Beginning of History*, London: Pluto Press.

De Brunhoff, Susanne 1976a, *Marx on Money*. New York: Urizen.

—— 1976b, 'Punti di vista marxisti sulla crisi monetaria', *Primo Maggio*, 6, now in Primo Maggio (eds.) 1978.

—— 1978, *The State, Capital and Economic Policy*. London: Pluto Press.

De Masi, Guido 1979, 'Composizione di classe e progetto politico', *Primo Maggio*, 13.

De Neve, Geert 2005, *The Everyday Politics of Labour: Working Lives in India's Informal Economy*, New Delhi: Social Science Press.

Del Monte, C. 1980, 'Denaro e valore (per una rettifica della forma-denaro in Marx)', *Collegamenti Wobbly*, 8.

Denby, Charles 1978, *Indignant Heart: A Black Worker's Journal*, Boston: South End Press.

Desai, A.R. (ed.) 1971, *Essays on Modernization of Underdeveloped Societies*, Vol. 1, Bombay, Thacker.

Deyo, Frederic, Stephan Haggard and Hagen Koo 1987, 'Labor in the Political Economy of East Asian Industrialization', *Bulletin of Concerned Asian Scholars*, 19, 2: 42–53.

Di Vico, Dario 2004, 'Le badanti, il nuovo welfare privato. Aiutano gli anziani e lo Stato risparmia', *Corriere della Sera*, June 13.

Dockès, Pierre 1982, *Medieval Slavery and Liberation*. London: Methuen.

Donoghue, John (forthcoming), 'Fire in the Ashes': The English Revolution and the Atlantic World, Chicago: University of Chicago Press.

Douglas, Paul H. 1918, 'The Problem of Labor Turnover', *The American Economic Review*, 8, 2: 306–16.

—— 1959, 'Labor Turnover', in Seligman and Johnson (eds.) 1959.

Duden, Barbara 1977, 'Das schöne Eigentum. Zur Herausbildung des bürgerlichen Frauenbildes an der Wende vom 18. zum 19. Jahrhundert', *Kursbuch*, 47: 125–40.

Duffy, Michael 1980a, 'Introduction', in Duffy (ed.) 1980.

—— 1987, *Soldiers, Sugar, and Seapower: The British Expeditions to the West Indies and the War against Revolutionary France*, Oxford: Clarendon Press.

—— (ed.) 1980, *The Military Revolution and the State 1500–1800*, Exeter: Exeter Studies in History, 1.

Dufrancatel, Christiane *et al.* 1979, *L'Histoire sans qualités*, Paris: Galilée.

Dummer, Ingeborg 1997, *Die Arbeitskraft – eine Ware? Eine werttheoretische Betrachtung*, Hamburg.

Eaton, Susan E. 2007, 'Eldercare in the United States: Inadequate, Inequitable, but Not a Lost Cause', in Folbre, Shaw and Stark (eds.) 2007.

Ebbinghaus, Angelika 1978, 'Taylor in Russland', in Bergmann *et al.* (eds.) 1978.

Egan, Pierce 1823, *Grose's Classical Dictionary of the Vulgar Tongue, Revised and Corrected, With the Addition of Numerous Slang Phrases, Collected from Tried Authorities*, London (no pagination).

Ehrenberg, Alain 2004, *Das erschöpfte Selbst*, Frankfurt am Main: Suhrkamp. [English: Ehrenberg 2010, *The Weariness of the Self: Diagnosing the History of Depression in the Contemporary Age*, Montreal: McGill-Queen's University Press.]

Ehrenreich, Barbara and Arlie Russell Hochschild (eds.) 2002, *Global Woman. Nannies, Maids and Sex Workers in the New Economy*, New York: Metropolitan Books.

Einführung der Bearbeiter 1992, Einführung der Bearbeiter von Karl Marx, Ökonomische Manuskripte 1863–1867, Text, Teil 2, in MEGA², II/4.2, Berlin and Amsterdam: Akademieverlag.

—— 2003, Einführung der Bearbeiter von Karl Marx/Friedrich Engels, Manuskripte und redaktionelle Texte zum dritten Buch des 'Kapitals', 1871 bis 1895, in Marx 1976–2008, Volume 14, Berlin and Amsterdam: Akademieverlag.

Eliot, T. S. 1962, *Collected Poems and Plays 1909–1950*, New York: Harcourt, Brace & World, Inc.

Ellingstad, Marc 1997, 'The Maquiladora Syndrome: Central European Prospects', *Europe-Asia Studies*, 49, 1: 7–21.

Elson, Diane (ed.) 1979, *Value: The Representation of Labour in Capitalism*. London: CSE Books.

Elson, Diane 1979a, 'The Value Theory of Labour', in Elson (ed.) 1979.

Elster, Jon 1985, *Making Sense of Marx*, Cambridge: Cambridge University Press.

Eltis, David 1983, 'Free and Coerced Translatlantic Migrations: Some Comparisons', *American Historical Review*, 88: 251–80.

Elwert, Georg and Diana Wong 1979, 'Thesen zum Verhältnis von Subsistenzproduktion und Warenproduktion in der Dritten Welt', in Arbeitsgruppe Bielefelder Entwicklungssoziologen 1979.

Elwert, Georg and Richard Fett (eds.) 1982, *Afrika zwischen Subsistenzökonomie und Imperialismus*, Frankfurt am Main and New York: Campus.

Emmer, P.C. (ed.) 1986, *Colonialism and Migration: Indentured Labour Before and After Slavery*, Dordrecht: Springer.

Emsley, Clive (ed.) 1978, *North Riding Naval Recruits: The Quota Acts and the Quota Men, 1795–1797*, Northallerton: North Yorkshire County Council.

Engels, Frederick 1975–2004a[1852], 'Revolution and Counter-Revolution in Germany', in Marx and Engels 1975–2004, vol. 11.

—— 1975–2004b[1844–5] 'The condition of the working class in England', in Marx and Engels 1975–2004, vol. 4.

—— 1975–2004c[1885], 'Preface to the First German Edition of *The Poverty of Philosophy*', in Marx and Engels 1975–2004, vol. 26.

—— 1975–2004d[1891], 'Introduction to Karl Marx's *The Civil War in France*', in Marx and Engels 1975–2004, vol. 27.

—— 1975–2004e[1893], 'Can Europe Disarm?', in Marx and Engels 1975–2004, vol. 27.

—— 1975–2004f[1849], 'The Magyar Struggle', in Marx and Engels 1975–2004, vol. 8.

—— 1975–2004g[1884], 'Marx and the *Neue Rheinische Zeitung* (1848–49)', in Marx and Engels 1975–2004, vol. 26.

—— 1975–2004h[1872], 'The Housing Question', in Marx and Engels 1975–2004, vol. 23.

—— 1975–2004i[1874], 'Refugee Literature', in Marx and Engels 1975–2004, vol. 24.

—— 1975–2004j[1877], 'Anti-Dühring: Herr Eugen Dühring's Revolution in Science', in Marx and Engels 1975–2004, vol. 25.

Ertman, Thomas 1994, '*The Sinews of Power* and European State-Building Theory', in Stone (ed.) 1997.

Esquieu, Louis and Louis Delourmel (eds.) 1909, *Brest pendant la Révolution (documents inédits): Correspondance de la Municipalité avec les Députés de la Sénéchaussée de Brest aux États Généraux et à L'Assemblée Constituante, 1789–1791*, Brest: Union rép. du Finistère.

Evans, Richard J. 1979, *Sozialdemokratie und Frauenemanzipation im deutschen Kaiserreich*, Berlin: Dietz.

Ewald, Janet J. 2000, 'Crossers of The Sea: Slaves, Freedmen, and Other Migrants in the Northwestern Indian Ocean, c. 1750–1914', *The American Historical Review*, 105, 1: 69–91.

Falconer, William 1784, *An Universal Dictionary of the Marine*, 5th edition, London: T. Cadell.

Fanon, Frantz 1963, *The Damned*, foreword by Jean-Paul Sartre, translated by Constance Farrington, Paris: Présence Africaine.

Fardon, Richard 1987, '"African Ethnogenesis": Limits to the Comparability of Ethnic Phenomena', in Holy (ed.) 1987.

Federici, Silvia 1990, 'The Debt Crisis, Africa and the New Enclosures', *Midnight Notes*, 10: 10–17.

—— 1999, 'Reproduction and Feminist Struggle in the New International Division of Labor', in Dalla Costa and Dalla Costa (eds.) 1999.

—— 2004, *Caliban and the Witch: Women, the Body and Primitive Accumulation*. Brooklyn, NY: Autonomedia.

—— 2006. 'Prostitution and Globalization: Notes on a Feminist Debate', in Davies and Ryner (eds.) 2006.

Ferguson, Ann and Nancy Folbre 2000, 'Women, Care and the Public Good: A Dialogue', in Anton, Fisk and Holmstrom (eds.) 2000.

Ferguson, Niall 2001, *The Cash Nexus. Money and Power in the Modern World, 1700–2000*, New York: Basic Books.

Fernandes, Leela and Patrick Heller 2006, 'Hegemonic Aspirations: New Middle Class Politics and India's Democracy in Comparative Perspective', *Critical Asian Studies*, 38, 4: 495–522.

Fernández-Kelly, Maria Patricia 1983, 'Mexican Border Industrialization, Female Labor Force Partecipation, and Migration', in Nash and Fernández-Kelly (eds.) 1983.

Fiameni, Gianfranco (ed.) 2006, *Danilo Montaldi (1929–1975): Azione politica e ricerca sociale*, Cremona: Biblioteca statale.

Finardi, Sergio and Elena Moroni 2001, *Stati d'eccezione. Zone e porti franchi nell'economia-mondo*, Milan: Angeli.

Fink, Leon 2001, *Major Problems in the Gilded Age and the Progressive Era*, second edition, Boston: Houghton Mifflin.

Fischer, Lewis R. Harald Hamre, Poul Holm, and Jaap R. Bruijn (eds.) 1992, *The*

North Sea: Twelve Essays on the Social History of Maritime Labour, Stavanger: Maritime Museum.

Fisher, Boyd 1917, 'Methods of Reducing the Labor Turnover', Bulletin of the United States Bureau of Statistics, 208 (Proceedings of Employment Managers' Conference).

Florida, Richard 2002, The Rise of the Creative Class, New York: Basic Books, 2002.

Flying Pickets (eds.) 2007, Sechs Monate Streik bei Gate Gourmet, Hamburg: Assoziation A.

Fogleman, Aaron S. 1996, Hopeful Journeys: German Immigration, Settlement, and Political Culture in Colonial America, 1717–1775, Philadelphia: University of Pennsylvania Press.

Folbre, Nancy 2006, 'Nursebots to the Rescue? Immigration, Automation and Care', Globalizations, 3, 3: 349–60.

Folbre, Nancy, Lois B. Shaw and Agneta Stark (eds.) 2007, Warm Hands in Cold Age, New York: Routledge.

Folbre, Nancy, Lois B. Shaw and Agneta Stark 2007, 'Introduction: Gender and Aging', in Folbre, Shaw and Stark (eds.) 2007.

Food and Agriculture Organization of the United Nations 2011, The State of Food and Agriculture 2010–11, Rome: FAO.

Foote, Christopher L., Warren C. Whatley and Gavin Wright 2003, 'Arbitraging a Discriminatory Labor Market: Black Workers at the Ford Motor Company, 1918–1947', Journal of Labor Economics, 21, 3: 493–532.

Forester, C.S. (ed.) 1954, The Adventures of John Wetherell, New York: Doubleday.

Fortunati, Leopoldina 1981, L'Arcano della Riproduzione. Casalinghe, Prostitute, Operai e Capitale, Venice: Marsilio Editore.

Foster, Richard and Kaplan, Sarah 2001a, Creative Destruction: Why Companies That Are Built to Last Underperform the Market – And How To Successfully Transform Them, New York: Doubleday.

—— 2001b, 'Creative Destruction', in the McKinsey Quarterly, 3: 41–51.

Foucault, Michel 2001, Dits et Écrits, vol. 2, Paris: Gallimard/Seuil.

—— 2001a, 'Le sujet et le pouvoir', in Foucault 2001.

—— 2001b, 'Foucault', in Foucault 2001.

Fröbel, Folker, Jürgen Heinrichs and Otto Kreye 1977, Die neue internationale Arbeitsteilung. Strukturelle Arbeitslosigkeit in den Industrieländern und die Industrialisierung der Entwicklungsländer, Reinbek: Rowohlt.

—— 1980, The New International Division of Labor, Cambridge: Cambridge University Press.

—— 1984, Umbruch in der Weltwirtschaft. Die globale Strategie: Verbilligung der Arbeitskraft/Flexibilisierung der Arbeit/Neue Technologien, Reinbek: Rowohlt.

Fuller, Thomas 2005, 'China Feels a Labor Pinch', International Herald Tribune, 20 April.

Gaius 1904, Institutions or Institutes of Roman Law, Oxford: Clarendon. Online at files.libertyfund.org/files/1154/0533_Bk.pdf.

Galenson, David W. 1981, White Servitude in Colonial America: An Economic Analysis, Cambridge: Cambridge University Press.

Galison, Peter 2003, Einstein's Clocks. Poincare's Maps: Empires of Time, New York: W.W. Norton & Co.

Gambino, Ferruccio 2003, Migranti nella tempesta. Avvistamenti per l'inizio del nuovo millennio, Verona: ombre corte.

Gandhi, Leela 2006, Affective Communities: Anticolonial Thought, Fin de Siecle Radicalism and the Politics of Friendship, Durham: Duke University Press.

Geertz, Clifford 1973, Interpretation of Cultures: Selected Essays, New York: Basic Books.

—— 1973a, 'Thick Description: Toward an Interpretive Theory of Culture', in Geertz 1973.

Geierhos, Wolfgang 1977, Vera Zasulič und die russische revolutionäre Bewegung, Munich: Oldenbourg.

George, Susan 1999, 'Eine kurze Geschichte des Neoliberalismus: Zwanzig Jahre einer elitären Volkswirtschaftslehre und Chancen für einen Strukturwandel', Infobrief Nr. 1 des Netzwerks gegen Konzernherrschaft und neoliberale Politik: Cologne.

Gerhardt, Sebastian 1997, 'Politbürokratie und Hebelwirtschaft in der DDR. Zur Kritik einer moralischen Ökonomie', Helle Panke, No. 45.

—— 2002, 'Linke Wirtschaftspolitik – Theorie oder Praxis?', in Bisschoff and Steinitz (eds.) 2003.

—— 2003, 'Arbeitswert, Kreislaufbetrachtung und Profit', unpublished paper.

—— 2003a, Wenn Du Dich selbst nicht kennst . . . Linke Wirtschaftspolitik – Theorie oder Praxis? Ein Diskussionsbeitrag available at <"http://planwirtschaft.files. word press.com/2011/07/2_kennen_korr .pdf>.

—— 2005, 'Auf der Suche nach der historischen Tendenz. Mangelnde Vergesellschaftung wissenschaftlicher Produktionsmittel und Marx' Vorarbeiten zum Dritten Band des Kapital. Anmerkungen zum MEGA Band II/14', *junge Welt*, 13 June.

Gerhardt, Volker (ed.) 1996, *Eine angeschlagene These. Die 11. Feuerbach-These im Foyer der Humboldt-Universität Berlin*, Berlin: Akademie-Verlag.

Germer, Claus 2005, 'The Commodity Nature of Money in Marx's Theory', in Moseley (ed.) 2005.

Gikas, Michael 1985, *Arbeitsbewertung – Entlohnungsverfahren oder ideologisches Instrument? Eine ideologie-und verfahrenskritische Analyse anhand ausgewählter aktueller Entwicklungstendenzen der betrieblichen Lohndifferenzierung*, Münster.

Gilbert, Arthur N 1976a, 'An Analysis of Some Eighteenth Century Army Recruiting Records', *Journal of the Society for Army Historical Research*, 54, 217.

—— 1976b, 'Army Impressment during the War of the Spanish Succession', *The Historian*, 38, 4: 689–708.

—— 1978, 'Charles Jenkinson and the Last Army Press, 1779', *Military Affairs*, 42, 1: 7–11.

Glazer, Nona 1993, *Women's Paid and Unpaid Labor. Work Transfer in Health Care and Retail*, Philadelphia: Temple University Press.

Glete, Jan 1993, *Navies and Nations: Warships, Navies and State Building in Europe, 1500–1860*, 2 vols., Stockholm: Almqvist & Wiksell International.

Godelier, Maurice 1980, 'Work and its Representations: A Research Proposal', *History Workshop Journal*, 10, 1: 164–74.

Goffmann, Erving 1968, *Asylums: Essays on the Social Situation of Mental Patients and Other Inmates*, Harmondsworth: Penguin Books.

Goldner, Loren 2008, 'Fictitious Capital and Today's Global Crisis: Part 1', The Whitechapel Centre, London, 22 January, available at <http://blip.tv/file/667781>.

Gori, Franco 1976, 'Per una ricerca sul bilancio dello stato', *Primo Maggio*, 6, now in Primo Maggio (ed.) 1978.

—— 1978, 'Chi scava che cosa', *Primo Maggio*, 9–10, Winter, now in Bologna (ed.) 1978.

Gorter, Herman 1910, *Der historische Materialismus*, Stuttgart: Dietz.

Gorz, André 2003, *L'immatériel. Connaissance, valeur et capital*, Paris: Galilée.

Graeber, David 2001, *Towards an Anthropological Theory of Value: The False Coin of Our Dreams*. New York: Palgrave.

Grandjonc, Jacques 1975, 'Die deutsche Binnenwanderung in Europa 1830 bis 1849', in Büsch *et al.* (eds.) 1975.

Graziani, Augusto 1979, 'Introduzione', in Graziani (ed.) 1979.

—— (ed.) 1979, *L'economia italiana dal 1945 a oggi*, Bologna: Il Mulino.

—— 1983a, 'Let's Rehabilitate the Theory of Value', *International Journal of Political Economy*, 27, 2.

—— 1983b, 'The Marxist Theory of Money', *International Journal of Political Economy*, 27, 2.

Green, Carole A. 2007, 'Race, Ethnicity and Social Security Retirement Age in the US', in Folbre, Shaw and Stark (eds.) 2007, *Warm Hands in Cold Age*, New York: Routledge.

Green, Marcus 2002, 'Gramsci Cannot Speak: Presentations and Interpretations of Gramsci's Concept of the Subaltern', *Rethinking Marxism*, 14, 3: 1–24.

Greenspan, Alan 2007, *The Age of Turbulence. Adventures in a New World*, New York: Penguin Press.

Grey, Mark A. 1999, 'Immigrants, Migration, and Worker Turnover at the Hog Pride Pork Packing Plant', *Human Organization*, Spring: 16–27.

Grilli, Liliana 1982, *Amadeo Bordiga: capitalismo sovietico e comunismo*, Milan: La Pietra.

Grober, Ulrich 1998, *Ausstieg in die Zukunft. Eine Reise zu Ökosiedlungen, Energie-Werkstätten und Denkfabriken*, Berlin: Christoph Links.

Grossberg, Lawrence, Cary Nelson and Paula Treichler (eds.) 1992, *Cultural Studies*, New York: Routledge.

Großer Duden 1985, Leipzig: Bibliographisches Institut.

Gruppe Berliner Dozentinnen (eds.) 1976, *Frauen und Wissenschaft. Beiträge zur Berliner Sommeruniversität für Frauen*, Berlin: Courage.

Guha, Ranajit 1983, *Elementary Aspects of Peasant Insurgency in Colonial India*, New Delhi: Oxford University Press.

—— 1989a, 'Domination with Hegemony and its Historiography', in Guha (ed.) 1989.

—— (ed.) 1989, *Subaltern Studies VI*, New Delhi: Oxford University Press.

Guha, Sumit 1999, *Environment and Ethnicity in India, 1200–1991*, Cambridge: Cambridge University Press.

Gutman, Herbert G. 1977, *The Black Family in Slavery and Freedom, 1750–1925*, New York: Vintage Books.

—— 1987, *Power and Culture: Essays on the American Working Class*, edited by Ira Berlin, New York: Pantheon.

Gutman, Herbert G. and Steve Brier (eds.) 1992, *Who Built America?*, vol. 2, New York: Pantheon Books.

Gutiérrez, David G. (ed.) 1996, *Between Two Worlds: Mexican Immigrants in the United States*, Wilmington: Scholarly Resources.

Guyer, Jane I. (ed.) 1995, *Money Matters: Instability, Values and Social Payments in the Modern History of West African Communities*, Portsmouth, NH: Heinemann.

—— 2004, *Marginal Gains: Monetary Transactions in Atlantic Africa*. Chicago: University of Chicago Press.

Hachtmann, Rüdiger 1997, *Berlin 1848. Eine Politik- und Gesellschaftsgeschichte der Revolution*, Bonn.

—— 2002, *Epochenschwelle zur Moderne. Einführung in die Revolution von 1848/49*, Tübingen: edition diskord.

Hagel, John and John Seely Brown 2005, *The Only Sustainable Edge*, Boston: Harvard Business School Press.

Halary, Isabelle 2004, 'Ressources immatérielles et finance de marché: le sens d'une liaison', paper presented on 14 October at the workshop 'Approches économiques et pluridisciplinaires du patrimoine', University of Reims/INRA-MONA Paris.

Hall, Michael and Verena Stolcke 1983, 'The Introduction of Free Labour on São Paulo Coffee Plantations', *Journal of Peasant Studies*, 10, 2/3: 170–200.

Hardt, Michael and Antonio Negri 2000, *Empire*, Cambridge, MA: Harvard University Press.

—— 2004, *Multitude: War and Democracy in the Age of Empire*, New York: Penguin Press.

—— 1994, *Labor of Dionysus*, Minneapolis: University of Minnesota Press.

Harkins, S.G. 2001, 'Performance Among Individuals and Groups: The Implications of Parallel Research Traditions for Social Loafing', in: S.G. Harkins (ed.) 2001.

—— (ed.) 2001, *Multiple Perspectives on the Effects of Evaluation on Performance*, Norwell: Kluwer Academic Publishers.

Harland, John 1985, *Seamanship in the Age of Sail*, Annapolis, MD: Naval Institute Press.

Harman, Chris 2007, 'Gramsci, the Prison Notebooks and Philosophy', *International Socialism*, 114: 105–23.

Harrington Meyer, Madonna, Douglas A. Wolf, and Christine L. Himes 2007, 'Linking Benefits to Marital Status: Race and Social Security in the US', in Folbre, Shaw and Stark (eds.) 2007.

Harriss, J. 2006, 'Middle Class Activism and the Politics of the Informal Working Class: A Perspective on Class Relations and Civil Society in Indian Cities', *Critical Asian Studies*, 38, 4.

Harriss-White, Barbara 2003, *India Working: Essays on Society and Economy*, Cambridge: Cambridge University Press.

Harriss-White, Barbara and Aseem Prakash 2009, *Outcastes and Modern Indian Capitalism*, New Delhi: Oxford University Press.

Hartmann, Detlef 1987, *Leben als Sabotage*, Berlin: Schwarze Risse/Rote Straße.

—— 1994, 'Revolutionäre Gegenmacht und die Probleme der metropolitanen Linken', *analyse & kritik*, 362, 12 January. [Also published in: Roth (ed.) 1994.]

—— 2006, *Empire. Linkes Ticket für die Reise nach Rechts. Umbrüche der Philosophiepolitik. Hardt/Negri, Sloterdijk, Foucault*, Hamburg: Assoziation A.

—— 2008, 'Cluster. Die Organisation des sozialen Kriegs', in Hartmann and Geppert 2008.

—— 2009, 'Die Krise, SFB 700 und die NATO', *analyse & kritik*, 539.

—— and Dirk Vogelskamp 2003, *Irak. Schwelle zum sozialen Weltkrieg*, Berlin/Hamburg: Assoziation A.

—— and Gerald Geppert 2008, *Cluster. Die neue Etappe des Kapitalismus*, Berlin/Hamburg: Assoziation A.

Harvey, David 1993, *The Condition of Postmodernity: An Enquiry into the Origins of Cultural Change*, Oxford: Blackwell.

—— 2003, *The New Imperialism*, New York: Oxford University Press.

Hatton, Timothy J. and Jeffrey G. Williamson 1994, 'International Migration 1850–1939: An Economic Survey', in Hatton and Williamson (eds.) 1994.

Hatton, Timothy J. and Jeffrey G. Williamson (eds.) 1994, *Migration and the International Labour Market 1850–1939*, London and New York: Routledge, 1994.

Hauck, Gerhard 1990, 'Modernisierung, Dependencia, Marxismus – Was bleibt?', *Peripherie. Zeitschrift für politische Ökonomie der Dritten Welt*, 39/40: 68–81.

Hausen, Karin 1976, 'Die Polarisierung der "Geschlechtscharaktere" – eine Spiegelung der Dissoziation von Erwerbs- und Familienleben', in Conze (ed.) 1976.

Hegel, G.W.F. 1892, *The Logic of Hegel*, second edition, Oxford: Oxford University Press.

—— 1970a, *Wissenschaft der Logik*, volumes 1–2, Frankfurt am Main: Suhrkamp.

—— 1970b, *Grundlinien der Philosophie des Rechts*, Frankfurt am Main: Suhrkamp.

—— 1986, *Enzyklopädie der philosophischen Wissenschaften im Grundrisse*, volumes 1–3, Frankfurt am Main: Suhrkamp.

Heim, Susanne and Ulrike Schaz 1996, *Berechnung und Beschwörung. Überbevölkerung – Kritik einer Debatte*, Berlin: Schwarze Risse.

Heinrich, Michael 1999, *Die Wissenschaft vom Wert*, Münster: Westfälisches Dampfboot.

Heller, Patrick 2005, 'Re-inventing Public Power in the Age of Globalisation: Decentralisation and the Transformation of Movement Politics in Kerala', in Ray and Katzenstein (eds.) 2005.

Henkel, Martin and Rolf Taubert 1979, *Maschinenstürmer. Ein Kapitel aus der Sozialgeschichte des technischen Fortschritts*, Frankfurt am Main: Syndikat.

Henninger, Max 2007, 'Doing the Math: Reflections on the Alleged Obsolescence of the Law of Value under Post-Fordism', *ephemera* 7, 1 available at <www.ephemeraweb.org/journal/7-1/7-1henninger.pdf>.

—— 2010, 'Die Wiederentdeckung der Subsistenz: Dahm und Scherhorn propagieren eigenverantwortliche Selbstversorgung mit Wohlfahrtsleistungen', *analyse & kritik*, 547: 18.

Hermlin, Stefan 1979: *Abendlicht*, Berlin: Wagenbach.

Herring, Ronald and Rina Agrawala 2006, 'Restoring Agency to Class: Puzzles from the Subcontinent', *Critical Asian Studies*, 38, 4: 323–56.

Herz, Barbara 1988, *Briefing on Women in Development*, paper presented at the World Bank Meeting in West Berlin.

Hess, Moses 1961 *Philosophische und sozialistische Schriften 1837–1850*, Berlin: Akademie-Verlag.

Hess, Moses 1961a, 'Die europäische Triarchie', in Hess 1961.

Hillert, Andreas and Michael Marwitz 2006, *Die Burnout-Epidemie, oder, Brennt die Leistungsgesellschaft aus?*, Munich: C.H. Beck.

Hobsbawm, Eric J. 1964, *Labouring Men. Studies in the History of Labour*, London: Weidenfeld and Nicolson.

—— 1964a, 'The Machine Breakers', in Hobsbawm 1964.

—— 1964b, 'Custom, Wages and Workload in Nineteenth-Century Industry', in Hobsbawm 1964.

Hobsbawm, Eric J. and Georges Rudé 1969, *Captain Swing*, London: Lawrence and Wishart.

Hochschild, Adam 2008, 'Introduction', in Marchal 2008.

Hochschild, Arlie and Barbara Ehrenreich 2002, *Global Women: Nannies, Maids and Sex Workers in the New Economy*, New York: Holt.

Hodgskin, Thomas 1813, *An Essay on Naval Discipline*, London: Sherwood, Neely & Jones.

Hoerder, Dirk 2002, *Cultures in Contact: World Migrations in the Second Millennium*, Durham: Duke University Press.

Holloway, John 1996, 'The Abyss Opens: The Rise and Fall of Keynesianism', in Bonefeld and Holloway (eds.) 1996.

Holtgrewe, Ursula 2003, 'Informatisierte Arbeit und flexible Organisationen: Unterwerfung, Distanzierung, Anerkennungskämpfe?' in Schönberger and Springer (eds.) 2003.

Holy Ladislav (ed.) 1987, *Comparative Anthropology*, Oxford: Blackwell.

Hondagneu-Sotelo, Pierrette (ed.) 2003, *Gender and US Immigration: Contemporary Trends*, Berkeley: University of California Press.

Honig, Emily 1984, 'Burning Incense, Pledging Sisterhood. Communities of Women Workers in the Shanghai Cotton Mills, 1919–1949', *Signs*, 10: 700–14.

Hughes, Craig *et al.* for the Team Colors Collective (eds.) 2010, *Uses of a Whirlwind. Movement, Movements, and Contemporary Radical Currents in the United States*, Oakland, CA: AK Press.

Hutchinson, John R. 1914, *The Press Gang Afloat and Ashore*, New York: E.P. Dutton & Co.

Hutchinson, S.T., J.R. Villalobos and M.G. Beruvides 1997, 'Effects of High Labour Turnover in a Serial Assembly Environment', *International Journal of Production Research*, 35, 11: 3201–23.

Illich, Ivan 1981, *Shadow Work*, London: Marion Boyers.

Informationsstelle Militarisierung (eds.) 2008, *Studien zur Militarisierung Europas*, 34.

International Labour Office (ILO) 1972, *Employment, Incomes and Equality. A Strategy for Increasing Productive Employment in Kenya*, Geneva: ILO.

—— 1998, *Economic and Social Effects of Multinational Enterprises in Export Processing Zones*, Geneva: ILO.

—— 2003, *Employment and Social Policy in Respect of Export Processing Zones (EPZs)*, Geneva: ILO.

—— 2007, *ILO Database on Export Processing Zones (Revised)*, Geneva: ILO.

—— 2010, *Global Employment Trends for Youth*, Geneva: ILO.

International Labour Organization 2009, *World of Work Report 2009. The Global Jobs Crisis and Beyond*, Geneva: ILO.

—— 2010, *World of Work Report 2010. From One Crisis to the Next?*, Geneva: ILO.

IOM 2008, *World Migration Report 2008: Managing Labour Mobility in the Evolving Global Economy*, Geneva: IOM.

Jacobs, Sylvia M. 1981, *The African Nexus: Black American Perspectives on the European Partitioning of Africa, 1880–1920*, Westport, CT: Greenwood Press.

James, C.L.R. 1970, 'The Atlantic Slave Trade and Slavery: Some Interpretations of their Significance in the Development of the United States and the Western World', in Williams and Harris (eds.) 1970.

—— 1980[1938], *The Black Jacobins: Toussaint L'Ouverture and the San Domingo Revolution*, London: Allison & Busby.

James, Francis 1973, *Ireland in the Empire 1688–1770: A History of Ireland from the Williamite Wars to the Eve of the American Revolution*, Cambridge, MA: Harvard.

James, Selma 1985, *The Global Kitchen*, London: Housewives in Dialogue.

Jerome, Harry 1926, *Migration and Business Cycles*, New York: National Bureau of Economic Research.

Johansen, Hans Chr. 1997, 'Danish Sailors, 1570–1870', in Van Royen, Brujin and Lucassen (eds.) 1997.

Johnson, Richard 2007, 'Post-hegemony? I don't think so', *Theory, Culture and Society*, 24, 3.

Jones, Gareth Stedman 1995, 'Class, "Experience" and Politics', in Joyce (ed.) 1995.

Joyce, Kelly and Laura Mamo 2006, 'Greying the Cyborg. New Directions in Feminist Analyses of Aging, Science and Technology', in Calasanti and Slevin (eds.) 2006.

Joyce, Patrick 1995, 'A People and a Class' and 'Narratives of Class', in Patrick Joyce (ed.) 1995.

—— (ed.) 1995, *Class*, Oxford: Oxford University Press.

Jurczyk, Karin and G. Günter Voß 1995, 'Die Modernisierung moderner Lebensführung', available at <http://www.arbeitenundleben.de/downloads/Juvo_ModAlf.pdf>.

Jütting, Johannes P. and Juan R. de Laiglesia (eds.) 2009, *Is Informal Normal?* Paris: OECD.

Kaldor, Mary 1999, *New and Old Wars: Organised Violence in a Global Era*, Cambridge: Polity Press.

Kandel, William and Emilio A. Parrado 2005, 'Restructuring of the US Meat Processing Industry and New Hispanic Migrant Destinations', *Population and Development Review*, 31, 3: 447–71.

Kant, Immanuel, 2007. *Critique of Pure Reason*, Oxford: Oxford University Press.

Katholische Arbeitnehmerbewegung (eds.) 1999, *Frauenfrust – Frauenlust: Beiträge zu einer Ökonomie aus feministischer Sicht*, Bornheim: KAB.

Kautsky, Karl 1909, *Der Weg zur Macht. Politische Betrachtungen über das Hereinwachsen in die Revolution*, Berlin: Buchhandlung Vorwärts. [English translation: *The Road to Power*, Chicago: S.A. Bloch, 1909.]

Keck, Margaret and Kathryn Sikkink 1998, *Activists Beyond Borders: Advocacy Networks in International Politics*, Ithaca NY: Cornell University Press.

Keiler, Peter 1993, 'Kritische Bemerkungen zum Marxschen Konstrukt "Ware Arbeitskraft": – ein Nachtrag zum Thema "125 Jahre Das Kapital" ', *Dialektik. Enzyklopädische Zeitschrift für Philosophie und Wissenschaften*, 3, 1: 145–50.

—— 1997, *Feuerbach, Wygotski & Co.*, Hamburg: Argument.

—— 1997a, 'Die verborgenen Quellen des leontjewschen Vergegenständlichungs-Aneignungs-Konzepts', in: Keiler 1997.

Kelly, J.N.D. 1975. *Jerome. His Life, Writings and Controversies*, New York: Harper & Row.

Kemp, Peter 1970, *The British Sailor: A Social History of the Lower Deck*, London.

Kendrick, John W. 1994, 'Total capital and economic growth', *Atlantic Economic Journal*, 22, 1: 1–18.

Kerblay, Basile 1971, 'Chayanov and the Theory of Peasantry as a Specific Type of Economy', in Shanin (ed.) 1983.

Khagram, Sanjeev *et al.* (eds.) 2002, *Restructuring World Politics: Transnational Social Movements, Networks and Norms*, Minneapolis: University of Minnesota Press.

Kiær, Henning F. 1961, 'Flådens Mandskap, Nyboder', in Steen Steensen (ed.) 1961.

Klein, Bernhard and Gesa MacKenthun (eds.) 2003, *Sea Changes: Historicizing the Ocean*, New York: Routledge.

Klemp, Ludgera 1993, 'Frauen im Entwicklungs- und Verelendungsprozess', in Nohlen and Nuscheler (eds.) 1993.

Klíma, Arnošt 1979, 'Agrarian Class Structure and Economic Development in Pre-Industrial Bohemia', *Past and Present*, 85: 49–67.

Kluge, Alexander 2008, ' "Unser Problem ist der Zeitbedarf für soziale Veränderungen". Ein Gespräch mit Alexander Kluge über Karl Marx, den Kapitalismus und die Kraft des Eigensinns', *Neue Zürcher Zeitung*, 286, 6–7 December: 25.

Kluge, Jürgen, Wolfram Stein and Thomas Licht 2001, *Knowledge Unplugged: The McKinsey & Company Global Survey on Knowledge*, New York: Palgrave.

Kohout, Michael 2009, 'The Maquiladora Industry and Migration in Mexico: A Survey of Literature', *Geography Compass*, 3, 1: 135–53.

Kolonko, Petra 2007, 'Wachsende Wut auf die Reichen', *Frankfurter Allgemeine Zeitung*, 6 March.

Kommunistisches Korrespondenzkomitee 1979: Das Kommunistische Korrespondenzkomitee in London an das Kommunistische Korrespondenzkomitee in Brüssel, London, 17. Juli 1846, in Marx 1976–2008, III/2.

Kondo, Dorinne K. 1990, *Crafting Selves: Power, Gender, and Discourses of Identity in a Japanese Workplace*, Chicago: University of Chicago Press.

Korsch, Karl 1967, *Karl Marx*, Frankfurt am Main/Vienna: Europäische Verlagsanstalt/Europa-Verlag.

—— 1974, 'The Crisis of Marxism', translated by Otto Koester, *New German Critique*, 3: 7–11.

—— 1996, *Gesamtausgabe*, vol. 5, Amsterdam: IISG.

—— 1996a [1929], 'Thesen zur Diskussion über "Krise des Marxismus" ' (1929), in Korsch 1996.

Kotlikoff, Laurence J. and Scott Burns 2004, *The Coming Generational Storm. What You Need to Know About America's Economic Future*, Cambridge, MA: MIT Press.

Kragh, Helge 1999, *Quantum Generations: A History of Physics in the Twentieth Century*, Princeton: Princeton University Press.

Krahl, Hans-Jürgen 1971, *Konstitution und Klassenkampf. Zur historischen Dialektik von bürgerlicher Emanzipation und proletarischer Revolution*, Frankfurt am Main: Verlag Neue Kritik.

Krätke, Michael R. 2007, 'Erneuerung der Politischen Ökonomie – Wo Marx unersetzlich bleibt', *Zeitschrift für marxistische Erneuerung*, 18/70: 123–37.

Krell, Gertraude 1993, 'Vergemeinschaftung durch symbolische Führung', in Müller-Jentsch (ed.) 1993.

Kropotkin, Peter 1998[1902], *Mutual Aid. A Factor of Evolution*, London: Freedom Press.

Kuczynski, Thomas 1996a, 'Auf der Suche nach dem verlorenen Prestige', *SoZ Magazin*, 26, 6.

—— 1996b, 'Von der Natur der Arbeit oder Das Ende der Arbeitsgesellschaft – ein soziologisch-politologisches Mißverständnis', in Friedrun Quaas and Georg Quaas (eds.) 1996.

—— 2007, 'Vom Wert der Natur', in van der Linden and Lieber (eds.) 2007.

Kühl, Stefan 2001, 'Über das erfolgreiche Scheitern von Gruppenprojekten', *Zeitschrift für Soziologie*, 30, 3: 199–222.

Kühne, Lothar 1971a, 'Über die Historizität des Subjektiven', in Kühne 1971b.

—— 1971b, *Dissertation B, Band II, Arbeiten zur Philosophie, Kunst- und Architekturtheorie*, Berlin.

—— 1979, 'Zu Marx' Bestimmung des "menschlichen Wesens" in der 6. Feuerbachthese', *Deutsche Zeitschrift für Philosophie*, 7.

—— 1981, *Haus und Landschaft*, Dresden: Verlag der Kunst.

Kula, Witold 1986, *Measures and Men*. Princeton: Princeton University Press.

Laclau, Ernesto and Chantal Mouffe 1985, *Hegemony and Socialist Strategy: Towards a Radical Democratic Politics*, London: Verso.

Latouche, S. 1993, *In the Wake of the Affluent Society: An Exploration of Post-Development*, London: Zed Books.

Lauricella, R. *et al.* 1981, *Crisi delle politiche e politiche nella crisi*, Naples: Libreria L'Ateneo di G. Pironti.

Lavery, Brian 1989, *Nelson's Navy: The Ships, Men and Organization, 1793–1815*, Annapolis, MD: Naval Institute Press.

Lebert, Didier and Carlo Vercellone 2004, 'L'économie de la connaissance et de l'immatériel, entre théorie et histoire: du capitalisme industriel au capitalisme cognitif', *Cahiers lillois d'économie et de sociologie*, Paris: L'Harmattan.

Lebowitz, Michael 1992, *Beyond 'Capital': Marx's Political Economy of the Working Class*, Basingstoke, Macmillan.

—— 2003. *Beyond Capital*. Second edition. New York: Palgrave-Macmillan.

—— 2009, *Following Marx: Method, Critique and Crisis*, Leiden: Brill.

Lee, Ching Kwan 1998, *Gender and the South China Miracle: Two Worlds of Factory Women*, Berkeley: University of California Press.

Leech, Samuel 1999, *A Voice From the Main Deck: Being a Record of the Thirty Years Adventures of Samuel Leech*, Annapolis, MD: Naval Institute Press.

Lefebvre, Georges 1970 [1932], *La Grande Peur de 1789*, Paris: A. Colin.

LeGoff, T.J.A. 1980, 'Offre et productivité de la main d'œuvre dans les armaments français au 18éme siècle', in Paul Adam (ed.) 1980, *Seamen in Society/Gens de mer en société*, s.l.: Perthes.

—— 1984, 'Les origines sociales des gens de mer français au XVIIIᵉ siècle', in *La France d'Ancien Régime: Études réunies en l'honneur de Pierre Goubert*, Toulouse: Privat.

—— 1985, 'L'impact des prises effectuées par les Anglais sur la capacité en hommes de la marine française au XVIIIᵉ siècle', in Acerra, Merino and Meyer (eds.) 1985.

—— 1997, 'The Labour Market for Sailors in France', in van Royen, Bruijn and Lucassen (eds.) 1997.

Lekas, Padelis 1988, *Marx on Classical Antiquity. Problems of Historical Methodology*, Sussex: Wheatsheaf Books.

Lenin, V.I. 1914, 'Conspectus of Hegels Logic', in Lenin, *Collected Works*, vol. 38.

Lenz, Ilse 1980, 'Frauen und das globale Fließband', *Beiträge zur feministischen Theorie und Praxis*, 1, 3: 90–104.

Lerche, Jens 1999, 'Politics of the Poor: Agricultural Labour and Political Transformations in Rural India', *Journal of Peasant Studies*, 26, 2–3: 182–241.

—— 2008, 'Transnational Advocacy Networks and Affirmative Action for Dalits in India', *Development and Change*, 39, 2.

Lerner, Gad *et al.* 1978, *Uno strano movimento di strani studenti. Composizione, politica e cultura dei non garantiti*, Milan: Feltrinelli.

Lev, Baruch and Suresh Radhakrishnan 2003, 'The Measurement of Firm-Specific Organization Capital', National Bureau of Economic Research Working Paper 9581, New York: National Bureau of Economic Research.

Licht, Walter 1992, *Getting Work: Philadelphia 1840–1950*, Cambridge: Harvard University Press.

Linebaugh, Peter 1982, 'All the Atlantic Mountains Shook', *Labour/Le Travailleur* 10: 87–121.

—— 1992, *The London Hanged: Crime and Civil Society in the Eighteenth Century*, Cambridge: Cambridge University Press.

—— 2008. *The Magna Carta Manifesto*. Berkeley: University of California Press.

Linebaugh, Peter and Marcus Rediker 2000, *The Many-Headed Hydra: Sailors, Slaves, Commoners, and the Hidden History of the Revolutionary Atlantic*, Boston: Beacon Press.

Lloyd, Christopher 1970, *The British Seaman, 1200–1860: A Social Survey*, Cranbury, NJ: Associated University Presses.

Loess Kurt, Van V. Miller and David Yoskowitz 2008, 'Offshore Employment Practices: An Empirical Analysis of Routines, Wages and Labour Turnover', *International Labour Review*, 147, 2/3: 249–73.

Luatti, Lorenzo, Serena Bracciali, Roberta Renzetti 2007, *Nello Sguardo dell'Altra. Raccontarsi il Lavoro di Cura*, in collaboration with Donne Insieme, Arezzo: Collana Briciole.

Lucas, Erhard 1983, *Vom Scheitern der deutschen Arbeiterbewegung*, Basel: Stroemfeld.

Lucassen, Jan 1997, 'The International Maritime Labour Market (Sixteenth to Nineteenth Centuries)', in van Royen, Bruijn and Lucassen (eds.) 1997.

Ludden, David (ed.) 2002, *Reading Subaltern Studies. Critical History, Contexted Meaning and the Globalisation of South Asia*, London: Anthem.

Lüthje, Boy 2001, *Standort Silicon Valley: Ökonomie und Politik der vernetzten Massenproduktion*, Frankfurt am Main: Campus.

Luxemburg, Rosa 1925, *Einführung in die Nationalökonomie*, Berlin: E. Laub.

—— 1972, 'The Accumulation of Capital: An Anti-Critique', in Tarbuck (ed.) 1972.

—— 2003, *The Accumulation of Capital*, London: Routledge.

Lybeck, Otto Emil 1945, *Svenska Flottans Historia, Andra Bandet, Tredje Perioden: Från Frihetstidens Slut till Freden i Kiel*, Malmö: Allhem.

Mackillop, Andrew 2000, *'More Fruitful than the Soil': Army, Empire and the Scottish Highlands, 1715–1815*, East Linton, Lothian: Tuckwell Press.

Mahbubani, Kishore 1992, 'The West and the Rest', *The National Interest*, Summer: 3–13.

Makdisi, Saree, Cesare Casarino and Rebecca E. Karl (eds.) 1966, *Marxism Beyond Marxism*, New York: Routledge.

Malcolmson, Robert W. 1981, *Life and Labour in England 1700–1780*, London: Hutchinson.

Malone, Dumas and Basil Rauch 1960. *Crisis of the Union, 1841–1877*, New York: Appleton Century Crofts.

Maloney, Thomas N. and Warren C. Whatley 1995, 'Making the Effort: The Contours of Racial Discrimination in Detroit's Labor Market, 1920–1940', *The Journal of Economic History*, 55, 3: 465–93.

Malthus, Thomas R. 1992, *An Essay on the Principle of Population*, Cambridge.

Mamozai, Martha 1982, *Herrenmenschen: Frauen im deutschen Kolonialismus*, Reinbek: Rowohlt.

Mandarini, Matteo 2003, 'Translator's Introduction', in Negri 2005a.

Marazzi, Christian 1977, 'Money in the World Crisis: The New Basis of Capitalist Power', *Zerowork*, 2: 91–112.

—— 1978a, 'La crisi del "doppio mulinello"', in Bologna (ed.) 1978.

—— 1978b, 'Sulla relativa autonomia dello Stato mondiale', *Aut Aut*, 164, March–April.

—— 1978c, 'Alcune proposte per un lavoro su denaro e composizione di classe', now in Primo Maggio (eds.) 1978.

—— 1986, 'Aspects internationaux de la recomposition de classe', in Blanche-Tahon et Corten (eds.) 1986.

—— 2002, *Capitale e linguaggio: Dalla New Economy all'economia di guerra*, Rome: Derive Approdi.

—— 2007, 'Amortissement du corps-machine', *Multitudes*, 27: 27–37.

Marchal, Jules 2008, *Lord Leverhulme's Ghosts: Colonial Exploitation in the Congo*, London: Verso.

Marciniak, Piotr and Wojciech Modzelewski 1989, *Studia nad ruchami spolecznymi*, vol. 2, Warsaw: Uniwersytet Warszawski; Instytut Socjologii.

Marcus, G.J. 1975, *Heart of Oak: A Survey of British Sea Power in the Georgian Era*, London.

Märke, Erika 1986, *Ein Weg aus der Abhängigkeit? Die ungewisse Zukunft des informellen Sektors in Entwicklungsländern*, Heidelberg: Forschungsstätte der evangelischen Studiengemeinschaft.

Marshall, Alfred 1920, *Principles of Economics*, London: Macmillan.

Marshall, P.J. 1998, 'Introduction', *The Oxford History of the British Empire*, vol. II, *The Eighteenth Century*, Oxford: Oxford University Press.

Marx Karl, 1976–2008, *Marx-Engels Gesamtausgabe, Zweite Abteilung: Das 'Kapital' und Vorarbeiten*, Vols. 1–15 (cited below as *MEGA²*, Volumes 1–15).

—— 1975–2004a[1858], 'Letter to Friedrich Engels, 2 April, 1858', in Marx and Engels 1975–2004, vol. 40.

—— 1975–2004b[1858], 'Letter to Ferdinand Lassalle, 22 February 1858', in Marx and Engels 1975–2004, vol. 40.

—— 1975–2004c[1859], 'A Contribution to the Critique of Political Economy', in Marx and Engels 1975–2004, vol. 29.

—— 1975–2004d[1857], 'Letter to Friedrich Engels 8 December 1857', in Marx and Engels 1975–2004, vol. 40.

—— Marx 1975–2004e[1865], 'Value, Price and Profit', in Marx and Engels 1975–2004, vol. 20.

—— Marx 1975–2004f[1846], 'Letter to Carl Friedrich Julius Leske, 1 August 1846', in Marx and Engels 1975–2004, vol. 38.

—— Marx 1975–2004g[1881] 'Letter to Vera Zasulich, 8 March 1881', in Marx and Engels 1975–2004, vol. 46.

—— Marx 1975–2004h[1853], 'The British Rule in India', in Marx and Engels 1975–2004, vol. 12.

—— Marx 1975–2004i[1844], 'The economic and philosophic manuscripts of 1844', in Marx and Engels 1975–2004, vol. 3.

—— Marx 1975–2004j[1857–8] 'Economic manuscripts of 1857–58', in Marx and Engels 1975–2004, vol. 28.

—— Marx 1975–2004k[1850], 'The class struggles in France 1848 to 1850', in Marx and Engels 1975–2004, vol. 10.

—— Marx 1975–2004l[1843], 'Contribution to the Critique of Hegel's Philosophy of Right. Introduction', in Marx and Engels 1975–2004, vol. 3.

—— Marx 1975–2004m[1847] 'The Poverty of Philosophy', in Marx and Engels 1975–2004, vol. 6.

—— Marx 1975–20004n[1861–3], 'A Contribution to the Critique of Political Economy', in Marx and Engels 1975–2004, vol. 31.

—— Marx 1975–20040[1862–3] 'Theories of Surplus Value', in Marx and Engels 1975–2004, vol. 31.

—— Marx 1975–2004p[1853], 'Revelations Concerning the Communist Trial in Cologne', in Marx and Engels 1975–2004, vol. 11.

—— Marx 1975–2004q[1871], 'The Civil War in France', in Marx and Engels 1975–2004, vol. 22.

—— Marx 1975–2004r[1857–8], 'Economic Manuscripts of 1857–58', in Marx and Engels 1975–2004, vol. 29.

—— Marx 1975–2004s[1852] 'The Eighteenth Brumaire of Louis Bonaparte', in Marx and Engels 1975–2004, vol. 11.

—— 1975–2004t[1848], 'German Foreign Policy and the Latest Events in Prague', in Marx and Engels 1975–2004, vol. 7.

—— 1975–2004u[1868], 'Letter to Frederick Engels, 10 October 1868', in Marx and Engels 1975–2004, vol. 43.

—— 1975–2004v[1845], 'Theses on Feuerbach', in Marx and Engels 1975–2004, vol. 5.

—— 1975–2004w[1857–8], 'Outlines of the Critique of Political Economy', in Marx and Engels 1975–2004, vol. 28.

—— 1975–2004x[1868], 'Letter to Dr. Ludwig Kugelmann, 11 July 1868', in Marx and Engels 1975–2004, vol. 43.

—— 1975–2004y[1875], 'Critique of the Gotha programme', in Marx and Engels 1975–2004, vol. 24.

—— 1975–2004z[1858], 'Letter to Ferdinand Lassalle in Berlin, 11 March 1858', in Marx and Engels 1975–2004, vol. 40.

—— 1975–2004aa[1862], 'Letter to Engels, 2 August 1862', in Marx and Engels 1975–2004, vol. 41.

—— 1975–2004bb[1856], 'The monetary crisis in Europe', in Marx and Engels 1975–2004, vol. 15.

—— 1975–2004cc[1881], 'Drafts of the Letter to Vera Zasulich', in Marx and Engels 1975–2004, vol. 24.

—— 1973, *Grundrisse. Foundations of the Critique of Political Economy (Rough Draft)*, translated with a foreword by Martin Nicolaus, Harmondsworth: Penguin.

—— 1976, *Capital* Volume I, trans. Ben Fowkes, Harmondsworth: Penguin.

—— 1979, *Capital* Volume II, trans. David Fernbach, Harmondsworth: Penguin.

—— 1981, *Capital* Volume III, trans. David Fernbach, Harmondsworth: Penguin.

Marx, Karl and Friedrich Engels 1975–2004, *Marx and Engels Collected Works*, 50 vols., Moscow: Progress Publishers.

——1956, *Werke*, 39 volumes, Berlin: Dietz Verlag

—— 1973, *The Revolutions of 1848. Political Writings*, vol. I, trans. David Fernbach, Harmondsworth: Penguin.

—— 1973a, 'Manifesto of the Communist Party' (1848), in: Marx and Engels 1973.

—— 1975–2004a, 'The German Ideology' in Marx and Engels 1975–2004, vol. 5.

—— 1975–2004b, 'The Communist Manifesto' in Marx and Engels 1975–2004, vol. 6.

—— 1975–2004c, 'Address of the Central Committee to the Communist League', in Marx and Engels 1975–2004, vol. 10.

—— 1975–2004d, 'Review', in Marx and Engels 1974–2005, vol. 10.

—— 1975–2004e, 'The Holy Family, or Critique of Critical Criticism. Against Bruno Bauer and Company', in Marx and Engels 1975–2004, vol. 4.

—— 1983, 'Preface to the Second Russian edition of the *Manifesto of the Communist Party*', in Shanin (ed.) 1983.

Massey, Douglas S. and J. Edward Taylor (eds.) 2004, *International Migration: Prospects and Policies in a Global Market*, Oxford: Oxford University Press.

Materialien 1993: *Materialien für einen neuen Antiimperialismus: Strategien der Unterwerfung, Strategien der Befreiung*, Berlin: Assoziation A.

Mathiez, Albert 1973 [1927], *La vie chère et le mouvement social sous la terreur*, Paris.

Mattick, Paul 1972, 'Nixon's "New" Economic Policy', *Radical America*, 6, 1.

—— 1980, *Economics, Politics and the Age of Inflation*, London: Merlin Press.

Mayr, Ernst 2006, *Das ist Evolution*, Munich: Goldmann, 2006.

McCrimmon, Mitch 2008, 'How to Tame the Alpha Male Leader', *Ivey Business Journal*, March-April: available at <http://www.iveybusinessjournal.com/article.asp?intArticle_ID=744>.

McCulloch, J.R. (ed.) 1859, *Scarce and Valuable Economical Tracts*, London.

Meadows, Bonella H. 1997, 'Cuba Keeps its People Fed through a New Agriculture', *Canadian Centre for Policy Alternatives Monitor*, October.

Medick, Hans 1977, 'Die proto-industrielle Familienwirtschaft', in Peter Kriedte/Hans Medick/Jürgen Schlumbohm, *Industrialisierung vor der Industrialisierung. Gewerbliche Warenproduktion auf dem Land in der Formationsperiode des Kapitalismus*, Göttingen: Vandenhoeck und Ruprecht.

*MEGA*² = Karl Marx and Friedrich Engels, *Gesamtausgabe*, Berlin: Akademie-Verlag (in progress).

Meier, August and Elliott Rudwick 1979, *Black Detroit and the Rise of the UAW*, Oxford: Oxford University Press.

Meillassoux, Claude 1982, 'Historische Bedingungen der Ausbeutung und Überausbeutung von Arbeitskraft', in: Elwert and Fett (eds.) 1982.

—— 2005, *Femmes, greniers et capitaux*, Paris: L'Harmattan.

Melville, Herman 1990, *White-Jacket, or The World in a Man-of-War*, Oxford: Oxford University Press.

Merl, Stephan 1993, 'Bauernprotest in Sowjetrußland zwischen 1917 und 1941', *1999. Zeitschrift für Sozialgeschichte des 20. und 21. Jahrhunderts*, 8,4: 11–36.

MES/DARES 2000, Ministère de l'emploi et de la solidarité (MES)/Direction de l'animation de la recherche, des études et des statistiques (DARES), *Efforts, risques et charge mentale au travail. Résultats des enquêtes. Conditions de travail 1984, 1991 et 1998*, Paris: La documentation française.

Messori, Marcello 1997, 'The Theory of Value Without Commodity Money? Preliminary Considerations on Marx's Analysis of Money' (1984), *International Journal of Political Economy*, 27, 2.

Messori, Marcello and Marco Revelli 1978, 'Centralità operaia', *Primo Maggio*, 9–10.

—— 1980, 'Teoria del valore-lavoro e composizione di classe', *Unità Proletaria*, 1–3.

Meyer, Ahlrich 1977, *Frühsozialismus. Theorien der sozialen Bewegung 1789–1848*, Freiburg and Munich: Alber.

—— 1992, 'Die Subsistenzunruhen in Frankreich 1846–47', *Francia. Forschungen zur westeuropäischen Geschichte*, 19, 3: 1–45; reprinted in Meyer 1999.

—— 1999, *Die Logik der Revolten. Studien zur Sozialgeschichte 1789–1848*, Berlin: Schwarze Risse.

Meyer, Jean 1980, 'Forces navales et puissances économiques', in Adam (ed.) 1980.

Mezzadra, Sandro 2008, *La condizione postcoloniale. Storia e politica nel presente globale*, Verona: ombre corte.

Mies, Maria 1982, *The Lace Makers of Narsapur: Indian Housewives Produce for the World Market*, London: Zed Books.

—— 1983, 'Subsistenzproduktion, Hausfrauisierung, Kolonisierung', in: *Beiträge zur feministischen Theorie und Praxis*, 9–10: 115–24.

—— 1986a, *Indische Frauen zwischen Unterdrückung und Befreiung*, Hamburg: Hanseatische Verlagsanstalt.

—— 1986b, *Patriarchy and Accumulation on a World Scale: Women in the International Division of Labour*, London: Zed Books.

—— 1997, 'Hausfrauisierung', in Volger (ed.) 1997.

—— 1999, 'Globalisierung der Wirtschaft und Gewalt gegen Frauen', in Kath-olische Arbeitnehmerbewegung (eds.) 1999.

—— 2000, 'Globalisierung von unten: Seattle 29.11.–3.12.1999', *Infobrief 2* (January 2000), published by Netzwerk gegen Konzernherrschaft und neoliberale Politik, Cologne.

—— and Vandana Shiva 1993, *Ecofeminism*, London: Zed Books.

Miller, James (undated), 'Memoirs of an Invalid', Amherst Papers, U1350 Z9A, Centre for Kentish Studies, Maidstone, England.

Ministerium 2003 = Ministerium für Wirtschaft und Arbeit des Landes Nordrhein-Westfalen, *Inititativ in NRW. Case-Management. Theorie und Praxis*, Neuss: Ministerium für Wirtschaft und Arbeit des Landes Nordrhein-Westfalen.

Minssen, Heiner 1999, *Von der Hierarchie zum Diskurs? Die Zumutungen der Selbstregulation*, Munich: Hampp.

Mirabaud, M. [Paul Henri Thiry, Baron d'Holbach] 1853, *The System of Nature; or, the Laws of the Moral and Physical World*, Boston: J.P. Mendum.

Misra, Joya, Jonathan Woodring and Sabine N. Merz 2006, 'The Globalization of Care Work: Neoliberal Economic Restructuring and Migration Policy', *Globalizations*, 3, 3: 317–32.

Mitrany, David 1951, *Marx Against the Peasant: A Study in Social Dogmatism*, London: Weidenfeld and Nicholson.

Monnier, Jean-Marie and Carlo Vercellone 2007, 'Travail, genre et protection sociale dans la transition vers le capitalisme cognitif', *European Journal of Economic and Social Systems*, 20, 1: 15–35.

Montague, Peter 1999, 'Wealth and Health', *Third World Resurgence* (Penang), 108–9: 4–6.

Montaldi, Danilo 1961, *Autobiografie della leggera*, Turin: Einaudi.

—— 1971, *Militanti politici di base*, Turin: Einaudi.

—— 1994, *Bisogna sognare. Scritti (1952–1975)*, Paderno Dugnano: Cooperativa Colibri.

Moreau de Jonnès 1929, *Adventures in the Revolution and under the Consulate*, London.

Morgan, Lewis Henry 1876, 'Montezuma's Dinner: An Essay on the Tribal Society of North America', *North American Review*, 122.

Morrison, Toni 1992, *Playing in the Dark: Whiteness and the Literary Imagination*, Cambridge, MA: Harvard University Press.

Morton, Adam D. 2007, *Unravelling Gramsci: Hegemony and Passive Revolution in the Global Economy*, London: Pluto.

Moseley, Fred 2005a 'Introduction', in Moseley (ed.) 2005.

—— (ed.) 2005, *Marx's Theory of Money. Modern Appraisals*. New York: Palgrave Macmillan.

Moulier Boutang, Yann 1998, *De l'esclavage au salariat. Économie historique du salariat bridé*, Paris: Presses universitaires de France.

Moynihan, Daniel P. 1973, *The Politics of a Guaranteed Income. The Nixon Administration and the Family Assistance Plan*, New York: Vintage Books.

Müller-Jentsch, Walter (ed.) 1993, *Profitable Ethik – Effiziente Kultur*, Munich: Rainer Hampp.

Murphy, Rachel 2002, *How Migrant Labor Is Changing Rural China*, Cambridge: Cambridge University Press.

Murphy, Timothy S. (ed.) 2005, *Books for Burning: Between Civil War and Democracy in 1970s Italy*, London: Verso.

Musto, Marcello 2007, 'The Rediscovery of Karl Marx', *International Review of Social History*, 52, 3: 477–98.

Na'aman, Shlomo 1979, *Gibt es einen 'wissenschaftlichen Sozialismus'?*, Hannover: SOAK.

Napoleoni, Claudio *et al.* 1978, 'Riposta a Napoleoni', in Primo Maggio (eds.) 1978.

Nash, June and Maria Patricia Fernàndez-Kelly (eds.) 1983, *Women, Men and the International Division of Labor*, Albany: State University of New York Press.

Naval Documents 1935: *Naval Documents Related to the Quasi-War Between the United States and France: Naval Operations from February 1797 to October 1798*, Washington, DC.

Neal, Larry 1978, 'The Cost of Impressment during the Seven Years War', *Mariner's Mirror*, 64: 45–56.

Neale, Jonathan 1990, 'Forecastle and Quarterdeck: Protest, Discipline and Mutiny in the Royal Navy, 1793–1814', Ph.D. diss., University of Warwick.

Negri 1974a, 'Tesi sulla crisi', in Bologna, Carpignano and Negri 1974.

—— 1974b, *Partito operaio contro il lavoro* (1973), in Sergio Bologna *et al.*, *Crisi e organizzazione operaia*, Milan: Feltrinelli. [English translation in Murphy (ed.) 2005.]

—— 1976, *Proletari e Stato*, Milan: Feltrinelli. [English translation in Murphy (ed.) 2005.]

—— 1979a, *Marx oltre Marx*, Milan: Feltrinelli.

—— 1979b, *Dall'operaio massa all'operaio sociale: Intervista sull'operaismo*, Milan: Multhipla edizioni.

—— 1988, *Revolution Retrieved: Selected political writings on Marx, Keynes, capitalist crisis and New Social Subjects, 1967–83*, trans. Ed Emery and John Merrington, London: Red Notes.

—— 1988a[1968], 'Marx on Cycle and Crisis', now in Negri 1988.

—— 1992, 'Valeur-travail: crise et problèmes de reconstruction dans le postmoderne', *Futur Antérieure*, 10: 30–6.

—— 1994, 'Keynes and the Capitalist Theory of the State' (1967), now in Hardt and Negri 1994.

—— 1996a, 'Twenty Theses on Marx: Interpretation of the Class Situation Today', in Makdisi, Cesarino and Karl (eds.) 1996.

—— 1996b, *Marx Beyond Marx: Lessons on the Grundrisse*, Brooklyn: Autonomedia.

—— 1997, *Prefazione*, in Negri 1998.

—— 1998, *Marx oltre Marx*, Rome: Manifesto libri, first published in 1978.

—— 1999, *Insurgencies: Constituent Power and the Modern State*, Minneapolis: University of Minnesota Press.

—— 2005, *Time for Revolution*, London: Continuum.

—— 2005a, 'Crisis of the Planner-State: Communism and Revolutionary Organisation' (1971), now in Murphy (ed.) 2005.

—— 2005b, 'Proletarians and the State' (1976), now in Murphy (ed.) 2005.

—— 2005c, 'Toward a Critique of the Material Constitution' (1977), now in Murphy (ed.) 2005.

—— 2005d, 'Preface to the Italian Edition: 1997 – Twenty Years Later' (1997), now in Murphy (ed.) 2005.

—— 2006a, *Fabrique de porcelaine*, Paris: Stock.

—— 2006b, *Goodbye Mr. Socialism*, Milan: Feltrinelli.

—— and Carlo Vercellone 2008, 'Le rapport capital-travail dans le capitalisme cognitif', *Multitudes*, 32: 39–50.

Nelson, Carey and Lawrence Grossberg (eds.) 1988, *Marxism and the Interpretation of Culture*, Urbana, IL: University of Illinois Press.

Nelson, Richard R. (ed.) 1962, *The Rate and Direction of Inventive Activity*, Princeton: Princeton University Press.

Nesporova, Alena 2002, *Why Unemployment Remains so High in Central and Eastern Europe*, Employment Paper 2002/43, Geneva: ILO.

Neumann, Franz 1944, *Behemoth: The Structure and Practice of National Socialism 1933–1944*, Oxford: Oxford University Press.

Neusüß, Christel 1988, *Die Kopfgeburten der Arbeiterbewegung, oder die Genossin Luxemburg bringt alles durcheinander*, Hamburg: Rasch und Röhring.

—— 1992, *Die Kopfgeburten der Arbeiterbewegung, oder: die Genossin Luxemburg bringt alles durcheinander*, second edition, Osnabrück: Montage Verlag.

Ngai, Pun 1999, 'Becoming Dagongmei: The Politics of Identity and Difference in Reform China', *China Journal*, 42: 1: 1–18.

—— 2005, *Made in China*, Durham and London: Duke University Press.

—— and Li Wanwei 2008, *Dagongmei. Arbeiterinnen aus Chinas Weltmarktfabriken erzählen*, Berlin/Hamburg: Assoziation A.

Nicol, John 1997, *The Life and Adventures of John Nicol, Mariner*, New York: Grove Press.

Nigam, Aditya 2006, 'Radical Politics in the Age of Globalisation: Notes on Recent Indian Experience' available at <http://www.sephis.org/pdf/nigam1.pdf>.

Nilsen, Alf G. 2008, 'Political Economy, Social Movements and State Power: A Marxian Perspective on Two Decades of Resistance to the Narmada Dam Projects', *Journal of Historical Sociology*, 21, 2–3.

Nimtz, August 2002, 'The Eurocentric Marx and Engels and Other Related Myths', in Crystal Bartolovich and Neil Lazarus (eds.) 2002.

Nisbet, Robert 1971, 'Ethnocentrism and the Comparative Method', in: Desai, A.R. (ed.) 1971.

NN 2009, 'Failing Sciences – Embedded Stakeholders. Wider den SFB 700', Karlsruhe: Paul Revere.

Nohlen, Dieter and Franz Nuscheler (eds.) 1993, *Handbuch der Dritten Welt 1: Grundprobleme Theorien Strategien*, Bonn: Dietz.

Nonaka, Ikujiro (ed.) 2005, *Knowledge Management. Critical Perspectives on Business and Management*, 3 volumes, London and New York: Taylor and Francis.

Nørlit, Axel 1942–3, 'Tvangsudskrivning og Presning af Mandskap til Flaaden og Defensionen (1800–07)', *Historiske Meddelelser om København*, 3: 353–82.

OECD (ed.) 2008, *Growing Unequal? Income Distribution and Poverty in OECD Countries*, Paris: OECD.

OECD Health Project 2005, *Long Term Care For Older People*, Paris: OECD.

Oelsnitz, Dietrich von der and Michael Busch 2008, 'Faulenzen in der Gruppe', *Frankfurter Allgemeine Zeitung*, 7 April.

Okishio, Nobuo 1993, *Essays on Political Economy*, Frankfurt am Main: Peter Lang.

Olson, Mancur 1971, *The Logic of Collective Action: Public Goods and the Theory of Groups*, Cambridge, MA: Harvard University Press.

Ong, Aihwa 1987, *Spirits of Resistance and Capitalist Discipline: Factory Women in Malaysia*, New York: State University of New York Press.

Oppenheimer, Franz 1912, *Die soziale Frage und der Sozialismus. Eine kritische Auseinandersetzung mit der marxistischen Theorie*, Jena: Fischer.

Osterkamp, Ute 1976, *Motivationsforschung*, volume 2, Frankfurt am Main: Campus.

Owen, Laura J. 1995, 'Worker Turnover in the 1920s: What Labor-Supply Arguments Don't Tell Us', *The Journal of Economic History*, 55, 4: 822–41.

Paasch, Armin 2007, 'Schöne neue Landwirtschaft', *Blätter für deutsche und internationale Politik*, 52, 10: 1168–72.

Palmer, Bryan D. 2003, 'Hydra's Materialist History', *Historical Materialism*, 11: 373–94.

Palmer, Sarah and David M. Williams 1997, 'British Sailors, 1775–1870', in Van Royen, Bruijn and Lucassen (eds.) 1997.

Panitch, Leo *et al.* (eds.) 2010, *The Crisis this Time* (*Socialist Register 2011*), London: Merlin.

Pannekoek, Anton 2003, *Workers' Councils*, Edinburgh, AK.

Panzieri, Raniero 1994, 'Plusvalore e pianificazione', in Panzieri, *Spontaneità e organizzazione*, Pisa: Serantini.

—— 1994a, 'Sull'uso capitalistico delle macchine nel neocapitalismo', in Panzieri 1994.

Papastergiadis, Nikos 2000, *The Turbulence of Migration*, Cambridge: Polity Press.

Parker, Geoffrey 1996, *The Military Revolution: Military Innovation and the Rise of the West, 1500–1800*, Cambridge: Cambridge University Press, 2nd edition.

Parrenas, Rhacel Salazar 2002, *Servants of Globalization. Women, Migration and Domestic Work*, Stanford: Stanford University Press.

Pasinetti, Luigi 1977, *Lectures on the Theory of Production*, Basingstoke: MacMillan.

—— 1993, *Structural Economic Dynamics: A Theory of the Economic Consequences of Human Learning*, Cambridge: Cambridge University Press.

Peña, Leticia 2000, 'Retaining a Mexican Labor Force', *Journal of Business Ethics*, 26: 123–31.

Perrot, Michelle 1979, 'La Femme populaire rebelle', in Christiane Dufrancatel *et al.* 1979.

Perry, J. and S. Power 2007, 'In Eastern Europe, Low Pay Is Driving Workers Away', *The Wall Street Journal Europe*, 1, 34, 10 July.

Peters, Arno 1996, *Das Äquivalenzprinzip als Grundlage der Global-Ökonomie*, Vaduz: Akademische Verlagsanstalt.

Philipps, Lisa 2008, 'Silent Partners: The Role of Unpaid Market labor in Families', *Feminist Economics*, 14, 2: 37–57.

Phillips, Carla Rahn 1997, 'The Labour Market for Sailors in Spain, 1570–1870', in Paul C. van Royen, Jaap R. Bruijn and Jan Lucassen (eds.) 1997.

Pirker, Theo 1949, 'Kleine Arbeitstheologie', *Frankfurter Hefte*, 4: 149–66.

—— *et al.* 1995, *Der Plan als Befehl und Fiktion: Wirtschaftsführung der DDR*, Opladen: Westdeutscher Verlag.

Pittock, Murray G.H. 1997, *Inventing and Resisting Britain: Cultural Identities in Britain and Ireland, 1685–1789*, London: MacMillan.

Piven, Frances Fox and Richard Cloward 1972, *Regulating the Poor: The Functions of Public Welfare*, New York: Vintage.

—— 1977, *Poor People's Movements*, New York: Pantheon.

Pongratz, Hans J. and G. Günter Voß 2003, *Arbeitskraftunternehmer. Erwerbsorientierungen in entgrenzten Arbeitsformen*, Berlin: edition sigma.

Pope, Dudley 1981, *Life in Nelson's Navy*, London: Allen & Unwin.

Portes, Alejandro, Manuel Castells and Lauren A. Benton (eds.) 1989, *The Informal Economy. Studies in Advanced and Less Developed Countries*, Baltimore: Johns Hopkins University Press.

Potere Operaio 1969, 'A Struggle that Costs So Much Must Pay Much More', *Potere Operaio*, 6, 23–29, also in Potere Operaio (not dated).

—— 1971, 'Crisi del sistema monetario: "Ben scavato, vecchia talpa!"', *Potere Operaio*, 43, 25.

—— 1972a, 'La classe operaia americana è dalla nostra parte: Lettera da New York', *Potere Operaio*, 47–8.

—— 1972b, 'Produzioni di merci a mezzo di commando', *Potere Operaio*, 49.

—— not dated, *Potere Operaio: A Selection (September 1969–April 1970)*, Milan: Potere Operaio.

Potts, Lydia 1990, *World Labour Market: A History of Migration*, London: St. Martin Press.

Preobrazhensky, Evgeny 1971, 'Peasantry and the Political Economy of the Early Stages of Industrialization', in Shanin (ed.) 1983.

Primo Maggio (eds.) 1978, *Saggi sulla moneta, Quaderni di Primo Maggio*, 2.

Pürschel, G. Bent 1961, 'Træk af Flådens Retsvæsen', in Steen Steensen (ed.) 1961.

Pyle, Jean L. 2006a, 'Transnational Migration and Gendered Care Work: Introduction', *Globalizations*, 3, 3: 283–96.

—— 2006b, 'Globalization and the Increase in Transnational Care Work: The Flip Side', *Globalizations*, 3, 3: 297–315.

Quaas, Friedrun and Georg Quaas (eds.) 1996, 'Jenseits des Transformationsproblems. Vorläufiges Resümee einer Diskussion zum werttheoretischen Ansatz von Fritz Helmedag', *Jahrbücher für Nationalökonomie und Statistik*, 215–6: 714–31.

Ranci, Costanzo 2001, *Il mercato sociale dei servizi alla persona*, Rome: Carocci.

Rancière, Jacques and Patrick Vauday 1975, 'En allant à l'expo: L'ouvrier, sa femme et les machines', *Révoltes logiques*, 1: 5–22. [English translation: 'Going to the Expo: the Worker, his Wife and Machines', in Rifkin and Thomas (eds.) 1988.]

Ray, Raka and Mary Katzenstein (eds.) 2005, *Social Movements in India: Poverty, Power and Politics*, Lanham, MA: Rowman and Littlefield.

Ray, Raka 1999, *Fields of Protest: Women's Movements in India*, Minneapolis: University of Minnesota Press.

Rifkin, Adrian and Roger Thomas (eds.) 1988, *Voices of the People. The Politics and Life of 'La Sociale' at the End of the Second Empire*, translated by John Moore, London: Routledge & Kegan Paul.

Recueil 1797–8: *Recueil des lois relatives à la marine et aux colonies*, 18 vols, Paris.

Red Notes (eds.) 1978, *Italy 1977–8: 'Living with an Earthquake'*, second edition, London: Red Notes.

Reddy, Sanjay G. 2007, 'Zählung der Armen: Die Wahrheit über die Welt-Armuts-Statistiken', *Peripherie. Zeitschrift für politische Ökonomie der Dritten Welt*, 107: 269–79.

Rediker, Marcus 1987, *Between the Devil and the Deep Blue Sea: Merchant Seamen, Pirates, and the Anglo-American Maritime World, 1700–1750*, Cambridge: Cambridge University Press.

—— 2003, 'The Red Atlantic, or, "a terrible blast swept over the heaving sea"', in Bernhard Klein and Gesa Mackenthun (eds.) 2003.

—— 2004, 'The Revenge of Crispus Attucks; Or, the Atlantic Challenge to American Labor History', *Labor: Studies in the Working-Class History of the Americas*, 1: 35–45.

—— 2007, *The Slave Ship: A Human History*, New York: Viking-Penguin.

Redlich, Fritz 1964, *The German Military Enterpriser and his Work Force, A Study in European Economic and Social History and Social History*, 2 volumes, Wiesbaden: Franz Steiner.

Reichardt, Tobias 2004, 'Marx über die Gesellschaft der klassischen Antike', *Beiträge zur Marx-Engels-Forschung*, New Series: 194–222.

Revelli, Marco 1975, 'Fascismo come "rivoluzione dall'alto" (1920–1925)', *Primo Maggio*, 5.

Ricardo, David 1951[1817], *On the Principles of Political Economy and Taxation*, edited by Piero Sraffa, Cambridge: Cambridge University Press.

Rieber, Robert W. and Aaron S. Carton (eds.) 1987–, *The Collected Works of L.S. Vygotsky*, six volumes, New York: Plenum.

Rinehart, James 1999, 'The International Motor Vehicle Program's Lean Production Benchmark: A Critique', *Monthly Review*, 50, 8: 19–27.

Roberts, M. 1956, *The Military Revolution, 1560–1660*, Belfast.

Robertson, R.T. 1993, '"The Greenery of Well-Engineered Factory Complexes": Fiji's Garment-led Export Industrialization Strategy', *Bulletin of Concerned Asian Scholars*, 25, 2: 31–41.

Robinson, William 1973, *Jack Nastyface: Memoirs of an English Seaman*, Annapolis, MD.

Rockman, Seth 2008, *Scraping By: Wage Labor, Slavery, and Survival in Early Baltimore*, Baltimore: Johns Hopkins University Press.

Rodger, N.A.M. 1992, 'Shipboard Life in the Old Navy: The Decline of the Old Order?', in Fischer, Hamre, Hol, and Bruijn (eds.) 1992.

—— 1995, 'La mobilisation navale au XVIIIᵉ siècle', in Acerra, Pousson, Vergé-Franceschi and Zysberg (eds.) 1995.

—— 2006, *The Command of the Ocean: A Naval History of Britain, 1649–1815*, New York: Penguin.

Rodney, Walter 1972, *How Europe Underdeveloped Africa*, London: Bogle-L'Ouverture Publications.

Roesler, Jörg 2007, 'Ausbeutung berechnet', *junge Welt*, 180, 6 August: 10–1.

Rogers, Nicholas 2002, 'The Hidden History of the Revolutionary Atlantic', *Australian Journal of Politics & History*, 48: 412–15.

Röhr, Werner, Brigitte Berlekamp and Karl Heinz Roth (eds.) 2001, *Der Krieg vor dem Krieg. Politik und Ökonomik der 'friedlichen' Aggressionen Deutschlands 1938/39*, Hamburg: VSA.

Rolling Thunder 2008, 'The Importance of Support. Building Foundations, Creating Community Sustaining Movements', *Rolling Thunder*, 6: 29–39.

Roodhuyzen, Thea 1998, *In woelig vaarwater: Marineofficieren in de jaren 1779–1802*, Amsterdam: De Bataafsche Leeuw.

Roos, Carl 1953, *Prisonen: Danske og Norske Krigsfanger i England, 1807–1814*, Copenhagen.

Röpke, Jochen 2004, 'Blinde Flecken der Wirtschaftspolitik. Von der Theorie der Parallelwelten und der Notwendigkeit einer De-Ontologisierung der Wirklichkeit', available at <http://www.uni-marburg.de/fb02/makro/forschung/gelbereihe/artikel/2004-02-Roepke-Blinde-Flecke.pdf>.

Rosdolsky, Roman 1977, *The Making of Marx's 'Capital'*, London: Pluto.

Rosenberg, Hans 1974, *Die Weltwirtschaftskrise 1857–1859*, Göttingen: Vandenhoeck und Ruprecht.

Ross, Andrew 2006, *Fast Boat to China*, New York: Pantheon Books.

Rossanda, Rossana 1975, 'Gierek und die polnischen Arbeiter', in: Rossanda, *Über die Dialektik von Kontinuität und Bruch*, Frankfurt am Main: Suhrkamp.

Rote Fahnen über Polen 1972, *Rote Fahnen über Polen. Seit wann schießt die Arbeiterklasse auf sich selbst?*, Munich: Trikont.

Roth, Karl Heinz (ed.) 1994, *Die Wiederkehr der Proletarität. Dokumentation der Debatte*, Cologne: Neuer ISP Verlag.

—— 2001, 'Von der Rüstungskonjunktur zum Raubkrieg: Die Ursachen der deutschen Aggressionspolitik 1938/39', in Röhr, Berlekamp and Roth (eds.) 2001.

—— 2005, *Der Zustand der Welt. Gegenperspektiven*, Hamburg: VSA.

—— 2007, 'Empirie und Theorie: Die Marxsche Arbeitswertlehre im Licht der Arbeitsgeschichte', *Sozial.Geschichte*.

Zeitschrift für historische Analyse des 20. und 21. Jahrhunderts, 22, 2: 45–67 and 22, 3: 147–68.

—— 2009, *Die globale Krise*, Hamburg, VSA.

Roth, Karl Heinz and Marcel van der Linden 2007, Position paper for this volume, unpublished.

Roux, Jacques 1793, *Manifesto of the Enragés* available at [www.marxists.org].

Rovatti, Pier Aldo 1975, 'Il problema del comunismo in Panzieri', *Aut-Aut*, 149–50: 75–101.

Rudé, Georges 1959, *The Crowd in the French Revolution*, Oxford: Clarendon.

—— 1964, *The Crowd in History. A Study of Popular Disturbations in France and England 1730–1848*, New York: John Wiley and Sons.

Ruge, Arnold 1840, 'Europa im Jahre 1840', *Hallische Jahrbücher*.

Rule, John 1986, *The Labouring Classes in Early Industrial England, 1750–1850*, London: Longman.

—— 1992, *The Vital Century: England's Developing Economy, 1714–1815*, London: Longman.

Sætra, Gustav 1997, 'The International Labour Market for Seamen, 1600–1900: Norway and Norwegian Participation', in van Royen, Bruijn and Lucassen (eds.) 1997.

Saint-André, Jean-Bon n.d., *Rapport sur la Trahison de Toulon*, no publisher.

Sainte Croix, Geoffroy E.M. de 1975, 'Karl Marx and the History of Classical Antiquity', *Arethusa*, 8: 7–41.

Salinger, Sharon V. 1987, *'To Serve Well and Faithfully': Labor and Indentured Servants in Pennsylvania, 1682–1800*, Cambridge: Cambridge University Press.

Salleh, Ariel 1997, *Ecofeminism as Politics of Nature: Marx and the Postmodern*, London: Zed Books.

Samuel, Raphael 1981, *People's History and Socialist Theory*, History Workshop Series, London: Routledge & Kegan Paul.

Sandbrook, Richard *et al.* 2007, *Social Democracy in the Global Periphery: Origins, Challenges, Prospects*, Cambridge: Cambridge University Press.

Sargent, John and Linda Matthews 2006, 'China versus Mexico in the Global EPZ Industry: Maquiladoras, FDI Quality, and Plant Mortality', Edinburg, Texas: University of Texas Pan American/

Department of Management, Marketing, and International Business.

Sarkar, Sumit 1997, *Writing Social History*, New Delhi: Oxford University Press.

Sassen, Saskia 1996, 'US Immigration Policy toward Mexico in a Global Economy', in Gutiérrez (ed.) 1996.

Scherhorn, Gerhard *et al.* 1999, 'Subsistenzwirtschaft: Mehr als nur ein Schattenmarkt', *Hoechst Magazin*, 3.

Schmidt, U. 2000, 'Chinas Kommunisten fürchten Falun Gong', *Neue Zürcher Zeitung*, 25 April.

Schönberger, Klaus and Stefanie Springer (eds.) 2003, *Subjektivierte Arbeit. Mensch, Organisation und Technik in der entgrenzten Arbeitswelt*, Frankfurt am Main: Campus.

Schröder, Jörg-Peter 2006, *Wege aus dem Burnout*, Berlin: Cornelsen.

Schuler, Monica 1986, 'The Recruitment of African Indentured Labourers for European Colonies in the Nineteenth Century', in Emmer (ed.) 1986.

Schuman, Michael *et al.* 2006, 'In diesem Werk lernt Deutschland', *Die Zeit*, 14 June.

Schumpeter, Joseph 1934, *The Theory of Economic Development: An Inquiry Into Profits, Capital, Credit, Interest, and the Business Cycle*, Cambridge, MA: Harvard University Press.

—— 1939, *Business Cycles: A Theoretical, Historical, and Statistical Analysis of the Capitalist Process*, 2 volumes, New York: McGraw Hill.

—— 1942, *Capitalism, Socialism and Democracy*, New York, Harper & Brothers.

—— 1950, *Capitalism, Socialism, and Democracy*, New York: Harper & Brothers.

Scott, James C. 1976, *The Moral Economy of the Peasant*, New Haven: Yale University Press.

Seccombe, Wally 1993, *Weathering the Storm. Working-Class Families from the Industrial Revolution to the Fertility Decline*, London: Verso.

Seifert, Andreas 2008, 'Testfall China', in Informationsstelle Militarisierung (eds.) 2008.

Seiwert, Hubert 2001, 'Falun Gong als Herausforderung für Peking', *Neue Zürcher Zeitung*, 5 July.

Selden, Mark 1975, 'American Global Enterprise and Asia', *Bulletin of Concerned Asian Scholars*, 7, 2: 15–33.

Selement, George 1973, 'Impressment and the American Merchant Marine, 1782–1812', *Mariner's Mirror*, 59: 409–18.

Seligman, Edwin R.A. and Alvin S. Johnson (eds.) 1959, *Encyclopaedia of the Social Sciences*, New York: MacMillan.

Seligson, Mitchell A. and Edward J. Williams 1981, *Maquiladoras and Migration: Workers in the Mexico-United States Border Industrialization Program*, Austin: University of Texas Press.

Senghaas-Knobloch, Eva 1979, *Reproduktion von Arbeitskraft in der Weltgesellschaft. Zur Programmatik der Internationalen Arbeitsorganisation*, Frankfurt am Main: Campus.

Sethuraman, S.V. 1976, 'The Urban Informal Sector: Concept, Measurement and Policy', *International Labour Review*, 114: 69–81.

Shaikh, Anwar and Ertugrul A. Tonak 1994, *Measuring the Wealth of Nations: The Political Economy of National Accounts*, Cambridge: Cambridge University Press.

Shanin, Teodor (ed.) 1983, *Late Marx and the Russian Road: Marx and the Peripheries of Capitalism*, New York: Monthly Review Press.

Shaw, Lois B. and Sunhwa Lee 2007, 'Growing Old in the US: Gender and Income Inadequacy', in Folbre, Shaw and Stark (eds.) 2007.

Shepperd, J.A. 2001, 'Social Loafing and Expectancy-Value Theory', in Harkins (ed.) 2001.

Sherlock, Stephen 1996, 'Class Re-formation in Mumbai: Has Organised Labour Risen to the Challenge?', *Economic and Political Weekly*, 31, 52: L34–L38.

Shiva, Vandana (no date), 'The Historic Significance of Seattle', available at <http://www.converge.org.nz/pma/apshiva.htm>.

Shorter, Edward 1975, 'Der Wandel der Mutter-Kind-Beziehung zu Beginn der Moderne', *Geschichte und Gesellschaft*, 1, 2–3: 256–87.

Silver, Beverly J. 2003, *Forces of Labor*, Cambridge: Cambridge University Press.

Simmel, Georg 1950, 'The Stranger', in Kurt Wolff 1976.

—— 1978. *The Philosophy of Money*. London: Routledge and Kegan Paul.

Singh, Sangeeta *et al.* 1984, 'Subaltern Studies II: A Review Article', *Social Scientist*, 12, 10.

Sinha, Subir 2008, 'Lineages of the Developmentalist State: Transnationality and Village India, 1900–1965', *Comparative Studies in Society and History*, 50, 1: 57–90.

Sklair, Leslie 1989, *Assembling for Development: The Maquila Industry in Mexico and the United States*, Boston: Unwin Hyman.

Smeeding, Timothy M. and Susanna Sandström 2007, 'Poverty Income Maintenance in Old Age: A Cross-National View of Low Income Older Women', in Folbre, Shaw and Stark (eds.) 2007.

Smith, Adam 1776, *An Inquiry into the Nature and Causes of the Wealth of Nations*, London: W. Strahan and T. Cadell.

—— 1937, *An Inquiry into the Nature and Causes of the Wealth of Nations*, New York: Random House.

Spinoza, Benedictus de 1678, *Ethica Ordine Geometrico Demonstrata*, available at <www.ac-nice.fr/philo/textes/Spinoza-Ethica/html/Ethica.htm>. [English translation: *Ethics Spinoza*, London: J.M. Dent & Sons, 1934.]

—— 1891, *The Chief Works of Benedictus Spinoza*, vol. 2, London: George Bell.

—— 1891a, 'On the Improvement of the Understanding', in Spinoza 1891, vol. 2.

Spivak, Gayatri 1988, 'Can the Subaltern Speak?', in Nelson and Lawrence (eds.) 1988.

—— 2000, 'Discussion: An Afterword on the New Subaltern', in Chatterjee and Jeganathan (eds.) 2000.

Springer, Roland 1999, *Rückkehr zum Taylorismus?*, Frankfurt am Main: Campus.

Stalin, J.V. 1952, *Economic Problems of Socialism in the USSR*, Moscow: Foreign Languages Publishing House.

Stalker, Peter 2000, *Workers Without Frontiers: The Impact of Globalization on International Migration*, Boulder: Lynne Rienner.

Stamatis, Georgios 1977, *Die 'spezifisch kapitalistischen Produktionsmethoden' und der tendenzielle Fall der allgemeinen Profitrate bei Karl Marx*, Berlin: Autorenpublikation im Verlag Mehrwert.

Sandstedt, Fred (ed.) 2000, *Between Imperial Eagles: Sweden's Armed Forces during the Revolutionary and Napoleonic Wars, 1780–1820*, Stockholm.

Stanley, Kathleen 2005, 'Immigrant and Refugee Workers in the Midwestern Meatpacking Industry: Industrial Restructuring and the Transformation of Rural Labor Markets', *Review of Policy Research*, 11, 2: 106–17.

Stark, Agneta 2007, 'Warm Hands in Cold Age – On the Need of a New World Order of Care', in Folbre, Shaw and Stark (eds.) 2007.

Staudenmaier, John M. 1994, 'Henry Ford's Big Flaw', *American Heritage of Invention and Technology*, 10, 2: 34–44.

Steedman, Ian 1977, *Marx after Sraffa*, London: New Left Books.

Steele, Sir Robert 1840, *The Marine Officer, or, Sketches of Service*, London: Henry Colburn.

Steen Steensen, R. (ed.) 1961, *Flåden Gennem 450 År*, second edition, Copenhagen: Martins Forlag.

Steinfeld, Robert J. 1991, *The Invention of Free Labor: The Employment Relation in English and American Law and Culture, 1350–1870*, Chapel Hill: University of North Carolina Press.

Sternberg, Fritz 1926, *Der Imperialismus*, Berlin: Malik.

Sternhell, Zeev, Mario Sznajder and Maia Ashéri 1989, *Naissance de l'idéologie fasciste*, Paris: Gallimard.

Stiglitz, Joseph 2010, *Freefall. America, Free Markets, and the Sinking of the World Economy*, New York, W.W. Norton.

Stockhammer, Engelbert and Paul Ramskogler 2007, 'Uncertainty and Exploitation in History', Vienna Economic University Working Paper, no. 104.

Stoddard, Ellwyn R. 1987, *Maquila: Assembly Plants in Northern Mexico*, El Paso: Texas Western Press.

Stone, Lawrence (ed.) 1994, *An Imperial State at War: Britain from 1689 to 1815*, London: Routledge.

Sull, Donald 2005, *Made in China: What Western Managers Can Learn From Trailblazing Chinese Entrepreneurs*, Boston: Harvard Business School Press.

Synonymwörterbuch 1973, Leipzig: Bibliographisches Institut.

Tahon, Marie-Blanche et André Corten (eds.) 1986, *L'Italie: le philosophe et le gendarme*, Montreal: VLB Éditeur.

Taillemite, Etienne 2003, *Histoire ignorée de la Marine française*, Paris: Perrin.

Tarbuck, Kenneth J. (ed.) 1972, Rosa Luxemburg and Nikolai Bukharin, *Imperialism and the Accumulation of Capital*, London: Penguin Press.

Tarski, Alfred 1935, 'Der Wahrheitsbegriff in den formalisierten Sprachen', *Studia Philosophica Commentarii Societatis philosophicae Poloniae*, 1, Lwow: Leopoli

—— 1956, *Logic, Semantics and Metamathematics. Papers from 1923 to 1938*, Oxford: Clarendon.

Taylor, Peter K. 1994, *Indentured to Liberty: Peasant Life and the Hessian Military State*, Ithaca, NY: Cornell.

The Economist 1996, 'A Global Poverty Trap', in *The Economist* July 20 1996.

Thielbeer, Siegfried 2000a, 'Unzufriedenheit auf dem Land', *Frankfurter Allgemeine Zeitung*, 23 October.

—— 2000b, 'Pekinger Blutopfer', *Frankfurter Allgemeine Zeitung*, 13 March.

Thompson, E.P. 1963, *The Making of the English Working Class*, London: Gollancz.

—— 1967, 'Time, Work-discipline and Industrial Capitalism', *Past and Present*, 38: 56–97.

—— 1971, 'The Moral Economy of the English Crowd in the Eighteenth Century', *Past and Present*, 50: 76–136.

—— 1978, *The Poverty of Theory and Other Essays*, London, Merlin.

—— Thompson, E.P. 1991a, *Customs in Common*, New York: The New Press.

—— 1991b, 'Time, Work-Discipline, and Industrial Capitalism', Thompson (ed.) 1991.

—— (ed.) 1991, *Customs in Common: Studies in Traditional Popular Culture*, London: Merlin.

Thompson, William 1850, *Inquiry into the Principles of the Distribution of Wealth*, London: W.S. Orr and Co.

Thorner, Daniel 1966, 'Chayanov's Concept of Peasant Economy', in Chayanov 1966.

Thörner, Klaus 2008, *"Der ganze Südosten ist unser Hinterland". Deutsche Südost-europapläne von 1840 bis 1945*, Freiburg: ça ira.

Tilly, Charles, Louise Tilly and Richard Tilly 1975, *The Rebellious Century, 1830–1930*, Cambridge, MA: Harvard University Press.

Tjaden, Karl Hermann 1990, *Mensch Gesellschaftsformation Biosphäre*, Marburg: Verlag Arbeit und Gesellschaft.

Tomba, Massimiliano 2007, 'Differentials of Surplus-Value in the Contemporary Forms of Exploitation', *The Commoner*, 12: 23–37, available at <http://www.commoner.org.uk/>.

Tomlins, Christopher 2001, 'Reconsidering Indentured Servitude: European Migration and the Early American Labor Force, 1600–1775', *Labor History*, 42, 1: 1–43.

Transforming Knowledge 2003, *Transforming Knowledge into Action*, Marburg: Philips-Universität Marburg.

Trivedi, Nirmal 2005, 'Biopolitical Convergences: Narmada Bachao Andolan and Homo Sacer, *Borderlands*, 5, 3.

Tronti, Mario 1966, *Operai e capitale*, Turin: Einaudi.

—— 1968, 'Internazionalismo vecchio e nuovo', *Contropiano*, 3.

—— 1971, *Operai e capital*, second edition, Turin: Einaudi.

Trotta, Giuseppe and Fabio Milana (eds.) 2008, *L'operaismo degli anni sessanta. Da 'Quaderni rossi' a 'classe operaia'*, Rome, DeriveApprodi.

Tuchscheerer, Walter 1968, *Bevor 'Das Kapital' entstand*, Berlin: Dietz.

Tully, K. 1999, 'A State of Change', *Corporate Location*, September: 104–7.

Turgot, A.R.J. 1859, *Reflections on the Formation and Distribution of Wealth*, in J. R. McCulloch (ed.) 1859.

Tyner, James A. 2003, 'The Global Context of Gendered Labor Migration from the Philippines to United States', in Hondagneu-Sotelo (ed.) 2003.

Tynjanow, Juri 1982, *Poetik*, Leipzig and Weimar: Kiepenheuer.

Tynjanow, Juri 1982a, 'Chlebnikow', in Tynjanow 1982.

Unger, Richard W. 1980, 'Regulation and Organization of Seamen in the Netherlands and Germany before the Industrial Revolution', in Adam (ed.) 1980.

United Nations 2009, *World Economic and Social Survey 2009*, New York: UN.
—— 2010, *The Millennium Development Goals Report 2010*, New York: UN.
Ursula Holtgrewe 2003, 'Informatisierte Arbeit und flexible Organisationen: Unterwerfung, Distanzierung, Anerkennungskämpfe?', in Schönberger and Springer (eds.) 2003.
Van der Linden, Marcel 1995, 'Forced Labour and Non-Capitalist Industrialization: The Case of Stalinism (c. 1929 – c. 1956)', in Brass and van der Linden (eds.) 1995.
—— 1998, 'Socialisme ou Barbarie: A French Revolutionary Group (1949–65)', *Left History*, 5, 1: 7–37.
—— 2005, 'Plädoyer für eine historische Neubestimmung der Welt-Arbeiterklasse', *Sozial.Geschichte*, 20, 3: 7–28.
—— 2007a, *Western Marxism and the Soviet Union. A Survey of Critical Theories and Debates since 1917*, Leiden: Brill.
—— 2007b, 'The "Law" of Uneven and Combined Development: Some Underdeveloped Thoughts', *Historical Materialism*, 15, 1: 145–65.
—— 2007c, 'Labour History: The Old, the New, and the Global', *African Studies*, 66, 2–3: 169–80.
Van der Linden, Marcel and Christoph Lieber (eds.) 2007, *Kontroversen über den Zustand der Welt*, Hamburg, VSA.
—— 2008, *Workers of the World: Essays toward a Global Labor History*, Leiden: Brill.
Van Gelder, Roelof 1997, *Het Oost-Indisch Avontuur: Duitsers in Dienst van de VOC (1600–1800)*, Nijmegen: SUN.
Van Royen, Paul C., Jaap R. Bruijn and Jan Lucassen (eds.) 1997, *'Those Emblems of Hell'? European Sailors and the Maritime Labour Market 1570–1870 (Research in Maritime History*, 13), St. John's, Newfoundland.
Van Treeck, Till, Eckhard Hein and Petra Dünhaupt 2007, *Finanzsystem und wirtschaftliche Entwicklung: Tendenzen in den USA und in Deutschland aus makroökonomischer Perspektive*, Düsseldorf: Hans-Böckler-Stiftung.
Veltz, Pierre 2000, *Le nouveau monde industriel*, Paris: Gallimard.

Vercellone, Carlo (ed.) 2006, *Capitalismo cognitivo*, Rome: Manifestolibri.
—— 2007, 'La nouvelle articulation entre salaire, profit, rente dans le capitalisme cognitif', *European Journal of Economic and Social Systems*, 20, 1: 45–64. [English translation: 'The new articulation of wages, rent and profit in cognitive capitalism', available at <http://hal-parısı.archives-ouvertes.fr/halshs-00265584/en/>].
—— 2008, 'La thèse du capitalisme cognitif. Une mise en perspective historique et théorique', in Colletis and Paulré (eds.) 2008.
Vester, Michael 1970, *Die Entstehung des Proletariats als Lernprozeß. Die Entstehung antikapitalistischer Theorie und Praxis in England 1792–1848*, Frankfurt am Main: Europäische Verlagsanstalt.
Vickers, Daniel (with Vince Walsh) 2005, *Young Men and the Sea: Yankee Seafarers in the Age of Sail*, New Haven, CT: Yale University Press.
Virno, Paolo 1980, 'Lavoro e conoscenza', *Pre-print*, 3: 2.
—— 1990, 'Edizione semicritica di un classico Frammento. Citazioni di fronte al pericolo', *Luogo comune*, 1: 9–13.
Vogel, Berthold 2009, *Wohlstandskonflikte. Soziale Fragen, die aus der Mitte kommen*, Hamburg: Hamburger Edition.
Volney, Constantin François 1991, *The Ruins, or, Meditation on the Revolutions of Empires*, Baltimore: Black Classic Press.
Voloshinov, V.N. 1975 [1930], *Marxismus und Sprachphilosophie*, Frankfurt am Main: Ullstein.
Voltaire 2010, *Philosophical Dictionary*, New York: Dover.
von Baeyer, Hans Christian 1998. *Maxwell's Demon: Why Warmth Disperses and Time Passes*, New York: Random House.
Voß, G. Günter and Hans J. Pongratz 2002, 'Der Arbeitskraftunternehmer', in: Bröckling, Ulrich *et al.* (eds.) 2003.
Vygodskij, V.S. 1974, *Introduzione ai 'Grundrisse' di Marx*, translated by Cristina Pennevaja, Florence: Nuova Italia, 1974. [Originally: Vygodskij, V.S. 1965, *Istorija odnogo velikogo okrytija Karla Marksa*, Moscow: Mysl].

Vygotsky, Lev Semenovič 1987a, *Thinking and Speech* in Vygotsky 1987b.

—— 1987b, *Problems in the Theory and History of Psychology* [Robert W. Rieber and Aaron S. Carton (eds.) 1987, vol. 3].

—— 1999, *Scientific Legacy* [Robert W. Rieber and Aaron S. Carton (eds.), The Collected Works of L.S. Vygotsky, vol. 6], New York: Plenum.

Wallerstein, Immanuel 1986, 'Societal Development, or Development of the World-System?', *International Sociology*, 1, 1 (March): 3–17.

Walpen, Bernhard 1996, '"Neu" Liberalismus als Problematik: Grenzen und Un/Möglichkeiten', discussion paper written for a seminar on 'church ethics and the neoliberal credo', Appenberg (Switzerland).

—— 2004, *Die offenen Feinde und ihre Gesellschaft. Eine hegemonietheoretische Studie zur Mont Pèlerin Society*, Hamburg: VSA.

Ward, C. Osborne 1888, *The Ancient Lowly: A History of the Ancient Working People from the Earliest Known Period to the Adoption of Christianity by Constantine*, Chicago: Charles H. Kerr & Co.

Waring, Marilyn 1989, *If Women Counted: A New Feminist Economics*, London: Macmillan.

Warnke, Camilla and Peter Ruben 1979, 'Arbeit – Telosrealisation oder Selbsterzeugung der menschlichen Gattung?', *Deutsche Zeitschrift für Philosophie*, 27, 1.

Wasserzieher, Ernst 1971, *Kleines etymologisches Wörterbuch der deutschen Sprache*, Leipzig: Bibliographisches Institut.

Watson Elizabeth A. and Jane Mears 1999, *Women, Work and Care of the Elderly*, Burlington, VT: Ashgate.

Way, Peter 1993, *Common Labor: Workers and the Digging of North American Canals, 1780–1860*, Cambridge: Cambridge University Press.

—— 2000, 'Rebellion of the Regulars: Working Soldiers and the Mutiny of 1763–1764', *William and Mary Quarterly*, 3rd Series, 57, 4: 761–92.

—— 2003, 'Class and the Common Soldier in the Seven Years' War', *Labor History*, 44, 4 (December): 455–81.

Wehler, Hans-Ulrich (ed.) 1966, *Moderne deutsche Sozialgeschichte*, Cologne.

Weiner, Norbert 1965, *Cybernetics*, Cambridge, MA: MIT Press.

Weinholz, Erhard 1993, 'Plädoyer für einen unwissenschaftlichen Sozialismus', *Neues Deutschland*, 9–10.

Weisbrot, Mark *et al.* 2010, *The Scorecard on Globalization, 1980–2000: Twenty Years of Diminished Progress*, Washington, DC: Center for Economic and Polical Research.

Welke, Ulrich 1997, *Der Kapitän: Die Erfindung einer Herrschaftsform*, Münster: Westfälisches Dampfboot.

Werlhof, Claudia von 1985, *Wenn die Bauern wiederkommen. Frauen, Arbeit und Agrobusiness in Venezuela*, Bremen: Edition CON.

—— 1978, 'Frauenarbeit: Der blinde Fleck in der Kritik der politischen Ökonomie', *Beiträge zur feministischen Theorie und Praxis*, 1, 1: 18–31.

—— 1998, 'The Proletarian is Dead: Long Live the Housewife!', in Bennholdt-Thomsen, Mies and von Werlhof 1998.

—— 1999, 'Frauen und Globalisierung', in Crenz *et al.* 1999.

Whitelaw, Ian 2007, *A Measure of All Things. The Story of Man and Measurement*, New York: St. Martin's Press.

Whitman, Stephen T. 1993, 'Industrial Slavery at the Margin: The Maryland Chemical Works', *Journal of Southern History*, 59, 1: 31–62.

Whittaker, W.G. 2006, *Labor Practices in the Meat Packing and Poultry Processing Industry: An Overview*, CRS Report for Congress.

Wichterich, Christa 1998, *Die Globalisierte Frau*, Reinbek: Rowohlt.

Wicker, Tom 1991, *One of US: Richard Nixon and the American Dream*, New York: Random House.

Williams, Edward J. and John T. Passe-Smith 1989, *Turnover and Recruitment in the Maquila Industry: Causes and Solutions*, Las Cruces: Joint Border Research Institute/New Mexico State University.

Williams, John A. and Charles F. Harris (eds.) 1970, *Amistad*, 1.

Wilson, Kathleen 1994, 'Empire of Virtue: The Imperial Project and Hanoverian Culture c.1720–1785', in Stone (ed.) 1994.

518 • Bibliography

Wilson, Peter H. 1998, *German Armies: War and German Politics, 1648–1806*, London: University College London Press.

Wittgenstein, Ludwig 1966, *Tractatus logico-philosophicus*, Frankfurt am Main.

Wolf, Dorothee, Kai Eicker-Wolf and Sabine Reiner (eds.) 1999, *Auf der Suche nach dem Kompaß*, Cologne: PapyRossa Verlag.

Wolf, Eric R. 1969, *Peasant Wars of the Twentieth Century*, New York: Harper & Row.

Wolff, Kurt (trans.) 1976, *The Sociology of Georg Simmel*, New York: Free Press.

Wolff, Michael 1981, *Der Begriff des Widerspruchs. Eine Studie zur Dialektik Kants und Hegels*, Königstein: Hain.

Woodall, Pam 1994, 'The Global Economy', *The Economist*, 1 October.

World Bank 2007: World Bank, *World Development Report 2008: Agriculture for Development*, Washington.

Wörter und Wendungen 1962, Leipzig: Bibliographisches Institut.

Wright, Steve 2002, *Storming Heaven: Class Composition and Struggle in Italian Autonomist Marxism*, London: Pluto.

Wrigley, E.A. 1994, 'Society and the Economy in the Eighteenth Century', in Stone (ed.) 1994.

Wygotski, Lew S. [Lev S. Vygodsky] 1985, *Ausgewählte Schriften*, vol. 1, Berlin: Volk und Wissen.

Zajicek, Toni Calasanti, Cristie Ginther and Julie Summers 2006, 'Intersectionality and Age Relations. Unpaid Care Work and Chicanas', in Calasanti and Slevin (eds.) 2006.

Zeiseweis, Kurt 1995, 'Es gab für uns kein zurück', *Zwiegespräch*, 31.

Zimmerman Mary K., Jacquelyne S. Litt, and Christine E. Bose. (2006), *Global Dimensions of Gender and Carework*, Stanford: Stanford University Press.

Index[1]

---

1. Marx's writings have been listed as separate entries.